Nonunion Employee Representation

ISSUES IN WORK AND HUMAN RESOURCES

Daniel J.B. Mitchell, Series Editor

BEYOND UNIONS AND COLLECTIVE BARGAINING
Leo Troy

CYBERUNION
Empowering Labor Through Computer Technology
Arthur B. Shostak

WORKING IN THE TWENTY-FIRST CENTURY
Policies for Economic Growth Through Training,
Opportunity, and Education
David L. Levine

INCOME INEQUALITY IN AMERICA
An Analysis of Trends
Paul Ryscavage

HARD LABOR
Poor Women and Work in the Post-Welfare Era
Joel F. Handler and Lucie White

NONUNION EMPLOYEE REPRESENTATION
History, Contemporary Practice, and Policy
Bruce E. Kaufman and Daphne Gottlieb Taras, editors

Nonunion Employee Representation

History, Contemporary Practice, and Policy

Edited by
**Bruce E. Kaufman and
Daphne Gottlieb Taras**

M.E. Sharpe
Armonk, New York
London, England

Library of Congress Cataloging-in-Publication Data

Nonunion employee representation : history, contemporary practice, and
policy / Bruce E. Kaufman and Daphne Gottlieb Taras, editors.
p. cm. − (Issues in work and human resources)
Includes bibliographical references and index.
ISBN 0-7656-0494-9 (hardcover : alk. paper)
ISBN 0-7656-0495-7 (paper : alk. paper)
1. Employee rights—United States. 2. Employee rights—Canada.
3. Labor laws and legislation—United States. 4. Labor laws and
legislation—Canada. I. Kaufman, Bruce E. II. Taras, Daphne
Gottlieb, 1956–   . III. Series.
HD6971.8.N66 2000
331'.01'10973—dc21   99-32610
                                      CIP

Printed in the United States of America

BM (c)	10	9	8	7	6	5	4	3	2	1
BM (p)	10	9	8	7	6	5	4	3	2	1

Contents

International Perspectives

Practitioner Commentary: Employers

Practitioner Commentary: Employees

List of Tables and Figures

Tables

Figures

Foreword

Daniel J.B. Mitchell

Around the developed world, unionization rates have been declining. Influences behind the decline vary from country to country. However, the global nature of the decline suggests that there are some overriding factors affecting many countries. Global competition in product markets—with its indirect labor-market impact—certainly would be one factor to be cited.

Within the United States there is now a contradiction in public policy. When the Wagner Act of 1935 was adopted, collective bargaining was assumed to be THE vehicle for worker participation and voice. Workers did not have to choose to be represented. But their choice was supposed to be unimpeded by management. Thus, alternative forms of nonunion representation were seen as suspect and viewed as a probable sign of managerial interference with worker choice about unionizing.

Much has changed since 1935. The Great Depression, a major factor in the passage of the Wagner Act, has become a distant memory. During the 1930s, workers with jobs had few labor market alternatives. Bargaining power was therefore tilted toward employers since management controlled access to scarce jobs. The social safety net that exists today, including unemployment insurance, was just being created. Employers could say "if you don't like it here, go somewhere else" with full knowledge that there was nowhere else to go.

Although there have been ups and downs of the business cycle since the Great Depression—and although concerns about corporate restructuring and downsizing certainly still lead to job insecurity—pressure for employee voice is not what it once was. Many workers who are nonunion would undoubtedly choose to be union-represented if a completely free choice were offered. But, if poll data are to be believed, many workers would not. Such nonunion-oriented employees would like some degree of voice but through mechanisms other than traditional collective bargaining.

This volume, edited by Bruce E. Kaufman and Daphne Gottlieb Taras, explores such alternative mechanisms, taking a multifaceted approach. The various chapter contributors look at nonunion representation in historical perspective and in international perspective. An historical viewpoint is always valuable since it illuminates the path by which current realities came to be. And the international perspective is valuable because it focuses attention on other options. In the matter of employee representation, as in many other aspects of the employment relationship, there is not necessarily one right way of carrying out a critical function.

As the editors note in their introduction, declining unionization has led to calls for legal remedies of various sorts. But even if no legislation is enacted, the legal system itself provides an alternative form of employee voice. The drop in the unionization rate in the United States has been accompanied by a rise in various types of workplace-related litigation. Unfortunately, lawsuits are a crude tool for providing employee representation and voice. Thus, if options can be developed privately to provide satisfactory representation, both sides of the employment relationship—management and employee—will benefit. The Kaufman-Taras volume should be a major reference in the future as issues of employee voice and representation are debated.

Nonunion Employee Representation

1

Introduction

Bruce E. Kaufman and Daphne Gottlieb Taras

The subject of this volume, nonunion employee representation (NER), until recently has languished in relative obscurity and neglect, particularly in Canada and the United States. Indeed, we are unaware of any book published in several decades in either country that deals explicitly with NER, while journal articles in business and the social sciences on this topic are sparse in number, nearly all historical in nature, and usually focused on the American experience with "company unions" of the 1915–35 period. When the National Labor Relations Act (NLRA, or Wagner Act) banned company unions and most other forms of NER in the United States in 1935, the subject abruptly passed from a major issue of contemporary research and policy debate to a peripheral topic in the field of labor history.

NER has returned as an important and contentious issue in both academic and policymaking circles. Four trends and developments of recent years have infused new life into the subject. The first is the marked long-term decline in the organized labor movement in the United States and, to a lesser degree, Canada and most other industrialized nations in the world. Certainly in the U.S.–Canada context, independent trade unions have for five decades or more been established by law and public policy as the principal and even preferred organizational form for representation of employee interests. When one-third or more

of U.S. private-sector workers in the 1940s and 1950s belonged to unions, and an even larger proportion in Canada, making unions the primary or even sole agency for collective employee representation did not seem unduly narrow or restrictive. But in the late 1990s only slightly more than 10 percent of private-sector employees in the United States are union members, and the Canadian private-sector figures have declined to fewer than 22 percent. Concern is growing over the large and apparently widening gap between the substantial proportion of the workforce that desires representation at work and the dwindling proportion that has such representation through membership in independent labor unions (Freeman and Rogers 1993). There are two main proposed public policy responses to this "representation gap" (Commission on the Future of Worker-Management Relations 1994). The first is to bolster the membership and coverage of unions, both by changing the laws to make organization swifter and surer and by devising more effective union organizing strategies; the second is encouragement of alternative, nonunion forms of representation in the workplace. This second option, such as joint industrial councils, peer-review dispute-resolution panels, joint labor-management safety committees, European-style works councils, and nonunion professional employee associations, is the subject of this volume.

3

A second trend having much the same effect is the popularization of new forms of management and work organization, variously referred to as participative management, employee involvement, and the "high performance" workplace (Lawler 1986; Lawler, Albers, and Ledford 1992; Levine 1995). In years past, management tended to organize work in a top-down, "command-and-control" system. At the top of the organizational pyramid were high-level executives who designed strategy and established broad company policy directives. In the middle of the pyramid were gradations of staff and management who executed policy, supervised shop floor employees, and reported operational results and problems back up the chain of command. At the bottom were the mass of employees who followed orders and produced goods and services.

Although popular with managers and economically successful for a number of decades, this traditional form of organization increasingly is regarded as anachronistic in an era of heightened global and domestic competition, information and skill-intensive production systems, shortened product and technology life cycles, and greater employee expectation of involvement and satisfaction at work. As a result, leading companies have been developing and implementing new work systems, often called high-performance workplaces. The traditional command-and-control system has given way to decentralized decision making, team forms of production, and enhanced opportunities for employee involvement and participation. In most medium- to large-size work situations, this participation necessarily must be representational in nature for reasons of cost and efficiency. Traditional collective bargaining provides one mechanism for such representation and involvement, but many business executives have neither the basic inclination nor economic incen-

tives to recognize and bargain with trade unions, nor do the majority of workers express a desire for union representation. As a consequence, interest in and experimentation with alternative nonunion representational structures has proliferated in recent years among both management advocates of employee involvement and labor advocates of industrial democracy. By promoting greater opportunities for employee voice in nonunion situations, these representational groups not only serve management interests in improved productivity and communication, but also ensure that employee interests in equitable terms and conditions of employment are factored into management decision making.

A third, and uniquely American, development that has given much greater saliency to the subject of nonunion representation is the ongoing political debate over reform of the NLRA (Estreicher 1994; LeRoy 1996). The Wagner Act contains statutory restrictions that have had the effect of banning most forms of nonunion employee representation. As stated in the NLRA, it is an unfair labor practice for management to participate in, dominate, or interfere with a labor organization. Forbidden forms of labor organization include various committees, teams, and councils that are of a representational nature and are created, financed, or operated by the employer and involve bilateral discussions about the terms and conditions of employment. Table 1.1 includes the relevant sections of the Wagner Act that pertain to NER. For comparison purposes, Table 1.1 also contains the provisions relating to NER from the U.S. Railway Labor Act (RLA), and an amalgam of twelve Canadian statutes, blended for convenience into what we term "the Canadian approach."

Critics of the NLRA (and, to a lesser degree, the RLA) claim that its strictures inhibit the abil-

Table 1.1

Statutory Treatments of Nonunion Representation in the United States and Canada

Statute	Definition	Prohibition
National Labor Relations Act (Wagner Act, 1935)	Section 2(5). A labor organization is "any organization of any kind, or any agency or employee representation committee or plan in which employees participate and which exists for the purpose, in whole or in part, of deal-ing with employers concerning griev-ances, labor disputes, wages, rates of pay, hours of employment, or conditions of work."	Section 8(a)(2). It is an unfair labor practice for an employer "to dominate or interfere with the formation or administration of any labor organization or contribute financial or other support to it."
Railway Labor Act (1926)	Section 1. "Representatives" means only persons or entities "designated either by a carrier or group of carriers or by its or their employees to act for it or them."	Section 2(2). Representatives for both management and labor "shall be designated by the respective parties and without interference, influence, or coercion by either party over the designation of representatives of the other; and neither party shall in any way interfere with, influence, or coerce the other in its choice of representatives."

Section 3(4). It shall be unlawful for any carrier to interfere in any way with the organization of its employees, or to use the funds of the carrier in maintaining or assisting or contributing to any labor organization, labor representative, or other agency of collective bargaining. |
| Canadian Approach (blending 12 statutes: federal, public service, and 10 provincial labor codes) | Definitions Sections: "Trade union," "bargaining agent," "union," "association of employees," or "labor organization" means an entity that has as one of its purposes the regulation of relations between employers and employees through collective bargaining. | Unfair Labor Practice Sections: It is an unfair labor practice for any employer or employer representative to participate in or interfere with the formation or administration of a trade union, or representation of employees in a trade union.

Prohibitions against Certification Sections. Labor boards (or in Quebec, the commissioner-general) shall not certify a trade union if it is employer dominated. |

ity of American companies to form and operate employee involvement and participation programs in nonunion workplaces and thereby harm both national competitiveness and cooperative employer-employee relations. For several years running, a coalition of Republican and conservative Democrats in Congress have sought to enact legislation, popularly known as the "TEAM Act," that would weaken significantly the NLRA's Section 8(a)(2) restrictions on "dominated" labor organizations. TEAM Act legislation was passed by both houses of Congress in 1996, was vetoed by President Clinton, and was reintroduced by its congressional supporters. The ongoing debate engendered by this proposed legislation, as well as that precipitated by the hearings and final report of the Clinton-appointed Commission on the Future of Worker-Management Relations (Dunlop Commission), have put the subject of NER squarely on the front burner of the American labor policy debate.

Proponents of the law claim Sections 2(5) and 8(a)(2) are crucial to protecting employee free choice in matters of union representation by preventing employers from manipulating and coercing workers through "sham" company unions. There also are those who agree that the NLRA treatment is problematic, but are gravely concerned that a movement to change the NLRA with respect to nonunion representation will merely allow management to lawfully employ new techniques to defeat unions. Another group would consider a change to the NLRA only if it was accompanied by more sweeping reform to the act in ways that would facilitate an easier transition to unionization where it is desired by employees.

By contrast, Canadians are not engaged in a similar debate. Canadian legislation, which observers would consider similar in most respects to the Wagner Act, diverged in its treatment of nonunion representation. NER is legal in Canada provided it is not designed to thwart union organizing. In Table 1.1, we blended a variety of Canadian statutes to demonstrate the Canadian approach. At first glance, it appears that the Canadian treatment is quite similar to the American. In Canada, it also is an unfair labor practice for management to participate in, dominate, or interfere with a union. A union that has been influenced by management cannot be certified as a bona fide bargaining agent and will not enjoy the protections of any collective bargaining statutes. Where Canada deviates from the Wagner Act is in the definition of a labor organization. A labor organization means a union, or at the least, a collective entity whose purpose includes regulation of relations through collective bargaining. Management must not interfere with a union, but management may deal openly with groups of nonunion employees on any issue of concern, including the terms and conditions of employment. It is not an unfair labor practice to run a NER plan because Canadian labor boards do not have the reach given to the U.S. National Labor Relations Board by the wording of NLRA Section 2(5). The critical distinction between Canada and the United States rests in the definitions sections of the statutes and not in any departure from the American Section 8(a)(2).

Aside from the contribution the Canadian approach can make in identifying an alternative wording to the NLRA, the Canadian-American divergence has provided scholars with a unique "natural experiment" that hitherto has remained unexploited. Here we have neighboring countries—in broad strokes similar in social, political, and economic institutions and labor policy approaches—that diverged greatly on NER within the corpus of similar labor laws. We think this provides a remarkable opportunity to shed considerable light on issues that otherwise would remain only topics of speculation. For example, what would have happened to the U.S. nonunion employee representation movement if the Wagner Act ban had not been enacted, and would union membership today be higher or lower?

Finally, a fourth trend that has worked to raise interest in NER is the important role that such representation plays in the industrial relations systems of other major industrial countries outside North America (Rogers and Streeck 1995; Wever 1995). Of most relevance in this regard is the European system of works councils, which are found in countries such as Germany, the Netherlands, Italy, and Norway. These councils typically are mandated or highly encouraged by law. They are plant- or establishment-level bodies of elected worker representatives that exist to promote dialogue and negotiation between management and employees, and formally are independent of trade unions (although the two often have a close relationship). Less well known, but also of interest for a North American audience, are the several forms of NER found in Japanese companies.

Although works councils and various forms of NER have existed in these countries for many years, they have captured noticeably greater attention in North America in the past decade. Certainly a major impetus is the widespread conviction that an important determinant of competitive success in the global economy is each nation's system of industrial relations practices and institutions, a perception that has fueled interest in learning more about alternative systems of employee representation and their impact on important economic and social outcomes. Also important is the Works Council Directive issued in 1996 by the policymaking body of the European Union, which mandates that all member countries establish joint management-labor consultative bodies in large enterprises. In 1997 the Labor government in Britain accepted these accords, requiring implementation within British firms by the end of the century (Younson 1998).

Thus, the "representation gap," new managerial practices, American public policy debate, and developments abroad have led to a convergence of interest in NER.

Employee Representation: Union and Nonunion Alternatives

This book is about collective representation. We use the term representation to mean that employees have the ability and venue to make their collective needs and opinions known to management. One or more persons must act in an agency function for other employees and communicate, negotiate and/or bargain with company managers over workplace issues of mutual interest and concern. Many companies—even those with high-performance worksites—have no form of employee representation, either because they choose not to as a matter of company policy or because they have not been organized by a labor union.

Employee representation in North America takes one of two basic forms: union or nonunion. The two systems diverge dramatically in a number of key respects.

In a union setting, employees are represented by an independent labor organization, typically a local affiliate of a national or international trade union. In the United States and Canada, the union becomes the exclusive, legally-recognized representational agent of the employees only after it has demonstrated that a majority of the employees desire that it serve this function. In the United States, this typically occurs when a union wins a majority vote of the employees in the designated bargaining unit in a representation election supervised by the National Labor Relations Board (or National Mediation Board in the transportation industries covered under the Railway Labor Act). The Canadian picture is complicated by the decentralization of labor law in the form of separate provincial and federal government statues. In all Canadian jurisdictions, unions may gain legal recognition through board-supervised votes, and in some jurisdictions, it is possible for unions to become certified to represent the bargaining unit after demonstration of a majority of authorization cards signed by the workers.

Nonunion forms of employee representation, by contrast, usually are created, structured, and operated by the employer. They are not independent labor organizations but, instead, are one part of a firm's larger system of personnel/human resource management practices. They can be established and terminated at the employer's discretion and in the United States and Canada require neither formal employee approval in a government-supervised representation election nor a grant of recognition by a labor board. In the prohibitions section of Table 1.1, it is clear that public policymakers in Canada never contemplated that nonunion representation would exist within the statutory framework accorded to relations between unions and management.

Labor unions and employer-created representational bodies also fundamentally differ in their structure, operation, and methods. Local union affiliates, for example, usually are chartered and governed by a national or international labor organization. They have written constitutions, elected officers, elected or appointed shop stewards, membership dues, and an independent treasury. They engage in bargaining with employers over wages, hours, and other terms and conditions of employment. They negotiate and sign often lengthy written contracts with employers. Unless expressly forbidden by law, they may strike to win their demands. They also have a formal grievance process that culminates in binding arbitration of disputes arising during the term of the collective agreement.

Nonunion forms of representation in North America are quite different, although some of the more formal arrangements mirror in a number of respects features of bona fide labor unions. Most often, employer-created representational groups are relatively informal, although some are quite well developed. Only a minority have some kind of written charter, constitution, or set of bylaws, while the majority are established and operated with only informal written policy guidelines, a brief written description in an employee handbook, or verbal directives from management. Very few charge any form of dues or initiation fee, and many have no official officers other than an appointed team leader or plant human resources manager.

The structure and purpose of nonunion representational groups are considerably more heterogeneous than is the case with labor unions. Many are limited to only the employees in a particular work area or department of a plant, such as a quality circle or safety committee (the former may or may not be representational in nature, while the latter typically is). In other instances, nonunion councils or committees represent all the employees in an individual plant, mill, or worksite, and on rarer occasions all employees across a large division or entire multiplant company. Almost never, however, do the membership and activities of these groups extend beyond the boundaries of an individual company, unlike many labor unions, which explicitly try to coordinate bargaining and labor standards across firms.

The breadth of issues dealt with by the typical nonunion representational body also differs considerably from the typical labor union. As implied by the terms "quality circle," "safety committee," and "peer review panel," the mission of many nonunion representational groups is to deal with one specific, narrowly defined process or activity. Common examples arise from production and quality concerns, personnel/human resource issues related to safety, dispute resolution, or information sharing. Nonunion representational groups may also handle issues related to traditional bread-and-butter concerns of employees, such as wages, benefits, hours and job security less frequently. There are also instances, although this occurs particularly in Canada, where NER forums handle more issues than would be the case in comparable unionized workplaces and assist in the development and implementation of a wide range of human resource and productivity-enhancing initiatives.

Issues are treated differently in union and nonunion approaches. Nonunion representation plans are much more likely to involve mutual discussion and deliberation between the parties than overt negotiation and bargaining. Nonunion forums adopt problem-solving approaches and usually work by consensus. The taking of votes, or articulation of rigid positions, tends to be discouraged for fear of polarizing dissent between employees and managers.

This last point raises a fundamental difference between union and nonunion forms of representation. A basic premise of trade unions and labor laws is that, to a significant degree, the interests of employers and employees conflict (Hyman 1997). The concern is that in the absence of collective bargaining, individual employees cannot amass sufficient bargaining power to secure their interests; as a result, there might be undesirably low rates of pay, excessive work hours, unsafe working conditions, and arbitrary and unfair discipline. The purpose of a union, then, is to protect and advance the interests of employees, a process that might introduce significantly more adversarialism into employer-employee relations than would be countenanced by management in a nonunion system. Exacerbating the element of conflict is the use by both unions and management of various coercive tactics to win collective bargaining objectives, including strikes and lockouts, and work slowdowns or speed-ups.

One of the fundamental reasons that employers create nonunion organizations is to avoid what they regard as the negative features of trade unions and, at the same time, attain more of the positive outcomes that flow from in-house forms of worker-management cooperation. While leery of unions, employers also recognize that collective forms of worker organization can contribute to a number of positive outcomes. For example, NER promotes improved two-way communication between management and shop floor employees, serves as an organizational vehicle to increase worker participation and involvement in the enterprise, provides a mechanism for identifying areas of management practice or policy that need improvement, and rapidly surfaces employee complaints and grievances. NER can be more acutely sensitive to local issues than a large national labor organization. Management also hopes for higher morale and loyalty among employees. NER is well suited to the types of employees who wish to participate in the enterprise, but for whom unions provide little appeal.

Critics claim that these purported benefits of NER are substantially overstated in most cases and usually work only to the advantage of employers. The basic problem, they say, is that employers deliberately structure nonunion representational bodies in ways that render them relatively powerless and unable to pose a threat to management interests. We hear of many nicknames for NER from this perspective, including "toothless dog," "donkey council," and "pet bear." Proponents of NER argue that a closer look reveals that many nonunion groups exert real influence and win numerous improvements at the workplace for employees that they otherwise would not obtain. This independent power comes from two sources: management's belief that these employee groups will contribute to increased employee loyalty, commitment, and hard work only if the workers also get visible, tangible benefits; and management's fear that dissatisfied workers will turn to bona fide trade unions if management does not act in an honest, equitable manner. The union threat generates positive outcomes for workers. In this regard, the name "pet bear" is most revealing: "To keep a pet bear in your house," said one senior Canadian industrial relations manager, "you have to keep sweets in your pocket and never turn your back for a second" (Taras and Copping 1996).

Trade unionists and other critics of NER stoutly reject that on balance there are any net benefits and criticize any purported advantages as wishful thinking or employer propaganda. Critics note, for example, that companies create NER forums only when it is in the interest of companies, while employees are unable to initiate nonunion representation systems when they clash with company objectives or philosophies. Thus, what is touted as greater worker-management "cooperation" is really a facade behind which lurks continued unequal bargaining power and inferior terms and conditions of employment for workers. That nonunion forms of representation are relatively powerless to protect employee interests is further demonstrated, say the critics, by their lack of in-

dependent financial resources, absence of a credible strike threat, negligible access to outside legal counsel or professional negotiators, and the vulnerability of employee representatives to employer retaliation with any attempt to deal over a truly contentious dispute.

NER also has adverse social and economic effects, say the critics. For example, because nonunion representational groups are limited to individual plants or companies, they cannot stabilize or standardize wages and labor conditions across firms in a particular product market, maintain aggregate purchasing power by making sure that wages grow in line with increased profits, or offset the power of business interests in the legislative and regulatory process. Indeed, without resources of their own, the only time that nonunion groups can enter the political arena is to lobby on behalf of employer interests. Finally, it is charged that the main reason employers establish nonunion employee groups is to thwart organizing by outside labor organizations, an action that violates widely accepted legal and ethical principles of freedom of association and due process in the workplace. For all these reasons, critics of nonunion forms of employee representation feel they are aptly called "sham organizations" and "sucker's unions."

Unlike Canada and the United States, many European countries make provision for the establishment of works councils in individual plants. Works councils offer, in effect, a "middle course" in employee representation. As noted earlier, these bodies are organized on an individual plant basis without regard to unionization, but at the same time employers are required by law to recognize and deal with the councils upon request of their employees and to discuss and gain their approval regarding changes in a wide range of in-plant employment practices. Although a seemingly attractive mix of union and nonunion systems of representation, often non-European business people and trade unionists express serious reservations. To many North American business executives, for example, works councils are excessively bureaucratic, cumbersome, and political. To North American unionists, who are accustomed to a system that grants exclusivity to union representation, works councils frequently are seen as pale substitutes for real industrial democracy, potential threats to union organization and bargaining success, and vehicles for coopting employee discontent before it can be transmuted into genuine worker power.

Then, finally, North Americans know much less about the various forms of employee representation that exist in other industrial countries. One case in point is the United Kingdom, where nonunion forms of representation have only recently appeared in any number—due in part to the recent arrival of a number of Japanese manufacturers. And then there is Japan itself. Approximately one-third of the Japanese workforce is represented by labor unions, but often these unions are "enterprise unions," which encompass only a particular firm, represent lower-level managers as well as wage earners, and emphasize cooperation and consensus over adversarial bargaining and strikes. Among nonunion companies, a number have voluntarily created various forms of employee representation committees and councils, but these neither are mandated by law nor are employers required to deal with them.

The conclusion that emerges from this brief survey is one of great variation across nations and cultures in the kind and extent of employee representation, as well as significant changes over time in the mix of representational forms in a number of individual countries. Also apparent are the significant similarities and differences that emerge when comparing the structures, purposes, and methods of the two major forms of employee representation in North America—union and nonunion. Considerable divergence of opinion exists about their relative advantages and shortcomings for employers, employees, and the broader economy and society. Probably the only thing that can safely be said is that the debate over alternative forms of employee representation and their associated legal regimes will intensify in coming years in the respective worlds of academic research, business and trade union practices, and public policy, both in North America and other parts of the world.

Overview of the Book: Issues, Research Design, and Philosophy

Given this brief introduction to the subject, we next want to describe the major issues to be addressed in the chapters that follow; explain the research design that motivated the choice of topics and focus of analysis; and discuss the intellectual philosophy that guided our selection of authors, choice of topics, and editorial policy regarding alternative perspectives and opinions on this controversial subject.

Issues and Research Design. Since little research of modern vintage has been done on NER, the range of important and unanswered issues relating to practice and policy is broad indeed— a fact reflected in the sizable number of chapters in this volume. Following this introduction there are eighteen academic chapters, eleven practitioner contributions, and a concluding chapter. We chose to emphasize coverage of three different dimensions of NER: history, contemporary practice, and policy, and to utilize a comparative, cross-country research design.

An emphasis on the history of NER might at

first seem an odd choice, since it is the one area of the subject that has been extensively investigated, and upon which a rough consensus appears to exist. After our own in-depth review of this literature, we became convinced that there is much more that can and needs to be said about the historical dimension. Here is why.

We believe that a thorough, balanced assessment of the present-day potentialities and pitfalls of NER hinges critically on an accurate knowledge and evenhanded interpretation of the historical record. For example, were early twentieth-century nonunion plans largely motivated by antiunion animus, or did employers instead create them primarily as a means to promote employee involvement and fair dealing? Were these plans ineffective, employer-manipulated "shams," or did they provide genuine voice and a demonstrable record of achievement for both employees and employers? Finally, what were the reasons behind the statutory treatment of NER? Why was the Wagner Act so forceful in rejecting the possibility of NER, while the Canadian approach allowed NER practices to persist? The extant historical literature falls considerably short of providing the needed answers. The problem areas are several.

First, American labor historians have done the great bulk of historical research on NER. While ably done and richly detailed, this literature nonetheless suffers from shortcomings that together result in an overly negative assessment of NER. The focus of labor history, as the name suggests, tends to favor the worker side of the employment relationship and, most particularly, the role and development of the organized union movement. The role of employee representation in management thought and practice (for example, as an instrument of strategic human resource management) is

slighted in favor of its impact—typically thought to be quite negative—on the union movement. There also exist studies, we note, commissioned or sponsored by companies that are unduly celebratory of the in-house NER systems (e.g., Chase 1947; Kline 1920), presenting unrealistically fawning accounts that cannot withstand serious scrutiny.

A second problem is that nearly all of the historical literature focuses on the United States. But these plans also appeared in Canada at approximately the same time (1915 to 1920) and then rose and fell in numbers and social approval in more or less lock-step fashion with their American counterparts through the mid-1930s. Very little in-depth analysis of the early Canadian experience with employee representation has been done, despite the obvious opportunity to learn more about the dissemination of these plans and set the context for some Canadian companies' continued use of NER.

Third, and most startling, is the almost complete neglect in the historical literature of the dramatically different fortunes of NER in the two countries in the post-1935 period. While the United States banned most forms of NER with the passage of the Wagner Act, Canada continued to allow employers to maintain and operate these plans. Hence, history has provided scholars with a unique opportunity to perform comparative research on two countries with industrial relations regimes that are broadly similar except for their notably different treatment of nonunion employee representation groups. Such research can shed light on a number of interesting questions. What, for example, might have happened to the American NER movement had the Wagner Act not contained the restrictive Sections 2(5) and 8(a)(2)? Would NER have remained a niche phenomenon, or grown in numbers and influence? What would have been the relationship between NER and the organized labor movement? A major purpose of this volume is to utilize the natural experiment created by the divergent histories of the two countries to begin formulating responses to these important questions.

Not only is little comparative U.S.–Canada research available, but there also exists a dearth of comparative analyses among other industrial countries. Several previous studies have noted that the subject of NER suddenly burst into prominence at roughly the same time—the years surrounding World War I—in most of the industrial countries of the world. But little beyond commentary on this fact has to date been published, a lacuna this volume makes an initial step toward filling.

The first five chapters of the volume are devoted to the historical record on the origins and evolution of NER. There are three U.S. chapters and two Canadian chapters. Bruce Kaufman provides an extensive review and reevaluation of the American experience in the pre–Wagner Act years. Daniel Nelson analyzes the evolution of thinking on the part of the American union movement. Sanford Jacoby examines the transition from "company unions" into "independent labor unions" after the Wagner Act. Attention then switches to Canada, where in the fifth chapter Laurel Sefton McDowell provides a thorough review of the birth of the Canadian employee representation movement in the 1910s and traces the waxing and waning of its fortunes through the 1940s. In the final chapter of the history set Daphne Gottlieb Taras reviews the development of labor law on NER in Canada, examines the current status of a sample of Canada's early employee representation plans, and demonstrates that some prominent Canadian companies practice

precisely the types of NER that the Wagner Act banned in the United States.

The historical experience with NER also is covered in several later chapters, although it is not their primary focus. In particular, each of the three "international" chapters on Germany (by John Addison, Claus Schnabel, and Joachim Wagner), Japan (by Motohiro Morishima and Tsuyoshi Tsuru), and the United Kingdom and Australia (by Paul Gollan) provide insight into the origins and development of NER in these countries.

We now come to the second and third major issues of the volume: the contemporary practice of NER and the nature of public policy toward it. We chose to make these major themes of the volume for several reasons.

First, there is a great need to explore and extend a largely neglected subject in the now burgeoning literature on employee involvement and participation (EIP) programs. Numerous studies describe the reasons companies adopt EIP, its various forms, and its benefits and costs. So far, however, very few studies examine the role of representation in the structure and delivery of EIP and even fewer have investigated the extent to which companies make use of various types of representational committees, teams, councils, and so on. But, we think, it is an interesting and timely issue both from an academic and practitioner perspective to understand better why and under what conditions an organization will want to implement EIP and, concomitantly, utilize some form of employee representational body to help structure and deliver the program.

This consideration immediately leads to what has become a major subject of debate in American legal and policymaking circles. In their search for a competitive edge, American companies are considering greater employee involvement and an increased willingness to incorporate employee input into strategic thinking. Great concern is voiced in certain quarters that the nation's labor law, and most particularly Sections 2(5) and 8(a)(2) of the NLRA, hamstring the ability of nonunion companies to implement EIP and other high-performance work practices effectively lest they run afoul of the law's restrictions on "dominated" labor organizations. The contentious 1992 NLRB *Electromation, Inc.* decision has served as an exemplar in this debate. The NLRB's ruling that forced the company to disband employee committees in the aftermath of an unfair labor practice complaint by the Teamster's Union, as well as several subsequent cases, fueled a major controversy over the extent to which American labor law impedes legitimate efforts of nonunion companies to promote EIP.

The American law is relatively clear, but its implications for American managerial practice are not. Studies are urgently needed that provide hard empirical evidence on questions such as these: Are nonunion companies actually constrained in their ability to respond to changes in managerial philosophy and the challenges of global competition? If yes, how serious a problem is this? Are these concerns acting as a subterfuge for weakening the NLRA's protection of employee free choice in the matter of union organization? The volume provides such evidence through several field-level studies that examine the interface between EIP in nonunion companies, the role played therein by employee representation, and the degree to which the NLRA is a significant constraint on employers. Particularly noteworthy in this regard is the inclusion of a chapter on EIP programs in Canada by Anil Verma. Since Canada does not have impediments to NER, we can infer that differences in the extent, scope, and function of such representation in Canadian companies, as compared to American, reflect the influence of divergent statutory treatments of NER.

We begin our scrutiny of contemporary issues with an attempt to build a firmer conceptual and theoretical foundation. Toward that end, we commissioned academic researchers from three different disciplines—Bruce Kaufman and David Levine from economics, Tove Hammer from organizational theory and behavior, and Samuel Estreicher from law—to use the extant theory of their respective fields to derive insights and predictions about NER.

Next come seven empirical chapters on NER in the United States and Canada, all by academics. To set the stage, Seymour Martin Lipset and Noah Meltz present the first-ever quantitative evidence on the extent of NER in both Canada and the United States, gathered from a recently completed survey in the two countries. Then, a discussion of contemporary American experience begins with the chapter by Bruce Kaufman, David Lewin, and John Fossum. They investigate through field research and detailed case study evidence the extent to which the NLRA appears to constrain the ability of nonunion companies to structure and operate advanced EIP programs. Next is the chapter by Michael LeRoy, which also examines the impact of the NLRA, but with a particular focus on the scope and operation of employee teams in nonunion companies. The third American chapter is by Roy Helfgott, who examines a relatively new and specialized forum of employee voice—diversity caucuses—and the lessons they have for NER.

The volume also features three empirical chapters using the Canadian setting. Daphne Gottlieb Taras begins with the results of an in-depth study of the Joint Industrial Council at Imperial Oil Limited. This formal and highly developed representation plan, long assumed defunct in American circles, has been in continuous operation in Canada for over seven decades. Of particular interest in her chapter are the bargaining relationships and tactics that are used in a complex and enduring NER plan. Next is the chapter by Anil Verma, which parallels the Kaufman, Lewin, and Fossum chapter in that he too examines the role and scope of employee representation in advanced EI programs. His objective was to determine to what extent NER is more frequently and/or extensively done in Canada in the absence of American NLRA-like legal impediments. Finally, Richard Chaykowski provides a detailed examination of the history and performance of NER in the Canadian federal public sector, with particular emphasis on the evolving relationship between the coexistent systems of union and nonunion representation.

The set of academic chapters is completed by the three on NER in Germany, Japan, and the United Kingdom and Australia. We thought it important to examine contemporary practice and policy regarding NER beyond the borders of North America. There is potentially much to learn from other countries in Europe and Asia, even though their economic, social, and political systems differ from our own, and from each other. John Addison, Claus Schnabel, and Joachim Wagner provide a detailed account of the origins and development of the German works council system and an in-depth review and evaluation of the empirical evidence on the outcomes of that system vis-à-vis both economic performance and improved employer-employee relations. They find, in particular, that works councils are associated with higher wages, lower profits, and reduced turnover. They conclude that the economic case for works councils is decidedly mixed and certainly less persuasive than claimed by some of their proponents.

To date virtually nothing has been written on Japan's NER in the English language. Filling this gap is the chapter by Motohiro Morishima and Tsuyoshi Tsuru, who first describe the various forms of NER found in Japan and their structure, function, and status under Japanese labor law. Morishima and Tsuru then present results from an analysis of several recent survey datasets regarding the impact of NER in Japanese companies on outcomes such as productivity, wages, and employee satisfaction. They find that while NER does strengthen employee voice, it does not lead to improvements in either employee separation rates or reported satisfaction with the company.

The third international chapter by Paul Gollan on the United Kingdom and Australia yields evidence from the Anglo-Saxon system of nation-states and industrial relations systems. He provides for each country an overview of the historical development of NER, its current status and treatment, the place of NER in contemporary industrial relations, and findings on the relative effectiveness and performance of NER as revealed in recent surveys and quantitative studies.

There are of course many other selections we might have made besides these three, but each of our international chapters offers evidence of NER within systems whose union-management relations are relatively accessible to a North American audience and whose national contributions to the global economy are widely acknowledged.

In an unusual and, we think, innovative step, we also asked a number of practitioners and policymakers to write eleven short chapters on the twin issues of contemporary practice and policy regarding NER. These people have been "in the trenches" and thus have firsthand knowledge of the subject that is an important complement to the evidence assembled from academic research.

The practitioner/policymaker section begins with three essays by employers and managers. Chris Fuldner, chief executive officer of EFCO Manufacturing Co. in Monet, Missouri, reports on his company's system of nonunion employee committees and teams and discusses the charges subsequently filed against EFCO for violation of NLRA Section 8(a)(2) and the lengthy litigation that ensued. Next is a chapter by David Boone, manager of Production Operations for Imperial Oil, giving his perspective on Imperial's purposes in encouraging NER and the pros and cons of the Joint Industrial Council system in Canada. A third employer essay is by Mark Harshaw, then acting director of human resources for one of Canada's largest steel companies, Dofasco. Harshaw describes Dofasco's long history with a type of NER known in Canada as "the Dofasco way."

Next are three essays by employees who serve as worker representatives or delegates in NER systems. The first is by Cathy Cone of Delta Air Lines, headquartered in Atlanta, Georgia. She serves as one of seven employee representatives on a companywide employee committee called the Personnel Board Council. The second essay is by Rod Chiesa and Ken Rhyason of Imperial Oil, who are top elected employee delegates on the company's Joint Industrial Council. The third essay in this cluster is by Kevin MacDougall of the Royal Canadian Mounted Police, who serves as a full-time employee representative on the RCMP's Division Staff Relations Representation Program.

Representatives of organized labor contribute two essays. The first is by Reg Basken, until recently vice president of the Canadian-based Communication, Energy and Paperworkers Union. He has had considerable experience in dealing with NER in Canada, and he provides a candid assessment of their purposes, strengths, weaknesses, and potential as a source of new union membership. He reviews union organizing strategies that work to attract employees represented by nonunion systems. The second essay is by Jonathan Hiatt and Lawrence Gold, general counsel and assistant general council, respectively, of the AFL-CIO. They explain why, from the perspective of the AFL-CIO, employer-created "company unions" are neither socially desirable nor serve to meet employees' interests, and why the NLRA does not adversely interfere with legitimate employee involvement programs at nonunion companies.

The way in which American law has been crafted to ban company unions poses intriguing problems for labor law practitioners. In his commentary, Andrew Kramer of Jones, Day, Reavis & Pogue describes some of the difficulties faced by attorneys when advising their clients of the pitfalls of operating nonunion representation systems.

The volume concludes with two essays on public policy. John Raudabaugh is a former member of the U.S. National Labor Relations Board, and he wrote an opinion in the *Electromation, Inc.* decision. He reflects on the events leading up to *Electromation, Inc.* and provides an assessment of the key policy issues involved in the case, and offers recommendations for future public policy. Andrew Sims, a former labor board chair in Alberta and head of a recent major Canadian federal government task force into labor law reform in the federal arena, expresses his thoughts on the current needs of nonunion employees and the bigger picture of crafting public policy to incorporate the needs of both union and nonunion employees in the face of major changes in the nature of employment.

Philosophy and Values

We end this introduction with a brief statement of the philosophy and values that guided our choice of topics, authors, and perspectives. This is important, we believe, so that readers can more accurately assess and evaluate the content and conclusions of the book, as well as to allay possible fears that the volume is intended to promote a partisan position either for or against nonunion employee representation.

Our conviction as editors is that the topic of NER is of growing importance in North American industrial relations and merits a more detailed, analytical investigation. That the topic is so highly controversial should attract, rather than dissuade, scholarly attention. In putting the volume together, we have striven to present a diverse but balanced set of views and opinions. Toward that end, we carefully selected authors who are well known, respected, and representative of a range of disciplines, countries, and policy positions. We also sought to achieve a balance between theory and practice by inviting academics and practitioners and policymakers to participate.

This volume by no means is the last word on nonunion employee representation, but it does, we think, materially advance the state of knowledge and debate on the subject.

Acknowledgments

These articles originated from a conference on Nonunion Employee Representation we co-organized in Banff, Canada, in September 1997. The conference was generously funded by the Labour-Management Partnerships Program of Human Resources Development Canada, Imperial Oil Limited, the John M. Olin Institute for Employment Practice and Policy, Industrial Relations Counselors, Inc., the Industrial Relations Research Group at the University of Calgary, and the Faculty of Management at the University of Calgary. The views expressed in this volume do not necessarily reflect those of our sponsors. In bringing together a large and international group of scholars, practitioners, and policymakers, the conference provided fertile terrain for the exchange of views and the advancement of knowledge. We gratefully acknowledge the vital role played by the Banff Conference sponsors and participants.

Earlier versions of chapters 1, 2, 6, 13, 17, and 18 appeared in a "Symposium on Nonunion Employee Representation" in *Journal of Labor Research* 20, no 1 (Winter 1999). A different version of chapter 4 will appear in *Industrial Relations* (forthcoming). An early version of chapter 11 was published in Samuel Estreicher's edited volume *Employee Representation: Proceedings of New York University's 50th Annual Conference on Labor* (Kluwer Law 1998). We thank these journals and editors for permissions to publish these materials in our volume.

References

Chase, Stuart. 1947. *A Generation of Industrial Peace: Thirty Years of Labor Relations at Standard Oil Company (N.J.).* New Jersey: Standard Oil Company.

Commission on the Future of Worker-Management Relations. 1994. *Report and Recommendations.* Washington, D.C.

Estreicher, Samuel. 1994. "Employee Involvement and the 'Company Union' Prohibition: The Case for Partial Repeal of Section 8(a)(2) of the NLRA." *New York University Law Review* 69 (April): 125–161.

Freeman, Richard, and Joel Rogers. 1993. "Who Speaks for Us? Employee Representation in a Nonunion Labor Market." In *Employee Representation: Alternatives and Future Directions*, ed. Bruce E. Kaufman and Morris M. Kleiner, pp. 13–80. Madison, Wis.: Industrial Relations Research Association.

Hyman, Richard. 1997. "The Future of Employee Representation." *British Journal of Industrial Relations* 35: 309–336.

Kline, Burton. 1920. "Employee Representation in Standard Oil." *Factory and Industrial Management*, May, pp. 355–360.

Lawler, Edward. 1986. *High Involvement Management*. San Francisco: Jossey-Bass.

Lawler, Edward, Susan Albers, and Gerald Ledford. 1992. *Employee Involvement and Total Quality Management: Practices and Results in Fortune 1000 Companies*. San Francisco: Jossey-Bass.

LeRoy, Michael. 1996. "Can TEAM Work? Implications of an Electromation and Du Pont Compliance Analysis for the TEAM Act." *Notre Dame Law Review* 71, no. 2: 215–266.

Levine, David. 1995. *Reinventing the Workplace*. Washington, D.C.: Brookings Institution.

Rogers, Joel, and Wolfgang Streeck. 1995. *Works Councils: Consultation, Representation, and Cooperation in Industrial Relations*. Chicago: University of Chicago Press.

Taras, Daphne Gottlieb, and Jason Copping. 1996. "When Pet Bears Go Wild: Triggering Certifications from Joint Industrial Councils." Paper presented at the Canadian Industrial Relations Association annual conference.

Wever, Kirsten. 1995. *Negotiating Competitiveness: Employment Relations and Industrial Adjustment in the United States and Germany*. Boston: Harvard Business School Press.

Younson, Fraser. 1998. "Collectivism Returns." *People Management* 4, no. 5 (March 5): 21–24.

History: The United States and Canada

2

Accomplishments and Shortcomings of Nonunion Employee Representation in the Pre–Wagner Act Years: A Reassessment

Bruce E. Kaufman

Recent years have seen a major revival of interest in methods that promote greater employee involvement and participation (EIP) in the workplace. To provide an organizational infrastructure for EIP, companies often create various kinds of teams, councils, committees, and review boards that are representational in nature and are intended to facilitate information exchange and two-way communication, improve efficiency and product quality, promote joint problem solving, decentralize decision making, delegate power and responsibility to lower-level employees, and increase morale and organizational commitment. In some instances, the structure and operation of EIP is jointly negotiated by a company and labor union through the collective bargaining process. Given, however, that today only one out of ten private-sector workers in the United States is covered by a union contract, most EIP initiatives are in nonunion firms and are thus management designed and operated.

Provisions of the National Labor Relations Act (NLRA, or Wagner Act) enacted in 1935 place significant constraints on the form and operation of EIP programs in nonunion companies. Although not discussed further in this chapter, the same is true of amendments made in 1934 to the Railway Labor Act. Section 8(a)(2) of the NLRA makes it an unfair labor practice for a company to "dominate or interfere with the formation or administration of any labor organization or contribute financial or other support to it." Section 2(5), in turn, defines a labor organization quite broadly as "any organization of any kind, or any agency or employee representation committee or plan, in which employees participate and which exists for the purpose, in whole or in part, of dealing with employers concerning grievances, labor disputes, wages, rates of pay, hours of employment, or conditions of work."

In a series of cases extending from 1937 to the present—but most notably in *Electromation, Inc.* (1992) and *E.I. Du Pont de Nemours & Co.* (1993), the National Labor Relations Board (NLRB) has ruled that a wide variety of EIP teams, councils, and committees in nonunion companies violate these provisions of the NLRA and are thus illegal (see the Estreicher, Kaufman, Lewin, and Fossum and LeRoy chapters in this volume). Great concern has been voiced by employer groups and a number of policymakers that these decisions, and the provisions of the NLRA that underlie them, harm American competitiveness and undermine efforts to improve employer-employee relations (Maryott 1997). Many others, however, support the NLRB decisions as a necessary bulwark against coercion of employees and the reappearance of the sham "company unions" of the 1920s-30s that Sections 8(a)(2) and 2(5) were meant to eliminate (Morris 1994).

The chapters in this volume all seek to provide additional perspective and evidence on the role and operation of nonunion forms of employee representation in the workplace and, in particular, on the pros and cons of the NLRA's ban on most types of these organizations. Since the impetus for passage of the NLRA and inclusion of Sections 8(a)(2) and 2(5) grew out of the economic and political events of the 1910s-30s, it seems appropriate that this chapter should reexamine and reassess the historical record on nonunion representation. Accordingly, in what follows I sketch the origins, development, and operation of the nonunion employee representation plans (NERPs); assess both their accomplishments and shortcomings; and conclude with implications from this analysis for both contemporary practice and public policy.

Origins and Development of Nonunion Employee Representation

Employee-formed trade unions date from the early 1800s in the United States, and by 1900 they had a membership of roughly 1 million. Company-established employee organizations, in contrast, emerged almost a century later. The first appearance of a formal plan of employee representation is uncertain. Hogler and Grenier (1992) claim the first NERP was established in the late 1870s at the Straiton and Storm Co., while Nelson (1982) cites the Filene Cooperative Association, established by the Wm. Filene Sons Co. in Bos-

ton in 1898. Yet another source—a report by the National Industrial Conference Board (NICB 1933)—states that the first NERP was a nonunion shop committee established in 1904 at the Nernst Lamp Co. in Pittsburgh. Whatever the case, in the early years of the twentieth century only a handful of nonunion representation plans existed in American industry. The most notable was the "industrial democracy" plan created by John Leitch in 1912 at the Packard Piano Company (Brandes 1976).

By common assent, one of the most influential developments in the history of employee representation took place in 1915 when the "Rockefeller plan" was inaugurated at the Colorado Fuel & Iron Company (CF&I) in the aftermath of a bloody miners' strike popularly known as the "Ludlow Massacre" (Gitelman 1988). The Rockefellers were the largest shareholders in CF&I, and John D. Rockefeller Jr. was widely criticized in the aftermath of the strike for the calamitous state of labor relations at the company. In order to restore order at the company and burnish his public image, Rockefeller hired a Canadian labor expert and future prime minister, William Lyon Mackenzie King, to investigate labor conditions at CF&I and make recommendations. King's advice, which was radical at the time, was to establish a formal plan of employee representation in which workers elected delegates who then met with management on an ongoing basis to discuss mutual workplace problems and issues. Rockefeller agreed to King's suggestion, and a representation plan was installed amid great national publicity. Rockefeller shortly thereafter became a convinced advocate of employee representation and strongly promoted it in speeches and meetings with fellow businessmen (see Rockefeller 1924).

Further stimulation to both union and nonunion

employee representation resulted from conditions created by World War I. At the start of American involvement in the war in 1917, trade union membership stood at 3 million, while nonunion representation plans covered a few thousand workers in a dozen or so plants (see Figure 2.1). Soon the combination of tight labor markets and rapidly rising prices spawned by the war set in motion numerous strikes, increased union organizing activity, and tremendously high levels of labor turnover. As indicated in Figure 2.1, by 1920 unions had added over 2 million new members. But the number of workers covered under nonunion employee representation plans also grew quickly. The impetus came from five factors (Wolf 1919; NICB 1922; French 1923):

- Rulings of various government wartime emergency boards, such as the National War Labor Board and the Shipbuilding Labor Adjustment Board, that mandated establishment of nonunion works councils and shop committees in over 125 firms threatened by strikes and other forms of labor unrest.
- The onrush of union organization caused a number of employers to establish a NERP as a stopgap union avoidance device.
- The wartime drive to "make the world safe for democracy" in the political sphere led to an upsurge of public sentiment in favor of "industrial democracy" in the economic sphere, motivating some employers to experiment with formal plans of employee representation.
- Rampant employee turnover, mounting labor unrest, and falling rates of productivity led a number of employers to become interested in more modern, progressive methods of personnel management, and NERPs were thus attractive as a means to promote improved two-way communication, greater opportunities for employee participation, and more equitable resolution of employment disputes.
- A palpable sense of fear spread among business interests in the late 1910s that worker unrest was plunging the nation toward socialism, Bolshevism, or "IWWism" (i.e., revolutionary unionism, as espoused by the Industrial Workers of the World) and NERPs were seen as an antidote that provided employees a modicum of greater power and influence without threatening the underlying system of property rights and management control of the workplace.

As a result of the combined impact of these five factors, by 1919 employers had established 225 nonunion plans covering over 400,000 workers (NICB 1922).

The boom in employee representation in America during World War I was also mirrored in a number of other countries (Miller 1922; Burton 1926). In reaction to widespread labor unrest and calls for greater democratization of industry, laws mandating some form of works council were enacted in Austria, Germany, Czechoslovakia, and Norway. Responding to similar conditions, the English government created a multiple-tier system of industry and national joint company-union representative boards called Whitley Councils. The Whitley plan influenced the early development of NERPs in the United States (Wolf 1919), although the American version did not provide a formal role for unions. As detailed in the chapter by MacDowell in this volume, numerous NERPs similar to those in America also appeared among Canadian firms at about this time and were likewise influenced by the English Whitely Council plan.

After the war, the fortunes of trade unions and NERPs diverged sharply. As a result of a combination of factors, including the lifting of wartime

Figure 2.1 **Trends in Membership: Trade Unions and Employee Representation Plans, 1900–1940**

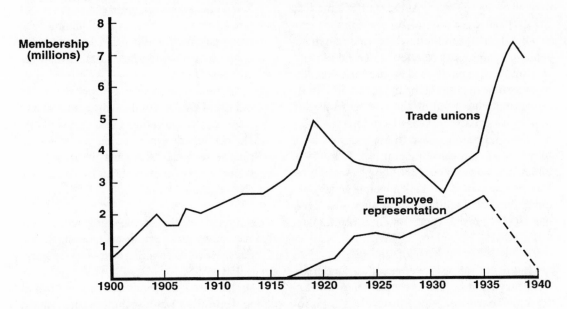

Sources: Nelson (1982); Bureau of the Census, Historical Statistics of the United States, 1789–1945, Part 1, p. 177.

protections of collective bargaining, the sharp depression of 1920–21, and an open-shop drive by antiunion employers, union membership plummeted from 5 million in 1920 to 3.6 million in 1923. At the same time, a survey by the National Industrial Conference Board revealed a net increase in the number of NERPs (NICB 1922). In 1922, for example, 385 companies had active employee representation plans that covered 690,000 workers. The bulk of these employee representation plans were in manufacturing, railroads, and utilities, but a few were found among such diverse groups as postal employees, teachers, and office and clerical workers. Although many of the wartime shop committees imposed by the government had already disappeared by the early 1920s, several hundred new plans emerged during the same time.

Over the course of the 1920s, the era of "Wel-

fare Capitalism," union membership continued on a path of slow decline with the loss of several hundred thousand more workers by the end of the decade. Although the number of firms with NERPs reached a high point in 1926 and then also declined (from 432 in 1926 to 399 in 1928), in terms of workers covered the Conference Board surveys revealed substantial growth—from 690,000 in 1922 to 1.5 million in 1928 (NICB 1933). This divergent pattern was the result of the growth of NERPs among a modest number of large firms and a simultaneous abandonment of NERPs by a greater number of small- to medium-size employers.

The Great Depression began in late 1929, and economic activity dropped sharply until the nadir of the slump was reached in the winter of 1932–33. Both trade union membership and workers covered under NERPs decreased during this period, an outcome not unexpected given the steep decline in employment. Given the low and falling level of union membership and power, the extreme pressure on companies to reduce costs, and the reluctance of employees to push grievances in an environment of great job insecurity, it would not have been surprising to see many employers abandon NERPs during this period. Although some did, a surprising number maintained their plans, albeit at a less active level in a number of cases. The Conference Board found, for example, that from 1928 to 1932 workers covered by NERPs dropped only 18 percent, compared to a decline in manufacturing employment of 40 percent.

In March 1933 Franklin Roosevelt became president, and in June he signed into law the centerpiece of his legislative program to spur economic recovery—the National Industrial Recovery Act (NIRA). The purpose of the NIRA was to restore confidence and boost purchasing power and aggregate demand (Kaufman 1996). To do so, the NIRA sought to end the deflationary spiral of wage and price cuts, increase jobs by reducing weekly work hours, promote a gradual increase in wages and household income, and "prime the pump" through increased public works spending. One method adopted to accomplish these aims was to promote collective bargaining, reflected in Section 7(a) of the NIRA, which stated that employees had the right to "organize and bargain collectively through representatives of their own choosing" free from coercion by the employer (Farr 1959).

Passage of the NIRA, and Section 7(a) in particular, precipitated a largely unexpected and tumultuous period of union organizing, strikes, and government intervention in employee-employer relations. Unions, which only a few short months previously had been largely moribund, sprang into action and in a year's time recruited nearly a million new members (see Figure 2.1). A portion of the union resurgence arose from mounting worker discontent and sense of grievance over the deprivations caused by the depression and real and perceived injustices at the hands of employers. Another portion arose from a desire to promote the president's economic recovery plan, a widespread belief that the NIRA either strongly encouraged or mandated collective bargaining, and the perception of employees that they needed to organize in order to have political clout in Washington to offset the influence exercised by employer groups in the determination of the minimum-wage and maximum-hour provisions mandated by the NIRA (Kaufman 1996). At the same time as membership in trade unions rebounded sharply, numerous companies rushed to establish some form of NERP. According to one estimate, by the middle of 1934 workers covered under some form of "company union" amounted to 1.8 million and rose to 2.5 million by 1935 (Bernheim and Van Doren 1935). As in the World War I period, the motivation driving employers to establish NERPs were diverse, but a consensus opinion was that the primary motive in many cases was to forestall union organization.

The proliferation of nonunion employee representation plans in 1933–35, their evident role as union-avoidance devices, and the belief of the Roosevelt administration that the spread of NERPs was impeding the economic recovery process envisioned in the NIRA (a process predicated upon higher wages) led to a growing crescendo of criticism against them. The foremost critic of NERPs was Senator Robert Wagner, who repeatedly referred to them as "sham" organizations. In early 1935 Wagner introduced new legislation in Congress that was aimed at substantially increasing the protection of workers' Section 7(a) rights contained in the NIRA and outlawing the "dominated" form of company union. To many people's surprise, this legislation—called the National Labor Relations Act—passed both houses of Congress and was signed into law by Roosevelt in the summer of 1935. As enacted, the NLRA contained both the Sections 8(a)(2) and 2(5) previously described.

Most companies with NERPs maintained them, given their expectation that the NLRA would be declared unconstitutional (as had the NIRA). When in 1937 the Supreme Court on a 5-4 vote ruled in favor of the NLRA in the *Jones and Laughlin* decision, the NLRB aggressively moved to disestablish nearly every type of employer-sponsored representation plan. The board's actions were supported by the Supreme Court in the first major Section 8(a)(2) case to come before it. In *Newport News Shipbuilding and Dry Dock Co.* vs. *NLRB*, the Court ruled in 1939 that the company's in-house representation plan was illegal even though the plan had been in existence since 1927, the company had ceased paying the employee representatives wages for time spent on council business, and the employees had voted in a secret ballot election in favor of the employer's representation plan over outside union representation. This decision effectively foreclosed the ability of companies to maintain a NERP, and by the end of the decade the plans had for all intents and purposes disappeared, either from abandonment, transformation into a local unaffiliated union, or absorption into a national or international labor union (see Jacoby 1989; Jacoby and Verma 1992; the Jacoby chapter in this volume). The movement spawned by the Rockefeller plan in 1915 had thus come to an abrupt and largely unexpected end in the relatively short time span of two decades.

The Structure of Nonunion Employee Representation

Although there is a sizable case study literature on nonunion employee representation in individual firms and industries, as well as a number of interpretative and overview pieces by modern-day scholars, no recent study I am familiar with provides a detailed cross-section "portrait" of the structure and operation of these plans. Knowledge of these organizational details, however, is crucial for both understanding the strengths and weaknesses of NERPs and evaluating the degree to which modern-day EIP programs parallel the NERPs of six decades earlier. Accordingly, this section provides a brief overview of the structure of NERPs and the next section examines their purpose and operation.

Nomenclature

When the NERP movement began in the mid-1910s, these employee organizations were most often referred to as either a *works council* or *shop committee*. Other names, such as *industrial council* and *employee association*, were also sometimes used. The National Industrial Conference Board (NICB 1922, pp. 1–2) defined a works council as "a form of industrial organization under which the employees of an individual establishment, through representatives chosen by and from among themselves, share collectively in the adjustment of employment conditions in that establishment."

By the early- to mid-1920s the terms works council and shop committee began to be replaced by two other names. The first, favored by management spokesmen, was *employee representation plan*, a terminology gradually adopted because it was more generic and inclusive. The second, originally used by trade unionists and other critics of NERPs in the 1920s, was *company union*. As noted in a Bureau of Labor Statistics study (BLS 1937), the term "company union" had by the mid-1930s become the most widely used label for these organizations, even though it was misleading in certain respects and carried a strong connotation of opprobrium. As described below, NERPs in a number of cases were, for example, not companywide, were not intended to function as a bargaining agent for dues-paying members, nor were they the toothless creatures of management domination as so often portrayed. These caveats notwithstanding, the company union label has stuck and is the term most often used today to describe these management-sponsored employee organizations. To keep the discussion on neutral ground, the term "nonunion employee representation plan" (NERP) is used in this study, although on occasion "company union" will also be used for descriptive convenience.

Structure

At the beginning of the employee representation movement in the mid- to late-1910s, it was customary to distinguish between two different organizational forms of NERPs (NICB 1922; BLS 1937).

The first was the *governmental* or *federal* type plan (also known as an *industrial democracy*-type plan) popularized by management consultant and "industrial evangelist" John Leitch. Modeled on the U.S. government, the Leitch plan called for a cabinet composed of upper-management executives, a Senate of management-selected foremen and supervisors, and a House of Representatives of elected employee representatives. Matters of interest to employees could be introduced in the House and, once passed on a majority vote, transmitted to the Senate for its deliberation and vote. If passed there, the proposal would go to the cabinet, where the company executives could approve the proposal, veto it, or send it back for further consideration. Although not a necessary part of a federal-type NERP, Leitch also maintained that the success of employee representation depends on some form of gain-sharing with employees, and thus many Leitch plans contained a profit-sharing arrangement called a Collective Economy Dividend (Leitch 1919).

In practice, the Leitch plan proved cumbersome and time-consuming, and firms that adopted it often collapsed the cabinet and Senate into one body or went even further and integrated the management and employee representatives into one joint deliberative body (Carpenter 1928a), a form of organization that became indistinguishable from the "committee" type of NERP discussed next. Of the several dozen Leitch plans put into operation, one of the best known and most enduring was the Industrial Assembly at Goodyear (Carpenter 1928b; Nelson 1982, 1988).

The second type of early NERP was the *committee* or *Rockefeller*-type plan pioneered by MacKenzie King at the Colorado Fuel & Iron Co. King's system proved far more popular than Leitch's and in one form or another became the standard organizational structure for formal plans of employee representation. In this plan, a plant or company committee was established with an equal number of management and employee delegates. The management representatives were appointed by the senior executives of the company, and the employee delegates were typically elected through a secret ballot process by all the nonsupervisory employees of the firm, including in a number of cases office and clerical workers. Sometimes, however, eligibility requirements were stipulated, such as over eighteen years of age or American citizenship. In small firms the employee representatives were often chosen in a companywide election, while in larger firms the employees were subdivided into election units, such as individual departments or mines, and then chose delegates (generally based on some formula stipulating the number of representatives per hundred employees) to represent them on the companywide or establishmentwide NERP.

Like the Leitch plan, the Rockefeller plan evolved in a number of directions and developed numerous permutations (NICB 1922; Burton 1926; Carpenter 1928b; BLS 1937). Some firms, for example, established a hierarchy of committees to deal with issues at, respectively, the department, plant, and company level. In some cases, the employee representatives also reported to the board of directors or were given a seat on the board (Selekman 1924). Other plans established special standing committees, sometimes a half dozen or more in number, with responsibility for particular issues, such as wages, grievances, company housing, safety and health, and recreation. Temporary or ad hoc committees were also frequently established to deal with special issues (what are today often called *project teams*). Other plans made provision for the employee delegates to hold separate meetings without management in attendance (a feature that became more common after passage of the NIRA). As described more fully in a moment, some committee-type NERPs were intended to function solely as advisory bodies or conduits for two-way communication, but in the majority of cases they were given varying degrees of authority to investigate problems, make proposals, and in some cases render a decision or request arbitration of disputes.

Other forms of nonunion employee representation appeared in several firms or industries, but none proved as popular as the committee type. Several NERPs were established, for example, on a multicompany basis (BLS 1937). The largest and most publicized was a World War I vintage organization called the Loyal Legion of Loggers and Lumbermen. It grew to include over 100,000 employees from numerous lumber firms located in the states of the Pacific Northwest. During the NIRA period, Saposs (1936) reports that a movement for confederating company unions emerged in several industries and that a district council of company unions had been established in the steel industry. Another permutation was the employee representation plans on many railroads during the 1920s and early 1930s (BLS 1937). These came the closest to fitting the label "company union" in that they were organizations solely for employees, were companywide and company created, collected dues from members, and negotiated written agreements. Although they had a number of unionlike features, these NERPs were not independent unions because their existence was at the pleasure of the company, the workers' representatives were limited to only company employees, and they eschewed strikes and other forms of economic coercion.

The formal plans of employee representation discussed here were the most visible and highly publicized forms of EIP in the 1920s, but they were only the tip of the iceberg. The final report of the second labor-management conference organized by President Wilson in 1919 noted that recent events "reveal a desire on the part of workers to exert a larger and more organic influence upon the processes of industrial life" (quoted in *Industrial Management* 5, no. 20: 349). Unwilling or unable to institute a formal plan of representation, many companies instead opted for more informal and small-scale employee committees—per the observation of one personnel management executive (Benge 1927, p. 125) that "committees are dotted throughout most industrial organizations, with varying degrees of responsibility and authority." Little else is known about their structure or operation, however.

The Operation of Nonunion Employee Representation

The next dimension of employee representation plans to be examined is their operation.

Establishment

NERPs were established both by government compulsion and as a voluntary decision by management. Indeed, it is possible to distinguish three distinct periods in the NERP movement in this regard (Nelson 1982, 1993). The first is the World War I period when the majority of shop committees and works councils were forced upon oftentimes reluctant companies by wartime government agencies. The second is the period roughly from 1920 to 1932 when NERPs were established as a matter of voluntary management action. The third period is the NIRA period from 1933 to 1935 when the majority of newly established NERPs were hastily erected either to comply with employers' belief that Section 7(a) required or strongly encouraged some form of collective bargaining and/or as a deterrent to union organization. In the overwhelming number of cases where NERPs were voluntarily established, it was at the instigation of management, although scattered examples arose where employees took the initiative in proposing a NERP.

Nearly all consultants and writers on employee representation strongly advised management to avoid unilateral imposition of the plan, as this practice undercut the spirit of cooperation that was the desired end product (NICB 1922; Cowdrick 1924; Myers 1924). Approximately two-thirds of employers heeded this advice in some form (BLS 1937). Most often it was by asking employees to vote yes or no on a proposal that management had already drawn up and was presenting for approval. The more liberal or progressive employers went further and included employees on the drafting committee or solicited their advice before presenting the plan for a vote (Carpenter 1921). Proponents of NERPs, sensitive to the charge of management domination, noted that the elections on plan adoption were often by secret ballot, and on occasion the employees voted down the proposal and the plan was shelved. Critics, on the other hand, noted that management frequently exerted both subtle and not-so-subtle pressure on employees to vote yes, and the choice on the ballot was limited to the status quo (individual bargaining) or a company union and almost never included the option of trade union representation (Dunn 1926).

Larger-size NERPs frequently had some form of written constitution or bylaws. These would typically explain the purpose of the plan, describe the structure of representation, the procedure for elections, and so on. Many began with some type of mission statement. The purpose of the employee representation plan on the Pennsylvania Railroad, for example, was stated to be "To give all employees an opportunity to have a voice in the management in all matters affecting their wages, working conditions, and welfare, and in other matters of mutual concern affecting the welfare of the company and the public which the company serves" (Pennsylvania System 1922, p. 3). Among plans adopted prior to the New Deal, constitutions exhibited a good deal of variation in terms of specific provisions and procedures; after passage of the NIRA, however, firms in their haste to set up representation plans often copied nearly verbatim a constitution or set of bylaws provided by an industry association or dominant firm (Saposs 1936).

An important provision included in many constitutions was a statement of nondiscrimination against union members with respect to election to the shop council and to the administration of shop rules. Some went further and mandated that no employee representative could be discharged without top-management approval, realizing that employee fear of retribution for speaking up is a major deterrent to successful operation of a NERP. As with most other aspects of employee representation, the farsighted, progressive employers generally followed this policy, partly in order to preserve the legitimacy of the plan in the workers' eyes and partly because they came to learn that putting the union supporters and "kickers" (chronic complainers) on the shop council turned many into conservative "company" men (Ozanne 1967). Other employers, however, mouthed nondiscrimination but made sure that only "safe" employees were elected or otherwise exerted pressure on worker representatives not to rock the boat. Such efforts could backfire, however, as employees who felt the system was rigged responded by either showing their disdain, say by electing representatives who could not speak English, or their anger, say by electing union militants in the hopes of using the council as a springboard for organizing (Myers 1924).

Employee representation, if done properly and with the right spirit, was a costly undertaking for firms. Typically the company paid all expenses, such as providing a meeting place and paying for employee time spent at council meetings. In the best plans the representatives were also given time off from work to handle grievances, talk with constituents, and so on. These hours, coupled with the frequently high demand on executive time, entailed significant costs and redirection of management attention. At International Harvester (Ozanne 1967, p. 145), for example, senior executives met frequently with the councils, and three to five management staff persons of the industrial relations department were assigned full-time to council activities. Likewise, over 8,500 hours of employee and management time were reportedly devoted to one year's operation of the works council turned independent local union at Jersey Standard's Bayway refinery (Chase 1947). Another not inconsequential element of cost is that the employee committees surfaced thousands of requests for wage increases, piece-rate adjustments, reduction of hours, improved working conditions, and reinstatement of discharged employees. Again, in the better-operated plans the employees won substantially more than half of these requests (Burton 1926; Leiserson 1929), which in most instances represented additional expense to the company.

Finally, managers also found that employee representation restricted their flexibility of operation. In some cases management would propose a change in policy only to encounter strong employee opposition, forcing either abandonment of the proposal or a scaling back. In other cases it might take several months or longer for the council to deliberate the matter and reach an agreement. A prime example of both occurred in the 1920–21 depression, when firms in most industries started cutting wages soon after the slump began. In this situation, and others similar to it, companies with NERPs typically reacted in one or a combination of three ways. One was to bypass the council and unilaterally implement the change in policy, a practice that accomplished management's goal but at the cost of undercutting the continued viability of the representation plan (NICB 1922). A second was to accept the time delays and inflexibilities as the price that had to be paid to gain the long-term benefits of employee cooperation. A third, longer-term option was to redesign the structure of the plans in order to speed up decision making. Not only did companies pursue this by abandoning the bicameral structure of the "federal" plan in favor of a unicameral "committee" plan, but during the course of the 1920s they also decentralized the latter by creating standing and/or ad hoc subcommittees, such as for grievances, safety, or company housing, that could meet more frequently and handle routine business that did not need to come before the full council (Carpenter 1928b).

Issues Covered

The majority of employee representation plans permitted joint consultation on all matters of concern to the employer and employees, including wages, hours, and working conditions. Many constitutions contained a "management rights" clause, however, that stipulated certain matters, such as the right to hire and fire, were sole prerogatives of management.

One contemporary study of employee representation concluded that the issues discussed could be grouped into four categories (Burton 1926): wages, hours, and other terms of employment; adjustment of grievances and complaints; production; and living and working conditions. The author of this study interviewed a large number of managers and workers involved with NERPs and examined the minutes from numerous meetings of different councils. The typical pattern was that during the first year or so, a flood of individual and group grievances were put on

the table, as well as numerous requests for wage adjustments and wage increases (also see NICB 1922). After this "break-in" period, however, a wider range of issues came to the fore in the successful councils, while the meetings in the less successful ones degenerated into forums for making announcements or consideration of minutiae.

A sense of the type of issues that came before the NERPs, and their relative numerical importance, can be gleaned from data presented by the National Industrial Conference Board (1922) and Burton (1926). The former presents data on issues considered by the NERPs of the Bethlehem Steel Co. Over a two-year period (1918–20), for example, 1,045 issues were considered by the NERPs in the company's five plants (p. 78); 31 percent involved some aspect of wages, 28 percent involved working conditions, 12 percent involved production methods, and 10 percent involved safety issues; and 71 percent were decided in favor of the employees (46 percent in the case of wages). The latter study provides data on issues considered by an unidentified "large manufacturing company" for the years 1918–25 (Burton 1926, p. 269). A total of 2,664 issues were put on the table; the distribution by topic is employment and working conditions (24 percent), wages (23 percent), safety (14 percent), production (10 percent), sanitation (7 percent), pensions (6 percent), housing (4 percent), and other (12 percent). Two-thirds of these were decided in the employees' favor.

These numbers, and the substance of the issues considered, may perhaps be made more concrete with a third example. The National Industrial Conference Board (1922, p. 82) listed all the agenda items considered over the course of a year by an unidentified western agricultural machinery manufacturer. Here are the first eight of forty-two: wage differentials of certain molders, drinking fountains needed, change in method of paying shop employees, exhaust fan needed in main plant, suggestion for starting foundry oven one hour earlier, better tools needed in machine shop, wheel trucks for foundry bull ladles needed, and clean-up on Saturday nights needed. All are reported as approved or satisfactorily adjusted.

Authority and Power

As on other dimensions, the amount of authority and power possessed by NERPs varied tremendously. On one extreme, some NERPs were set up solely as an advisory body or communication device and had no authority and little power over any issue of administration or policy. On the other extreme, a handful of companies placed significant portions of the management function in the hands of the employee representatives, including seats on the board of directors and final say over discharges. The great bulk of NERPs, however, were located somewhere in the middle of this spectrum.

Authority and power are separate concepts. Authority is a right to do, power is the ability to influence. Whatever authority was given to NERPs, it was always understood to be a delegated authority from the owners of the companies to the employees (Cowdrick 1924). Thus, employee representatives might have authority to bring grievances up before the joint committee, but this authority was unilaterally bestowed by management and could be unilaterally withdrawn or disregarded at its pleasure. On their part, most employers with NERPs realized that once the rules and expectations concerning these groups were in place, they either had to abide by them (or appear to be doing so) or risk destroying management's credibility and the viability of the NERP (Ozanne 1967). Indeed, it was for this reason that many employers felt deep ambivalence about employee representation in the knowledge that breaking the implicit contract established with the employees concerning joint dealing and due process would certainly cause anger and demoralization and possibly a drive for union representation. Most concluded that the costs and risks were too great, or the benefits too small or uncertain, and elected not to go down the road of employee representation. Certainly many concluded that if union avoidance is the chief goal there are easier, less costly, and more effective ways to accomplish it (e.g., firing union activists, labor spies, yellow-dog contracts) than forming an employee representation plan. Not only were there cheaper and more effective methods of antiunionism, a number of employers objected to the notion of sharing management with the employees as a dangerous experiment tinged with Bolshevism (Ching 1973). To a significant degree, NERPs were thus caught in the middle of an ideological tug of war—damned by organized labor as toothless shams of employer control and rejected by the traditionalists in the business community as agents of creeping socialism.

On the part of employees, they generally entered into employee representation with considerable skepticism, knowing that their newly bestowed "rights" were not rights at all but privileges given at management's discretion—a skepticism compounded by the conviction that no matter how good something sounds, if management proposes it, then the chances are good that the company's gain will be at the workers' expense. To overcome this skepticism, managers knew that it was crucial in the beginning of employee representation to live up to the expectations and responsibilities they had created so as to create an atmosphere of trust and credible commitment. Not infrequently, they also gave the employees a few strategically timed "wins" to further promote the image of genuine joint dealing. From a trade union perspective, however, the "bottom line" was always that these commitments were likely to be honored only as long it was profitable to do so, and hence the promise of nonunion industrial democracy was, in a memorable phrase, a "delusion and a snare" (wording in a resolution condemning company unions passed at the 1919 AFL convention in Atlantic City, New Jersey).

Given that the grant of authority to the employees was conditional, it was in a number of cases nonetheless shared in some meaningful ways. According to accounts written by firsthand observers, for example, the two largest sources of employee dissatisfaction came from the petty tyrannies of the foremen and the ever-present threat of discharge without recourse to appeal (NICB 1922; Burton 1926). A significant number of NERPs were given authority over grievances and discharges in an effort to curb these abuses. In a 1935 government survey of company unions (BLS 1937), for example, 70 percent were given authority to review grievances and two-thirds could review complaints over safety and health. Arbitration of unresolved disputes was provided for in 40 percent of the company unions surveyed, although in half of these cases both management and the employees had to give agreement. The government investigator concluded that approximately one-third of the company unions that dealt with grievances did an "effective" job and another one-third did a "modestly effective" job.

NERPs were also given authority in a number of other areas of the business. A common practice, for example, was to give the NERP some role in administering the welfare, safety, and recreation programs (Brandes 1976). A number of firms with company housing delegated all or a portion of its management to the employee representatives, reportedly with considerable satisfaction on both sides.

Perhaps no issue associated with employee representation plans was in the end to generate as much controversy as their power, or lack thereof, in furthering the interests of employees. A basic division of opinion existed over the years on the purpose of employee representation. Some maintained that NERPs were mainly a method of "group dealing" and were intended to foster greater cooperation and integration through improved communication, mutual understanding, and grievance resolution (Hicks 1941). From this perspective, the entire purpose of employee representation is to shift the focus of labor and capital away from an adversarial struggle over terms and conditions of employment to cooperation and mutual gain. While power is the key consideration for both sides in an adversarial "we versus them" game, promoting effective teamwork is the key consideration if the game is instead framed as "win-win." To put it another way, the distribution of intraorganizational power is irrelevant if both sides have the same interests and are pulling in the same direction.

Other people among both proponents and critics of employee representation maintained that the purpose of NERPs was not only collective dealing but also collective *bargaining*. The term "bargaining" implies a process of haggling or negotiating between two sides whose interests are not identical and the outcome of which has a large element of win-lose (a zero-sum game). From this perspective, conflicts of interest between labor and management are inevitable, and those who propose otherwise are engaged in wishful thinking or self-delusion. The key question then becomes how best to represent and protect the interests of both sides.

The answer of the critics of employee representation is that workers need independent trade unions (Dunn 1926). The starting place for their position is that the individual employee suffers from a distinct inequality of bargaining power vis-à-vis the employer (Kaufman 1989, 1993). This inequality arises from the basic fact that the worker needs the job more than the company needs the worker, and thus the company can drive the harder bargain. The end result is lopsided terms and conditions of employment, such as poverty-level wages, few benefits, lack of job security, and harsh treatment at the hands of supervisors. The solution to the worker's lack of individual power is to form a trade union and gain collective power through group action, such as striking. Only when power confronts power on equal terms will the outcome be a reasonable one, in this view.

To the critics of employee representation, it is manifestly clear that NERPs dismally fail the test of equal power. Ozanne (1967, p. 123) described the councils at International Harvester as "weak and dependent" and (p. 153), "reek[ing] of paternalism." No person was more eloquent on this matter than Senator Robert Wagner. He said, for example, "I cannot comprehend how people can rise to the defense of a practice so contrary to American principles as one which permits the advocates of one party to be paid by the other . . . collective bargaining becomes a sham when the employer sits on both sides of the table or pulls the strings behind the spokesman of those with whom he is dealing" (National Labor Relations Board 1985, p. 2489). As he saw it, NERPs were indeed a sham because the employee representatives were fearful of being discharged if they pressed the employees' interests too forcefully, companies stage-managed the agenda and meetings, management was far better informed about

prevailing conditions at other firms than were the employee representatives (asymmetric information in modern-day terms), strikes were forbidden, and the company was free to abrogate at its pleasure any agreement or understanding with the employees.

Other people, including many proponents of employee representation (e.g., Teagle 1933), adopted the "bargaining" perspective but nonetheless maintained that NERPs were good for employees as well as employers. Their case was built on two premises. The first is that trade unions and collective bargaining are in certain respects deficient and thus need to be supplemented or replaced by employee representation. Here the schools of thought branched off in two directions. The basic dividing line was whether employee representation and trade unions are viewed as *complements* or *substitutes* (Douglas 1921; Seager 1923). Proponents of the former view maintained that NERPs and trade unions both serve useful, albeit quite different, functions in the industrial relations system. This group was sympathetic to organized labor, but recognized that in-plant shop committees are the superior mechanism for promoting efficiency of production and adjusting the myriad of day-to-day problems and grievances because they are closer to the shopfloor and less adversarial in approach. Trade unions, in contrast, are far superior in dealing with industrywide conditions, such as wage rates and hours of work, because of their marketwide coverage and substantially greater bargaining power. Thus, this school of thought favored a two-tier system of bargaining: in-plant bargaining by some form of employee representation and marketwide bargaining by trade unions (Seager 1923; Tead and Metcalf 1933).

Proponents of the "substitute" view were more critical of unions and believed that, on net, they did not serve the long-run interests of employers, workers, or the community. The substitute they endorsed in place of the trade union was employee representation. From their perspective, unions are an outside "third party" that depend on conflict and acrimony for their survival, are driven by internal political dynamics to "milk the cow" (the company) for "more, more, more" at the expense of future jobs and company well-being, and are too often led by people who are overly militant and/or unscrupulous, autocratic, and corrupt. As one person put it: "Why should we overthrow the autocracy of the employer, an autocracy which doubtless oftener than not is a benevolent autocracy . . . in order to establish a meddlesome oligarchy whose interests are frequently quite different from the interests of the workers for whom it speaks?" (Hotchkiss 1920, pp. 113–114).

Putting aside the "substitute versus complement" issue, and given the consensus opinion that some form of joint dealing is necessary in large-scale enterprises, the second premise of those holding the "bargaining" perspective is that employee representation is superior because it provides a middle level of power between two unworkable extremes: domination by the employer in a system of nonunion individual bargaining and domination by the trade union in a system of collective bargaining. That some NERPs did indeed have power and sometimes exerted it in ways that favored employee interests over employer interests is clear from the case study literature. At the Dan River Mills, for example, Smith (1960, p. 277) notes: "in 1922, despite the disapproval of management, the House and Senate voted to close the mills for two weeks at Christmas time." Later, a company executive remarked about the incident: "I was confident that the legislative bodies would take their cue from the implied wish of the management and vote for the shorter shut-down. But democracy is no mere form at Danville; it is not a game of 'follow the leader' but a business of building up independent thought and action" (p. 277).

As in this example, sophisticated managers of firms with representation plans realized that a certain degree of power sharing is actually in the company's best interests, as it promotes enhanced organizational effectiveness. Thus, giving employees some say over discipline and discharge cases; a forum for communicating to higher management about production problems, poor supervisory practices, or sources of employee discontent; and an opportunity to participate in decision making and develop personal leadership qualities helps build improved employee morale, plant efficiency, and the quality of management, and at the same time it reduces the rampant apathy and sometimes simmering discontent that pervades most workplaces (NICB 1922; Hall 1928). Thus, from this perspective, it is true that NERPs do not have as much power as trade unions, but the converse is that to be successful, a NERP must confer some power to employees or it will have a short half-life and this power, limited as it may be, will in the long-run gain for the employees more of the high wages, job security, and self-respect that workers want and that trade unions claim to gain. Thus, NERPs do engage in collective bargaining, but in a limited manner that avoids the economic costs and hard feelings that go with adversarial-style trade union collective bargaining.

Evidence, as documented below, can be adduced to support all sides of this argument—a fact noted by Leiserson (1928, p. 119) six decades ago when he observed: "almost anything that may be said about employee representation will be true." Thus, in some employee representation plans, the employee delegates seldom spoke out in meetings or lobbied for redress of grievances on the part of their fellow workers (Ozanne 1967). They were, in effect, the puppets of management that Senator Wagner railed against. Many of these plans, as indicated above, soon fell into disuse or later germinated into full-fledged trade unions, such as in the steel industry in the mid-1930s (Hogler and Grenier 1992). But in other companies the power of the NERP was real and visibly exercised, as evidenced by the vociferous debates in council meetings, the large proportion of grievances and proposals decided in employees' favor, and the choice of employees to keep their representation plans even when given the opportunity in a secret ballot election to have union representation (Bruere 1927, 1928; Chase 1947; Gray and Gullett 1973).

To a degree that only a few prescient observers then realized (e.g., Commons 1919, 1921), the issue of power and the efficacy of NERPs versus trade unions as a protector of employee interests hinged critically on the macroeconomic environment and, in particular, the level of unemployment. In a prosperous, relatively full-employment economy, such as the 1920s, firms had both the financial wherewithal and the incentive to "do the right thing" by employees, part of which took the form of joint dealing/bargaining with employees through employee representation plans. But in a depression economy, such as the 1930s, where companies face the imminent threat of bankruptcy and a sea of desperate job seekers, incentives for voluntary power sharing disappear for all but the most forward-looking employers, and it is "every man for himself." In this environment, inequality of bargaining power becomes transparent, and NERPs inevitably appear impotent in the face of declining wages, speed-ups, and the inevitable harshness and arbitrariness that creep into management practices during hard times (Asher, Edsforth, and Boryczka 1995).

Why Firms Adopted Employee Representation: A Closer Look

The discussion just completed highlights the fact that any assessment of the pros and cons of employee representation must come to terms with what exactly was its purpose. Whether this purpose was improved communication, union avoidance, or participative management makes a big difference. Hence, in what follows I take a closer look at this subject.

The more candid writers on employee representation were quite frank in admitting that management adopted NERPs largely on the basis that it was a good business decision (Cowdrick 1924). As previously noted, ethical and philosophical considerations associated with the industrial democracy movement during and shortly after World War I also played a role in the initial spread of NERPs (Derber 1970; Lichtenstein and Harris 1993), but typically bottom-line survival considerations of profit and control were dominant over the longer term and in the large corporations where the executive function was vested in salaried managers rather than an owner/entrepreneur.

Appreciation of the reasons why a NERP might be a good business decision for firms of that era, and the objectives that management hoped NERPs would accomplish, requires a brief examination of the nature of work, methods of personnel management, and state of labor-management relations in 1915 to 1930.

Initial Conditions

Prior to World War I, the management function of personnel administration was practically nonexistent (Jacoby 1985; Kaufman 1993, 1998). A few scattered firms had some form of employment office or an employment manager, but in the great bulk of companies the plant manager or mill superintendent set the broad outlines of personnel policy and then delegated the administration of this policy to the various department foremen, supervisors, and gang bosses. They generally had a high degree of autonomy and authority to run their departments as they saw fit, including decisions about hiring, firing, pay, discipline, and the organization and performance of work. Hiring was often done at the plant gate by the individual foreman in a fairly haphazard, arbitrary manner (e.g., selecting only those men who had calluses on their hands, who came from a particular country or ethnic group, or who had family or friendship ties); employment was "at will," and workers were routinely laid off or fired with little or no reason or advance warning; rates of pay were also determined arbitrarily and frequently differed markedly between gender and ethnic groups and even for people working side by side at the same job; the typical form of motivation used by front-line supervisors was the "drive system," which relied on tactics such as shouting, cussing, pushing, and threatening the workers; and although executives often professed that they had an "open door" for those who had a grievance, the workers quickly discovered that this door was all too often a one-way exit to unemployment (Williams 1920; Gibb and Knowlton 1956).

This system of personnel management, when combined with large-scale plants employing hundreds and thousands of workers; a growing trend toward absentee ownership by dispersed stockholders; long work hours (twelve-hour shifts in steel); fatiguing, dirty, and dangerous work; lack of even the most basic amenities (e.g., clean drinking water, bathrooms); and a workforce composed of numerous immigrants, many of whom spoke no English and came from a preindustrial, peasant background; resulted in tremendous rates of employee turnover, labor unrest, low productivity, and waste of human and physical resources. Prior to World War I, most employers were either ignorant or insensitive to the large costs and amount of conflict this system generated. When the nation entered the war in 1917, however, events quickly coalesced in a manner that forced employers to rethink fundamentally the way they managed people. Out of this rethinking was born a new human resource management (HRM) paradigm and the employee representation movement (Kaufman, 2001).

A New HRM Paradigm

The wartime economy had a number of negative repercussions upon employers. As previously described, productivity declined precipitously, and employee turnover, strikes, and union organizing all rose substantially. Added to employers' woes was the fact that government policy shifted toward accommodation with organized labor and support of collective bargaining, evidenced in new promulgations that asserted workers' legal right to organize and rulings of the National War Labor Board that forced employers to recognize and deal with trade unions (French 1923).

These problems led to a major transformation in management thinking about labor. The most visible sign was the emergence and popularization of a new field of management, variously called *industrial relations*, *employment management*, *personnel management*, or *personnel administration* (Jacoby 1985, 1997; Kaufman 1993, 1998). The idea expressed by the early founders of personnel management was that the plethora of labor problems experienced by employers was the inevitable outgrowth of a system of labor management suffering from a lack of sound, scientific principles about work organization, efficient administration, and human psychology; little systematization and formalization of personnel policy; excessive decentralization of authority to foremen; a "commodity" view of workers and a "hire and fire" approach to employment; loss of personal contact and communication between management and the workers; the blind eye turned to the numerous injustices and petty tyrannies inflicted upon employees; and the lack of elementary workplace rights and procedures for assuring due process and fairness in the resolution of disputes. A flavor of the labor philosophy embedded in this system, and the practices associated therewith, is given in these remarks of a company executive in 1920 (Smith 1960, p. 263): "One of the great evils that grew out of [the prewar] system, was the tendency of those who employed labor to buy it just exactly as they would the machinery and materials required; to obtain it at the lowest possible price and get as much out of it as they could. . . ."

An outgrowth of the "new thinking" was the establishment of the first personnel departments by a number of medium-large firms and the creation of a new executive position responsible for development of personnel policy and its administration. Another outgrowth was a new and rapidly expanding literature written by both academics and practitioners that expounded the new themes of this movement—the importance of scientific principles in "man management" and "human engineering," the importance of taking into account the "human factor" in designing work and managing people, the payoff to be gained by replacing adversarial relations with cooperative relations, the benefits of eliciting employee goodwill and participation, and the necessity of ensuring both sides of the employment relationship some channel for voice in the enterprise and a "square deal" in the administration of justice.

The intellectual groundwork for employee representation was thus laid in the late 1910s in a series of books, such as John R. Commons' *Industrial Goodwill* and *Industrial Government* (1919, 1921), Mackenzie King's *Industry and Humanity* (1918), John Leitch's *Man-to-Man* (1919), Paul Litchfield's *Industrial Republic* (1920), William Basset's *When the Workmen Help You Manage* (1919), John D. Rockefeller's *The Personal Relation in Industry* (1924), and Whiting Williams's *What's on the Worker's Mind* (1920), as well as a host of articles in management publications, such as *Factory and Industrial Management* and *Bulletin of the Taylor Society*, by consultants such as Ordway Tead (1917) and Mary Parker Follett (in Urwick and Metcalf 1940) and personnel practitioners. No one label was attached to the new HRM paradigm espoused in these publications, but frequently it was referred to as the "employee goodwill" model—a term popularized by Commons in *Industrial Goodwill* to connote a new strategic perspective on labor management (Kaufman 1998, 2001). The proponents of the goodwill model touted it as a superior way to do business because it would lead to greater work effort, loyalty, and harmonious relations and, thus, greater profit. In addition, it was in keeping with American political principles of democracy and due process and Christian ethics of "do unto others."

At a practical level, the impetus for employee representation came from two different sources. One was the necessity of dealing with the host of labor problems previously detailed. The second was to rid the workplace of the interference of third parties, most particularly labor unions. Most employers were antiunion as a matter of principle, and their experience during World War I with numerous sympathy strikes, jurisdictional disputes, demands for a closed shop, and union leaders who too often, from the employers' perspective, preached class warfare and acted in a high-handed, irresponsible manner only further stiffened their antiunion resolve.

Given this historical context, the reasons employers established nonunion employee representation plans and the purposes they were to serve come into better focus (Kaufman 2000). Without question, union avoidance was a strong, ever-present motive. During periods of aggressive, widespread union activity, such as 1917–20 and 1933–35, union avoidance was typically the salient motive (see Bernstein 1970; Ozanne 1967). Other motives of course figured in the decision to set up employee representation, as a period of crisis is often a catalyst for moving managers to adopt labor reforms that are long overdue, but the historical evidence is clear that absent the overt threat of unionization, it would have been "business as usual" for many of these new converts to employee representation.

During periods of union stagnation or quiescence, such as 1921–32, other motives came to the surface as the primary reason for the establishment of NERPs. Union avoidance was of course still an important goal, but the lack of a tangible union threat meant that it could remain largely latent and out of sight, while managers focused on other issues. And these other issues were the labor problems that the World War I experience, and its immediate aftermath, had so painfully and clearly brought to the surface.

Modern academic research in management and industrial relations has notably failed to appreciate two aspects of the employer response to the resolution of these labor problems in the late 1910s and early 1920s. The first is that this re-

sponse was, at least in the liberal/progressive wing of the employer community, to put together a well-thought-out, systematic *human resource strategy* (Kaufman 2001). The second aspect is that the new HR paradigm they attempted to implement is in many respects a 1920s version of today's much discussed *high-performance workplace* model (Commission on the Future of Worker-Management Relations 1994; Kochan and Osterman 1994; Kaufman 1997).

A business strategy is an integrated, comprehensive plan that identifies one or more objectives of significance to the growth and survival of the organization and a set of methods or actions that, if successfully executed, will achieve the objectives. The conventional wisdom is that in this historical era companies' HR practices and policies, to the degree they existed, were largely piecemeal, administrative, and reactive in nature—which is to say the antithesis of "strategic" (Dulebohn, Ferris, and Stodd 1995). But this view is seriously misleading.

The evidence is clear-cut that a new paradigm of labor management emerged during World War I; that it entailed major changes in organizational structure, management practices, and the treatment and utilization of labor; and that the executives realized full well that adopting this new paradigm was a strategic decision of the highest kind (Gibb and Knowlton 1956). As described below, only a minority of companies, generally from the progressive/liberal wing of the business community, actually adopted this new paradigm. Examples include Standard Oil of New Jersey, U.S. Rubber, General Electric, International Harvester, and Bethlehem Steel. These firms were part of the "leading edge" of employers—a minority of employers that Commons estimated to be 10 to 25 percent of the total. The apex of the employee representation movement, and the

Welfare Capitalism movement in general, was composed of ten firms, including those listed above, that were members of a then-secret group called the Special Conference Committee (Ozanne 1967; Scheinberg 1986; Jacoby 1997). These firms had close links to the Rockefeller interests, to the Rockefeller-supported consulting firm Industrial Relations Counselors, and they promoted adoption and development of progressive employment practices through monthly meetings of top executives and extensive sharing of information and personnel.

In contrast, most small-to-medium-size firms, and many large ones too, chose to travel a different path (Jacoby 1997). Examples include most of the member companies of the National Association of Manufacturers (preponderantly small-to medium-sized firms) and large corporations, such as General Motors and U.S. Steel. Unlike the progressive, leading-edge firms, once the union threat of 1917–20 had passed, these companies largely reverted to traditional labor-management practices, albeit sometimes shorn of their more egregious rough edges. This, too, was a strategic decision for many of these companies, as they concluded that traditional methods of organization and personnel management could more easily and inexpensively accomplish their profit goals.

It is also noteworthy, as previously stated, that this new paradigm of HR management involved many of the conceptual underpinnings and management practices associated with what today is called a high-performance workplace. In their description of the new paradigm of HR management, for example, Beer and Spector (1984) list fourteen guiding principles, including a systems perspective, a mutuality of interests, extensive communication and information sharing, a problem-solving approach to dispute resolution, gain sharing, and power equalization. Similarly, Levine and Tyson (1990) conclude that successful employee participation programs involve four fundamental components: assured individual rights, gain sharing, employment security, and a reduction in status differentials.

Many of these same principles were essential parts of the new HR paradigm that emerged in the late 1910s and were then implemented in the 1920s under the banner of Welfare Capitalism (Jacoby 1997; Kaufman 2001). The starting point of the new paradigm was a three-part hypothesis: (1) that the employment relationship contains elements of both cooperation and conflict, (2) superior organizational performance and job satisfaction come from a cooperative relationship, and (3) it is possible through appropriate management policies and practices to turn a conflictual employer-employee relationship into a cooperative one. *Cooperation* was the touchstone theme of the new management paradigm. The Conference Board (NICB 1922, p. 53) echoed this theme in stating: "the ultimate objective of employee representation may be regarded as the achievement of cooperation between management and men—the substitution of cooperation for antagonism."

And how was cooperation to be achieved? Here the proponents of the new HR paradigm took, per the advice of Beer and Spector, a systems perspective. They argued that achievement of a cooperative model requires that labor and management recognize that they have a mutuality of interests (Hicks 1941). Given such a recognition, workers and managers will conclude that they are members of the same team, that they win or lose together, and thus that they have every incentive to cooperate for the best interests of the organization. High levels of work effort, output, product quality, attendance at work, and so on, will inevitably flow, leading to a "win-win" combination of growth in profits, wages, and employment.

Consonant with a strategic systems perspective, the pioneers of the new HR paradigm developed a comprehensive, integrated set of new management practices and policies. And at many companies employee representation was the crown jewel of this new paradigm (Leiserson 1929; Brandes 1976; Gitelman 1992).

One prong of the new paradigm was, following Frederick Taylor, to apply *scientific management principles* to the organization and performance of work and labor management (Nelson 1980). Accordingly, during this period progressive firms took the lead in establishing the first personnel departments. The function of these departments was to centralize, standardize, and professionalize the management of the workforce. This meant, among other things, application of scientific principles and theories from fields such as engineering, psychology, and economics to the design and administration of production methods, employee selection procedures, incentive and gain-sharing pay programs, and dispute-resolution procedures. These scientific-based practices, it was thought, would increase both efficiency and equity in the workplace and, by fostering both greater loyalty to the company and a larger financial stake in its success, create a mutuality of interests.

A second prong went under the rubric of *human relations*. Contrary to conventional wisdom, the term "human relations" and the essence of human relations as an intellectual construct were not the product of Elton Mayo and the Hawthorne experiments in the late 1920s and early 1930s but emerged in the late 1910s in the writings and speeches of various business practitioners and consultants (Kaufman 1993). Their essential point was that relations between labor and capital are, in fact, relations between human beings and that

a cooperative employment relationship thus requires systems of leadership, motivation, and interpersonal and group relations that maintain dignity, foster human development, and promote justice. Accordingly, an essential element of the new HR paradigm was to move away from "hard" methods of labor discipline, the drive system, and the commodity treatment of labor toward more humane and democratic methods. Examples included the first training classes for foremen in human relations, establishment of "just cause" procedures for discipline and discharge, and extensive company-sponsored communication and recreation programs.

The third prong of the new paradigm was extensive provision of *employee welfare benefits* (Gitelman 1992). The Industrial Welfare movement had originated at the turn of the twentieth century, so the provision of benefits to employees, such as company housing, accident insurance, and a company doctor, was not a new idea by the 1920s. What was new was the notion that the welfare benefits should not be a relatively autonomous activity the company does for paternalistic motives; instead, they are a strategic part of the company's overall labor policy and are offered and structured in ways that are better linked to profit and loss.

The fourth prong of the new paradigm was employee representation. Some progressive/liberal employers implemented the other components of the new HRM model but did not adopt representation. Examples include Western Electric (Cohen 1990), Endicott-Johnson (Zahavi 1988), and International Business Machines (IBM). Nonetheless, among the firms in the vanguard of the new HRM movement, such as Standard Oil of New Jersey, Procter and Gamble, Goodyear, Du Pont, Eastman Kodak, and Swift, employee representation was ubiquitous. These employers believed that NERPs served several valuable functions (Calder 1924; Hall 1928). One was to improve two-way communication between management and workers. Another was to promote efficiency and economy in production. Yet another was to educate employees on the problems and perspectives of management and at the same time sensitize managers to the problems and perspectives of wage earners. Also important was extinguishing the smoldering fire of resentment and injustice among employees caused by unsettled grievances and perceived injustices. Finally, firms saw that providing employees with voice and participation in company affairs promoted loyalty and work effort.

Companies realized two important benefits from these considerable expenditures of time and money on improved employer-employee relations. The first was lower operating cost, higher product quality, and greater organizational learning (NICB 1922; Burton 1926; Bruere 1927, 1928); the second was union avoidance. Both are discussed in more detail below.

The Evolution of Employee Representation Up to the New Deal

The nation experienced a short but very sharp depression in 1920–21. This event represented an effective end to the wartime economy and the labor unrest that followed in its wake. The union movement was quickly deflated and put on the defensive, a position which it would occupy until mid-1933. In contrast, the decade of the 1920s was a period of sustained growth for NERPs and represented the "mature" phase of the employee representation movement. By the mid-1920s almost all of the compulsory World War I works councils had disappeared and what remained were 800–900 NERPs, many of which were operated by roughly forty large multiplant companies.

A detailed look at the experience of NERPs in the period from 1921 to 1932 is instructive because it is during this period of relative normalcy that an accurate assessment of both their accomplishments and shortcomings can best be made. In addition to the growth of employee representation, some consideration must also be given to the reasons for the decline in the organized labor movement, given the frequent charge that the latter is often a function of the former. Several aspects of this record, I argue, have too often been ignored or misinterpreted by contemporary scholars.

NERPs: A Mixed Record of Performance

The historical evidence suggests that the record of employee representation in the 1920s was a mixed one. Employee representation in some companies was quite successful; in others the performance was mediocre; and yet in others representation accomplished very little. I present four cases to illustrate the diversity of experience.

One of the most successful experiments in employee representation was at the Standard Oil Co. of New Jersey. Employment conditions at Jersey Standard prior to World War I were primitive and arduous, and supervisors and foremen administered personnel policy in a largely autocratic and oftentimes discriminatory fashion (Gibb and Knowlton 1956). The result was simmering discontent that erupted into large-scale, bloody strikes in 1915 and 1916. Jersey Standard was a Rockefeller company, and John D. Rockefeller Jr., based on his experience at Colorado Fuel & Iron Co., decided that fundamental change was needed in the company's approach to employee relations. Toward that end, he installed Walter Teagle—a proponent of more modern and progressive management practices—as president. Under Teagle, the company became a leading example of the Welfare Capitalist HRM model. The company established a personnel and training department, inaugurated a host of new employee benefits, reduced hours and increased wages, established an extensive new internal communications program with the workforce, and created an employee representation plan at its various facilities. Of these changes, Gibb and Knowlton state (1956, pp. 578–579), "No one of the many measures adopted in this first year of great transitions was unprecedented, but the comprehensive scope and the total effect of all the efforts imparted to company policy an almost revolutionary character." They go on to say (pp. 594–595, emphasis added), "In labor relations as in technology the company deliberately set as its goal the attainment of an *entirely new performance level*"—language clearly evocative of the goals of today's high-performance workplace model.

To administer the new labor relations program, Jersey Standard hired Clarence Hicks—the person Mackenzie King had earlier recruited to manage the NERP at CF&I—and made him an executive assistant reporting directly to Teagle. Under Hicks's guidance, employee representation plans were established in 1918 at the company's various refineries and facilities and operated continuously until 1937 when the company was forced by the newly enacted NLRA to disband them. According to Gray and Gullett (1973), who examined minutes of local council meetings at several refineries and interviewed workers, the representation plan

> contributed significantly and positively to harmonious industrial relations within the company. The plan influenced the development and usage of new formal channels of communication between management and the workforce. Through these channels employees filed grievances and made requests

for improvements in wages, hours, and working conditions. Using these same channels for transmitting information to the operating employees management explained its position on numerous matters of concern to the workforce. Evidence was presented which suggests that both sides were fairly successful in influencing the attitudes and actions of the other. (p. 38)

The evident satisfaction of the employees with the representation plans is illustrated by the fact that in numerous plant elections ordered by the NLRB during the late 1930s and again in the early 1940s over 97 percent of Jersey employees elected to keep their company unions in the form of "independent local unions," rather than join an AFL- or CIO-affiliated national union (Chase 1947).

A second example of progressive employment practices and successful employee representation is the Leeds and Northrup Company. *Forbes* magazine sponsored a competitive selection process in 1931 to identify companies with "the soundest worker-management relations" (Balderston 1935, p. v). Leeds and Northrup won first prize. In describing why the company was selected, Balderston says: "It is natural to expect that a program honored in this signal fashion would have the usual arrangements that one expects to find in a firm with advanced personnel policies, that is, *employee representation*, retirement annuities, group insurance, and systematic guidance of wage rates and promotion" (p. 141, emphasis added). Fittingly, the name chosen for the representation plan was the "Cooperative Association." As an indication of the work of the Council, Balderston relates that "since old age without income is another threat of insecurity that preys on the minds of workers of advancing years, the employee representatives in council requested, in 1926, that this subject be considered. A joint committee, on which council members predominated, worked on it assiduously for many months, finally reporting a plan of old age retirement allowances which was approved and put into operation in 1927" (p. 147).

Other employee representation plans achieved more mediocre results. One example is the plan established by Mackenzie King at the Colorado Fuel & Iron Co. According to Benjamin Selekman and Mary Van Kleeck (1924), who spent over five months in Colorado interviewing managers, miners, and union officials, the plan was still "an incomplete experiment" eight years after its inauguration (p. 398). In some areas employee representation had made a noticeable contribution, principally with regard to living conditions and settlement of individual grievances. Selekman found, however, that most miners expressed apathy toward the plan and voted in elections for representatives only at management's insistence. One major source of discontent with the NERP, according to Selekman, was that it gave the miners no voice in the determination of wages. (The plan mandated that the company would pay competitive wages, but it was reserved to management to determine what these were.) Another was that the plan allowed certain first-level supervisors to serve as employee representatives, but the miners did not trust that they would fairly represent their interests. Perhaps of most importance, despite Rockefeller's vow that the plan would establish a "partnership" between management and the miners, Selekman and Van Kleeck found that the employees were given no real opportunity to develop a sense of participation. Instead, management simply solicited the workers' suggestions or listened to their complaints and then announced a decision. That these shortcomings were real was evidenced, first, by several strikes in the early 1920s and, finally, by union organization of the company in 1933.

Finally we come to an example of a NERP that did little more than engender resentment and dissatisfaction among the employees. Margaret Meyer, a master's student at Cornell University under Sumner Slichter, studied the operation of the works council at the Schenectady, New York, plant of the General Electric Co. (Meyer 1927). During the World War I period the skilled workers at the plant were organized into several unions. The unions were militant and used their strike threat to settle most grievances in favor of the workers. But after the war the company ousted the unions after a long strike and operated the plant on an open-shop basis. In 1922 the plant manager presented a plan for employee representation to the workers, but they voted it down by a large margin. After letting some time go by, in 1924 the manager announced without taking a vote that a new works council plan was being put in effect. Its purpose was limited to "facilitating an exchange of views" and did not even provide a role for representatives in settling individual grievances. The most substantive issue put before the council was an employee request for establishment of old-age pensions. After the plant manager initially gave the go-ahead and a draft proposal was worked up, he changed his mind and stated that a pension program was not feasible at that time and that a jointly funded relief and loan program for employees was preferable anyway. Accordingly, such a plan was prepared and adopted, despite repeated statements by council members that they continued to desire the pension system. Other reasons why the shop council was not favorably viewed by employees included the fact that the company refused to distribute the minutes of council meetings, questions concerning wage rates were ruled out of order, and alleged discriminatory layoffs of older workers was met with a pledge of "we'll investigate it," after which nothing more was heard.

The Central Motive: Union Avoidance or Mutual Gain?

If NERPs were largely antiunion avoidance devices, it is reasonable to predict that during the course of the 1920s, when the labor movement was in marked decline, many employers would let their representation plans lapse, and few new ones would be established. The facts are just the opposite. As previously noted, the number of NERPs and employees covered by representation plans was higher in 1929 than ten years earlier. Perhaps more remarkably, even during the darkest days of the depression in 1931–33, relatively few companies (at least the solvent ones) disbanded their NERPs even under the pressure of extreme financial exigency and a close-to-zero probability of union organization.

The more compelling explanation for the expansion of NERPs during the 1920s has to do with the spread and consolidation of the new HR paradigm born during the World War I years and its central business motive: cooperation and mutual gain. If adoption of this new paradigm was indeed a *strategic* decision by these companies, they would be likely to stick with it over the long haul, unless of course it either proved ineffective or external conditions changed radically. And the evidence, I believe, is that most did stick with the new paradigm and, indeed, further refined and strengthened it.

The central purpose of employee representation and all other accoutrements of Welfare Capitalism was universally agreed by management spokespeople to be *cooperation* and *unity of interests*. W.T. Holliday (1934), president of Standard Oil of Ohio, states: "It [employee representation] originated as a part of the development of modern management, for the realization that mutual understanding and cooperation between management and the men were necessary for sound and efficient operation; that there could not be a proper and effective organization unless its men felt that they were being fairly and justly treated and had proper opportunity for their complaints and advice to be heard" (p. 100). In a similar spirit, E.K. Hall (1928), vice president of personnel at AT&T, said that employee representation originated from "the theory that it ought to be possible to unite every element in industry and tie it up tight for coordinated, effective action" (p. 77).

Skeptics are right to discount management rhetoric on this subject as tainted with self-interest, but according to outside and largely impartial observers at the time the goal of increased cooperation through "mutual gain" employee relations was indeed the central animating motive of Welfare Capitalism. Certainly two of the most credible eyewitnesses to employee representation are Sumner Slichter and William Leiserson, former students of John R. Commons and noted scholars, consultants, and arbitrators in the 1920s and 1930s.

The fact that labor's cooperation and goodwill, rather than overt and suppressive union avoidance, was the animating motive behind the personnel management is testified to by Slichter (1929) when he states: "*In short, every aspect of the post-war labor situation might be expected to cause employers to abandon their newly acquired interest in labor's goodwill and to revert to pre-war labor policies.* And yet this has not happened. On the contrary, the efforts to gain labor's goodwill have steadily grown" (pp. 396–397; emphasis in original). He goes on to say that "dread of labor troubles" remains an ever-present concern, but that "possibly the most important determinant of post-war labor policies during the last four or five years has been the growing realization by managers of the close relationship between industrial morale and efficiency" (p. 401).

Leiserson echoes this theme and also addresses the impact of Welfare Capitalism on the labor movement in these words:

> The trade unions may pooh-pooh the idea that there can be any other labor leaders than those who are officials of bona fide labor organizations, and they heap derision on welfare workers and organizers of company unions. But the facts are there for all who view them disinterestedly: that the Personnel Managers are leading the great masses of unskilled, semiskilled, and clerical workers away from the official labor movement, and attaching them with various devices more or less loyally to the management of the corporations which employ them. These personnel workers whom industry has put into the field know as well as the union leaders that injustice, exploitation, low wages, unfair discharges, overspending, and overwork cause resentment, discontent, strikes, and unionization. They know also that it is bad for business, leads to low productivity and high costs. They therefore make the prevention of such conditions their main tasks, and they try to impress on the managers of industry their responsibilities in this respect. (1929, p. 141)

Explicit in Leiserson's remarks is the proposition that improved employee relations leads to two valuable outcomes for management—higher profit through reduced cost and increased productivity and union avoidance. Critics of management, both then and now, decry the pacifying effect Welfare Capitalism and NERPs had on workers' desire for union representation, but in the view of Commons, Slichter, and Leiserson, the "bottom line" is that the employment conditions for workers were far superior to a decade earlier and often superior to what unions could obtain. The enviable status of workers at Welfare Capitalist firms was noted by Commons (1921,

p. 263) when he stated, "From 10 per cent to 25 per cent of American employers may be said to be so far ahead of the game that trade unions cannot reach them. Conditions are better, wages are better, security is better, than the unions can actually deliver to their members."

The fact that good treatment would quench the desire of workers for union representation was, of course, part of management's calculations. At Standard Oil of New Jersey, for example, Gibb and Knowlton (1956, p. 585) acknowledge that "there was a ready, if unspoken, appreciation of the fact the new plans and practices were suffocating by sheer weight of generosity the forces of unionism within the company." But most people—even persons sympathetic to the labor movement—find it difficult to see evil in this outcome. In this vein, Leiserson states:

> The weakening of trade unionism that has resulted is an undesirable consequence, but who will say then that we should go back to the days when management neglected its social responsibilities toward its employees. . . . The labor movement must have a mission beyond the program which personnel management has shown itself willing to adopt. If it is weakened by the activities of personnel management, it needs to look to its larger program. (1929, pp. 146–147)

Trade Unions Not a Viable or Attractive Option for Many Workers

As noted earlier, critics of employee representation and Welfare Capitalism claim these management programs are largely motivated by antiunion animus. Robert Bruere (1928), a trade unionist and associate editor of *Survey* magazine, sums up the view of organized labor on this matter in these words: "Welfare work and the company union in particular were singled out as the most insidious of all the devices invented by hostile employers to frustrate the aspirations of the labor movement" (p. 545). This line of argument is also subscribed to by a number of contemporary labor historians (e.g., Bernstein 1960; Brandes 1976; Gitelman 1988) and is used, in part, to explain the significant decline in union membership that took place during the 1920s.

Under closer scrutiny, however, it is clear that company unions and Welfare Capitalism were not the central problems bedeviling the labor movement of that period. In a private letter written to Leiserson in 1925, Sumner Slichter states: "I do not regard the company union as a very satisfactory explanation for the continuous decrease in membership of the A.F. of L. during the last three years" (quoted in Kaufman 2000). Then, writing four years later, Slichter (1929) makes the same point but then asks: "But have not the new personnel policies at least prevented the spread of unionism and thus are they not *indirectly* responsible for the fall in union membership?" And he answers: "To this question the answer must be that the effectiveness of the new labor policies in checking the spread of unionism has not been tested, because in few cases has a determined effort been made to organize plants in which the new policies are found" (p. 427).

Slichter's point—one amplified on by Nelson in his chapter in this volume—is that most of the companies in the vanguard of the Welfare Capitalism movement were in industries that had little or no unionism and in which organized labor had hitherto directed relatively little organizing activity (exceptions existed, such as railroads and steel). While in practice the two forms of employee representation in the 1920s were largely noncompeting groups, the spread and apparent success of Welfare Capitalism and NERPs did nonetheless strike fear into the hearts of the AFL leadership because they threatened not only to contain the advance of the organized labor movement within the narrow perimeter of industries and skilled trades already organized (e.g., construction, printing, the needle trades) but also to provide the means for organized employers at some future date to rid themselves of their unions. Given these unwelcome prospects, the AFL and its supporters launched a steady drumbeat of vitriolic criticism against company unions from 1919 until the passage of the NLRA in 1935. (Early in World War I, the AFL endorsed shop committees in the hope that they would provide a springboard to unionization, but then switched to a hostile position when this hope appeared fruitless.)

What is too often neglected, both then and now, is that on a number of counts the organized labor movement was itself responsible for the loss of membership and momentum it suffered in the 1920s. It must be remembered, for example, that most unions were craft unions that catered to skilled, native-born male workers. A number actively discriminated against workers who were foreign born, female, or members of minority racial or ethnic groups, leading Leiserson (1929) to remark that "the history of handling of these workers by the trade unions is not something to impress on their minds that the unions are particularly desirous of promoting their interests" (p. 157).

Likewise, most unions of this period expressed little interest in organizing the unskilled and semi-skilled workers of American industry. Looking back on the 1920s, for example, Cyrus Ching (1973), a vice president of industrial relations at U.S. Rubber and an influential exponent of progressive personnel practices, said in this regard: "The A.F. of L. at that time was not interested in that type of work or in the mass production industry worker at all. Sam Gompers made it very plain that he was only interested in skilled crafts and the so-called aristocracy of labor, and they didn't have the necessary administrative ability or the staff to really organize mass industry. They didn't want to in the first place" (pp. 91–92). Indicative of the AFL's lack of interest and gumption in organizing industrial workers was the fact that General Electric's progressive chairman, Gerard Swope, invited William Green (AFL president) to his office in the late 1920s and indicated that the company would not oppose union organization if it was on an industrial basis (Loth 1958). He never heard back from Green.

Unions of that era had other liabilities that reduced employee demand for representation. Several unions, particularly in the building trades and local services (e.g., dry cleaning, building maintenance) had significant elements of corruption and racketeering (Hostetter and Beesely 1929). Public approval of unions was also hurt by frequent jurisdictional disputes, sympathy strikes, and high initiation fees and other devices that limited membership (Daugherty 1934). The internal governance of some unions of the 1920s was also rife with cronyism and autocracy. Another factor was the quality of union leadership, often judged by outside observers to be mediocre and unimaginative (see citations in Kaufman 1996). Also of relevance is the fact that it was employers, not unions, who were in the front line of innovation with regard to new employment practices, such as paid vacations and promotion from within. And, as supporters of progressive trade unionism ruefully noted at the time, it was the employers, not the unions, that were in the forefront of popularizing a "vertical" (industrial) form of labor organization (Bruere 1927). Finally, many labor unions of that period did not have well-developed shop committees but relied on a business agent or "walking delegate" to check periodically on conditions and intervene in case

of a dispute, an arrangement that tended to isolate union officials from the day-to-day concerns of the employees and needs of the company (Bernheim and Van Doren 1935).

Indicative of the moribund state of organized labor in the 1920s and early 1930s are the recollections of Thomas Eliot, a self-professed "New Dealer" who worked in the Roosevelt administration as a deputy to Labor Secretary Francis Perkins. He recounts in his autobiography:

> While I was all for upholding the workers' rights under Section 7(a), and highly critical of employers who denied them those rights, I was not automatically pro-union. Far from it. Frequently I wrote [to his family in 1933] about the leaders of some of the major A.F. of L. craft unions, especially in the building trades, calling them "a bunch of racketeers in league with a lot of the building contractors." And again, "It's hard to be enthusiastic about organized labor." Those were early comments, but in 1934 I still felt the same way: "I'd like to see equality of bargaining power, but I doubt the efficacy of any program designed to increase the strength of the A.F. of L. as presently constituted. There is a dearth of disinterested labor leaders. If some of the top men could be deported, and Sydney Hillman and Phillip Murray and a few like that put in charge, then maybe we'd have a worthwhile labor movement." (Eliot 1992, pp. 56–57)

Seen in this light, company unions—despite their acknowledged defects—were not as evidently inferior to trade unions as the critics of the employee representation often maintain. The surest proof of this statement is that even at the height of union organizing activity in the 1933–35 period over one-third of workers voted for company union representation in secret ballot elections conducted by the two labor boards created by executive order of President Roosevelt (Wolman 1936). These results, it should be noted, understate the demand for company-sponsored plans among the total workforce because the elections were held only at companies where union organizing was under way.

Employee Representation Delivered Tangible Benefits to Both Employers and Employees

Some company unions, such as the General Electric example described above, were little more than window dressing or a stopgap device to keep out a trade union. A significant number, however, established a clear record of accomplishment and measurably improved the working life of employees and at the same time delivered smoother, more productive employment relations for companies.

Observers (e.g., Leiserson 1929) were agreed that the single most important accomplishment of employee representation was to curb the arbitrary, sometimes tyrannous power of the foreman over the rank and file worker. As noted earlier, up to the time of World War I, the individual shop foreman or gang boss was given considerable autonomy and authority to manage labor as he saw fit. The injustices, resentments, and conflicts bred by this system need not be further elaborated. Of all groups in the workplace, it was typically the front-line cadre of supervisors and foremen who most disliked employee representation, resisted its introduction, and overtly or covertly sabotaged its effectiveness. And the reasons were simple: employee representation curbed their power, gave employees an alternative channel to obtain redress to grievances, and made their actions not only accountable to others but also subject to outside investigation and criticism.

It is true, as critics charge, that the effectiveness of NERPs in protecting workers' rights and giving them voice was frequently compromised by fear of retribution and lack of independent representation. But, on the other hand, the pro-

tection they afforded was still much superior to that under traditional arrangements. Bernheim and Van Doren (1935) testify to this mixed record when they say that "employee associations have been very efficient sources of getting at petty difficulties but have in numerous instances been deficient in the handling of major issues" (p. 106) but then later state: "Company unions often supply effective machinery for adjusting grievances and correcting abuses. . . . In this respect they afford the employee a means of protection which he can seldom achieve under conditions of individual bargaining" (p. 331). Leiserson (1929) reaches a similarly upbeat conclusion when he states, "An examination of the grievances adjusted under employee representation plans reveals that the vast majority of cases are settled in favor of the workers when the plans are first adopted. Later more care is taken to prevent injustice to workers" (p. 160).

Both case studies (e.g., Selekman 1924; Smith 1960; Schatz 1983; Schacht 1985) and quantitative empirical analyses (Fairris 1997) reveal that NERPs led to a variety of other benefits for employees. Examples include lower accident rates, rehabilitation of rundown company housing; provision of locker rooms, eating facilities, and clean restrooms and drinking water; medical services, legal help; employees' magazines; and company sports teams. Fairris (1997) also finds that companies with NERPs experienced higher rates of productivity growth. An additional indirect benefit of NERPs was that they often caused companies to set up a personnel department, or to strengthen it considerably. (Only one-third of companies with 250 or more employees had a personnel department as of 1929. See Jacoby 1985.) Indeed, observers of employee representation were nearly unanimous in noting that employee representation led to a significant improvement in the overall professionalism and skills of management (Burton 1926).

It is easy in hindsight to dismiss many of the employee benefits listed above as inconsequential, tools of management control, or a product of a degrading management paternalism. But in the context of the 1920s many of these things represented a substantial improvement in the quality of work life. Leiserson (1928) attests to this when he observed:

> The unskilled and semi-skilled working people of this country, in the last six years, have obtained more of the things . . . out of employee representation plans than they have out of the organized labor movement. . . . There is even evidence that these workers sometimes deliberately prefer company unions to the regular trade unions. The reason is that they think employee representation is doing what the unions have failed to do. (p. 127)

Finally, a common criticism of NERPs is that they were powerless to win improvements in wages and hours for workers. Certainly they lacked the bargaining power of an independent union. But companies that created NERPs were also subject to two other forces besides raw bargaining power. One was that the NERPs represented incipient unions and, in order to keep employees loyal (or at least docile), the companies would more readily grant a wage advance, delay a wage reduction, or adjust piece rates or work hours than they would have without a NERP. A second was that the payoff to a NERP was winning labor's goodwill and cooperation, and managers knew that there was a "price tag" attached to this in the form of above-average wage levels.

Perhaps the clearest example of the impact on wages of management's new labor policy in general, and NERPs in particular, was the difference in wage behavior in the 1920–21 depression and

a decade later in the Great Depression (Bernstein 1960; Kaufman 1996). In the former, the bulk of firms quickly started cutting wages when the downturn came. In the latter, the large, progressive firms resisted wage cuts even though the plants were operating at only 10–25 percent of capacity (Ozanne 1967; Brody 1980) and profits were decimated. Only in the fall of 1931, after two full years of depression, did these companies finally succumb and institute wage reductions. This may be reckoned as the price employers were willing to pay for labor's loyalty and cooperation.

The New Deal and the Demise of Employee Representation

The evidence indicates that the experience of American workers in the 1920s with company unions was, on net, positive, but nonetheless fraught with ambivalence and burdened by expectations that were only partially fulfilled. On one hand, workers gained tangible benefits from NERPs and appreciated management's oftentimes sincere effort to forge better labor-management relations, while on the other hand they distrusted management's motives, chafed at the workers' lack of power and control, and resented paternalism and manipulation.

Even with this mixed record, it is significant and impressive that in the course of a single decade leading-edge American employers went from a situation in which they had no formal personnel programs or policies to one featuring a professionally staffed personnel department, a plethora of employee benefits, and, most remarkably, a joint council where management met with worker representatives to discuss employment and production problems of mutual concern. Both the promise and accomplishments of Welfare

Capitalism seemed sufficiently bright that Leiserson (1929) was moved to end his review essay of the personnel management movement with these words: "But with all due allowances made, when the contributions of Personnel Management are recapitulated in some such fashion as we have attempted, the result is bound to be an imposing sum" (p. 164).

But six years later, Welfare Capitalism lay in ruins, and Leiserson was testifying before Congress in support of the Wagner Act and its ban on company unions. How could events and public opinion take such a drastic turn? The answer rests with the economic calamity of the Great Depression and the New Deal economic recovery program adopted by the Roosevelt administration in response to it.

The NIRA and Section 7(a)

The downfall of nonunion employee representation is inextricably linked with the Great Depression and passage of the National Industrial Recovery Act (NIRA) in June 1933 (Brody 1980; Kaufman 1996). When Franklin Roosevelt assumed office in March of that year, the American economy was on the verge of collapse. Roosevelt's most important, far-reaching economic recovery measure was the National Industrial Recovery Act, a piece of legislation partially written by Senator Robert Wagner, sponsored by Wagner in the Senate, and enacted into law with only a relatively short debate in Congress.

In 1933, opinion on what caused the depression was fragmented and confused, leading to an equally diverse and conflicting body of proposals on how to spur economic recovery. Some people blamed foreign financial crises, others cited maladroit monetary policy on the part of the U.S. Federal Reserve Bank, while yet others pointed to unbridled stock market speculation and excessive debt. Whether coincidence or rooted in some common experience, two of the most powerful and influential men in the U.S. government held the same view on these questions and shaped economic policy with this view in mind. These two men were Franklin Roosevelt, the president, and Senator Robert Wagner, widely acknowledged as one of the Senate's most astute politicians and its most articulate spokesman on domestic economic affairs.

In Senate testimony on the NIRA, Wagner outlined his (and, implicitly, Roosevelt's) diagnosis for the origins of the depression. He stated that the depression was the product of a growing imbalance between aggregate demand and supply. During the 1920s, profits grew far faster than wages, which caused, in turn, the nation's ability to produce goods and services to outstrip consumer's ability to purchase them; also, there was an excessive inflow of speculative capital into the stock market. The end result was overproduction, a growing glut of unsold products, and an eventual stock market crash. The initial slump was aggravated by a series of wage and price cuts that began in 1930 and gathered downward momentum the next year. Wagner labeled this process "destructive competition" because the desperate attempt by firms and workers to maintain sales and employment through price and wage cuts only further intensified the downturn, in his view, by precipitating a cascading series of bankruptcies and an additional shrinkage of household income and purchasing power.

Given this diagnosis, Wagner and Roosevelt sought to reverse the downturn through a three-pronged attack embodied in the NIRA: stabilization of the wage-price structure in the near term to short-circuit the process of destructive competition; an increase in household purchasing power and aggregate spending in the medium to long run through a redistribution of income from capital to labor; and a spur to job creation through a "spread the work" program of reduced work hours and a large public works program (Farr 1959).

The first two objectives were to be attained through provisions contained in "codes of fair competition" adopted and implemented by each industry. The NIRA suspended portions of the antitrust laws so that employers could work out price and production stabilization procedures through industry trade associations. If employers were to be allowed and encouraged to combine to set prices collectively, then it was both a matter of equity and good economics similarly to encourage combination and wage setting on the part of labor (good economics in that wage rates needed to be maintained and even increased relative to prices if a redistribution of income was to occur). Hence, at Senator Wagner's insistence, a Section 7(a) was included in the NIRA that mandated that every code of competition contain a statement affirming as national policy that workers had the right to join labor organizations of their own choosing and engage in collective bargaining without interference or coercion (Bernstein 1950; Farr 1959). Section 7(a) also mandated that every code of competition establish minimum-wage rates and maximum hours applying to all workers in the industry. Both the minimum-wage and collective bargaining mandates were aimed at stabilizing wages and augmenting consumer purchasing power and aggregate demand.

Given this overview, the key points bearing on the issue of employee representation are these:

1. Until the drafting of the NIRA was well under way in the late spring of 1933, scant evidence exists that Roosevelt planned on asking for legislation to encourage collective bargaining. He had not mentioned such legislation in his campaign speeches, it was not mentioned in the 1932 Democratic Party platform, and most of his economic and political advisers, with the notable exception of Wagner, were not particularly enthusiastic about the cause of organized labor. Equally important, there is little evidence that the bulk of American workers had a strong, preexisting demand for union representation, at least of the AFL variety. Even after Roosevelt was elected, but before the NIRA was announced, union organizing remained in the doldrums, and union activists despaired of making headway when workers were so apathetic and disinterested (Bernstein 1970; Zieger 1984). Instead, the fact that Section 7(a) was included in the NIRA was due to (1) the conviction of Roosevelt and his advisers that wage stabilization and wage increases were needed to promote recovery, (2) the threat by Wagner that "no Section 7(a) no bill," and (3) the need to assuage the AFL after FDR opposed the Federation's pet recovery program based on a maximum thirty-hour workweek (the "thirty-hour" bill, introduced by Senator Hugo Black earlier in 1933).

2. The NIRA was launched with great fanfare, including parades and patriotic speeches across the nation. Organized labor, and particularly the United Mine Workers (UMW) union, touted in speeches, placards and car caravans that "the president wants you to join the union." Although the NIRA was actually neutral on this matter (Section 7(a) protected the right to join a union, but also made clear that workers could join a company union or no union at all), the message had a powerful effect and thousands of workers across the country rushed to join unions. Without question, a portion of this demand for union representation was organic, much like the World War

I rush to join unions, and arose from the deterioration in labor conditions during the depression, a mounting sense of grievance and injustice, and disillusionment with employers and the broken promises of Welfare Capitalism. (A particular grievance was that many companies, such as International Harvester, maintained stockholder dividends at pre-depression levels even as they repeatedly cut wages and hours.) Equally clear, however, was that another portion arose from quite different motives, including patriotic duty and a belief that collective bargaining would spur economic recovery. Zieger (1984) nicely captures the melange of influences when he states: "Workers in every sector seized upon the NRA promise, as a means both of bettering their individual lot and of revitalizing the economy. Patriotism fused with self-interest" (p. 71). Also operative was the growing belief among workers that they needed to organize in independent trade unions if labor's interests were to be given due weight in Washington, D.C., where the labor provisions in the NIRA's codes of fair competition were being drafted—per economist David McCabe's remark (1934, p. 77) that "the Recovery Act has to date given less impetus to organization for collective bargaining . . . than to organization for political action."

3. Most employers did not anticipate the climactic effect that Section 7(a) would have on labor relations, evidenced in part by the fact that little business lobbying effort had gone into deleting Section 7(a) from the NIRA bill (Farr 1959). Given the belated perception of many employers that some form of collective bargaining was now heavily favored, if not mandated (per the comment of Dale Yoder [1938, p. 477] that "the Act was widely described as having made collective bargaining compulsory . . ."), and their palpable fear of bona fide trade unions, hun-

dreds of companies rushed to form employee representation plans, others resuscitated NERPs that had atrophied in years gone by, and those with functioning NERPs often modified them in ways that would, they hoped, allow the plans to pass as agencies of collective bargaining (e.g., instead of employees and management meeting jointly, the employees now met separately; some type of written agreement between the NERP and company was drafted and signed). Some management representatives (e.g., Ching 1973) candidly acknowledged that most of these company unions were established expressly for union-avoidance purposes or as a way to stay in compliance with Section 7(a)'s perceived sanction of collective bargaining and were "frauds" if alleged to serve any other purpose.

4. Employers' rush to install company unions, coupled with widespread discrimination against union activists and refusals to bargain with outside unions, led to a growing adverse public and political reaction. Part of this negative reaction was fueled by a sense that employers were engaged in rank hypocrisy when, on one hand, they supported the NIRA provisions that let companies collectively determine product prices and sales quotas and yet, on the other hand, so stoutly resisted in both principle and practice the ability of workers to combine in trade unions to set wages and other terms and conditions of employment. The public also had a difficult time reconciling employers' adamant resistance to unions when these same companies had for more than a decade preached the virtues of what was then called "the doctrine of high wages" (e.g., that high wages are good for business because it gives consumers the means to purchase the products of industry).

5. So many disputes arose over the administration and enforcement of Section 7(a) that Roosevelt was forced in August 1933 to estab-

lish by executive order a new agency, the National Labor Board (NLB). Early in 1934 the NLB was replaced by a new board, the National Labor Relations Board (NLRB). Both boards were chaired by Senator Wagner and were empowered to mediate disputes and hold secret ballot elections to determine workers' choice of bargaining agent. Wagner became involved in hundreds of disputes and became increasingly radicalized as he came face to face with repeated cases where employers refused to consent to secret ballot elections, engaged in blatant antiunion discrimination, and foisted hastily built employee representation plans on their reluctant workers (Huthmacher 1968). Not only did this offend Wagner's sense of fair play, but it also seemed to undercut the viability of the president's economic recovery program, depending as it did on raising wages.

6. In reaction, Wagner set to work in 1934 to draft new legislation, which subsequently became the National Labor Relations Act, that would strengthen and clarify Section 7(a) of the NIRA. He stated repeatedly that the cause of the depression was the marked inequality of bargaining power that existed between capital and labor and that economic recovery depended on equalizing bargaining power in order to restore a balance between wages and profits. He thus viewed the proliferation of company unions as the greatest threat to the Roosevelt economic program because they were set up explicitly to thwart union organization, which he viewed as essential to recovery. His position in this matter is clearly stated in a 1934 article he authored in the *New York Times* (reprinted in National Labor Relations Board 1985, pp. 22–26). He states:

> The company union has improved personal relations, group-welfare activities, discipline, and other matters that may be handled on a local basis. But it has failed dismally to standardize or

improve wage levels, for the wage question is a general one whose sweep embraces whole industries, or States, or even the Nation. Without wider areas of cooperation among employees there can be no protection against the nibbling tactics of the unfair employer or of the worker who is willing to degrade standards by serving for a pittance.

It is noteworthy that in these remarks Wagner explicitly recognizes that NERPs provide positive benefits in terms of in-plant employment conditions. Yet he advocates banning them for economic reasons—in particular because they cannot take wages out of competition.

7. Wagner repeatedly stated that he did not object to "company unions" as long as they were independent employee organizations free of any management influence. The nonunion form of employee representation plan, however, was inevitably dominated by management and thus, in his words, "real collective bargaining becomes impossible when management sits on both sides of the table." In order to root out all forms of employer domination, he included Section 8(a)(2), which prohibits employers from *dominating or interfering with the formation or administration of any labor organization or contributing financial support to it*. And to make sure that employers could not wiggle around this prohibition, he drafted the language of Section 2(5) very broadly so that a labor organization is defined expansively to include *any type of committee or plan which employees participate in on a representational basis* and that engages in *any type of dealing with employers over grievances, labor disputes, wages, rages of pay, hours of employment, or conditions of work*. As a result, early NLRB and court rulings declared illegal nearly all of the various types of NERPs established by employers up to that point. By the early 1940s, as Jacoby describes in his chapter in this

volume, NERPs had either been disbanded, transformed by employers into independent plant-level labor unions, or organized into locals of national or international trade unions. The employee representation movement, which began in earnest in 1915 with the founding of the Rockefeller Plan at CF&I, had come to an unexpected and inglorious end only two decades later.

Conclusions

My conclusion from a review of the historical evidence is that the employee representation plans that emerged and proliferated in American industry during the 1915–35 period were, on net, a constructive, positive development for improved industrial relations. Instead of being "sham" organizations, "little more than a facade," or a "misadventure," as charged by critics (e.g., Brandes 1976; Gitelman 1988; Cohen 1990; Barenberg 1993; Brody 1994), NERPs were a signal step in the evolution of management from a commodity model of labor toward a more humane, strategic, and participative model. In this respect, employee representation and the Welfare Capitalist HRM model were the first steps on the road to what is often called today a *high-performance, mutual-gain workplace*. Although this assessment of employee representation is at odds with the conclusions that most labor historians reached, it is consistent with the observations of the foremost labor historian of that period—John R. Commons—and the foremost academic experts on the practice of personnel management in the 1920s—Commons's students-turned-professors Sumner Slichter and William Leiserson (Kaufman 2000a).

My positive evaluation of employee representation is not meant, however, to be an apologia for company unions. The historical record is clear that the performance of NERPs in many cases fell significantly short of the results touted by their most ardent proponents. It is also equally clear that many employers, particularly in the World War I and NIRA periods, established NERPs for the primary purpose of union avoidance. Nor is there any disputing the contention that NERPs are inherently management dominated and nondemocratic. But these charges, in my view, do not constitute grounds for a blanket condemnation of NERPs nor for their legal banishment, as currently contained in the National Labor Relations Act.

Consider, for example, the charge that NERPs are management dominated and nondemocratic. To critics of employee representation, it is patently obvious that any organization established and operated by the employer is unable to serve the interests of the workers effectively (Morris 1994; Herrnstadt 1997). But such is not necessarily the case. Upon reflection, it is clear that every aspect of a nonunion firm's human resource policy and practice is management dominated. It is the management, after all, that establishes the rules and regulations that determine compensation, training, hiring and firing, and the administration of discipline. Although all these dimensions of human resource practice are unilaterally determined by management, and are not subject to any kind of democratic vote by the workers, no one seriously recommends that they be declared illegal for this reason or that they are necessarily detrimental to the interests of employees. Parallel reasoning suggests that if it is legitimate for management unilaterally to determine these other parts of human resource practice, then it should also be legitimate for firms to establish and operate employee representation committees and councils. The other side of liberty, however, is responsibility. Just as it is incumbent on nonunion employers to operate their compensation, training, and staffing functions in a nonexploitative, nondiscriminatory manner, so too is it incumbent on them to operate employee councils and committees in a manner that promotes socially advantageous, mutual-gain outcomes. The challenge of social policy, therefore, is to create the appropriate system of checks and balances that protects and promotes employee interests and at the same time allows nonunion firms as much flexibility as possible in the design and operation of their human resource programs.

In my view, the best approach for social policy in this regard was enunciated sixty years ago by Slichter in testimony before Congress on Senator Wagner's proposed Labor Disputes Act (the forerunner to the NLRA). He states:

> The problem which impresses me as overwhelmingly important is not one of preventing the formation of the so-called "company union," because as a practical matter I do not believe that can be done . . . even if it were desirable to do it. But the problem is giving the independent labor organization a fair opportunity to compete with the employee committees and to provide a method by which, in an impartial manner, the wishes, the preferences of the employees can be ascertained. (National Labor Relations Board 1985, p. 92)

Slichter's position is that both union and nonunion forms of employee representation should be permitted by law and that the guarantor that both serve the public interest is *competition and free choice*. I believe Slichter is correct on this matter and on two counts. First, competition and free choice are bedrock principles in the American social ethos and thus a policy toward nonunion employee representation based on these principles is most likely to gain public support and social legitimacy. Second, Slichter's position is also in accord with abundant theoretical and empirical evidence that competition and free

choice in both the economic and political spheres best promotes economic progress and protect the rights and interests of all parties. The reason is that competition and free choice prevent individuals or social institutions from taking advantage of the public by exploiting a monopoly position and, at the same time, motivate them to serve their "customers" (consumers or citizens) in the most efficient, highest-quality manner.

The lesson to be learned from the history of employee representation prior to the Wagner Act is that the abuses and shortcomings of NERPs are *not* best solved by banning them but by creating conditions of competition and free choice so that employers are effectively constrained from using them for opportunistic, exploitative purposes. As I have argued elsewhere (Kaufman 1999; also see Kaufman and Levine in this volume), greater competition and free choice with respect to forms of employee representation can be promoted in two ways. The first is by using monetary, fiscal, and training policies to ensure conditions of full employment in labor markets; the second is to use labor law to ensure that employees have a relatively unobstructed, low-cost access to an alternative form of representation (including no representation) if they are dissatisfied with the system currently at their workplace. Both policies effectively prevent employers from using NERPs for antisocial, opportunistic purposes, such as union avoidance, since workers can readily exit the firm for other employment or vote for independent union representation. Likewise, when nonunion companies face effective competition for the loyalty of their workers in both the labor market and the "market" for alternative forms of representation, they are far more motivated to structure and operate NERPs (and all other HR practices) in a manner that promotes mutual gain, win-win outcomes.

Seen in this light, the National Labor Relations Act was a much-needed step toward accomplishing the second part of this policy agenda (promoting employee free choice in the market for alternative representation), but it seriously erred in banning nonunion representation in an effort to promote the first (macroeconomic recovery). Not only was this bad economics (Bernstein 1987), but it robbed nonunion companies of a valuable device for improving both productivity and employee well-being. The correct policy response today is to further strengthen the NLRA where necessary in order to protect employee free choice (e.g., stronger financial penalties for employer acts of antiunion discrimination), maintenance of the social commitment to full employment, and a substantial relaxation of the NLRA's strictures on NERPs.

The weight of the historical evidence is that nonunion employee representation plans in the 1920s, and the Welfare Capitalist HRM model of which they were a part, were a significant, positive development in industrial relations and promoted the interests of both employers and employees. Certainly the performance on employee representation fell short of the hopes and pronouncements of its most ardent proponents, and equally certain is the fact that NERPs were used as explicit tools of union avoidance. But these shortcomings and abuses were magnified by inadequate protections of the right to organize, the debacle of the Great Depression, and the misguided efforts of the Roosevelt administration to stimulate economic recovery through cartelization of markets and increased unionization. Had labor law and macroeconomic policy been structured along the lines suggested here, NERPs most certainly never would have been banned and, indeed, would most likely remain a central component of the human resource practices of progressive, high-involvement nonunion

employers (see the chapters by Taras in this volume for evidence from Canada). I further conjecture that even the organized labor movement would benefit from the modified deregulation of NERPs advocated here. Unions, like nonunion employers, would be motivated by greater competition to develop and implement more effective programs in order to recruit and retain workers. And unions would also find that NERPs provide a fertile source of new organizing opportunities. Just as happened in the 1930s, some nonunion employers would run their NERPs in a maladroit, opportunistic manner, and their workers, like workers in steel, auto, and other industries sixty years ago, would quickly become disillusioned and seek union representation.

References

Asher, R., R. Edsforth, with R. Boryczka. 1995. "The Speedup: The Focal Point of Workers' Grievances, 1919–1941." In *Autowork*, ed. R. Asher and R. Edsforth, pp. 65–98. Albany: SUNY Press.

Balderston, Canby. 1935. *Executive Guidance of Industrial Relations*. Philadelphia: University of Pennsylvania Press.

Barenberg, Mark. 1993. "The Political Economy of the Wagner Act." *Harvard Law Review* (May) 106: 1381–1496.

Basset, William. 1919. *When the Workmen Help You Manage*. New York: Century.

Beer, Michael, and Bert Spector. 1984. "Human Resource Management: The Integration of Industrial Relations and Organizational Development." In *Research in Personnel and Human Resource Management*, vol. 2, ed. Gerald Ferris and Kenneth Rowland, pp. 261–297. Greenwich, Conn.: JAI Press.

Benge, Eugene. 1927. "Trends in Labor Management." *Industrial Management* 73, no. 2: 124–125.

Bernheim, Alfred, and Dorothy Van Doren, eds. 1935. *Labor and the Government*. New York: Twentieth Century Fund.

Bernstein, Irving. 1950. *The New Deal Collective Bargaining Policy*. Berkeley: University of California Press.

———. 1960. *The Lean Years: A History of the American Worker, 1920–1933*. Boston: Houghton Mifflin.

———. 1970. *The Turbulent Years: A History of the American Worker, 1933–1941*. Boston: Houghton Mifflin.

Bernstein, Michael. 1987. *The Great Depression: Delayed Recovery and Economic Change in America, 1929–1939.* New York: Cambridge University Press.

Brandes, Stuart. 1976. *American Welfare Capitalism, 1880–1940.* Chicago: University of Chicago Press.

Brody, David. 1965. *Labor in Crisis.* New York: Lippincott.

———. 1980. *Workers in Industrial America: Essays on the Twentieth Century Struggle.* New York: Oxford University Press.

———. 1994. "Section 8(a)(2) and the Origins of the Wagner Act." In *Restoring the Promise of American Labor Law,* ed. Ronald Sieber, Sheldon Friedman, and Joseph Uehlein, pp. 29–44. Ithaca, N.Y.: ILR Press.

Bruere, Robert. 1927. "32,000 R.P.M." *The Survey,* January 1, pp. 443–448, 472–473.

———. 1928. "A Quaker Builds a Company Union." *The Survey,* September 1, pp. 545–547, 567–573.

Bureau of Labor Statistics, U.S. Department of Labor. 1937. *Characteristics of Company Unions, 1935.* Bulletin No. 634. Washington, D.C.: U.S. Government Printing Office.

Burton, Ernest. 1926. *Employee Representation.* Baltimore: Williams and Wilkins.

Calder, John. 1924. *Modern Industrial Relations.* New York: Longmans, Green.

Carpenter, O.F. 1921. "Instituting Employee Representation." In *Industrial Government,* ed. John Commons, pp. 340–364. New York: Macmillan.

———. 1928a. "Experiments in Industrial Democracy: The Evolution of a Pioneer Democracy." *Factory and Industrial Management,* February, pp. 289–293.

———. 1928b. "Experiments in Industrial Democracy: A Combination of Legislative and Conference Plans." *Factory and Industrial Management,* April, pp. 766–769.

Chase, Stuart. 1947. *A Generation of Peace: Thirty Years of Labor Relations at Standard Oil Company (N.J.).* New Jersey: Standard Oil Company.

Ching, Cyrus. 1973. *Reminiscences of Cyrus Ching.* New York: Columbia University Oral History Project.

Cohen, Lizabeth. 1990. *Making a New Deal: Industrial Workers in Chicago, 1919–1939.* New York: Columbia University Press.

Commission on the Future of Worker-Management Relations. 1994. *Fact-finding Report.* Washington, D.C.: U.S. Department of Labor and U.S. Department of Commerce.

Commons, John. 1919. *Industrial Goodwill.* New York: McGraw-Hill.

———. 1921. *Industrial Government.* New York: Macmillan.

Cowdrick, Edward. 1924. *Manpower in Industry.* New York: Henry Holt.

Daugherty, Carroll. 1934. *Labor Under the N.R.A.* New York: Houghton Mifflin.

Derber, Milton. 1970. *The American Ideal of Industrial Democracy.* Urbana: University of Illinois Press.

Douglas, Paul. 1921. "Shop Committees: Substitute for, or Supplement to, Trade-Unions." *Journal of Political Economy* 29, no. 2: 89–107.

Dulebohn, James, Gerald Ferris, and James Stodd. 1995. "The History and Evolution of Human Resource Management." In *Handbook of Human Resource Management,* ed. Gerald Ferris, Sherwin Rosen, and Darold Barnum, pp. 18–41. New York: Blackwell.

Dunn, Robert. 1926. *American Company Unions.* Chicago: Trade Union Educational League.

Eliot, Thomas. 1992. *Recollections of the New Deal: When the People Mattered.* Boston: Northeastern University Press.

Fairris, David. 1997. *Shopfloor Matters: Labor-Management Relations in Twentieth Century American Manufacturing.* London: Routledge.

Farr, Grant. 1959. *The Origins of Recent Labor Policy.* Boulder: University of Colorado Press.

French, Carroll. 1923. *The Shop Committee in the United States.* Baltimore: Johns Hopkins University Press.

Gibb, George, and E. Knowlton. 1956. *The Resurgent Years, 1911–1927.* Vol. 2 in *History of Standard Oil (N.J.).* New York: McGraw-Hill.

Gitelman, H.M. 1988. *Legacy of the Ludlow Massacre.* Philadelphia: University of Pennsylvania Press.

———. 1992. "Welfare Capitalism Reconsidered." *Labor History* 33, no. 1: 5–31.

Gray, Edmund, and C. Ray Gullett. 1973. "Employee Representation at Standard Oil Company of New Jersey: A Case Study." Occasional Paper 11. Baton Rouge: College of Business Administration, Louisiana State University.

Hall, E.K. 1928. "What Is Employee Representation?" *Personnel* 4 (February): 71–84.

Herrnstadt, Owen. 1997. "Section 8(a)(2) of the NLRA: The Debate." *Labor Law Journal* 48, no. 2: 98–112.

Hicks, Clarence. 1941. *My Life in Industrial Relations.* New York: Harper & Bros.

Hogler, Raymond, and Guillermo Grenier. 1992. *Employee Participation and Labor Law in the American Workplace.* Westport, Conn.: Quorem.

Hostetter, Gordon, and Thomas Beesley. 1929. *It's a Racket!* Chicago: Les Quin Books.

Hotchkiss, Willard. 1920. "Participation in Management—Discussion." *American Economic Review* 10: 110–115.

Huthmacher, J. 1968. *Senator Robert F. Wagner and the Rise of Urban Liberalism.* New York: Athenaeum.

Jacoby, Sanford. 1985. *Employing Bureaucracy: Managers, Unions, and the Transformation of Work in American Industry, 1900–1945.* New York: Columbia University Press.

———. 1989. "Reckoning with Company Unions: The Case of Thompson Products, 1934–1964." *Industrial and Labor Relations Review* 43, no. 1: 19–40.

———. 1997. *Modern Manors: Welfare Capitalism Since the New Deal.* Princeton: Princeton University Press.

Jacoby, Sanford, and Anil Verma. 1992. "Enterprise Unions in the United States." *Industrial Relations* 31, no. 1: 137–158.

Kaufman, Bruce. 1989. "Labor's Inequality of Bargaining Power: Changes Over Time and Implications for Public Policy." *Journal of Labor Research* 10, no. 3: 185–199.

———. 1993. *The Origins and Evolution of the Field of Industrial Relations in the United States.* Ithaca, N.Y.: ILR Press.

———. 1996. "Why the Wagner Act?: Reestablishing Contact with Its Original Purpose." In *Advances in Industrial and Labor Relations*, vol. 7, ed. David Lewin, Bruce Kaufman, and Donna Sockell, pp. 15–68. Greenwich, Conn.: JAI Press.

———. 1997. "The Emergence and Growth of a Nonunion Sector in the Southern Paper Industry." In *Southern Labor in Transition, 1940–1995*, ed. Robert Zieger, pp. 295–329. Knoxville: University of Tennessee Press.

———. 1998. "John R. Commons: His Contributions to the Founding and Early Development of the Field of Personnel/HRM." In *Proceedings of the Fiftieth Annual Meeting*, vol. 1, pp. 328–341. Madison: Industrial Relations Research Association.

———. 1999. "Does the NLRA Constrain Employee Involvement and Participation Programs in Nonunion Companies? A Reassessment." *Yale Law and Policy Review* 17, no. 2: 729–811.

———. 2000. "The Case for the Company Union." *Labor History*.

———. 2001. "The Practice and Theory of Strategic HRM and Participative Management: Antecedents in Early Industrial Relations." *HRM Review* (forthcoming).

King, William Mackenzie. 1918. *Industry and Humanity.* Toronto: University of Toronto Press.

Kochan, Thomas, and Paul Osterman. 1994. *The Mutual Gains Enterprise.* Cambridge: Harvard Business School Press.

Leiserson, William. 1928. "The Accomplishments and Significance of Employee Representation." *Personnel* 4 (February): 119–135.

———. 1929. "Contributions of Personnel Management to Improved Labor Relations." In *Wertheim Lectures on Industrial Relations*, pp. 125–164. Cambridge: Harvard University Press.

Leitch, John. 1919. *Man-to-Man: The Story of Industrial Democracy.* New York: Forbes.

Levine, David, and Laura D'Andrea Tyson. 1990. "Participation, Productivity, and the Firm's Environment." In *Paying for Productivity: A Look at the Evidence*, ed. Alan Blinder, pp. 183–244. Washington, D.C.: Brookings Institution.

Lichtenstein, Nelson, and Howell Harris, eds. 1993. *Industrial Democracy: The Ambiguous Promise.* New York: Oxford University Press.

Litchfield, Paul. 1920. *The Industrial Republic: A Study in Industrial Economics.* Boston: Houghton Mifflin.

Loth, David. 1958. *Swope of GE: The Story of Gerard Swope and General Electric in American Business History.* New York: Simon and Schuster.

McCabe, David. 1934. "The Effects of the Recovery Act upon Labor Organization." *Quarterly Journal of Economics* 42 (November): 52–78.

Maryott, Michele. 1997. "Participate at Your Peril: The Need for Resolution of the Conflict Surrounding Employee Participation Programs by the TEAM Act of 1997." *Pepperdine Law Review* 24, no. 4: 1291–1326.

Meyer, Margaret. 1927. "A Study of the Works Council of the General Electric Company at Schenectady." Unpublished Master's Thesis, Cornell University.

Miller, Earl. 1922. *Workmen's Representation in Industrial Government.* Urbana: University of Illinois Press.

Morris, Charles. 1994. "Deja vu and 8(a)(2):What's Really Being Chilled by Electromation?" *Cornell Journal of Law and Public Policy* 4, no. 3: 25–32.

Myers, James. 1924. *Representative Government in Industry.* New York: George Doran.

National Industrial Conference Board. 1919. *Works Councils in the United States.* Research Report No. 21. Boston: National Industrial Conference Board.

———. 1922. *Experience with Works Councils in the United States.* Research Report No. 50. New York: National Industrial Conference Board.

———. 1933. *Collective Bargaining Through Employee Representation.* New York: National Industrial Conference Board.

National Labor Relations Board. 1985. *Legislative History of the National Labor Relations Act, 1935*, vols. 1 and 2. Washington, D.C.: U.S. Government Printing Office.

Nelson, Daniel. 1980. *Frederick W. Taylor and the Rise of Scientific Management.* Madison: University of Wisconsin Press.

———. 1982. "The Company Union Movement, 1900–1937: A Reexamination." *Business History* Review 54 (Autumn): 335–357.

———. 1988. *American Rubber Workers & Organized Labor, 1900–1941.* Princeton: Princeton University Press.

———. 1993. "Employee Representation in Historical Perspective." In *Employee Representation: Alternatives and Future Directions*, ed. Bruce E. Kaufman and Morris Kleiner, pp. 371–390. Madison, Wis.: Industrial Relations Research Association.

Ozanne, Robert. 1967. *A Century of Labor-Management Relations at McCormick and International Harvester.* Madison: University of Wisconsin Press.

Pennsylvania System. 1922. *Employee Representation on the Pennsylvania Railroad System.* Philadelphia: Pennsylvania System.

Rockefeller, John D. Jr. 1924. *The Personal Relation in Industry.* New York: Boni and Liveright.

Saposs, David. 1936. "Organizational and Procedural Changes in Employee Representation Plans." *Journal of Political Economy* 44, no. 6: 803–811.

Schacht, John. 1985. *The Making of Telephone Unionism, 1920–1947.* New Brunswick, N.J.: Rutgers University Press.

Schatz, Ronald. 1983. *The Electrical Workers: A History of Labor at General Electric and Westinghouse, 1923–60.* Urbana: University of Illinois Press.

Scheinberg, Stephen. 1986. *The Development of Corporation Labor Policy, 1900–1940.* New York: Garland.

Seager, Henry. 1923. "Company Unions vs. Trade Unions." *American Economic Review* 13: 3–13.

Selekman, Ben. 1924. *Sharing Management with the Workers.* New York: Russell Sage Foundation.

Selekman, Ben, and Mary Van Kleeck. 1924. *Employees' Representation in Coal Mines.* New York: Russell Sage Foundation.

Slichter, Sumner. 1929. "The Current Labor Policies of American Industries." *Quarterly Journal of Economics* 43 (May): 393–435.

Smith, Robert. 1960. *Mill on the Dan: A History of Dan River Mills, 1882–1950.* Durham: Duke University Press.

Tead, Ordway. 1917. "Employees' Organizations and Their Helpful Uses." *Industrial Management*, November, pp. 249–256.

Tead, Ordway, and Henry Metcalf. 1933. *Labor Relations Under the Recovery Act.* New York: McGraw-Hill.

Teagle, Walter. 1933. "Employee Representation and Collective Bargaining." Pamphlet. New York: A Report to the Business Advisory and Planning Council for the Department of Commerce.

Urwick, L., and Henry Metcalf, eds. 1940. *Dynamic Administration: The Collected Papers of Mary Parker Follett.* New York: Harper and Brothers.

Williams, Whiting. 1920. *What's on the Worker's Mind.* New York: Scribner's.

Wolf, A.B. 1919. *Works Committees and Joint Industrial Councils.* Philadelphia: United States Shipping Board, Emergency Fleet Corporation.

Wolman, Leo. 1936. *Ebb and Flow of Trade Unionism.* New York: National Bureau of Economic Research.

Yoder, Dale. 1938. *Personnel and Labor Relations.* Englewood Cliffs, N.J.: Prentice-Hall.

Zahavi, Gerald. 1988. *Workers, Managers, and Welfare Capitalism: The Shoeworkers and Tanners of Endicott Johnson, 1890–1950.* Chicago: University of Illinois Press.

Zieger, Robert. 1984. *Rebuilding the Pulp and Paper Workers Union, 1933–1941.* Knoxville: University of Tennessee Press.

3

The AFL and the Challenge of Company Unionism, 1915–1937

Daniel Nelson

The 1919 American Federation of Labor convention spelled out the deficiencies of a recent industrial innovation: the company union. "With hardly a pretense of organization, unaffiliated with other groups of workers in the same industry, destitute of funds, and unfitted to use the strike weapon, the company union is a complete failure . . . a delusion and a snare" (AFL 1919, p. 303). Adopted without debate, the resolution was similar to many union proclamations of the post–World War I years, when the labor movement enjoyed unprecedented power and élan. But this statement proved to be more than a routine expression of union militancy. The 1919 attack was the first blow in what would be a long and effective campaign against company unionism. Ultimately, it would result in a successful legislative assault on the company union as it had been known since the mid-1910s.

Most industrial relations experts of the 1930s and after assumed that conventional unions and company unions were incompatible rivals, locked in battle for worker loyalties. That assumption reflected union propaganda, such as the 1919 resolution, and the events of the mid-1930s, rather than familiarity with the operations of company unions. Before 1933, most unions and company unions occupied separate industrial spheres, rarely competing or even addressing the same issues. The most formidable company organizations, at

firms such as Goodyear, AT&T, Du Pont, Standard Oil of New Jersey, and Leeds & Northrup, emerged in industries that had little or no history of union activity and no current organizing activity; they were alternatives to individual bargaining, not collective bargaining (Nelson 1982, 1993; "Employee Representation" 1925. Also see French 1923, pp. 92–101; Fairris 1997, ch. 1–2. For company union contributions to improved production management, see Gray and Gullett 1973; Williamson et al. 1963). With few exceptions, they were not an immediate threat to the labor movement.

A larger but less consequential group of company unions appeared during World War I in response to government efforts to diffuse labor unrest and maximize production. The National War Labor Board and other agencies required or encouraged some type of shop organizations, though they did not spell out the details (French 1923, pp.15–32; Conner 1983; Haydu 1997, pp. 48–84; McCartin 1997, pp. 163–165). Alert union leaders saw an opportunity to make inroads in industry. In 1918 the AFL Executive Council called for large plants to have "a regular arrangement . . . whereby . . . a committee of workers would regularly meet with the shop management . . . and . . . carry . . . to the general manager or to the president any important grievance" (AFL 1918, p. 85). President Samuel Gompers was more forthcoming. He wrote: "the shop committees must be made strong effective agencies. Trade unions should have an important part in accomplishing this purpose" (Gompers 1918, p. 810). In short, once the employer had conceded the desirability of a formal workers' voice, workers—with the assistance of organized labor—would convert the committees into conventional unions, presumably affiliated with the AFL.

Employers were equally alert to this possibility. They were largely powerless to prevent union inroads as long as the government boards remained active. A prolonged dispute at Bethlehem Steel, which introduced shop committees but resolutely refused to deal with the AFL, was a measure of the impact of public policy on recalcitrant employers (Brody 1965, pp. 82–85; Montgomery 1987, pp. 414–416; McCartin 1997, pp. 158–164). When wartime controls ended, many industrial firms quickly abolished their committees. Others followed the lead of Bethlehem Steel and recast their committees as union substitutes in a campaign to reverse the union gains of the war period. Instead of halfway houses on the road to collective bargaining, these company unions became features of the postwar open-shop crusade.

AFL leaders were taken aback. Union militants responded by attacking all nonunion committees; the 1919 AFL resolution was their declaration of war on company unionism. As the open-shop movement gained momentum, Gompers and other union leaders had little choice but to endorse the radicals' position. At President Woodrow Wilson's First Industrial Conference, in October 1919, Gompers reluctantly attacked company unionism (French 1923, pp. 82–84; Taft 1957, pp. 394–400; Hurvitz 1977). Thereafter, Federation leaders became increas-

ingly outspoken. Before their new hostility had any immediate significance, however, the severe postwar recession decimated the industries that had expanded most rapidly during the war years. Employment and union membership dropped precipitously. Most of the company unions that had been created to satisfy government demands or preserve the open shop also disappeared (NICB 1922).

The revival of the economy in 1922 raised fundamental questions about the future of worker representation in industry. Would the AFL find a way to reestablish its wartime foothold in manufacturing? Would the remaining company unions (at AT&T, Goodyear, etc.) become halfway houses to union recognition or bulwarks against outside organizations? Would the AFL oppose them, or would it conclude, with contemporary analyst Carroll French, that "a moderation of this policy would be . . . best [for] . . . the shop committee and the trade union and ultimately for the general progress of industrial relations" (French 1923, p. 92). The answers to these questions were not long in coming. In the following years, AFL fortunes in manufacturing continued to decline, and the Federation abandoned any effort to encourage or influence company unionism. Most company unions in turn operated wholly apart from organized labor. The two movements might have remained separate and distinct except for a handful of high-profile challenges to powerful, entrenched unions that revived the hostility of the immediate postwar years. Indeed, AFL efforts to cope with the most serious of them, in the railroad industry, persuaded union leaders that even more decisive action was necessary. By the mid-1920s, they had concluded that the only satisfactory long-term solution was the legislative abolition of company unionism.

Colorado Fuel and Iron

The first major contest occurred at the Colorado Fuel and Iron Company, the largest western coal and steel producer and a company union pioneer, largely owned by the Rockefeller family. CFI's influential Rockefeller Plan of 1915 was a result of one of the most violent labor conflicts of that era, a strike by the United Mine Workers that culminated in the infamous Ludlow Massacre of 1914. Altogether, at least seventy-four people died in the conflict (Taft and Ross 1969, p. 332; McGovern and Guttridge 1972). The plan, however, was not explicitly or inevitably antiunion. In the late 1910s no one, certainly not John D. Rockefeller Jr. or W.L. MacKenzie King, his industrial relations adviser, knew what its effect would be. They hoped to avoid a union contract and even eliminate the union, but their primary concern was to restore peace and stability and stop the avalanche of unfavorable publicity that followed the Ludlow Massacre (Gitelman 1988; McCartin 1997, pp. 54, 212–213).

It would be difficult to imagine a more unfavorable setting for such an experiment. The coal and steel industries were noted for poor working conditions, authoritarian management, and labor conflict; Colorado was famous for its hostility to miners' unions; and CFI managers and workers were deeply suspicious of each other. Superintendents and foremen had virtually unlimited authority in personnel matters, and despite a noteworthy company welfare program, CFI had no personnel department or industrial relations program. Only the embarrassment of the Ludlow Massacre and John D. Rockefeller Jr.'s personal intervention suggested that the future might be different from the past.

There were good reasons, then, for union leaders to view the Rockefeller Plan as a surrogate union designed to thwart the growth of the United Mine Workers and steelworkers' organizations. This theme appeared in most contemporary writing about the plan and is perpetuated in many historical studies (Bernstein 1960, pp. 157–161). Accounts of the workers' roles provide some support for this interpretation. Most of the elected representatives were inexperienced and easily intimidated. They were afraid to raise controversial issues and disregarded legitimate grievances. Apparently they made few suggestions for improvements in working conditions, an important function of successful company unions. Even the men who were current or former union officers complained about their powerlessness. Writing in the early 1920s, Ben B. Selekman and Mary Van Kleeck blamed these problems on the company's failure to establish a personnel department, which meant that the employee representatives had no staff to turn to for day-to-day assistance (Selekman and Van Kleeck 1924, p. 197).

But that was only part of the story. Like most effective and durable company unions, the Rockefeller Plan had a greater impact on management than on labor. It forced supervisors to be more sensitive to their responsibilities as labor managers and leaders. Selekman and Van Kleeck ably summarized the impact of the plan on CFI executives and their subordinates.

> Opening up the channels of communication between employees and higher officials of the company had at once the effect of letting in the light on the practice and policy of superintendents. . . . The superintendent, no longer believing that the grievances of miners were small matters which would never become known to his superior officers, gained a new conception of his responsibility for keeping his relations with his men harmonious. A company which adopts a plan of employees' representation cannot afford too many blunders by foremen or superintendents. . . . [The]

company gained a new realization of the necessary qualifications of a superintendent . . . he must
know how to secure efficiency not by authority
conferred upon him by virtue of his office . . . but
by leadership recognized by the men as the result
of fair dealing. (Selekman and Van Kleeck 1924,
pp. 106–107)

Selekman and Van Kleeck cited several cases
of superintendents who were transferred or discharged for failing to live up to the spirit of the
plan. Though most foremen and other subordinate managers were initially skeptical, they too
adapted or left.

This change of attitude and approach had tangible results. Working conditions improved. CFI
housing, already among the best in the region,
was better maintained. Safety work received
greater emphasis. Wage inequities diminished,
and supervisors lost their power to discharge
employees. Most notable, in view of CFI's history, was the company's permissive attitude toward union activity. UMW organizers had free
access to the mine villages (though critics made
much of a brief crackdown, in 1919, on the eve
of the national coal strike), and steelworkers' organizers often visited the Pueblo steel plant. In
another break with tradition, plant managers met
with union leaders. During the coal and steel
strikes of 1919, and the coal strikes of 1921 and
1922, CFI officials refused to hire guards or replacement workers, and those conflicts remained
peaceful. A few of the miners' strike leaders were
not reemployed in 1919; otherwise, the strikers
returned to their jobs at the end of the disputes
(Selekman and Van Kleeck 1924, pp. 284–363;
Selekman 1924, pp. 168–195; Conner 1983, pp.
109–111).

Despite this restraint, the unions remained
antagonistic. As early as 1918, the UMW had
adopted a rule banning union members from participating in Rockefeller Plan activities. In the
following years, it tried to maintain a parallel
organization. Union opposition did not deter CFI
managers or revive the UMW, but it did deprive
the plan of the services of some of the most assertive employees. The steelworkers' unions took
the opposite tack and tried to gain control of the
plan. They had no greater success in the brief
period before the unsuccessful national strike of
1919–20 demoralized their members and undermined their organizations.

Though there was no systematic study of the
Rockefeller Plan after 1924, it apparently operated with reasonable success. Four joint committees considered complaints and grievances
regarding wages, safety, housing, and recreation.
The steel plant wage committee, for example,
made periodic trips to eastern mills to ensure that
CFI met or exceeded industry averages.[1] In the
meantime, CFI followed the example of other
Rockefeller-dominated companies, introducing a
personnel department and various employee programs. In 1928, Rockefeller hired a prominent business professor, Elton Mayo, to assess the plan's
progress. Mayo spent three weeks in Colorado, interviewing company officials and inspecting the
plants and company towns. He concluded that the
managers supported the plan and had won the confidence of most of the workers, particularly the
miners. Despite disputes between Mexican and
American workers, and the emergence of a small
Industrial Workers of the World (IWW) faction, the
mines were operating smoothly, with "mutual understanding." An IWW-inspired strike in 1927 had
attracted little support. The UMW local also declined, partly because of the chaotic state of the
national organization. The steelworkers, though
nonunion, were more contentious. Their joint meetings still featured arguments over petty issues.[2]

The CFI record was troubling to AFL leaders.

Without resorting to the traditional union-avoidance tactics of the coal industry, the company had thwarted the largest and most powerful American union at the height of its power. Was there any reason to believe that Goodyear or Standard Oil did not have the same potential? From the AFL perspective, CFI and other elite corporations were antiunion employers who had adopted a "sophisticated" approach to union avoidance; their tactics were gentler than those of most open-shop employers, but the results were identical.[3]

The collapse of the economy in the 1930s reopened the issue of union representation at CFI. As business declined, the company cut production and laid off many employees, but to no avail; it declared bankruptcy in 1933. Although the ensuing reorganization did not directly affect the plan, it persuaded many CFI miners that they could no longer rely on the company for improved wages, benefits, or employment security. When the United Mine Workers took advantage of Section 7(a) of the National Industrial Recovery Act to launch a new organizing drive, they were ready to listen. CFI managers, eager to be included in the industry code, which would enable them to raise prices, agreed to a government-supervised employee election. In late October 1933, CFI miners voted 877 to 273 for the UMW. Union officials declared that "the company union is dead and goes into history" (*New York Times*, March 21, 1941).

That judgment was premature. The miners' decision apparently had no influence on the much larger group of CFI steelworkers. In the Pueblo plant, the Rockefeller Plan continued to operate without significant change until 1937, when CFI lawyers concluded that it violated the Wagner Act. The plan became an independent union, though it retained informal ties to the company. In 1940, at the urging of the Steel Workers Organizing Committee (SWOC), the NLRB ruled it company dominated and voided its agreement with CFI.[4] A union organizing campaign followed. In the ensuing representation election the SWOC received a third of the votes and an independent organization that included many plan leaders attracted a smaller number. A large majority of the workers, however, opted for no organization (*New York Times*, March 21, 1941). Though this outcome probably pleased CFI managers, its meaning for the labor movement and company unionism was less clear. If the plan had proven to be a halfway house for CFI miners, it was something else for steelworkers. They followed the example of many employees at elite corporations who preferred individual bargaining or unaffiliated local unions.

Pennsylvania Railroad

The most important additions to the ranks of company unions in the 1920s came from the railroad industry, the most highly unionized industry of the immediate postwar years. Unlike the elite firms that introduced employee representation to improve shop management, enhance company loyalty, and reduce turnover, railroads embraced company unionism to create a nonunion voice in an increasingly deregulated environment. Led by the Pennsylvania, the largest and most influential railroad, they created union substitutes. But their goal was not simply union avoidance; they sought to obliterate the unwelcome events of the preceding decade, notably the heavy-handed government regulation that had culminated in the federalization of the industry in 1918.

On the eve of U.S. involvement in World War I, unions had had an important but restricted role in the railroad industry. Operating employees had long had powerful organizations and agreements with their employers. Other groups, such as switchmen, telegraphers, and clerks, were organized on some roads but not on others. Less-skilled employees and shopcraft workers such as machinists and boilermakers were unorganized. In all, about one-third of railroad employees were union members (NICB 1934b, p. 9). The government takeover of the industry in early 1918 opened the door to unions of less-skilled employees such as the railway clerks and maintenance-of-way employees and to broader-based unions like the machinists and blacksmiths. By the end of 1919, more than three-quarters of all railroad employees were union members. No other major industry had a comparable level of organization.

To railroad executives, the increase in union membership symbolized an erosion of managerial prerogatives at a time of unprecedented challenges from government and the nascent automobile and trucking industries. To many, recovery and modernization meant not only the introduction of improved technology and rationalized services but also fewer external restrictions. The company union was part of the modernization process.

To union leaders, federal operation of the railroads had been a remarkable stimulus to membership growth, proof of the power of government to open doors that resisted private initiatives. Even the independent and generally conservative operating brotherhoods were impressed. Forsaking their customary independence, they joined other rail and metal trades unions, coordinated by the AFL Railway Employees Department, to support the postwar Plumb Plan, which sought government ownership of the industry. When that effort failed, they turned to elective politics and launched a vigorous political campaign that culminated in support for Robert LaFollette's third-party presidential candidacy in 1924. Rail union

leaders believed that their fortunes were tied to government; if government retreated, they would lose power and members. The company union thus became a symbol of privatization and the likely end of the labor movement's most significant inroad into large-scale industry (MacKay 1947; Waterhouse, 1991).

The conflict over company unionism dated from the Transportation Act of 1920, which restored the railroads to their stockholders and created a Railroad Labor Board to resolve disputes. Although the act privatized the industry, it also strengthened the Interstate Commerce Commission and created the Labor Board, which was to preserve some features of the wartime regime. This combination maximized bureaucratic red tape and ultimately discredited the government. Beginning in 1921, the Pennsylvania and other opponents of wartime concessions by the government systematically attacked the Labor Board; by 1924 they had destroyed it. In 1925–26 they played major roles in creating a new labor-management system that gave them almost complete freedom to manage day-to-day employee relations. The result, the Railroad Labor Act of 1926, marked a return to the status quo antebellum with one major exception: it gave de facto recognition to company unionism (Huibregtse 1995, pp. 159–194; Bernhardt 1923).

Pennsylvania executives focused on the shopcraft workers. Pennsylvania Railroad shopworkers had no prewar history of organization, and the largest concentration, at Altoona, Pennsylvania, was highly susceptible to company influence. Vice President W.W. Atterbury, in charge of operations, terminated relations with the AFL shopcraft organizations in the spring of 1921 and introduced a new representation system. Atterbury's plan was based on the negotiating procedures that had grown up between the company and the operating brotherhoods. Each occupational group elected representatives who discussed wages, working conditions, and other issues with an appropriate management committee. If an impasse resulted, the dispute went to a regional management-employee board. The board required a two-thirds vote to act. Atterbury insisted that the plan was not antiunion. He noted that the elected representatives of the operating employees and switchmen were union officers. In other occupations, however, the AFL did "not really [provide] the kind of representation our employees desired." Unions gave them "no real voice." On the other hand, his plan provided an "outlet for the expression of opinions." It also ensured that supervisors "deal justly" with employees (Atterbury 1924, p. 108). To most outside observers the Atterbury plan was a pale replica of a conventional union agreement, a transparent effort to displace the least-secure unions (Dunn 1926a, pp. 1–5; Dunn 1926b, pp. 15–19).

The shopcraft organizations immediately protested. They ordered union members not to vote in the ratification elections and held their own elections. When the Labor Board rejected both tallies and ordered new elections, Atterbury refused to cooperate. The company's refusal to comply with the order led to a suit and ultimately a 1923 Supreme Court decision that the Board had no enforcement powers.

In the meantime, union leaders at the Pennsylvania and other railroads were mobilizing to oppose wage reductions during the postwar recession. The wage issue soon became a critical test of union power. Union hostility to wage cuts, including Labor Board–approved reductions, ultimately led to the great shopcraft strike of the summer and fall of 1922. The strikers' eventual defeat devastated the unions. Striking employees of many railroads lost their jobs or their seniority (Davis 1992; Murray 1969, pp. 240–263; Zieger 1969, pp. 109–143).

The Pennsylvania suffered less than other railroads, at least in part because of the Atterbury plan. Initially, the elected employee representatives, many of whom were union members, refused to agree to the company's plan to reduce wages. To their chagrin, they were unable to persuade their constituents to join them in striking. Only one-third of Pennsylvania Railroad shopcraft employees walked out, the lowest proportion of any major railroad. Atterbury quickly replaced them (McPherson 1924, pp. 47–50). He attributed his success to the influence of the company union, now reconstituted with nonstrikers. Other antiunion railroad managers were equally impressed. After the strike collapsed, the Atterbury plan spread quickly. By some accounts, more than half of all major railroads had some form of employee representation by the late 1920s.[5] They accounted for more than 10 percent of all company unions and a larger percentage of employee members. As late as 1934, after a substantial decline, they still represented more than 17 percent of employees of the largest railroads (NICB 1934b, p. 16).

The relationship of the Atterbury plan and other company unions of railroad employees to the plight of the shopcraft unions and the Labor Board is clear. What is not clear is whether they became more than surrogate unions. Did railroad managers follow the path of the large manufacturing companies and CFI in utilizing company unions to improve management and morale? Atterbury's statements emphasize grievance settlements, a point that most company union advocates deemphasized. The Pennsylvania's welfare program, including its well-known pension plan, was consistent with the activities of the elite manufacturing firms, but there is little evidence that

Pennsylvania executives used, or even sought to use, the company union to curb supervisors' powers, improve communications, solicit suggestions, or involve employees in decision making.[6] Atterbury's vague references to its responsibilities and the absence of other information suggest that it was at best a flaccid version of the Goodyear, Standard Oil, and CFI plans. Employee representation plans at the Santa Fe, Burlington, and other railroads were equally obscure (Bryant 1974, p. 243; Waters 1950, pp. 324–325). In the absence of contrary evidence, it is likely that they remained largely what they had been in 1922–23, substitute unions designed to deflect the employees' interest in a formal voice and keep the AFL at bay.

This conclusion is strengthened by the experiences of shopcraft workers at the Baltimore & Ohio and other "progressive" railroads that maintained collective bargaining relationships with the AFL after the 1922 strike. Spurred by Otto Beyer, an engineer who had worked for the U.S. Railroad Administration, the B & O and several other railroads introduced formal cooperative plans in 1922 and 1923. Railroad managers and local union leaders met frequently to discuss ways to increase productivity. By most measures, the Beyer plan was a notable success, suggesting that improved communications, greater efficiency, and improved morale were also possible with AFL organizations (Vrooman, 1991, ch. 2–3; McPherson 1924, pp. 76–81; Wood 1931).

As one of the few industries where unions and company unions directly competed, railroads had a substantial impact on the thinking of union leaders of the late 1920s and early 1930s. While the halfway house metaphor remained appealing, company unions in practice were obstacles and even rivals. Not only had CFI had been lost to the labor movement, but the railroads had re-versed the advances of the war years, eliminating hundreds of thousands of union members. It is hardly surprising that AFL leaders continued to dismiss company unions as "the advanced, refined method of opposing unions" ("Company Unions" 1934, p. 131).

What was to be done? The Atterbury plan had appeared in the wake of privatization and deregulation. Regardless of the relationship between government and labor in other sectors of the economy, government and union influence in the railroad industry had been closely and positively correlated. Anything that revived federal controls was likely to be beneficial to the AFL. In 1918 and 1919, railroad unions, including the brotherhoods, had agitated for government ownership. As the railroad managers' attack on union power became more intense and successful in the 1920s, the unions again turned to the federal government for assistance. Anything as ambitious as nationalization was almost certain to fail. But narrower, less controversial goals, such as the abolition of company unionism, might be attainable.

Union Political Campaigns

In the mid-1920s, AFL leaders formulated a new legislative plan. They had had moderate success in defeating congressional proponents of the Transportation Act in 1920 and 1922. After the failed shopcraft strike, they launched an aggressive campaign to eliminate the Labor Board and create a mediation system similar to the one that had operated during the war. Donald Richberg, the unions' attorney, drafted the 1924 Howell-Barkley bill, which abolished the Labor Board, created union-management boards to mediate disputes, and prohibited railroad corporations from assisting or interfering in the operation of labor organizations. Though railroad executives were critical of the Labor Board, they adamantly opposed Howell-Barkley. Their hostility undermined congressional support and the bill failed in the House of Representatives by a narrow margin (Huibregtse 1995, pp. 90–125; Vadney 1970, pp. 49–65; Richberg 1954, pp. 129–130).

This defeat proved to be only a temporary setback. In the 1924 election campaign the Republicans sought to placate organized labor in order to undercut the LaFollette campaign. Accordingly, President Coolidge expressed his dissatisfaction with the Labor Board and, in a surprise, election-eve meeting with leaders of the brotherhoods, pledged his support for the principles of Howell-Barkley. His reelection provided new impetus to the legislative campaign (Huibregtse 1995).

By early 1925, railroad executives realized that some legislation was inevitable. They formed a committee, headed by Atterbury, to negotiate with a union committee dominated by leaders of the operating brotherhoods. Using Howell-Barkley as a starting point, the joint committee gradually worked out a compromise. It agreed to scrap the Labor Board and accept the Howell-Barkley structure for mediating disputes, but not the Howell-Barkley restrictions on company unions. The final bill included general language forbidding interference with the selection of bargaining agents but no specific ban on company unions. Union representatives disingenuously hailed these provisions as the death knell of "Atterburyism." In fact, Atterbury supported the compromise and even testified in favor of it (Richberg 1954, pp. 129–130). With labor and management support, the new bill passed by wide margins in early 1926 (Huibregtse 1995, p. 177).

Not surprisingly, the Railway Labor Act was a boon to the operating brotherhoods but not to the shopcraft organizations. By promoting mediation and arbitration, it diffused unrest among the op-erating employees (Moulton 1933, p. 197). But it also split the union coalition and gave de facto sanction to company unions, since there was no way to enforce the ban on employer interference. Thereafter, the AFL organizations had to look out for themselves. They made little progress until the depression undermined the industrial and political foundations of the postwar era.

As Congress began to address the issues raised by the collapse of the economy, the AFL and the Railway Employees Department resumed their campaign to enlist government as an ally. Their aggressive efforts were a notable example of AFL pragmatism and an even more compelling example of the effectiveness of determined special-interest lobbies. The contrast between the achievements of the railroad unions and those of other unions operating under the supposedly permissive Section 7(a) of the National Industrial Recovery Act, could not have been sharper. Whereas Section 7(a) inspired temporary union gains, together with a new generation of company unions, the railroad unions greatly expanded their membership and curtailed the influence of company unions.

The railway unions' first success came in early 1933, when Congress adopted a new federal bankruptcy act. Although the legislation generally reflected the interests of railroad managers and investors, Senator George Norris, an AFL ally, added a provision forbidding bankrupt corporations from providing financial assistance to labor organizations. The railroads accepted the Norris amendment because it did not include an enforcement mechanism. They had no reason to believe it would be any more effective than the Railway Labor Act.

A few months later, however, the new Roosevelt administration sponsored "emergency" legislation to help the Interstate Commerce Commission cope with the effects of the depression. The railroad companies tried to exclude any labor reforms from the emergency bill, but they were no match for the railway unions. Led by George M. Harrison of the Railway Clerks and A.F. Whitney of the Trainmen, union representatives "tramped the corridors" of Congress, "carrying on an intense campaign of education." They also had "three or four" meetings with the president, who finally agreed to their demands (*Labor*, June 6, 1933). The labor provisions of the act included restrictions on layoffs and a ban on support for company unions, now extended to all railroads. In addition, the law provided for the appointment of a federal "coordinator" to oversee the implementation of the law. In the office of the coordinator the unions had a government agency with enforcement powers.

Roosevelt appointed Joseph Eastman, a veteran civil servant and ICC member, as coordinator. Known as a friend of organized labor, Eastman soon came under sustained pressure to enforce the company union restrictions. His biographer reports that "he discovered that labor officials could be just as aggressive, just as ruthless . . . as the employers had ever been." Eastman told a friend that "labor executives are drunk with power" (Fuess 1952, p. 203).

Political pressures and devotion to duty nevertheless forced Eastman to insist that the railroads adhere to the letter of the law. In September 1933 he reminded railroad executives to keep "hands off." He also sent a questionnaire to each company soliciting information about company union finances. Where AFL organizations were challenging company unions, he proposed elections to determine who would represent the workers. Many railroads—notably bankrupt companies that required continued government assistance—cooperated, publicly disavowing any intention to influence their employees. In November, after conferring with Eastman, the managers of the Pere Marquette agreed to an election, a breakthrough for the Eastman approach (*Labor*, October 10, 1933). In December, Eastman lectured rail executives on their responsibilities under the law. Many company unions, he charged, "have been tainted . . . with coercion or influence on the part of carrier management" (*Labor*, December 19, 1933). Meanwhile, the railway unions took advantage of their position to recruit many company union members, either individually or in groups. Eastman's influence also deterred railroad companies from introducing additional organizations. The number of company unions in the railroad industry declined at the same time the number in manufacturing was growing rapidly (NICB 1934b, p. 9).

By early 1934, the railroad unions had formulated an ambitious legislative plan to consolidate their gains and win additional concessions, including a six-hour workday and a government-administered retirement plan. Though Eastman opposed many of these provisions and succeeded in sabotaging some of them, such as the six-hour day, the unions successfully guided the measure through Congress. President Roosevelt reluctantly agreed to support it. The Railroad Labor Act of 1934 included restrictions on company unions similar to those introduced in 1933 and added a powerful enforcement mechanism, the National Mediation Board, which was given the power to resolve representation disputes. The act provided that "a majority of any craft or class of employees shall have the right to determine who shall be the representative of the class or craft" (NMB 1935, p. 15). The unions hailed the act as the "greatest legislative victory ever scored by organized labor in America" (*Labor*, June 26, 1934).

Beginning in the summer of 1934, the NMB conducted representation elections or signature checks on many railroads. By the end of June 1935—two years before the Wagner Act became fully effective—the NMB had held contested elections on forty-five railroads (NMB 1935, p. 15). The AFL unions had decisive advantages in these contests: greater resources, the implied imprimatur of the federal government, and undisputed control of the National Railroad Adjustment Board, the labor-management body created by the 1934 act to resolve grievances. They won approximately three-quarters of the elections and in aggregate received nearly 70 percent of the ballots. Notable victories occurred on the Illinois Central; the Delaware, Lackawanna and Western; the Union Pacific; and the Southern Pacific. (Except for three small groups of maritime workers, Pennsylvania Railroad employees remained off-limits to the AFL.) Yet because the elections were by occupational groups, there were exceptions. Northern Pacific workers, for example, voted four-to-one for the AFL, but NP electrical employees backed their company union. Rock Island blacksmiths and electrical workers similarly opted for company organizations over AFL organizations (NMB 1935, pp. 16–17; *Labor*, September 4, 18, and 25, October 16, 1934; McKillips 1936, pp. 48–50). Despite the unions' advantages, some company unions survived.

This little-known chapter in the labor history of the mid-1930s, featuring assertive AFL leaders and a peaceful expansion of union power, bears little resemblance to the more familiar parts of that story. In manufacturing, the NRA years were marked by an upsurge of worker militancy and an increasingly violent employer backlash. Strikes, violent confrontations, and ruthless contests for worker allegiance punctuated the ensuing struggles. The difference lay in the railroads' prior acceptance of a formal employee voice, however attenuated, and the presence of well-

organized, politically active AFL organizations. Union triumphs in railroad shops and roundhouses in 1933 and 1934 simply marked a return to the representation system of the early 1920s. Apart from Atterbury and a few diehards, most railroad managers were prepared to live with these changes.

From the Railroad Labor Act to the Wagner Act

By 1933, the labor movement had a comprehensive answer to the challenge of company unionism. It would discourage company unions whenever possible, deprive them of employer resources, and aggressively recruit their members. If union influence had been decisive, Section 7(a) would have included a ban on employer interference similar to the ban in the 1933 bankruptcy and transportation acts, together with a meaningful enforcement mechanism. But AFL influence was limited, and company unions gained new life. When Congress passed the Railroad Labor Act, the railroad industry appeared to be an isolated exception to the broader pattern. Within a year, however, Congress enacted the Wagner-Connery Act, complete with Section 8(a)(2) and a reinvigorated National Labor Relations Board. The Supreme Court's *Jones & Laughlin* decision two years later gave official sanction to the union view of company unionism.

The story of the origins of the Wagner Act, told often and well, highlights several factors that help explain this dramatic change of policy (Bernstein 1950, 1970; Gross 1974; Tomlins 1985; Dubofsky 1994; Kaufman 1996). First, as most historians of the act have emphasized, Wagner succeeded in portraying his proposal as a stimulus to economic recovery, rather than a concession to the labor movement. Second, the ideas and proposals that Wagner incorporated in the bill were all familiar to contemporary industrial relations experts. The railroad legislation was one important source; the NIRA and the New Deal labor boards were others. Wagner's contribution was to package these well-known but controversial proposals in a politically palatable form (Kaufman 1996). Third, the Wagner Act was a product of the political environment of 1935. It probably could not have been passed before 1935 or after 1937. A wary Roosevelt refused to endorse it until the spring of 1935 and many politicians, including many who voted for it, viewed it as a prolabor gesture that would not survive a court challenge. Employers generally disregarded it. The eventual *Jones & Laughlin* decision inspired a repeal movement that gained substantial momentum in the late 1930s and continued to enliven political debate through the 1940s (Gross 1981; Tomlins 1985, pp.148–246).

A final factor was the changing character of the company union movement after 1933. The most authoritative surveys, by the National Industrial Conference Board, reported a doubling in the number of plans and a large membership increase; 45 percent of employees at the NICB's sample firms in 1933 and 1934 were company union members (NICB 1933, 1934a, b). A Labor Department study in 1935 also reported dramatic increases in company union membership after 1933. In six of the seven manufacturing industries with the largest increases, two-thirds or more of the members had been added in 1933 and 1934 (BLS 1938, p. 54). Most employers who introduced company unions in 1933 sought to satisfy the requirements of Section 7(a) while avoiding the AFL. In this respect, they resembled many World War I–era employers. However, there were no counterparts to CFI or Goodyear in the new generation of company union con-

verts; indeed, the discussions of internal communications and employee loyalty, which had given variety and nuance to company unionism in the 1910s, seemed irrelevant in the economically depressed 1930s (Jacoby 1985, pp. 227–228; Fairley 1936). Whereas company unionism at elite firms had required major commitments of money and time, the new organizations operated on a shoestring.

If these company unions did little to improve productivity or morale, they were effective agents of the open shop. Typically, a small group of favored employees, often directed by supervisors, would form a representation plan that met the letter of the law and was available to help thwart outside organizers. Company union officers often formed extralegal groups that disrupted union activities, attacked picket lines, assaulted organizers, and testified against prolabor legislation (Fine 1963; Nelson 1988; Auerbach 1966). They also alienated their members. Many of the new company unions collapsed because of rank-and-file apathy or hostility. Others became halfway houses. Like the CFI miners, many factory employees were skeptical of their employers' motives. The sudden appearance of a company union, particularly one that seemed devoted mostly to deflecting union organizing efforts, did little to reassure them. In the auto, rubber, and steel industries, company unions contributed to the rise of AFL and CIO organizations.

As a result of these developments, the AFL critique of company unionism acquired new credibility and popularity. Employers who had well-established and effective company unions found themselves on the defensive. Henry S. Dennison, perhaps the best-known representative of the elite manufacturers, told a Senate committee that he and other employers welcomed the evolution of company unions into "true and independent" unions. Yet he strongly objected to any plan of "forcing" union growth "beyond the rate at which capable leaders can be discovered and can gain experience." Such a misguided policy would result in "enough fool trouble, bitter strife, and bloodshed to set the whole country blindly against unionism in any form." The results would "last a generation" (U.S. Senate 1934, pp. 434–437). Given the contemporary understanding of company unionism, few politicians were willing to oppose Wagner's plan of "forcing" union growth.

The result was a political and ideological victory for the labor movement, symbolized by the Wagner Act's Section 8(a)(2). Political restrictions on company unions paid important dividends in the late 1930s as the NLRB adopted Eastman's role and played it with even greater vigor. As Sanford Jacoby notes in his chapter, only the most effective company unions survived, usually as unaffiliated local unions. The longer-term effect of the union achievement was to publicize and legitimize a view of company unionism that reflected the assumptions and perspectives of the 1930s.

The AFL campaign against company unionism is thus a story of bungled opportunities and striking achievements. By resolutely rejecting any positive relationship with company unions in the 1920s, the AFL may have forfeited whatever chance it had to encourage a formal workers' voice and regain a meaningful presence in manufacturing. But if it failed to grasp one opportunity, it successfully exploited another. The AFL political campaign against company unionism was one of the most notable successes of the labor movement of the 1920s and early 1930s. Without forsaking their traditional interests, unions enlisted and used government to achieve goals that were difficult or impossible to attain through private, voluntary action. By 1933, they had demonstrated

that both political parties, the Congress, and the president were sensitive to union pressures. As a result, the labor movement was able to leave its stamp on the emerging industrial relations system of the 1930s. Substitute unions became unacceptable and collective bargaining, policed by the federal government in the interests of economic prosperity, employer neutrality, and worker democracy, became the law of the land.

Notes

1. "Colorado Fuel and Iron and International Union of Mine, Mill and Smelter Workers, Local 442"; also "S.W.O.C. Cases C-983-4, R1100, March 29, 1940," *Labor Relations Reference Manual* 6 (1940) (Washington, D.C., 1941), pp. 198–199.

2. Elton Mayo to Arthur Woods, November 20, 1928, Elton Mayo Papers, Box 10, Harvard Business School.

3. See "More Sophisticated Methods," *American Federationist* 42 (May 1935): 470.

4. "Colorado Fuel and Iron and International Union of Mine, Mill and Smelter Workers, Local 442," pp. 198–201.

5. L.M. Graham to Frances Perkins, n.d. (1935), Pennsylvania Railroad Presidential Correspondence, WWA, 1925–35, 38, 97/30E, vol. 1, Hagley Library. Also Elva M. Taylor, "Employee Representation on American Railroads," *American Federationist* 33 (December 1926): 1484–1487.

6. See "Proceedings of a Meeting Held in Pennsylvania YMCA Building," April 16, 1923, and "Meeting Held in General YMCA Auditorium," December 29, 1925, Pennsylvania Railroad Papers, ff5 and ff18, PDGOF.

References

American Federation of Labor. 1918. *Report of the Proceedings of the 38th Annual Convention, 1918.* Washington, D.C.

———. 1919. *Report of Proceedings of the 39th Annual Convention, 1919.* Washington, D.C.

Atterbury, W.W. 1924. "How We Brought Management and Workers Together." *System, the Magazine of Business,* January, p. 42.

Auerbach, Jerold S. 1966. *Labor and Liberty: The LaFollette Committee and the New Deal.* Indianapolis: Bobbs-Merrill.

Bernhardt, Joshua. 1923. *The Railroad Labor Board: Its*

History, Activities, and Organization. Baltimore: Johns Hopkins University Press.

Bernstein, Irving. 1950. *The New Deal Collective Bargaining Policy*. Berkeley: University of California Press.

———. 1960. *The Lean Years: A History of the American Worker, 1920–1933*. Boston: Houghton Mifflin.

———. 1970. *Turbulent Years: A History of the American Worker, 1933–1941*. Boston: Houghton Mifflin.

Brody, David. 1965. *Labor in Crisis: The Steel Strike of 1919*. Philadelphia: Lippincott.

Bryant, Keith L. Jr. 1974. *History of the Atchison, Topeka and Santa Fe Railway*. New York: Macmillan.

"Company Unions." 1934. *American Federationist* 31 (February): 130–132.

Conner, Valerie Jean. 1983. *The National War Labor Board; Stability, Social Justice, and the Voluntary State in World War I*. Chapel Hill: University of North Carolina Press.

Davis, Colin J. 1992. "Bitter Conflict: The 1922 Shopmen's Strike." *Labor History* 33 (Fall): 433–455.

———. 1997. *Power at Odds: The 1922 National Railroad Shopmen's Strike*. Urbana: University of Illinois Press.

Dubofsky, Melvyn. 1994. *The State and Labor in Modern America*. Chapel Hill: University of North Carolina Press.

Dunn, Robert W. 1926a. " 'General' Atterbury's Company Union." *Labor Age*, January, pp. 1–5.

———. 1926b. "More About Atterbury 'Company Union' Camouflage." *Labor Age*, February, pp. 15–19.

"Employee Representation." 1925. *Proceedings of the Cleveland Conference of the Production Executives Division, November 13 and 14, 1924*. New York: American Management Association.

Fairley, Lincoln. 1936. "The Company Union in Plan and Practice." New York: Affiliated School for Workers.

Fairris, David. 1997. *Shopfloor Matters: Labor-Management Relations in Twentieth-Century Manufacturing*. London: Routledge.

Fine, Sidney. 1963. *The Automobile Under the Blue Eagle: Labor Management and the Automobile Manufacturing Code*. Ann Arbor: University of Michigan Press.

French, Carroll E. 1923. *The Shop Committee in the United States*. Baltimore: Johns Hopkins University Press.

Fuess, Claude Moore. 1952. *Joseph B. Eastman: Servant of the People*. New York: Columbia University Press.

Gitelman, H.M. 1988. *The Legacy of the Ludlow Massacre: A Chapter in American Industrial Relations*. Philadelphia: University of Pennsylvania Press.

Gompers, Samuel. 1918. "Labor Representation Essential." *American Federationist* 26 (September): 81.

Gray, Edmund R., and C. Ray Gullett. 1973. *Employee Representation at Standard Oil of New Jersey: A Case Study*. Baton Rouge: Division of Research, College of Business Administration, LSU.

Gross, James A. 1974. *The Making of the National Labor Relations Board: A Study in Economics, Politics, and the Law*. Albany: SUNY Press.

———. 1981. *The Reshaping of the National Labor Relations Board: National Labor Policy in Transition, 1937–1947*. Albany: SUNY Press.

Haydu, Jeffrey. 1997. *Making American Industry Safe for Democracy: Comparative Perspectives on the State and Employee Representation in the Era of World War I*. Urbana: University of Illinois Press.

Huibregtse, Jon Roland. 1995. "Years of Transition: American Railroad Labor, 1919–1934." Ph.D. dissertation, University of Akron.

Hurvitz, Haggai. 1977. "Ideology and Industrial Conflict: President Wilson's First Industrial Conference of October 1919." *Labor History* 18 (Fall): 509–524.

Jacoby, Sanford M. 1985. *Employing Bureaucracy: Managers, Unions, and the Transformation of Work in American Industry, 1900–1945*. New York: Columbia University Press.

Kaufman, Bruce. 1996. "Why the Wagner Act? Reestablishing Contact with Its Original Purpose." In *Advances in Industrial and Labor Relations*, ed. David Lewin, Bruce Kaufman, and Donna Sockell, vol. 7, pp. 15–68. Greenwich, Conn.: JAI Press.

MacKay, Kenneth C. 1947. The Progressive Movement of 1924. New York: Columbia University Press.

McCartin, Joseph A. 1997. *Labor's Great War: The Struggle for Industrial Democracy and the Origins of Modern Labor Relations, 1912–1921*. Chapel Hill: University of North Carolina Press.

McGovern, George, S., and Leonard F. Guttridge. 1972. *The Great Coalfield War*. Boston: Houghton Mifflin.

McKillips, Budd L. 1936. "Company Unions on the Railroads." *The Nation*, January, pp. 48–50.

McPherson, William Heston. 1924. "Employee Representation for Shop Craft Employees on the Pennsylvania Railroad System." Master's thesis, Ohio State University.

Montgomery, David. 1987. *The Fall of the House of Labor: The Workplace, the State, and American Labor Activism, 1865–1925*. New York: Cambridge University Press.

Moulton, Harold G. 1933. *The American Transportation Problem*. Washington, D.C.: The Brookings Institution.

Murray, Robert K. 1969. *The Harding Era: Warren G. Harding and His Administration*. Minneapolis: University of Minnesota Press.

National Industrial Conference Board. 1922. *Experience with Works Councils*. New York: NICB.

———. 1925. *The Growth of Works Councils in the United States*. New York: NICB.

———. 1933. *Collective Bargaining Through Employee Representation*. New York: NICB.

———. 1934a. *Individual and Collective Bargaining in May, 1934*. New York: NICB.

———. 1934b. *Individual and Collective Bargaining in Public Utilities and on Railroads, October, 1934*. New York: NICB.

National Mediation Board. 1935. *First Annual Report, National Mediation Board, 1935*. Washington, D.C.

Nelson, Daniel. 1970. "'A Newly Appreciated Art,' the Development of Personnel Work at Leeds & Northrup." *Business History Review* 44, no. 4: 520–535.

———. 1982. "The Company Union Movement, 1900–1937: A Reexamination." *Business History Review* 56, no. 3. 335–357.

———. 1988. *American Rubber Workers & Organized Labor, 1900–1941*. Princeton: Princeton University Press.

———. 1993. "Employee Representation in Historical Perspective." In *Employee Representation: Alternatives and Future Directions*, ed. Bruce E. Kaufman and Morris M. Kleiner, pp. 371–390. Madison: Industrial Relations Research Association.

Richberg, Donald. 1954. *My Hero: The Indiscreet Memoirs of an Eventful but Unheroic Life*. New York: Putnam.

Selekman, Ben M. 1924. *Employees' Representation in Steel Works*. New York: Russell Sage Foundation.

Selekman, Ben M., and Mary Van Kleeck. 1924. *Employees' Representation in Coal Mines*. New York: Russell Sage Foundation.

Taft, Philip. 1957. *The A.F. of L. in the Time of Gompers*. New York: Harper.

Taft, Philip, and Philip Ross. 1969. "American Labor Violence: Its Causes, Character, and Outcome." In *The History of Violence in America*, ed. Hugh Davis Graham and Ted Robert Gurr, pp. 281–344. New York: F.R. Praeger.

Tomlins, Christopher L. 1985. *The State and the Unions: Labor Relations, Law, and the Organized Labor Movement in America, 1880–1960*. New York: Cambridge University Press.

U.S. Bureau of Labor Statistics. 1938. "Characteristics of Company Unions, 1935." Bulletin 634.

United States Senate. 1934. Committee on Education and Labor. 73rd Cong., 2nd sess.

Vadney, Thomas. 1970. *The Wayward Liberal: A Political Biography of Donald Richberg*. Lexington: University Press of Kentucky.

Vrooman, David M. 1991. *Daniel Willard and Progressive Management on the Baltimore & Ohio Railroad*. Columbus: Ohio State University Press.

Waterhouse, David L. 1991. *The Progressive Movement of 1924 and the Development of Interest Group Liberalism*. New York: Garland.

Waters, L.L. 1950. *Steel Trails to Santa Fe*. Lawrence: University of Kansas Press.

Williamson, Harold F., Ralph Andreano, Arnold R. Daum, and Gilbert C. Klose. 1963. *The American Petroleum Industry: The Age of Energy, 1899–1950*. Evanston: Northwestern University Press.

Wood, Louis Aubrey. 1931. *Union-Management Cooperation on the Railroads*. New Haven: Yale University Press.

Zieger, Robert H. 1969. *Republicans and Labor, 1919–1929*. Lexington: University of Kentucky Press.

4

A Road Not Taken: Independent Local Unions in the United States Since 1935

Sanford M. Jacoby

Although most European and some Asian countries have shop committees or works councils that are independent of national unions, the United States does not. In a few U.S. companies, however, one finds independent local unions, which are single-employer unaffiliated unions that represent employees of a plant or company. Most of the independent local unions in existence in the 1940s started out as employee representation plans, or "company unions," which, as Daniel Nelson (1982) has shown, were popular in the 1920s (when they were associated with progressive welfare capitalism) and once again in the mid-1930s (when employers rapidly established them in the wake of the 1933 National Industrial Recovery Act). Few of these company unions survived until the 1940s, however. Either they became part of national unions affiliated with the AFL and CIO, or the National Labor Relations Board (NLRB), which initially implemented the Wagner Act's company union ban with draconian stringency, disestablished them. Precisely how many company unions disappeared in the period between 1935 and 1940 has never been calculated; this chapter provides such an estimate.

The surviving company unions evolved into relatively autonomous organizations that were financially independent of the employer; these became known as independent local unions

(ILUs). The ability of these former company unions to withstand both NLRB scrutiny and raiding attempts by affiliated (national) unions encouraged new groups of employers and workers to establish ILUs during the war. Later, when the Taft-Hartley Act of 1947 signaled that the NLRB would take a more lenient approach, there was an increase in the rate of ILU formation, a spurt that lasted into the 1950s. A number of ILUs became feisty organizations during those years, successfully fending off raids by affiliated unions and even engaging in some successful raids of their own. ILUs appealed to white-collar workers and to employees in smaller firms outside the big cities. Because these constituted the main sectors where unionism did not reach in the 1950s, observers forecast a rosy future for ILUs: they would "more than hold their own" (Troy 1960, p. 503).

In fact, however, after the late 1950s, ILUs went into a decline from which they never recovered. Few new ILUs appeared; NLRB disestablishments persisted; and affiliated unions (now part of the merged AFL-CIO) became more adept at raiding ILU members. While ILUs never completely disappeared, by the 1970s they had become a relatively insignificant feature of American industrial relations.

After providing a statistical analysis of ILU

membership trends between 1935 and 1967, this chapter takes a closer look at the factors that influenced those trends: changes in labor law; the characteristics of ILUs; worker attitudes toward ILUs; and, especially, employers' industrial relations policies. On this last point, some new evidence is presented that suggests that even those employers who were still forming ILUs in the 1950s were orienting them away from collective bargaining and toward something resembling the "new nonunion model" of the 1960s and 1970s. Whether this same reorientation would have occurred if Congress and the NLRB had been more tolerant of ILUs remains an open question. Whatever the answer, today Congress and the NLRB have an opportunity to moderate their long-standing hostility to ILUs and other employer-assisted organizations by providing a larger space for experimentation with representational forms.

Company and Independent Union Trends, 1935–1967

According to a survey done by the Twentieth Century Fund (1935, pp. 79–80), there were about 2.5 million workers represented by company unions in early 1935, shortly before passage of the Wagner Act. If the average size of a company union was the same in 1935 as it had been in 1932 (i.e., 1,645 workers per union), then there were about 1,515 company unions in 1935 (Millis and Montgomery 1945, p. 835). Many of these company unions disappeared after passage of the Wagner Act, which made it an unfair labor practice for an employer to dominate, interfere with, or provide financial assistance to a labor organization.

Note that while the Wagner Act did not ban company unions, the NLRB interpreted the act to mean that any company union that had been created with employer support—nearly all of them—was tainted and liable for disestablishment. The Wagner Act's antipathy to company unions stemmed from the act's economic rationale: the belief held by Senator Wagner and other congressional underconsumptionists that only massive wage increases would prevent future depressions and that company unions could never raise wages as effectively as national unions could (Jacoby 1993; Kaufman 1996; Mitchell 1986). The Wagner Act specified that a labor organization was one that "dealt," rather than "bargained," with the employer. Had Congress adopted the latter terminology, as proposed by the secretary of labor in 1935, it would have legitimized employer-supported organizations that did not engage in bargaining (Millis and Brown 1950; *Cabot Carbon* 1959). The result might have been something like the two-tier industrial relations systems found in Europe, where works councils coexist with national unions and industrial bargaining. As for the NLRB, its animosity toward company unions—almost a missionary zeal—stemmed from the political proclivities of the board's early members and from a strict interpretation of its congressional mandate.

Initially, many employers paid little attention to the Wagner Act's section 8(2), fully expecting that the Supreme Court would find the act unconstitutional. In 1937, however, the Supreme Court upheld the act. Now the NLRB picked up the pace of disestablishments and applied a harsh rule: a disestablished company union was not permitted to appear on an election ballot even if the employer withdrew his support. To the annoyance of company union supporters, the NLRB did not apply this same stricture to tainted locals of an affiliated union, as in a "sweetheart" situation. In these instances, an affiliated union could appear on the ballot if it could prove the employer had ceased his support (Crager 1942). On top of all this, a growing number of company unions were taken over by national union affiliates, as in the automotive, steel, and agricultural equipment industries. Company unions made tantalizing targets for national unions because it was easier to take over a company union than to organize a group of nonunion employees.

In response to these developments, some company unions transformed themselves into new organizations—independent local unions (ILUs)—that were financially and otherwise independent of employers and that had other features modeled after trade union organizations and procedures (Saposs 1936; Rosenfarb 1940). Although employers gave implicit winks and nods—and frequently more—to the loyal employees who formed these ILUs, most employers were careful not to involve themselves directly in the process.

National union leaders were skeptical that any worker would willingly choose to create an ILU in the absence of employer support or coercion. An Oil Workers' (OCAW-CIO) organizer described employee loyalists as if they were zombies: In the oil industry, he said, the "concept of company unionism had become so well grounded that certain employees, as if in a trance, went through the motions of creating [a new] series of company unions" (O'Connor 1950, p. 97). NLRB officials often took this view as well, leading to an extremely hostile environment for the new ILUs.

Membership Estimates, 1935–1940

Of the roughly 1,500 company unions in existence in 1935, how many of them survived to 1940? To answer this, we would have to know the number of disestablishments that occurred from 1935 to 1940 and also the number of successful raids by affiliated unions. The number of disestablishments is relatively easy to obtain: al-

most 700 through fiscal year 1940, followed by 502 disestablishments in 1940–41, the peak year for all time, making for a total of 1,200 disestablishments from 1935 to 1940–41 (Millis and Montgomery, 1945, pp. 850–851; *NLRB Annual Reports*). If all of these were disestablishments of company unions in existence in 1935 and none involved double-counting, then by mid-1941 the NLRB had disestablished about 80 percent of all company unions in existence six years earlier—a colossal achievement.

Neither of these conditions obtained, however. Some disestablishments involved company unions formed after 1935, while other disestablishments (as at Thompson Products' main plant in Cleveland) involved multiple incarnations of the same original company union (Jacoby 1989). The latter occurrence was probably not of great quantitative significance, but it is difficult to say how prevalent was the former, since, as mentioned, a number of new company unions appeared between 1935 and 1939. Even with these qualifications, it is still true that the NLRB eliminated a vast number of company unions from 1935 to 1940.

As for raids, company and independent unions participated in 1,101 elections between 1935 and 1940–41 and of these they lost half, or 556 elections (Millis and Montgomery 1945, p. 853). Unfortunately, we cannot simply add this figure to the 1,200 NLRB disestablishments to get a total number of company union "deaths" because in a few instances an independent union defeated during an election refused to concede or was in the midst of legal proceedings and subsequently was disestablished by the NLRB. What we can say is this: administrative decisions by the NLRB eliminated twice as many ILUs as were eliminated by NLRB elections from 1935 to 1940, and of those ILUs in existence in 1935 or created after that date, a very large number had disappeared by 1940.

There is, however, another way of determining what happened to company unions between 1935 and 1940: estimate the number of ILUs in existence in 1940 by counting backward from survivor data available for 1967. We can form this estimate by looking at survivors of the 1940 ILU population cohort still alive in 1967 and adding to them the number of cohort deaths that occurred between 1940 and 1967. While the calculations that follow involve several assumptions, the adjustments are made conservatively, so as to bias downward the final result.

The starting place is a comprehensive BLS survey of 884 ILUs in existence in the United States in 1967. The BLS asked these ILUs for their founding dates. Of those specifying a date (12 percent did not say), 171 had been formed prior to 1940; these 171 ILUs had 192,000 members in 1967. If those not reporting a founding date contained the same proportion (22 percent) of pre-1940 foundings as the reporting group, then in 1967 there were 194 ILUs with 204,000 members that were survivors of the 1940 population cohort (BLS 1969, p. 14).

The chief causes of death for the 1940 cohort were disestablishments and raids. Again, disestablishments are easy to determine: there were 2,167 disestablishments between 1940 and 1967, with the bulk of these—1,554—coming between 1940 and 1947 (*NLRB Annual Reports*). Of course, not all of these disestablishments were of ILUs from the 1940 cohort; some were ILUs "born" after that date. Using the BLS founding-date data, we can infer that ILUs formed prior to 1941 constituted about 40 percent of all ILUs in the 1940s, 24 percent of all ILUs in the 1950s, and 22 percent of all ILUs in the 1960s (through 1967). If disestablishments of the 1940 cohort

were proportional to their weight in the total ILU population over time, then about 700 of the disestablishments occurring between 1940 and 1967 involved ILUs from the 1940 cohort.

How many workers belonged to these disestablished ILUs? In 1967 the average unit size of ILUs founded before 1941 was about 1,122 members. These survivor ILUs were probably larger than the average ILU in existence in 1940. If we conservatively estimate average unit size at 700 members, which is the average number of workers per unfair labor practice case in 1947, then about 490,000 workers were affected by disestablishments of the 1940 cohort.

Next we need to estimate how many of those ILUs alive in 1940 were subsequently raided by affiliated unions. To get this figure, I first calculate the total number of successful raids by affiliated unions and then estimate how many of these raids involved ILUs from the 1940 cohort. The chief source of raiding data is Krislov (1954, 1955, 1960), whose studies combine ILUs and "left-wing" unions for the time period of 1940 to 1948 and separately identify ILUs for 1948 to 1960.

According to Krislov, the number of raids on independent and left-wing unions rose and then fell in the 1940s: from 16 (1940) to around 200 (1943 and 1946), down to 98 (1948). In the early 1950s, ILUs made up about half the raids on ILUs and left-wing unions combined, so if we apply this ratio to the 1940s and smooth Krislov's data to derive annual figures, the result is an estimated 624 raids on ILUs from 1940 to 1948. How many raids were successful? In the 1950s ILUs lost 46 percent of all raids initiated against them (Troy 1960). If this proportion was the same in the 1940s—a conservative assumption—then raids accounted for 287 ILU "deaths" from 1940 to 1948, a period during which the 1940 cohort comprised 33 percent of the total ILU population. The bottom line: there were 95 deaths from the 1940 cohort due to raids in the 1940s, with a total loss of members of 47,500 (based on the average unit size of all units affected by raids in the 1940s of 500 members).

We have better data on raids for the 1948 to 1958 period, when ILUs lost 308 of the 671 raids initiated against them. Applying the 1940 cohort population weights of .46 in 1948 and .25 in 1958 gives a total loss due to raids on the 1940 cohort of 111 units. The average unit size in all ILU raids, successful or not, during this period was about 300. Hence the total loss due to raids was 33,000 members.

In short, if we add to the 194 cohort survivors in 1967 the sum of losses due to disestablishments (700) and losses due to raids (206), we arrive at an estimated number of ILUs in 1940 of 1,100, which is about 73 percent of the total existing in 1935; following the huge number of disestablishments (502) in 1940–41, there would have been in 1941, *ceteris paribus*, 598 ILUs in existence, about 40 percent of the total existing in 1935. As for membership, if we add to the 192,000 cohort survivors in 1967, the losses due to disestablishments (490,000) and to raids (80,500), we arrive at an estimated membership in 1940 of 762,500, which is 31 percent of the total from 1935; following the disestablishments of 1940–41, there would have been, *ceteris paribus*, 411,000 ILU members. Thus the number of company unions shrank dramatically from 1935 to 1941, with much of this shrinkage the result of actions by the NLRB and, to a lesser extent, to raids by affiliated unions.

In the rest of this section, I present an overview of membership trends for the 1941–47, 1947–53, and 1953–67 subperiods.

Membership Estimates, 1941–1947

Net membership did not change very much, if at all, from 1941 to 1947: Troy (1960, 1961) calculates that in 1947 there were about 469,000 ILU members in 222 ILUs. The stabilization of ILU membership during and immediately after the war reflected, in part, a steady decline in the number of disestablishments—from 283 in 1942 to 101 in 1944 to an average of only 47 per year from 1945 to 1947. Based on the number of workers per unfair labor practice case in these years, I estimate total losses due to disestablishments at 511,000 members for the 1941–47 period.

In this period one begins to see raids by ILUs against AFL and CIO unions, though such activity remained "sporadic" (Krislov 1954, p. 20). In contrast, raids by affiliated unions against ILUs continued at a steady pace; about 96,000 ILU members switched to affiliated unions during and after the war.

Disestablishments and raids against ILUs (accounting for 600,000 "deaths") were roughly offset by ILU births during these years. The BLS data show that of the ILUs in existence in 1967, 146 had been founded between 1940 and 1945 and an additional 115 between 1946 and 1950. The first cohort in 1967 had 127,000 members; the second cohort had 56,000 members. If we interpolate the latter cohort, we come up with a figure of 139,000 new ILU members joining in 1940–47 and surviving to 1967. We know that the 1940 population cohort had a survival rate of .25 to 1967. If we conservatively apply the same survival rate to the 1940–47 birth cohort, it suggests that 556,000 new members joined ILUs during this period.

Thus, from 1941 to 1947, net ILU membership either increased slightly (based on the difference between my 1941 figure and Troy's for 1947) or decreased slightly (based on my rough comparisons of deaths minus births). But this appearance of stasis in fact masks the intersection of two sizable flows: deaths and births of about a half million individuals each.

Membership Estimates, 1947–1953

According to Troy (1960, 1961), ILU membership rose between 1947 and 1953 from 469,000 to 706,000, a huge net gain of 237,000 members. Although Troy's figure may be on the high side—my estimates show a net gain of only 136,000—it is plausible because, as during the preceding period, the ILU death rate continued to drop due to a decline in disestablishments, while the birth rate rose.

The post–Taft-Hartley years saw a brief acceleration in the rate of ILU formation. The BLS (1969) survivor figures show an average of twenty-four ILUs being formed each year from 1940 to 1950 and twenty-nine ILUs formed each year from 1951 to 1960. Averaging these figures yields an estimate of 179 ILUs with 63,000 members established from 1947 to 1953 and surviving to 1967. Applying a survival rate of .25 yields an estimate of 252,000 members joining 700 new ILUs during this period, a marked increase.

What is distinctive about postwar ILU growth is that it occurred at smaller establishments than previously. According to the survivor data, the average size of a unit formed prior to 1940 was 1,122 employees; new unit size fell in the late 1940s to 487, and dropped even more in the 1950s to only 211 members.

Another postwar characteristic was the greater ability of ILUs to win elections. ILUs did well against national unions, winning a majority of all representation elections and a majority of votes

from 1948 to 1958 (only in 1953 was this not the case). ILUs also won a majority of all raids against them: an average of 54 percent for the 1948–58 period (Troy 1960).

A sign of heightened ILU confidence were the raids launched during this period by ILUs against national unions, of which ILUs won about two-thirds (Krislov 1954). Belying their reputation for quiescence, a number of ILUs also engaged in organizing activity during these years. This activity remained modest—the number of elections for unorganized workers in which ILUs participated hit a peak of only twenty-two in 1958—but it was yet another indication "of increasing strength of local independents in competition with 'legitimate' unions" (Krislov 1960, p. 219).

Deaths during this period occurred chiefly through disestablishments and raids by national unions: 358 such raids occurred between 1948 and 1953, and national unions won 163 of them. With an average unit size of about 300 members, such raids accounted for a loss of about 49,000 ILU members (Troy 1960). As for disestablishments, they continued on a steady downward trend. There were 134 disestablishments from 1948 to 1953, accounting for ILU losses of about 67,000 members. In short, my estimates show a net increase of 403 ILUs during this period (higher than Troy's figure; see Table 4.1) and a net membership gain of 136,000 (smaller than Troy's).

Membership Estimates, 1953–1967

The vitality shown by ILUs in the early 1950s did not last. The total number of elections involving ILUs fell from 294 in 1953 to 205 in 1958; the number of voters dropped from 68,000 to 35,000; to put this another way, the average size of an ILU election unit fell from 231 to 170 (Troy

Table 4.1

Company Unions and ILUs: 1935–1967

	ILUs	Membership
1935	1,515	2,500,000
1940	1,100	762,500
1941	598	411,000
1947	222	469,000[a]
1953	625	605,000
1953	365	706,000[a]
1956	385	709,000[a]
1961	1,277	452,000[b]
1967	884	475,000[b]

Source: Unless otherwise indicated, figures are estimated in the text.
[a]From Troy (1961).
[b]From BLS (1969).

1960). Because the ILUs created in the 1950s
were relatively small, they were less stable entities than in earlier years. Many were one-shot
organizations created in response to a union organizing drive and then allowed to dwindle away
(Shostak 1962). When the BLS (1961) conducted
its first comprehensive investigation of ILUs in
1961, it could find only 452,000 members belonging to 1,277 ILUs, the majority of which had
fewer than 100 members.

During the 1960s, the formation of new ILUs
slowed to a crawl in nearly all industries and geographic areas. The survivor data show that only
fifty-six ILUs with 11,000 members were created between 1961 and 1967 (BLS 1969). Moreover, the disestablishment rate rose: from about
twenty-seven per year under the Eisenhower
NLRB to thirty-seven per year under the
Kennedy-Johnson board. Other signs of weakness included membership losses in the telephone

industry, where large ILUs in New York and California succumbed to raids by the Communications Workers (CWA), and in the electrical
machinery industry, where the International
Union of Electrical Workers (IUE) raided large
ILUs at Stromberg-Carlson, Sprague, and Wagner
Electric (Shostak 1962, p. 67; BLS 1969, p. 12).

Changes in Labor Law

The shrinkage of ILUs after 1935 and their subsequent brief revival reflected a confluence of
causal factors, chiefly the interaction between ILU
characteristics, the evolving labor law, worker
attitudes, and employer strategies. Without doubt,
the rapid decline of ILUs from 1935 to 1940 was
principally caused by the Wagner Act's language
on company unions and the way this language
was interpreted by the early NLRB. At the 1939–
40 hearings on the Smith bill (a proposal to reform the Wagner Act that anticipated Taft-Hartley)
employers bitterly complained about the NLRB's
hostility to company unions and its practice of
disestablishing them even when they no longer
received employer support. The Smith committee took up this line and excoriated the NLRB
for having "consistently pursued a policy aimed
at the extermination of these nationally unaffiliated organizations" (Millis and Brown 1950, pp.
176, 348–353; Gross 1981).

Although Pearl Harbor curtailed legislative
reform efforts in Congress, employers kept beating the drums for more lenient NLRB treatment
of company unions. At a Conference Board
roundtable held in New York in 1942, the head
of the National Association of Manufacturers,
Frederick Crawford, urged the audience to "find
a way of putting into the field a greater awareness of independent unions, Wagner or not," and
then assailed the NLRB for its "prejudiced atti-

tude" (*New York Times*, May 21, 1942). The NLRB was sensitive to these criticisms, to charges aired at the Smith hearings, and to the prospect of renewed legislative activity when the war ended. Under Harry Millis, who became chairman in November 1940, the NLRB steered a more centrist course. As noted, the number of disestablishments dropped steadily: from 502 in 1941 down to 54 in 1945. Doctrinal changes also occurred. In cases where the only charge was that the ILU had grown out of an employer-supported company union and where the parties had been bargaining for at least two years, the NLRB now permitted the ILU to appear on the ballot if employer domination had ceased—the same rule the NLRB had been applying to affiliated "sweetheart" locals (Gross 1981; Millis and Brown 1950).

When the Taft-Hartley Act was passed in 1947, its company union provisions codified what had already become NLRB procedure. The act forbade the NLRB from discriminating between affiliated and unaffiliated unions. Now, in contrast to the situation under the Wagner Act, the NLRB interpreted the law in ways favorable to ILUs. When judging cases of employer support to unions, it no longer paid attention to affiliation status. Instead, the distinction was between employer domination (the remedy for which still was disestablishment) and lesser forms of illegal employer interference. If the employer ceased the latter, the NLRB would allow the ILU to appear on the ballot. Taft-Hartley also forced the NLRB to apply weaker fracture rules: unfair labor practices committed more than six months prior to the filing of an election petition by a company union were not allowed to bear on the petition. These changes effectively grandfathered the legal status of existing company unions.

Another provision of Taft-Hartley was interpreted by some employers (and courts) to permit the formation of employee committees to discuss grievances, wages, and working conditions in the absence of a certified union. Language specifically permitting such committees was contained in the House version of the act—section 8(d)(3) of the Hartley bill—but the Senate version contained no such provision. Instead, the Senate bill added to the existing section 9(a), which read that "any individual employee or group of employees shall have the right at any time to present grievances to their employer" the words "*and to have such grievances adjusted without the intervention of the bargaining representative, as long as the adjustment is not inconsistent with the terms of a collective-bargaining contract or agreement in effect.*" After a conference with the Senate, the House conferees reported to their colleagues that section 8(d)(3) would be unnecessary because the revised section 9(a) "permits individual employees and groups of employees to meet with the employer." With Taft-Hartley thus appearing to sanction employee committees and with the NLRB meting out milder remedies for employer interference, the stage was set for an upsurge in ILU formation. Between 1947 and 1953, ILUs grew at a more rapid pace than either AFL or CIO membership (Note 1957; Millis and Brown 1950; *Cabot Carbon* 1959, pp. 215–217).

Rulings favoring ILUs continued to appear in the 1950s, as the first Republican-appointed board since the NLRB's inception steered a more conservative course than its predecessors. The Eisenhower board was reluctant to order disestablishments, preferring instead to order employers to cease illegal support. Disestablishments under Eisenhower averaged only twenty-six per year. As one appellate court said approvingly, the NLRB no longer had to "baby along employees in the direction of choosing an outside union as their bargaining representative" (*Coppus Engineering*, 1957, p. 2315).

The federal courts generally approved of the NLRB's more lenient treatment of ILUs. In *Chicago Rawhide* (1955), which current NLRB chairman William Gould (1996) recently termed a "landmark" case, an appellate court upheld the legality of an employee association formed at a new nonunion plant in the early 1950s. Straining to find a formula that would permit the association's legality—even though the employer had given assistance of various kinds to it—the court drew a distinction between "support" and "cooperation." Support was impermissible because "even though innocent, [it] can be identified because it constitutes at least some degree of control or influence." Cooperation, however, "only assists the employees or their bargaining representative in carrying out their independent intention." Assistance, in other words, "does not always mean domination . . . and the Board must prove that the employer is actually creating company control over the union." Hence the test of whether an employer action was support (unlawful) or cooperative assistance (lawful) was not clear-cut. As the court admitted, using language from another case, it was "not an objective [test] but rather subjective, from the standpoint of the employees." From the early 1940s through the late 1950s, then, the legal atmosphere increasingly was tolerant of ILUs, and this permitted the formation of a substantial number of new ILUs, with over 800,000 new members.

ILU Characteristics

One feature common to ILUs in the 1940s and 1950s was their identification with a single company. Affiliated locals were similarly oriented, but they had other, more diffuse, concerns: with the craft, occupation, or industry, and with the national union itself. Inside large companies, the unitary link between the ILU and the employer reinforced personnel policies intended to foster a career-type employment relationship. Hence there was a strong association between the presence of ILUs and progressive welfare capitalism, with the latter comprising such enterprise-oriented policies as systematic personnel management and fringe benefits. If anything, the association was even stronger in the 1930s, when two-thirds of the firms with company unions offered benefit and welfare plans (Nelson 1982; BLS 1938, p. 201).

As compared to industrial unions, ILUs were conservative organizations, suspicious of "big" government and "big" labor and relatively supportive of small business. After the war, this conservatism helped ILUs to proliferate in smaller companies outside the big cities, places that traditionally were suspicious of outsiders. Because of their almost exclusive focus on a single firm and their isolation from other unions, many ILUs revolved around the personalities of their leaders. The ILU's person-based culture meshed smoothly with—indeed, reinforced—the family-oriented and charismatic type of management existing in companies dealing with ILUs. Yet ILU informality had its downside: it tended to create oligarchies that were less tolerant of dissent than the more bureaucratic, but also more democratic, leadership of affiliated unions.

When Shostak (1962) studied ILUs in the 1950s, he found around half the ILUs in his sample to be "weak." They were organizations that prepared poorly for negotiations and rarely challenged the employer's authority. Many of them were small, semirural, and inexperienced. Few were survivors dating back to the 1920s or the 1930s; instead, most had been created in the 1940s and early 1950s. Typically employers started them in response to a union organizing drive, but the employers acted with support from employees who were loyal to them and, as noted, suspicious of outsiders. In one plant, for example, the employees were scared of the Teamsters; in another, the ILU leader was a former small businessman whose company had been fatally damaged by the Ladies' Garment Workers Union.

On the other hand were the "strong" ILUs, which were more independent than other ILUs but less militant than most national union affiliates. These ILUs almost never struck, but they had other ways of pressuring the employer, such as rejecting a contract or threatening to affiliate with a national union. Strong ILUs were often found in urban areas, where they were exposed to regular raids from national unions. Because of this—and because of their internal structure—these ILUs often did a better job of "servicing" their members than did business agents who had to deal with numerous affiliated locals. For example, at Thompson Products, which had both types of unions, the grievance rate inside one ILU plant was lower than inside an affiliated-union plant represented by the United Auto Workers (UAW), but the ILU pressed a greater number of these grievances through to arbitration. At Swift & Company, which also had both types of unions, the ILU plant had a higher grievance rate and steward ratio than the AFL-affiliated plant (the Meatcutters) but lower than the plant represented by the CIO's Packinghouse Workers (Jacoby and Verma 1992; Purcell 1960).

One selling point for ILUs was that they offered these services for dues that were much lower than those charged by a national union. While this meant that ILUs had fewer resources for information and education, their financial and organizational autonomy permitted a vigorous, almost Jeffersonian, kind of democracy that gave members more influence than in larger unions and certainly allowed more participation than the quasi dictatorships found inside some affiliated unions. Many of these ILUs had started out looking like their weaker counterparts, but competition with national unions and situational factors caused them to evolve over time. In fact, the "strong" unions in Shostak's sample were almost all much older than the "weak" unions (Shostak 1962; Jacoby 1997; *Personnel* 1955).

The same evolution occurred at Thompson Products (today TRW), when what once had been quiescent company unions initiated by management in the early 1930s were transformed in the 1940s and 1950s into relatively independent, though cooperative, ILUs (Jacoby 1989, 1997). The largest of Thompson's ILUs was the Aircraft Workers Alliance, which represented workers at Thompson's factories in the Cleveland area. Over time the AWA developed a cadre of leaders who were adept at contract administration and bargaining. These leaders usually tried to be fair to management, though they were far from obsequious. Unlike, say, a Japanese company union, the AWA assertively disagreed with management, stubbornly pressed grievances, and effectively persuaded the company to change its policies and plans. Nevertheless, the AWA's leaders rarely displayed the belligerence typical of many affiliated union locals. Some of this can be traced to the use of joint council meetings, which permitted a regular airing of differences, instead of letting them build up to eruptions at contract expirations. The council meetings had a collaborative, collegial, and amiable atmosphere. (Not without reason had the old IWW slogan averred, "Feet which meet under a mahogany table don't kick.") Then there was the fact that the AWA, in contrast to an affiliated local, offered no opportunities for retiring officers to move into union staff positions.

Leaders returned to their old jobs when their terms expired, unless they were promoted into management, and they knew promotion was not likely if they had been too contentious.

One striking feature of the AWA was its isolation from other unions. It had few contacts with, and no formal ties to, company unions at Thompson Products plants outside Cleveland. Within Cleveland, the local AFL and CIO were contemptuous and suspicious of the AWA, which repaid those feelings in kind. Too small to train its own officers and cut off from mainstream labor education programs, the AWA had to rely on management to meet some of its basic organizational needs. The company held classes for newly elected stewards, where they received basic information on Thompson's personnel practices, financial situation, and markets. Company managers sought to "integrate" new AWA officers by taking them to conferences of the American Management Association and by holding training sessions for them on such technical subjects as job evaluation. Given all this, it is not surprising that when the UAW reappeared at Thompson's Cleveland plants in the 1960s, its organizers castigated the AWA's "cozy relationship" with management. From a trade union perspective, there was something odd about the AWA's isolation and its dependence on management. But the AWA seems less peculiar when viewed from within, that is, when set in the context of Thompson's own evolving species of progressive welfare capitalism.

Not every ILU was as isolated as the AWA. Throughout the nation were federations composed of ILUs from the same company, city, geographic region, or industry. Examples of single-company federations included the National Brotherhood of Packinghouse Workers (NBPW) at Swift and the Central States Petroleum Union, which in the 1950s represented about 5,000 employees belonging to several ILUs at Standard Oil of Indiana. The oil refining industry also provided examples of multiemployer federations, such as the Federation of Independent Oil Unions, started in 1955 by six ILUs facing organizing drives from the CIO-affiliated Oil, Chemical, and Atomic Workers (Brandt 1960; Marshall 1961; Purcell 1960; Shostak 1962). The largest multiemployer federations came from the telephone companies. In the late 1930s and 1940s, the National Federation of Telephone Workers (NFTW) comprised numerous ILUs in the Bell System, most of them former company unions started by management. After the CWA emerged out of the NFTW in 1947, some of the Bell ILUs—especially those representing white-collar office personnel and high-wage employees on the Pacific Coast and in the Northeast— chose to remain independent, although they formed federations like the Alliance of Independent Telephone Unions, the New England Federation of Telephone Operators, and the Federation of Women Telephone Workers. There also were several multiemployer federations of ILUs representing white-collar and professional employees, including the National Federation of Salaried Unions, which claimed 40,000 members in the early 1950s, and the Engineers and Scientists of America (ESEA), composed of ILUs representing engineers and draftsmen at Boeing, Douglas, Sperry, Honeywell, and other firms (Schacht 1985; Barbash 1952; Troy 1958; Waters 1954; *Fortune* 1956, p. 203; Walton 1961).

Resembling the AFL and CIO were the multi-industry federations, of which the largest was the National Independent Union Council, started by the NBPW in 1950 and including ILUs at companies in Illinois, Kansas, and Missouri. Similar organizations included the Confederated Unions of America, started in 1942, and the National Federation of Independent Unions (NFIU). The three federations merged in 1960 to form the Congress of Independent Unions which, in addition to the Swift locals, included ILUs at Zenith Electronic, ARMCO Steel, Elgin Watch, and other firms. Among the services these federations provided for their members was a staff of skilled negotiators, information on contracts and wages, a monthly magazine, and the "advantage of membership in a bona fide labor federation which protects them from the dangers of isolation; NFIU affiliates cannot be labeled 'company unions' or be accused of being under management or any other domination" (*Union Labor News Review*, March 6, 1964: 2).

Most ILUs were too small to provide themselves with a permanent staff, so they depended heavily on the advice given to them by labor lawyers who specialized in representing ILUs. Occasionally these lawyers amalgamated their clients into a federation, though these "federations" usually were nothing more than a clever entrepreneurial gimmick to garner new clients. Milton Roemisch of Cleveland was one of the new breed of lawyers who emerged during the 1930s and 1940s as advisers to, and often de facto leaders of, ILUs. Roemisch represented independent unions at a number of Cleveland-area firms, including Ohio Tool, Sherwin-Williams Paint, Thompson Products, and Ohio Crankshaft. In the early 1940s Roemisch affiliated twenty-six of these independents into a federation he called the National League of American Labor (Jacoby 1997).

Worker and Management Attitudes

That ILUs could win a majority of NLRB elections during the 1950s suggests that workers had some consistent reasons for preferring ILUs to national unions or no representation. One important factor was the desire of ILU members to preserve compensation premiums that might otherwise be eliminated by national unions. Union organizers readily admitted that ILUs frequently paid at or above the union rate; an OCAW official acidly commented that ILU members "have everything that union men do in wages and working conditions, everything—except freedom" (O'Connor 1950, p. 97; also see Jacoby 1997). These premiums were endogenous—they were due to preexisting skill or geographic wage differentials—but they were threatened by the wage standardization policies pursued by national unions. Troy (1960) cites examples drawn from the Bell System—where ILUs were found in high-wage cities such as Chicago, New York, and Los Angeles, while the CWA had its locals in lower-wage cities such as Atlanta, Cleveland, and Philadelphia—and from other industrial unions such as the Transit Workers and the Automobile Workers, which periodically experienced defections of their skilled trades into ILUs. Hostility of the NLRB to craft severance, despite protests from the AFL prior to its merger with the CIO, thwarted what might otherwise have been a source of additional ILU members (Tomlins 1985).

Another reason ILUs had support from their members was the simple fact that they offered essentially the same benefits as a national union but at a much lower cost. The ratio of ILU-to-national union dues ranged from one-quarter at Swift to one-sixth at Thompson Products, and even less in some small companies (Purcell 1960; Jacoby 1997). Along with lower dues came a direct kind of union democracy. All of an ILU's officers—from the president on down—were from the plant and were usually well known by the members (Robinson 1968; Shostak 1962). At Thompson Products, for example, ILU elections were hotly contested and highly publicized. Unlike an affiliated local of a national union, the ILUs were masters of their own fate. They did not have to answer to a higher authority or conform to policies that were not of their choosing. Because they had no staff and only a simple hierarchy, the ILUs tended to be less formal than a national union, and although the UAW faulted Thompson's ILUs for failing to hold regular meetings, the latter's small size and numerous social activities kept its officers in close touch with the rank and file. There were no outside experts or business agents telling members how to run the union. The ILU's claim to be "your union" may have conjured up a more appealing image than the UAW's promise of providing "one big union, coast to coast." Realizing this, the AWA referred to the UAW as "the octopus" and urged Thompson workers not to feed it (Jacoby 1997).

Because ILUs often were found in small firms outside urban centers, their members tended to be conservative and promanagement. Members often nurtured dreams of self-employment that caused them to identify with the interests of the small businessmen who employed them. They shared the producerist values espoused by the managers of these small firms, who were a daily presence on the shopfloor and in the community. With a high degree of loyalty to management, ILU members were reluctant to strike and, in fact, strikes by ILUs were a rare occurrence. For example, the ILUs at Swift four times refused to join in strikes called by national unions in the late 1940s and 1950; the ILUs complained that the nationals relied too heavily on the strike as a bargaining tactic. National unions were disliked for other reasons: their liberal proclivities, communist affiliations, or simply the fact they were large bureaucratic organizations from the "outside." Alongside the story of the CIO's victories in Chicago, Detroit, and Pittsburgh, there is a

different tale to be told about the conservative and isolationist values that united managers and workers outside the cities, even in labor's Midwest stronghold. Think, for example, of the five ILUs formed by the Christian Labor Association, all of whose members belonged to the Dutch Reformed Church and lived in and around Holland, Michigan (Purcell 1960; Shostak 1962; Millis and Montgomery 1945, p. 869; Nelson 1995).

Finally, ILUs drew support from groups who felt that national unions were insensitive to their needs and concerns. Despite national unions' claim to be inclusive—to possess what one historian terms a "culture of unity" (Cohen 1990)—the climate inside the new CIO unions frequently was similar to that of the AFL's, that is, dominated by the concerns of white, male, manual workers. Although the leadership of the CIO unions often condemned racial discrimination, matters were different at the plant level, where white workers viewed the union as their special preserve and tried to keep blacks out. This was the case at Thompson Products, where white UAW members discriminated against black workers, turning the latter into stalwart supporters of the ILU, and of management, which went out of its way to hire black workers during the 1940s. At Swift, black workers much preferred the ILU to the AFL's Meatcutters Union, which had a long history of discrimination (Purcell 1960; Jacoby 1997).

Female workers were another group that gave disproportionate support to ILUs. Data from the late 1960s show that the percentage of women in ILUs was nearly twice as high as in national unions (BLS 1969). While there is no research on the subject, it is likely that the strength of ILUs in the Bell System owed something to the fact that women preferred these organizations to national unions. Sixty-five percent of the phone companies' employees were female and while many explanations exist for the correlation between ILUs and female employment (Schacht 1985, p. 75), surely one of them is the fact that women were turned off by the "macho," take-charge attitudes of national union organizers, who could be insensitive to the needs of women workers. Telephone ILUs sometimes made explicit recognition of gender, as with the Federation of Women Telephone Workers, which had nearly 13,000 members in California in the 1950s (Troy 1958). For a variety of reasons, women could be extremely loyal to top management. When Purcell (1960, p. 67) surveyed Swift employees, he found that women at the ILU plants demonstrated the highest level of corporate loyalty among all groups of Swift employees.

Reinforcing gender was the fact that women, including those at the telephone company, were disproportionately employed in white-collar occupations. The BLS (1969) data show that the proportion of white-collar workers in ILUs was more than twice as high as in national unions. One of the more interesting examples of this phenomenon were the various ILUs representing engineers and technicians at companies like General Electric, Lockheed, Boeing, RCA, Westinghouse, and other firms. Most of these unions were formed after the war to avoid inclusion in larger industrial unions dominated by blue-collar workers. As noted, several of them federated into the Engineers and Scientists of America. The professionals and semiprofessionals in these ILUs found themselves between a rock and a hard place: subject to occasional raids by national unions, while under constant criticism from the national engineering societies, who argued that professionalism and unionism, even of the ILU variety, were wholly incompatible (Walton 1961; Shostak 1962).

Management Perspectives

How did managers regard ILUs? The question is difficult to answer because management's usually positive appraisal of ILUs was based on consideration of the next worst alternative, that is, an affiliated union. In a world without affiliated unions, managements would never have tolerated organizations as independent and unpredictable as ILUs. But they still might have sought workplace institutions for handling employee grievances, for securing employee participation in enterprise affairs, and for organizing other employee-related activities. In fact, this combination of functions—voice, governance, and welfare—was the basis for the first representation plans that appeared at the turn of the century, many of them at companies that had little to fear from trade union organization (Jacoby 1985).

To the extent that ILUs sustained the employer-initiated thrust of representation plans and company unions, managers were happy with them. And even when ILUs displayed some mettle—in bargaining and grievance handling—managers were tolerant because an ILU was preferable to an affiliated union, especially a union affiliated with the CIO, an organization dreaded by most managers. This was the situation for most of the 1940s and early 1950s. But several events changed managerial preferences in the 1950s. First, the CIO shed its communist wing in the late 1940s and then merged with the AFL in 1955. Second, the capacity of the labor movement to attract new members began to weaken around this time. And, third, as we later see, managers developed an alternative to ILUs that was less "unionesque" while still providing a mechanism for employee participation. As a result of these events, management interest in ILUs gradually faded.

One of the reasons that managers of the 1940s and early 1950s preferred an ILU to an affiliated union was the ILU's conservative orientation, its divorce from politics, and the fact that it harbored no left-wing "eggheads" on its staff (Shostak 1962). Also, the ILU was more inclined to take a cooperative, problem-solving approach in its relations with management. Part of this reflected the simple fact that an ILU's top officers were always available to make adjustments on the spot. There were also cooperative incentives arising from the existence of a bilateral monopoly: the ILU had no other company to bargain with, and management preferred it to any other union (Jacoby 1989). Evidence of cooperation could be seen in many dimensions—from the absence of strikes to the organization of work. For example, in the oil refinery industry of the 1950s, only ILUs—not affiliated unions—had developed craft consolidation plans for reducing the rigidity of craft demarcations. And at TRW (the successor to Thompson Products), the ILU plants had fewer job classifications than the affiliated union plants (Brandt 1960, p. 148; Jacoby and Verma 1992).

Managers also had reasons to be skeptical of ILUs, however. The primary problem was that many ILUs, in management's eyes, were a species of Trojan horse. ILU members were tempting organizing targets for national unions because, unlike workers in nonunion firms, they already were a collectivity and were familiar with the arcana of contracts and grievance procedures. Even though national unions did not always succeed in raids against ILUs, they tried repeatedly. Raids against ILUs increased in the 1950s as the number of easily organized nonunion enterprises (i.e., blue-collar operations outside the South) steadily shrank. Ten percent of all ILUs experienced an organizing raid each year in the 1950s, surely an annoyance to management. One ILU at

Swift experienced no fewer than seven raids from 1943 to 1959, even though it won all of them by comfortable majorities (Krislov 1960; Shostak 1962; Purcell 1960).

Many managers also began to appreciate just how costly was the ILU strategy. ILU labor costs were equal to—and in some instances higher than—they would have been with an affiliated union. In part, this reflected the aforementioned skill or geographic premium that ILUs were seeking to preserve. In other cases it showed the power of ILUs to extract rents from management in return for maintaining their unaffiliated status. There is considerable evidence of ILUs strategically playing on management's affiliation fears in the studies I have done of Thompson in the 1940s and 1950s, and the work I did with Anil Verma on TRW in the 1970s and 1980s. The increase in raiding activity in the 1950s no doubt gave ILUs greater leverage in this regard (Jacoby and Verma 1992).

Faced with these immediate problems—and with the growing perception that unions, especially militant CIO unions, were a declining threat—some companies that earlier had pursued an ILU strategy began to step back from it. Take, for example, the experience of Du Pont. Throughout the 1930s and the war, Du Pont established company unions at its U.S. facilities; by 1946 85 percent of its employees were represented by them. After the war, however, Du Pont made a significant shift. Over the course of the next decade it opened twenty-five new plants, many in the South and all without ILUs. By 1960, ILUs represented only 59 percent of Du Pont's employees, and the percentage has fallen steadily since then (Rezler 1963).

Not every company was as quick as Du Pont to shed the ILU strategy. Thompson Products stuck with it after the war, establishing ILUs (or something akin to them) at all of the new plants it built or acquired in the late 1940s and 1950s. Unlike Du Pont, Thompson's plants were concentrated in the Midwest and Northeast, where organizing drives remained a threat. Also, Thompson's ILUs were demonstrably less militant than Du Pont's. Between 1944 and 1959, Du Pont's ILUs carried out four strikes and filed sixteen unfair labor practice charges against management, while not one of Thompson's ILUs struck or complained to the NLRB. This record, as well as its ILU's willingness to cooperate in boosting efficiency, convinced Thompson management that ILUs raised productivity sufficiently to offset their wage costs (Rezler 1963; Jacoby 1997).

This is not to say that Thompson management was entirely satisfied with its company unions. Wage costs were high, and raids—and the legal expenses that went with them—were a perennial issue. So in the early 1950s Thompson began to experiment with an alternative to traditional company unionism—the committee system—at three small plants acquired after the war. While the impetus for seeking an alternative to ILUs may have been internal, the fact that the Taft-Hartley Act now appeared to allow the formation of employee committees was a permissive, if not directly causal, factor. Employee committees were more decentralized and informal than ILUs, making it harder for organizers to transform them into national union affiliates. Also, the committee system explicitly ruled out collective bargaining, thus eliminating the labor-cost pressures associated with ILUs. On the other hand, management hoped that the new system would replicate what it saw as the positive features of company unions and ILUs: two-way communication, rapid dispute resolution, and a cooperative approach to problem solving. Thus Thompson was trying to

create new institutions to preserve the communicative features of company unions without an excess of independence or bargaining power.

In keeping with Thompson's diversification into technology-intensive defense products, two of the three "new system" plants were electronics factories: Bell Sound Systems, a Columbus, Ohio, manufacturer of amplifiers and communications equipment, and Dage Television, which made closed-circuit televisions for the military in Michigan City, Indiana. (The third plant was an automotive valve factory in Fruitport, Michigan.) Over a three-year period, from 1953 to 1956, Thompson management introduced virtually identical organizations in all three plants: the Voice of the Plant (Bell Sound), the Frontiersmen Association (Fruitport), and the Dage Employees' Association. Neither the Bell nor the Fruitport organization met directly with management. Instead, their elected officers spent their time directing the plants' numerous recreation and welfare activities. Separate from these organizations, however, were "human relations committees" that met with management to discuss problems and complaints. In order to avoid coming under NLRB purview, the purpose of the committees was described as "the exchange of ideas on matters affecting human relations . . . and good living within the company" (Jacoby 1997).

The Dage plant, smallest of the three, did things a bit differently. As at the other two plants, acquisition by Thompson brought a rapid expansion of employee recreational activities and regular use of advanced personnel techniques such as attitude surveys. But local management felt that the Dage employees would not be satisfied with the vagaries of the Bell-Fruitport model and pressed company officials for something that would "provide as many advantages of a union-type organization as possible in order to avoid possible outside interference." The end result, the Dage Employees' Association, was a hybrid combining some features of an ILU (regular meetings with management) and others taken from the new committee system (handling welfare activities autonomously and carefully refusing to "deal" with management on wages or working conditions) (Jacoby 1997).

The new approach received legal sanction from the courts. The more lenient legal environment prevailing after Taft-Hartley, as reflected in decisions like *Chicago Rawhide* (1955) and *Coppus Engineering* (1957), no doubt encouraged Thompson to stay the course and caused other firms to imitate Thompson. For example, General Electric in the 1950s pioneered the use of employee associations known as "sounding boards." These brought together engineers and managers in a single association to consider mutual problems. The National Society of Professional Engineers gave its imprimatur to these associations, viewing them as more suitable for engineers than a bargaining group like the ESEA (Shostak 1962). It is difficult to say how prevalent these committees were in the 1950s, although one study done in the late 1950s of two dozen nonunion firms in an unidentified midwestern city found that nine of them (40 percent) had some kind of representation plan, and only one of these was an ILU. The other eight were employee committees whose rotating membership was appointed by, and met with, management on a regular basis to discuss workplace issues (Conant 1959).

All this activity came to a sudden halt after 1959, however, when the Supreme Court, in its *Cabot Carbon* decision, ruled emphatically that an employee committee that does not bargain with management nevertheless is a labor organization governed by section 8(a)(2). After analyzing the legislative history of section 9(a) as amended, the Court concluded that Congress had never intended to authorize an employer to deal with an employer-supported committee (*Cabot Carbon* 1959).

The consequences of *Cabot Carbon* were swift and wide. Employers who utilized the committee system immediately proposed a federal law that would explicitly exclude committees and "sounding boards" from the law's definition of labor organizations; the parallels to recent events *(Electromation* and the TEAM Act) are striking (Shostak 1962, p. 85). But legislative efforts were fruitless, and the NLRB and lower courts followed the Supreme Court's lead. One of the first companies affected was TRW, where a 1960 organizing drive at Dage resulted in unfair labor practice charges being filed against the plant's committee system. In a decision later upheld by the Seventh Circuit, the NLRB ruled that the Dage committees were a labor organization and that they were dominated by management (*TRW* 1961, 1962). Although the company asserted that the committees never bargained and merely "expressed views and conveyed information to management," the board rejected the claim and ordered TRW to get rid of the committees. Other decisions in the 1960s were equally inimical to employee committees, including *Walton Manufacturing* (1961) and *Dennison Manufacturing* (1967)—the latter being one of the first U.S. firms to experiment with company unions.

Not every post-*Cabot* decision involving employee committees held them unlawful. In cases like *Modern Plastics* (1967) and *Hertzka & Knowles* (1974), the courts found committees to be permissible, usually because there was insufficient evidence that the employer dominated the committees. And even where committees were held unlawful, one heard dissenting opinions, like those of one appellate justice, who argued: "an inflexible attitude of hostility toward employee committees defeats the Act. It erects an iron curtain between employer and employees, penetrable only by the bargaining agent of a certified union, if there is one, preventing the development of a decent, honest, constructive relationship between management and labor" (*Walton Manufacturing* 1961, p. 182).

In spite of these exceptions, for most employers prudent conduct was to abandon employee committees. With its resounding defeat in *Dage*, TRW shifted gears and gave up on both ILUs and the new committee system. During the 1960s, it built or acquired thirty-nine new plants and created company unions at none of them (Verma and Kochan 1985). The 1960s saw the introduction at TRW of yet another hybrid, this one combining a new "small group" approach (sensitivity groups and other team-building programs) together with a bevy of communications programs whose roots stretched back to the 1930s (attitude surveys, "sensing" sessions, and leadership training).

The new approach was more individualized, emotionally engaging, and rooted in the behavioral sciences than ILUs or the committee system. Combined with attitude surveys and other psychological techniques, it would become the basis for the "new" nonunion model of the 1960s and 1970s (Kochan, Katz, and McKersie 1986). But the new approach was also more passive, less democratic, and less of a threat to managerial prerogatives. Still, few in either management or labor mourned the passing of the ILU. And most managers saw the new approach as consistent with the thrust of earlier efforts. As TRW's vice president for personnel told *Business Week* (1966, p. 92), "Openness, leveling, listening therapy, conflict resolution—all this talk by behavioral scientists. Hell, we've been doing these things for 30 years. They're just elegant terms for principles we practiced years ago—old wine in new bottles."

Conclusions

Company unions represented more than 2 million workers in 1935, but by the end of World War II most of these company unions had disappeared. One of the driving forces behind the demise of company unions was the NLRB, which, especially in its early years, worked hard to disestablish a large number of them. Others were taken over by national unions, which offered a more militant and innovative form of representation.

Yet company unions did not entirely disappear from the scene. Several hundred evolved into relatively independent organizations—ILUs—that offered an alternative to national unionism in the 1940s and 1950s. For employers, the benefits of ILUs were clear: they were less aggressive, strike-prone, and politicized than most affiliated unions. For ILU members, the story is more complex. Some no doubt were bullied or misled into supporting ILUs, which is the traditional union perspective. There was some of that, to be sure, but there was more. ILU members were a relatively conservative group—loyal to their union and to the companies that employed them. And the ILUs they belonged to were dynamic institutions, which, due to situational incentives and to pressure from government and national unions, evolved into organizations that met their members' needs. Compared to a national union, ILUs were less independent and powerful; in contrast, they were also less bureaucratic and remote.

By the 1950s, however, a paradox began to emerge: just when the law was making it easier for employers to start ILUs, companies that already had them began to lose interest. The explanation is straightforward: with the threat from organized labor fading, the benefits of company unionism faded too; meanwhile, the growing independence of company unions made them more costly to deal with. Management eventually found a cheaper alternative, one that channeled employee participation through committees and, later on, through small groups instead of through elected bodies. Thus the ILU was a precursor to some of the more innovative participatory schemes developed by behavioral scientists in the 1960s and 1970s.

Nevertheless, something was lost during the transition from ILUs to the "small group" approach. Company unions, however imperfect, at least relied on formally democratic methods and were able to influence management at the corporate level. In contrast, the behavioral sciences—both in their early (human relations) and modern (small group) manifestations—discouraged self-organization, while focusing employee influence primarily on the work group. Hence, in spite of enormous differences between the workplace of the 1920s and today, one may still ask, as Slichter (1929) did seventy years ago, whether there is not a need among employees "for more initiative and enterprise, for more mental independence, and for more disposition to rely on cooperative self-help than modern personnel practice is disposed to encourage?"

References

Barbash, Jack. 1952. *Unions and Telephones: The Story of the Communications Workers of America.* New York: Harper.

Brandt, Floyd S. 1960. "Independent and National Unionism in the Oil Refining Industry." Ph.D. dissertation, Harvard University.

Bureau of Labor Statistics (BLS). 1938. *Characteristics of Company Unions.* Bulletin no. 634. Washington, D.C.: BLS.

———. 1961. *Unaffiliated and Single-Employer Unions.* Bulletin no. 1348. Washington, D.C.: BLS.

———. 1969. *Unaffiliated Intrastate and Single-Employer Unions, 1967.* Bulletin no. 1640. Washington, D.C.: BLS.

Cabot Carbon et al. v. NLRB. 1959. 360 U.S. 203.

Chicago Rawhide Mfg. v. NLRB. 1955. 221 F. 2d (7 CCA).

Cohen, Lizabeth. 1990. *Making a New Deal: Industrial Workers in Chicago, 1919–1939.* Cambridge, U.K.: Cambridge University Press.

Conant, Eaton H. 1959. "Defenses of Nonunion Employers: A Study from Company Sources." *Labor Law Journal* 10 (February): 100–109.

Coppus Engineering v. NLRB. 1957. 240 F. 2d 564 (1 CCA).

Crager, Burton. 1942. "Company Unions Under the National Labor Relations Act." *Michigan Law Review* 40 (April): 831–855.

Dennison Manufacturing and United Papermakers and Paperworkers. 1967. 168 NLRB 1012.

Gould, William. 1996. "Remarks on Workplace Cooperation." *Daily Labor Report*, October 28, E1–E3.

Gross, James A. 1981. *The Reshaping of the National Labor Relations Board: National Labor Policy in Transition, 1937–47.* Albany: SUNY Press.

Hertzka & Knowles v. NLRB. 1974. 503 F. 2d 625.

"Independents Begin to Huddle." 1956. *Fortune*, March, pp. 203–206.

Jacoby, Sanford M. 1985. *Employing Bureaucracy: Managers, Unions, and the Transformation of Work in American Industry, 1900–1945.* New York: Columbia University Press.

———. 1989. "Reckoning with Company Unions: The Case of Thompson Products, 1934–1964." *Industrial and Labor Relations Review* 43 (October): 19–40.

———. 1993. "Reflections on Labor Law Reform and the Crisis of American Labor." *Chicago-Kent Law Review* 69, no. 1: 219–227.

———. 1997. *Modern Manors: Welfare Capitalism Since the New Deal.* Princeton: Princeton University Press.

Jacoby, Sanford M., and Anil Verma. 1992. "Enterprise Unions in the United States." *Industrial Relations* 31 (Winter): 137–158.

Kaufman, Bruce. 1996. "Why the Wagner Act? Reestablishing Contact with Its Original Purpose." *Advances in Industrial and Labor Relations* 7: 15–68.

Kochan, Thomas, Harry C. Katz, and Robert B. McKersie. 1986. *The Transformation of American Industrial Relations.* New York: Basic Books.

Krislov, Joseph. 1954. "Raiding Among the 'Legitimate' Unions." *Industrial and Labor Relations Review* 8 (October): 19–29.

———. 1955. "The Extent and Trends of Raiding among American Unions." *Quarterly Journal of Economics* 69 (February): 145–152.

———. 1960. "Organizational Rivalry among American Unions." *Industrial and Labor Relations Review* 13 (January): 216–226.

Marshall, F. Ray. 1961. "Independent Unions in the Gulf Coast Oil Petroleum Refining Industry." *Labor Law Journal* 12 (September): 823–840.

Millis, Harry, and Emily Clark Brown. 1950. *From the Wagner Act to Taft-Hartley*. Chicago: University of Chicago Press.

Millis, Harry, and Royal E. Montgomery. 1945. *Organized Labor*. New York: McGraw-Hill.

Mitchell, Daniel J.B. 1986. "Inflation, Unemployment, and the Wagner Act: A Critical Reappraisal." *Stanford Law Review* 38 (April): 1065–1095.

Modern Plastics v. *NLRB*. 1967. 379 F. 2d 201.

National Labor Relations Board (NLRB). Various years. *Annual Report of the National Labor Relations Board*. Washington, D.C.

Nelson, Daniel. 1982. "The Company Union Movement, 1900–1937: A Reexamination." *Business History Review* 56, no. 3: 335–357.

———. 1995. *Farm and Factory: Workers in the Midwest, 1880–1990*. Bloomington: Indiana University Press.

Note. 1957. "Section 8(a)(2): Employer Assistance to Plant Unions and Committees." *Stanford Law Review* 9 (March): 351–365.

O'Connor, Harvey. 1950. *History of the Oil Workers International Union (CIO)*. Denver: OWIU.

Personnel. 1955. "The Case for the Local Independent Union." 32 (November): 226–233.

Purcell, Theodore V. 1960. *Blue Collar Man: Patterns of Dual Allegiance in Industry*. Cambridge: Harvard University Press.

Rezler, Julius. 1963. "Labor Organization at Du Pont: A Study in Independent Unionism." *Labor History* 4 (Spring): 178–195.

Robinson, James W. 1968. "Structural Characteristics of the Independent Union in America." *Labor Law Journal* 19 (July): 417–437.

Rosenfarb, Joseph. 1940. *The National Labor Policy and How It Works*. New York: Harper.

Saposs, David J. 1936. "Organizational and Procedural Changes in Employee Representation Plans." *Journal of Political Economy* 44 (December): 803–811.

Schacht, John. 1985. *The Making of Telephone Unionism, 1920–47*. New Brunswick, N.J.: Rutgers University Press.

Slichter, Sumner H. 1929. "The Current Labor Policies of American Industries." *Quarterly Journal of Economics* 43 (May) 393–435.

Shostak, Arthur B. 1962. *America's Forgotten Labor Organization*. Princeton: Industrial Relations Section, Princeton University.

Thompson Ramo Wooldridge (TRW) and Teamsters Union. 1961. 132 NLRB 995.

Thompson Ramo Wooldridge (TRW) v. *NLRB*. 1962. 50 LRRM 2759.

Tomlins, Christopher L. 1985. *The State and the Unions: Labor Relations, Law, and the Organized Labor Movement in America, 1880–1960*. Cambridge, U.K.: Cambridge University Press.

Troy, Leo. 1958. "The Course of Company and Local Independent Unions." Ph.D. dissertation, Columbia University.

———. 1960. "Local Independent and National Unions: Competitive Labor Organizations." *Journal of Political Economy* 68 (October): 487–506.

———. 1961. "Local Independent Unions and the American Labor Movement." *Industrial and Labor Relations Review* 14 (April): 331–349.

Twentieth Century Fund. 1935. *Labor and the Government*. New York: McGraw-Hill.

Union Labor News Review. Various issues.

Verma, Anil, and Thomas A. Kochan. 1985. "The Growth and Nature of the Nonunion Sector Within a Firm." In *Challenges and Choices Facing American Labor*, ed. Thomas A. Kochan. Cambridge: MIT Press.

Walton Mfg. v. *NLRB*. 1951. 289 F.2d 177 (5 CCA).

Walton, Richard E. 1961. *The Impact of the Professional Engineering Union*. Boston: Graduate School of Business Administration, Harvard University.

Waters, Elinor. 1954. "Unionization of Office Employees." *Journal of Business* 27 (October): 285–292.

"Where Diversity Is the Tie that Binds." 1966. *Business Week*, September 24, p. 92.

5

Company Unionism in Canada 1915–1948

Laurel Sefton MacDowell

The current debate in academic and business circles in the United States over section 8(a)(2), the National Labor Relations Act's ban on "dominated" labor organizations (company unions), the fact of dramatic union decline in the United States, and the post-NAFTA atmosphere in labor relations that features employer confidence, management aggressiveness against unions, an active search for a nonunion environment either through plant shutdowns or the encouragement of nonunion representation forms, has heightened business interest and renewed curiosity about company unions.

This chapter reviews the history of company unionism in Canada from 1915, the year William Lyon Mackenzie King, who in 1900 became the first deputy minister of labor in the new federal Department of Labor, was hired by the Rockefeller Foundation (See Figure 5.1). It concludes in 1948 when the federal government passed the Industrial Relations Disputes Investigation Act and the provinces, which constitutionally resumed paramountcy in labor relations following the war, either opted into it or passed similar legislation within their jurisdictions. All of these laws incorporated wartime labor relations developments, especially the collective bargaining clauses of war order P.C. 1003 (1944), which was Canada's Wagner Act, and were the basis of a new postwar legal framework for industrial relations. The Ca-

Figure 5.1 **A Young W.L. Mackenzie King, 1927**

Source: W.L. Mackenzie King. 1927. *The Message of the Carillon*. Toronto, Ontario: Macmillan.

nadian system favored collective bargaining and unions but did not totally exclude other forms of representation. I examine the development of nonunion representation forms, conclude that employee representation is desirable, that nonunion and union representation forms are different, and that collective bargaining through independent unions has been preferred by most employees in Canada, in a legal environment that is less restrictive of company unions and more liberal toward independent unions than that of the United States.

An Overview

The rise and fall of company unions in Canada roughly paralleled developments in the United States, with relatively little activity until the end of World War I, when there was a burst of new employee representation plans (ERPs). These continued into the prosperous 1920s, as some employers launched an active open-shop drive and initiated a movement of "Welfare Capitalism." During the Great Depression most of these schemes failed or stagnated, but a few emerged in the 1930s in reaction to the stirrings of workers, who were fed up with depressed conditions and began organizing industrial unions. As union membership grew in Canada a little later than in the United States, so too did employer support for the ERPs, until near the end of World War II the passage of collective bargaining legislation facilitated trade union organization and outlawed employer-dominated organizations. Some nonunion representation forms persisted, at Dofasco steel company for example, but were not certified. Some ERPs evolved into trade unions, such as a local independent union at Algoma, which in 1942 joined the Steelworkers' union. But most ERPs disappeared and were replaced by certified unions, which in the 1950s developed mature bargaining relationships with employers and won real gains for their members. The few ERPs that became genuinely independent of employers and were certified by a labor board, negotiated agreements that except for preambles about the desir-ability of labor-management cooperation, were indistinguishable from collective agreements in that they dealt with the same range of issues and had grievance procedures that provided for final dispute resolution through arbitration by an outside person mutually agreed upon by the parties or appointed by the minister of labor.

The first influential company union scheme was the result of Canadian-American collaboration. After he was defeated temporarily in politics in 1911, Mackenzie King, who had been Canada's minister of labor, an effective mediator, and author of Canada's compulsory conciliation legislation in 1907, developed his "American Plan" between 1915 and 1917, when he worked for the Rockefeller Foundation. King was hired following the brutal suppression in the 1914 Ludlow Massacre of 9,000 miners and their families. They lost their strike against the Rockefeller-owned Colorado Fuel and Iron Company in the Colorado mining district, led by their union the United Mine Workers (UMWA). King produced an alternative representation plan, based on industrial councils, guarantees of certain basic rights, and a defined grievance procedure, which sidestepped the issue of union recognition, was imposed on the miners, and successfully eliminated the union for eighteen years. It achieved industrial peace in Colorado, however, and the plan was adopted by large American corporations in the United States and Canada including General Electric, International Harvester, and Standard Oil. As a result, in the emerging field of industrial relations King acted as a labor consultant between 1917 and 1920 and later, as prime minister, became influential in developing labor policy, but in Canadian union circles King was seen as "the father of company unionism" in North America (King 1973, p. xi; Ferns and Ostry 1976, p. 214).

King was Canada's prime minister from 1921

to 1930 and again from 1935 to 1948 when significant developments in labor relations policy were introduced. His ideas on class relations as expressed in his book *Industry and Humanity* (1918) and his experience with the Rockefeller Foundation may have predisposed him to be sympathetic to representative institutions other than unions. He certainly delayed implementing collective bargaining legislation because he associated that process with conflict, which he strenuously sought to avoid. At any rate, as labor relations law developed in Canada and in the United States, company-dominated unions were outlawed in the United States in 1935 and examined in Canada near the end of World War II. Nonunion forms of employee representation in Canada could exist "provided they are not deliberately designed to thwart union organizing," but in the United States the Wagner Act ban on nonunion representation has been enforced more firmly (Taras 1997, p. 1, and Taras in chapter 6 of this volume explains the legality of Canadian nonunion representation).

Industrial Councils in the Immediate Post–World War I Period

Many industrial council proposals were first introduced in Canada in 1918 and 1919 as the level of industrial conflict and worker dissatisfaction increased, as soldiers returned and war plants converted to peacetime production. At International Harvester, Imperial Oil, Swift's, Bell Telephone, and such smaller firms as McLary Manufacturing in London, Ontario, workers' councils were formed, and worker and management representatives discussed matters of mutual interest (Thompson and Seager 1985, p. 141). Some of the details about the origins and working of these schemes were revealed in testimony in 1919 be-

fore a Royal Commission, often called the Mathers Commission after its chair, which the federal government created to investigate the causes of industrial unrest in Canada. Between April and June it toured the country, held open hearings in Canadian cities, and received submissions from business, unions, and workers of varying trades and skill levels at a time when there was concern about working-class discontent and fear of the Bolshevist threat in the aftermath of the Russian Revolution.

The Mathers Commission reported in June 1919 when strike activity was at its peak. It concluded that serious unrest in Canada was general but "most pronounced" in the West and attributed such conflict to reaction to European events and "the disturbed state of the public mind generally owing to the war" (Royal Commission 1919, Ontario evidence, p. 13). It found that a minority of radical workers sought to control the production process, but most simply wanted higher wages and union recognition. It attributed unrest to fear of unemployment, the high cost of living resulting from wartime inflation, which some workers attributed to excessive profiteering by "middle men," the universal desire for shorter work hours, employers' refusal to recognize unions or engage in collective bargaining, workers' mistrust of the government for restricting their freedom of speech during the war, the gap between rich and poor, and the lack of enough adequate housing or equal educational opportunities for working people. Canadian workers believed that they did not receive a fair share of remuneration for their labor, and in 1919 their discontent led to unprecedented conflict. But some workers and businesses sought cooperation and industrial peace as a more complex system of industrial production evolved.

The commissioners agreed on the social problems and the goal of industrial peace, but they divided over solutions. The majority proposed that employees should have a right to collective bargaining and legislative reforms including unemployment insurance, old-age pensions, minimum wages, and an eight-hour day. They also praised the development of industrial councils, both the Rockefeller and Whitley models. The minority report favored only the Rockefeller schemes (Naylor 1991, p. 188). No substantive legislation resulted.

The hearings themselves were revealing because the commission was interested in witnesses' opinions of industrial councils. It solicited views on the Whitley scheme (the result of a report of a British Parliamentary Committee on Joint Industrial Councils headed by J. H. Whitley, which in 1917 proposed a system of national, regional, and enterprise-level committees that would include employers and, wherever possible, trade unions) and the Rockefeller plan (Mackenzie King's plan for employees' committees in industry that explicitly excluded unions). Most of the witnesses—both workers and management—were remarkably well informed about such proposals. Workers preferred the British model, while management wanted no plan or the Rockefeller plan (Naylor 1991, p. 164).

The Rockefeller scheme was adopted primarily by large American corporations with branch plants in Canada as an alternative to unions and became fairly prevalent in the 1920s. At International Harvester, for example, works councils were introduced in about twenty plants in North America in the 1920s and early 1930s, and some functioned for over twenty years. They were introduced following strikes in 1918–19, because Harvester President Cyrus McCormick III knew of Mackenzie King's work in "rescuing the Rockefellers from the United Mine Workers in 1915"; he eulogized the plans as a step toward "sharing management with labour" and implemented works councils to forestall labor organization (Storey 1981, p. 201). The new system could deal with day-to-day grievances, but the councils' role was largely ceremonial concerning major issues such as layoffs or pay scales.

When the plan was introduced in its Ontario plant, only a small number of skilled workers in the tool room were unionized; the majority of unskilled workers had no say in decision making. The men had instructed the industrial council to demand an eight-hour day which council member William McKinley said had "been simmering in the minds of the people for a long time." The workforce split over the issue as the skilled union men were dissatisfied with the length of the day, but the unorganized men were concerned with wages. McKinley noted, "I don't think it is leisure the men are after so much as it is bread, it is food." Most of them were on piecework making an average of 37 cents an hour for nine hours—about $20 a week. "The hard struggle for existence is such that there are lots of men who would work twelve hours a day for the sake of easing off the struggle to make ends meet" (Royal Commission 1919, Ontario evidence, pp. 74, 78).

McKinley recognized that the council had relatively little power and told the commission, "now suppose we were all red-hot revolutionaries and we insisted on impossible things, there is nothing to stop the company from annulling the council." The council had refused a shorter workday because management said trade was bad, and it admitted that it could deal with small grievances but large problems were decided by the head office. Nevertheless, in McKinley's view, International Harvester's industrial council resulted in some improvements. "Under the old system, the foreman was a little god, a little kaiser in his own department." But with the council, if there was discrimination, a man could approach his council rep to get a hearing.

Trade unionists had no use for industrial councils because, they argued, a council was not necessary if an employer dealt fairly with an elected representative shop committee. They wanted their own union organization, which, as Hamilton machinist Richard Riley told the commission, "was perfectly capable of looking after them and they don't desire schemes introduced by the company." In his view, industrial councils could work only where workers were already organized and had some support. "In those industrial councils, there is nothing at the back of the worker, and when he presents his demands and the employer can't see it, there is nothing for him to do but go back to work" (Royal Commission 1919, Ontario evidence, pp. 12–13, 86). Fred Stucberry, an engineer on the council at Imperial Oil in Sarnia, would have preferred representation through a union. He poignantly described the dilemma of all industrial council representatives where there was no union behind them. "A man might be a good enough man to talk to the men," he said, "but when he gets before these big guys he falls down."

Following the Mathers Commission report, the federal government announced that it was holding a National Industrial Conference with union, employer, government, and "public" representatives to debate issues confronting industry. Interestingly, this pattern of a commission report followed by a government-sponsored conference paralleled similar events in 1919 initiated by President Wilson's administration. For six days in September, in Ottawa, Canadian labor was accorded an unprecedented opportunity to express its concerns and be consulted, as it had requested from the start of the war. The Canadian Industrial Reconstruction Association (CIRA), an organization of large business interests established in 1918, also supported the conference on problems and the consequences of postwar conflicts (Naylor 1991, p. 190).

Delegates were selected by the Canadian Manufacturers' Association (CMA) and the Trades and Labour Congress of Canada (TLC). The minister of labor, Gideon Robertson, chose as delegates members of the Borden government's labor subcommittee and the Mathers Commission. Newly selected Liberal Party leader Mackenzie King attended as an "interested party" and spoke about his recent book, *Industry and Humanity.* A delegate talked about Whitleyism, and the American National War Labor Board was represented. All emphasized the need for cooperation.

The government's strategy, which was consistent with its actions to end the Winnipeg General strike in 1919 and oppose the radical One Big Union movement, was to focus on cooperation with conservative craft unionists. This approach was reflected in the labor delegation's composition, made up of the nonsocialist leaders of the Trades and Labour Congress of Canada (TLC). The business delegation represented large and small business, and many did not share the CIRA view that a new industrial relations regime was necessary or desirable (Naylor 1991, p. 193). The CMA was sympathetic to the National Association of Manufacturers (NAM) in the United States, which was identified with an open-shop drive against unions, and ultimately it rejected all Mathers Commission recommendations except a minimum-wage law for women and youth, if it was necessary (Naylor 1991, p. 195). So employers were divided between those establishing "progressive" welfare programs and representation schemes in their own industries (along the lines of the Rockefeller model) and those focused on opposing unions and radicals; but both groups were individualistic, confident, and opposed to widespread collective bargaining or an expanded role for the state in social welfare or industrial relations.

Some firms organized industrial councils as a substitute for what they viewed as "outside organizations." Bruce Scott's detailed study of the industrial council at Massey-Harris from 1919 to 1929 found that it was a modified version of the International Harvester plan established in March 1919, and both exemplified the employees' committees that emerged after the war. The Massey-Harris council was established in 1919 during the May Day strike of the Toronto metal trades council, which involved 300 of its employees. It had an equal number of representatives elected by the workers or appointed by the company and met once a month on the company's "home ground" in its plush boardroom. The meetings were conducted using elaborate parliamentary procedure, which had the effect of subduing the workers' representatives whose leaders were deferential (Scott 1976, pp. 164, 173). From the company perspective, the council was useful for public relations purposes as it published the minutes of meetings in the company newsletter, the *M-H Weekly*, usually highlighting the unity of council discussions. Issues such as wages and vacations with pay, which could be contentious, were withdrawn, postponed, or avoided by elaborate procedures that unnerved worker representatives, allowed the company to control discussion, but gave their employees the appearance that they were participating in making decisions.

The Massey-Harris council enabled management to consult its employees and provide information about issues that might create problems. Thus it was useful as a communication device, which could encourage harmony, as in 1920, when 200 workers struck over the appointment of an assistant foreman. The foreman told them to refer the matter to council and, once that was done, the matter was settled quickly. "The majority of the council voted in favour of maintaining the services of the assistant foreman, who was known to be a capable workman and voted in favour of the men returning to work" (*Financial Post*, May 8, 1920). On the whole, management was pleased with the council because workers had made no exorbitant demands since its establishment, and individual employees, both workmen and foremen, were careful not to bring up petty complaints that upon investigation might injure their standing with the company.

Thus, in a subtle way, the Massey-Harris council did control employee behavior and had the effect of continuing to vest more authority in higher management and keep it from the shopfloor. The council provided workers with more knowledge of the company and experience in meetings, and it gave them, in circumscribed circumstances, limited control over their conditions of work. The health and safety subcommittee was active, and over the years it introduced guards on machines, renovations in the plant, a visiting nurse, a plant doctor, the introduction of lockers, work shoes paid for by the company, and showers.

It is debatable how much the council stimulated loyalty to the company. Workers generally ignored its "Suggestion Card" scheme; between 1920 and 1924, only thirty-seven rewards for suggestions were made, and they averaged seven dollars each. There was low attendance at the annual company picnics, even though their planning absorbed a great deal of council's time. As time passed, few sought election to the council and the number of acclamations increased. On production, wages, and employment issues, the company made decisions alone. Indeed, in 1927, when a worker representative tried to get time and a half for overtime after forty-eight hours for a minority of staff not covered by the accepted overtime arrangement, management manipulated his motion to decrease overtime pay to time and a quarter for everyone in the plant. "The employees' one serious attempt at bargaining in the council thus resulted in a deterioration of conditions even compared to pre-council years" (Scott 1976, pp. 170, 182). Workers' representatives at Massey-Harris never again tried to challenge the management in such a direct manner.

The Massey-Harris council and many in other industries ceased to exist in hard economic times. In the 1921–22 recession, the company shut down for an extended period, instituted a wage cut of 20 percent unilaterally, and cut its Toronto workforce to one-third its 1920 level. In 1923 when the economic situation improved, the company revived the council, by which time the threat of a union had diminished, as union membership in Canada was declining and the level of conflict had dropped dramatically. The revived council again functioned as a means of improved communication between employees and management. With the onset of the Great Depression, the poor state of the economy adversely affected the council, which limped along for two years and ceased to exist in 1931. Not until 1943 did the company renew consultation with its employees, who, by then, had organized a union.

Industrial Councils in the 1920s

The industrial council was an employer initiative to maintain industrial harmony, create "a spirit of goodwill toward the management on the part of the workers" (*Financial Post*, May 8, 1920), and ensure productive, loyal, and unorganized workforces. By such arrangements, workers could be consulted individually or on advisory committees, but such consultation did not impact on managements' prerogative to run industry as it saw fit. Workers were to be pacified with in-house programs that encouraged loyalty; if they tried to act independently to form their own organizations, they were punished. "Thus an illusion of democracy was offered," according to David Bercuson, "unsupported by any substantive share in the process of making key decisions" (King 1973, p. xi). This approach was unsatisfactory to unionists, who wanted through collective representation to negotiate corporate policies that most affected workers.

During the 1920s, in a political environment where business was praised for creating prosperity and better consumer goods, employers felt secure. Consequently, as in the United States, Canadian business attacked unions aggressively and called publicly for the "open shop" in the name of individual freedom. Managers, particularly of American-owned branch plants in Canada, argued that unions were old-fashioned and that adversarial relations between employers and employees that had caused class confrontation in 1919 were being replaced by cooperative labor-management relations (Thompson and Seager 1985, p. 141). Their promotion of plant-level industrial councils and various programs of corporate welfarism spawned company proposals for employees committees, which were not independent and did not originate with the workers themselves. Some such plans originated at the end of the war, while others continued to be introduced "as a means of curbing unrest in the ranks of labor" (*Financial Post*, October 1, 1920).

Businesses' establishment of employees' representation committees was supported by the federal Department of Labor which, in February 1921, assembled employers from firms that had established industrial councils to discuss their operation at a national conference. The department estimated that Canadian workers covered by some form of industrial council numbered 145,000 in July 1920, which was a considerable movement in that it amounted to about 40 percent of the number of workers organized in trade unions, but this figure may have been overstated (Scott 1976, p. 160; Naylor 1991, p. 206). At the conference, with no employee or union representatives in attendance, "the manufacturers spoke frankly about their success in getting the employee members on their work councils to withdraw demands for wage increases and even approve wage cuts" (McCallum 1990, p. 59). By 1921, companies felt less threatened by unions than in 1919, and much of the conference discussion concerned reducing the influence of foremen and centralizing administration, a trend noted by American historians as also occurring in the United States (Jacoby 1985; Nelson 1982, p. 336).

In the 1920s, the department's journal, *Labour Gazette*, was filled with articles and reports about employee welfare, methods of increasing workers' efficiency, profit-sharing schemes, group insurance plans, joint councils, and "prophecies of industrial peace," a phrase which was used by Harvard Emeritus President Dr. Charles W. Eliot (*Labour Gazette*, April 1925, p. 358), a friend of Liberal Prime Minister Mackenzie King. Both men were enthusiastic about such plans, but from the union point of view, their shortcoming was that they failed to take account of the nature of corporate power. They neither recognized employers' power over employees nor compelled management to abide by agreements, and though the plans sometimes offered protection to workers, they were only of value if employers voluntarily followed the rules that they themselves had set (King 1973, p. xii).

Such schemes proliferated particularly in Canada's industrial heartland, where American investment in Canadian industries and resources increased. The industrial council idea appealed to Canadian employers who adopted American business philosophies of efficiency like the "scientific management" ideas Frederic Winslow Taylor popularized before the war, and who professionalized and centralized their personnel relations. In a period sometimes referred to as the "second industrial revolution," the locus of decision-making power shifted permanently to new managers administering company rules pronounced by management, and away from work rules formulated among skilled workers hired by small firms.

Also in the 1920s, an interesting variation of the industrial council movement developed in the railway industry. There, the rail running trades, which were craft unions affiliated with the TLC, were entrenched and were among the oldest unions in Canada. Their members were skilled workers who, in the nineteenth century, consulted with their employers and developed mature relationships with them. There was no question of breaking these unions and no advantage to the companies to do so, but the new trends in the 1920s influenced the Canadian National Railway (CN) to introduce a cooperative scheme complementary with its collective bargaining relationship with employees in its major repair shops and roundhouses. The plan, which was established in 1924 across the country, consisted of local joint committees of management and employees and one central joint committee with jurisdiction over the entire railway system. CN wages, hours, and work rules were negotiated and fixed by collective agreement. The new cooperative plan was additional; it recognized the unions as necessary and constructive, but it was to increase efficiency. In contrast to employers who refused to deal with unions, CN used union officials to represent the employees on the joint committees.

The effects were mainly positive, despite some friction between a few officials and union representatives. Foremen noticed both a higher quality and reduced cost of repair and maintenance work. The men were rewarded with better working conditions and steadier employment, for the railroad provided jobs of remodeling and rebuilding rolling stock during slow repair periods. H. M. Cassidy wrote in a laudatory article, "shops and grounds have been cleaned up, additional drinking water and toilet facilities provided" and other improvements made (Cassidy 1926, p. 43). Grievances decreased by 75 percent and were dealt with more quickly. Through the plan, the men participated in finding solutions to management problems and shared actual production policy decisions. By using collective bargaining methods, trade union representation, and material incentives, the CN experimental industrial policy achieved greater efficiency in production while working within an existing collective bargaining tradition.

The CN approach was laudatory, but it developed as a result of some exceptional circumstances. Its president, Henry Thornton, was seen as a radical by other business leaders. His philosophy of cooperation was genuine, but he headed a railway that he sometimes referred to as "the people's railway," and in 1925 he described as "the greatest experiment in public ownership that the world has ever seen" (Seager 1992, p. 3). He was sensitive to his employees' needs and got on with their union leaders. When the AFL convention met in Toronto in 1929, Thornton was a guest speaker, as AFL leaders favored the CN plan. It was similar to the B&O plan introduced in 1922 in the United States, which was "sold" to the AFL leaders as an alternative to open-shop conditions. They had accepted it because it offered employees harmony, stable employment, and a voice in policy, and offered employers efficiency and higher productivity, but it was also based on union strength, not weakness, which was unusual in such plans (Seager 1992, p. 27). Thornton's application of it in Canada succeeded because he presided over the railway as its fortunes rose, when between 1925 and 1928 freight and passenger rates and railway wages all increased so that the economic situation favored his approach to labor-management relations. While this variation of employee representation combined with aspects of welfare capitalism worked and looked to the future, it was based on two features of the past—employer paternalism and craft unionism (Seager 1992, p. 38). When Thornton left the company, the plan lapsed.

In the 1920s in Quebec, the cooperative approach to labor-management relations was unique in North America and resulted in the creation of the Catholic union movement by the Roman Catholic church. Some locals emerged after 1901 when an archbishop arbitrated a shoe workers' dispute, and workers agreed to have a chaplain assigned to their union (*Labour Organizations* 1928, p. 14). In 1907 the Quebec Catholic church conceived of a coordinated policy consciously to encourage the organization and expansion of Catholic unions as an alternative to "neutral" American unions, which were perceived as materialistic, foreign, and militant or even radical. In keeping with its interpretation of the church's social policy embodied in Pope Leo XIII's 1891 encyclical *Rerum Novarum* on "The Conditions of the Working Classes," which Pope Pius X proclaimed in 1912 as the fundamental rules for workers' associations, the priests created and controlled unions of Catholic workers that favored harmony over improved wages and working conditions, and arbitration over strikes. Business and the Quebec government favored and even promoted them over AFL unions.

By 1921, when local Catholic unions united in the Federation of Catholic Workers of Canada, they represented about one-third of organized workers in Quebec (Isbester 1971, p. 242). Because of their close relations with employers, the church, and Quebec politicians, the nonconfessional labor movement viewed them as company unions until the asbestos strike in 1949, when lay Catholic union leaders conducted a militant strike against the Canadian Johns Manville company and the government (which supported management). The strike split the church, gained the support of the rest of the labor movement, and the Catholic unions thereafter became more secular, independent, and nationalistic. But up to and including the 1920s, as Bruno Ramirez has noted, "the local clergy played a crucial role as a midwife in that process that saw the transformation of thousands of rural Quebecers into an industrial proletariat, setting ideological and organizational parameters for the nascent workers' movement and insuring that the workers' social consciousness be nurtured by submission to authority and respect for the sacrosanct doctrine of class harmony" (Ramirez 1989, p. 124).

Another aspect of the environment in which company unions grew in the 1920s involved the introduction by many managements of corporate welfarism. Such initiatives often but not always accompanied the introduction of industrial councils. At Imperial Oil, for example, where the relationship between paternalism and profit was clearly articulated and its determination to maintain an open shop was clear, the company introduced its industrial council in 1919, accompanied by a package of welfare benefits, a pension plan, and in 1920 started its "Cooperative Investment Trust," a share-purchase plan (Grant 1998, pp. 82–87). Such welfare benefits resulted from the same management philosophy behind industrial councils and were designed to improve the situation of employees and decrease the turnover of personnel simultaneously. The results "included everything from putting a picnic table outside the factory to providing employees and their dependents with comprehensive insurance coverage in the event of sickness, disability or death" (McCallum 1990, pp. 47, 67) and varied from providing bathing facilities and lunchrooms to promote healthier, more sanitary work environments to establishing recreational programs such as sports teams, workers' clubs, music and gardening programs, and social outings. In isolated northern company towns like Espanola, Copper Cliff, or Abitibi, corporations viewed such company projects as necessary to maintain a workforce (Goltz 1974). They could involve industrial training, domestic service education for women workers, or English and citizenship classes for immigrant workers. Certain companies provided financial aid at low interest rates to assist employees in the purchase of a home. John Cummings, a metal polisher at McLary's in London, who favored a representative grievance committee, was buying his home from his employer, but he feared discrimination if he complained as an individual (Royal Commission 1919, Ontario evidence, p. 227).

Many companies introduced profit-sharing schemes and stock-purchase plans based on employee contributions to encourage workers to identify their interests with the employers. At Stelco, which formed an industrial council later, a profit-sharing scheme was first introduced in 1913 and reorganized in 1919, in which the company bought shares at par and sold them to their workers at a lower rate. It expected "every employee to come and buy stock that he may be a continuous employee with us" (Royal Commission 1919, Ontario evidence, p. 35). Procter and Gamble in Hamilton, which employed 200 people and had an industrial council, also engaged the interest and money of its workers this way, and viewed their participation in its plan as an intention to stay. James Howarth, a pipefitter with the firm, thought the men liked the profit-sharing scheme, viewed it as an incentive to thrift and as an investment. Procter and Gamble also had a sick benefits plan in effect for thirty years, in which 1 percent of company income was allocated to take care of the needy, and an elected committee of the men administered the fund (Royal Commission 1919, Ontario evidence, pp. 90, 110). In 1919 the large Toronto department store, the Robert Simpson Company, introduced an employees savings plan; Ford Motor Company started a profit-sharing plan in 1920, as did Lever Bros. Ltd., an English soap manufacturer and the John Morrow Screw and Nut Co. of Ingersoll. In most share-purchase plans, employees' shares were held in trust so that they did not acquire voting rights (McCallum 1990, pp. 54, 56). Other plans had simple annual bonus payments.

Life insurance, pensions, sickness benefits, and workers' savings plans, first introduced in 1919, increased, and by March 1920, at least forty Canadian employers had purchased group life insurance plans from Sun Life. Some of these plans excluded immigrant workers, as at International Harvester, or female employees, as at Goodyear (Naylor 1991, p. 170), but not always. Joan Sangster argued that Westclox in Peterborough secured the allegiance of its predominantly female labor force with relatively high wages by community standards, paid vacations, group insurance, and sick-leave plans. In a patriarchal atmosphere that was palpable, the women nevertheless participated

in the process of accommodation (Sangster 1995, p. 139). Pension schemes developed slowly in few companies, so most workers continued to demand state pensions (McCallum 1990, pp. 51, 72; *Labour Gazette* 1921, p. 549; 1923, pp. 829, 1345). Workers appreciated the improvements. By 1922, about 3,000 Imperial Oil employees participated in its stock-purchase plan, as did 55 percent of General Motors' eligible employees by 1924. Unions remained hostile because firms were unwilling to deal with them; they viewed the stock-purchase schemes as risky and as a substitute for wages. Trade unionists found the paternalism underlying both industrial councils and these plans distasteful, for despite consultative committees, in all cases, the form and limits of employee benefits were determined by management alone. Unions also opposed wage-incentive plans such as those established at the Knechtel Furniture Co. in Hanover, Doo Twine Mills in Kitchener, American Optical in Belleville, and Coleman Stove and Lamp in Toronto. In some cases, when employees worked faster and longer under such plans to increase their wages, they lost interest in unions. But, in 1929 at Canadian Cottons Ltd., 700 workers struck unsuccessfully for a return to procedures "before the efficiency experts came along" (McCallum 1990, pp. 53, 56, 64).

All variants of corporate welfarism, like the industrial councils, were to promote closer management-employee relations. Employers introduced these benevolent paternalistic schemes to stabilize their workforces, as they further rationalized and integrated their production processes, increased efficiency, lowered costs, and improved their machinery. To become more competitive, many employers abandoned the nineteenth-century strategy of working people excessively long hours and paying them subsistent wages. Instead, they saw advantages in shortening the workday, raising wages to increase workers' purchasing power, and making jobs more attractive to discourage absenteeism and turnover and to increase productivity. Some schemes promoted better health, all aimed to tie workers to their jobs by limiting their mobility, and all discouraged strike activity—sometimes by threatening to cut off benefits as a deterrent. The goal was a stable, productive, loyal workforce.

Thus, in the 1920s this philosophy of corporate liberalism and its varied "progressive" schemes transformed many businesses in Canada. Its penchant for efficiency and professionalism in management deprived workers of any control over many aspects of their working conditions, but this approach might have become the basis for relatively harmonious if unequal labor-management relationships had it not been for the searing experience of the Great Depression. It was the depression that not only ended most company-sponsored employees' committees and corporate welfare reforms but also steeled workers' determination to gain independent representation in industry.

Industrial Councils in the Depression Years

Most industrial schemes could not be sustained at a time when employers were trying to survive by implementing wage cuts and layoffs. An exception to this scenario was Imperial Oil where company unionism persisted because that corporation had the capacity to purchase labor harmony even in the 1930s, was able to maintain a union-free environment until 1946 when one plant, at Ioco, unionized, but where today the majority of Imperial Oil's refineries remain nonunion (Grant 1998, pp. 94–95). The more usual situation oc-

curred in Sydney, Nova Scotia, in the steel industry, where a local of the Amalgamated Association of Iron, Steel and Tin Workers (hereafter called the Amalgamated) lost a strike in 1923 and thereafter an ERP existed for thirteen years. In 1936 SWOC (Steelworkers' Organizing Committee) Local 1064 was chartered following publicity about its successful American organizing activities; it undermined the nonunion representation system and "prepared its leaders to make a change" (Logan 1948, p. 251). The industrial council voted itself out of existence, expressing some regret to the company, which had dealt with it for years. The employer refused to meet with the union, and a collective agreement was not signed until 1940.

Inadvertently, some employees' committees provided workers with experience that served them well in the 1930s when they organized trade unions. In Sault Ste. Marie for example, in 1914 the Amalgamated first entered Algoma, reorganized in 1916, but when it and the AFL carved up the union in 1919, the company refused to deal, posted a wage increase, and the workers lost interest in union representation. After two steep wage reductions in the 1920 recession, the plant had no representation for fifteen years. Then in 1935, some workers organized the Algoma Steelworkers Union (ASU) as an independent union. The company recognized it, and the parties negotiated improved wages and working conditions. In 1937 the ASU achieved the status of a national union and briefly affiliated with the All Canadian Congress of Labour. In 1938, it was courted by the SWOC, which had to confront its distrust of internationalism after its experiences with the Amalgamated and the AFL, and its suspicion about SWOC's reputation for radicalism, but in 1940, it joined the SWOC, which in 1942 became the United Steelworkers of America.

Canadian workers in the largely unorganized mass production industries followed the example of American workers, who were joining CIO unions in droves, and began to organize a bit later than in the United States, around 1936. With the exception of a major victory at GM in Oshawa in 1937, winning first agreements with hostile employers was difficult, and the number of unionized employees to 1939 increased gradually (MacDowell 1993). Canadian workers did not experience the rapid growth of the CIO unions in the 1930s that occurred in the United States because in Canada there was no Franklin Roosevelt, no New Deal, no Wagner Act, and a more repressive response by the state when workers engaged in sit-down strikes, a dramatic and effective tactic identified with the CIO movement. Out of office from 1930 to 1935 during the most severe conditions of the decade, Mackenzie King was reelected in 1935, but he concentrated on fiscally conservative stratagems that involved ad hoc, underfunded relief measures. Social policies were not introduced until 1940 when an Unemployment Insurance Act was passed.

Between 1937 and 1939, union organizing continued slowly; informal relationships with some managements developed even where there was not full recognition; the union movement influenced community organizations and local politics in many working-class communities, and workers' expectations about their future place in industry and society began to rise. Associated with these developments was greater unity between immigrant and Canadian workers, less emphasis on craft unionism with more attention paid to organizing industrial unions, less elitism among the skilled workers, solidarity, and a belief in industrial and political democracy.

With greater working-class activism, it is not surprising that managements established employees' committees from the mid-1930s and in the 1940s as a substitute for independent unions, but workers trying to organize unions distrusted these initiatives. A number of different scenarios emerged. The large steel plant in Hamilton Ontario, Stelco, established an ERP in 1935 at the first sign of a union, and it persisted into the war years with management's backing. Union activists developed a successful strategy of running for election to the works council and taking it over (Freeman 1982, p. 38). Briefly, prounion employees worked independently but then sought a SWOC charter, and after years of work and a titanic struggle in 1946, with a still divided workforce, the company finally accepted the union, negotiated a contract, and granted a union dues checkoff.

In the same city, one of the longest-lasting alternatives to unions emerged at another steel plant, Dominion Foundries (Dofasco), and the program exists to this day. Dofasco management was antiunion and as soon as SWOC gained a contract with U. S. Steel, it acted. To instill fear, it responded to the union threat by firing workers on the existing union executive and other union sympathizers. At the same time, the company introduced various innovative employee welfare programs such as annual picnics and Christmas parties, a new company magazine with a soothing paternalistic tone that went into workers' homes and was read by their spouses. It sponsored sports teams, a band, and a choir to create a sense of community and company loyalty. It restructured its personnel department and started a welfare department that paid close attention to safety. This was a significant change for a company known in the early 1930s as a "slaughterhouse of accidents." Most importantly, in 1938, it created the "Employee Profit-Sharing and Savings Fund" to which all employees contributed and the company matched such contributions from its profits.

The plan was voluntary, but the company wanted employees in it. It soon was 100 percent subscribed, and it did stabilize the workforce. Many profit-sharing schemes, which tied payments to the market and wages to company profits, failed and the workers lost. The Dofasco plan had fund trustees who invested in bonds and recognized securities. After canvassing over 200 profit-sharing plans, the company based its own on Joslyn Manufacturing Co. in Chicago, which matched employee contributions to the savings fund up to 10 percent of its net earnings and not more than four times the amount of the employees' savings. Each worker invested 3 to 5 percent of his yearly earnings and not more than $150 (Storey 1981, pp. 227, 230). In this way, workers built up retirement savings and with wartime prosperity, the growing fund benefited its subscribers. The employees were grateful to the company and afraid of losing the fund, which the company made clear would disappear if they opted for a union. Basically they chose the fund over a union (Storey 1981, pp. 12, 14, 181, 220–237).

Dofasco management also adopted an open style, in contrast to Stelco management's, which remained much more arbitrary. It solved individual problems and reduced the powers of foremen and supervisors by removing their authority to hire and fire. Periodically it also paid wage increases. With no sheet mill at Dofasco, which at Stelco had provided some early union leaders, and with the Steelworkers' Union (USWA) focusing on Stelco, Dofasco remained union free, despite a brief organizing drive there, which sociologist R. H. Storey determined was too short to be effective. As unionization advanced at Stelco and within Hamilton, Dofasco management introduced new programs for "cooperative rela-tions" with its employees that extended its previous welfarist approach so that "the Dofasco way" became associated with an effective alternative nonunion representation approach to labor-management relations. During the large 1946 strike at Stelco, Dofasco's strategy then and thereafter was to match any gains negotiated for workers by the USWA, and thus Dofasco workers benefited from the Stelco workers' struggle for a union and from their negotiations with Stelco over the years.

Company Unionism During World War II

In Canada, the major growth of the industrial union movement occurred during World War II. In contrast to the United States, Canada entered the war in 1939; the direction of the war economy was centralized and managed as never before, so that workers could not shop around for jobs and employers could not fire rabble-rousers. Wages rose and then were controlled, unemployment disappeared, and the government hired many dollar-a-year men from business to assist in organizing the war production effort—the level of production, the distribution of materials and workers, and the delivery of war material. Most of these men were as antiunion as the minister of munitions and supply, C. D. Howe. It was an opportunity for workers to organize but, predictably, determined hostile employers opposed independent unions. During World War II, despite wage-and-price controls, industrial unions grew 400 percent in membership; industrial unrest accelerated and peaked in 1943; the major unions rejected a policy of no-strike pledges despite their acceptance by the American labor movement, which had a better relationship with Roosevelt's government than Canadian workers had with

King's administration. Indeed, labor's support of the social democratic party, the CCF, which supported its demands for collective bargaining legislation and for greater representation in wartime policymaking, resulted in some dramatic victories for that party, particularly provincially.

In 1943, the federal government felt pressured on both the political and industrial fronts by a dramatic increase in industrial conflict that included a national steel strike; the National War Labour Board (NWLB) decided to conduct a public inquiry into labor relations and wage conditions in Canada. Its majority and minority reports recommended collective bargaining legislation, which the Canadian government finally introduced in 1944.

The Canadian war order (P.C. 1003) was similar to the American Wagner Act (passed in 1935 and judged constitutional in 1937) in that it recognized workers' right to organize independent trade unions and to bargain collectively; it outlawed company-dominated unions, defined unfair labor practices, and established a labor board to certify independent unions and generally administer and enforce the policy. It also retained the practice of compulsory conciliation introduced by Mackenzie King in the Industrial Disputes Investigation Act (1907), which became a distinctive characteristic of the Canadian system. It differed from the Wagner Act in that it was not passed as a recovery measure in the depression and had no preamble that stated that collective bargaining was a good thing. The federal government passed it reluctantly, after extreme pressure, because the prime minister viewed collective bargaining as conflict inducing (Whitaker 1977).

This legislation was its only concession to the labor movement. At the same time the government continued wage controls, and at the end of the war tried to impose contracts in many indus-

tries that limited wage levels to increases of 10 percent. In 1946, organized labor led a strike wave across the country that effectively ended the controls policy it had opposed. In 1945 the federal government also introduced the Family Allowances Act, which labor saw in part as a substitute for higher wages. As a result, although unions had always supported social reforms like standards legislation, unemployment insurance, and universal medical insurance, they remained ambivalent about family allowances.

During the war, many employees' committees developed in response to the changing labor relations situation. Where managements did not want to recognize a union (and there was no legislation to compel them), they sought to defeat unions by soliciting support among their employees for an alternative mechanism in competition with a union already on the scene. Many examples of this union-avoidance strategy were described in union briefs before the 1943 NWLB inquiry, whose hearings demonstrated the existing polarization of labor relations in Canada. Prior to P.C. 1003, two cases in 1941—at National Steel Car Corporation (Nasco) in Hamilton and in the gold mines in Kirkland Lake—gained national attention, demonstrated many managements' antiunion strategy and also that they had government support.

Nasco's workers had experience with both unions and nonunions. In the early 1930s, when its management announced a speed-up and wage reduction, members of a newly formed National Steel Car Workers Industrial Union struck for six weeks in protest, but failed to win either recognition or any demands. In 1937 there were two brief spontaneous work stoppages that resulted in small wage increases and thereafter SWOC began distributing its leaflets at the plant regularly. In 1941 a strike at Nasco became the first significant test of industrial unionism in Hamilton (Storey 1981,

p. 277). The steelworkers' union organized the plant and sought union recognition. When the company refused to meet, the union applied for a conciliation board, which recommended a plantwide, government-supervised representation vote, and if the union won, that the company negotiate with it. It also advised the company to reinstate union president George Tanner, who had been fired. When nothing happened, the workers in April 1941 voted to strike. Immediately, the government acted by appointing a government controller, Ernest Brunning, to implement the conciliation report recommendations. Tanner was rehired and a vote taken, which the union won. Instead of meeting with the union, the controller, acting on advice from the government and specifically from the minister of munitions and supply (which was unusual), indicated that he did not intend to negotiate with the union "to the surprise, I would be inclined to suggest, of everybody" wrote the conciliation board's union nominee to the minister of labor (Cohen file 2854a, v. 24). Controller Brunning stimulated the establishment of an employees' committee, which met with him and agreed to his proposals regarding wages and hours. Thus the union and collective bargaining procedures were ignored.

A second strike was threatened, and no negotiations with the union took place until a new controller was appointed. He held talks with both the union and the employees' committee, each of whom represented their own members. Despite the representation vote, the union did not achieve recognition as the exclusive bargaining agent until it was finally certified in September 1945. The government had intervened actively to support the nonunion representation committee over the union after a vote that clearly chose the union, and as a result the situation produced workers' protests and disillusionment within the labor movement (MacDowell 1983, pp. 31–32).

In Kirkland Lake, the mines were 95 percent organized when the Mine Mill union embarked on a legal strike for union recognition in 1941–42, having gone through all the required wartime procedures of a government inquiry, compulsory conciliation and a government-supervised strike vote, before a work stoppage was permissible. In the absence of Wagner-type legislation, obdurate mine managers won the long strike, despite overwhelming support for the union. The strike took place in very cold winter temperatures because of delays resulting from the lengthy procedures. The future minister of labour, Humphrey Mitchell, had investigated the dispute prior to the strike and recommended that management recognize local employees' committees rather than the Mine Mill union, and this proposed solution became known as "the Kirkland Lake Formula" (Cohen 1941, ch. 6).

Following the loss of the strike and the blacklisting of union activists, the mine operators persisted in creating nonunion representation committees to compete with the union. These committees at each mine discussed closer ties in one organization and affiliated to the Amalgamated Unions of Canada, centered in Hamilton, whose president, D.V. Mitchell, had been an officer of the National Union of Railwaymen and a former director of the Canadian Federation of Labour (CFL). The CFL broke away from the All Canadian Congress of Labour in 1936; it was promanagement, anti-American, politically conservative, and opposed in all trade union circles (both craft and industrial union). The Amalgamated claimed to be a national union but, unlike the CIO or TLC international unions, as it wrote in a brief, it "agrees that the local union should be supreme and not have to take orders from the parent body" (RG7-60, box 3, file 26).

In September 1942, after the Kirkland Lake

strike, Ontario Minister of Labor Peter Heenan promised to introduce collective bargaining legislation before a Canadian Congress of Labour convention. Immediately, fifty-five major Hamilton employers addressed an open letter to Premier Gordon Conant to express concern for the fate of "independent unions." In February 1943 the CFL and the Associated Workers' Organizations—established in November 1942 to represent nonunion groups—presented the Ontario government with a memorandum that expressed apprehension lest the new legislation "be patterned after the methods adopted elsewhere," which would "impede or prevent the formation and operation of free labor unions," by which they meant nonunion organizations in single workshops as opposed to unions that had in their words "acquired monopolistic control of a whole trade or industry" (Jackson, file 1–51, v. 1).

The existence of the Amalgamated Unions of Canada and the Associated Workers' Organizations indicated a business-supported alternative to unions, whose affiliates included both certified and uncertified employees' committees. Employers learned that the Ontario Labour Court administering the Ontario Collective Bargaining Act of 1943, which outlawed company unions, would certify committees it considered independent of an employer and it was flexible in its criteria of "independence," so that employer-dominated committees persisted. For example, in eight certification applications before the Labour Court in 1943–44 from the Kirkland Lake mining area, which sometimes were initiated by an employees' association with the union as intervener and on other occasions were brought by the union, the Labour Court awarded five certifications to the employees' committees and three to the union. It evidently was convinced that the committees were independent of management. Only after the proc-

lamation of federal war order P.C. 1003 (Canada's Wagner Act) in February 1944, and as a result of overwhelming support for the union and its continuous and determined organization, was Mine Mill finally certified in 1945 in the mines of Kirkland Lake.

In 1943, both an Ontario select committee and the federal NWLB inquiry on labor problems heard of many cases of employers' use of employees' committees to counteract trade union activity and to combat the introduction of collective bargaining into the workplace. A detailed UEW brief presented by the District 5 director in Canada, C.S. Jackson (NWLB Proceedings, p. 808), described the problem. In the previous six months, the UEW had been organizing in about thirty war plants in Ontario and was established in fourteen major plants in the province including Westinghouse in Hamilton, and Canadian G.E. in Toronto. Jackson told the board, "We can cite examples where employers daily disrupted the harmony of their plant, spent huge sums of money directed from the war, to fight their employees legitimate right to self-organization; where companies attempted to foist on their employees . . . company unions, plant councils and so-called independent unions in the hope of being able to turn the employees away from bona fide trade unionism and full labour management co-operation" (NWLB Proceedings, p. 825).

He outlined cases, like Taylor Electric Co. in London, where in July 1942 workers asked the UEW to help them organize a local, which in two weeks was 90 percent unionized. "The manager virtually threw the organizer out of the office" when he requested an interview. In August the union applied for conciliation after the company promoted a company union by holding meetings in the plant and fired the president of the local union. A federal government investigator recommended reinstatement with full back wages, but the company stalled. The company president secured a letter from the Department of Munitions and Supply (DMS) ordering him to cancel munitions production temporarily, and on this basis he discharged forty employees including the union leadership. A conciliation board then met, ordered the reinstatement of the twenty-two union people and a representation vote. Most union supporters had secured other jobs, so the vote was lost. Union employees were unprotected, and by using intimidating and discriminatory tactics, the company undermined support for the union. An unusual aspect of this case was the apparent collusion between DMS and the company management for "the temporary cancellation of a war order in order to give the manufacturer a weapon which could be used to reduce the majority position of the union in the shop by layoffs and dismissals arising out of the cancellation of that order" (NWLB Proceedings, p. 829). As soon as the conciliation case was over, war production resumed.

Jackson presented numerous examples of other Ontario companies, such as the Sawyer Massey company in Hamilton, Robbins and Meyers in Brantford, Parker Pan in Toronto, and Atlas Steel in Welland. At Atlas Steel, the UEW union claimed that as soon as it began to organize "the company called a meeting, had an agreement signed by a selected few to be ratified by the meeting." The meeting voted against the agreement, so the company started an "independent" union and hired an American expert to promote their phony union. The company achieved no great gains and "in the past few weeks U.E. signed up 50 percent of the plant" (Jackson, file 1–51, v. 1).

At Sawyer Massey in Hamilton, the Sawyer Massey Employees' Association was founded after the union organized the plant and won a rep-

resentation vote by a margin of two to one. The company's lawyer, R.R. Evans, drafted its constitution at the same time he was negotiating with the union. The company did not intend to sign a collective agreement and introduced through the company union some of the union proposals on the table. The company's refusal to recognize the union created unrest and chaos in production (NWLB Proceedings, p. 830), but other unions encountered similar problems.

Other large Hamilton companies had antiunion open-shop policies, and Evans had played a role in setting up the company union at Nasco. Jackson charged that the Niagara Institute of Industrial Relations assisted its member companies to block unions in the Welland-Niagara-St. Catharines area and had promoted plant councils. Its employer members, Jackson claimed, had "been the worst offenders in dealing with their employees as a whole and in completely ignoring the fact that employees at any time had any fundamental rights" (NWLB Proceedings, p. 831).

After collective bargaining legislation passed in Ontario in 1943 and federally in 1944, employers such as Imperial Oil successfully lobbied against the exclusion of company unions and sought to have the new laws recognize its employees' committees. The early boards did so, as long as they were "independent" of employer influence. This condition was not always easy to verify. During its tenure of about a year, the Ontario Labour Court in Ontario in its first six months handled 130 certification cases representing 80,000 workers before a board replaced it to administer representation votes and determine bargaining units (RG7-60, box 3, file 26). In these proceedings, unions often faced employees' committees as interveners or themselves intervened in certification cases brought by employees' committees. When leading union lawyer, J. L. Cohen, presented thirty certification cases on behalf of several clients before the Ontario Labour Court in 1943, he won fifteen, lost eleven to employees' committees, withdrew three, and one was caught in the changeover from the court to the board that replaced it and had to be restarted, so he won only about 73 percent of the cases (RG7-60, box 3, file 26). Thus the management strategy of supporting employees' committees against unions remained somewhat effective in these early years of legislation, but unions worked to strengthen the legislative prohibition of company unions with some success. Cohen wrote to a union client in August 1944 that company unions were still not banned or illegal. "I have just been able to get from Finkelman's Board for the first time a judgment ruling a company union off the ballot because of employer interference, but this is very new" (Cohen, file 3065, v. 36).

In a postwar strike wave in Canada's major industries over wages, union recognition, and union security as employers like Ford in 1945 and Stelco in 1946 squared off against the unions, what was at stake was the future role of unions in Canadian labor relations. Was there to be a return to the prewar days of the 1920s or were the gains of large independent unions—increased union membership, collective bargaining legislation, union security and checkoff provisions in many contracts, and shop steward systems and grievance-arbitration procedures in place in many workplaces—to be retained? Were managements to have an unfettered prerogative to operate in hierarchical structures as they saw fit with perhaps occasional consultation with in-house employees' committees about secondary issues? Or were managements expected to deal with trade unions in a consultative structure about issues that were determined as bargainable by the parties during contract talks and through grievance-ar-

bitration procedures between contract talks? In the battle of 1946, the unions won on the issue of collective bargaining. Most of the wartime employees' committees disappeared, presumably because they no longer served employers as union-avoidance mechanisms. The climate of opinion defeated employees' committees because workers decided to join unions, which in the prosperous postwar economy raised the real wages of their members and negotiated benefits. The few employees' committees that were certified and negotiated a first contract appeared to be independent not only because a board had certified them but because the contracts they negotiated were virtually identical to collective agreements negotiated by unions (RG7-33, box 1).

After the war, prosperity and considerable industrial peace lasted for nearly twenty years, during which time many bargaining relationships between companies and unions matured into workable arrangements. In 1948 the federal government passed legislation to replace its temporary war order of 1944, which recognized the new labor relations system that had developed during World War II. The provinces, most of which decided to pass their own acts rather than opt into the federal legislation, resumed jurisdiction over labor relations that had been centralized for the wartime crisis. The balkanization of labor legislation and policies that some observers feared at the time did not result, but a centralized labor relations system that would have required a constitutional amendment was rejected and, except for minor regional differences, the basic new principles were in place.

Conclusion

Historically, Canadian nonunion representation schemes were primarily union-avoidance mechanisms. Employers, rather than employees, initiated them, though some briefly evolved into independent local organizations or were considered as such for the purposes of certification (whether or not they in fact were). They often did not represent workers' interests and, as a result, when given a choice, workers rejected them. In certain situations, where there was no possibility of a union and there was employer support for ERPs, workers accepted them on the basis that something was better than nothing. In virtually all such cases of accommodation, workers understood the extent of employer involvement and management motives, and either they were hostile or they could see certain advantages to themselves regardless of management aims. Such committees, while stigmatized as antiunion, had other aims—the promotion of loyal, efficient, and productive workforces. For employees, some ERPs improved safety standards and communications with management. Some, such as Algoma's, evolved into independent local committees and developed workers' leadership skills, but these often were an intermediate form of employee representation preceding unionization.

Employers did not intend ERPs to deal with wages or grievance procedures but established them to consult and communicate with employees. Thus, they were not the same as unions, but were a different, limited, and weaker form of employee representation. In 1941 J.L. Cohen, in his book *Collective Bargaining in Canada*, defined all variants of "company unions," explained how unions differed from ERPs, why unions objected to them, and why "union recognition" was such an important issue in Canadian strikes in the 1940s.

He wrote:

> The essential feature of collective bargaining, without which it cannot be said that collective bargaining exists, is the independence of the bargaining medium operating on behalf of the workers so that it meets on *equal* terms with the employers. Anything which destroys that independence violates the first essential of collective bargaining. Any form of employee representation or employee recognition which destroys the independence of the bargaining medium, and which is acquiesced in by the workers, not on their own volition, but only because of the influence, or control, or dictate of the employer, is a *collective bargaining form which emanates from the company and not from the worker.* [Emphasis added.] That form of arrangement, whatever the variation, is therefore a form of company unionism. (Cohen 1941, p. 59)

ERPs were paternalistic representation mechanisms that discussed a relatively limited range of issues; unions were independent, had bargaining power, and engaged employers on basic issues of pay, job security, seniority and decision-making procedures in industry through collective bargaining and grievance/arbitration procedures. Workers of the day understood the difference, that ERPs were a management-backed alternative form of representation to independent unions and fought many strikes over the "union recognition" issue.

Most ERPs emerged in the relatively prosperous periods of the 1920s and 1940s, and many could not survive the Great Depression. Some were started in the 1930s by managements responding to immediate situations that involved union activity. Thus the longevity of nonunion representation forms depended on the economic situation. In all the ERPs there were limits on the scope of issues discussed; there was not equal power between the parties, and decision making in companies that had such plans remained hierarchical, though a greater element of consultation with employees was introduced.

In the past, historians paid scant attention to company unions. Recently, as a result of union decline in the United States, academics and businesses have examined other representation forms in industry and reevaluated company unions in the modern context. They focus on cooperation in industry and mutual gains, and thus view ERPs as progressive, but this is not primarily how they were viewed in the past. Current critics see sections 8(a)(2) and 2(5) of the Wagner Act as confining and seek to liberalize it to allow for nonunion representation schemes. The offending clauses obviously have not protected unions, and their existence may inhibit representation where the chance of unionization is low. As unions are in decline in the United States, the motive for starting representation plans today may be only partly union-avoidance, and may reflect a shift back to paternalism and welfare capitalism similar to a time when there was no welfare state, in a period when the current welfare state is being cut back, restructured, and downsized.

The decline in American union membership reflects the way in which the industrial relations systems in North America have evolved since their introduction. Historically, the collective bargaining system in North America was partly an accident. It emerged from the Great Depression and the war, when deplorable conditions motivated workers to pressure determinedly for collective bargaining rights against considerable employer opposition in both countries. In the United States, unions were assisted by Franklin Roosevelt and New Deal legislation, which was challenged in the courts but eventually declared constitutional. In Canada, there was no collective bargaining legislation in the 1930s, with the result that relatively little union growth occurred until the war, when all-out production and the existence of full employment created conditions favorable to union organization. Canadians caught up to the American workers and achieved their "Wagner Act," but not until 1944.

After the war in the United States, the Taft-Hartley Act was passed as a "correction" for some of the "imbalances" in the Wagner Act, and it was followed by right-to-work laws accompanied by political support for the weakening of the collective bargaining system. Public-sector employees never achieved the goals of their industrial counterparts in the United States, partly for lack of political support, as demonstrated in 1981 by President Reagan's firing of air traffic controllers (Estreicher 1994, p. 19).

In Canada, because collective bargaining legislation came later, there was no backlash or Taft-Hartley Act. Also, the politics were different because the association of the labor movement with a "third party" on the left maintained pressure on mainstream politicians to be conciliatory (Bruce 1989). The constitutional structure in the two countries is different, and the more decentralized administrative approach to labor relations in Canada at the provincial level has proven to be a more efficient and flexible system than the centralized system in the United States. As a result, the gains won in Canada during and after the war by blue-collar industrial workers in the private sector and eventually recognized in legislation were extended to public-sector employees in the 1960s with minor adaptations suited to their particular needs. The transformation of independent associations (not certified) of public and professional employees into certified unions engaged in collective bargaining with employers substantially increased union membership in Canada. This in turn resulted in greater public acceptance of collective bargaining because about 35 percent or more of the nonagricultural labor force participated in the process.

The Canadian labor relations environment became both more permissive toward nonunion representation mechanisms and more liberal toward trade union development. In such an atmosphere, trade unions have increased membership.

Truly independent organizations could be certified by labor boards or not as they wished, and such independent associations evolved often at the halfway point between being consultation mechanisms and collective bargaining entities. The different approaches of the two countries has resulted in a divergence that has been much analyzed, as in Canada the number of workers engaged in the collective bargaining process rose and stabilized, but in the United States, union membership figures eroded and then plummeted. (Lipset 1986; Adams 1989; Chaykowski and Slotsve 1996; Rose and Chaison 1996).

In the 1990s the issue of employees' committees has reemerged particularly in the United States, because in the North American labor relations systems, many workers, especially in expanding private service-sector industries, have not unionized. In the present competitive global economy, a resurgence of absolute management rights, opposition to unions and collective bargaining, and attention to the "bottom line" has accompanied unilateral downsizing of companies and plant shutdowns by mobile capital. The result has been unemployment, the weakening of labor and standards legislation, an overall decrease in union membership in North America, and exploitation of the people and the environment of less developed countries by North American investors and multinational corporations. Such measures increase the power imbalance between workers and employers and have been protested in Canada by trade unionists and others.

While the future of collective bargaining by independent unions has led to pessimistic analyses, even among those concerned about an employee voice in workplaces (Gottesman 1994), industrial committees remain a partial solution to employee representation in industry. In the absence of representative unions with bargaining power, workers are left with an option that was

pursued in the nineteenth century, namely, to look for other work. Only today, with fewer jobs, that is more difficult.

Today, the low level of unionization in the United States and the rapid transformation of the global economy, supplemented by continuous technological innovation and the dominance of the powerful is enough to give anyone pause, but such changes influence people, and their responses are not always predictable. Presumably as industrial development occurs elsewhere, workers' expectations in such places will rise, as they did when North American employees were at the same stage, and they will become every bit as dissatisfied with economic, political, gender, and racial inequalities as workers in the past have been. While some employees may find appeal in nonunion representation forms that give them a "voice" as a kind of therapy in a situation with little "exit" potential in today's market, others undoubtedly will opt for collective bargaining mechanisms to achieve a more satisfying position in the modern labor market.

The discussion of alternatives to democratically elected trade unions that bargain collectively with their employers in a framework backed up by legislation may be an expression of realism for some in the current political and economic climate, given the existing power imbalance in our two societies. But it reflects skepticism about a type of industrial democracy that seemed feasible and suitable just after a war fought, as workers pointed out at the time, for those same principles of democracy. The current debate not only recognizes that the industrial relations system left out many workers, but advocates a modern variant of industrial councils and a system that is tolerant of both unions and industrial councils as a solution to some current problems.

The irony of the comparative history of company unions in Canada and in the United States,

Figure 5.2 **Union Density in North America 1921–1993**

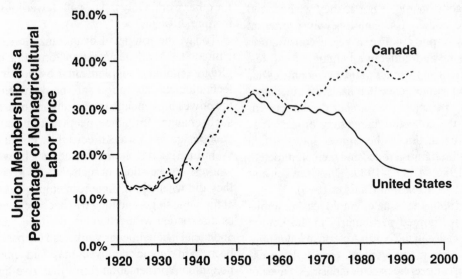

Sources:

United States:

1921–84: Troy and Sheflin membership series (Hirsch and Addison 1986, pp. 46–47).

1985–93: Current Population Survey membership series (U.S. Bureau of the Census 1993; U.S. Bureau of Labor Statistics 1993).

Canada:

Labour Canada, various years, *Directory of Labour Organizations in Canada*; Labour Canada 1994.

Joseph B. Rose and Gary N. Chaison. "Linking Union Density and Union Effectiveness: The North American Experience," *Industrial Relations* 35, no. 1 (January 1996): 80.

is that in Canada, where there has been a more "permissive" legal framework that allowed ERPs to exist (albeit without certification unless they could prove their independence), there has been less promotion of company unions in recent years, more independent associations engaged in consultation with employers have evolved into unions and have adopted collective bargaining, particularly but not exclusively in the public sector, and since 1948 a consistently higher level of unionization in Canada than in the United States has been the result.

References

Adams, Roy. 1989. "North American Industrial Relations: Divergent Trends in Canada and the United States." *International Labour Review* 128, no. 1: 47–64.

Bruce, Peter G. 1989. "Political Parties and Labor Legislation in Canada and the U. S." *Industrial Relations* 28, no. 2 (Spring): 115–141.

Canada, Department of Labour. *Labour Gazette*, (1921, p. 549; 1923, pp. 829, 1345; 1925, p. 358. Ottawa: Department of Labour.

———. 1928. *Labour Organizations in Canada*. Ottawa: King's Printer.

Canada, Royal Commission on Industrial Relations (Mathers Commission). 1919. Ontario evidence. Ottawa: King's Printer.

Cassidy, H.M. 1926. "Labour Co-operation on the Canadian National." *Canadian Forum* 7, no. 74 (November): 42–45.

Chaykowski, Richard, and George Slotsve. 1996. "Union Wage Premiums and Union Density in Canada and the United States." *Canadian Business Economics* 4, no. 3 (Spring): 46–57.

Cohen, J.L. 1944. Papers, file 2854a, 24; file 3065, 36, National Archives of Canada (NAC), Ottawa, Ontario.

———. 1941. *Collective Bargaining in Canada.* Toronto: SWOC.

Estreicher, Samuel. 1994. "Labour Law Reform in a World of Competitive Product Markets." In *The Legal Future of Employee Representation*, ed. Matthew W. Finkin, pp. 13–56. Ithaca, N.Y.: ILR Press.

"Factory Forum, a Preventive of Labor Troubles," May 8, 1920, p. 2; "Workers Share on Fifty-Fifty Basis in Profits," October 1, 1920, p. 2. *Financial Post.*

Ferns, H.S., and B. Ostry. 1976. *The Age of Mackenzie King.* Toronto: Lorimer.

Freeman, Bill. 1982. *1005: Political Life of a Union Local.* Toronto: Lorimer.

Goltz, Eileen. 1974. "Espanola: The History of a Pulp and Paper Town." *Laurentian University Review* 6, no. 3 (June): 75–104.

Gottesman, Michael H. 1994. "In Despair, Starting Over: Imagining a Labour Law for Unorganized Workers." In *The Legal Future of Employee Representation*, ed. Matthew W. Finkin, pp. 57–94. Ithaca, NY: ILR Press.

Grant, H.M. 1998. "Solving the Labour Problem at Imperial Oil: Welfare Capitalism in the Canadian Petroleum Industry, 1919–1929." *Labour/Le Travail* 41 (Spring): 69–95.

Isbester, Fraser. 1971. "Quebec Labour in Perspective 1949–69." In *Canadian Labour in Transition*, ed. Richard U. Miller and Fraser Isbester, pp. 240–266. Scarborough, Ont.: Prentice-Hall.

Jackson, C.S. 1943. Papers, "Company Unions," file 1–51,1, NAC, Ottawa.

Jacoby, Sanford M. 1985. *Employing Bureaucracy: Managers, Unions and the Transformation of Work in American Industry, 1900–1945.* New York: Columbia University Press.

King, William Lyon Mackenzie. 1973. Introduction by David Jay Bercuson. *Industry and Humanity.* Toronto: University of Toronto Press.

———. 1927. *The Message of the Carillon.* London, Ont.: Macmillan.

Lipset, Seymour Martin. 1986. "North American Labor Movement:A Comparative Perspective." In *Unions in Transition*, ed. S.M. Lipset, pp. 421–452. San Francisco: ICS Press.

Logan, H.A. 1948. *Trade Unions in Canada.* Toronto: Macmillan.

McCallum, Margaret E. 1990. "Corporate Welfarism in Canada 1919–1939." *Canadian Historical Review* 71, no. 1: 46–79.

MacDowell, Laurel S. 1983. *"Remember Kirkland Lake": The Gold Miners' Strike of 1941–42.* Toronto: University of Toronto Press.

———. 1993, "After the Strike: Labour Relations in Oshawa, 1937–39." *Relations Industrielles/Industrial Relations* 48, no. 4: 691–712.

NWLB Proceedings. 1943."Labour Relations and Wage Conditions in Canada," v. 34, J.L. Cohen Papers, NAC, Ottawa.

Naylor, James. 1991. *The New Democracy: Challenging the Social Order in Industrial Ontario 1914–25.* Toronto: University of Toronto Press.

Nelson, Daniel. 1982. "The Company Union Movement, 1900–1937: A Reexamination." *Business History Review* 56 (Autumn): 335–357.

Ontario, Department of Labour. 1943. RG7-33, box 1, company and union agreements 1946–48, Provincial Archives of Ontario (PAO), Toronto.

———. "Summary of Activities of the Labour Court, June 14, 1943 to December 31, 1943." RG7-60, Ontario Labour Court files, PAO, Toronto.

———. RG7-60, box 3, file 26, Lakeshore Workmen's Council and Lakeshore Mines Ltd. and Local 240 IUMMSW, PAO, Toronto.

Ramirez, Bruno. 1989. "Migration and Regional Labour Markets 1870–1915: The Quebec Case." In *Class Community and the Labour Movement: Wales and Canada 1850–1930*, ed. D.R. Hopkin and G.S. Kealey. St. Johns, Newfoundland: Society for Welsh Labour History and Canadian Committee for Labour History.

Rose, Joseph, and Gary Chaison. 1996. "Linking Union Density and Union Effectiveness: The North American Experience." *Industrial Relations* 35, no. 1 (January): 70–105.

Sangster, Joan. 1995. *Earning Respect: The Lives of Working Women in Small-Town Ontario, 1920–1960.*Toronto: University of Toronto Press.

Scott, Bruce. 1976. "A Place in the Sun: The Industrial Council at Massey-Harris 1919–1929." *Labour/Le Travailleur* 1, no. 1: 158–192.

Seager, Allen. 1992. "'A New Labor Era'? Canadian National Railways and the Railway Worker, 1919–1929." Paper read at the annual meeting of the Canadian Historical Association, Charlottetown, P.E.I., June.

Storey, R. H. 1981. "Workers, Unions and Steel: The Shaping of the Hamilton Working Class, 1935–48." Ph.D. dissertation, Toronto, University of Toronto.

Taras, Daphne Gottlieb. 1997. "Why Nonunion Representation Is Legal in Canada." Paper read at the Nonunion Employee Representation Conference, Banff, Alberta. September.

Thompson, J.H., and A. Seager. 1985. *Canada 1922–1939: Decades of Discord*. Toronto: McClelland and Stewart.

Whitaker, Reginald. 1977. "The Liberal Corporatist Ideas of Mackenzie King." *Labour/Le Travailleur* 2: 137–169.

6

Portrait of Nonunion Employee Representation in Canada: History, Law, and Contemporary Plans

Daphne Gottlieb Taras

While the national labor law of the United States was designed to eradicate company unions and most forms of employer-promulgated employee representation plans, Canada took a different approach. Canadian labor laws across all jurisdictions affirmed the primacy of bona fide unions but maintained a deliberate silence on the status of nonunion employee representation plans. There are few legal impediments that prevent Canadian employers from dealing with nonunion employees, and nonunion employees who would prefer to represent their own interests without unionizing may meet and deal with their employers on any topic salient to the employment relationship, including items such as wages and working conditions that normally characterize union-management bargaining relations. As long as such behavior within Canadian workplaces does not thwart union organizing activities or interfere with collective bargaining at unionized locations, it is lawful. As a result, nonunion forms of employee representation constitute an important, though little known, part of the Canadian industrial relations landscape. Canadian companies practice many permutations of nonunion representation that would be considered unlawful in the United States.

In the United States the combination of Section 8(a)(2) and Section 2(5) of the 1935 Wagner Act (1935, 49 Stat. 449) prohibits most nonunion collective representation. This issue is well documented in the American literature (Estreicher and LeRoy chapters in this volume; Jenero and Lyons 1992; Finkin 1994). Nonunion representation as an issue reached a zenith after the contentious National Labor Relations Board's (NLRB) *Electromation* decision (December 1992) and became one of the most difficult items examined by the Commission on the Future of Worker-Management Relations (1994). The arguments were starkly laid out by both proponents and opponents of the Teamwork for Employees and Management (TEAM) Act proposal to loosen 8(a)(2) restrictions against nonunion representation, which was vetoed in 1996 by President Clinton (Flynn 1996, pp. 70–74). The American approach was affirmed in the NLRB's recent *EFCO* decision (December 1998). Through this extremely turbulent examination, there was little knowledge or examination of the Canadian approach. This chapter demonstrates that in Canada, formal nonunion forms of employee representation are lawful, provided they are not deliberately designed to thwart union organizing. They continue to exist today, alongside a viable union presence and without legal challenge under Canada's collective bargaining statutes.

What explains this discrepancy in approaches between the two countries? I document that the company union movement was at least as significant in Canada as it was in the United States in the years prior to the passage of the Wagner Act. Deliberate but subtle adjustments to the Wagner model allowed company unions to flourish lawfully in Canada. The array of factors that fostered the design of Canadian laws relating to the company union question are described (summarizing the findings of a more detailed study of the origins of Canada's approach in Taras 1997a).

The precise statutory mechanisms that allow the persistence of nonunion forms are presented and analyzed. In Canada, the federal government has jurisdiction over labor relations matters in a relatively narrow range of industries (e.g., interprovincial transport, banking, military, federal civil service). Each of the ten provinces has jurisdiction over nonfederal employment within its provincial boundaries. Thus, the Canadian approach, which in practice is an amalgam of multiple exclusive jurisdictions, is noteworthy because none of the many labor laws followed the Wagner Act wording that banned nonunion representation plans. That is not to say that the Canadian statutes are identical in their treatment of this issue; rather, despite the differences in wording of the various Canadian statutes, they are united in their departure from the American approach.

Many American scholars and practitioners naturally wonder what might have happened to the American industrial relations setting in the absence of a Wagner Act ban? The Canadian experience is instructive in this regard. I draw upon the historic record to trace the fate of a number of early plans in Canada and speculate on the reasons for the continued existence or demise of the plans. The only cross-country and contemporary estimates of the penetration of nonunion representation into the industrial relations landscape is a survey completed by Lipset and Meltz in 1997 (and reported in this volume). Their evidence is that Canada and the United States did not diverge appreciably as a result of their different public policies regarding nonunion representation. Nineteen percent of Canadians and 20 percent of Americans who work for enterprises that are not unionized report that their employer has a formal nonunion employee representation plan of one kind or another.

This chapter is organized chronologically, starting at the turn of this century, stopping at the World War II period to describe the statutory disjuncture between Canada and the United States and the subsequent legal framework for nonunion representation, and continuing with an examination of current practices. The chapter ends with speculation about the topic as we enter the next millennium.

Early Canadian Experiences with Nonunion Representation

By the end of World War I, Canadians had considerable experience in operating formal nonunion plans of employee representation, and there was broad support for the idea in public policy circles. In 1919 the federal government convened a National Industrial Conference to examine the recommendations of the 1919 Royal Commission on Industrial Relations with respect to joint councils. A resolution was unanimously adopted by conference delegates (comprising employers, employees, and the public) approving the formation of "joint industrial councils as a means of furthering greater co-operations between employer and employees." Tom Moore, president of the Trades and Labour Congress (TLC, an umbrella organization for craft unions similar to the American AFL), even cautiously endorsed JICs (joint industrial councils) with the stipulation that they include, rather than replace, trade unions (Logan 1948, p. 512). Mackenzie King, Canada's premier labor policymaker (and future prime minister), argued that there was a natural evolution on a continuum from no representation to formal unions. Management must be taught to work with labor first, he argued, before unions could achieve gains at the worksite. Nonunion representation plans were "an initial step to condition employers to the necessity of giving representation to employees . . . as a final step extend the employees recognition through their trade union organizations" (quoted by Martin 1954, p. 256).

Mackenzie King strongly believed in collective bargaining, but with a caveat: collective bargaining was an idea worthy of promotion particularly in the absence of strong unions. Thus, the Department of Labour embarked on a policy to encourage joint councils and other forms of nonunion collective representation but remained silent on whether unions should be included or bypassed altogether. This is a key point, since in Canada employers were not compelled to recognize or bargain with unions until the final days of World War II. Mackenzie King helped formulate a stance that presumed the superiority of collective action, as he accepted that individuals in an employment relationship were too weak to exert any power to improve their wages and working conditions.

In 1921 the Department of Labour commissioned a study entitled "Joint Councils in Industry," which found these forms of representation

to have merit. Information was collected throughout the country about plans that had these two objects: "(1) to provide means whereby on the one hand employees may crystallize their thoughts, and present their views to the management, with respect to wages and working conditions, and on the other hand to provide the management with a means whereby it may better know the preferences and appreciate the points of view of the workers; (2) to provide means for exchanging ideas and suggestions and to develop further a spirit of co-operation; in short, to secure the largest possible measure of joint action between employer and employee in any matters pertaining to their common welfare" (p. 6). The report provided details of the structure of the plans:

In most cases, worker representatives were elected by secret ballot.

The number of workers per representative averaged at a ratio of 30:1.

In practically all cases, management selected an equal number of management appointees to meet with workers.

Most plans involved the director of personnel, the welfare supervisor, or employment manager, in a support function.

Most plans provided that employees were free to join labor or other lawful organizations.

No foreman or official with authority to hire or discharge was allowed to represent employees.

Meetings were held once a month and usually on company premises.

In some cases, the plan allowed for the creation of standing committees which investigated and reported on matters of concern (e.g., health, safety, sanitation, recreation, libraries, athletics).

In several cases, the plans' constitutions provided for multistep grievance procedures resulting in binding arbitration by a senior manager or management representative within the companies.

The minutes of meetings were kept and were freely available to workers.

The plans dealt with a broad range of subjects,

including wages and benefits, working conditions, quality of production, and various items within the welfare capitalist philosophy at the time (Brandes 1976), including church work, education, gardens, and thrift.

The diffusion of nonunion plans in Canada was broad, with documentation of the installation of joint councils or committees in many industries and in the civil service. Such dominant companies as Bell Telephone of Canada, Imperial Oil, International Harvester of Canada, Kerr Lake Mining, Manitoba Bridge & Iron Works, and Massey Harris were ardent practitioners of nonunion plans and proudly testified as to the benefits of their various plans to the 1919 Canadian Royal Commission on Industrial Relations. In some cases, the plans had spread directly to Canada from the United States due to Rockefeller ownership of Canadian companies (Gitelman 1987). In the public sector, the Saskatchewan Civil Service Joint Council made a favorable report.

Joint councils were being used by unionized industries to operate as sectoral councils, including a Canadian Railway Board of Adjustment (formed from the railway companies and six of its unions to address war-related productivity, though by mutual consent of unions and management, it continued after the war was over), and the National Joint Conference Board of the Building and Construction Industries of Canada (organized in 1920) set up to harmonize employment conditions across the country. The Province of Manitoba passed an Industrial Conditions Act of 1919 that established a "Joint Council of Industry" that acted in very similar ways as our contemporary labor relations boards.

It is worth noting that the report made no distinction between union and nonunion representation plans; instead, it adopted the Mackenzie King approach of considering unions as existing along a continuous spectrum of possibilities for employee representation. These were the days before the labor law was crafted to bring exclusivity of bargaining to a single union, which achieved majority support within the entire bargaining unit.

The situation in the United States was similar. The Executive Council of the AFL endorsed union-management shop committees established to confer with management and process important grievances. In remarkably contemporary language, the council further argued: "It is fundamental for efficiency in production that the essentials of team work be understood and followed by all. There must be opportunity for intercourse and exchange of viewpoints between workers and managers" (Canada, Department of Labour 1921, p. 17). American employers and policymakers also endorsed employee representation and, as in the Canadian case, sidestepped the central question of union recognition and bargaining. The Committee on Industrial Relations of the U.S. Chamber of Commerce at its Reconstruction Congress of American Industries (Atlantic City, December 1918) declared that "employees should be accorded a voice in determining the conditions under which their work is performed by the untrammeled election of plant and shop committees to deal with these matters in conjunction with management" (ibid.). President Wilson's Industrial Congress of 1920 seemed satisfied with the development from 1914 through 1920 of joint industrial councils in the Rockefeller industries, as they brought industrial harmony and greater worker participation and seemed to have broken the violent state of war between major industrialists and their workforces.

Until the Wagner Act ban attempted to eliminate the U.S. company union movement, Canada and the United States were running on roughly parallel tracks. The early reports of nonunion plan penetration documented that by mid-1919 about half a million American workers were covered by works councils or joint councils (U.S. National Industrial Conference Board 1919, p.1). A comparable figure for Canada was that by July 1920, the number of Canadian workers coming within the scope of joint councils and committees was approximately 145,000, and growing rapidly (Canada, Department of Labour 1921, p. 6). On a per capita basis, Canada had about twice the penetration of nonunion systems than the United States. In 1920 nonunion systems covered up to half as many Canadian workers as did unions (Grant 1998, p. 71).

In Canada, as in the United States, some nonunion plans arose from management paternalism but applied to foster genuine worker representation, while other nonunion plans clearly were an attempt to sidestep union representation using a smokescreen of benevolent cooperation (Douglas 1921, pp. 92–93). The differentiation between the two motives is obscured in Canada because of the impact of American ownership of major Canadian firms. While the American parent company might have been warding off union drives in the United States, the same need not have been true in Canada. Subsidiaries of American corporations practicing nonunion systems included International Harvester, General Motors, General Electric, and U.S. Rubber (McCallum 1990). Thus, the effects of cross-border ownership were an important factor in the development of nonunion practices in Canada.

While the private sector in Canada took its cue from south of the border, the burgeoning Canadian civil service drew its model from a bastardized application of the British Whitley Committee Plan, first promulgated in 1917 and adopted by the British civil service in 1919 (Seymour 1932; White 1933). British Whitleyism was intended to spread through various industries to ensure labor-management consultation, and the intent of the British government was that

> the Councils will be recognized as the official standing consultative committees to the Government on all future questions affecting the industries which they represent and that they will be the normal channel through which the opinion and experience on an industry will be sought on all questions with which the industry is concerned. It will be seen, therefore, that it is intended that Industrial Councils should play a definite and permanent part in the economic life of the country. . . . (Canada, Joint Councils 1921, p. 13)

British Whitleyism incorporated union participation, but in Canada the model was promoted as a substitute for unions. Furthermore, the adoption of Whitleyism in Canada was confined primarily to the civil service (which until the mid-1960s did not have the right to unionize) and despite considerable interest, actual implementation did not occur until the final years of World War II. The NJC met for the first time in June 1944. Mackenzie King defanged the NJC, however, by ensuring that it had neither the authority to deal with wage and salary issues nor a mechanism to enforce its decisions. It was to have an advisory and consultative role only, a major departure from the British Whitley Council mandate (Barnes 1974, p. 101; Frankel 1960, p. 382). Parenthetically, when the public sector finally was given the right to unionize in the Public Service Staff Relations Act of 1967, the nonunion forms that permeated the civil service were transformed immediately into unions and gave an enormous boost to Canadian union density (Ponak and Thompson 1995).

In the 1930s the Canadian labor movement noted with considerable interest the passage of the Wagner Act and heartily embraced its guarantees of recognition, compulsory bargaining, and explication of unfair labor practices. The Canadian federal government, however, was sluggish in its response to union pressures, and allowed the provinces to take the lead in drafting "mini-Wagner" statutes (Woods 1973, pp. 25–28, 83–85).

The institutional setting for the passage of labor laws differed between the two countries. The decade that intervened between the adoption of the American Wagner Act and Canada's federal attempt at comparable legislation involved a basic realignment of economic and political forces. These years were characterized by the emergence of union organizing along industrial (Congress of Industrial Organizations [CIO] affiliated) lines, which threatened business and political interests. Preoccupation with Canadian participation in World War II meant a fierce emphasis on uninterrupted productivity at precisely a point when industrial unrest reached a peak (MacDowell 1978, p. 176). The constellation of forces that had an impact on the drafting of Canadian laws were different from the pressure points which underpinned the Wagner Act.

Statutory Treatment of Nonunion Representation in Canada

While the United States enacted its principal labor law in 1935 during a period of domestic reform on the heels of the depression, various factors caused delays in Canada (Taras 1997a). When finally Canada prepared a federal Wagner Act equivalent in 1944, the political environment was profoundly altered, rendering the company union debate quite distinguishable from that experienced in the United States. Canada was at war in Europe, and Canadian industries were being organized by the CIO at home. There was considerable pressure on governments to avoid any legis-

lation that would force management to recognize and deal with "radical" unions. The government was preoccupied with unemployment and did not see the passage of prolabor laws as an instrument of macroeconomic planning, as was the case in the United States (Kaufman 1996). Indeed, there is no evidence from Mackenzie King's diaries or his industrial relations scholarship that he ever viewed labor policy as anything other than a moral imperative. Instead, Canada was inclined to favor strong state intervention, which tended to sideline the union movement (MacDowell 1978; Rudin 1972).

Canada was finally prepared to pass its comprehensive labor legislation, PC 1003, only after considerable political pressure was applied to Mackenzie King's Liberal government. The two most critical reasons for the passage of the new labor statute seem to be the rise of the "socialist" CCF, which was potentially disastrous to Liberal party electoral prospects (Pickersgill 1960, p. 571; Taras 1997a, p. 771), and organized labor's disagreement with the government's approach to solving labor disputes (MacDowell 1978; Martin 1954; Coates 1973). Disaffected labor found an excellent ally in the CCF. The labor movement felt that it was being betrayed by the federal government's Industrial Disputes Inquiry Commission's (IDIC, created in June 1941) consistent mishandling of four contentious struggles (Canadian General Electric, National Steel Car [NASCO], Canada Packers, and Kirkland Lake). The IDIC intervened in the General Electric case by attempting to persuade union representatives of the advisability of bypassing union recognition in favor of a one-plant employee committee. Commenting on the similar NASCO intervention, MacDowell said that "not only was the government unprepared to support union recognition . . . it also had condoned the establishment of an employer-dominated committee which had been used to undermine the existing union [United Steelworkers, which ultimately certified the plant in 1945]" (1978, p. 183). The IDIC then broke the Canada Packers strike by bypassing the union and mandating elections of worker representatives to meet in a Committee of Employees (Cohen 1941, p. 92). The IDIC's Kirkland Lake solution was equally odious to organized labor: "That each company respectively will enter into a signed agreement to be negotiated between the officers and a committee of employees of each company to govern the rates of pay and working conditions of the employees of the said company, exclusive of superintendents, foremen, technical staff and office staff" (quoted in Cohen 1941, p. 90). The commission's approach of substituting nonunion forums in place of trade unions to end recognition strikes was viewed as an assault on the legitimate trade union movement (Martin 1954, pp. 341–344; Cohen 1941, p. 59). Kirkland Lake became a call to arms for organized labor, which began fervently clamoring for the passage of Wagner-style protective legislation to guarantee union recognition (MacDowell 1983).

Mackenzie King had to act quickly. Under the War Measures Act (R.S.C. 1927, chap. 206), the federal government could draft comprehensive legislation. In 1944 after the National War Labour Board (NWLB) Hearings were held, the Wartime Labour Relations Regulations, commonly referred to as PC 1003, were promulgated (February 17, 1944). A landmark in Canadian labor policy, it contained many features of the U.S. Wagner Act, alongside Mackenzie King's traditional emphasis on conciliation and dispute resolution. Because of the federal government's sweeping wartime powers, PC 1003 covered most areas of economic activity in Canada, superseding provincial jurisdiction. Except in wartime

emergencies, the regulation of labor matters falls within the jurisdiction of the provinces in Canada. When the wartime powers of the federal government ended, the main elements of PC 1003 were adopted by most provinces (and eventually by all) and set the basic framework for a common Canadian approach to labor law.

While enormous pressure was brought to bear in support of comprehensive labor legislation modeled on the Wagner Act, PC 1003 was never intended explicitly to ban nonunion forms of employee representation. Though the fundamentals within PC 1003 mirrored the Wagner Act (e.g., giving employees the right to organize, be represented, be recognized, bargain, and strike), there was no resolve among policymakers to eradicate company unions. Indeed, both federal and provincial jurisdictions eventually found language (in Table 6. 1) that removed nonunion representation from the scope of labor relations tribunals and courts. Five explanations are reviewed.

First, Prime Minister Mackenzie King had not changed his early sentiments favoring nonunion representation. He remained silent in the wake of the contentious recommendations of the IDIC, and he continued to endorse a nonunion forum for the civil service. Indeed, he is credited with authorship of the "Rockefeller Plan" of joint industrial councils that diffused nonunion representation throughout North American private industry. In a number of provinces, and particularly Ontario, the governments of the day were fearful of powerful international unions. Thus, while in the United States, Senator Wagner was a staunch adversary of company unions and had a strong hand in drafting legislation that reflected his antipathy (Kaufman 1996), similar backing for a company union ban did not emerge in Canada.

Second, World War II brought about calls for

Table 6.1

American and Canadian Labor Law Provisions with Regard to Definitions and Prohibitions

Labor relations acts	Definitions	Prohibitions
	U.S. FEDERAL LABOR RELATIONS ACTS	
National Labor Relations Act (Wagner Act provisions in 1935)	Section 2(5). A labor organization is "any organization of any kind, or any agency or employee representation committee or plan in which employees participate and which exists for the purpose, in whole or in part, of dealing with employers concerning grievances, labor disputes, wages, rates of pay, hours of employment, or conditions of work."	Section 8(a)(2). It is an unfair labor practice for an employer "To dominate or interfere with the formation or administration of any labor organization or contribute financial or other support to it."
Railway Labor Act of 1926	Section 1. "Representatives" means only persons or entities "designated either by a carrier or group of carriers or by its or their employees to act for it or them."	Section 2(2). Representatives for both management and labor "shall be designated by the respective parties and without interference, influence, or coercion by either party over the designation of representatives of the other; and neither party shall in any way interfere with, influence, or coerce the other in its choice of representatives."
		Section 3(4). It shall be unlawful for any carrier to interfere in any way with the organization of its employees, or to use the funds of the carrier in maintaining or assisting or contributing to any labor organization, labor represesntative, or other agency of collective bargaining.
	CANADIAN FEDERAL AND PROVINCIAL ACTS	
PC 1003 (Wartime Labour Relations Regulations, issued under the authority of the War Measures Act, Ch. 206 of R.S.C. 1927), effective from 17 February 1944 until the very early post–World War II period. PC 1003 is now defunct, although its	Section 2 (i) "employees' organization" means an organization of employees formed to regulate relations between employers and employees; Section 2 (n) "trade union" means a provincial, national or international employees' organization, or a local branch chartered by, and in good standing with, such an organization.	Section 19 (1) No employer shall dominate or interfere with the formation or administration of a trade union or employees' organization or contribute financial or other support to it; but an employer may, notwithstanding the foregoing, permit an employee or representative of a trade union or an employees' organization to confer with him during working hours to attend to the business of the

clauses were adopted by many of the provinces and appear in the federal labour code.

organization or union during working hours without deduction of time so occupied in the computation of the time worked for the employer and without deduction of wages in respect thereof.

Section 7. Upon such application [by an employees' organization for certification] the Board shall by an examination of records, by a vote or otherwise, satisfy itself that ... the unit of employees concerned is one which is appropriate for collective bargaining; and if the Board is not so satisfied, it shall reject the application.

Section 22 (2) The Board may require any employers' organization or trade union or local branch thereof, or an employees' organization affected by any application for certification of bargaining representatives, or affected by an existing collective agreement, to file with the Board: (a) a statutory declaration stating the names and addresses of its officers; or (b) a copy of its constitution and bylaws.

Canada Labour Code Part 1. [R.S.C. 1985, c. L-2] *Note:* This act covers employees working in federal undertakings, estimated to make up approximately 10% of working Canadians.

Section 3 (1) "Bargaining agent" means (a) a trade union that has been certified by the Board as the bargaining agent for the employees in a bargaining unit and the certification of which has not been revoked.

"Bargaining unit" means a unit (1) determined by the Board to be appropriate for collective bargaining or (b) to which a collective agreement applies.

"Trade union" means any organization of employees, or any branch or local thereof, the purposes of which include the regulation of relations between employers and employees.

Section 25(1) "Notwithstanding anything in this Part [the Labour Relations Code], where the Board is satisfied that a trade union is so dominated or influenced by an employer that the fitness of the trade union to represent employees of the employer for the purpose of collective bargaining is impaired, the Board shall not certify the trade union as the bargaining agent for any unit comprised of employees of the employer and any collective agreement between the trade union and the employer that applies to such employees shall be deemed not to be a collective agreement. . . ."

Section 94. No employer or employer representative shall participate in or interfere with the formation or administration of a trade union or the representation of employees by a trade union, or contribute financial or other support to a trade union.

Alberta Labour Relations Code [R.S.A., 1988, Ch. L-1.2, as amended 1995]

Section 1 (b) "Bargaining agent" means a trade union that acts on behalf of employees in collective bargaining or as a party to a collective agreement with an employer or employers' organization, whether or not the bargaining agent is a certified bargaining agent;

Section 36(1) Prohibited Practices. "A trade union shall not be certified as a bargaining agent if its administration, management or policy is, in the opinion of the Board, (a) dominated by an employer, or (b) influenced by an employer so that the trade union's fitness to represent employees for the purposes of collective bargaining is impaired."

(continued)

Table 6.1 (*continued*)

Labor relations acts	Definitions	Prohibitions
	(x) "Trade union" means an organization of employees that has a written constitution, rules or bylaws and has as one of its objects the regulation of relations between employers and employees.	Section 146(1) No employer or employers' organization and no person acting on behalf of an employer or employers' organization shall (a) participate in or interfere with (i) the formation or administration of a trade union, or (ii) the representation of employees by a trade union, or (b) contribute financial or other support to a trade union.
British Columbia Labour Relations Code [R.S.B.C. 1996, Ch. 244]	Section 1(l) "Bargaining agent" means (a) a trade union certified by the board as an agent to bargain collectively for an appropriate bargaining unit.	Section 6(1) Unfair Labour Practices. "An employer or person acting on behalf of an employer must not participate or interfere with the formation, selection or administration of a trade union or contribute financial or other support to it."
	Section 1(l) "Trade union" means a local or Provincial organization or association of employees, or a local or Provincial branch of a national or international organization or association of employees in British Columbia, that has as one of its purposes the regulation in British Columbia of relations between employers and employees through collective bargaining, and includes an association or council of trade unions, but not an organization or association of employees that is dominated or influenced by an employer.	Section 31. No employer-dominated association of employees shall be certified as a bargaining agent. An agreement between such an organization or association of employees and an employer shall not be considered as a collective agreement.
Manitoba Labour Relations Act [R.S.M. 1987, C. L-10, as amended]	Section 1: A "union" is an organization of employees formed for purposes which include "the regulation of relations between employers and employees."	Section 6(1). There is a strict prohibition against participation or interference by an employer or employers' organization or person acting on behalf of an employer or employers' organization in the formation or administration of a union or in the representation of employees by their certified bargaining agent. An employer is also prohibited from contributing financial or other support to a union. Section 43. Certification is prohibited where the Board is satisfied that the administration, management, or policy of a union is dominated by an employer to the extent that its fitness to represent employees is impaired. Any collective agreement entered into by the union and the employer is deemed not to be an agreement for the purposes of the Act.

Act	Definition	Provisions
New Brunswick Industrial Relations Act [consolidated to June 30, 1997. C.S.N.B., Ch. I-4.]	Section 1(1). A "trade union" includes any organization of employees formed for purposes that include the regulation of relations between employers and employees, has a written constitution and bylaws which define the conditions under which persons may be admitted to membership, and includes a provincial, national or international union, but does not include an employer-dominated organization.	Section 3 (1) No employer or employers' organization shall participate in or interfere with the formation, selection, or administration of a trade union or council of trade unions or representation of employees in the union, or contribute financial support to a trade union or council of trade unions. Section 18. The Board shall not certify a trade union if any employer or employers' organization has participated in its formation, selection or administration or has contributed financial or other support to it.
Newfoundland Labour Relations Act [R.S.N. 1990, C. L-1, as amended]	Section 2(1) A "trade union" or "union" means a local or provincial organization or association of employees, or a local or provincial branch of a national or international association of employees within the province that has as one of its purposes the regulation in the province of relations between employers and employees through collective bargaining but does not include an organization or association of employees or a council of trade unions that is employer influenced or dominated.	Section 23. The participation or interference with the selection, formation, or administration of a trade union by an employer or an employers' organization is forbidden, as are financial contributions or other support. Section 44. If the Board believes the administration, management, or policy of a trade union or council of trade unions is (a) influenced by the employer so that its fitness to represent employees in collective bargaining is impaired, or (b) dominated by an employer—such trade union or council of trade unions is not entitled to certification and any agreement entered into between the parties shall be held not to be a collective agreement for the purposes of the Act.
Nova Scotia Trade Union Act [R.S.N.S. 1989, ch. 475, amended 1994, c. 35]	A "trade union" or "union" means any organization of employees formed for purposes that include regulating relations between employers and employees which has a constitution and rules or bylaws setting forth its objects and purposes and defining the conditions under which persons may be admitted as members thereof and continued in membership.	Section 53 (1) No employer and no person acting on behalf of an employer shall (a) participate in or interfere with the formation or administration of a trade union or the representation of employees by a trade union; or (b) contribute financial or other support to a trade union. Section 25(15) Notwithstanding anything contained in this Act, no trade union, the administration or policy of which is, in the opinion of the Board, dominated or influenced by an employer, so that its fitness to represent employees for the purpose of collective bargaining is impaired or which discrimin-

(continued)

Table 6.1 *(continued)*

Labor relations acts	Definitions	Prohibitions
		...ates against any person [on grounds prohibited by Human Rights legislation], shall be certified as the bargaining agent of the employees, nor shall an agreement entered into between that trade union and the employer be deemed to be a collective agreement.
Ontario Labour Relations Act [1995 S.O. Ch. 1, Sched. A; as amended by 1997, Ch. 4, S. 83; 1997, Ch.31, S. 151; 1998, Ch. 8, SS. 1–23]	Section 1: A "trade union" includes a provincial, national or international organization as well as a certified council of trade unions.	Section 65: An employer is prohibited from participating in or interfering in the formation of, or representation of employees by, a trade union. Section 13. The Board will not certify a union which has been financed or supported by the employer, or which has been organized or administered with the assistance of the employer, and will deny certification to any union which discriminates against any person on grounds prohibited by the Human Rights Code, 1981, or Canadian Charter of Rights and Freedoms.
Prince Edward Island Labour Act [R.S.P.E.I. 1988, C. L-1, as amended]	Section 7(1): A "trade union" or "union" means any organization of employees formed for purposes which include the regulation of relations and collective bargaining between employees and employers and includes a council of trade unions which have been vested with appropriate authority by any of its constituent unions to enable it to discharge the responsibilities of a bargaining agent.	Section 10(1)(b) An employer, or employers' organization, or any person acting on their behalf is prohibited from participating in or interfering with the formation or administration of a trade union or contributing financial support to such a trade union. Section 15. The Board shall not certify a trade union if an employer or employers' organization participated in its formation or administration, or contributed financial support to it.
Quebec Labour Code [R.S.Q., c. C-27]	Section 1. An "Association of employees" is defined as a professional syndicate, a union, brotherhood or other group whose object is the promotion of the interests of its members, particularly in the negotiation and application of collective agreements. *Note:* A 1969 amendment aimed at eliminating company unions removed voluntarily "recognized" associations from the Code's protection. Only certified associations may make binding agreements.	Section 12: Employers are prohibited from interfering in any manner in the formation or activities of an association of employees. Section 149: Where this prohibition has been violated, the Labour Court may order its dissolution after giving it an opportunity to be heard. Section 29. If there is an allegation of employer interference in the formation or conduct of an employees' association, the labour commissioner-

Saskatchewan: The Trade Union Act [R.S.S. 1978, Chapter T-17]	Section 2 (e) "company dominated organization" means a labour organization, the formation or administration of which an employer or employer's agent has dominated or interfered with or to which an employer or employer's agent has contributed financial or other support, except as permitted by this Act. Section 2 (j) "Labour organization" means an organization of employees, not necessarily employees of one employer, that has bargaining collectively among its purposes. Section 2(l) "Trade union" means a labour organization that is not a company-dominated organization.	general shall order the certification agent [delegated by the commissioner-general to investigate applications for certification] to suspend the investigation. Section 9: "The board may reject or dismiss any application made to it by an employee or employees where it is satisfied that the application is made in whole or in part on the advice of, or as a result of influence of or interference or intimidation by, the employer or employer's agent. Section 11(1) "It shall be an unfair labour practice for an employer, employer's agent or any other person acting on behalf of the employer: (b) to discriminate or interfere with the formation or administration of any labour organization or contribute financial or other support to it. . . . (k) to bargain collectively with a company dominated organization. . . ."
Public Service Staff Relations Act [R.S., c. P-35, s. 1.] *Note:* This Act covers employee relations in the federal Public Service of Canada.	Section 2(1) "Employee organization" means any organization of employees the purposes of which include the regulation of relations between the employer and its employees for the purposes of this Act, and includes, unless the context otherwise requires, a council of employee organizations.	Section 8(1) No person who occupies a managerial or confidential position, whether or not the person is acting on behalf of the employer, shall participate in or interfere with the formation or administration of an employee organization or the representation of employees by such an organization. Section 40 (1) The Board shall not certify as bargaining agent for a bargaining unit, any employee organization in the formation or administration of which there has been or is, in the opinion of the Board, participation by the employer or any person acting on behalf of the employer of a such a nature as to impair its fitness to represent the interests of employees in the bargaining unit.

Note: Prohibitions on employer domination in the third column are followed in most legislation by provisions that allow for certain exemptions, for example, conferring with the employer is allowed, as are the provision of such items as transportation, employer contributions to pensions or welfare trust funds, and time off for employees to attend to union matters.

greater cooperation between labor and management. World War I spurred both the U.S. National War Labor Board and the Canadian 1919 Royal Commission to encourage employee representation. World War II had the same effect in Canada (McInnis 1996). The first agitation for joint production committees apparently occurred in 1942 at the August convention of the TLC, where a resolution was passed requesting that government establish Labour Management Production Committees (Logan 1948, p. 527). According to the Department of Labour, "Official sponsorship of labour-management production committees began in Canada with the wartime need for all-out production. In the early years of the war the Department of Munitions and Supply and National Selective Service endorsed the idea of joint committees of employers and employees to deal with production problems" (*Labour Gazette*, March 1948). Joint committees were struck in the unionized essential war industries such as steel, and in nonunion agriculture and the TLC's NWLB submission lists other joint committees representing nonunion workers (1944, p. 65). During the war, any form of worker-management participation was encouraged. A ban on nonunion forms would have only impeded these measures. When the civil service won the right to be represented through the NJC, Mackenzie King commented that "it was becoming increasingly difficult to deny the requests of the civil service that the government, in its role of employer, should make available to its own staff the procedures and approaches which, in its legislative and executive roles, it was advising or even directing industry to follow" (Barnes 1974, p. 27).

Third, proponents of company unions were able to make persuasive cases as they provided evidence to both the Select Committee of the Legislative Assembly of Ontario Hearings of 1943 and the National War Labour Board inquiry of 1943. There were a number of themes that seemed to recur (Taras 1997a). Fear was expressed that a blanket prohibition against all company unions would abrogate employees' freedom of association. There also were sentiments that Canadian-born company unions were preferable to foreign-controlled (American) unions, which might disrupt Canadian industries to their own advantage. Furthermore, company union success stories were described in detail. The Wagner Act's disbanding of "several excellent organizations" such as International Harvester's JIC system was criticized at the NWLB Hearings (p. 269). A number of companies and nonunion plans described their records of achievement using nonunion systems.

These arguments did not go unchallenged. *Canadian Tribune* (the labor newspaper) spoke out at the hearings with examples of the prominent companies that used company unions to avoid genuine labor unions, including National Steel and Car Corporation of Hamilton, de Havilland Aircraft of Toronto, Welland Chemical Works of Niagara Falls, Underwood Elliott Fisher of Toronto, Atlas Steel of Welland, Otis-Fensom of Hamilton, Aluminum Company of Kingston, Sawyer-Massey Ltd. of Hamilton, Canadian Marconi of Montreal, and Stelco and Inco of Sudbury (NWLB Hearings, pp. 227–231). Strong arguments against company unions and employer domination of labor organizations also were made by a host of international (CIO) union affiliates.

The employer arguments proved more persuasive to the National War Labour Board commissioners. Their majority report criticized the "new type of labour leader," who irresponsibly refused to represent the long-term interests of his constituents and who preferred to stoke his ambition by attempting "to organize quickly by stirring up labour unrest" (NLRB Report in *Labour Gazette*, February 1944, p. 4). The concept of union responsibility guided the future federal and provincial statutory provisions that required unions to demonstrate their financial accountability, their legal status, and their purpose of bargaining with employers to effect agreement rather than foment revolution. The Wagner Act–type prohibition on company unions was diluted. At the same time, the certification of trade unions influenced or dominated by management was prohibited. Thus, Canadian laws retained the Wagner Act's Section 8(a)(ii) provisions, but eventually rewrote the Wagner Act's Section 2(5) definition of a labor organization so that only real unions (not small groups of "agitators") could qualify for the protections afforded by labor laws.

The fourth reason for Canada's failure to ban nonunion forms of representation was that some of the more conservative Canadian unions were preoccupied by the issue of how to achieve statutory protection for "responsible" unions. The TLC was not as opposed to company unions as might be expected. According to MacDowell (1983), in 1937 the TLC responded to the pressure of its industrial unions for protective legislation by drafting a "model bill" and presenting it to various provincial governments. The bill was criticized at TLC conventions because it did not compel collective bargaining, did not prohibit company unions, and did not include a mechanism to determine the bargaining agent. The TLC expelled CIO-affiliated unions in 1939, but remained wary of the company union issue. This is speculative, but there is a possibility that the TLC was ambivalent about banning company unions because that might give organizing momentum to its bitter rival, the CIO-affiliated Canadian Congress of Labour. Company unions clearly were more of a substitute for industrial unions

than traditional craft unions.

The TLC's submission to the 1943 NWLB Hearings includes the TLC policy on company unions. It focuses, with hard rhetoric, on barring company unions from certification and collective bargaining rights. A close reading reveals that the TLC does not advocate an outright ban on their existence (as in the Wagner Act).

> Only bona fide trade unions or genuine employees' organizations should be accorded benefits under any proposed collective bargaining legislation. We are firm in our view that the counterfeit species of so-called employee-organization, usually known as the "company union" (and also known as a plant council or works council, or employees' committee), should be denied any standing under a collective bargaining act. The company union (the phrase incidentally is a contradiction in terms) is a device for forestalling or undermining genuine trade union organization. In one aspect, it is the application of the principle of the yellow dog contract on a large scale. . . . (p. 69)

The TLC then states that collective bargaining status should be denied to nonunion plans:

> It is essentially a parasitic organization enjoying and feeding on the gains of genuine trade unionism and seeking to camouflage its real purposes by imitating trade union organization and techniques. . . . A collective bargaining act cannot by its very nature, if truly a collective bargaining act, give any status to any group of employees in the organization and activities of which the employer is directly or indirectly concerned. We cannot have true collective bargaining between an employer and his shadow. . . . (p. 71)

By contrast, it was the more radical, less influential CCL (CIO-affiliated) unions that called for a total ban on company unions (pp. 1013–1014). Company unions obviously were more of a substitute to industrial organizing and hence a greater threat to the CIO than to the TLC. In the end, the TLC approach prevailed.

A fifth and extremely circumstantial case might be made that powerful companies sought to buy influence from politicians. Many ardent practitioners of nonunion plans were significant players on the electoral stage, through generous contributions to political campaigns. It might indeed be significant that the top sixteen funders of the federal Liberal Party in 1940 (accounting for 60 percent of the total campaign purse) included the union-resistant mining companies. A number of companies cited in the War Labour Board's hearings as operating nonunion plans, or thwarting union organizing attempts, funded the Liberal campaign. Among the top seven companies, which pledged between $25,000 and $30,000 each and accounted for almost 35 percent of funds raised, were Eaton's, Dominion Foundries and Steel, Imperial Oil, International Nickel, Hamilton Bridge, and Canada Packers (Whitaker 1977, pp. 123–125). Significant practitioners of nonunion employee representation appear on this list, as do companies that had mounted aggressive campaigns against union organizing. There is absolutely no proof of any connection between monetary contributions and labor policy; it is mentioned as more of an intriguing curiosity than an assertion of fact.

How Were Canadian Statutes Constructed?

To avoid banning nonunion forms, Canadian lawmakers concentrated on creating narrow and structural definitions of labor organizations. In most Canadian statutes, a labor organization is a trade union, and the terms are used synonymously in the majority of codes. A comprehensive table listing the construction of the definitions sections of

the major contemporary Canadian labor law statutes, the defunct PC 1003, plus two major American statutes, is found in Table 6.1. The earliest provincial legislation, the Nova Scotia Trade Union Act (S.N.S.1937) defined trade unions and required them to file constitutions, rules, bylaws, and other documents containing their objectives (s. 9), provide yearly financial statements to the Provincial Government (s. 10), and offer "a just and true" statement of accounts on demand by the union membership (s. 11).

PC 1003 focused on trade unions, but allowed for the notion of a looser "employees' organization." Unlike the Wagner Act definition of a "labor organization," however, PC 1003 limited the meaning of an employees' organization to encompass one that was "formed to regulate relations between employers and employees." In subsequent post–World War II labor legislation, it was common that to demonstrate trade union status and seek protection in the collective bargaining statutes, a labor organization or employees' organization was required to have a constitution, bylaws, and officers, and to file financial statements and exist for the primary function of bargaining with management over terms and conditions of employment.

Where Canadian legislation was silent on these requirements, as a practical matter the various labor boards used them as tests of union bona fides prior to issuing certification. The Public Service Staff Relations Act defines "employee organization" as meaning "any organization of employees the purposes of which include the regulation of relations between the employer and its employees for the purposes of this Act," the latter phrase most often interpreted by the Public Service Staff Relations Board to mean the authority to enter into a collective agreement. Federal and English-Canadian provincial statutes bar the *certification* of any employee organization that is influenced or dominated by management, but have no provisions prohibiting their existence or empowering the labor boards to order their dissolution. Among the many jurisdictions, only Quebec specifies that where employers interfere in the formation or activities of an association of employees, the Labour Court may order a dissolution of the association after giving it an opportunity to present arguments.

By contrast, Section 2(5) of the Wagner Act defines a labor organization broadly to include not only labor unions but "any organization of any kind or any agency or employee representation committee or plan" that features employee participation, employee representation, and deals with the employer regarding any traditional subjects of collective bargaining. When Section 8(a)(2) is invoked in tandem with the definitions section, there is a clear prohibition on the continued existence of any company-dominated labor organization, and the NLRB can order the disbanding of a nonunion plan. The U.S. law has a reach and sweep that in Canada was severely curtailed.

In Canadian legislation, the existence of a Section 8(a)(2) equivalent obscured the fuzziness of the treatment of nonunion forums. The union movement, and in particular the TLC, had achieved such significant fundamental guarantees in the creation and diffusion of PC 1003 that the murky treatment of nonunion forms of representation received little criticism.

All Canadian jurisdictions contain provisions similar or identical to the American Section 8(a)(2). These provisions are critically important to prevent "rat unions," which are really representing management interests, from achieving the statutory protections offered to legitimate trade unions. These include the right to be the exclusive bargaining agent and the shield against being raided by rival unions except during a very narrow window of opportunity after the expiration of the collective agreement.

A review of relevant cases in the five decades since labor laws were first passed in Canada (Taras 1997a, p. 780) reveals a fairly consistent application of these basic premises: (1) employer-dominated employee associations cannot be certified; (2) only organizations that have constitutions, bylaws, election of officers performed in a fair manner, and that exist for the purposes of collective bargaining can be certified; (3) bona fide unions capable of achieving certification can conduct organizing campaigns against noncertified employer-dominated associations at any time: the usual no-raid period does not apply, even when these associations have entered into agreements with employers; and (4) labor boards issue decisions that prevent certification but do not order the dissolution of nonunion associations.

The practical result is that Canadian firms may freely operate formal nonunion plans that may include many or all of the characteristics that were specifically targeted for eradication in the United States (e.g., having worker elections to select worker representatives, meeting on company time and company premises, having significant representation by management within the plan and in decision-making roles, formally discussing wages and working conditions, and drawing up documents that on their face strongly resemble collective agreements). But even if nonunion representation results in drawing up binding written documents that are applied to all employees, these agreements do not enjoy the legal status that true collective agreements have under labor relations legislation, or are they subject to the constraints (such as the requirement of mandatory grievance arbitration provisions and, in some provinces, mandatory union dues checkoffs) that apply to true collective agreements. Nonunion agreements do not confer any right to strike or engage in a concerted work stoppage, and there is no lawful means for nonunion employees to strike (except where health and safety is a serious concern). Many of their terms are, however, considered to be incorporated into individual contracts of employment and are enforceable as part of those individual contracts.

A brief caveat is in order. Not all Canadian employers have the unfettered right to initiate new work arrangements. The legal situation is more complex in worksites that involve the coexistence of employee involvement schemes and collective bargaining arrangements. Canadian laws bestow exclusive bargaining rights to unions that achieve certification. Various kinds of employee involvement programs currently are in vogue in Canada, all of which require more collaborative work arrangements between managers and workers. However, an employer cannot implement an initiative "in a manner which disregards a union's statutory bargaining rights" (Gleave 1998, p. 199). While nonunion employers may freely communicate with employees, the situation is more complex in worksites that contain unions. Employer communication in a unionized setting is constrained by a number of principles: for example, there can be no promises of reward, intimidation, threats or coercion to interfere with, undermine, or derogate the union; employers may not negotiate directly with workers on matters within the purview of the collective bargaining relationship; and the union must not be maligned or demeaned by the employer (listed in Canada Labour Relations Board case *Sedpex Inc.* 1988). In unionized worksites, firms cannot employ "union substitution" strategies designed to marginalize the unions' role in representing workers (Wright 1998). Canadian labor relations boards have suf-

ficient powers under the various labor statutes that they are empowered to safeguard the role of unions. Employers cannot use consultative programs to "subvert, circumvent or replace the union it its legitimate role as exclusive bargaining agent" (*CUPE* v. *CBC* 1994, pp. 121–122). On the other hand, the Canada Labour Relations Board commented in this leading CBC case that employee involvement initiatives were commendable and that on their own would not violate labor laws provided that management first attempts to deal with employees through the union. (The difficult position unions find themselves in as a result of management's employee involvement initiatives is described from the union position by Hargrove 1998 and Wright 1998. The management perspective is offered by Heenan 1998, and Gleave 1998). Because Canada has significantly greater union penetration than the United States (currently about 34 percent of employed Canadians in nonagricultural settings, compared to under 14 percent of Americans), the stream of cases dealing with employers' change initiatives in the presence of unions is very important and is closely monitored. There remains in Canada little scrutiny of labor-management relations in union-free settings.

The larger issue in this chapter is why nonunion employers enjoy greater maneuverability in Canada than in the United States. Much of the attention in the United States is focussed on the impact of Section 8(a)(2) of the NLRA, and concerted attempts have been made to amend that section, most recently through the TEAM Act. Yet Canada has virtually the identical provisions in its various labor codes, without encountering the same difficulties as those in the United States. What was different in Canada?

The critical section is not, as it is most frequently argued in the United States, Section

8(a)(2), but rather NLRA Section 2(5), which defines labor organizations broadly and functionally. In Canada, the definitions section is used to confine the jurisdictional reach of labor boards to matters affecting bona fide unions. Nonunion forms of representation exist in the realm of individual contracts of employment. Unions are free to raid nonunion plans at any time, as any agreements reached between management and its nonunion workers cannot be used as a shield against union organizing. Many Canadian unions (e.g., steelworkers, communication, energy, and paperworkers) have been successful in courting nonunion plans and winning union certification (Basken in this volume).

The Contemporary Stage

Nonunion employee representation has never vanished from Canadian industrial relations practices. This section of the chapter first traces the fate of random sample of nonunion plans that were mentioned in the 1919 commission and again in the 1943 War Labour Board Hearings. Second, it provides examples of contemporary plans. Finally, it gives estimates of the current penetration of nonunion plans.

What happened to Canada's original "company unions"? Table 6.2 provides the results of my efforts to trace the evolution of a number of significant plans. Aside from the number of companies that ceased to exist as separate entities over time, Table 6.2 demonstrates that a large number of plans were successfully wooed by unions. Nonunion plans that were accused in the National War Labour Board Hearings of 1943 of being established for the sole purpose of thwarting unionization were those that were most easily won by unions.

In every case that I could find, when unionized, the workforce went directly from a nonunion plan to a large national or international union. They did not follow the American pattern of establishing local independent unions after being forced to disband nonunion forums in the wake of the Wagner Act (e.g., Jacoby and Verma 1992). This might help to explain why only 3.7 percent of Canadian union membership encompasses certified independent local unions, and only 352 ILUs are listed by Human Resources Development (HRDC 1998, p. 16). By contrast, a number of American companies including Bell/AT&T and Standard Oil of New Jersey/Exxon experienced a transition from company unions to independent unions (and often again to large national unions) (see Koch et al. 1989; Gibb and Knowlton 1956). This possible divergence between the two countries deserves further investigation.

Table 6.3 is a summary of some plans currently operating in Canada, derived both from a review of the literature and from telephone interviews conducted in the summer of 1997. The company names were selected through a word-of-mouth process, since companies are not required to report their use of such plans to any central body such as a labor ministry, and Statistics Canada does not ask for information about employee involvement plans that involve representation. Thus, no generalizations can be made from Table 6.3 about the situation across Canada. What can be said with absolute confidence, however, is that virtually all of the plans described in Table 6.3 would be unlawful under American law, and all are practiced "in the sunlight" in Canada.

Contemporary nonunion plans exist, as evinced in Table 6.3, and most have attributes remarkably similar to those detailed in the 1921 Report of the Canadian Department of Labour described earlier. Generally, they use elected worker delegates who meet with management on paid time

Table 6.2

Fate of "Company Unions" Mentioned in 1919 or 1943

Bell Canada	Joint Research Councils adopted by subsidiary, Bell Northern Research. Other subsidiaries unionized
Borden Incorporated (Farm Machinery)	Company no longer operating as such
Canada Packers	Unionized (now Maple Leaf Foods)
Canadian National Railway	Unionized
Canadian Broadcasting Corporation	Unionized
Consolidated Mining and Smelting	Company no longer operating as such
Dominion Iron and Steel	Company no longer operating as such
Dominion Foundries and Steel (DOFASCO)	Company remains committed to nonunion employee representation via Advisory Council on Profit-Sharing, joint committees, and focus groups
Du Pont	No longer has joint councils
General Motors	Unionized
Gray-Dart Motors	Company no longer operating
Imperial Oil	Company remains committed to Joint Industrial Councils. About 5% of workforce currently unionized
Inco	Unionized
International Harvester	Company no longer operating as such
Kerr Lake Mining Company	Company no longer operating as such
Manitoba Bridge and Ironworks Ltd.	Company no longer operating as such
Massey Harris (Massey Ferguson)	Company no longer operating as such
Public Service of Canada	Continued to use National Joint Council until public service given right to unionize in 1960s. Now heavily unionized
Robb Engineering Works	No company reference available
Spanish River Pulp & Paper Mills Ltd.	No company reference available
Steel Company of Canada (Stelco)	Unionized
Westinghouse	Unionized

to represent the interests of their worker constituencies. They discuss a broad range of topics, and meetings are "on the record" in that minutes are distributed to workers or agreements are drawn that become the basis of employment relations. In many cases, there is an ongoing union organizing threat, and I believe that in all cases the company carefully matches or exceeds the wages and benefits negotiated within unionized sectors of the comparable industry.

Not only are some of the older firms such as Dofasco and Imperial Oil continuing to foster their nonunion systems, but there also are no barriers to the entry of new practitioners. Since the 1970s, a number of companies have initiated such plans, including Husky Manufacturing (headquartered in Bolton, Ontario) and the Town of Banff. Industry giants such as Petro-Canada, Imperial, and Dofasco continue to operate nonunion vehicles for employee participation for their nonunion workforces, occasionally alongside some union penetration of their companies and constant union organizing activities, without incurring labor board complaints by unions. For a union to mount a successful legal challenge would require demonstrable proof that the company has an antiunion animus and operates the plans to thwart employees' ability to exercise their rights under various labor codes. These cases are extremely rare and are aimed at the renegade, overtly

Table 6.3

Companies Currently Operating Nonunion Representation Plans

Company	Date plan founded	Characteristics of plan
Amoco	Early 1970s	Joint Industrial Councils have elected worker representatives serving two year terms, acting as "ombudsmen" on behalf of constituents. Ratio is about 1 rep per 20 workers. Managers are selected. Four meeting per year, paid time for workers. No budget available to JIC directly. Issues include working conditions, procedures, policy changes, interpretation of procedures, but *not* wages or benefits. Decisions reached by senior management. Agreements result in an hourly employee handbook. JIC body review handbook, but management determines final content. Grievances ultimately resolved by senior company officials. Benefits include formal open lines of communication, constant interaction between workers and managers. Disadvantages are that some supervisors and managers feel the JIC meetings are an "imposition." One plant became unionized in mid-1980s and two years later became disenchanted with the union and decertified.
Dofasco	Profit sharing since 1938	Widely known as the "Dofasco Way, " a comprehensive philosophy on employee treatment. Advisory Council on Profit Sharing; Joint Health and Safety Committees (required by legislation), and extensive use of Focus Groups on issues such as pay. There are elected employees who meet with appointed management representatives. The bulk of representation happens through cross-functional work teams, but some representational teams are constituted to deal with projects, in which case, it is assigned a project number and project budget. Company is divided into 9 areas, with one worker rep fro each area, with equal number of management reps. (Company has about 7,000 employees.) Advisory Council meets monthly, on paid time. Issues dealt with are profit sharing, and *not* wages. Meetings are very formal, with minutes kept and guided by a charter. Grievances settled through "open door" policy, and ultimately decided by CEO and HR directors. Benefits are "taking care of people" to be successful; disadvantages are involving employees who may not be comfortable with process, leading to frustration, and the cost factor. There have been unionization attempts since 1912; and currently there are two unions actively campaigning. Dofasco always has matched the wages of its heavily unionized rival company, Stelco. (See Livesey 1997a; Weiner 1980; Storey 1983.)
Husky Manufacturing	Early 1970s	Employee Council consisting of a dozen company workers who meet directly with Husky president (and founder), who listens to problems and answers questions. The rotating employee council meets monthly. Employee reps must poll fellow workers on what issues they want put to the president. Detailed meeting minutes are included in every pay slip. Issues raised include parking lot lighting, speed bumps on access roads, tightened security, and an on-site fitness center. Company has a $5 million child-care center for employees. Company uses profit-sharing, and about 25% of shares are held by employees. Workers sit on five resource management teams that control company expenditures. Employee salaries are at high end of industry (Livesey 1997b).
Imperial Oil	1918	Joint Industrial Councils with equal numbers of elected (worker) and selected (management) delegates. Details of the plan are in Taras (in this volume).

(continued)

(continued)

Table 6.3 *(continued)*

Company	Date plan founded	Characteristics of plan
Pembina Pipelines	Acquired as company purchased sites post–World War II	Joint Industrial Councils consist of 4 elected worker representatives for 50 workers who meet with management reps. An Employee Association has 3 representatives for 50 workers (in 1996; no divestitures have changed staffing). Meetings are monthly; Reps meet their constituents prior to meetings each month. Paid time for workers; No budget. Issues discussed include holidays, seniority, hours of work, working conditions wages, overtime, shift scheduling, vacations, call-in policies, etc. Decisions are made by management. Senior management has ultimate power to dispose of grievances. Advantages are better communication. Disadvantage is that people "don't want to stir anything up" in these meetings.
Petro-Canada	Late 1970s; came into the company via acquisitions of sites during aggressive expansion	Employee-Management Advisory Committees, a four-tier system of representation. The rest of the company is heavily unionized. Worker delegates meet managers, supported by IR manager. Meetings result in drawing up of the Information Booklet which outlines rates of pay and allowances, hours of work, holidays, etc. Company initiated peer-review grievances in 1995. Many plants unionized in early 1990s, and now the EMACs cover only about 240 employees.
Royal Canadian Mounted Police	1972	Division Staff Relations Representative Program initiated when members began bringing employment-related grievances to media attention, and sought mechanism for representation while ban against unionization of RCMP in effect (between 1918 and 1974). Twenty-nine democratically elected reps service 17,300 nonunion workers across the country. Paid, full-time positions, with budget. First term is 2 years; if reelected, successive terms are 3 years. Twenty-eight reps are elected by constituents and one is elected nationally. RCMP members must be nominated to serve; elections held in accordance with Canada's Elections Act. Candidates have 3 days to campaign at RCMP's expense, provided up to 3 pages of literature to be distributed through the ranks. Generally a 90% rate of voting in elections. Management side consists of selected senior managers of RCMP. Meetings are held every 6 months. Issues include pay and benefits, discipline, clothing and equipment design, travel benefits, isolation, discharge, etc. Decisions usually made by consensus. Written policy results from meetings. The commissioner of the RCMP has ultimate authority to resolve grievances. Unionization efforts are ongoing: estimates are that about 10% of RCMP would prefer union. Currently 3,000 are unionized as public sector employees (out of 20,300).
Town of Banff	1990, with incorporation of the Town of Banff	Liaison Groups consist of elected worker representatives who meet with management representatives. HR manager is used as a resource. Six reps for 80 workers. Groups meet every 2 months, on paid time. No budget. Matters discussed include personnel policy, hours of work, flex time, sick leave, cost of living allowances but *not* hourly wages. Decisions are made by consensus. Town Manager has ultimate responsibility to determine grievance outcomes. Benefits include better communication. Disadvantages include failure to resolve issues quickly.

antiunion employer rather than at companies that operate sophisticated nonunion systems as part of their elaborate human resource management practices.

Many of the companies listed in Table 6.3 operate nonunion representation as a component of a larger philosophy of employee relations. These companies, and Dofasco and Husky are exemplars, provide benefits that the unions in their industries could not deliver: significant profit-sharing schemes and, in Husky's case, a lavish child-care center for employee families. The founder and president of Husky insists that "I think you build something to last if you treat workers well. . . . You build a stronger operation. Look at Rockefeller [Senior?]; he treated his employees like s—. He treated everybody like s—. The question is, is that the way you want to live? I don't think it would give me satisfaction . . ." (Livesey 1997b, p. 44). Imperial Oil managers are committed to their Joint Industrial Council and speak of it with pride. The "Dofasco Way" is an integrated system of Welfare Capitalist measures. By contrast, in the case of Petro-Canada, which is heavily unionized and has no strong commitment to its Employee-Management Advisory Committees, many of its nonunion plants have become unionized as a result of 1990s downsizing and worker frustration with the EMACs as a form of representation. The Stelco Employee Representation Plan, designed as a union substitution scheme in the midst of union organizing in 1935, did not survive (Storey 1987). Plans that persisted over time, and that repelled sustained union organizing efforts, were operated by employers who are not merely avoiding unions, although certainly this was and continues to be a goal. Dofasco CEO Mayberry admits in the widely distributed *Globe and Mail's Report on Business Magazine*, "I would

take it as a very significant personal failure if we became unionized" (Livesey 1997a, p. 26).

To provide estimates of the penetration of nonunion representation plans I rely exclusively on data recently made available by Lipset and Meltz. Table 6.4 provides cross-country comparative estimates from a telephone survey conducted in 1997. At first glance, what is most surprising about Table 6.4 is the similarity between Canada and the United States, notwithstanding considerable differences in public policy regarding nonunion representation.

The most significant difference in Table 6.4 that can be readily explained by public policy treatments of nonunion plans is that more Canadians participate in nonunion plans that involve the election of worker delegates than in the United States. This conclusion clearly is supported by the information provided in Table 6.3, which shows that most Canadian plans seem to involve the election of worker delegates.

Table 6.4 must be interpreted with caution, however, as collective representation remains substantially greater in Canada than in the United States. The two countries start with different bases. Almost 34 percent of Canadians are unionized, compared to under 14 percent of Americans, so only 66 percent of Canadians are "eligible" for nonunion representation, compared to 86 percent of Americans.

Less readily explained are (1) the extent to which American companies are practicing nonunion representation even in the presence of legal restrictions, and (2) the extent to which Canadian companies are *not* availing themselves of opportunities for formal worker participation. I would argue on the basis of my interviews, the literature available on companies that run sophisticated nonunion plans, and my prior study of the Joint Industrial Council (see Taras in this vol-

Table 6.4

Comparison of Canada and U.S. Contemporary Nonunion Representation Using Lipset and Meltz 1997 Survey

	Canada (%)	United States (%)
If your worksite is not unionized: Do you have any formal nonunion employee representation at your workplace? (N = 528 Canada; 669 U.S.)		
Yes	19	20
No	77	78
Don't know	4	2
(If yes: N = 102 Canada; 140 U.S.): Are you covered by nonunion employee representation?		
Yes	51	63
No	44	35
Don't know	6	3
Does this nonunion employee representation provide a:		
Joint Health & Safety Committee		
Yes	67	66
No	24	28
Don't know	9	6
Committee Discussing Compensation and Benefits of Employment		
Yes	63	65
No	24	30
Don't know	13	5
Are the nonunion employee representatives:		
Elected by employees	31	25
Appointed by management	27	28
Chosen in some other way	32	41
Don't know	10	6

Source: Survey on Attitudes Towards Work and Unions conducted by Seymour Martin Lipset and Noah Meltz in June 1996.

Note: The sample size for the survey was 1,400 Canadians and 2,100 Americans, for a total sample of 3.500. Only those employees who are not part of a unionized worksite are included in this table. The data were kindly provided by Noah Meltz.

ume) that formal nonunion employee representation requires a level of commitment and a philosophical approach to employee relations that few companies are willing to make. Companies that botch their approaches to nonunion representation will find themselves either disbanding the plans or having workers seek union representation. Companies that failed to meet union wage and compensation patterns, or existed in indus-

tries that suffered significant business downturns that caused erosion in their treatment of workers, were quickly unionized (Storey 1987). On the other hand, companies that are genuinely interested in involving their workers will find ways (sometimes creative, sometimes running afoul of the American law) of doing so, and perhaps there is a threshold or saturation level for nonunion representation. Clearly, loosening the American restrictions against nonunion representation might allow the companies that already have incorporated strong employee involvement initiatives and forestalled union organizing to broaden the scope of topics dealt with officially, and allow a more democratic selection of workers to participate in issues affecting their cohorts.

As to whether other American companies would set up sham company unions and weaken the union movement further, I am in no position to speculate, for two reasons. First, Canada does not have a prosperous union-busting consulting industry that has jumped on nonunion representation as a further tool in the arsenal of union-avoidance techniques. Second, Canadian labor laws are much more protective of union organizing in that management is prohibited from campaigning, and workers can select the union either by cards or by election after a very fast organizing period (Taras 1997b, pp. 321–326). Workers who are dissatisfied with any company-sponsored plan can make the transition to the union with considerable speed. Thus, generalizing on the basis of Canadian experience is a risky venture.

The most paradoxical aspect is that in Canada a relatively strong union movement coexists with a relatively healthy environment for nonunion collective representation, while in the United States the union movement has weakened alarmingly even in the presence of legal restrictions designed to help unions penetrate industry.

References

Barnes, L. 1974. *Consult and Advise: A History of the National Joint Council of the Public Service of Canada.* Queen's University, IR Centre, Research and Current Issue Series No. 26.

Basken, Reg. 2000. "My Experience with Unionization of Nonunion Employee Representation Plans in Canada." In *Nonunion Employee Representation*, ed. B.E. Kaufman and D.G. Taras. Armonk, N.Y.: M.E. Sharpe.

In this volume.

Brandes, Stuart D. 1976. *American Welfare Capitalism 1880–1940.* Chicago: University of Chicago Press.

Canada, Department of Labour. 1921. "Joint Councils in Industry." *International Labour Review*, supplement to the *Labour Gazette*, February, pp. 1–24.

———. 1965. "Today's Need for Joint Consultation." Labour-Management Cooperation Service.

———. 1970. "Handbook for Labour-Management Consultation Committees." Labour-Management Cooperation Service.

———. Multiple years. *Labour Gazette.*

Canada, 1919. Royal Commission on Industrial Relations. Report of Commission, pp. 13–18.

———. 1943. *National War Labour Board Proceedings.*

Coates, D. 1973. "Organized Labour and Politics in Canada: The Development of a National Labour Code." Ph.D. dissertation, Cornell University, Ithaca, N.Y.

Cohen, J.L. 1941. *Collective Bargaining in Canada.* Toronto: Steel Workers Organizing Committee.\

CUPE v. *Canadian Broadcasting Corporation*, 1994, 27 C.L.R.B.R. (2d) 110 (Canada Labour Relations Board).

Douglas, P.H. 1921. "Shop Committees: Substitute for, or Supplements to, Trade Unions?" *Journal of Political Economy* 29, no. 2: 89–107.

EFCO Corporation, 371 NLRB 1998. Issued December 31, 1998 on NLRB website.

Electromation, Inc. 309 NLRB 1992 @ 990.

Estreicher, Samuel. 2000. "Nonunion Employee Representation: A Legal/Policy Perspective." In *Nonunion Employee Representation*, ed. B.E. Kaufman and D.G. Taras. Armonk, N.Y.: M.E. Sharpe. In this volume.

Finkin, M.W., ed. 1994. *The Legal Future of Employee Representation.* Ithaca, N.Y.: ILR Press.

Flynn, G. 1996. "Is Pro-worker Good Business?" *Workforce* 75: 66–74.

Frankel, S. 1960. "Staff Relations in the Canadian Federal Public Service: Experience with Joint Consultation." In *Canadian Public Administration*, ed. J.E. Hodgetts and D.C. Corbett, pp. 370–385. Toronto: Macmillan.

Gibb, G.S., and E. Knowlton. 1956. *History of Standard Oil Company* (New Jersey). New York: Harper & Row.

Gitelman, H.M. 1987. *The Legacy of the Ludlow Massacre: A Chapter in American Industrial Relations.* Philadelphia: University of Pennsylvania Press.

Gleave, Stephen F. 1998. "Worker Involvement Initiatives: A Management Viewpoint." *Labour Arbitration Yearbook*, pp. 195–204.

Grant, Hugh. 1998. "Solving the Labour Problem at Imperial Oil: Welfare Capitalism in the Canadian Petroleum Industry, 1919–1929." *Labour/Le Travail* 41 (Spring): 69–95.

Hardy, J. Fred, and Allen Ponak. 1983. "Staff Relations in

Hardy, J. Fred, and Allen Ponak. 1983. "Staff Relations in the Royal Canadian Mounted Police." *Journal of Collective Negotiations* 12: 87–97.

Hargrove, Buzz. 1998. "Decision-Making in the Workplace: A Union Viewpoint." *Labour Arbitration Yearbook*, pp. 205–215.

Heenan, Roy L. 1998. "Decision-Making in the Workplace: A Management Viewpoint," *Labour Arbitration Yearbook*, pp. 189–193.

Human Resources Development Canada. 1998. *Directory of Labour Organizations in Canada*. Hull, Quebec: Workplace Information Directorate.

Jacoby, Sanford, and Anil Verma. 1992. "Enterprise Unions in the United States: A Case Study." *Industrial Relations* 31 (Winter): 137–158.

Jenero, K.A., and C.P. Lyons. 1992. "Employee Participation Programs: Prudent or Prohibited?" *Employee Relations Law Journal* 17, no. 4: 535–566.

Kaufman, B.E. 1996. "Why the Wagner Act? Reestablishing Contact with Its Original Purpose." *Advances in Labor and Industrial Relations* 7: 15–68.

Koch, Marianne, David Lewin, and Donna Sockell. 1989. "The Determinants of Bargaining Structure: A Case Study of AT&T." In *Advances in Industrial and Labor Relations* 4.

LeRoy, Michael H. 2000. "Do Employee Participation Groups Violate Section 8(a)(2) of the National Labor Relations Act?" In *Nonunion Employee Representation*, ed. B.E. Kaufman and D.G. Taras. Armonk, N.Y.: M.E. Sharpe. In this volume.

Livesey, Bruce. 1997a. "Heart of Steel." *Report on Business Magazine*, August, pp. 20–26.

———. 1997b. "Provide and Conquer." *Report on Business Magazine*, March, pp. 34–44.

Logan, H.A. 1948. *Trade Unions in Canada*. Toronto: Macmillan.

MacDowell, L.S. 1978. "The Formation of the Canadian Industrial Relations System during World War Two." *Labour/Le Travailleur* 3: 175–196.

———. 1983. *Remember Kirkland Lake: The Gold Miners' Strike of 1941–42*. Toronto: University of Toronto Press.

Mackenzie King, W.L. 1973, 1980. *The Mackenzie King Diaries 1893 to 1950*. Toronto: University of Toronto Press.

Martin, W.S. 1954. "A Study of Legislation Designed to Foster Industrial Peace in the Common Law Jurisdictions of Canada." Ph.D. dissertation, University of Toronto.

McCallum, Margaret E. 1990. "Corporate Welfarism in Canada, 1919–39." *Canadian Historical Review* 71: 46–79.

McInnis, P.S. 1996. "Teamwork for Harmony: Labour-Management Production Committees and the Postwar Settlement." *Canadian Historical Review* 77: 317–352.

Pickersgill, J.W. 1960. *The Mackenzie King Record, 1939–1944*. Chicago: University of Chicago Press.

Ponak, A., and M. Thompson. 1995. "Public Sector Collective Bargaining." In *Union-Management Relations in Canada*, 3d ed., ed. M. Gunderson and A. Ponak, pp. 415–454. Toronto: Addison-Wesley.

Rudin, B. 1972. "Mackenzie King & the Writing of Canada's Anti Labour Laws." *Canadian Dimension* 8: 42–48.

Sedpex Inc., 1988, 72 di 148 (Canada Labour Relations Board No. 667).

Seymour, J.B. 1932. *The Whitley Councils Scheme*. London: P.S. King and Sons.

Storey, Robert H. 1983. "Unionization Versus Corporate Welfare: The Dofasco Way." *Labour/Le Travail* 12: 7–42.

———. 1987. "The Struggle to Organize Stelco and Dofasco." *Relations industrielles/Industrial Relations* 42: 366–385.

Taras, D.G. 1997a. "Why Nonunion Employee Representation Is Legal in Canada." *Relations industrielles/Industrial Relations* 52: 763–786.

———. 1997b. "Collective Bargaining Regulation in Canada and the United States: Divergent Cultures, Divergent Outcomes." In *Government Regulation of the Employment Relationship*, ed. B.E. Kaufman, pp. 295–341. Madison, Wis.: Industrial Relations Research Association.

———. 2000. "Contemporary Experience with the Rockefeller Plan: Imperial Oil's Joint Industrial Council." In *Nonunion Employee Representation*, ed. B.E. Kaufman and D.G. Taras, Armonk, N.Y.: M.E. Sharpe. In this volume.

U.S. Department of Labor and Department of Commerce. Commission on the Future of Worker-Management Relations. 1994. *Report and Recommendations*. Washington, D.C.: U.S. Government Printing Office.

U.S. National Industrial Conference Board. 1919. "Works Councils in the United States." Research Report Number 21.

Weiner, Andrew. 1980. "In the Family Way." *Canadian Business*, November, pp. 113–124.

Whitaker, R. 1977. *The Government Party: Organizing and Financing the Liberal Party of Canada 1930–58*. Toronto: University of Toronto Press.

White, L.D. 1933. *Whitley Councils in the British Civil Service*. Chicago: University of Chicago Press.

Woods, H.D. 1983. *Labour Policy in Canada*, 2nd ed. Toronto: Macmillan of Canada.

Wright, Michael D. 1998. "Worker Involvement Initiatives: A Union Viewpoint." *Labour Arbitration Yearbook*, pp. 217–229.

Theory

7

An Economic Analysis of Employee Representation

Bruce E. Kaufman and David I. Levine

The economic analysis of employee representation (ER) has followed two very different tracks. The economics literature on trade union forms of employee representation is voluminous and dates back more than a century. In contrast, nonunion forms of employee representation, such as shop committees, works councils, and company unions, have received only scant attention in recent years from American economists. The most noteworthy exception is the recent paper by Freeman and Lazear (1995) that applies economic theory to an examination of European-style works councils. Also relevant is a small but growing literature in economics, such as studies by Levine and Tyson (1990), Ben-Ner and Jones (1995), and Levine (1995), which examines the theoretical underpinnings of employee involvement programs. As noted there, participation can take two forms: direct participation, in which employees communicate and interact with management; and indirect participation, in which employees are represented by certain of their peers through various forms of committees and councils in dealings with management. It is the latter form that is examined here, although a number of the implications and conclusions also apply to the former.

In this chapter we formalize and extend the theory of nonunion employee representation in several directions, building on the literature cited above. The central conceptual contribution is to ground the study of employee representation in a theoretical approach not hitherto applied to this subject—transaction cost economics. From this model we generate a number of insights and predictions about employee representation, such as the determinants of an employer's demand for ER and the variation in extent of nonunion ER forms across firms, market structures, and macroeconomic environments. We also take a more in-depth look at the private versus social dimension of both the benefits and costs of nonunion representation. The chapter concludes with a discussion of policy implications.

An Economic Model of Employee Representation

The generic employment practice considered here is some form of employee representation in a nonunion workplace. By employee representation we mean any kind of organizational structure that has one or more employees in it that (a) represents in some agency capacity other employees in the workplace, (b) meets and discusses workplace issues with company management, and (c) is established, financed, and operated by the company. Examples include safety committees, problem-solving teams, peer-review panels, departmental production and quality review committees, plant-wide joint industrial councils, or employee representatives on a board of directors. Later we extend the analysis to consider representational forms mandated by law, such as European works councils. We do not, however, discuss forms of employee representation that are instigated by employees; see Bishop and Levine (1999) for an example and additional citations.

The first task is to identify the factors that influence a firm's desired level of employee representation. One approach is to model ER as a factor input that provides a flow of services for use in the production process, analogous to capital and labor services. Assuming the firm's goal is maximum profit, the job of management is to choose the optimal level of employee representation, which it does by comparing the marginal revenue and cost of additional ER expenditures.

More specifically, assume that along with capital and labor, a firm uses employee representation as a factor of production. In the case of ER services, we assume a firm can increase employee representation in small amounts from the zero level (no representation of any type or kind) by continuously expanding and formalizing the extent of representation. We do not specify the details, but note only that a company can expand employee representation to successively broader levels in the organization, pay for extra time at ER meetings, increase the authority of the employee representatives, or broaden the range of issues the ER plan deals with. Each factor input also has an associated unit cost, denoted by V in the case of ER services.

The first-order condition for employee representation services that emerges from maximizing profits sets the marginal revenue product of employee representation equal to its cost:

$$V = MP_{ER} \times P, \qquad [1]$$

where P is product price (on the assumption of a perfectly competitive product market) and MP_{ER} is the marginal physical product of ER services. In words, this first-order condition states that a firm should utilize successive amounts of employee representation as long as representation's marginal revenue product is equal to or greater than its marginal cost.

This simple model provides a useful schema for thinking about the various factors that influence a firm's decision to adopt some form of employee representation, as well as its breadth and depth of activities. Specifically, we first analyze the factors that influence employee representation's productivity, and then its cost (the right-hand and left-hand sides of equation 1).

A Transaction Cost Analysis of Employee Representation

A relatively new theoretical framework in economics—*transaction cost economics*—provides considerable insight on the determinants of a firm's demand for employee representation. Transaction cost economics begins by asking why economic activity is sometimes organized through markets and other times through firms, and what variables or factors influence the choice of one organizational form over the other. Intuitively, market failures must exist to make firms viable. At the same time, the market failures that lead to firms can also lead to a role for employee representation.

The Transaction Cost Framework

The starting point in transaction cost economics (TCE) is the observation that the division of labor inherent in a complex, multiperson economy requires that goods and services be exchanged between individuals in both the processes of production and distribution. Society has alternative choices as to how this exchange process can be organized, such as a market economy versus a centrally planned economy or through markets versus within a business firm, and thus the issue is to determine why one organizational form is chosen over another.

As viewed in TCE, every transaction takes place in the context of an explicit or implicit contract made between two or more economic agents that stipulates the terms and conditions of trade. The fundamental postulate of TCE is the *efficiency principle*—that economic activity is largely organized in ways that minimize the total costs of entering into and executing these contracts (Williamson 1985). Most TCE analyses assume that whether production and exchange takes place through markets or within one large firm, or whether a firm is organized as a single business unit or a multidivisional company, depends on which organizational form is the most efficient in carrying out these transactions (Cheung 1983). We start with this framework, and extend the analysis to cases where profit maximization leads managers to sometimes trade off efficiency and bargaining power.

In TCE, the ultimate source of transaction costs arises from one or more forms of *market failure*. A perfectly competitive market corresponds to all the assumptions of the neoclassical general equilibrium competitive model, including perfect information, people with unbiased and costless computational capacities, numerous buyers and sellers who act as price takers, zero mobility costs, and absence of externalities and public goods. In such an environment, all transactions take place through markets, and multi-person firms do not exist (Milgrom and Roberts 1993, p. 73).

To the extent that one or more of these assumptions are violated, transaction costs exist. Imperfect information, for example, gives rise to a host of contracting problems, such as adverse selection and opportunism, that add to the cost of exchange. Whether transactions are still carried out in markets or are internalized within firms turns on which institutional form minimizes the sum of production and transaction cost. And if exchange takes place within firms, entrepreneurs will be motivated to organize the firm and structure its production and human resource practices to attain high efficiency through reduction of transaction cost.

The Employment Relationship

A positive demand for employee representation necessarily presupposes the existence of firms, since only in firms is there an employer-employee relationship. We do not detail further the nature of the transaction costs that give rise to firms but simply accept that various forms of market failure provide an efficiency rationale for them (see Milgrom and Roberts 1993; Demsetz 1995). The nature of the employment relationship within firms does require further analysis, however.

Three fundamental features of the employment relationship affect the firm's demand for employee representation. The first is that the employment relationship is an example of an *incomplete contract*. The employment relationship is a contractual one in nature, for the buyer of labor (the firm) agrees to pay the seller of labor (the worker) a certain amount of money in return for the seller's labor services over some period of time. The employment relationship is an incomplete contract in that it is typically impossible for the two parties to draw up an agreement that specifies the course of action to be taken under every possible eventuality. Instead, the customary practice is that certain key provisions (e.g., base rate of pay, attendance policy) are agreed to by the employer and employee orally or in writing. At the same time, many other aspects are left open-ended because it is impossible to anticipate certain future contingencies and/or to draft language to cover them fully (e.g., the job tasks and pace of work a worker will be asked to perform in future weeks). Because of the incomplete nature of the employment contract, there are numerous opportunities for misunderstanding and opportunistic behavior and a concomitant need for ongoing communication and problem solving between employer and employee.

The second fundamental feature of the employment contract is that the relationship has traditionally been one of *at-will employment.* In most commercial contracts the buyer and seller cannot unilaterally abrogate the agreement once it is legally entered into. The employment contract is different, however, in that either the employer or employee can declare the (largely implicit) contract null and void "at will" by the employee quitting or the employer firing the worker. Employment-at-will, even when modified and restricted by laws such as those banning discrimination, means that both parties face uncertainty concerning whether the other will honor its commitments.

The third fundamental feature of the employment contract is that it establishes an *authority relation* between employer and employee. In market exchange, both the buyer and seller of labor are treated as equals before the law. But once an employment contract has been agreed upon, the legal relationship between buyer and seller changes to that of "employer" and "employee." (Many aspects of the law are derived from a time when the participants were still referred to as the "master" and "servant.") The

owners of the firm and appointed management assume the role of employer (or "boss") and gain the right to use the labor of the worker as desired. The employee, in turn, agrees to submit to the authority of the employer and execute in good faith the employer's directives. The opportunity to quit, coupled with various court rulings and laws, provide the employee with some protection. At the same time, in most cases the presence of unemployment and of wages and benefits linked to tenure imply that employees have a high cost of job loss. Thus, the authority relation places most employees in a relatively vulnerable position with regard to the execution of the terms and conditions of the employment contract.

These three features of the employment relationship would provide no incentive for either party to demand employee representation if it were not for the presence of significant forms of market failure and, hence, transaction cost. Perfect information and costless, omniscient human cognitive capabilities would eliminate the problem of incomplete contracting, as all future contingencies could be foreseen, and language could be drafted to cover them. Likewise, with complete information, numerous buyers and sellers, and zero costs of mobility, the existence of at-will employment would pose no hardship on either party, as new buyers and sellers could be located instantly and with zero cost. And, finally, the existence of numerous alternative job opportunities and zero costs of job search means that employers could never abuse their authority over workers, since workers would immediately exit the firm for other employment. The reality, however, is that all labor markets contain, to one degree or another, market failures. Thus, the possibility exists that employee representation may reduce transaction costs and improve efficiency.

Benefits of Employee Representation

The existence of transaction costs, and the market failures that underlie them, are the basic factors that make employee representation a productive investment for some firms. Thus, employers will demand employee representation, *ceteris paribus*, whenever the presence of employee representation reduces the transaction costs associated with the employment contract (subject to not being offset by losses in bargaining power). We decompose the efficiency effects of employee representation into three distinct (but not necessarily independent) parts: improvement in organizational coordination, improvement in employee motivation, and reduction in supervisor moral hazard.

Improvement in Organizational Coordination

One challenge facing the owners of the firm is to coordinate the activities of all employees. This coordination process can be performed by the price mechanism when production is organized and performed through markets. When production is instead organized and performed within firms, the coordination task relies on a different mechanism—the exercise of authority through management command.

Statute and common law give the firm's owners ultimate authority to determine what products are produced, how they are produced, and who will perform the individual tasks of production. These decision-making rights are usually delegated by the owners to a cadre of employees known as "management." The management of the firm typically takes the form of a pyramid-shaped hierarchy, extending from a single top decision maker (the chief executive officer) to a large number of first-line supervisors at the base. The supervisors interface with the nonmanagement, production workers. It is the task of the production ("front-line") employees to make the product or deliver the service in accordance with the directives of management.

There are several channels through which employee representation can reduce the transaction costs that arise in coordinating the process of production. Three examples illustrate employee representation's potential.

One source of transaction cost is imperfect information and bounded rationality. The impact of these factors on firm structure can be analyzed by modeling the firm as a communication network and information-processing mechanism (Radner and Marschak 1972; Radner 1992; Boulton and Dewatripont 1994). From this perspective, firms are structured in part to reduce the costs of moving information to decision makers and in processing this information. In a world of perfect information and unbounded rationality, the chief executive officer (CEO) would be able to acquire and process all necessary information needed for coordination of the firm and communicate it to each production worker directly. But with imperfect information and bounded rationality, any attempt of the CEO to perform this task singlehandedly quickly results in information overload.

As a result, in some settings efficiency can be enhanced by having a pyramid-shaped hierarchy in which the task of information collection and processing is decentralized among many people at the base of the organization, who in turn pass on their reports to designated superiors who winnow, condense, and interpret the information and pass it on to their superiors, who perform the same function, pass on their reports to the next layer of management, and so on until the information in a much compacted form reaches the CEO at the top. Once the CEO makes a decision based on this information, the decision is then passed down the chain of command, where at each step it is elaborated upon and fleshed out in operational detail until finally implemented by the production workers at the bottom of the organization.

Employee representation can improve the efficiency of this process if it performs "skip-level" reporting in organizations that facilitates the flow of strategically important information to top decision makers (Boulton and Dewatripont 1994). Particularly in very large organizations, information may flow through a dozen or more levels of management hierarchy before reaching the top executive level. The virtue of this process is that at each stage of the hierarchy the information is processed and condensed so that only the portion pertinent to decision makers at the next higher level of the hierarchy is sent forward, thus economizing on the demands placed on the information handling and decision-making capabilities of top management. The negative consequence, however, is that the greater are the layers of hierarchy, or the more voluminous and complex the information received by the production workers, the more the information is filtered and the weaker and more delayed is the "signal" that eventually reaches the top from any point at the base of the pyramid.

For nonstrategic issues, this filtering process will generally not pose a problem, as such issues can effectively be handled by lower levels of the hierarchy. For strategic issues that bear heavily on the long-run success of the organization, however, this filtering process may deprive top decision makers of the quantity, quality, and immediacy of information needed for efficient coordination decisions. Some form of employee representation, then, may provide a more direct and speedier channel for the flow of such strategic information to higher-level decision makers. An industrial council, for example, may provide a forum for selected production workers to report directly to a vice-president, the CEO, or board of directors on important matters such as the state of employee morale or problems in customer service or production efficiency. For this to be an efficient use of the time and scarce cognitive resources of these top decision makers, the information provided by the employee representatives must be of a strategically important nature. Thus, employee morale would be of strategic concern only in organizations where employee dissatisfaction has the potential for imposing significant costs on the organization, such as where the quality of employee service to customers is of major importance or where employees have major discretion in the performance of key production tasks.

A second example of where employee representation may reduce coordination costs involves the framing of decisions. Part of the coordination challenge for organizations is to ensure that managers fully and accurately factor into their reports and decisions the perspective, interests, and needs of the various agents (or departments, divisions, etc.) reporting to them. At the same time, "framing effects" arising from bounded rationality often impart a systematic bias into this process (Tversky and Kahneman 1986). In particular, people assign greater saliency to certain pieces of information received by their sensory organs and downgrade or ignore other pieces of information. The pieces of information given a greater and lesser weight are determined by the particular mental picture, or "frame," used by the decision maker in ordering and interpreting the incoming information. By their nature, these mental frames are selective and subjective interpretations of reality. Thus, they are influenced by each person's personal characteristics (gender, race, age, etc.) and socioeconomic background (income, occupation, nationality, etc.).

Framing effects are likely to be important in management-worker relations. Because of the division of labor in production, the authority relation between managers and employees, and the significant conflict of interests that often exists between the firm and its workforce, managers and workers come to have quite distinct attitudes and perspectives regarding the performance, evaluation, and remuneration of work.

The problem this poses for effective coordination is that, due to framing effects, managers' decisions often give excessive weight to the management perspective and insufficient weight to the employees' perspective. Employee representation, for example, through a safety committee, can be an institutional device to ensure that employee perspectives get adequately factored into management decision making. Moreover, just the addition of new perspectives can often increase creativity in looking for solutions to problems (Nemeth and Owens 1996).

Finally, employee committees can reduce coordination costs when they permit decisions to be decentralized. Consider the case when production employees in two departments have the information needed to make an effective decision. When a hierarchy is used to coordinate, the information must be passed up the hierarchy to the lowest-level manager who supervises both work groups. A cross-department committee of employees can pool the same information with lower costs of managerial time and cognitive effort.

Improvement in Employee Motivation

Firms not only have to coordinate economic activity, they also have to motivate employees. A variety of market failures, and hence transaction costs, can impede motivation. This fact opens the door for employee representation to have a positive productivity effect. Here are several examples.

The first concerns public goods in the workplace. A public good is any good or service in which no one can be denied access on account of nonpayment for use (nonexcludability) and in which greater consumption by one person does not reduce the amount available for others (nonrivalrous consumption). National defense is an oft-cited example of a public good. There are also many public goods in the workplace, such as reduced noise pollution, lower speed of an assembly line, and elimination of health hazards. The problem with all types of public goods is that individual consumers or employees have an incentive to free-ride—that is, to consume the good but not pay for it. This free-riding, in turn, leads to a market failure in that public goods are underproduced relative to the socially optimal level.

Similar to national defense, a solution to a public goods problem in the workplace is to create some form of "industrial government," say in the form of an employee representation committee (Commons, 1921). All workers might desire more expenditure by the firm on noise abatement or a reduced line speed but be unwilling to voice this opinion for fear of individually suffering the costs while colleagues reap the benefits. Likewise, no single employee has an incentive to investigate suspected health hazards in the workplace or the extent to which the employer is properly measuring performance in calculating a gain-sharing bonus. But employee representation changes the incentives by, in effect, collectivizing the costs. That is, every employee now has a greater incentive to reveal his or her true demand for the public good, partly because representation shields the individual worker from being identified by management as a "troublemaker" and partly because all workers share the financial or work-related costs arising from greater provision of the public good.

While the employees clearly gain from having more of the public good, the effect on the firm is ambiguous. When public goods are valued by employees, the firm can save money through lower wages or turnover costs by having a more accurate understanding of employees' preferences. But this saving to employers may be more than offset by the higher cost associated from rectifying the public-good problem.

A second motivational benefit of employee representation may be higher trust and cooperation between workers and management. The desire of management is that employees exert maximum work effort and attention to quality in the production process. Doing so could also be to the self-interest of workers *if* they share in the higher profits that result. But in a traditional hierarchically organized firm, many employees typically hold back out of fear of management opportunism. That is, employees fear that once they give their utmost in production, the management will renege on the implicit contract; for example, by laying off employees or refusing to increase wages.

As illustrated by the well-known prisoner's dilemma game, without some mechanism to strengthen the bond of trust between the two parties, the incentives are for one or both sides to opt for outcomes that are individually rational but suboptimal relative to what could be achieved with cooperation (see Miller 1992). The prisoner's dilemma game also suggests that two alternative mechanisms can help make it possible for exchange partners to achieve the superior cooperative outcome. One is to provide a channel for greater two-way communication so that each side

gains trust in the intentions of the other; the second is to commit the parties to repeated plays of the game so that each side gains a greater stake in engaging in fair dealing over the long run, rather than opportunistic behavior in the short run.

Employee representation can serve as a useful instrument in solving prisoner dilemma problems in the employment relationship. On one hand, employee representation provides a valuable mechanism to strengthen communication and trust between management and employees. Monthly meetings of an industrial council, for example, provide a forum for management to keep worker representatives informed about production and employment-related matters affecting them. If employees learn ahead of time of the necessity of layoffs or outsourcing, they may be less likely to take these actions as a breach of trust. Likewise, firms that go to the expense of establishing an employee representation program signal to workers that management sees employee relations as a major concern.

Not only does employee representation strengthen trust, but it communicates to workers that the firm is interested in a longer-term relationship with its employees in which "voice," rather than "exit," is the vehicle for resolving differences. To the extent that employees can voice complaints to management when they are dissatisfied, they have an alternative to quitting (Freeman and Medoff 1984). The ensuing lower turnover lengthens both employee and employer horizons; in a repeated prisoner's dilemma, longer horizons make it easier to support the high-trust outcome of cooperation.

A third example in which employee representation can reduce the costs of motivation in the employment relationship concerns promoting employees' perceptions that they are dealt with fairly. In the face of both cost of job loss and contract terms that are left unspecified, management is provided with an opportunity, and sometimes an incentive, to take actions that employees feel are unfair or exploitative. At the same time, when employees perceive that their reward or treatment is less than that received by comparable others or relative to that justified by work performance, feelings of inequity arise (Adams 1963). The aggrieved party reacts, in turn, by trying to redress the imbalance in perceived effort and rewards, for example, by confronting management with a demand for shorter hours or reducing their level of work effort.

In traditionally organized firms, no formal voice mechanism exists for employees to present grievances to management, nor does there exist a formal judicial process within the firm to assure due process in the resolution of disputes. The consequence, particularly in poorly managed firms, can be high employee resentment, which reduces productivity and increases turnover.

Employee representation is one mechanism that can help firms develop and maintain a sense of fair dealing and equitable treatment among the employees. It does this in two ways. One is that an employee representation plan, such as a peer review dispute resolution panel or a joint industrial council, provides a formal structure through which employees can voice complaints and seek redress. The second is that workers have greater faith in the fairness of the process when some of their peers serve as members of the body that hears the evidence and renders a decision. Substantial evidence indicates that these forms of voice can enhance individuals' sense of procedural justice; moreover, perceptions of procedural justice increase employee commitment and effort (Lind and Tyler 1988).

Ensuring that employees perceive procedures as fair will probably have its largest effect on or-ganizational citizenship behaviors (OCB) and other forms of activity that are not necessarily part of a job description (Organ 1988). Organizational citizenship behaviors are above and beyond the call of duty that are discretionary and are not rewarded by an organization's formal reward structure. A number of studies have found that OCB is higher when employees perceive more fairness, especially procedural justice (e.g., Farh, Podsakoff, and Organ 1990; Konovsky and Pugh 1994; Moorman 1991). Other studies provide fairly consistent evidence that OCB relates to organizational performance (e.g., MacKenzie, Podsakoff, and Fetter 1991; MacKenzie, Ahearne, and Podsakoff, 1997). The implication is that organizations have an incentive to maintain what employees perceive to be a fair employment contract. Given employee representation's positive effects on perceptions of fair procedures, this link to higher discretionary effort provides an additional benefit to employers.

Finally, many employees like to participate in decisions (Lawler 1986). To the extent that employee representation provides opportunities for these employees to participate, it can raise their motivation and utility. Employers may also be able to improve their sorting of employees if ER provides a subset of employees' exposure to higher-level tasks and managers. For example, NUMMI, an auto assembly plant famous for high levels of employee involvement, frequently promotes members of an important ER team of union members—the "Pilot Team"—into lower levels of management (Levine 1995).

Reduce Supervisor Opportunism

Motivation issues arise for supervisors as well as for employees. In the communication network of the hierarchical organization described above, efficiency declines when the reports assembled and passed on by agents at one layer of the hierarchy are inaccurate or biased. In the presence of imperfect information and different preferences on the part of superiors and subordinates it is typically impossible to construct an incentive mechanism that perfectly aligns the interests of owners and mid-level managers (Barney and Ouchi 1986; Miller 1992). The result is that mid-level managers opportunistically engage in acts that promote their interests at the expense of top executives and owners, a process known as moral hazards.

The supervisors and foremen are at the interface of the conflict of interest that exists between management and workers over the pace of work, the assignment of job tasks, the evaluation of performance, and the administration of discipline. Because supervisors and foremen are evaluated, in part, on the achievement of higher production and lower cost, as well as the fact that many prefer to exercise unilateral authority over subordinates, their treatment of production workers can sometimes be arbitrary or self-interested. The result can be higher costs resulting from higher employee turnover, lower work effort, and even production sabotage.

In a world of perfect information, top executives would immediately detect these deviations from firm policy and stop them. But with imperfect information, front-line supervisors can indulge their own preferences by imposing overly harsh discipline or unequal treatment, while disguising from top management the negative responses from production workers.

It is not surprising, in this light, that front-line foremen and supervisors have typically been the people in the management hierarchy that have most strenuously opposed employee representation (Burton 1926). Employee representation gives production workers a direct channel of communication to upper-level management and a way to report heavy-handed or inequitable treatment by supervisors and foremen. Employee representation can thus reduce firms' problems that arise when supervisors use private information to promote their individual interests.

The Costs of Employee Representation

Firms' demand for employee representation depends on its costs as well as its benefits. In this section we briefly consider the determinants of both the direct and indirect sources of employee representation's marginal cost.

Direct costs include the compensation of employees for the time they spend in training and in meetings, the implicit rental of the office space they use, the cost of distributing documents, the costs of consultants, and so forth.

Indirect costs of involving employee representatives in decisions can occur when decision making is slowed and when managers lose flexibility. Indirect costs can also include higher labor costs. For example, firms that institute an employee representation system are often making an investment for purposes of achieving greater trust and cooperation with the workforce. As a way to signal their good intentions, and to further cement the bonds of loyalty and goodwill, they may also decide to pay above-market wages and benefits (Akerlof 1982). In addition, when firms utilize a plant- or companywide form of nonunion representation council or committee, they are shifting the locus of wage determination, at least in part, from an individual basis to a collective basis. Even in a nonunion situation, workers as a group typically possess more bargaining power vis-à-vis management than they do as individuals.

Costs and benefits of employee representation also depend on whether employee representation hinders or facilitates the organization of employees by an independent labor union. We discuss this complex issue after sketching out the basic model.

Equilibrium and Comparative Statics

Equation 1 at the beginning of this chapter defined the firm's equilibrium level of employee representation. This same equilibrium condition can be represented graphically, as in Figure 7.1. The vertical axis measures both the monetary return and cost of a unit of employee representation services; the horizontal axis measures units of ER services used by the firm. A representative marginal revenue product (demand) curve for ER services is given by the line D; a representative ER marginal cost (supply) curve is given by S. The demand curve has a rising and then falling portion, illustrating that in this hypothetical firm additional units of ER at first yield increasing returns in production, followed later by diminishing returns. The supply curve slopes upward, illustrating that higher levels of ER lead to increasing marginal costs of employee representation, on the presumption that as ER becomes more formal and extensive in the firm, both the direct and indirect unit costs rise (e.g., going from a joint safety committee to a companywide industrial council brings with it higher wage and benefit payments). The intersection of the demand and supply curve, at the point where the marginal cost (V_1) and marginal revenue product (MRP_1) of ER are equal, yields the firm's profit maximizing level of employee representation, ER_1.

The demand and supply curves for employee representation services will vary across firms, market structures, and macroeconomic environments, giving rise to both cross-section and time-series variation in the extent of employee representation. The prior discussion of the determinants of the benefits and costs of employee representation imply a number of predictions about the cross-section and time-series variation in ER. Here are some examples.

Large Scale of Production

Economies of scale are a source of market imperfection and give rise to large-size organizations. As organizations increase in size, their coordination costs rise. In addition, the costs of direct forms of employee participation become larger or, to state it the other way, indirect forms of employee representation become increasingly cost effective. Other things equal, therefore, the demand for some form of nonunion employee representation increases with the size of the economic organization.

Greater Complexity of Production

Employee representation yields a larger marginal product in certain types of production processes. Where production is technologically complex or knowledge intensive, for example, tasks often cannot be tightly specified or monitored by management. Management therefore has an incentive to set up forms of employee representation to improve coordination. Employee representation also can play a larger role in motivation because employees have task-specific knowledge and information that managers need. Thus, nonpecuniary incentives can be important to promote feelings of equity among employees and thus increased effort and knowledge revelation.

Figure 7.1 **Demand and Supply of ER Services**

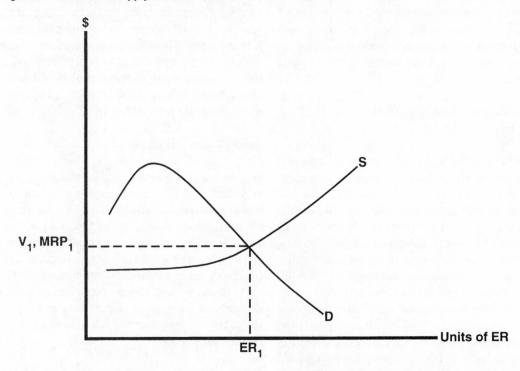

Interdependent (Team) Forms of Production

Employee representation also has a larger marginal product in production processes characterized by significant interdependencies and nonseparabilities. In such situations, the level of production of each individual worker is dependent on the work effort and conscientiousness of the others in the work group or team (Alchian and Demsetz 1972). This interdependency gives rise to a form of externality and free-rider problem in production, since lack of work effort on one person's part affects the performance of the others. One method management has to solve the externality problem is to create some form of

employee representational body. This body can facilitate an interchange of information (thus helping identify free riders) and the promulgation and enforcement of work norms (thus providing a sanction against free riders).

Working Conditions and Employment Practices Subject to the Public-Goods Problem

Employee representation may also help firms gain more accurate knowledge about employee preferences regarding working conditions and employment practices in the company. As noted above, many working conditions and employment practices have a public-goods aspect because they affect workers as a group, are nonexcludable in coverage, and are thus subject to the free-rider problem. Examples include health and safety hazards and calculation of team-based gain-sharing bonuses. Because of the free-rider problem, employees are inhibited from fully revealing their desired levels and types of working conditions and employment practices, leading to dissatisfaction on their part with existing practices and consequent problems for the firm, such as high turnover rates and low work effort. The problem of discovering employee preferences is compounded for firms by factors such as heterogeneous worker preferences and firm-specific working conditions and employment practices (so no market data exists on their value to workers). Employee representation helps solve the free-rider problem by providing a mechanism for group expression of employee preferences and also helps firms identify the extent of diversity in employee preferences (i.e., identifying the mean and variance of the distribution of preferences). For these reasons, firms with a larger proportion of working conditions and employment practices subject to a significant public-goods problem are also those most likely to find some form of employee representation to be a worthwhile investment.

Employees Are a Strategic Asset

Wherever labor is crucial to the long-run success of the business enterprise, management will have a greater incentive to invest time and resources into good employer-employee relations. Important determinants of the tenor of employer-employee relations are perceptions of employees that the firm listens to them, they have an opportunity to participate in decisions affecting the performance of their jobs, and the firm deals with them in a fair and equitable manner. All of these attributes are potentially enhanced by some form of employee representation.

Imperfectly Competitive Product Markets

Firms that operate in imperfectly competitive product markets (e.g., oligopoly) typically earn higher profits. Because work effort and commitment are influenced by perceptions of equity, these firms often find it in their self-interest to share a portion of above-normal profits in the form of higher wages in order to enhance employee motivation (Groshen 1991). This can be done through various types of gain-sharing programs, but often firms find that the payoff is larger if employees are allowed to participate in the design and administration of these programs (enhanced procedural justice). One convenient vehicle for doing so is some form of employee representation.

Internal Labor Markets

The marginal product of employee representation is likely to be higher in firms with well-developed internal labor markets. Internal labor markets typically arise where employees' skills are company specific and acquired through on-the-job training (Williamson, Wachter, and Harris 1975). Since such employees are not readily obtainable from external labor markets, companies hire new workers into entry-level jobs and then promote them to higher, more responsible jobs as they acquire the necessary skills and training. Important features of internal labor markets are that employees tend to have a long tenure with the firm; the existence of specialized, company-specific skills creates a condition of bilateral monopoly between the worker and employer; and firms have more discretion over pay rates and other human resource management practices. All of these conditions make it important that management pay particular attention to maintaining positive employee morale and motivation, because poorly motivated workers will be with the firm a long time, and the costs of exit are large for both workers and firms. One method firms with well-developed internal labor markets are likely to find attractive for this purpose is employee representation, since it fosters cooperation and fair dealing through joint communication and decision making.

High-Performance Human Resource Management Practices

Studies find that successful employee participation and involvement programs are seldom stand-alone activities but are part of a larger system of complementary human resource management practices (Levine and Tyson 1990; Huselid 1995). The same can be expected of employee representation programs. The productivity gains from employee representation are dependent not only on the level of ER services used in production but also on the level of complementary HR practices that support and promote cooperation, fair dealing, and gain sharing. These human resource practices, such as a formal dispute resolution system, profit-sharing, team-based forms of production, and an egalitarian culture, interact synergistically and thus are typically found as a package or bundle in modern high-performance workplaces. Where such HR practices are found, and particularly in larger-size work units, one can predict (*ceteris paribus*) that some form of employee representation body is also more likely to be present.

Full Employment

Nonunion forms of employee representation are more successful in a full-employment macroeconomic environment. When substantial involuntary unemployment exists in labor markets, employers can use the threat of job loss to motivate employee work effort and loyalty. Not only does the threat of job loss provide an alternative source of motivation, it is typically less costly to implement than high-performance human resource practices, such as profit-sharing and employee representation. Conversely, during periods of full employment the threat of job loss loses its motivational force and firms must find another, more positive inducement to attract and retain employees and get them to work hard. One such approach is to use high-performance HR practices, such as employee representation, to motivate workers by appealing to their sense of mutual gain and shared enterprise.

Macroeconomic Stability

Cyclical instability in the macroeconomy reduces the financial payoff firms gain from employee representation. Successful employee representation requires considerable up-front investment in training, management time, and legal and organizational development consulting services, while the payoff is only realized later—often many years later. The size of the payoff, in turn, is heavily dependent on creation and maintenance of a spirit of cooperation, gain-sharing, and fair treatment. When the macroeconomy slides into recession, firms often have little choice but to institute layoffs, wage reductions, and other cost-saving measures. Not only do these measures weaken the spirit of cooperation and fair dealing built up at much expense, but they also result in the loss of the firm's investment in ER to the extent that the employees who have received training are let go.

Unions and the Demand for Employee Representation

To this point we have examined firms' demand for employee representation solely as a function of the contribution employee representation makes to production. But firms may adopt ER for non-production reasons. One example is government mandate, a second is to thwart the organization of the firm's workforce by an independent labor union. It is the latter motive we examine in more detail in this section.

An independent labor union is an alternative form of employee representation that can either serve as a substitute or complement to a nonunion form of ER. Labor unions also act as an agent for employees in dealing with the employer. But their goals, structure, and mode of operation are quite different. Nonunion forms of ER, for example, are established and operated by employers and have as their central objective greater profit. Independent labor unions, in contrast, are formed by employees and operate to further the interests of employees rather than the interests of the firm's owners (although the two interests are to some extent complementary). Both forms of ER have the potential to redistribute revenues from profits to wages, but the probable amount of redistribution is substantially greater with a union because of its greater amount of collective bargaining power and its objective of promoting employees' welfare rather than the firm's.

Labor unions can improve the efficiency of firm production for the same reasons that nonunion forms of employee representation do (Freeman and Medoff 1984). To the extent that the benefits of ER depend on credible commitments from the firm, labor unions may actually have a larger impact on productivity because of their power to enforce employer compliance and the legal enforceability of written agreements. These benefits notwithstanding, nearly all firms, at least in North America, desire to remain union free and resist efforts of unions to organize their workers. This opposition is partly because most employers believe that unionization leads, on net, to reduced profits—a conclusion supported by most academic research (Addison and Hirsch 1997). In addition, most managers prefer to maintain their prerogatives and to avoid the adversarialism they associate with collective bargaining.

To avoid unionization, employers utilize two different strategies, or a mix thereof. The first is *union substitution*; the second is *union suppression* (Kochan and Katz 1988). Union substitution is a positive approach that endeavors to prevent unionization by removing the sources of employee dissatisfaction, such as low wages, job insecurity, and harsh treatment. Union suppression, on the other hand, is a negative approach that prevents unionization largely through fear and intimidation—say, by firing unionist activists and spreading rumors of moral turpitude about the union leaders.

Nonunion employee councils and committees can be utilized as part of either type of union-avoidance strategy (Kaufman 1999). A company pursuing a union-substitution strategy, for example, may create various representational committees and councils to promote improved communication between management and the workers, provide an opportunity for greater employee involvement in workplace decision making, and ensure a more equitable resolution of employment disputes. These uses of nonunion representational bodies typically promote not only greater efficiency and profit for employers but also a more equitable and satisfying workplace for employees.

Nonunion representational bodies can also be part of a union-suppression program. Employers, for example, may quickly establish an employee committee once they learn that a union organizing drive has commenced, not for purposes of improving the long-run quality of labor relations, but to buy time to defeat the union. Committees can facilitate this goal in a number of ways, such as serving as a base to learn the identity of union activists, for spreading procompany propaganda or disinformation about the union, and as a belated (but false) signal that the employer intends to deal with the sources of employee dissatisfaction.

Both types of union avoidance create an increased demand for nonunion ER by employers. At the same time, committees can create a collective identity among workers and provide a focal point for expressions of employee discontent, a training ground for worker leaders, and an organizing base for outside unions. In some instances, when the employer's union-avoidance program alienates the workers, they are able quickly to turn a nonunion council into a launching pad for unionization (Summers 1997; Taras 1998). For these reasons, some employers perceive that nonunion forms of ER can promote unionization, rather than retard it, and this belief reduces their demand for ER.

Two conclusions emerge from this analysis. First, economic theory does not predict whether employers' desire to avoid unions will, on net, increase or decrease their use of nonunion employee representation. Second, the economic and social ramifications of nonunion representation for union avoidance differs depending on whether employers pursue a substitution or suppression strategy. The former is far more likely to benefit the interests of both employers and employees, while the latter benefits employers at the expense of workers. At the same time, differentiating employers' motives for ER is not easy.

Private Versus Social Optima of Nonunion Employee Representation

Absent legal regulation to either encourage or restrict its use, the amount of nonunion ER available in the economy is determined by firms in their pursuit of maximum profit. An important question to consider is whether this level of nonunion ER is also optimal for economic efficiency and social welfare.

An individual firm decides on the profit-maximizing level of employee representation by comparing the marginal benefit and the marginal cost of an additional unit, where the benefit and cost include only those that accrue to the firm. Positive or negative externalities can cause the marginal benefits and costs of ER experienced by society to diverge systematically from those experienced by firms, leading to either an undersupply or oversupply of nonunion ER relative to the social optima.

There are a number of reasons why a competitive, free market system may produce either too little or too much nonunion employee representation. Listed below are seven of the most important. The first six result in an undersupply of nonunion employee representation, while the seventh leads to an oversupply relative to the social optima.

Prisoner's Dilemma Problems

As earlier noted, one reason firms adopt employee representation is to overcome prisoner's dilemma problems arising from a low trust–low cooperation syndrome between the firm and its workers.

But the very adoption of employee representation may itself be hampered by the same prisoner's dilemma problem. That is, both management and workers must trust that once they enter into an employee representation program the other side will not use ER in an opportunistic way to increase their short-run gain at the expense of the other. Workers, for example, may believe that once they share ideas, the firm will renege on its commitment to the ER program and increase the pace of work without sharing the gains. Alternatively, they may fear that employers will only go through the motions of empowerment with no change in working conditions. Conversely, firms may fear that once they empower workers through an ER program that the employees will treat the improved working conditions as an entitlement, and the program will cease to improve motivation. Because of these fears, in some situations the firm will decide not to adopt ER, even though from a social perspective doing so would increase economic efficiency.

These problems are amplified by a negative externality created by the actions of employers. Each employer that sets up a poorly conceived ER plan, or that establishes one largely to avoid an independent union, hurts the credibility of other employers' plans.

Adverse Selection

Firms that adopt an employee representation program typically modify or attenuate traditional "hire and fire" employment-at-will policies standard at other, traditional firms. Because of the promise of increased job security and fair dealing in matters of discipline, these firms will attract numerous job applicants. The problem for an ER firm is that a disproportionate share of the job applicants will be "lemon" employees who are at risk of being dismissed for lower performance—a process known as *adverse selection* (Levine 1995). Such employees are attracted to this firm because of its more lenient policies in dismissal. Unless government policy mandates similar employment practices at other firms, ER firms will end up with a more problem-prone workforce. The result is reduced incentive to adopt employee representation in the first place.

Workplace Safety

To the extent that a safer workplace has positive externalities, and employee safety committees can raise safety, the free market will underprovide safety committees. Underprovision of safety may be due to incomplete experience rating of workers' compensation and disability insurance, market imperfections, or the fact that some employees have no health insurance. In such cases, third parties will often bear some of the costs engendered by deficient safety and health conditions in firms. Eliminating third-party subsidization of health cost, say, by forming a nonunion safety committee that improves safety and health conditions, will benefit society but is often not in the individual interest of firms. In addition, workplace injuries can lead to psychic costs that citizens bear when they know their compatriots are injured at work, but this social cost is also disregarded by profit-maximizing firms.

Unemployment and Macroeconomic Instability

Conditions of involuntary unemployment and cyclical instability in the macroeconomic environment can also reduce the incentive for firms to adopt employee representation relative to that which would exist in a more stable, high-employment economy (Levine 1992). As previously described, with involuntary unemployment, the threat of job loss provides the firm with an alternative, often cheaper way to motivate current employees to work hard. Likewise, frequent and/or deep recessions reduce the expected value of the firm's return on enhanced equity and trust building because layoffs and other cutbacks inevitably corrode the spirit of cooperation that ER systems are meant to promote.

Industrial Democracy

It is a widely held belief in most Western industrial countries (and many others) that all employees deserve certain democratic rights related to due process, fair dealing, and freedom of association. Although nonunion firms with employee representation systems do not provide as strong a protection of these rights as do independent trade unions and government legislation, generally the number and enforcement of such rights is greater with employee representation than without. From a social perspective, therefore, it may be desirable that some nonunion firms that do not find employee representation profit-maximizing nevertheless provide representation to increase rights at work.

Bargaining Problems

Employee representation may increase productivity for the firm yet still not be adopted if the private costs of employee representation for the firm rise even more. A prime concern in this regard is that strengthened ER will increase the bargaining power of workers and allow them to capture more of the surplus (rents) of the firm (Levine 1995; Freeman and Lazear 1995). In effect, from the firm's perspective the growth in

the size of the "pie" from ER is more than outweighed by larger share of the pie going to labor. In this case, a profit-maximizing management rationally forgoes employee representation. But from a social perspective the calculus looks different because although the employer sees higher wages as a cost, from a social point of view they simply redistribute from one factor input to another. Thus, in this case, free-market forces will lead to an undersupply of ER relative to what is optimal for society.

Union Avoidance

The bargaining problem implies that companies may inefficiently provide too little employee representation if ER increases employer bargaining power. Conversely, companies may provide inefficiently too much employee representation to maximize employer bargaining power if the representation reduces the probability of unionization.

As noted earlier, some nonunion firms will establish employee representation largely to remain nonunion, even though the employee representation does not contribute to greater production efficiency or to employee satisfaction. Whenever the costs of union avoidance outweigh any efficiency costs of unions, then the cost of resources used to provide ER services in these firms is greater than the social benefit. At the same time, from the private perspective of firms, the benefit of remaining union-free may justify the costs. The divergence between social and private calculations is due to the fact that higher union wages are an expense to the firm, but are in many cases an income transfer from a social point of view. Thus, union avoidance may cause nonunion firms to provide more ER services than is warranted on the basis of social benefit and cost.

* *

Underconsumptionist Arguments Against Nonunion Employee Representation

In the 1930s, Senator Robert Wagner and allies argued that nonunion forms of representation impose an additional cost on society that is not factored into firms' calculation of private benefit and cost. They believed that the Great Depression was caused by lack of consumer purchasing power and that the slump was then exacerbated by a cascading series of wage and price cuts—a deflationary process they called "destructive competition" (Kaufman 1996). Wagner thought a solution to both underconsumption and destructive competition was to promote greater trade unionism and collective bargaining. The logic is that union bargaining power redistributes income from profits to wages (raising consumption) and, in a recession, puts a floor under wages and prices (ending harmful deflation). Because, in Wagner's view, nonunion forms of representation retard the spread of trade unionism, they at the same time promote both underconsumption and destructive competition. Although he did not use the language, in today's terms one would phrase his arguments that nonunion employee representation plans create a negative externality; thus, they should be restricted by public policy.

Most modern-day economists (e.g., Mitchell 1986; Bernstein 1987) dismiss underconsumption and destructive competition arguments for the Great Depression, so Wagner's macroeconomic rationale for banning nonunion employee representation finds sparse support from this quarter (but see Sherman 1991). Moreover, it is not even clear if nonunion forms of representation do indeed impede union growth, as noted above. Nevertheless, Wagner's macroeconomic arguments

were highly influential in 1935 in gaining Congressional support for banning most forms of nonunion employee representation in the NLRA.

* *

Policy Implications

Governments in the industrial world have adopted very different policy stances toward nonunion employee representation. For example, the United States restricts nonunion employee representation; Japan and Canada take a more neutral "hands-off" position; while the continental European countries require or highly encourage employers above a modest size to have a nonunion form of employee representation (usually a works council). In this section we consider what the theory developed in this chapter implies about the advantages and disadvantages of each approach. We also consider what (if any) government policies or regulations could improve the operation and social benefits of nonunion employee representation.

No to Universal and Compulsory Employee Representation

Mandatory companywide or establishmentwide nonunion employee representation programs, either in the form of works councils in various countries of Europe, some form of joint industrial council as found in certain Canadian firms, or the "employee representation committees" proposed by Weiler (1990) for the United States, are not likely to be justifiable on strictly economic terms. The reason is that in many employment relationships it is unlikely that the improvements in productivity or justice outweigh the economic costs from employee representation programs.

The productivity gain from plant or companywide employee representation committees can be less than the costs for several reasons. One, for example, has to do with the nature of the production process. In lines of business where production is low-tech, work tasks are relatively simple, and individual work performance is easily measured and monitored, the coordination and motivation effects of employee representation (and employee participation more generally) may add little value. A second is that as the size of the representational body becomes larger, individual employees lose a sense of direct participation and ownership in its operation and, hence, the motivational impact of employee representation is progressively attenuated (Cotton 1993). The effectiveness of employee representation also depends in part on the presence of other high-involvement work practices, such as gain-sharing and an egalitarian culture, but only a subset of firms find it profitable to adopt the complete system. Finally, historical evidence indicates that firms that are compelled by government edict to implement employee representation systems rarely devote sufficient time, attention, and resources to make them successful (see the Kaufman chapter in this volume).

Employee representation in very large organizations can also be problematic. While to some degree there are economies of scale in the operation of employee representation programs (e.g., average fixed costs of employee representation may fall due to the spreading of overhead costs), sources of increasing direct and indirect costs probably soon dominate at many firms. Larger-size employee representation programs, for example, tend to be more formal and bureaucratic and take longer to deliberate and reach decisions. Equally of concern to firms, they tend to become more involved in, and impinge upon, strategic business issues. From a social perspective some of these costs, such as the redirection of firm investment expenditures toward lower-return activities, may be very costly.

Given these considerations, an economic case for mandatory plant or companywide employee representation councils has to rest on some type of argument of a public good or positive externality nature. As previously elaborated, an unregulated, competitive market system may undersupply the socially optimal amount of employee representation. While this suggests a case for public encouragement of nonunion employee representation at the margin, it does not suggest that universal mandates for employee representation will be cost effective.

Proponents of mandatory employee representation councils or committees also cite noneconomic rationales, however. Some maintain, for example, that every employee should as a matter of basic human right have some form of representation at the workplace (Adams and Friedman, 1998). Others argue, as previously noted, that employee representation in the workplace has positive external effects by educating and training the workforce in democratic values and processes. These arguments cannot be evaluated by economic analysis and thus ultimately rest on the social and political philosophy ascribed to by the citizens of each country. It appears that this type of noneconomic argument is compelling in many European countries that have a relatively strong social democratic ethos but is much less so in Anglo-Saxon countries with their stronger tradition of individualism. Consistent with this last observation is recent survey evidence that a significant number of American workers do not desire formal, large-size forms of employee representation (Freeman and Rogers 1999). At the same time, 90 percent of those with opinions wanted to have more involvement at work.

Universal and compulsory employee representation will hit some workplaces where the costs are high, and others where the benefits are low—

ideally, we want targeting to just those workplaces where the benefits outweigh the costs. This targeting can be improved by mandating employee representation only when the benefits are likely to be high, and by providing marginal incentives that permit employers to self-select when costs are low relative to benefits.

Selectively Mandate Employee Representation When the Benefits Are High

A greater case can be made for mandatory employee representation committees focused on specific workplace issues. The best example is some form of joint management-labor safety and health committee. The argument in favor of mandatory safety and health committees rests on the twin propositions that market imperfections lead to a significant undersupply of workplace safety and health in firms and that some form of joint management-labor employee representation committee is the most efficient method to correct this deficiency. With regard to the first, market imperfections such as imperfect information, restricted worker mobility, and externalities are likely to lead to a suboptimal provision of safety and health in the labor market (Burton and Chelius 1997). This conclusion is supported by research that often finds negligible compensating wage differentials for risk of injury and death (Brown 1980). Whether employee representation safety committees should be mandatory across all workplaces, or only a subset, depends on the extent to which these market failures affect all types of occupations and industries. The productivity payoff may be sufficiently small in certain low-risk industries, such as retail trade and financial services, that an argument can be made to exempt them, while all firms in, say, the mining, construction, and

manufacturing industries are required to have committees. In fact, the safety committees that are mandated by workers' compensation insurers typically follow this pattern (OSHA 1995).

Theory suggests that a regulatory approach that relies on targeted levels of safety and health performance ("output" measures), plant-level worker-management cooperation, and involvement of shopfloor employees is likely to outperform a system of mandated government standards on a myriad of specific workplace practices ("input" measures), periodic plant visits by government inspectors, and punitive fines for violations (Levine 1997). This conclusion is buttressed by empirical evidence (Watchman 1994) that joint labor-management safety committees, as mandated in thirteen American states, have typically led to greater improvements in workplace safety and health than has the federal government's system of inspections and fines as practiced by the Occupational Safety and Health Administration (OSHA).

A second area of workplace practice that some form of mandatory employee representation be justified on economic efficiency grounds is the resolution of employment disputes. As with safety and health, theory suggests that market imperfections will cause individual firms to underinvest systematically in resources devoted to the equitable resolution of disputes with employees. Particularly where firms operate under the legal regime of employment-at-will, and workers have general skills that are readily available in the market (say, due to involuntary unemployment), it may be cheaper for the management to terminate an employee with whom it has a dispute or argument and replace him or her with a new hire than to incur the costs of investigation, adjudication, and the possible ill-will of first-line supervisors (Lewin 1997). Noneconomic considerations, such as preserving and exercising management power and control over employees, reinforce this conclusion.

But what is optimal from the perspective of individual firms may well be suboptimal from a social perspective. In particular, as argued by Freeman and Medoff (1984) the "exit" option for resolving disputes entails a number of social costs, including support of unemployed workers during their job search (e.g., unemployment insurance), loss of worker skills, and inculcation of attitudes among both employers and employees that are inimical to trust and cooperation. Hence, from a social perspective, it may be justified on economic grounds to require that all firms implement some form of formal dispute-resolution process. One option might be to require that some form of employee participation and representation be a part of every dispute-resolution process, while another might be to mandate some form of formal dispute resolution but to allow choice over the specific method with some methods being of a nonrepresentative nature (e.g., arbitration, mediation) and others representational (e.g., peer review, ombudsperson). These considerations are then reinforced by noneconomic arguments, such as the belief in a democratic society that provisions for due process in the resolution of workplace disputes should be a guaranteed human right.

Provide Incentives for Greater Employee Representation

A number of situations exist where mandatory employee representation may not be desirable (or politically feasible), but where efficiency can nonetheless be improved by encouraging firms to make greater use of employee representation systems. To promote this end, public policy should provide selective incentives and subsidies that together increase the private benefits and/or reduce the private costs of employee representation to business firms.

Successful high-involvement work practices, for example, typically require much larger expenditures on worker training—expenditures many firms are unwilling to fund fully for fear that once trained, these workers, attracted by higher wage offers, will leave to work at other firms. Possible solutions include greater public funds devoted to workplace training in high-involvement skills, such as is required in operating sophisticated employee representation programs, and a new system of work-skill certification that gives employees a credential attesting to their proficiency in specific skill areas (Levine 1995). The latter provides greater incentives for employees to bear the cost of skill acquisition since the credential provides a more reliable signal to employers as to the person's actual level of skill, a fact that should translate into improved job offers.

Another set of policies that would encourage greater adoption of employee representation programs are those aimed at maintaining full employment and reducing turnover and layoffs. As previously noted, the cyclical "boom and bust" of the macroeconomy undermines firms' incentives to invest in employee representation, as does the presence of a substantial amount of involuntary unemployment. Solutions at the macro level include a stronger commitment on the part of fiscal and monetary authorities to maintaining full employment and greater federal funds devoted to reducing structural unemployment through employee relocation and training programs. At a micro level, possible solutions include mandatory "just cause" termination procedures (which would reduce turnover and layoffs at individual firms) and changes in the unemployment insurance system that encouraged job sharing (partial layoffs). Tax subsidies to companies that implement profit sharing may help if they lower the marginal cost of employees (Weitzman 1984; but see Levine 1989).

A third set of policies would be aimed at reducing the short-run focus of capital markets on quarterly and annual profits, a focus that works against firm investment in employee representation programs and other high-involvement work practices that typically have a longer payback period. (Porter 1992 reviews such suggestions.) One proposal that focuses on employee representation is to provide stronger tax incentives to the formation of ESOPs (employee stock ownership plans) only when they provide a mechanism for employee representation in decision making (say, by having one or more seats on the board of directors; Levine 1995). Such limits would reduce ESOPs formed solely for tax advantages and increase their presence at employers that are serious about transforming the workplace. Available evidence suggests only the latter experience productivity improvements from ESOPs.

Discourage Use of Employee Representation as a Union-Avoidance Device

While public policy should encourage nonunion employee representation in some situations, policy should restrict representation that is largely intended to suppress employees' desire for an outside union. To increase the likelihood that firms use nonunion employee representation systems for socially beneficial purposes, the best safeguard is that they face effective competition in both the labor market and the "market" for alternative forms of employee representation (Kaufman 1999). Effective competition in labor markets prevents firms from using nonunion employee representation forms for purposes in-

imical to worker interests because employees can readily quit and find alternative employment. Likewise, if workers can readily replace the employer's form of representation with an alternative—such as a trade union—then the existence of effective competition again protects the workers' interests.

Effective competition in labor markets is best promoted by maintenance of high employment. Appropriate public policy measures include expansionary fiscal and monetary policies and government training and education programs to combat structural forms of unemployment. Competition in labor markets is also promoted by effective antidiscrimination and equal opportunity laws.

To promote effective competition in the market for alternative forms of representation, public policy must ensure that workers are able to exercise relatively free choice with respect to union representation. The provisions in the National Labor Relations Act that create the secret ballot union representation election process and prohibit acts of antiunion discrimination such as dismissal of union activists are significant steps in this direction. Considerable evidence indicates, however, that employers can still thwart employees' desire for union representation because of weak penalties in the NLRA and sometimes lengthy administrative delays in holding elections and adjudicating cases (Commission on the Future of Worker-Management Relations 1994). A good case can be made, therefore, that public policy should increase the financial penalties for antiunion acts of discrimination by employers, speed up the process of holding representation elections, and make it easier for the NLRB to seek immediate injunctive relief in cases of egregious employer misconduct. To reduce further the likelihood that nonunion employee councils and committees are used to avoid a union, the NLRA might also be amended to make it an unfair labor practice for an employer to establish any employee representation body once a union has petitioned for a representation election.

Increase the Effective Operation of Employee Representation Committees

Public policy should also aim to improve the operation of nonunion forms of employee representation. The theoretical analysis presented earlier in this chapter indicates that one of the most important obstacles in this regard is each party's fear of opportunism. This fear adversely affects the desire of both management and workers to implement and participate fully in an employee representation system, but it is typically a greater consideration on the employee side because they are frequently the more vulnerable and less powerful of the two parties. As described earlier, the employment relationship has strong elements of a prisoner's dilemma game. By cooperating, both workers and the firm can gain an improved outcome and the larger share available to each is the incentive to do so. But workers are often reluctant to commit fully to the cooperative outcome because they fear management will renege on the sharing of benefits and costs when it is to the firm's advantage to do so (e.g., as when a firm abrogates a no-layoff pledge because of a sudden slump in sales). For this reason, employee representation systems are prone to suboptimal performance and often have a short life span.

The problem of opportunism stems from the incomplete nature of the employment contract, which is further exacerbated from the perspective of employees by the employment-at-will doctrine that makes employer promises noncredible. One way to reduce employer opportunism is to enforce employer commitments to employees. For example,

public policy might stipulate that firms are free to decide voluntarily whether or not to establish a form of employee representation, but if they choose to do so, the employee representation plan must meet certain minimum standards. These standards might include written procedures for selection of employee representatives; a written statement delineating the purpose of the employee representation plan, the range of workplace issues subject to joint consultation, and the process for resolution of disputes. A proposal along this line is by Richard Edwards (1997). He argues that all firms should be legally required to have an employee handbook, that these handbooks spell out procedures for dispute resolution, handling of grievances, and so on, and that they be considered by the courts as legally binding contracts. Employee representation systems would be one of the employment practices covered in the handbooks.

Conclusions

Nonunion forms of employee representation have received relatively little attention by economists. This chapter has endeavored to move the economic analysis of employee representation forward by applying a new conceptual framework to the issue. This framework is transaction cost economics. We treat employee representation as a factor input, and the decision facing the firm is how much of this factor input to utilize in production. As with other inputs, this choice turns on a comparison of benefits and costs.

The attractiveness of the transaction cost model is that it identifies certain key aspects of the employer-employee relationship that influence the benefits and costs of employee representation. Then we use these insights to derive comparative static predictions about the cross-section and time-series variation in employee representation forms, and to identify reasons why a free-market system probably underproduces employee representation (with the important exception that union avoidance can lead to inefficiently high nonunion representation).

We also use these insights to derive a number of policy conclusions. Our analysis suggests that social welfare is promoted by making available to firms and workers a wide range of alternative forms of representation, including no representation. Doing so will help close the gap in the amount of representation available at the workplace and the amount employees desire (Freeman and Rogers 1999). We thus favor revisions in the National Labor Relations Act to permit greater use of nonunion forms of representation. In addition, we advocate selective incentives to encourage such representation where the social benefits are likely to be particularly high. We do not believe, however, that a compelling case can be made on efficiency grounds that representation should be universally mandated.

Effective competition is crucial to the successful performance of nonunion forms of representation. Thus, we also favor a relaxation of the NLRA's ban on most forms of nonunion representation only if accompanied by measures that strengthen the act's protection of workers' right to organize. That is, workers need relatively free and unobstructed ability to obtain independent representation in order to ensure that employers structure and operate nonunion forms of ER in ways that serve the interests of both parties.

References

Adams, Roy, and Sheldon Friedman, 1998. "The Emerging International Consensus on Human Rights in Employment." *Perspectives on Work* 2, no. 2: 24–27.

Adams, Stacy. 1963. "Toward an Understanding of Inequity." *Journal of Abnormal and Social Psychology* 67: 422–436.

Addison, John, and Barry Hirsch. 1997. "The Economic Effects of Employment Regulation: What Are the Limits?" In *Government Regulation of the Employment Relationship*, ed. Bruce E. Kaufman, pp. 125–178. Madison: Industrial Relations Research Association.

Akerlof, George. 1982. "Labor Contracts as Partial Gift Exchange." *Quarterly Journal of Economics* 97, no. 4: 543–569.

Alchian, Armen, and Harold Demsetz. 1972. "Production, Information, and Economic Organization." *American Economic Review* 62 (December): 77–95.

Barney, Jay, and William Ouchi. 1986. "Agency Theory." In *Organizational Economics*, ed. Jay Barney and William Ouchi. San Francisco: Jossey-Bass.

Ben-Ner, Avner, and Derek Jones. 1995. "Employee Participation, Ownership, and Productivity: A Theoretical Framework." *Industrial Relations* 34, no. 4: 532–554.

Bernstein, Michael. 1987. *The Great Depression: Delayed Recovery and Economic Change in America, 1929–1939.* New York: Oxford University Press.

Bishop, Libby, and David I. Levine. 1999. "Computer-Mediated Communication as Employee Voice: A Case Study." *Industrial and Labor Relations Review* 52, no. 2: 213–233.

Boulton, Patrick, and Mathias Dewatripont. 1994. "The Firm as a Communication Network." *Quarterly Journal of Economics* 109, no. 4: 809–839.

Brown, Charles. 1980. "Equalizing Differences in Labor Markets." *Quarterly Journal of Economics* 94, no. 1: 113–134.

Burton, Ernest. 1926. *Employee Representation.* Chicago: Williams and Wilkins.

Burton, John, and James Chelius. 1997. "Workplace Safety and Health Regulations: Rationale and Results." In *Government Regulation of the Employment Relationship*, ed. Bruce E. Kaufman, pp. 253–294. Madison: Industrial Relations Research Association.

Cheung, Steven. 1983. "The Contractual Nature of the Firm." *Journal of Law and Economics* 26 (April): 1–21.

Commission on the Future of Worker-Management Relations. 1994. *Fact-Finding Report.* Washington, D.C.: U.S. Department of Labor and U.S. Department of Commerce.

Commons, John. 1921. *Industrial Government.* New York: Macmillan.

Cotton, John. 1993. *Employee Involvement.* Newbury Park, Calif.: Sage.

Demsetz, Harold. 1995. *The Economics of the Business Firm.* New York: Cambridge University Press.

Edwards, Richard. 1997. "Alternative Regulatory Approaches to Protecting Workers' Rights." In *Govern-*

ment Regulation of the Employment Relationship, ed. Bruce E. Kaufman, pp. 403–428. Madison: Industrial Relations Research Association.

Farh, Jiing-Lih, Philip M. Podsakoff, and Dennis W. Organ. 1990. "Accounting for Organizational Citizenship Behavior: Leader Fairness and Task Scope Versus Satisfaction." *Journal of Management* 16: 705–721.

Freeman, Richard, and Edward Lazear. 1995. "An Economics Analysis of Works Councils." In *Works Councils: Consultation, Representation, and Cooperation in Industrial Relations*, ed. Joel Rogers and Wolfgang Streeck, pp. 27–52. Chicago: University of Chicago Press.

Freeman, Richard, and James Medoff. 1984. *What Do Unions Do?* New York: Basic Books.

Freeman, Richard, and Joel Rogers. 1999. *What Workers Want.* Ithaca, N.Y.: ILR Press.

Groshen, Erica. 1991. "Sources of Inter-Industry Wage Dispersion: How Much Do Employers Matter?" *Quarterly Journal of Economics* 106, no. 3: 869–884.

Hammer, Tove H., Steven C. Currall, and Robert N. Stern. "Worker Representation on Boards of Directors: A Study of Competing Roles." *Industrial and Labor Relations Review* 44 (July): 661–680.

Huselid, Mark. 1995. "The Impact of Human Resource Management Practices on Turnover, Productivity, and Corporate Financial Performance." *Academy of Management Journal* 39, no. 3: 635–672.

Kaufman, Bruce E. 1996. "Why the Wagner Act: Reestablishing Contact with Its Original Purpose." In *Advances in Industrial and Labor Relations*, vol. 7, ed. David Lewin, Bruce Kaufman, and Donna Sockell, pp. 15–68. Greenwich, Conn.: JAI Press.

———. 1999. "Does the NLRA Constrain Employee Involvement and Participation Programs in Nonunion Companies?: A Reassessment." *Yale Law and Policy Review* 17, no. 2: 729–811.

Kochan, Thomas, and Harry Katz. 1988. *Collective Bargaining and Industrial Relations*, 2d ed. Homewood, Ill.: Irwin.

Konovsky, Mary A, and S. Douglas Pugh. 1994. "Citizenship Behavior and Social Exchange." *Academy of Management Journal* 37, no. 3: 656–669.

Lawler, Edward. 1986. *High-involvement Management.* San Francisco: Jossey Bass.

Levine, David I. 1989. "Efficiency Wages in Weitzman's Share Economy." *Industrial Relations* 28, no. 3: 321–334.

———. 1992. "Public Policy Implications of Imperfections in the Market for Worker Participation." *Economic and Industrial Democracy* 13, no. 2: 183–206.

———. 1995. *Reinventing the Workplace.* Washington, D.C.: Brookings Institution.

———. 1997. "They Should Solve Their Own Problems: Reinventing Workplace Regulation." In *Government Regulation of the Workplace*, ed. Bruce E. Kaufman, pp. 475–498. Madison: Industrial Relations Research Association.

Levine, David I., and Laura D'Andrea Tyson. 1990. "Participation, Productivity, and the Firm's Environment." In *Paying for Productivity: A Look at the Evidence*, ed. Alan Blinder, pp. 183–244. Washington, D.C.: Brookings Institution.

Lewin, David. 1997. "Workplace Dispute Resolution." In *Handbook of Human Resource Management*, ed. David Lewin, Daniel Mitchell, and Mahmood Zaidi, pp. 197–218. Greenwich, Conn.: JAI Press.

Lind, E. Allan, and Tom R. Tyler. 1988. *The Social Psychology of Procedural Justice.* New York: Plenum Press.

MacKenzie, Scott, Philip Podsakoff, and Michael Ahearne. 1997. "Moderating Effects of Goal Acceptance on the Relationship Bwtween Group Cohesiveness and Productivity." *Journal of Applied Psychology* 82, no. 6: 974–983.

MacKenzie, S.B., P.M. Podsakoff, and R. Fetter. 1991. "Organizational Citizenship Behavior and Objective Productivity as Determinants of Managerial Evaluations of Salespersons' Performance." *Organizational Behavior and Human Decision Processes* 50, no. 1: 123–150.

Milgrom, Paul, and John Roberts. 1993. *Economics, Organization, and Management.* Englewood Cliffs, N.J.: Prentice Hall.

Miller, Gary. 1992. *Managerial Dilemmas.* New York: Cambridge University Press.

Mitchell, Daniel J.B. 1986. "Inflation, Unemployment, and the Wagner Act: A Critical Reappraisal." *Stanford University Law Review* 38 (April): 1065–1095.

Moorman, Robert H. 1991. "Relationship Between Organizational Justice and Organizational Citizenship Behaviors: Do Fairness Perceptions Influence Employee Citizenship?" *Journal of Applied Psychology* 76, no. 6: 845–855.

Nemeth, Charlan, and P. Owens. 1996. "Making Work Groups More Effective: The Value of Minority Dissent." In *Handbook of Work Group Psychology*, ed. M.A. West, pp. 125–141. London: Wiley.

Organ, D.W. 1988. *Organizational Citizenship Behavior: The Good Soldier Syndrome.* Lexington, Mass.: D.C. Heath.

Occupational Safety and Health Administration (OSHA). 1995. *Review and Analysis of State-Mandated and Other Worker Protection Programs.*

Podsakoff, Philip M., Michael Ahearne, and Scott B. MacKenzie. 1997. "Organizational Citizenship Behavior and the Quantity and Quality of Work Group Performance." *Journal of Applied Psychology* 82, no 2: 262–270.

Porter, Michael, 1992. *Capital Choices*. Washington, D.C.: Council on Competitiveness.

Radner, Roy. 1992. "Hierarchy: The Economics of Managing." *Journal of Economic Literature* 30 (September): 1382–1415.

Radner, Roy, and Jacob Marschak. 1972. *The Economic Theory of Teams*. New Haven: Yale University Press.

Sherman, Howard. 1991. *The Business Cycle: Growth and Crisis Under Capitalism*. Princeton: Princeton University Press.

Summers, Clyde. 1997. "Works Councils in the American System." In *Proceedings of the Forty-ninth Annual Meeting*, pp. 106–112. Industrial Relations Research Association.

Taras, Daphne G. 1998. "Nonunion Representation: Threat or Complement to Unions?" In *Proceedings of the Fif-*

tieth Annual Meeting, pp. 281–290. Industrial Relations Research Association.

Tversky, Amos, and Daniel Kahneman. 1986. "Rational Choice and the Framing of Decisions." *Journal of Business* 59 (October): S251–278.

Watchman, Gregory. 1994. "Safe and Sound: The Case for Safety and Health Committees Under OSHA and the NLRA." *Cornell Journal of Law and Public Policy* 4, no. 3: 65–125.

Weiler, Paul. 1990. *Governing the Workplace*. Cambridge: Harvard University Press.

Weitzman, Martin. 1984. *The Share Economy*. Cambridge: Harvard University Press.

Williamson, Oliver. 1985. *The Economic Institutions of Capitalism*. New York: Free Press.

Williamson, Oliver, Michael Wachter, and Jeffery Harris. 1975. "Understanding the Employment Relation." *Bell Journal of Economics* 6 (Spring): 250–278.

8

Nonunion Representational Forms: An Organizational Behavior Perspective

Tove Helland Hammer

Workplace industrial relations systems serve three functions: conflict resolution and assurance of due process; the supervision, motivation, and participation of individual employees; and the determination and operation of work rules and work organization (Katz and Kochan 1992). When the workforce is unionized, these functions are negotiated between the employer and the union on behalf of the employees. Conflict management and protection of individual rights are ensured through grievance and arbitration procedures defined in a legally binding collective bargaining agreement. The terms of the labor exchange, in the form of the wages and benefits to be paid for hours of work, levels of job performance, work attendance, and adherence to organizational rules, are likewise specified in the contract, as are the ways in which work is designed and is to be distributed among groups of employees. Collective bargaining allows labor and management joint control over the terms and conditions of employment—workers join unions to be able to influence their employers' decisions about hiring and firing, hours and wages, job assignments, and assessment of job performance.

In nonunion work settings, management controls hiring and promotion, the administration of pay and benefits, and the establishment and maintenance of work rules. The employer's power to

act is not unlimited, of course. A series of legal statutes dictate employee rights with respect to equal opportunity, health and safety, unjust discharge, and protection of privacy (Wolkinson and Block 1996; Kaufman 1997). In addition, labor market demands for some workers, such as high-skilled technical employees, give a subset of the labor force leverage in setting their terms of employment. Many employers have also decided that some parts of managerial power should be shared with employees as a means of obtaining their cooperation and commitment to organizational goals or to avoid unionization (see, for example, Kochan, Katz, and McKersie 1986). Despite statutory, labor market, and voluntary constraints on unilateral managerial decision making, however, the nonunionized workplace affords management much more flexibility in setting long-range personnel policies and establishing day-to-day personnel practices.

The purpose of an industrial relations system is to improve organizational performance, usually defined as effectiveness and efficiency; ensure an equitable labor exchange; and provide employees with the opportunity for personal development and well-being (Kaufman 1993). Effectiveness is the degree to which the organization reaches its goals, a state determined by both internal factors and variables in the external environment. Organizations usually have multiple, sometimes conflicting, goals that reflect the interests of different stakeholders, such as stockholders, customers, creditors, and employees. Whether or not an organization is effective depends therefore on the criteria used in the assessment. Efficiency, in contrast, is an indicator of how well the organization functions internally—it has to do with the way the organization utilizes resources and can be thought of as the amount of resources used to produce a given unit (see, for example, Daft 1983; Jones 1998). With equity, I mean a labor exchange that is fair to both employer and employees, with mechanisms for adjusting the terms and conditions of employment when either party believes that it has been, or will be, taken unfair advantage of by the other or when adjustments are deemed necessary by both parties to ensure economic survival and prosperity. The meaning of employee well-being and personal growth is a bit more diffuse, but it includes being treated with dignity and respect in the workplace and having the opportunity to utilize one's abilities and learn new skills as part of employment.

The industrial relations system influences efficiency by creating or facilitating the internal conditions that allow the firm to operate with a workforce that is able and willing to exert effort toward the tasks specified by management, work rules and procedures that maximize production output per unit time, and a minimal amount of labor-management conflict. Whether unions help or hamper organizational efficiency has been hotly debated for many years (see Freeman and Medoff 1984; Addison and Hirsch 1997). There is more agreement with, and less controversy about, the view that unions serve to secure procedural and distributive justice in the workplace and protect workers' rights. With respect to the third goal of industrial relations, employee well-being and

personal growth, few would doubt the unions' commitment to having working men and women treated with dignity and respect, but there has been considerable debate about unions' interest in creating opportunities for psychologically fulfilling work for its members, especially when this has involved direct worker participation in decision making (see, for example, Kochan, Katz, and Mower 1984; AFL-CIO Committee on the Evolution of Work 1985).

In this chapter I examine theoretical and empirical foundations for different forms of nonunion representation from the field of organizational behavior. In particular, I draw from the research in organizational and social psychology and organizational sociology to examine the psychological processes that determine employees' behavior and attitudes in response to a set of industrial relations programs and practices, and the organizational forces that operate on a macro level to determine the effects of nonunion representational forms. One of the questions I address is how a nonunion industrial relations system should function to ensure organizational effectiveness; equity in the employer-employee relations, including the protection of employee rights and due process in the workplace; and personnel policies and practices that encourage labor-management cooperation, employee motivation, commitment, and job satisfaction. The focus of the chapter is on what we can learn about the value to workers and employers of different representation programs or structures from knowledge of psychological and sociological theory and research. I concentrate the analysis on three groups of programs and practices, each intended to serve a different function: (1) direct worker participation in organizational decision making, which should influence worker motivation, the quality of worklife, and employees' contribution to organizational effectiveness;

(2) employee representation (indirect participation) in decision making at the strategic level of the firm, intended to give workers a voice in decisions about broader issues of concern to them, such as the terms and conditions of employment; and (3) dispute-resolution mechanisms intended to secure workplace equity and due process. Where I consider it relevant, I compare these practices and programs with what is available to employees covered by collective bargaining agreements.

The Unitarist Model of Employment Relations

Within the framework of collective bargaining we assume a pluralist model of organizations in which a variety of groups and coalitions coexist, some with divergent interests, some with common goals (Fox 1973). While there is interest-group conflict, it can give way to collaboration and compromise when it is regulated through bargaining and negotiations that follow established rules. This perspective differs from the unitarist model of employment relations on which many policies and practices in the nonunionized workplace is based. Unitarists assume a true communality of interests between employers and employees, or management and labor. They do not deny the existence of labor-management conflict, but hold that conflicts are unnecessary and undesirable and can be avoided once the parties recognize that they share the same goals. In healthy work organizations there should be no need for collective bargaining to counterbalance the employer's power and for an elaborate grievance machinery to manage conflict because in an open, trusting employment relationship based on a communality of interests there will be no exploitation for private gain.[1]

Because interest-group conflict is not seen as an inevitable or even a natural part of the employment relationship in the unitarist model, establishing and maintaining formal systems or sets of procedures to manage conflict or adjudicate individual rights at the workplace have not, until recently, been a prominent feature of employment relations in the unitarist organization. Although many firms, especially larger ones, have human resources management programs designed to handle employee grievances and contain labor-management conflicts (e.g., Mahoney and Watson 1993; Applebaum and Batt 1994; Milkovich and Boudreau 1994), some based on union models of mediation and arbitration (Dunlop and Zack 1997; Stallworth 1997; Bingham 1998; Lipsky and Seeber 1998), the issue of individual rights and grievance processing is downplayed (Kochan, Katz, and McKersie 1986).

In contrast, policies and practices directed at worker motivation and the organization of work are firmly anchored in the unitarist model. The implementation of employee involvement and worker participation schemes, team production, and compensation programs that tie pay to individual, work group, or firm performance is based on the assumption that labor and management have joint interests in maximizing firm productivity and profits. As we later see, theories of work motivation and job satisfaction support the use of programs that include job redesign, high-involvement management, and team-based manufacturing for improving employee attitudes and performance (see, for example, Hackman and Oldham 1980; Lawler 1986; Hammer 1988).

In the following section, I analyze the formal programs and informal structures that involve employees in decisions about how work should be performed at the point of production and how work rules are determined and enforced. I give a brief description of different variants of direct worker participation and present the theories from organizational and social psychology that have either given rise to the programs or that allow us to evaluate program effectiveness. Finally, I ask if these structures afford workers real influence over decision making—that is, whether they are effective voice mechanisms in the nonunion workplace.

Because direct worker participation programs are usually limited to decision making at the shopfloor level, however, it could be argued that they are not a form of "real" worker representation, or at best, a very modest one. The counterargument is that such programs are a potential voice mechanism for the workforce in the sense that they can afford employees the opportunity for influence over decisions about what they do in the workplace and how they do it. In addition, if implemented correctly, the programs serve to improve employees' well-being and personal growth through expanded jobs, higher skill requirements, and opportunities for teamwork and leadership.

To place the analysis of nonunion representational forms in perspective, it is helpful to recall the "representation gap" identified by Freeman and Rogers (1994) in their national-level survey among unorganized private-sector employees. The survey data showed a widespread desire among workers for more involvement in and influence over workplace decisions than they reported they had, particularly with respect to benefits and pay raises. To get it, workers wanted to be represented by a group or an association that could negotiate on their behalf with management. The preferred type of association seemed to be one that would combine some characteristics of unions with those of employee committees found in many employee involvement programs. The ideal association should be independent of management, have elected representatives, and include a grievance system with outside arbitrators to adjudicate disputes that cannot be solved internally. These features are part of the union legacy. However, the association should have management support because workers do not want adversarial labor-management relations, and the employer should provide its budget and staff. The latter requirement makes the model employee association similar to an enterprise union, an illegal entity in the United States. The important aspect of these data is not that unorganized workers want company unions but that they want harmonious and collaborative relations with management and are reluctant to join unions in part because they fear that it will result in conflictive labor relations. Of course, a preference for a nonadversarial employment relationship does not negate the possibility of labor-management interest-group conflict. The fact that there is a representation gap means that workers do not trust their employers to make unilateral decisions about the terms and conditions of employment.

Worker Participation in Organizational Decision Making

The programs and institutions that enable employees' voice to be heard in a formal way within the enterprise differ in the scope of decisions they include, the amount of power workers can exercise vis-à-vis management, and the organizational level at which the decisions are made. Some are purposefully designed to give employees a very modest role in decision making; others are intended to give the workforce a substantial amount of power in organizational governance. Some programs were designed for other purposes, such as increasing worker motivation or staffing flexibility, and have provided opportunities for worker participation as a side benefit.

Worker participation in management can be direct or indirect (through representatives), and can be prescribed by law, established through contracts, or granted by an employer. It is convenient to place the different models or forms of participation in two categories based on their origins—legal statutes and employer grants (Hammer 1996). Legally based or prescribed structures such as worker representation on corporate boards of directors and works councils (in Europe), or collective bargaining, are formal systems with written rules and regulations that provide uniform guidelines for involving workers in decision making in all organizations that come under the jurisdiction of the law or contract. Employer granted or initiated participation usually does not specify employees' legal rights to be involved in decision making. To the extent that formal written agreements exist in granted programs, they are specific to a given enterprise. Examples of granted participation are shopfloor employee involvement programs; labor-management committees like the ones found in productivity gain-sharing plans; and autonomous, or self-directed, work teams.

Direct Participation

Two sets of theoretical arguments have been used to legitimate direct worker participation, *human growth and development theories* and a *productivity and efficiency* rationale (Dachler and Wilpert 1978). *Human growth and development theories* suggest that people have a psychological need to develop to their full potential and become independent, active, self-controlled individuals engaged in continuous learning. This need can be met, in part, in jobs that are intrinsically interesting and challenging and give the worker autonomy and responsibility. Direct worker participation can satisfy psychological growth

needs and by doing so increase worker motivation and job performance (McGregor 1960; Likert 1961; Argyris 1964). The theories emphasize how work should be organized and organizational structures should be created to facilitate the psychological growth of the individual worker. Worker participation is one means for doing so, but not the only one (Dachler and Wilpert 1978). The basic assumption underlying the theories is that workers have untapped energy and talent that will be released in the employer's service when opportunities for participation are available.

The *productivity and efficiency* rationale is an assumption that worker involvement in decision making will increase individual productivity and job satisfaction and decrease absenteeism and turnover because workers will develop a commitment to organizational goals and feel that they have a stake in the organization's future (Coch and French 1948; Morse and Reimer 1956). In addition, improved communication and coordination within and across work groups can contribute to increased efficiency (Hackman 1990).

The Motivation to Work and Job Redesign

Intrinsic Motivation

The idea that people have basic needs for psychological growth comes from what we call "need-motive-value" theories of motivation that emphasize the role of personality, stable dispositions, and values as determinants of behavior (Kanfer 1991). The set of theories includes Maslow's need hierarchy theory (Maslow 1970), Alderfer's existence-relatedness-and-growth (ERG) theory (Alderfer 1972), need achievement theory (McClelland 1961; Atkinson and Raynor 1974), and intrinsic motivation theory (White

1959; Deci 1975). The theories offer somewhat different definitions of the motivation construct, but all emphasize how people are motivated by curiosity, a need for challenge, self-determination, mastery, a need to achieve against standards of excellence, and the need to learn something new. The most important application of these theories has been efforts to design jobs that are intrinsically motivating by giving workers the opportunity to satisfy their needs for psychological growth and development. Intrinsically motivated behavior is that set of activities for which there is no apparent reward other than the behavior itself. This means that the motivation to work comes from the work content, that is, from the actual tasks people are given to do. The operational definitions of intrinsically motivating work can be found in models of job redesign.

Job Redesign Theories and Models

Job redesign or job characteristics models had their origins in sociotechnical systems theory, which stated that the goal in the design of organizations and the engineering of work processes should be the joint optimization of social work relations and technology. Instead of designing production processes around individual workers, as was the rule of Scientific Management, production, or manufacturing, processes should be engineered for *work groups*. Clusters of tasks should be tied together in bundles, or families, of jobs, to be executed by autonomous, or self-directed, work teams (Trist and Bamford 1951; Wild 1975; Emery and Thorsrud 1976; Kelly 1982).

A self-directed team is a multiskilled group of employees who have been cross-trained to do each of the jobs within the cluster assigned to the team and have the responsibility to manage the team's work schedules. Pay systems vary, but pay-for-

knowledge or team productivity bonus plans are common. The degree of autonomy varies as well, from the semiautonomous work group that has a supervisor, the self-managed team that elects its own leader, or the self-designing team with authority to determine its own composition (Sundstrom, DeMeuse, and Futrell 1990; Cotton 1993). The teams usually have authority to make decisions in two areas: personnel matters, such as the hiring, firing, and performance appraisal of team members, and some aspect of the work process, such as the allocation of tasks and how they should be carried out, to the extent that the latter is not fixed by engineering standards. Job redesign and teamwork mean that jobs are "broad-banded," that is, there are only a few job classifications, and team members can move among job tasks as needed.

Ideally, jobs in self-directed teams mean that workers (1) have to use a variety of different skills; (2) are involved in the completion of whole, identifiable pieces of work; (3) have a substantial impact on the work, or life, of others; (4) experience freedom, independence, and discretion; and (5) get direct feedback on how well they are performing. These five characteristics, *skill variety*, *task identity*, *task significance*, *autonomy*, and *feedback*, are the components of Hackman and Oldham's Job Characteristics Model (Hackman and Oldham 1980). There are other variants of job design models (see, for example, Sims, Szilagyi, and Keller 1976), as well as other forms of shopfloor participation programs, many tailor-made to suit the production technologies and management philosophies of the employer, but all are anchored in the "need-motive-value" theories.

Performance-Contingent Pay

Compensation programs that include productivity bonuses or other forms of gain- and profit-sharing are also supported by motivation theory, in particular, reinforcement theory (e.g., Komaki, Coombs, and Shepman 1996) and expectancy theory (Vroom 1964), both of which are derived from learning theory (Tolman 1932). The main tenet of learning theory is that behavior that is reinforced (followed by pleasurable consequences) will be repeated. According to expectancy theory, people will be motivated to perform when they believe that the performance will lead to outcomes they want or will allow them to escape outcomes they want to avoid, and they believe they will be able to reach and sustain a given performance level. It is assumed that people will value different outcomes, or desire them to different degrees, which means that not everyone will respond the same way to the same performance-outcome contingencies.

By making part of wages contingent on individual or team performance, the employer is capitalizing on individual differences in skills, abilities, and motivation levels, rewarding those who are capable and willing to exert more effort toward the attainment of organizational goals. Reward systems based on the recognition of individual differences are a better fit with theory and empirical data about human performance—years of psychological research have demonstrated the importance of individual differences in knowledge, skills, and abilities, in personality characteristics, and in interests and values (see, for example, Dawis 1991; Hogan 1991; Lubinski and Dawis 1992). Collective bargaining agreements that base wages only on job classifications and seniority trade individual differences for group solidarity. To be sure, there are benefits to wage solidarity for both the collective and individual, especially when seen against a history of employer control over the wage and effort bargain, but there are also costs to the individual employee

from not reaping the pecuniary benefits of effort and performance above the standard agreed to in collective bargaining.

The basic premise behind productivity bonuses and gain- and profit-sharing plans is that employees' contributions to organizational effectiveness beyond accepted and established levels will be returned to them in the form of money, either as wages or as deferred benefits. This premise also says that other positive outcomes for the employee that can follow work in high-involvement organizations, such as increased job satisfaction and intrinsic motivation and feelings of self-worth from participation in decision making, are not substitutes for pay in a redefined employment exchange. Performance-based wage systems therefore come closer to satisfying the prescriptions of equity theory (Adams 1963, 1965).

Is direct worker participation, as we observe it in the high-involvement work setting, an effective form of representation for nonunion employees? Does it give workers a meaningful voice in workplace governance?

Employee involvement in decision making based on sociotechnical systems principles in the nonunion firm is granted participation created on the employer's initiative. The goal of these programs is increased organizational effectiveness through improvements in employee job performance and job satisfaction, and more flexible staffing. Shopfloor programs provide opportunities for direct workplace participation by large numbers of workers over a small number of issues related to work at the point of production. Although some programs allow workers considerable opportunities for involvement in, and influence over, decisions about the execution of their work, there is considerable variation in the participation experiences in different firms (for examples, see Appelbaum and Batt 1994). Employer granted programs of worker involvement are unlikely to be effective labor voice mechanisms because the scope of topics over which employees may have some influence is very limited and the programs depend on the employer's willingness to maintain and support them.

This does not mean that employee involvement programs are without value for employees. In fact, the programs are very important. Nevertheless, we must realize that their value derives from their ability to satisfy basic psychological needs, not from what they might offer in the way of employee power. The term *empowerment*, used frequently in connection with shopfloor participation programs, does not mean a redistribution of power across hierarchies within the enterprise that will give workers a say in determining the content of the employment exchange. Empowerment means only the freedom of the individual worker to make decisions about how, and sometimes when, his or her work should be organized and carried out. If employee involvement programs offer the opportunity for employee voice of a broader scope, it is incidental. A number of large-scale evaluations of worker participation programs have shown that the kind of voice and the amount of power the participation programs offer employees are very limited, indeed (IDE 1981, 1991; Hammer 1996).

The programs are important for the psychological well-being of the individual employee, and they can also serve an economic function for the employer if they are designed and implemented correctly (see Hammer 1988; Cotton 1993). From a unitarist perspective, an employee involvement program represents a win-win situation. The participation must be direct, however; that is, it must be experienced by each worker. Indirect participation through representatives does not satisfy the same psychological needs. Therefore, employee involvement programs serve a set of worker needs that American unions have not chosen to prioritize. While such programs may be an important component of a nonunion program of worker representation, they cannot stand alone as effective forms of worker representation.

Indirect Forms of Participation

In this section, I discuss structures that could be used to give nonunion employees a voice in decisions about broader employment relations issues, such as the terms and conditions of employment. In theory, employee involvement in decision making above the shopfloor level should be better served by programs of representative participation, such as joint labor-management committees, adaptations of the European works council model, or representation on corporate boards of directors. This is because the scope of topics—the domain of decision making—in these bodies can go far beyond the topics usually addressed in direct employee involvement programs. For example, works councils are plant-level bodies of elected employees that meet regularly with management to discuss a wide variety of personnel issues, such as work and leave schedules, pay schemes, employee selection and training, safety, technological changes that affect the nature and pace of work and the work environment, and social welfare issues (IDE 1981, 1991). Joint consultative committees, or labor-management committees, usually have more open-ended mandates to deal with issues of common interest to labor and management. The works council model has been suggested as the most reasonable substitute for the local union in nonunion firms (e.g., Kochan and Osterman 1994), but before we get too enthusiastic about it we should remember that the effectiveness of the European works council as an employee voice mechanism depends on a whole set of integrated participation structures that ties shopfloor, board level, and trade union participation into a unified whole (Streeck 1984).

Research on representative participation in the United States (other than collective bargaining) is sparse. Case studies of labor-management committees have focused on how the committees have functioned to solve economic problems in unionized settings (see, for example, Whyte et al. 1983; Gerhart 1987), or as components in gain-sharing programs (Schuster 1984). There is, however, a small body of research on worker representation on corporate boards of directors that speaks to the question of what is likely to happen to this form of participation.

Boards of directors are charged by corporate law with protecting the financial interests of stockholders. According to agency theory, the board's chief function is to monitor and control the corporation's managers to ensure that they do not put their personal interests ahead of the owners' interests when these conflict (Fama 1980; Fama and Jensen 1983). In the United States there has been considerable debate about and research on the effectiveness of corporate boards as supervisory bodies, and the conclusions, particularly from managerial hegemony studies, are not encouraging. For example, boards have been described as rubber stamps of managerial decision making, in which directors are coopted by the firm's executives, who control their appointments to the board and the benefits that accrue from the directorships (Pfeffer 1972; Herman 1981; Vance 1983). Board reform efforts to make directors less subservient to management's interests and more responsive to the interests of other stakeholders, such as employees or institutional investors, include increasing the number of outside directors

(Mace 1971; Herman 1981; Freeman and Reed 1983). Employee representatives are considered stakeholder, or special-interest, directors.

Most studies conducted in Europe of both legally prescribed and voluntary experiments with worker directorships have concluded that this form of worker participation has had only limited impact on corporate decision making (see, for example, Engelstad and Qvale 1977; Batstone, Ferner, and Terry 1983; IDE 1981, 1991). The exception is Germany's system of codetermination (Streeck 1984). The explanation offered for the lack of worker director influence has been institutional constraints—being in a minority position and prohibited from communicating with their workforce constituents—and personal inadequacies, such as lack of the training, experience, and skills necessary to comprehend the complexities of the financial and legal information needed for strategic decision making. In contrast, Hammer, Currall, and Stern (1991) have suggested that worker board representation fails as an effective form of employee participation in large part because management prefers and thus tries to create a role for worker directors that will not threaten managerial power on the board. In a study of worker directorships in fourteen U.S. firms, they found that CEOs defined the worker directors' functions as explaining board decisions to a labor constituency after the decisions were made. This differed considerably from the way both the worker directors and the worker constituents defined the worker director role. The latter saw it as an advocate for and protector of workers' interests in the boardroom.

To examine why worker directors end up with such a limited role on the board and whether other outside directors share this experience, I turn to institutional theory (Scott, Mitchell, and Peery 1981; Scott 1991).

The Effects of Institutional Norms on Employee Board Representation

According to institutional theory, the patterns of behaviors, social relations, and rules about what is appropriate that develop over time in organizations come to be taken for granted and are therefore seen as legitimate (Scott 1991; Davis, Diekmann, and Tinsley 1994). On corporate boards, the behavior of directors is governed by a set of norms that covers both boardroom deliberations and interactions that take place outside the boardroom with the board chair, the CEO, and fellow directors. The norms include the decision-making model that the board follows. How the board goes about reaching its decisions has implications for the distribution of power on the board because control over decision-making processes dictates control over decision outcomes (Bachrach and Baratz 1970). If new directors have different definitions of their roles and different decision-making models, existing directors' control over board deliberations and decision-making outcomes is threatened. Therefore, it is in the interest of management directors to define new directors' roles so that they do not threaten or dilute managerial power and to ensure compliance with these role definitions through the enforcement of norms about board behavior.

The norms that prescribe appropriate behavior in and around the boardroom include a ban on public challenges to and criticisms of the CEO, the absence of open conflict in the boardroom, consensus decision making, and minimal interference in the day-to-day management of the organization (Lorsch and MacIver 1989; Pettigrew and McNulty 1995; McNulty and Pettigrew 1996). If the board includes directors representing stakeholders' groups, such as employees, customers, suppliers, or local communities, the norms also dictate that they refrain from stakeholder advocacy (Brannen et al. 1976; Hammer, Currall, and Stern 1991). These norms come from a consensus model of decision making that assumes that divergent group interests can be reconciled in overarching common goals (the unitarist model). To accommodate various interests and ensure commitment to common goals, decision making is often a long process involving extensive consultation among all parties, informal discussions, and quiet negotiations. The outcome is broad-based consensus (Hammer and Stern 1986).

The opposing decision-making model is a political, or pluralist, one that takes as given that conflict is an inevitable result of the existence of interest groups and a natural part of organizational life. The norms and rules that govern conduct and decision making according to the political model run counter to the behavioral expectations that operate in the boardroom. In the political model, interest-group advocacy is the norm, expressions of open conflict are accepted, and decisions are settled by majority vote (Pfeffer 1981). When the board norms are challenged, as they are likely to be with the presence of worker directors, management directors will first try to socialize the challengers to adopt "legitimate" behaviors, which means minimizing the employee stakeholder role and refraining from labor interest-group advocacy. If worker directors persist in defining workforce concerns and employment relations as topics that belong on the board's agenda, institutional theory predicts that management directors will respond with tactics designed to silence or limit labor advocacy. Similarly, open expressions of disagreement and conflict, which violate the norms against disagreeing with the CEO in the boardroom, will be suppressed.

There are very few studies of what actually happens in corporate boardrooms. Nevertheless, in one five-year observation study inside a corporate board, Hammer, Currall, and Stern (1999) examined how CEOs and management directors tried to socialize worker directors and other outside directors representing the workforce to existing board norms. Although the stakeholder directors were not blocked from introducing workforce issues into the board debate, this was a very small part of the board's business. Analyses of board discourse showed that management directors dominated board discussions on most topics in large part because they controlled information important to the board's deliberations and decision making. When the employee stakeholder directors brought their political model of decision making to the boardroom, challenging board norms, the CEO exercised increasingly intense power tactics to maintain control. The board never managed to integrate the different norms of conduct and therefore did not become an effective decision-making body.

Based on their findings, Hammer et al. (1999) argued that effective worker representation will require socialization and training to increase awareness of existing institutions and the potential for deviations from them among both original board members and new directors. Role expectations must be discussed and negotiated. Management directors need to learn, before it becomes apparent in the boardroom, that they cannot assume outsiders' adherence to a consensus model and also how they can incorporate different models into board decision making without destroying the effectiveness of the board. There should be a two-way education and training process for both worker directors and original board members that includes an acknowledgment of problems likely to face the new directors relative to the workers they represent and their lack of technical knowledge.

Those advocating reform in boards of directors have recommended both increased numbers of outside director appointments and stakeholder representation on boards. The outside director approach has been adopted widely in the United States, but shows only small effects because of information control by management directors. Special interest-group representation has yet a smaller chance to increase board accountability to outside stakeholders because the outsiders are unlikely to constitute a majority of board members, are unlikely to hold an alternative decision model that might be applied, and are unlikely to have social support inside a board for advocacy of an interest-group position. In fact, Hammer et al. (1991) have suggested that the value of worker directorships may be only as a form of symbolic representation, of utility to management and perhaps to union leaders who negotiate such an arrangement, but of little importance for the workforce.

Although both theory and data tell us that worker representation on boards of directors is unlikely to give the workforce much influence over corporate decisions, it does not mean that other forms of indirect participation will have the same limitations. The strong culture of conformity to norms and group cohesion that operates in the boardroom is unlikely to be replicated in labor-management committees or in works councils, if for no other reason that committees and councils will not be staffed with members who are beholden to the CEO for committee seats and monetary rewards. Committees and councils are also likely to have a more equal distribution of employee to management representatives. But some of the factors that limit worker influence on boards of directors will in all likelihood be present in other joint labor-management structures. These include a managerial advantage with respect to the knowledge and expertise needed to understand and solve complex problems at the strategic level, lack of access to information needed to make informed decisions, norms against labor interest-group advocacy, and the possibility that employee representatives can be coopted through group pressures for consensual decision making. Therefore, recommendations that come from the board research are applicable to committees and councils: worker representatives must be given adequate training and have sufficient access to firm-level information to participate as equal partners in discussions and decision making; both management and employee representatives must be clear about role expectations, role behaviors, and norms of conduct for all committee and council members; and there should be acceptable channels available for communication between the employee representatives and their workforce constituencies.

Conflict Resolution and Due Process

I suggested earlier that direct forms of employee participation are not a sufficient form of nonunion representation because they usually do not contain structures intended to ensure employees procedural and distributive justice. It is possible, of course, that workers will be treated fairly and that the employment exchange will be an equitable one without employee representation. As we later see, however, individuals' perceptions of justice are influenced by the amount of control they have over both processes and outcomes (Folger 1986), and beliefs about fair treatment are very much a part of people's psychological makeup. Why are employees' perceptions of justice so important?

Theories of Justice and Equity in Social Exchange

Distributive justice is the use of a normative rule for allocating resources to recipients. According to Homans (1974), who introduced the concept, the rule says that a person who is in an exchange relationship has two expectations: (1) the rewards each one will receive will be proportional to his or her costs, and (2) the net rewards (that is, profits) will be proportional to investments. Homans argued that this rule of proportionality is universal, but that individuals and societies will have different beliefs about what should be considered investments, rewards, and costs. Through their own experience in social exchanges, and by observing what happens to others, people learn what the relationships are between investments and profits, and they develop expectations that these relationships will hold in the future. From the basic learning process of operant conditioning (learning theory), people come to know that the outcomes, or consequences, that befall themselves and others will conform to the distributive justice rule.

Blau (1964) argued that beliefs in fairness had more of a social base and was learned as a norm or value during early socialization, instead of being acquired through operant conditioning. He also distinguished between what he called a "fair rate of exchange," which is a normative standard the defines a fair or just reward in return for a specified service, and the "going rate of exchange," which can fluctuate with the availability and market value of the service. A fair rate of exchange is a moral expectation.

Lerner (1975) anchored beliefs in distributive justice in a psychological need to believe that people generally get what they deserve—what he called "the belief in a just world." People not only want justice for themselves but also for others, and they become psychologically committed to the idea that people deserve to be treated fairly. Therefore they develop rules, or norms, for how outcomes should be distributed under different circumstances. The common rules of justice are equity, equality (parity), and need.

The equity rule says that outcomes (rewards) should be proportional to inputs (investments), and is exemplified in wage systems based on merit or performance. The equality rule demands that outcomes be shared equally among recipients, as is the case, for example, in the distribution of workgroup pay bonuses. On a societal level, the distribution of goods and services follow the equality rule. Distributions based on needs—quite often a topic of heated debate—are seen mostly in the case of medical care or welfare programs (Cohen and Greenberg 1982).

There has been considerable debate in the research literature about the primacy of one rule over the others (see Leventhal 1976; Walster, Walster, and Berscheid 1978), but this debate need not concern us here. Research has suggested that the equality rule is preferred in long-term exchange relationships with similar others, presumably because people believe that, over the long term, the equality rule will benefit each party. In the employment exchange, where the equity norm has predominated in the United States, an equality rule of distribution works better with interdependent task groups (such as work teams) because it is often not possible to determine who contributed what to a joint product. The use of the equality distribution rule also tends to reduce conflict, promote cooperation, and increase productivity in interdependent groups (Greenberg 1982).

It is the equity rule that has received most of the conceptual and empirical attention, starting with the development of a formal equity theory by Adams (1963, 1965). Adams argued that people make two sets of comparisons to determine if justice has been served. In the first comparison, people compare their outcomes with their inputs, for example, their wages, fringe benefits,

and working conditions with their contributions to the employer of education, effort, and experience. If the value of the inputs equals the value of the outcomes, people feel equitably treated. If outcomes exceed inputs, people experience guilt, and if inputs exceed outcomes, people experience inequity. Inequity leads to psychological tension, which must be reduced to restore a psychological equilibrium. If the inequity is experienced in the employment exchange there are different ways to reduce it depending on the worker's freedom of movement, such as reducing the quality or the quantity of one's work, being less willing to accommodate to the employer's requests for flexibility, or refusing to do general citizenship acts.

The second comparison process involves the calculation of the input/outcome equation of a "comparison other," someone in a similar position, or someone with similar characteristics. Recall that the belief in a just world means justice for both self and others. Equity in the comparison case means that both Self and Other should be treated fairly (outcomes should equal inputs), and failing that, their equations should be the same.

Equity theory is based on Festinger's (1954) social comparison theory and the theory of cognitive dissonance (Festinger 1957). Social comparison theory describes the psychological needs people have for knowing that they are right, while cognitive dissonance theory describes the need for cognitive consistency or balance. The frustration of these needs leads to a psychological tension that motivates behavior. I am not going to cover the details of the tension reduction mechanisms here. I have linked the model of distributive justice to the basic psychological processes of learning and tension reduction, as well as to the sociological concept of social norms only because I wanted to show that the need for justice, or fairness, is rooted deep in the individual psyche.

Because justice—being treated fairly—is a psychological need, there should be mechanisms or structures in the workplace that ensure fair treatment. Ideally, employees should have input into decisions about how dispute resolution mechanisms are used because perceptions of fairness depends so much on how one defines inputs and outcomes, neither of which are clear-cut (for example, is the autonomy one experiences in self-directed work teams an outcome, or is it something that requires more work and therefore an input?). Procedural justice—how fair the rules and processes are—has turned out to be just as important to people's beliefs about their experiencing justice as the outcomes they receive. Research on dispute resolution has shown that control over both the process of inquiry and control over the decision outcome are important (Folger 1986), and research on performance appraisals has demonstrated that the fairness of the procedures followed is more important than the outcome (Greenberg 1996). In a way, procedural justice is perceived to be a prerequisite for distributive justice.

The Ambiguities of the Psychological Contract

The question of what is fair, or equitable, in the employment exchange is often difficult to answer when the terms of exchange are not subject to collective bargaining. In the nonunion firm, the individual employee negotiates an agreement with an agent of the employer about (at least) the wages and fringe benefits to be paid by the employer for time worked or amounts produced, and, possibly, a set of general mutual obligations. There may be a written formal agreement that describes the terms and conditions of employment, as well as written rules of conduct prescribing employee behaviors, and a personnel handbook that spells out the rights or privileges granted by the employer—what Edwards (1997) has called enterprise rights. But it is also likely that many of the mutual obligations that should have been discussed during the negotiations of an individual employment contract were not, and therefore they exist only as a set of implicit and covertly held expectations about what the employer will provide in exchange for the employee's ability and willingness to work (Rousseau 1995).

These unwritten expectations become a *psychological contract*, a subjective perception of mutual obligations that can change over time during an employment relationship (e.g., Hiltrop 1995; Anderson and Schalk 1998). Because the psychological contract is subjective, there is no guarantee that employer and employee define it the same way. In fact, because individual employment contracts usually lack the detail and specificity of a collectively bargained agreement, the exact terms of the employment exchange often emerge over time as it is shaped by a series of formal and informal events around job structures and performance standards, including past practices, slowdowns, speed-ups, motivation programs, rewards systems, and so on. Psychological contracts are formed on the basis of trust, and when the terms and conditions of employment are redefined by one of the parties without consultation or consent of the other, it is seen as a violation and often accompanied by feelings of betrayal (Robinson and Rousseau 1994).

When conflicts arise in the employment relationship, either because written or psychological contracts are broken, or employees believe they are inequitably treated or that their rights in the workplace are violated, do the structures or programs available in the nonunion workplace offer procedural and distributive justice?

Nonunion Structures for Conflict Resolution

Federal legislation offers nonunion employees protection from discrimination, unjust treatment, and having to perform work that threatens their health and safety. There is general agreement, however, that going to court to get justice from one's employer is an excessively time-consuming and costly burden and an extraordinary inefficient way of solving disputes that arise over the wage and effort bargain or other clauses in an em-ployee's psychological contract. To resolve workplace disputes, many nonunion employers have implemented a variety of conflict-management systems, such as "open door" policies, in-house grievance procedures, peer-review of grievances, an ombudsman's office that offers employees the opportunity to bring their grievances to a third party or directly to management, or they have adopted alternative dispute resolution (ADR) programs, in which forms of mediation or arbitration are used as substitutes for the public judicial or administrative process available to resolve disputes (Lipsky and Seeber 1998).

In a recent study of Fortune 1,000 companies, Lipsky and Seeber (1998) found that ADR processes were well established, widespread in all industries, and covered many different types of disputes. Over 87 percent of the sample firms had used mediation—the preferred form of ADR— and 80 percent had used arbitration to solve disputes. In disputes over employment rights, that is, conflicts that arise over an already existing agreement, 79 percent of the firms reported using mediation while 62 percent used arbitration. As Edwards (1997) has argued, mediation may

be especially suitable in settling workplace disputes because so many of them involve strong emotions. The mediation process allows the parties to work through their anger and frustration with the help of a mediator before they start to solve their joint problem, which may be especially useful when disputes arise over "clauses" in psychological contracts that are based on misperceptions, untested assumptions, and misunderstandings.

There are a number of reasons why nonunion firms have adopted conflict-management systems, including the increased use and expense of litigation, especially of wrongful discharge complaints, the growth of a human resource management perspective that views employees as corporate assets to be managed with care, a concern about possible unionization, and a statutory and judicial encouragement of arbitration (Stallworth 1997). The most important reason given in the Lipsky and Seeber (1998) study for the use of ADR was its cost effectiveness—to save the time and expense of litigation.

The widespread use of ADR, at least in large firms, appears on the surface to offer the nonunion worker both procedural and distributive justice. Because these programs are established and controlled by the employer, however, there is an imbalance of economic and information power that places the employee at a disadvantage. Employees who are required to sign agreements to submit future employment disputes to arbitration as a condition for employment have neither the sophistication nor the power to prevail when the employer is likely to be a repeat player in the arbitration process with a built-in bias in his or her favor (Estreicher 1991; Bingham 1998).

The use of nonunion arbitration, in particular, has been criticized for granting employees neither form of justice. Getman (1979) has argued that one cannot transplant arbitration to the non-union setting because the principles that have developed in labor arbitration were based on consensual decision making and apply to disagreements over the interpretation of what has been negotiated in collective bargaining. The important issue here is control. We know from the psychological research on procedural justice that a person's control over the dispute-resolution process is a very important factor in perceptions of fairness (Greenberg 1996). We also know from analyses of dispute-resolution outcomes that procedures that deny the grieving employee a voice in the selection of arbitrator, an opportunity to be represented at an arbitration hearing, and limited or no access to information relevant to his or her case, do not ensure distributive justice (Edwards 1997; Stallworth, 1997).

The uneven playing field afforded employees with employer-controlled ADR programs has led to the development of ground rules, or due process protocols, for the mediation and arbitration of employment disputes. These include, among other recommendations, the right of the employee to participate in the selection of an arbitrator and to bring his or her own counsel to the hearing, and adequate prehearing discovery (Dunlop and Zack 1997).

As part of a debate about the utility of government regulation of the employment relationship (Kaufman 1997), it was suggested that one way to protect employee rights, without undue government regulation, would be to require employers to publish the rights they were granting their employees, including those related to due process procedures, in firm-specific employee handbooks that would be legally enforceable by statute (Edwards 1997, p. 421). I am not going to discuss the desirability of legally mandated em-

ployee handbooks here, but it is fair to say that psychological theory and research would support the public availability of as much detailed information about the mutual rights and obligations in an employment relationship as the employer is capable of committing to writing. It is far better for both parties in the employment exchange to have fewer clauses in their psychological contracts, and more clauses in publicly accessible documents, than the other way around.

Conclusion

In this chapter I have examined three different structures for worker representation in the non-union firm: direct participation of the "high-involvement work system" variety, indirect participation at the strategic level of the firm, and alternative dispute-resolution programs. I have argued that forms of worker participation of either the direct or indirect variety that are based on employer grants are not stable, or secure, voice mechanisms for employees. Any structure of non-union representation that is based on the principle of voluntarism can be dissolved at the employer's discretion. Even if the employer finds it unwise for practical or political reasons to dissolve programs adopted to involve employees in decision making, he or she can define the roles employees are expected to play within the programs in such a way that their influence over decision outcomes is severely restricted. While the use of formal ADR programs in nonunion firms can be considered an improvement over informal and ad hoc procedures for solving employment disputes, programs designed and controlled unilaterally by the employer do not ensure procedural and distributive justice.

The effectiveness of nonunion representation programs depends on the goodwill, trust, and power relationship between the parties. Trust is a brittle property of any relationship, easily broken and difficult to rebuild. A decision about whether or not to trust another person takes place in a situation where (1) one's fate is dependent on another person's actions, and (2) the other person's actions are free to vary (Deutsch 1958, 1962). In the nonunion firm, the actions of the employer, or management, are quite free to vary. This means that the effectiveness of nonunion representation depends on management policies and practices, and managers' beliefs about the utility of power sharing and commitment to programs that allow and encourage worker involvement and influence. When employers favor worker representation, it can improve organizational effectiveness, efficiency, and equity. As Heckscher (1996) points out, however, employment relationships based on pure voluntarism are inherently insecure.

Acknowledgment

I appreciate helpful comments from Bruce Kaufman and Wilfred Zerbe on earlier drafts of this chapter.

Note

1. There are two other well-known models that describe the employment relationship. The radical, or Marxian, view, considers labor-management conflict inevitable, a result of fundamentally opposed interests of employers and employees at the wage nexus. Because labor is always at a power disadvantage in this model, workers will be unable to withstand exploitation by employers. The opposite perspective comes from neoclassical economics, which also accepts as given a conflict of interest between workers and employers, but offers a different resolution in the form of the competition for labor and employment that is assumed to take place in a perfect free market. The competition equalizes the bargaining power of worker and employer and ensures an efficient and equitable employment relationship.

References

Adams, J.S. 1963. "Toward an Understanding of Inequity." *Journal of Abnormal and Social Psychology* 67: 422–436.

———. 1965. "Inequity in Social Exchange." In *Advances in Experimental Social Psychology*, ed. L. Berkowitz, p. 2. New York: Academic Press.

Addison, J.T., and B.T. Hirsch. 1997. "The Economic Effects of Employment Regulations: Are There Limits?" In *Government Regulations of the Employment Relationship*, ed. B.E. Kaufman, pp. 125–178. Madison: Industrial Relations Research Association.

AFL-CIO Committee on the Evolution of Work. 1985. *The Changing Nature of Workers and Their Unions.* Washington, D.C.: AFL-CIO.

Alderfer, C.P. 1972. *Existence, Relatedness, and Growth.* New York: Free Press.

Anderson, N., and R. Schalk. 1998. "The Psychological Contract in Retrospect and Prospect." *Journal of Organizational Behavior* 19: 637–647.

Appelbaum, E., and R. Batt. 1994. *The New American Workplace: Transforming Work Systems in the United States.* Ithaca, N.Y.: ILR Press.

Argyris, C. 1964. *Integrating the Individual and the Organization.* New York: Wiley.

Atkinson, J.W., and J.O. Raynor. 1974. *Motivation and Achievement.* New York: Wiley.

Bachrach, P., and M.S. Baratz. 1970. *Power and Poverty. Theory and Practice.* London: Oxford University Press.

Batstone, E., A. Ferner, and M. Terry. 1983. *Unions on the Board.* Oxford: Basil Blackwell.

Bingham, L.B. 1998. "An Update on Employment Arbitration and the Courts." *Perspectives on Work* 2, no. 2: 19–23.

Blau, P.M. 1964. *Exchange and Power in Social Life.* New York: Wiley.

Brannen, P., E. Batstone, D. Fatchett, and P. White. 1976. *The Worker Directors: A Sociology of Participation.* London: Hutchinson.

Coch, L., and J.R.P. French. 1948. "Overcoming Resistance to Change." *Human Relations* 1, no. 4: 512–533.

Cohen, R.L., and J. Greenberg. 1982. "The Justice Concept in Social Psychology." In *Equity and Justice in Social Behavior*, ed. J. Greenberg and R.L. Cohen. New York: Academic Press.

Cotton, J.L. 1993. *Employee Involvement. Methods for Improving Performance and Work Attitudes.* London: Sage.

Dachler, H.P., and B. Wilpert. 1978. "Conceptual Dimensions and Boundaries of Participation in Organizations:

A Critical Evaluation." *Administrative Science Quarterly* 23, no. 1:1–39.

Daft, Richard L. 1983. *Organization Theory and Design.* New York: West.

Davis, G.F., K.A. Diekmann, and C.H. Tinsley. 1994. "The Decline and Fall of the Conglomerate Firm in the 1980s: The Deinstitutionalization of an Organizational Form." *American Sociological Review* 59, no. 4: 547–570.

Dawis, Rene V. 1991. "Vocational Interests, Values, and Preferences." In *Handbook of Industrial and Organizational Psychology*, ed. M.D. Dunnette and L.M. Hough, vol. 2, pp. 833–872. Palo Alto: Consulting Psychologists Press.

Deci, E.L. 1975. *Intrinsic Motivation.* New York: Plenum Press.

Deutsch, M. 1958. "Trust and Suspicion." *Conflict Resolution* 2, no. 4: 265–279.

———. 1962. "Cooperation and Trust: Some Theoretical Notes." In *Nebraska Symposium on Motivation*, ed. M.R. Jones. Lincoln: University of Nebraska Press.

Dunlop, J.T., and A.M. Zack. 1997. *Mediation and Arbitration of Employment Disputes.* San Francisco: Jossey-Bass.

Edwards, R. 1997. "Alternative Regulatory Approaches to Protecting Workers' Rights." In *Government Regulations of the Employment Relationship*, ed. B.E. Kaufman, pp. 403–428. Madison: Industrial Relations Research Association.

Emery, F.E., and E. Thorsrud. 1976. *Democracy at Work.* Leiden: Martinus Nijhoff.

Engelstad, P.U., and T.U. Qvale. 1977. *Innsyn og innflytelse: Styre og bedriftsforsamling.* Oslo: Tiden Norske Forlag.

Estreicher, S. 1991. "Arbitration in Employment Disputes Without Unions." *Chicago-Kent Law Review* 66, no. 3: 753–797.

Fama, E.F. 1980. "Agency Problems and the Theory of the Firm." *Journal of Political Economy* 88, no. 2: 288–307.

Fama, E.F., and M.C. Jensen. 1983. "Separation of Ownership and Control." *Journal of Law and Economics* 26, no. 2: 301–325.

Festinger, L.A. 1954. "A Theory of Social Comparison Processes." *Human Relations* 7, no. 2: 117–140.

———. 1957. *A Theory of Cognitive Dissonance.* Evanston: Row, Peterson.

Folger, R. 1986. "Mediation, Arbitration, and the Psychology of Procedural Justice." In *Research in Negotiation in Organizations*, ed. R. Lewicki, B. Sheppard, and M. Bazerman, pp. 57–79. Greenwich, Conn.: JAI Press.

Fox, A. 1973. "Industrial Relations: A Social Critique of Pluralist Ideology." In *Man and Organization*, ed. J. Child, pp. 185–233. New York: Wiley.

Freeman, R.B., and J.L. Medoff. 1984. *What Do Unions Do?* New York: Basic Books.

Freeman, R.B., and J. Rogers. 1994. *Worker Representation and Participation Survey: Report on the Findings.* Princeton: Princeton Survey Research Associates.

Freeman, R.E., and D.L. Reed. 1983. "Stockholders and Stakeholders: A New Perspective on Corporate Governance." *California Management Review* 25, no. 3: 88–106.

Gerhart, P.F. 1987. *Saving Plants and Jobs. Union-Management Negotiations in the Context of Threatened Plant Closing.* Kalamazoo: W.E. Upjohn Institute for Employment Research.

Getman, J.G. 1979. "Labor Arbitration and Dispute Resolution." *Yale Law Journal* 88, no. 5: 916.

Greenberg, J. 1982. "Approaching Equity and Avoiding Inequity in Groups and Organizations." In *Equity and Justice in Social Behavior*, ed. J. Greenberg, and R.L. Cohen. New York: Academic Press.

———. 1996. *The Quest for Justice on the Job. Essays and Experiments.* Thousand Oaks, Calif.: Sage.

Hackman, J.R. 1990. *Groups That Work (and Those That Don't). Creating Conditions for Effective Teamwork.* San Francisco: Jossey-Bass.

Hackman, J.R., and G.R. Oldham. 1980. *Work Redesign.* Reading, Mass.: Addison-Wesley.

Hammer, T.H. 1988. "New Developments in Profit Sharing, Gainsharing, and Employee Ownership." In *Productivity in Organizations: New Perspectives from Industrial and Organizational Psychology*, ed. P. Campbell, R.J. Campbell, and Associates. San Francisco: Jossey-Bass.

———. 1996. "Industrial Democracy." In *International Encyclopedia of Business and Management*, ed. M. Warner, vol. 2, pp. 1921–1930. London: Thomson Business Press.

Hammer, T.H., S.C. Currall, and R.N. Stern. 1991. "Worker Representation on Boards of Directors: A Study of Competing Roles." *Industrial and Labor Relations Review* 44, no. 4: 661–680.

Hammer, T.H., S.C. Currall, and R.N. Stern. 1999. "Outsiders on the Corporate Board: A Study of Power and Conflict Among Management and Stakeholder Directors." Manuscript, New York State School of Industrial and Labor Relations, Cornell University.

Hammer, T.H., and R.N. Stern. 1986. "A Yo-Yo Model of Cooperation: Union Participation in Management at the Rath Packing Company." *Industrial and Labor Relations Review* 39, no. 3: 337–349.

Heckscher, C.C. 1996. *The New Unionism. Employee Involvement in the Changing Corporation.* Ithaca, N.Y.: ILR Press.

Herman, E.S. 1981. *Corporate Control, Corporate Power.* New York: Cambridge University Press.

Hiltrop, J.M. 1995. "The Changing Psychological Contract: The Human Resource Challenge of the 1990s." *European Management Journal* 13, no. 3: 286–294.

Hogan, R.T. 1991. "Personality and Personality Measurement." In *Handbook of Industrial and Organizational Psychology*, ed. M.D. Dunnette and L.M. Hough, vol. 2, pp. 873–919. Palo Alto: Consulting Psychologists Press.

Homans, G.C. 1974. *Social Behavior: Its Elementary Forms.* New York: Harcourt Brace Jovanovich.

IDE International Research Group. 1981. *Industrial Democracy in Europe.* Oxford: Clarendon Press.

———. 1991. *Industrial Democracy in Europe Revisited.* New York: Oxford University Press.

Jones, G.R. 1998. *Organizational Theory.* New York: Addison-Wesley.

Kanfer, R. 1991. "Motivation Theory and Industrial and Organizational Psychology." In *Handbook of Industrial and Organizational Psychology*, ed. M.D. Dunnette and L.M. Hough. Palo Alto: Consulting Psychologists Press.

Katz, H.C., and T.A. Kochan. 1992. *An Introduction to Collective Bargaining and Industrial Relations.* New York: McGraw-Hill.

Kaufman, B.E. 1993. *The Origins & Evolution of the Field of Industrial Relations in the United States.* Ithaca, N.Y.: ILR Press.

———, ed. 1997. *Government Regulations of the Employment Relationship.* Madison: Industrial Relations Research Association.

Kelly, J.E. 1982. *Scientific Management, Job Redesign and Work Performance.* London: Academic Press.

Kochan, T.A., H.C. Katz, and R. B. McKersie. 1986. *The Transformation of American Industrial Relations.* New York: Basic Books.

Kochan, T.A., H.C. Katz, and N.R. Mower. 1984. *Worker Participation and American Unions: Threat or Opportunity?* Kalamazoo: The W.E. Upjohn Institute for Employment Research.

Kochan, T.A., and P. Osterman. 1994. *The Mutual Gains Enterprise.* Cambridge: Harvard University Press.

Komaki, J.L., T. Coombs, and S. Shepman. 1996. "Motivational Implications of Reinforcement Theory." In *Motivation and Leadership at Work*, ed. R.M. Steers, L.W. Porter, and G.A. Bigley. 6th ed. New York: McGraw-Hill.

Lawler, E.E. III. 1986. *High Involvement Management.* San Francisco: Jossey-Bass.

Lerner, M.J. 1975. "The Justice Motive in Social Behavior: An Introduction." *Journal of Social Issues* 31, no. 3: 1–19.

Leventhal, G.S. 1976. "Fairness in Social Relationships." In *Contemporary Topics in Social Psychology*, ed. J. Thibaut, J. Spence, and R. Carson. Morristown, N.J.: General Learning Press.

Likert, R. 1961. *New Patterns of Management.* New York: McGraw-Hill.

Lipsky, D.B., and R.L. Seeber. 1998. "In Search of Control: The Corporate Embrace of ADR." *University of Pennsylvania Journal of Labor and Employment Law* 1, no. 1: 133–157.

Lorsch, J.W., and E. MacIver. 1989. *Pawns or Potentates.* Cambridge: Harvard Business School Press.

Lubinski, D., and R.V. Dawis. 1992. "Aptitudes, Skills, and Proficiencies." In *Handbook of Industrial and Organizational Psychology*, ed. M.D. Dunnette and L.M. Hough, vol. 3, pp. 1–60. Palo Alto: Consulting Psychologists Press.

McClelland, D. 1961. *The Achieving Society.* Princeton: Van Nostrand.

McGregor, D. 1960. *The Human Side of Enterprise.* New York: McGraw-Hill.

McNulty, T., and A. Pettigrew. 1996. "The Contribution, Power and Influence of Part-time Board Members." *Corporate Governance* 4, no. 3: 160–179.

Mace, M. 1971. *Directors: Myth and Reality.* Cambridge: Division of Research, Harvard Business School.

Mahoney, T.A, and M.R. Watson. 1993. "Evolving Modes of Work Force Governance: An Evaluation." In *Employee Representation. Alternatives and Future Directions*, ed. B.E. Kaufman and M.M. Kleiner. Madison: IRRA.

Maslow, A. 1970. *Motivation and Personality*, 2nd ed. New York: Harper.

Milkovich, G.T., and J.W. Boudreau. 1994. *Human Resources Management*, 7th ed. Homewood, Ill.: Richard D. Irwin.

Morse, N.C., and E. Reimer. 1956. "The Experimental Change of a Major Organizational Variable." *Journal of Abnormal Social Psychology* 52, no. 1: 120–129.

Pettigrew, A., and T. McNulty. 1995. "Power and Influence in and around the Boardroom." *Human Relations* 48, no. 8: 845–873.

Pfeffer, J. 1972. "Size and Composition of Corporate Boards of Directors: The Organization and Its Environment." *Administrative Science Quarterly* 17, no. 2: 218–228.

———. 1981. *Power in Organizations.* Marshfield, Mass.: Pitman.

Robinson, S.L., and D.M. Rousseau. 1994. "Violating the

Psychological Contract: Not the Exception but the Norm." *Journal of Organizational Behavior* 15, no. 3: 289–298.

Rousseau, D.M. 1995. *Psychological Contracts in Organizations. Understanding Written and Unwritten Agreements.* Thousand Oaks, Calif.: Sage.

Schuster, M.H. 1984. *Union-Management Cooperation. Structure. Process. Impact.* Kalamazoo: The W.E. Upjohn Institute for Employment Research.

Scott, W.G., T.R. Mitchell, and N.S. Peery. 1981. "Organizational Governance." In *Handbook of Organizational Design*, ed. P.C. Nystrom and W.H. Starbuck, pp. 135–151. New York: Oxford.

Scott, W.R. 1991. "Unpacking Institutional Arguments." In *The New Institutionalism in Organizational Analysis*, ed. W.W. Powell and P.J. DiMaggio. Chicago: University of Chicago.

Sims, H.P., A.D. Szilagyi, and R.T. Keller. 1976. "The Measurement of Job Characteristics." *Academy of Management Journal* 19, no. 2: 195–212.

Stallworth, L.E. 1997. "Government Regulation of Workplace Disputes and Alternative Dispute Resolution." In *Government Regulations of the Employment Relationship*, ed. B.E. Kaufman, pp. 369–402. Madison: Industrial Relations Research Association.

Streeck, W. 1984. "Codetermination: The Fourth Decade."

In *International Yearbook of Organizational Democracy*, ed. B. Wilpert and A. Sorge, pp. 391–422. New York: Wiley.

Sundstrom, E., K.P. DeMeuse, and D. Futrell. 1990. "Work Teams: Applications and Effectiveness." *American Psychologist* 45, no. 2: 120–133.

Tolman, E.C. 1932. *Purposive Behavior in Animals and Men.* New York: Century.

Trist, E.L., and K.W. Bamford. 1951. "Some Social and Psychological Consequences of the Longwall Method of Goal-getting." *Human Relations* 4, no. 1: 3–38.

Vance, S.C. 1983. *Corporate Leadership: Boards, Directors, and Strategy.* New York: McGraw-Hill.

Vroom, V.H. 1964. *Work and Motivation.* New York: Wiley.

Walster, E., G.W. Walster, and E. Berscheid. 1978. *Equity: Theory and Research.* Boston: Allyn and Bacon.

White, R. 1959. "Motivation Reconsidered: The Concept of Competence." *Psychological Review* 66, no. 5: 297–333.

Whyte, W.F., T.H. Hammer, C.B. Meek, R. Nelson, and R.N. Stern. 1983. *Worker Participation and Ownership. Cooperative Strategies for Strengthening Local Economies.* Ithaca, N.Y.: ILR Press.

Wild, R. 1975. *Work Organization.* New York: Wiley.

Wolkinson, B.J., and R.N. Block. 1996. *Employment Law. The Workplace Rights of Employees and Employers.* Cambridge, Mass.: Blackwell.

9

Nonunion Employee Representation: A Legal/Policy Perspective

Samuel Estreicher

Virtually alone among the developed nations, American labor law contains a provision barring employers from forming committees of their employees to engage in bilateral discussions over wages, hours, and other conditions of employment. Section 8(a)(2) of the National Labor Relations Act of 1935 (NLRA) prohibits employer domination or support of any "labor organization," broadly defined in Section 2(5) to reach "any organization of any kind" in which (1) "employees participate," and (2) "which exists for the purpose, in whole or in part, of dealing with employers" over (3) "grievances, labor disputes, wages, rates of pay, hours of employment, or conditions of work." Other countries, such as Canada (Taras 1997), bar company-dominated or -supported unions from being certified as bargaining agencies or from being used as a basis to deny employees the opportunity to petition for independent representation. No other country, however, seeks so deeply to entrench the position of independent unions by foreclosing all space for employer-sponsored vehicles for bilateral discussions over pay and working conditions with employees.

Owing in large part to changes in the organization of work, which now require a greater level of involvement of line employees in work processes and aspects of firm decision making, the employer community in recent years has launched a legislative campaign to relax the strictures of Section 8(a)(2). In 1996 the Teamwork for Employees and Managers Act of 1996 (TEAM Act) passed both Houses of Congress but was vetoed by President Clinton. A renewed effort is likely with a change in the administration. The TEAM Act would amend Section 8(a)(2) to permit employers to establish and support committees of supervisors and employees that would "address matters of mutual interest, including, but not limited to, issues of quality, productivity, efficiency, and safety and health. . . ." Such committees, under the proposal, could not claim or seek authority as exclusive bargaining representatives or negotiate collective agreements. In the union-represented sector, presumably they could not be established prior to bargaining with the union. The proposal faced considerable opposition from the labor movement (and its friends in Congress), who charged that it would bring back the "company union" abuses of the 1930s.

The "Company Union" Problem of the 1930s

Those who drafted the NLRA, principally Senator Robert F. Wagner of New York, offered two distinct explanations for Section 8(a)(2). The first—what we might call the "employer coercion" rationale—was that the provision would remove an effective management device for beating down unions even when the employees plainly preferred independent representation. The second—what we might term the "false consciousness" rationale—seeks to protect the preconditions for self-organization by stripping employers of any role in the process of deciding whether workers need representation and who their representative shall be. (The term "false consciousness" refers to explanations for Section 8(a)(2) that remove certain representational options (employer-promoted systems) from the menu of choices available to workers, either because of fears that workers will not be able to make truly uncoerced choices or because of legislator preferences for a particular representational form (independent, multifirm unions)).

The employer-coercion concern grew out of the industrial conflict that led to the NLRA's enactment. In the period between the National Industrial Recovery Act of 1933 (NIRA), which announced in Section 7(a) that employees had a right to organize and engage in collective bargaining and could not be compelled to join a company union or other labor organization, and the 1935 *Schechter Poultry* decision declaring the NIRA unconstitutional, employee representation plans mushroomed as companies sought to fend off union-organizing drives (Pederson 1937; Jacoby 1985). For many companies, the in-house representation plans were part of an arsenal of tactics that also included the use of spies, professional strikebreakers, and mass discharges of union supporters (Auerbach 1966; Bernstein 1950).

Because of his service on the National Labor Board (one of a number of agencies formed to adjust labor-management disputes during the NIRA period), Senator Wagner personally confronted a number of notorious cases in which employers openly defied the law. These companies insisted they would deal with their employees as a group only through the vehicle of the employer-sanctioned representation plan—even when the independent union enjoyed the overwhelming support of the workers. For example, in the *Edward G. Budd Mfg. Co.* case, "when management told the United Automobile Federal Labor Union, which claimed 1,000 Budd employees as members, that the company 'could not recognize the American Federation of Labor inasmuch as Budd had employee representation that was operating satisfactorily,' approximately 1,500 Budd employees went on strike on November 14, 1933" (Gross 1974, p. 37). Similarly, in the *Weirton Steel* case, facing a strike of "some 10,000 Weirton workers" seeking recognition of the Amalgamated Association of Iron, Steel and Tin Workers, Ernest T. Weir first negotiated a settlement providing for an election under National Labor Board auspices. He "waited until the men had returned to work and then repudiated the agreement" by holding his own company union election in which the outside union was not permitted on the ballot (Bernstein 1970, pp. 177–178). As then-Professor Paul H. Douglas of the University of Chicago observed in testimony on the bill that became the NLRA:

> There is good reason . . . why workers should prefer regular interplant unions instead of plant company unions. When, however, the workers attempted to assert this preference, they were frequently denied this opportunity by their employers who, in these cases, refused to recognize the right of the regular union to carry out the collective bargaining, and who *insisted that the company union should be the bargaining agency instead.* (1 NLRA Legis. His. 1975, p. 238; emphasis supplied)

Despite this history, however, the employer-coercion explanation does not explain the full breadth of the Section 8(a)(2) prohibition because other aspects of the 1935 legislation directly addressed the coercive tactics that often accompanied the installation of the NIRA-era employee representation plans. In place of the powerless NIRA labor boards, Congress established the NLRB, an independent federal agency with authority to conduct elections and issue judicially enforceable orders against employers who refused to comply with the law. The statute clearly commanded employers to recognize and negotiate exclusively with the majority representative of the workers and refrain from discharge of, or other discrimination against, union supporters. Hence, even without Section 8(a)(2), company unions could not be erected to block an independent union that was desired by the workers.

Section 8(a)(2)—and the definition of "labor organization" in Section 2(5) to which the prohibition refers—goes well beyond the particular evils of the NIRA period (and beyond the 1926 Railway Labor Act: see Appendix 1). The provision seeks to prevent any employer role in the formation and operation of workplace entities that "deal with" employers on wages and working conditions. It applies even when employees are not seeking to organize an independent union and do not have the slightest interest in doing so. Senator Wagner's reasons for this broader proposition remain a bit murky. The underlying rationale cannot be grounded, however, in a concern over protecting employees from deceptive employer practices. To deal with the problem of employers who install a minority union as an exclusive bargaining representative, provisions akin to Canadian law would have sufficed—a bar to employer support or domination of entities seeking Section 9 authority—without need for the sweeping definition of "labor organization" in Section 2(5).

But for Senator Wagner there was a broader objective—and here the "false consciousness" rationale for Section 8(a)(2) comes into play. In Wagner's view, employers had to be kept out of the picture altogether in order to preserve the preconditions for genuine employee free choice. Company-supported systems, he argued, were inherently flawed vehicles for workplace representation; representatives could not effectively advance worker interests because they could not form alliances with national labor organizations.

Although Wagner took pains to explain that his bill would not restrict independent organizations comprised only of the employees of a single employer, he objected to the employer-dominated union "which arbitrarily restricts employee cooperation to a single employer unit, and which habitually allows workers to deal with their employer only through representatives chosen from among his employees." Such organizations could not form "wider areas of cooperation among employees" to maintain labor standards across firms and, even for issues properly limited to a single company, would be bereft of the expert assistance of a national organization. (See 78 Cong. Rec. 4229 [article by Wagner on "Company Unions" in the *New York Times*, March 11, 1934], reprinted in 1 NLRA Leg. Hist., pp. 23–24.) In addition, Wagner viewed these plans as inherently deceptive because the representatives were beholden to the employer, who would thus be able "to exercise a compelling force over the collective activities of his workers." As Wagner noted:

> Only representatives who are not subservient to the employer with whom they deal can act freely in the interest of the employees. Simple common sense tells us that a man does not possess this freedom when he bargains with those who control his source of livelihood. I am well aware that many

employer-dominated organizations now permit their employees to choose outside representatives, and the National Labor Board has affirmed this policy in a recent case. But this right is a mockery when the presence of a company union firmly entrenched in a plant enables an employer to exercise a compelling force over the collective activities of his workers. Freedom must begin with the removal of obstacles to its exercise. (1 NLRA Leg. His., p. 24)

There is a bit of a leap here from the evidence and arguments marshaled to the breadth of the provision enacted. The inherent weakness of company unions and the employer's ability to show favoritism through its company union would support at most the statutory preference for independent unions, rules against discrimination, and a refusal to include company unions as alternative options on NLRB ballots (which had been the practice during the NIRA period).

Perhaps the reach of Section 8(a)(2) is best explained, not by epistemological concerns about whether workers could make free choices if employers were permitted to launch their own representational vehicles, but by the substantive preference of Wagner and his colleagues for a particular form of representation (independent multiemployer unions) that would be capable of raising wages and lifting the nation to economic recovery (Kaufman 1997). Brody (1994), on the other hand, emphasizes the failure of the employer community of the time seriously to put forth their internal systems as a viable supplement to collective bargaining.

Whatever the ultimate explanation may be, Congress in 1935 decided to deny employers any role in establishing a workplace structure for employee representation even when that structure could not be raised as a bar to independent organization. In the name of "employee free choice," workers were to be presented with a set of restricted alternatives. They had to be put to the stark choice of whether

they wanted unilateral management or an independent union—with nothing in between.

To the modern ear, legislation against "false consciousness" smacks of paternalism. Who is to say what workers want? Aren't they the best stewards of their own fate? Are intermediate forms of workplace representation—falling between the polar extremes of unilateral management and independent unionism—inherently "false" choices?

A modern defense has been offered by Barenberg (1993, 1994). Using social psychology theory and relying on participant-observer studies of Japanese transplants (e.g., Fucini and Fucini 1990), he maintains that employer involvement in workplace representation provides opportunities for manipulating employee sentiment and undermining formation of group opposition forces that are not available in the traditional hierarchical workplace. A similar view is taken in Parker (1993). Gold (1994), the AFL-CIO's former general counsel, agrees with this analysis and further argues that the availability of "free" (i.e., company-sponsored) alternatives distorts employee decision making and reduces incentives to recognize voluntarily independent unions. Whether the presence of a company union fatally deters independent organization is a debatable historical and factual issue, belied by the number of AFL-CIO affiliates that had their origin in company-supported structures (e.g., Hogler 1989; Nelson 1989; Schacht 1975). Other criticisms of Section 8(a)(2)'s modern defense are offered in Estreicher (1994b).

Pre-1990 Interpretation of Section 8(a)(2) by the NLRB and the Courts

Newport News

In the period immediately after the passage of the NLRA, which covers workers in all industries affecting commerce except for employees of rail and air carriers, the Labor Board was busy disestablishing employee representation plans that companies had formed during the NIRA period. In one case (*Newport News*, 1939), a company plan in effect since 1927 had been revised in 1937 to eliminate employer payments to elected employee representatives and provide for a secret-ballot referendum of the employees, who by a "sweeping majority" voted for the plan's continuance. Even though it was conceded that "the company had never objected to its employees joining labor unions [and] that no discrimination had been practiced against them because of their membership in outside unions," the Supreme Court agreed with the Board that disestablishment was required under Section 8(a)(2):

> While the men are free to adopt any form of organization and representation whether purely local or connected with a national body, their purpose so to do [*sic*] may be obstructed by the existence and recognition of an old plan or organization the original structure or operation of which was not in accordance with the provisions of the law. (*Newport News*, 1939, p. 250)

Attempt at Section 8(a)(2) Reform in 1947

In part because of favorable experience with employee committees established at the suggestion of the War Production Board during World War II, an attempt was made in 1947 to loosen up the strictures of Section 8(a)(2). The House of Representatives passed H.R. 3020, which contained language providing that it would not constitute, or be evidence of, an unfair labor practice for employers to "form" or "maintain"

> a committee of employees and discuss with it matters of mutual interest, including grievances, wages, hours of employment, and other working conditions, if the Board has not certified or the employer has not recognized a representative as their representative under Section 9. (H.R. 3020, 80th Cong., 1st sess. 26 [1947])

The Senate's bill (S. 1126) did not contain this provision, limiting any change to Section 8(a)(2) to the proviso currently in the law that allows individual employees or groups of employees to present grievances to their employees on company time. In conference, the Senate version prevailed.

Cabot Carbon's Definition of "Dealing With"

Section 8(a)(2)'s reach received its authoritative construction from the Supreme Court in its 1959 decision in *Cabot Carbon*. In that case, the company had continued its wartime "Employee Committees" into the postwar period for the purpose of handling grievances at its nonunion plants and for nonrepresented personnel at unionized plants. Even though the committees had no membership requirements, collected no dues, never attempted to negotiate collective agreements, and were not found to derogate from the authority of certified labor organizations where they existed, the Court agreed with the NLRB that the committees were "labor organizations" within the meaning of Section 2(5):

> [The Committees] made proposals and requests respecting such matters as seniority, job classification, job bidding, working schedules, holidays, vacations, sick leave, a merit system, wage corrections, and improvement of working facilities and conditions. [P]lant officials participated in the discussion of these matters and frequently granted the Committee requests. . . . [The Company argues that] the proposals and requests amounted only to recommendations and that final decision

remained with [the Company]. But this is true of all such "dealing," whether with an independent or a company-dominated "labor organization." The principal distinction lies in the unfettered power of the former to insist upon its requests (*Cabot Carbon*, 1959, pp. 213–214).

Some Loosening Up of Section 8(a)(2) in the Labor Board and the Courts of Appeals

The NLRB's "Complete Delegation" Approach

In the NLRB's 1977 ruling in *General Foods*, the Board established the principle that the "dealing with" element of a Section 2(5) statutory "labor organization" is not present where management delegates some portion of its authority to employee groups. General Foods—an early pioneer in the establishment of self-directed teams (Walton 1982)—organized its small testing and research facility at St. Anne, Illinois into four work teams that, acting by consensus of their members, made job assignments to individual team members, arranged job rotations, scheduled overtime, and interviewed job applicants. The Labor Board adopted the administrative law judge (ALJ)'s findings that the four teams were akin to "unstructured assemblies of employees, without spokesman or leadership and without any agency relationship to its components"; that the exercise of some managerial responsibilities by the teams involved a delegation from management rather than "dealing with the employer on a group basis"; and that any discussion of pay and working conditions arose from individual workers voicing their own views, rather than positions taken by the team.

In other rulings, the NLRB held that companies could establish committees comprised of management personnel and employees to adju-

dicate grievances. Thus, in *Sparks Nugget* (1977), the Board reasoned that

> the Employees' Council performs a purely adjudicatory function and does not interact with management for any purpose or in any manner other than to render a final decision on the grievance. Therefore, it cannot be said that the Employees' Council . . . "deals with" management. Rather, it appears to perform a function of management: i.e., resolving employee grievances. (p. 276)

The Board in that case did find that the employer violated the act in unilaterally establishing the adjudicative body without prior consultation with the Section 9 bargaining representative. (For a similar ruling, see *Mercy-Memorial Hospital*, 1977).

Some Disquiet with Adversarialism in the Courts of Appeals

In the 1980s, some of the Courts of Appeals (principally the Sixth and Ninth Circuits) strove to find some latitude for internal systems within the confines of Section 8(a)(2). The ruling in *Streamway Division* (1982) is illustrative of some judicial reluctance to find "labor organization" status. In that case, after one unsuccessful union organizing drive but before a second such campaign, the company formed a committee of elected employee representatives to meet with management personnel to identify problems and elicit suggestions for improving operations. The employee representatives served for three-month terms; the company thus sought to maximize employee participation through rotation. The Sixth Circuit, disagreeing with the Board, found that the committee did not constitute a "labor organization." The court identified three factors: (1) the "continuous rotation of Committee members . . . makes the Committee resemble more closely . . . employee groups speaking directly to management on an individual, rather than a representative basis"; (2) the absence of any antiunion animus or evidence "connecting the creation of the committee to the organization drive that occurred months afterward"; and (3) the fact that neither the employees nor the union involved in the election campaigns "considered that the Committee even remotely resembled a labor organization in the ordinary sense of the word" (*Streamway Division*, 1982, pp. 294–295).

In *Hertzka & Knowles* (1974), the Ninth Circuit found some flexibility, not in the definition of "labor organization," but in the required element of a Section 8(a)(2) violation that there be impermissible employer "support" or "domination." Following a union decertification, the employer, an architectural firm, acted on an employee's suggestion to form five in-house committees of employees and partners to address professional stature within the firm, remuneration, minimum standards, efficiency, and the physical environment. The court held that unlawful "domination" requires a showing that "the employees' free choice . . . is stifled by the degree of employer involvement at issue." Because the committees were formed at the suggestion of an employee, there was no evidence of "actual interference with the assertion of employee demands through the committees," and management did not exercise a formal veto over employee suggestions, they did not violate Section 8(a)(2) (*Hertzka & Knowles*, 1974, pp. 630–31).

Pressure on the Section 8(a)(2) Model: Changes in the Organization of Work

This is how the situation stood under the NLRA going into the 1990s. Whatever the conceptual and choice-inhibiting difficulties with Section 8(a)(2), for several decades the prohibition presented no real problems for American companies—given the prevailing theories on how best to utilize human resources. These theories, heavily influenced by the "Scientific Management" school of Frederick W. Taylor, emphasized hierarchal organization and stripping production and service workers of "brainwork," the latter to be the exclusive preserve of small armies of engineers and supervisors. Against this backdrop, Congress could plausibly assume that when companies instituted committee systems, they were interested more in union avoidance than in efficiency and productivity.

Today, Section 8(a)(2), as written, is problematic for American companies because they can no longer afford Taylorism. The "mass production" factory of the 1930s and 1940s is a relic of the past. Global competitive product markets put increasing pressure on managers to reduce the layers of supervisors and engineers that the old hierarchical structures required and to delegate increasing responsibility to front-line workers. American companies, particularly in the manufacturing sector, require "smart" workers who take "ownership" in their jobs—who (with minimal supervision) can operate computer controls, understand and engage flexibly in the production/service delivery processes, monitor quality, and tailor their work to the special requirements of customers and suppliers. To meet customer demands more effectively and reduce capital requirements, firms are utilizing general-purpose multifunctional or programmable equipment that requires workers to develop problem-solving and "debugging" capabilities, once the domain solely of layers of industrial engineers and supervisors (MacDuffie and Krafcik 1992; Kochan 1992; Adler 1988).

This ongoing transformation of the workplace requires a high level of commitment from front-line workers that is flatly inconsistent with the unilateral style of the Taylorist school of management. Workers cannot be treated as passive recipients of management dictates if they are at the same time expected to learn new tasks and skills; rotate among work assignments; interact with engineers, customers, and suppliers; and essentially supervise themselves.

Varieties of Employee Involvement Programs

"Employee involvement" appears in a variety of forms and should not be viewed as a unitary phenomenon.

Off-Line Systems

Employers are now experimenting with a variety of approaches for producing a high-commitment workforce. Some take the form of Japanese-style "quality circles," problem-solving or cross-functional teams that bring together workers and managers to solve operational issues and develop improvements in work design and processes (e.g., Ledford, Lawler, and Mohrman 1988; Lawler and Mohrman 1985; Mantz and Sims 1993). In these systems, employee involvement takes place "off-line" because the systems are parallel to the production or service delivery processes with which the workers are normally engaged, and hence leave undisturbed the pre-existing organization of work (Hill 1991).

On-Line Systems

Increasingly, leading companies such as Ford, Motorola, Texas Instruments, General Foods,

Procter & Gamble, General Electric, TRW, Inc., and Eastman Kodak, to name but a few, have moved to "on-line" systems that seek to integrate employee involvement with actual production or service processes, and thus to transform the organization of work. These companies have moved away from a functional organization that divided, say, production, engineering, and purchasing functions into separate departments, preferring instead to create divisions of production and support personnel that are dedicated to particular processes, such as new product development, or particular product or customer lines. Such reorganization seeks to promote interdependence among groups involved with the same product or in servicing the same customer, heighten responsiveness to customer needs, and facilitate measurement of performance and quality. Many of these firms have also sought to delegate authority downward by training front-line workers to function as "self-directed work teams" responsible for task assignments, scheduling of work, maintaining and improving performance levels, cost and quality controls, and safety—all with a minimum of supervision (e.g., Boyett and Conn 1991; Wellins, Byhan, and Wilson 1991; Goodman, Devadas, and Hughson 1988; Lawler 1986).

These developments have certainly not taken hold in all U.S. companies, and indeed the shift toward self-directed teams is still in its formative stages. Even within the same company some divisions and even buildings utilize traditional processes next door to those embarked on team-based systems (Estreicher 1994a, b). But considerable diffusion of these new approaches has already occurred. Osterman's (1994) survey of establishments with fifty or more employees reveals that over half use teams to some extent, and 40.5 percent involve at least half of their nonsupervisory front-line workforce in teams.

Some have argued that employee involvement

works best in union-represented environments (Appelbaum and Batt 1994; Eaton and Voos 1992; Kelley and Harrison 1992). These findings are sharply contested in McMahan and Lawler (1994). The comparative advantages (or disadvantages) of union representation for organizational performance are beyond the scope of this paper.

Uncertain Legal Status of Employee Involvement Programs

There is considerable concern in many, although not all, management circles that these workplace innovations may run afoul of Section 8(a)(2).

Off-line systems would appear to be in greatest jeopardy because they bring together workers and managers outside natural work groupings to address workplace problems. These systems would appear to be, at least facially, "organization[s]" within the meaning of Section 2(5) of the NLRA "in which employees participate and which exists for the purpose, in whole or in part, of dealing with employers. . . ."

To skirt legal difficulties, companies may take steps to avoid any give-and-take with employees and use the off-line system strictly as a one-way communications device (*Sears Roebuck* 1985) or as a task force to perform a managerial task (*General Foods* 1977), so as not to be said to be "dealing with" a statutory "labor organization" within Section 8(a)(2)'s strictures. Also, firms may attempt to steer clear of any discussion of compensation and working conditions by confining the quality circle or problem-solving group to issues of productivity and quality—however difficult such line-drawing may prove in practice.

On-Line Systems

Self-directed teams and other on-line systems stand a better chance of not being treated as "labor organization[s]" because of the Board's 1977 *General Foods* decision (discussed above). Despite academic criticism (Kohler 1986; Barenberg 1994), the decision remains good law.

However, even with a supportive ruling like *General Foods*—which a differently constituted Labor Board might decide differently—serious legal questions remain. First, the ALJ in that case was impressed by the fact that the *entire* bargaining unit was organized into teams, finding it difficult to ascribe labor-organization status to a group that was not "set apart from the totality of the bargaining unit which it has been called upon to represent." Does the analysis change where, as is true in many companies, self-directed teams have taken hold only in some divisions or parts of divisions? Team-based systems cannot be instantly implemented by managerial dictate. Successful systems require a learning process whereby employees take on increasing responsibilities only after they develop appropriate skills and have mastered less difficult assignments (MacDuffie and Krafcik 1992; Useem and Kochan 1992).

Second, does the rationale in *General Foods* apply only to situations where management can be said to have relinquished *all* control over the decisions delegated to the teams? For many companies, supervisors continue to play a guiding role on teams, either because the team members have not yet developed the capability to operate as fully self-directed units or because management believes it unwise yet to relinquish its guiding influence. In the absence of a complete delegation of managerial authority to the work teams, can such teams be said to "deal with" employers?

Another issue concerns the problem of line-drawing, for teams will not always be able to steer clear of discussions of pay and working conditions. The ALJ in *General Foods* dismissed evidence of such discussions between team members and supervisors as instances of individuals voicing their own grievances or as *de minimis* excursions into traditional areas of collective bargaining. At what point does a team's exercise of responsibility over matters like job assignments, peer performance review, safety, and recognition awards—which are commonly handled on a team basis in the more advanced companies— constitute "dealings" over Section 2(5) subjects?

Off-Line Systems

Beginning with its 1992 ruling in *Electromation*, the NLRB has engaged in a largely unsuccessful effort to clarify the law of employee involvement. *Electromation* involved an off-line system of employer-initiated committees that plainly dealt with Section 2(5) subjects. Responding to employee dissatisfaction with unilateral changes in its existing attendance bonus and wage policies— and well before any union appeared on the scene—Electromation formed employee "Action Committees" for dealings with management over absenteeism, pay progression, attendance bonus, and no-smoking policies. The committees were comprised of six employees who volunteered to sit in meetings with one or two management officials. There was no evidence that the employer initially was aware of an incipient Teamster union organizing drive when it formed the teams. After the union surfaced and demanded recognition, management informed the employees that it would no longer participate on the committees, but stated that the employees could continue to meet if they so desired. On these facts, the Labor Board found a violation of Section 8(a)(2) because the committees were a company-dominated "bilateral mechanism" for dealings with employees.

In its May 1993 ruling in *E.I. Du Pont & Co.*, the Board applied the reasoning in *Electromation* to invalidate Du Pont's employee safety and fitness committees at its Deepwater, New Jersey, facility. Because Deepwater was a union-represented facility, without reaching the Section 8(a)(2) issue, the Board could easily have found the committees to be an attempt at "direct dealing" with employees over mandatory bargaining subjects in violation of the employer's duty to bargain exclusively with the majority representative. Instead, the Board chose to rest its decision on Section 8(a)(2). The agency allowed—as akin to "brainstorming" sessions—the company's all-day safety conferences in which employees were encouraged to share safety-related suggestions without deciding on proposals for improved safety conditions. By contrast, Du Pont's safety and fitness committees were charged with developing such proposals and deciding on safety incentive awards for employees and hence, in the NLRB's view, constituted an employer-dominated bilateral mechanism for dealing with the employer on statutory subjects.

Both *Electromation* and *Du Pont* involved off-line employee involvement programs that treated Section 2(5) subjects, and thus arguably left open the question of the legality of off-line systems that avoid consideration of such subjects and of on-line systems like self-directed teams based on natural work groupings. Nevertheless, however faithful these rulings may be to the original understanding of the Wagner Act, they have cast a pall of uncertainty over such programs as well.

Arguments for Limiting the Reach of *Electromation*

A number of arguments have been offered for limiting the reach of *Electromation* and *Du Pont*, but they are not likely to withstand analysis or offer much shelter from NLRB litigation. (Appendix 2 contains post-*Electromation/Du Pont* rulings at the Labor Board.)

Representational Capacity

One limiting reading of the Board's rulings is that Section 8(a)(2) requires proof that the employees involved in the employer-initiated and -supported system functioned in a representational capacity (Perl 1994). The statute, however, does not expressly contain such a requirement. Read literally, Section 2(5) reaches "any organization of any kind" satisfying the "dealing with" and subject-matter elements. Indeed, although the Board in *Electromation* left this question open as a formal matter, it found a representational element present on the rather meager showing that the committee members (though volunteers selected by management) were supposed "to get their ideas from other employees regarding the subjects of their committees for the purpose of reaching solutions that would satisfy the employees as a whole." The employees serving on the safety and fitness committees in *Du Pont* were found to be acting in a representational capacity because they came from different functional areas in the plant and, in that sense, reflected a representative cross-section of the plant.

More recently, Polaroid's employee focus group, called the "Employee Owners Influence Council" (EOIC), was found to be a representative body because the company in fact "encouraged [EOIC] members to communicate with other employees about issues under consideration by the EOIC and to report back to the EOIC on the sentiments of these employees" (*Polaroid* 1996).

The Labor Board seems to be using an attenuated, elastic notion of representation. It is not necessary that employee representatives are designated or selected to act on behalf of others, or even affirmatively encouraged to canvass and poll the views of the represented. Indeed, formal selection by the larger group, standing alone, may be determinative of labor-organizational status under Section 2(5), even if employees on the committees are not expressly urged to, and do not in fact, poll and report back to their colleagues on the plant floor (*Webcor Packing* 1995).

Apparently all that is required for representational capacity is that committee members reflect a functional cross-section of the plant or department, and perhaps see their role as one of communicating views or suggestions from their particular area. Plainly, representational capacity will be readily found in virtually every off-line structure, whether it be a plant safety committee or cross-function grouping to discuss, say, work shifts or merit incentive awards (NLRB Gen. Counsel Mem. 1993). (Even for on-line systems, there may be a problem if the liaison role of the team leader is deemed to satisfy the representational element of Section 2(5) [Barenberg 1994].)

The Distinction Between Quality/ Productivity and Working Conditions

Board member Oviatt's concurrence in *Electromation* suggested that programs confined to narrowly conceived "productivity" and "quality" issues do not come within the subjects of "dealing" reached by Section 2(5) ("grievances, labor disputes, wages, rates of pay, hours of employment or conditions of work") (LeRoy 1993). Meyer (1993) argues that as long as committees confine themselves to permissive subjects of bargaining, these groups will not be held to satisfy the subject-matter element in Section 2(5).

Admittedly, from management's perspective, much of the business of employee involvement is directed to securing improvements in efficiency and quality. But the distinction between "productivity" or "quality" and Section 2(5) subjects is likely to prove ephemeral in many instances. This is because employee contributions to productivity and quality are likely to involve suggestions for altering wages, hours, and other terms and conditions of employment (Datz 1993). Safety issues, for example, will almost invariably involve work conditions (NLRB Gen. Counsel Mem. 1993). Similarly, a work group focusing on ways better to utilize existing personnel is bound to turn its attention to subjects such as shift schedules and job assignments. Sometimes, as in *Webcor Packing* (1995), the employees themselves will insist that the program take up matters of pay and working conditions.

Even if this proffered distinction were workable in practice, is it really desirable to curtail the capacity of employee involvement systems to address key motivational questions such as incentive compensation? For example, employee committees are an important feature of the "Scanlon Plan" gain-sharing strategy (Strauss 1990; Schuster 1983). Similar committees also play a role in IMPROSHARE, a leading alternative gain-sharing program that tends to deemphasize employee involvement (Interview with Mitchell I. Fein and Thomas Lennon of Mitchell Fein, Inc., Hillsdale, N.J., January 10, 1994).

The new model of worker involvement seeks generally to encourage a high level of commitment to the goals of the firm. But this objective is frustrated if legal strictures require avoiding any discussion of financial rewards for that commitment—a subject that must continue to be determined in the old-fashioned way via unilateral pronouncements from the human resources department.

Avoidance of Bilateralism

The NLRB rulings allow one-sided communication devices, like the all-day safety conferences sustained in *Du Pont*, at which employees are permitted to express ideas and suggestions, as long as management only listens. Such devices are surely useful, but like the quality-circle experiments of the 1970s and 1980s, they do not offer a model for sustained employee involvement. Workers are now expected to shoulder new responsibilities, bring to their jobs their full range of mental and interpersonal skills, and be aggressively and self-consciously concerned with product quality, customer satisfaction, and firm profits. And yet the law still requires one-sided conversations and unilateral management.

Structural Independence

Summers (1993), Klare (1994), Morris (1996), and Gould (1996) suggest that firms can avoid liability under Section 8(a)(2) if they are willing to allow the committees or teams to function as independent units free to select their own representatives, set their own agendas, and press disagreements with management. But this proffered limitation misstates the purpose of many employee-involvement systems that, while they also offer a vehicle for employees to have a say in workplace decisions, are not intended as a substitute for unions but as an aid to management in pursuit of its objectives. Even self-directed teams that have authority to hire new employees, to rotate job assignments, and to evaluate each other's performance operate within the sphere of authority delegated by management (Estreicher 1994a, b).

What Form Should Section 8(a)(2) Reform Take?

In sum, Section 8(a)(2), as it currently stands, erects significant obstacles for many employee involvement programs in nonunion firms. Paradoxically, it is precisely those features that we otherwise might most want to encourage in the nonunion sector—management "give and take," some sort of selection procedure to ensure representativeness, and wide-ranging discussion extending into matters of pay and working conditions—that are most likely to trigger regulatory difficulties.

Whatever its original justification, Section 8(a)(2) has not spurred union growth in over five decades and has had largely negative effects. From the perspective of a predominantly nonunion American workforce, Section 8(a)(2) affirmatively discourages what the law should encourage: enhanced employee voice and involvement. Moreover, under current social conditions—a better educated workforce, minimum wage and other protective legislation, and a rights-conscious legal culture—it is doubtful that permitting employers to institute committees for bilateral discussions over matters of mutual concern, including pay and working conditions, would have the effect of preventing employees from making an uncoerced decision over whether they wish to be represented by an independent union.

TEAM Act Proposal

What form should Section 8(a)(2) reform take? In my view, the current version of the proposed TEAM Act does not go far enough. (The text of the TEAM Act proviso is set out in Appendix 3.) First, it leaves undisturbed the definition of "labor organization" under Section 2(5) of the NLRA

and related labor laws. The safe harbor thought to be created by the TEAM Act may well not remove the cloud of legal uncertainty and potential liability that hangs over companies that provide financial assistance to employee committees or do not comply with the election, reporting, and disclosure requirements for unions under the Labor-Management Reporting and Disclosure Act of 1959 (LMRDA) (Morris 1996). The TEAM Act notably does not amend the definition of "labor organization" in Section 3(i) of the LMRDA (29 U.S.C. Section 402(i)). Polaroid's earlier legal difficulties with its "Employees' Committee" arose under the LMRDA, not the NLRA. (See Letter of June 11, 1992, from James B. Cannon, area administrator, Office of Labor-Management Standards, U.S. Dept. of Labor, to William Graney, chairman, Polaroid Corporation's Employees' Committee [preliminarily sustaining employee's complaint that she had been denied right to elect chairman and vice-chairman under Section 401(b) of the LMRDA, 29 U.S.C. Section 481(b)]).

Second, the proposed bill does not expressly make clear that the "matters of mutual interest" that companies can discuss with employee committees may include pay and working conditions. Especially in view of the fact that earlier versions of the TEAM Act proposal would have permitted discussion of what are now Section 2(5) subjects (LeRoy 1996), employers may still face liability for committees that stray into these otherwise prohibited areas "on more than [an] isolated or ad hoc basis" (Reno Hilton Resorts Corporation 1995).

From the other direction, the TEAM bill needs to make provision for situations where employers act strategically to put in place committees or other employee-involvement processes for the purpose of thwarting a pending or imminent union-organizing drive, with the intention of abolishing the committees when the union leaves the scene. Senator Bingaman had offered an amendment to the TEAM bill to curb such abuses (Bingaman Amend. 1996).

Also, as I have argued in a number of places (Estreicher 1993, 1994a,b, 1996, 1997), any change in Section 8(a)(2) should be part of an integrated package of reforms that also (1) bolsters the legal protections for employees wishing to be represented by independent unions, and (2) alters existing rules that unnecessarily encourage adversarial relations and stymie cooperative labor-management solutions in the union sector.

Evaluation of Alternative Proposals

Sawyer/Dorgan Substitute

In the September 1995 debates in the House, Representative Sawyer proposed a substitute for the TEAM Act (then H.R. 7543), (the text of which is set out in Appendix 3) that would allow (1) "employee-managed work units" to hold periodic meetings to discuss among themselves "conditions of work within the work unit"; (2) "supervisor-managed work units" to hold periodic meetings to discuss the unit's work responsibilities, in the course of which "conditions of work within the work unit" could be broached; and (3) committees created to decide methods of quality and production to discuss working conditions, but only "on isolated occasions" and only in the course of "considering design quality or production issues. . . ." Moreover, employers could not disband or alter work units or committees during union-organizing drives and could not punish employees for refusing to participate in such units or committees.

In the July 1996 debates on S.295, Senator Dorgan introduced a proposal similar to Representative Sawyer's.

The Sawyer/Dorgan substitute is problematic on a number of grounds. First, by protecting employees in their refusal to participate in employee-managed and employer-managed work units, this alternative measure would hamstring the effective operation of on-line forms of employee involvement. These programs are principally vehicles for getting the employer's work done. Here, employees should be subject to the usual rule that they have to meet work requirements if they are to be paid and retain their positions.

Second, even aside from this difficulty, the Sawyer/Dorgan proposal would not protect from Section 8(a)(2) systems that assign members of work teams to serve as liaisons to broader plantwide committees. For example, safety leaders of work teams might also sit on a plantwide safety council to consider issues of overall plant design and operations.

Third, with respect to off-line forms of employee involvement, the proposal would merely restate existing law. Off-line committees can already in isolated instances discuss work conditions in the course of addressing quality and process issues. Under the Sawyer/Dorgan substitute, a company that established a plantwide group of employees to elicit and respond to employee reactions to a proposed change in, say, medical insurance benefits would still be risking a violation of Section 8(a)(2).

Finally, the proposal was too rigid in preventing employees from altering or abandoning team processes units during organizational campaigns. No showing was required, contrary to present law (*Exchange Parts* 1964), that the employer was changing the status quo for the purpose of affecting the outcome of a NLRB representation election.

Moran Substitute—Election Requirements

Also in the course of the House's September 1995 debates, Representative Moran urged that members of any committee system that operates in a representational capacity be elected in a secret ballot by a majority of the employees. The Moran proposal echoes a common theme among the TEAM Act's opponents—an employer-initiated and -supported system that engages in any representational activity must provide for secret-ballot elections (e.g., Morris 1996; Kubasek et al. 1997).

Although elections make sense in certain situations, and we can count on employers in their self-interest to use them when they do, a legal mandate is unwise. An election requirement would be entirely unworkable for on-line systems where assignments within work teams are a function of employee skills and aptitude, rather than popularity, or where the team is an at an early stage of the learning process and some members are resisting their new responsibilities.

Elections are also problematic for some off-line systems. If a company wants a cross-functional team to discuss changes in incentive pay, is it clear that the best way to choose employee representatives for the team is on the basis of a popular vote, rather than an assessment of which employees are likely to make the most productive contribution to team deliberations?

More fundamentally, the Moran proposal and others like it mistakenly view employee-involvement programs as a substitute for unions. That was the position taken by employers in the early 1930s. It is not, however, the objective of companies establishing such programs or of the proponents of the TEAM Act.

Employers are not seeking to put in place independent—or, depending on your point of view, adversarial—structures of their own making.

Firms embark on such programs where they believe management goals will be furthered. If the cost of expanding worker roles is to invite a federal mandate, many firms will abandon or substantially curtail their employee-involvement programs. They may do so because of a fear of creating a beachhead for an independent union drive. Employers may also legitimately have concerns that their organizational culture and employee capability require continued management oversight of the involvement effort. These programs entail a learning process in which employees develop the skills to function effectively as a team and gradually come to see the benefits of meetings, cross-functional training, peer evaluation of performance, and related activities. The extent to which management releases its controls will often be a function of the success of the learning effort. In the end, election requirements and the like would affirmatively discourage experimentation in nonunion firms, particularly those companies that need to transform a low-productivity, low-morale workforce.

Some advocates of election requirements are less interested in perfecting nonunion employee involvement systems than they are in closing a perceived "representation gap" in the nonunion workforce (e.g., Rogers 1993). In a sense, the Section 8(a)(2) issue is thought to provide an opening wedge for promoting inside-the-firm institutions that might ultimately seek union representation. This is a mistaken strategy both for the practical reasons given above and because it is important to maintain conceptual and practical distance between company-initiated and -supported systems and independent employee organizations.

Employee involvement is a desirable goal whether or not it increases the demand for independent representation, as long it does not prevent workers from effectively deciding on their own whether they want such representation. Because employee involvement programs can enhance opportunities for worker participation and improve firm performance, but without foreclosing other options, legal restrictions should be lifted. Such programs are not a substitute for unions, however, and should not be made to do the work of unions. The "voice" benefits of employee involvement obtain only to the extent that management believes that organizational goals are furthered by such programs. Therefore, employees should clearly understand that the employer's committee system is a vehicle for participation in workplace decisions in aid of management's objectives, not an alternative form of union representation.

Bolstering the Exit Option

I do believe, as stated in previous writings, that a significant relaxation of the Section 8(a)(2) prohibition should be accompanied by changes in the law that make less hazardous the option to seek independent representation. Employees should not be confronted simply with the choice between a "free" form of representation under the employer's plan and the risk of job loss in opting for independent unionism. Some argue that union supporters face a 1 in 20 risk of retaliatory discharge (Weiler 1983); others would lower the estimate to 1 in 60 (LaLonde and Meltzer 1991). Either way, workers dissatisfied with their company's committee system or other aspects of their work lives should be able, without risk of losing their jobs, to choose independent unions. Reform, if it is to take place, should be part of an integrated package that includes additional penalties for proven retaliatory discharge, broadened union access to the employee electorate once a NLRB election has been scheduled, and dis-

incentives to pursue the representational dispute after an election through meritless litigation.

*

It is better to deal directly with the adequacy of Section 9 protections, rather than freight employee involvement programs with requirements that can serve only to stymie initiatives that hold the promise of enhancing worker participation and releasing the productive potential of American workers.

Acknowledgments

An earlier version of this chapter was presented at the Conference on "Nonunion Forms of Employee Representation: History, Contemporary Practice and Policy," Banff, Alberta, September 3–5, 1997. The views expressed here are solely those of the author and should not be attributed to NYU's Center for Labor and Emmployment Law or any other organization. I dedicate this paper to the memory of Alice Hanson Cook, a pioneer in the study of labor unions and gender issues and long a mainstay of the Cornell ILR faculty, who in 1970 first got me thinking about these issues by asking for a paper on "the role of the company unions in the formation of the United Steelworkers of America." All rights reserved. Copyright © 1999 by Samuel Estreicher.

References

Adler, Paul. 1988. "Managing Flexible Automation." *California Management Review* 30 (Spring): 34–56.
Aircraft Mechanics Fraternal Assn., 21 N.M.B. 229 (May 3, 1994).
Amendment to S. 295, The Teamwork for Employees and Management Act of 1997, 105th Cong., 1st Sess., intended to be proposed by Mr. Bingaman.
Appelbaum, Eileen, and Rosemary Batt. 1994. *The New American Workplace: Transforming Work Systems in the United States.* Ithaca, N.Y.: ILR Press.

Auerbach, Jerrold S. 1966. *Labor and Liberty: The LaFollette Committee and the New Deal.* Indianapolis: Bobbs-Merrill.

Barenberg, Mark. 1993. "The Political Economy of the Wagner Act: Power, Symbol, and Workplace Cooperation." *Harvard Law Review* 106, no. 7 (May): 1379–1496.

———. 1994. "Democracy and Domination in the Law of Workplace Cooperation: From Bureaucratic to Flexible Production." *Columbia Law Review* 94, no. 3 (April): 753–983.

Bernstein, Irving. 1950. *The New Deal Collective Bargaining Policy.* Berkeley: University of California Press.

———. 1970. *Turbulent Years: A History of the American Workers, 1933–1941.* Boston: Houghton Mifflin.

Boyett, Joseph, and Henry P. Conn. 1991. *Workplace 2000: The Revolution Reshaping American Business.* New York: Dutton Books, esp. pp. 234–265, 328–345.

Brody, David. 1994. "Section 8(a)(2) and the Origins of the Wagner Act." In *Restoring the Promise of American Labor Law*, ed. Sheldon Friedman, Richard W. Hurd, Rudolph A. Oswald, and Ronald L. Seeber, pp. 29–44. Ithaca, N.Y.: ILR Press.

Datz, Harold J. 1993. "Employee Participation Programs and the National Labor Relations Act—A Guide for the Perplexed." Reprinted in Bureau of National Affairs, Inc., *Daily Labor Report*, February 17, pp. E-1 ff.

Eaton, Adrienne E., and Paula B. Voos. 1992. "Unions and Contemporary Innovations in Work Organization, Compensation and Employee Participation." In *Unions and Economic Competitiveness*, ed. Lawrence Mishel and Paula B. Voos, pp. 173–215. Armonk, N.Y.: M.E. Sharpe.

E.I. Du Pont & Co., 311 N.L.R.B. 893 (1993).

Electromation, Inc., 309 N.L.R.B. 990 (1992), enforced, 35 F.3d 1148 (7th Cir. 1994).

Estreicher, Samuel. 1993. "Labor Law Reform in a World of Competitive Product Markets." *Chicago-Kent Law Review* 69, no. 1: 3–46.

———. 1994a. Statement of Samuel Estreicher, Professor of Law, New York University School of Law, Before the Commission on the Future of Worker-Management Relations (January 19, 1994).

———. 1994b. "Employee Involvement and the 'Company Union' Prohibition: The Case for Partial Repeal of Section 8(a)(2) of the NLRA." *New York University Law Review* 69, no. 1 (April): 125–161.

———. 1996. "Freedom of Contract and Labor Law Reform: Opening Up the Possibilities for Value-Added Unionism." *New York University Law Review* 71, no. 3 (June): 827–849.

———. 1997. Statement of Samuel Estreicher, Professor of Law, New York University School of Law, Before the U.S. Senate Committee on Labor and Human Resources (February 12, 1997).

"Former NLRB Chairman Miller Calls *Electromation* Problem 'Myth.'" 1993. Bureau of National Affairs, Inc., *Daily Labor Report*, October 20, p. A-5.

Fucini, Joseph J., and Suzy Fucini. 1990. *Working for the Japanese: Inside Mazda's American Auto Plant.* New York: Free Press.

General Foods Corp., 231 N.L.R.B. 1232 (1977).

Gold, Laurence. 1994. "The Legal Status of 'Employee Participation' Programs after the NLRB's *Electromation* and *Du Pont* Decisions." In *Contemporary Issues in Labor and Employment Law: Proceedings of New York University 46th Annual National Conference on Labor*, ed. Bruno Stein, pp. 329–351. Boston: Little, Brown.

Goodman, Paul S., Rukmini Devadas, and Terri L. Griffith Hughson. 1988. "Groups and Productivity: Analyzing the Effectiveness of Self-Managing Teams." In *Productivity in Organizations: New Perspectives from Industrial and Organizational Psychology*, ed. John P. Campbell, Richard J. Campbell, and Associates, pp. 295–327. San Francisco: Jossey-Bass.

Gould, William B. 1996. "Remarks of NLRB Chairman Gould on Workplace Cooperation." Reprinted in Bureau of National Affairs, Inc., *Daily Labor Report*, October 28, pp. E-1 to E-3.

Gross, James A. 1974. *The Making of the National Labor Relations Board: A Study in Economics, Politics, and the Law, 1933–1937.* Vol. 1. Albany, N.Y.: SUNY Press.

Hertzka & Knowles v. *NLRB*, 503 F.2d 625 (9th Cir. 1974).

Hill, Stephen. 1991. "Why Quality Circles Failed but Total Quality Management Might Succeed." *British Journal of Industrial Relations* 29, no. 4 (December): 541–568.

Hogler, Raymond L. 1989. "Worker Participation, Employer Anti-Unionism, and Labor Law: The Case of the Steel Industry, 1918–1937." *Hofstra Labor Law Journal* 87, no. 1 (Fall): 1–69.

Hogler, Raymond L., and Guillermo J. Grenier. 1992. *Employee Participation and Labor Law in the American Workplace.* New York: Qurorum Books.

Jacoby, Sanford M. 1985. *Employing Bureaucracy: Managers, Unions, and the Transformation of Work in American Industry, 1900–1945.* New York: Columbia University Press.

Kaufman, Bruce E. 1997. "Company Unions: Sham Organizations or Victims of the New Deal?" In *Proceedings of the Forty-Ninth Annual Meeting of the Industrial Relations Research Assn*, ed. Paula B. Voos. Madison: IRRA.

Kelley, Maryellen R., and Bennett Harrison. 1992. "Unions, Technology, and Labor-Management Cooperation." In

Unions and Economic Competitiveness, ed. Lawrence Mishel and Paula B. Voos, pp. 247–286. Armonk, N.Y.: M.E. Sharpe.

Klare, Karl E. 1994. Prepared statement of Karl E. Klare submitted to the Commission on the Future of Worker-Management Relations (January 19, 1994).

Kochan, Thomas A. 1992. "Employee Participation, Work Redesign, and New Technologies: Implications for Manufacturing and Engineering Practice." In *Handbook of Industrial Engineering*, ed. Gavriel Salvendy. New York: Wiley.

Kohler, Thomas C. 1986. "Models of Worker Participation: The Uncertain Significance of Section 8(a)(2)." *Boston College Law Review* 27, no. 2 (March): 499–551.

Kubasek, Nancy K., Westley J. Hiers, Shannon T. Browne, and Carrie Williamson. 1997. "Putting Worker-Management Relations in Context: Why Employee Representational Choice Needs Greater Protection in Reform of Section 8(a)(2) of the NLRA." *Harvard Journal on Legislation* 34 (Winter): 53 ff.

LaLonde, Robert J., and Bernard D. Meltzer. 1991. "Hard Times for Unions: Another Look at the Significance of Employer Illegalities." *University of Chicago Law Review* 58, no. 3 (Summer): 953–1014.

Lawler, Edward E. III. 1986. *High-Involvement Management: Participation Strategies for Improving Organizational Performance*. San Francisco: Jossey-Bass, esp. pp. 101–118, 170–190.

Lawler, Edward E. III, and Susan A. Mohrman. 1985. "Quality Circles After the Fad." *Harvard Business Review* 63 (January-February): 65–71.

Ledford, Gerald E. Jr., Edward E. Lawler III, and Susan A. Mohrman. 1988. "The Quality Circle and Its Variations." In *Productivity in Organizations: New Perspectives from Industrial and Organizational Psychology*, ed. John P. Campbell, Richard J. Campbell, and Associates, pp. 255–294. San Francisco: Jossey-Bass.

LeRoy, Michael H. 1993. "Employer Domination of Labor Organizations and the *Electromation* Case: An Empirical Public Policy Analysis." *George Washington Law Review* 61, no. 6 (August): 1812–1855.

———. 1996. "Can TEAM Work? Implications for *Electromation* and *Du Pont* Compliance Analysis for the TEAM Act." *Notre Dame Law Review* 71, no. 2: 215–266.

Legislative History of the National Labor Relations Act, 1935. 1985. Vols. 1 and 2. Washington, D.C.: National Labor Relations Board.

MacDuffie, John Paul, and John J. Krafcik. 1992. "Integrating Technology and Human Resources for High-Performance Manufacturing: Evidence from the International Auto Industry." In *Transforming Organizations*, ed. Thomas A. Kochan and Michael Useem, pp. 209–225. New York: Oxford University Press.

McMahan, Gary C., and Edward E. Lawler III. 1994. *Effects of Union Status on Employee Involvement: Diffusion and Effectiveness*. Washington, D.C.: Employment Policy Foundation.

Mantz, Charles C., and Henry P. Sims. 1993. *Businesses Without Bosses: How Self-Managing Teams Are Building High-Performance Companies*. New York: Wiley.

Mercy-Memorial Hospital Corp., 231 N.L.R.B. 182 (1977).

Meyer, Richard S. 1993. "Common Causes and Special Causes: Who Is Threatened by Deming—Labor or Management?" *Labor Law Journal* 44, no. 10 (October): 620–631.

Morris, Charles J. 1996. "Will There Be a New Direction for American Industrial Relations?—A Hard Look at the TEAM Bill, the Sawyer Substitute Bill, and the Employee Involvement Bill." *Labor Law Journal* 47, no. 2 (February): 89–107.

Nelson, Daniel. 1989. "Managers and Nonunion Workers in the Rubber Industry: Union Avoidance Strategies in the 1930s." *Industrial and Labor Relations Review* 43, no. 1 (October): 41–52.

NLRB v. *Exchange Parts Co.*, 375 U.S. 405 (1964).

NLRB v. *Newport News Shipbuilding & Dry Dock Co.*, 308 U.S. 241 (1939).

NLRB v. *Streamway Division, Scott & Fetzer Co.*, 691 F.2d 288 (6th Cir. 1982).

NLRB General Counsel GC 93–4. 1993. "Guideline Memorandum Concerning *Electromation, Inc.*, 309 N.L.R.B. No. 163 (April 15, 1993)." Reprinted in Bureau of National Affairs, Inc., *Daily Labor Report*, April 26, pp. G-1 ff.

The New Work Systems Network: A Compendium of Selected Work Innovation Cases. 1990. Washington, D.C.: U.S. Department of Labor, Bureau of Labor-Management Relations, BLMR 136, pp. 50–52, 247–248.

Oak Grove School District, Calif. PERB Decision No. 582 (1986).

Osterman, Paul. 1994. "How Common Is Workplace Transformation and Who Adopts It?" *Industrial and Labor Relations Review* 47, no. 2 (January): 173–188.

Parker, Mike. 1993. "Industrial Relations Myth and Shop-Floor Reality: The 'Team Concept' in the Auto Industry." In *Industrial Democracy in America: The Ambiguous Promise*, ed. Nelson Lichtenstein and Howell John Harris, pp. 176–205. Cambridge, U.K.: Cambridge University Press.

Pederson, Florence. 1937. *Characteristics of Company Unions 1935*. Washington, D.C.: U.S. Department of Labor, Bureau of Labor Statistics.

Perl, Arnold E. 1994. "Employee Participation Groups: A Management View of *Electromation* and Its Consequences." In *Contemporary Issues in Labor and Employment Law: Proceedings of New York University 46th Annual National Conference on Labor*, ed. Bruno Stein, pp. 353–361. Boston: Little, Brown.

Polaroid Corporation, et al., Cases 1–CA-29966, -30063 & -30211 (NLRB, Sept. 30, 1999), reprinted in Bureau of National Affairs, Inc., *Daily Labor Report*, October 7, P.E-30ff.

Redwoods Community College District, Calif. PERB Decision No. 650 (1987).

Reno Hilton Resorts Corporation, 319 N.L.R.B. No. 140 (December 18, 1995).

Rogers, Joel. 1993. "Reforming U.S. Labor Relations." *Chicago-Kent Law Review* 69, no. 1: 97–127.

Schacht, John N. 1975. "Toward Industrial Unionism: Bell Telephone Workers and Company Unions, 1919–1937." *Labor History* 16, no. 1 (Winter): 5–36.

Schechter Poultry Corp. v. *NLRB*, 295 U.S. 495 (1935).

Schuster, Michael. 1983. "Forty Years of Scanlon Plan Research." In *International Yearbook of Organizational Democracy*, ed. Colin Crouch and Frank Heller, vol. 1, pp. 35–52. New York: Wiley.

Sears Roebuck, Inc., 274 N.L.R.B. 230 (1985).

Sparks Nugget, Inc., 230 N.L.R.B. 275 (1977).

Strauss, George. 1990. "Participatory and Gain-sharing Systems: History and Hope." In *Profit Sharing and Gain Sharing*, ed. Myron J. Roomkin, pp. 1–45. Metuchen, N.J.: IMLR Press, Rutgers University.

Summers, Clyde W. 1993. "Employee Voice and Employer Choice: A Structured Exception to Section 8(a)(2)." *Chicago-Kent Law Review* 69, no. 1: 129–148.

Taras, Daphne Gottlieb. 1997. "Why Non-Union Representation Is Legal in Canada." *Relations Industrielles/Industrial Relations* 52, no. 4: 761–786.

U.S. Airways, Inc. v. *National Mediation Board*, 177 F.3d 985 (D.C. Cir. 1999).

Useem, Michael, and Thomas A. Kochan. 1992. "Creating the Learning Organization." In *Transforming Organizations*, ed. Thomas A. Kochan and Michael Useem, pp. 391–406. New York: Oxford University Press.

Walton, Richard E. 1982. "The Topeka Work System: Optimistic Visions, Pessimistic Hypotheses and Reality." In *The Innovative Organization: Productivity Programs in Action*, ed. Robert Zager and Michael P. Roso. New York: Pergamon Press.

Webcor Packing, Inc., 319 N.L.R.B. No. 142 (1995), enforced, 118 F.3d 1115 (7th Cir. 1997), cert. denied, 118 S.Ct. 1035 (1998)

Weiler, Paul C. 1983. "Promises to Keep: Securing Workers' Rights to Self-Organization under the NLRA." *Harvard Law Review* 96, no. 8 (June): 1769–1827.

Wellins, Richard S., William C. Byham, and Jeanne M. Wilson. 1991. *Empowered Teams: Creating Self-Directed Work Groups That Improve Quality, Productivity, and Participation.* San Francisco: Jossey-Bass.

Appendix 1

The "Company Union" Problem Under Other U.S. Labor Laws

The Railway Labor Act of 1926

The Railway Labor Act of 1926 (RLA) covers employees of carriers by railroad and air. To deal with the "company union" problem on the railroads, Congress provided for a prohibition similar in breadth to Section 8(a)2 of the NLRA. Section 2, Second, provides that representatives for both management and labor "shall be designated by the respective parties and without interference, influence, or coercion by either party over the designation of representatives of the other; and neither party shall in any way interfere with, influence, or coerce the other in its choice of representatives. . . ." In addition, under Section 3, Fourth, "it shall be unlawful for any carrier to interfere in any way with the organization of its employees, or to use the funds of the carrier in maintaining or assisting or contributing to any labor organization, labor representative, or other agency of collective bargaining. . . ."

In two respects, however, the RLA prohibition differs from the NLRA's. First, the RLA does not provide a definition of "labor organization"; instead, it defines "representative" to mean only persons or entities "designated either by a carrier or group of carriers or by its or their employees to act for it or them" (RLA, Section 1). Hence, representatives must act in a representational ca-

pacity, which is not true of "labor organization[s]" under Section 2(5), NLRA. Moreover, the context of the substantive prohibitions (RLA, Section 2, Second, and 3, Fourth), suggests that "representatives" are those who act for the parties in collective bargaining activities, rather than the broader "dealing with" concept of Section 2(5).

The second major distinction stems from the division of enforcement responsibilities under the RLA. The National Mediation Board (NMB, or Board) is the federal agency that deals with representational disputes. However, the NMB does not have jurisdiction over violations of the substantive prohibitions of the Act that do not vitiate the integrity of the election results; such violations are redressable only through a lawsuit in the federal courts. Thus, the NMB has ruled that employer-formed committees or similar conduct occurring before the "laboratory period" of the election campaign are outside its regulatory purview:

> In view of the absence of a demonstrated anti-union campaign, and the fact that the carrier did not attempt to form or encourage its employees to join the Employee Council during the laboratory period, the Board finds that the bare fact of the Council's existence did not taint the laboratory conditions. Moreover, [the union] has not shown that the carrier's and the Council's course of dealing was significantly altered in response to [the

union's] organizing drive or the Board's authorization of an election. (*Aircraft Mechanics* 1994, p. 254; also *U.S. Airways* 1999)

State Public-Sector Labor Relations Laws

A survey of fifty states would be impractical. We take California as an example. Under Section 3513(a) of California's general public-sector labor relations law (the Dills Act), "employee organization" is broadly defined to include "any organization which includes employees of the state and which has one of its primary purposes representing such employees in their relations with the state." Section 3540.1(d) of the state's Educational Employment Relations Act similarly defines "employee organization" as "any organization which include employees of a public school employer and which has one of its primary purposes representing those employees in their relations with that public school employer."

California's definition of covered "employee organization" requires a representational role and does not contain the "dealing with" language of Section 2(5) of the NLRA. However, the definition has been broadly construed to reach any group that has as a central focus the representation of employees on employment-related matters. Thus, a faculty forum, established to "improve communications and solve problems," qualified as an employee organization because negotiable subjects were discussed, even though actual negotiations never took place (*Oak Grove* 1986). On the other hand, employee groups that "engage in a mere discussion with management, rather than making recommendations to management" or "where management has delegated actual decisionmaking authority" to the groups fall outside of the statute's coverage (*Redwoods* 1987).

Appendix 2

Post–*Electromation*/*Du Pont* Rulings at the Labor Board

Ryder Distribution Resource, 311 N.L.R.B. 814 (1993)

The employer introduced a "Quality Through People" program as a mechanism for problem solving through "quality action" teams focusing on safety, maintenance and repair, communication, training, and wages and benefits. Employee volunteers were urged to poll the workforce and report results to management. The Board found that the central purpose of the wages and benefits committee was "to address the employees' dissatisfaction with their wages through the creation of a bilateral process . . . to reach bilateral solutions based on management and employee proposals."

Peninsula General Hospital, 312 N.L.R.B. No. 97 (1993) enforcement denied, 36 F.3d 1262 (4th Cir. 1994)

An employee organization in existence since 1968, the Nursing Services Organization, served as a forum to discuss practice issues and for continuing nurses education. The Board found that its purpose had changed in 1989 to address nurses' employment issues. The Court of Appeals held that the Board's order lacked substantial evidence of a "pattern or practice" of "dealing," making proposals to which the hospital responded.

Keeler Brass Co., 317 N.L.R.B. 1110 (1995)

The employer established a Grievance Committee. Employee representatives sat for two-year terms. The Board found that the committee addressed grievances but that the committee's resolutions were not in fact final. Rather, they were treated as recommendations that the employer was free to accept or reject hence, the committee did not excuse delegated authority but rather reflected a "bilateral mechanism" with Section 2(5).

Webcor Packaging, Inc., 319 N.L.R.B. No. 142 (1995), enforced, 118 F.3d 115 (6th Cir. 1997), cert. denied, 118 S.Ct. 1035 (1998)

A box manufacturer established a plant council of elected employee representatives to offer recommendations to management about proposed changes in working conditions, including the development of an employee handbook and grievance procedure. The Board ruled this was a "bilateral mechanism" within the reach of Section 2(5). The Court of Appeals, distinguishing *Streamway Division* (1982), agreed with the

Board that the fact that the company had made at least four significant policy changes as a result of the council's recommendations indicates "an active, ongoing course of dealings. . . ."

Dillon Stores, 319 N.L.R.B. No. 149 (1995)

The company's "In-Store Representative Program," involving elected employee representatives, was found to have as one of its purposes making proposals to which the company responded.

Stoody Co., 320 N.L.R.B. 18 (1995)

A Handbook Committee created by the employer was held not to be a "labor organization" because the employer made clear that the committee was to perform only an information-gathering role, even though there had been some isolated discussion of employee suggestions for changes in the employer's vacation policy. The Board explained:

> By requiring that "dealing" consist of a pattern or practice of making proposals to management on the subjects covered in Section 2(5), *Du Pont* allows for the isolated errors that may occur in any genuine attempt to change the interaction between employer and employees. Such errors or missteps will not result in a finding that an employee participation committee is a statutory labor organization. At the same time, *Du Pont* makes it clear that recurring instances of an employee participation committee making proposals to management on mandatory subjects constitutes "dealing" and the committee will be found to be a labor organization.

Vons Grocery Co., 320 N.L.R.B. 53 (1995)

A "Quality Circle Group" (QCG), which grew out of the employer's "roundtable" meetings, was found not to be a "labor organization" when it strayed beyond operational issues to consider a dress code and accident point system—subjects that previously had been addressed in discussions between the employer and the union. The company took immediate steps to assure the union that such incidents would not reoccur. The Board ruled that the QCG's dress code and accident point system proposals did not constitute the requisite "pattern or practice."

EFCO Corp., Case No. 17–CA-6911, 327 N.L.R.B. 71 (1998)

The company's "Employee Benefit Committee," "Employee Policy Review Committee" and "Safety Committee," established before the company became aware of union organizing activity among its employees, were found to be dominated "labor organization[s]" because they reviewed company policies and made recommendations for management action. However, the Safety Committee's mere reporting of safety hazards was a permissible "employer's delegation of safety duties" and the screening function of the Company's "Employee Suggestion Screening Committee" performed only an informational role.

Polaroid Corp., et al., Cases No. 1-CA-29966, -30063 & -30211 (1999)

The company's elected "Employee-Owners' Influence Council" (EOIC) was found to be a labor organization because EOIC members were expected to be representative of workforce views, and "the EOIC functioned on an ongoing basis as a bilateral mechanism in which that group of employees effectively made proposals to management, and management responded to these proposals by acceptance or rejection by word or deed."

Appendix 3
"TEAM Act" and Sawyer Substitute

"TEAM Act" (S.295)

The "Teamwork for Employees and Managers Act" would add the following proviso to Section 8(a)(2):

> That it shall not constitute or be evidence of an unfair labor practice under this paragraph for an employer to establish, assist, maintain, or participate in any organization or entity of any kind, in which employees participate to at least the same extent practicable as representatives of management participate, to address matters of mutual interest, including, but not limited to, issues of quality, productivity, efficiency, and safety and health, and which does not have, claim, or seek authority to be the exclusive bargaining representative of the employees or to negotiate or enter into collective bargaining agreements with the employer or to amend existing collective bargaining agreements between the employer and any labor organization, except that in a case in which a labor organization is the representative of such employees as provided in Section 9(a), this proviso shall not apply.

Sawyer Substitute Proposal

> Provided further, That it shall not constitute or be evidence of an unfair labor practice under this paragraph for an employer to establish, assist, maintain, or participate in—
> (i) a method of work organization based on employee-managed work units, notwithstanding that such work units may hold periodic meetings in which all employees assigned to the unit discuss, and subject to agreement with the exclusive bargaining representative, if any, decide upon the conditions of work within the work unit;
> (ii) a method of work organization based on supervisor-managed work units, notwithstanding the fact that such work units may hold periodic meetings of all employees and supervisors assigned to the unit to discuss the unit's work responsibilities and in the course of such meetings on occasion discuss conditions of work within the work unit; or
> (iii) committees created to recommend or to decide upon means of improving the design, quality, or method of producing, distributing, or selling the employer's product or service, notwithstanding the fact that such committees on isolated occasions, in considering design quality, or production issues, may discuss directly related issues concerning conditions of work: Provided further, That the preceding proviso shall not apply if—
> (A) a labor organization is the representative of such employees as provided in Section 9(a);
> (B) the employer creates or alters the work unit or committee during organizational activity among the employer's employees or discourages employees from exercising their rights under Section 7 of the Act;
> (C) the employer interferes with, restrains, or coerces any employee because of the employee's participation

in or refusal to participate in discussions of conditions of work which otherwise would be permitted by subparagraph (i), (ii), or (iii), or

(D) an employer establishes or maintains an entity authorized by subparagraph (i), (ii), or (iii) which discusses conditions of work of employees who are represented under Section 9 of the Act

without first engaging in the collective bargaining required by the Act: Provided, further, That individuals who participate in an entity established pursuant to subparagraph (i), (ii), or (iii) shall not be deemed to be supervisors or managers by virtue of such participation.

Contemporary Practice

10

Estimates of Nonunion Employee Representation in the United States and Canada: How Different Are the Two Countries?

Seymour Martin Lipset and Noah M. Meltz

There is a general awareness that, with the exception of the Scandinavian countries and a few others, the percentage of employees who belong to unions has been declining worldwide. The International Labour Organization (ILO), for example, in its *World Labour Report 1997–98,* estimates that worldwide trade union membership dropped sharply during the past decade. Membership declined in seventy-two of the ninety-two countries surveyed. In forty-eight of them union density dropped below the 20 percent level between 1985 and 1995.

What has not been examined in any systematic way, however, is the extent and direction of change in nonunion employee representation as a possible alternative. In the 1920s in the United States and Canada, nonunion employee representation plans, known in the United States as the "American Plan," were introduced by large corporations as substitutes or replacements for unions. Following the passing of the Wagner Act in the United States in 1935, these plans became fertile organizing grounds for unions on both sides of the border. In this chapter we present the results of a survey that provides information on the extent of nonunion representation in Canada and the United States. We also examine some possible hypotheses concerning where this representation is located and who belongs to these organizations. We end by raising some questions concerning the possible effect of these developments on labor relations in the two countries.

The Survey

The major focus of the binational telephone survey conducted in June and July 1996 was on the attitudes of Americans and Canadians toward work and unions.[1] The results are drawn from interviews with randomly generated samples of 1,750 adults in the United States and 1,495 in Canada. In one subsection we included several questions concerning nonunion representation.[2] Figure 10.1 sets out the survey questions on which the estimates of nonunion representation were based.

The General Results

To put the results in a general context, Table 10.1 indicates the extent of union representation in the

Figure 10.1 **Measures of Nonunion Employee Representation**

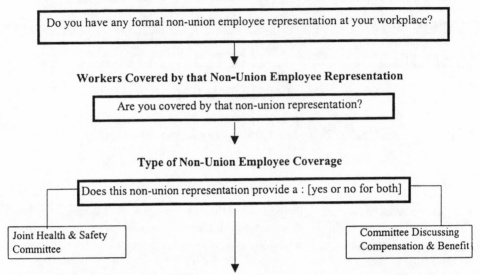

Presence of Non-Union Employee Representation at Workplace

Do you have any formal non-union employee representation at your workplace?

Workers Covered by that Non-Union Employee Representation

Are you covered by that non-union representation?

Type of Non-Union Employee Coverage

Does this non-union representation provide a : [yes or no for both]

Joint Health & Safety Committee

Committee Discussing Compensation & Benefit

Workers who are Members of Non-Union Organizations that Bargain Collectively

Are you a member of an organization other than a union that bargains collectively on behalf of you and other workers? [non-union workers only]:

two countries at the time of the survey and the proportion of individuals indicating that their workplaces had employees involved in decision making. Employee involvement included such things as the presence of self-directed work teams, total quality management, quality circles, and other employee involvement programs.

In June 1996, 35 percent of Canadians in our survey belonged to unions, compared with 16 percent in the United States. These results are virtually identical with the aggregate figures available from other sources in the two countries.

When employees were asked whether their employers had introduced decision making in new ways to get employees involved (a crude measure for "the high-performance workplace") half the workers in each country said they were involved in new forms of decision making (50 percent in the United States and 51 percent in Canada). Not surprisingly, the extent of employee involvement among workers increased with establishment size, reaching a maximum in both countries within firms employing 5,000 workers or more (90 percent in the United States and 71 percent in Canada).

Interestingly, in both countries a higher percentage of unionized workplaces involved their employees in decision making than did the nonunionized workplaces (58 percent vs. 49 percent in the United States, and 60 percent vs. 44 percent in Canada). Within the nonunionized sector, workplaces that had formal nonunion em-

Table 10.1

Union Density and Employee Involvement*

	United States (%)	Canada (%)
Union density	16	35
Presence of employee involvement among total workforce	50	51
Presence of employee involvement among total workforce by establishment size (# employees)		
1–5	29	30
6–10	31	33
11–50	37	41
51–100	51	56
101–500	60	65
501–1,000	70	69
1,001–5,000	73	70
5,000>	90	71
Employee involvement among unionized workforce	58	60
Employee involvement among nonunionized workforce	49	44
Employee involvement among nonunionized but employee-represented workforce	64	71
Employee involvement among nonunionized and nonrepresented workforce	43	36

Source: Lipset and Meltz, U.S.–Canada Angus Reid Survey of Employee/Employer Attitudes 1996.

Note: Nonunion employee representation is measured by those answering yes to the presence of nonunion representation at their workplace.

*Employee involvement includes using things like self-directed work teams, total quality management, quality circles, or other employee involvement programs.

ployee representation also had a higher percentage of workers involved in some form of employee involvement than did the nonrepresented sector (64 percent vs. 43 percent in the United States, and 71 percent vs. 36 percent in Canada).

Despite the huge differences between the countries in the extent of unionization, the amount of nonunion representation is very similar, as is shown in Table 10.2. One-fifth of nonunion employees in each country have formal employee representation other than unions present at their workplaces. In terms of coverage, the proportion of nonunion employees covered by that same formal nonunion representation is 15 percent in the United States and 14 percent in Canada.

An alternative measure of representation by substitutes for unions is the extent to which these organizations discuss compensation and benefits with their nonunion workforce. The percentages are 11 in the United States and 10 in Canada. Finally, if we look only at those who belong to (or who state that they are members of) nonunion organizations that bargain (rather than discuss) compensation and benefits, we find that roughly 5 percent of employees in each country are represented (5 percent in the United States and 5.5 percent in Canada).

No matter what set of figures is used, the results seem clear: the extent of nonunion representation is similar in both Canada and the United States. The range of estimates for nonunion representation is 5 percent for employees who say they are *members* of nonunion organizations (5.5 percent in Canada), 15 percent for those who claim to be *covered* (14 percent in Canada) by nonunion organizations, and 20 percent for employees who work in establishments where there is some form of nonunion representation present.

To fully compare the extent of nonunion employee representation with union representation,

Table 10.2

Nonunion Forms of Employee Representation*

	United States (%)	Canada (%)
Presence of formal nonunion employee representation among nonunion workforce	19.5	20.0
Nonunionized workforce covered by that formal nonunion employee representation	15.0	14.0
Type of nonunion employee representation among the nonunion workforce:		
Formal nonunion employee representation that discusses compensation and benefits among nonunion workforce	11.0	10.0
Formal nonunion employee representation that discusses joint and health safety among nonunion workforce	10.0	10.0
Nonunionized workforce who are members of an organization that bargains collectively on their behalf	5.0	5.5

Source: Lipset and Meltz, U.S.–Canada Angus Reid Survey of Employee/ Employer Attitudes (1996).
*Numbers are rounded to the nearest half (.5) percent.

we have to combine workplace nonunion representation, as reported by nonunion members, with nonunion representation as reported by union members. The combined figures show that in the United States workers report that almost as many workplaces have nonunion representation (20 percent) as have union representation (21.7 percent, 16 percent members and 5.7 percent nonunion with union coverage). In Canada almost twice as many employees have union representation (38.3 percent, 35 percent members and 3.3 percent nonunion with union coverage), as have nonunion representation (19.5 percent).

When we group employees into private and public sectors we again find a great similarity between figures for the United States and Canada.

In both countries 17 percent of private sector employees report the presence of nonunion representation in the workplace. For public-sector workers the nonunion representation is 33 percent in the United States and 40 percent in Canada. To explore the extent of nonunion representation in more detail, we confine our analysis to workplaces where nonunion employees report nonunion representation, and compare this with union membership.

Nonunion Representation by Industry

Tables 10.3 and 10.4 show actual union density by industry for the United States and Canada together with estimates for union density measures

Table 10.3

U.S. Estimates of Union and Nonunion Forms of Employee Representation by Industry, 1996*

Industry	BLS estimate of union membership (% of total employment)	Survey estimate of union membership (% of total employment)	Presence of nonunion employee representation (% among nonunion workforce)	Nonunion workforce covered by nonunion employee representation (% among nonunion workforce)	Nonunion employee representation discussing wages and benefits (% among nonunion workforce)
Total	14.5	16	19.5	15	11
(millions)	(16.3)	(17.9)	(18.3)	(14.1)	(10.3)
Agriculture	1.9	9	11	N/A	11
Construction	18.5	24	11	11	11
Mining	14.1	N/A	N/A	N/A	N/A
Manufacturing	17.2	17	17	10	12
Wholesale and retail trade	5.6	6	16	12	12
Transportation and storage industries	27.0	30	19	12.5	12.5
Communication and public utilities	25.9	33	21	14	14
Public administration	37.7	26	34.5	27.5	31
Finance, insurance, and real estate	2.4	4	7	3	3
Other services	5.7	9	12	9	3

Sources: Lipset and Meltz, U.S.–Canada Angus Reid Survey of Employee/Employer Attitudes, 1996; and data from the Bureau of Labor Statistics 1997.

*Survey data (columns 2 to 5) are rounded to the nearest half (.5) percent.

from our survey. For the most part, our survey results are similar to those of the government estimates. Tables 10.3 and 10.4 also contain three estimates of nonunion representation by industry. The estimates correspond to the first three rows of Table 10.2, which included the following measures: the presence of employee representation among nonunion workers; nonunion workers covered by nonunion employee repre-

sentation; and the percentage of nonunion workers covered by formal nonunion employee representation that discusses compensation and benefits.

There is a large and significant correlation between union density and our first measure of nonunion employee representation (the presence of formal nonunion representation across two-digit industrial classifications). When the figures for the United States and Canada are pooled, the cor-

Table 10.4

Canadian Estimates of Union and Nonunion Forms of Employee Representation by Industry, 1996*

Industry	LFS estimate of union membership (% of total employment)	Survey estimate of union membership (% of total employment)	Presence of nonunion employee representation (% among nonunion workforce)	Nonunion workforce covered by nonunion employee representation (% among nonunion workforce)	Nonunion employee representation discussing wages and benefits (% among nonunion workforce)
Total	33.9[a]	36.0	20	14	10
(millions)	(4.0)[a]	(4.0)	(1.4)	(1.0)	(0.7)
Agriculture	2.4	3	7	N/A	N/A
Construction	27.3	30	18	6	6
Mining	29.2	32	18	9	9
Manufacturing	33.3	36	33	18.5	20
Wholesale and retail trade	12.0	14	11	6	9
Transportation and storage industries; communication and public utilities	48.4	51.5	19	19	11
Public administration	65.8	73	22	17	11
Finance, insurance, and real estate	9.2	12	15	7	5
Community, business, and personal services	34.6	37.5	11.5	8	8

Sources: Lipset and Meltz, U.S.–Canada Angus Reid Survey of Employee/Employer Attitudes, 1996; and data from the Labour Force Survey, Statistics Canada (1997).

[a]Human Resources Development Canada (1997) for 1996. Union density of 31.0 percent in 1997 and union membership of 3.6 million in 1997 were reported by the Labour Force Survey 1997.

*Survey data (columns 2 to 5) are rounded to the nearest half (.5) percent.

relation of union density with that of nonunion representation (column 3 in Tables 10.3 and 10.4) is 0.59. For the United States separately, the figure is 0.67, and for Canada it is 0.57.

One possible avenue for analysis is to ask why industries with high union density also tend to have high nonunion representation density. Pre-sumably this is related to underlying factors (such as larger plant size and a manufacturing/blue-collar environment) that make some form of voice and dispute resolution more beneficial for workers and for employers.

Examining the data in more detail, however, shows different patterns in the United States and

Canada. In the United States, most of the low union density private-service sectors and agriculture have nonunion representation one and a half times or more greater than the union density figures (wholesale and retail trade, finance, insurance and real estate, and other services). For all the remaining industry sectors, union density exceeds nonunion representation. In Canada, union density by industry sector exceeds the percentage of nonunion representation in every industry except finance, insurance, and real estate, the sector with the lowest union density area (excluding agriculture). What these figures may mean is discussed in the next section.

Interpretation

Several observations can be made concerning the extent and industry location of nonunion representation. If we solely consider nonunion membership, nonunion business organizations have one-third the number of union members in the United States and one-seventh in Canada. If we consider coverage and the presence of nonunion representation at the workplace, the estimates of formal nonunion representation in the United States range from just below to more than union coverage (11 percent and 19.5 percent, vs. 16 percent). For Canada, nonunion representation is much less than union membership (10 percent and 20 percent vs. 35 percent).

These data underline the importance of knowing more about where the nonunion representation is located (industry, occupation and geographical location, size of organization, etc.); what factors gave rise to it; how close it is to union representation in terms of formally representing employee interests, such as grievance procedures, gain-sharing plans, and so on; and in what direction the numbers involved are going.

We also have to explore the extent to which nonunion representation includes professional associations that bargain with employers, but whose members do not consider themselves as belonging to a union.

Is nonunion employee representation simply a substitute for union representation, such that there is an inverse relationship between them? Or, alternatively, is there some complementarity, such that firms are more prone to introduce employee representation plans when the extent of unionization in an industry is high, rather than when it is low? The survey cannot answer all the questions, but it can shed light on some of them.

In terms of industry, it appears that in general, the higher the union membership, the greater the nonunion representation. What is most striking, however, is that the differences between union density and nonunion representation are the greatest for the low union density industries: agriculture, wholesale and retail trade (United States only), finance, insurance and real estate, and other services (United States only; community, business, and personal services in Canada). In the case of these industries it appears that nonunion representation is a substitute for unionization. For the other industries, the high correlation does not tell us whether greater union representation leads to greater formal nonunion representation or the reverse. Disentangling whether union representation in neighboring firms is the cause rather than the result of nonunion representation needs to be explored further.

Concluding Comments

Several tentative conclusions can be drawn from the data presented here. Particularly striking is the similarity in the extent of nonunion representation in the United States and Canada given the huge differences in union density. The fact that there is a high correlation between union membership by industry and formal nonunion representation suggests, as Riddell (1993) has found, that differences in union membership across countries are the result of differences in the "supply" of opportunities to join unions, rather than the demand for union services.

Overall, a majority of employees in both countries seem to want some form of "voice" in the workplace. This is consistent with the late Jack Barbash's (1987) "law of equilibrium," that is, when there is an equity function to be represented in the workplace and unions, employers and governments compete to represent this function. For American workers, however, our survey results seem to indicate that nonunion representation only partly substitutes in two industry sectors for interest in trade unions. Further analysis will explore in more detail the role of nonunion representation in substituting for interest in unions.

Acknowledgments

The authors are indebted to the William H. Donner Foundation of the United States for a grant to conduct this research. The analysis was facilitated by support from the John Olin Center for Labor Market Analysis of George Mason University. The authors also appreciate the advice of Bruce Kaufman and the assistance of Rafael Gomez, Ivan Katchanovski, Marcella Ridlen Ray, Scott Talkington, and the Angus Reid Group, one of the leading Canadian survey organizations, which handled the collection and coding of the data. We also want to thank Mag Burns of the Angus Reid Group for working with us on the development and carrying out of the survey.

Notes

1. For an overview of the results of this survey, please see Lipset and Meltz (1997).

2. Daphne Taras suggested these questions. We appreciate her advice and assistance.

References

Barbash, Jack. 1987. "Like Nature, Industrial Relations Abhors a Vacuum." *Relations Industrielles* 42, no. 1: 168–179.

Human Resources Development Canada. 1997. *Directory of Labour Organizations in Canada, 1997*. Ottawa: Minister of Public Works and Government Services Canada.

International Labour Organization. 1998. *World Labour Report 1997–98*. Geneva, Switzerland: ILO.

Lipset, S.M., and Noah Meltz. 1997. "Canadian and American Attitudes towards Work and Institutions." *Perspectives on Work* 1, no. 3 (December): 14–19.

Riddell, Craig. 1993. "Unionization in Canada and the United States: A Tale of Two Countries." In *Small Differences That Matter: Labor Markets and Income Maintenance in Canada and the United States*, ed. David Card and Richard Freeman. Chicago: University of Chicago Press.

11

Contemporary Experience with the Rockefeller Plan: Imperial Oil's Joint Industrial Council

Daphne Gottlieb Taras

Imperial Oil has been Canada's preeminent oil company throughout the twentieth century. There have been periods in which it has been larger than the petroleum industry's second and third competitors combined. Its 1997 net earnings were $847 million. First launched as a Canadian-owned company in the late 1800s, and deliberately named Imperial to signify its role as a bastion against foreign ownership, it was not long before the majority of the company was sold to American interests. Imperial Oil is an affiliate of Exxon Corporation, which holds almost 70 percent of its shares. Because of Imperial Oil's dominant position in the Canadian petroleum industry, it has been a natural pattern setter for all kinds of human resource practices. Until a period of turbulence in the 1990s threatened Imperial's position as the leading company, other industry managers tended to aspire to copy Imperial's wages, benefits, and working conditions. Among oil companies, however, Imperial remains unique in its fervent commitment to a plan of nonunion representation first developed for the Rockefeller interests and practiced without interruption throughout Imperial since 1919.

Imperial Oil's Joint Industrial Council (JIC) is the largest and most enduring private-sector formal nonunion employee representation plan in Canada. Arguably, the plan has the richest history and most significant provenance of any nonunion plan in North America. In this chapter I examine employee representation in Imperial Oil's upstream division, Production Operations (formerly known as Esso Resources). The purpose is (1) to describe the origins and longevity of the JIC and (2) to analyze the current operations of the JIC with particular attention to the nature of bargaining, the advantages and disadvantages associated with this form of representation for both employers and workers, and the current strains that threaten the foundations of this elaborate nonunion system.

This research is significant because it offers a contemporary examination of the intricacies of a popular nonunion system that was banned in the United States after the passage of the Wagner Act in 1935.[1] The majority of studies available on nonunion representation (Hogler and Grenier 1992, ch. 2) describe company plans outlawed by the Wagner Act and thus usually treated as historic relics of a bygone era by contemporary scholars (e.g., Nelson 1993). The literature is relatively silent on their current capacity to meet the needs of employees and managers, and their ability to adapt to the changes in workforce demographics and technological innovations. In short, there is little information that would assist us in determining the effectiveness of nonunion representation as a mechanism for workplace democracy.[2]

In addressing these gaps, Canada is an attractive site for research. Canadian labor laws permitted the continuation of nonunion representation plans in the years following the Wagner Act ban, and a variety of important Canadian organizations are ardent practitioners of nonunion forms. (See Taras 2000, in this volume, for a description of the Canadian laws.) There is little doubt that the JIC has characteristics that would be found objectionable under American law: workers are elected by their fellow workers to meet and deal with management on issues that are presumed to belong most appropriately within the realm of the collective bargaining regime. The JIC is the creation of management, and it is funded entirely by the company. It is guided in its deliberations by worker-management agreements that strongly resemble collective agreements in the unionized sector.[3] Although the contents of nonunion worker-management agreements are similar to collective agreements, the legal status is different. While collective agreements are protected by collective bargaining statutes throughout the many Canadian jurisdictions, the nonunion agreements technically are individual contracts of employment that happen to be applied collectively. Any redress for a breach of such an agreement would be sought through a civil suit. This contrasts markedly with the union system, where a typical dispute is settled through grievance arbitration. Though some highly evolved Canadian plans may be much closer to the union model than is the case in the United States, they are not protected by labor laws, and they exist outside the jurisdiction of labor boards.

This chapter is divided into two main sections. The first section sets the context for the detailed analysis of the JIC, which is contained in the second section. The first section reviews the history of the JIC and outlines how it was adopted by Imperial Oil. The current institutional features of the JIC are described. The second section examines the inner workings of the contemporary JIC. It begins with a brief description of the research methodology of the case study. It then explores the dynamics between employees and managers in the JIC: Is it a bargaining relationship? What are the sources of worker power? What are the tactics used by both workers and managers in order to achieve desired outcomes? The chapter then reviews the JIC's advantages and disadvantages, from both workers' and managers' perspectives. The chapter concludes by assessing the adaptability of nonunion plans, with a specific description of current strains that threaten JIC longevity.

Setting the Context

The Rockefeller Plan

The JIC has a rich history. After the labor relations disasters experienced by the Rockefeller-owned Colorado Fuel and Iron Company, reaching an apotheosis of misery in the Ludlow massacre of 1914, the Rockefeller interests commissioned the development of a new form of industrial relations (Gitelman 1988; King 1973; Rockefeller 1916; Kline 1920). The author of this plan (which can be found in Colorado Plan 1916 and Rockefeller 1916, pp. 63–95) was William Lyon Mackenzie King, then the former deputy minister of labour in Canada (and its future prime minister). Mackenzie King recommended that the company sidestep union recognition and implement a scheme of worker representation. The provenance of the plan can be traced to a letter from King to John D. Rockefeller Jr., dated August 6, 1914, written in the two days immediately following Canada's declaration that it was joining Britain in World War I. Excerpts from this historically significant letter are reproduced in Figure 11.1. Clearly, Mackenzie King had a clear idea of the attributes of nonunion representation, and the letter foreshadows the eventual JIC plan quite accurately.

King clearly believed, in concert with many industrialists of the time, that collective bargaining was desirable, even (and perhaps, particularly) in the absence of unions. As envisioned by King, the JICs guaranteed basic rights to unionize and offered to all employees a well-defined (though management dominated) grievance procedure, but evaded the central issues of union recognition and management's duty to bargain with unions. Like most other company union plans of that era, the JIC explicitly promised that there would be "no discrimination by the company or by any of its employees on account of membership . . . in a union" (Rockefeller 1916, p. 75). While the union movement vociferously denounced the JIC, nevertheless, the advantages of the JIC plan were widely touted by public policymakers and relatively more progressive managers. The presidentially appointed Federal Commission on the Labor Difficulties in the Coal Fields of Colorado lauded the JIC:

> Every employee has the absolute right openly to belong to a labor union or not, as he pleases; but in view of the fact that many men in the company's employ do not belong to labor unions, it offers the rights of representation, which are embodied in the company's plan to unorganized labor in its employ as well as to organized labor. In other words, as between the company and its employees, all have the right of representation, and not only those who are organized. (King 1918, p. 284, from 64th Cong., 1st sess., doc. 859)

JICs consisted of selected (management) and elected (worker) representatives in equal numbers who met regularly on matters such as health, sanitation, safety and accidents, recreation, education, and conciliation. In practice, JICs also became involved in the wage and compensation package by proffering advice and recommendations to management. The JIC plan called for secret-ballot votes for the election of representatives.

From the mines of Colorado, the JIC plan was diffused throughout the Rockefeller industrial empire. The Standard Oil plan became the exemplar of nonunion systems (Kline 1920; Chase 1947; Gibbs and Knowlton 1956; Gray and Gullett 1973). Imperial Oil was one of many Rockefeller-owned companies in which the JIC established a firm hold. The JIC became unlawful in the United States with the passage of the Wagner Act.

The Company: A Profile of Imperial Oil

For over 100 years, Imperial Oil Limited has been the preeminent integrated oil and gas company in Canada (Imperial Oil 1991; Imperial Oil's company magazine, *Review*; Imperial website 1999). Despite deep "right-sizing" waves throughout the 1990s, Imperial remains Canada's largest producer of conventional crude oil and controls the largest proved crude-oil reserves. It is the country's largest refiner and marketer of petroleum products, a major supplier of petrochemicals, and a significant producer of natural gas. In 1989 Imperial Oil purchased Texaco Canada at a cost of $5 billion, which was the second largest corporate acquisition in Canada.

Imperial adopted the JIC due to the cross-border

Figure 11.1 Mackenzie King Letter, August 6, 1914

Dear Mr. Rockefeller:

. . . Recognition, simply for the sake of recognition, is going to seem to be less pressing as an immediate end [after the war], than that of maintaining standards already existing, and [unions] may rightly come to regard as their friends and allies companies and corporations large enough and fair enough to desire to maintain these standards of their own accord. . . .

Between the extreme of individual agreements on the one side, and an agreement involving recognition of unions of national and international character on the other, lies the straight acceptance of the principle of Collective Bargaining between capital and labour immediately concerned in any certain industry or group of industries, and the construction of machinery which will afford opportunity of easy and constant conference between employers and employed with reference to matters of concern to both. . . .

A Board on which both employers and employed are represented, and before which at stated intervals questions affecting conditions of employment can be discussed, and grievances examimed, would appear to constitute the necessary basis of such machinery. . . .

[A] line might be drawn between those who are "paid salaries" on the one hand, and those who "earn wages" on the other. . . . [B]roadly speaking, men who have authority to give orders and to direct operations, fall into the salaried class, while men who have no authority to direct others, and whose own work is subject wholly to direction, fall into the category of wage-earners. The selection of representatives on such Boards should be made at a meeting or meetings of employees called expressly for the purpose. It might be left optional for the employees to say whether they desired a permanent form of organization of which their representatives on a Board would be the officers or whether they would prefer the selection of individuals at stated periods, without reference to any permanent form of organization. It could also be left optional with the workers themselves to say whether they wished to allow representatives so chosen, a salary in payment of their services, or whether such services would have to be voluntary. A company might, with propriety, offer to provide the place of meeting for the Boards, and possibly go the length of supplying the employees with permanent office accommodation for their representatives, leaving it, however, to the employees themselves to provide whatever might be necessary in the way of salaries and expenses in the keeping up of such offices.

It would not appear desirable at the outset that these Boards should have anything to do with benefit features . . . but should aim primarily at affording a guarantee of fair play in determining, in the first instance, the conditions under which men would be obliged to work and the remuneration to be paid, and secondly, the carrying out of these conditions in a spirit of fair play. One thing to be especially aimed at in the construction of such Boards would be the making virtually certain of the possibility of grievances or conditions complained of being made known to, and subject to the review of persons in authority over and above the parties immediately concerned, where the parties fail to adjust these differences between themselves; this is to be carried even to the point that directors, if need be, should have, where the numbers to be affected are likely to justify it, a knowledge of the situation, and the power to pass upon it. This feature will probably not appeal to pit bosses and managers who may desire absolute authority. . . .

[E]mployees, before taking up any questions with the officers of the company, would try to adjust or settle it among themselves. Failing adjustment in this manner, differences and difficulties would be presented to the officers of the company . . . by the duly constituted representatives chosen to safe-guard the

(continued)

interests of all. Having had a preliminary sifting in this manner, cases could be brought before a committee of the Board or before the whole Board in any one industry for adjustment. If it should be found that an individual Board could not definitely determine a matter of importance, there might be brought a further appeal on stated conditions to a Board chosen to represent the industry as a whole, or a group of allied industries. . . . This would make it an essential that all members of such Boards, excepting possibly, persons chosen as chairmen, referees, or umpires, should be persons actually employed in the industry or connected with it in some way, not persons chosen from outside. . . .

Source: National Archives of Canada MG 26J1, Volume 24.

influence of its owner. In 1898 the Rockefeller-owned Standard Oil purchased a majority share in then-Canadian-owned Imperial. Standard Oil Company (New Jersey) subsequently became Exxon Corporation. Standard Oil was an early and ardent proponent of JICs, but was forced to disband its JICs in the late 1930s (Chase 1947), replacing them with a multitude of local independent unions that remain in place today. Thus Imperial Oil might be a living laboratory of what might have happened in the United States petroleum industry in the absence of a ban.

Standard Oil faced concerted union organizing in the United States, and certainly there was a strong union-avoidance component to its initial adoption of the JIC. To a lesser degree this was true in Canada as well. The greatest challenge was at the Ioco refinery in British Columbia, where in February 1918 workers went on strike in support of wage demands and a reduction in the eighty-four-hour workweek. Though this twelve-day work stoppage netted modest gains for workers, and encouraged workers to join a short-lived chapter of an international oil union, in the end the organizing came to nothing because the company refused to recognize any fledgling union locals (Grant 1998, p. 81). Serious union organizing of the petroleum industry did not begin until the late 1940s (Roberts 1990).

Imperial Oil unveiled the JIC in 1918 and in-

troduced the plan into its Sarnia refinery in January 1919. According to a study by Grant (1998, p. 83), the fledgling JIC got off to a "rocky start": "The Employees Federation—a coalition of trade unions active in the plant—seized the opportunity to elect an active union member to the joint council, who promptly placed the union's salary demands on the table for discussion at the first meeting. He was subsequently dismissed and only reinstated following the threat of a walkout. . . . At a meeting convened by the Employees Federation, the 400 to 500 employees of the Sarnia refinery voted to press their wage demands through the union rather than the industrial council."

In response to a perceived union threat, the company began to consider methods to anticipate employee demands and forestall any deterioration in employee relations. The wage rates were improved, which initiated the long-standing management practice in the petroleum industry of paying premium wages (Taras 1997a, b). By the start of World War II, workers in petroleum refineries were averaging over 40 percent higher than the average manufacturing industry wage (Grant 1998, p. 83).

Imperial also began a series of progressive employee-oriented programs in the 1919 and 1920 period, including an eight-hour working day, life insurance policies, pension plans, and a benefit program to provide assistance to employees with illnesses or injuries. An employee share-purchase plan began in 1920 and was heavily subscribed (Grant 1998, p. 88). In 1932, Imperial was the second company in Canada to adopt the five-day workweek; in 1937, employees were given paid holidays; 1939 brought a company savings plan; in 1953, Imperial was the first Canadian company to employ a full-time industrial hygienist to address health and safety hazards; during the 1970s, compressed workweeks and flexible hours became possible for some employees (Imperial Oil 1991). Company practice consistently reflected the aims of Welfare Capitalism, whose precepts of cooperation and compassion, and union avoidance, are eloquently described by Brandes (1976) and Jacoby (1998).

When the Canadian federal government held National War Labour Board hearings in 1943 to investigate appropriate labor statutes for the war effort and afterward, Imperial Oil's Vice President Henry H. Hewetson delivered a submission vigorously defending the continued legality of the JIC against efforts to adopt an American-style ban on nonunion representation. He worried that

> the fact that there have been presented to the Board recommendations [identical to sections 2(5) and 8(a)(2) in the American Wagner Act] which if implemented might eliminate employee representation plans and the Joint Council as a legal means of negotiation between employees and employers has caused us to feel that presentation by us at this time is necessary. . . . [L]egislation should provide that the way be left open at all times for employees to deal co-operatively with their employer in their own way by any procedure they may choose even though such employees are a minority group. . . . We are here to recommend protection of the Joint Council as a well-tried procedure in industrial relations that is based upon co-operation, goodwill and the community of interest between employees and employers. There are many employees to-day who have achieved most desirable relations with their employers, and

> not only should they never be deprived of the result of their efforts, but the opportunity should be preserved for other employees, and their employers as well, to do likewise. It is essential, therefore, that the co-operative procedure as embodied in the Joint Council be protected by law for those who choose to make use of it. (Canada 1943, pp. 1106–1109)

Imperial was one of a number of prominent Canadian firms making such submissions. Because of the importance of wartime labor-management cooperation in all its forms—union and nonunion—as well as a variety of other factors (Taras 1997a, b), Imperial's view prevailed, and the JIC continued to be a lawful mechanism for employee representation.

Imperial Oil's corporate welfarism was within the norm of many large, prosperous companies throughout North America. However, the persistence of the JIC allows a longer scrutiny of the employee relations dynamics within Imperial. In addition to the longevity of the plan, it is distinctive because of the "high price that Imperial Oil was able and willing to pay" and that its workers had the capacity to extract " in order to maintain a loyal, union-free labour force" (Grant 1998, p. 90). The labor bill as a percentage of total costs of production was low, and the profits of the company were high. Therefore the costs of running nonunion, including generous benefits and premium wages, were borne easily from company profits.

The company has not been entirely immune from union inroads. During the first nationwide wave of organizing after World War II both a Calgary refinery and the Ioco refinery were eventually certified. After many decades of cooperative labor-management relations, both refineries were closed (Calgary in the 1970s and Ioco in the 1990s) due to technological obsolescence. Imperial Oil, including its subsidiaries, was the target of at least six post-1950 nationwide union organizing attempts by the Energy and Chemical Workers Union (which merged with two other unions to form the current Communication, Energy and Paperworkers Union). Despite what is obviously a determined effort on the part of the union to make Imperial the flagship of its membership, the union historically has failed to penetrate Imperial to any substantial degree. More recently, however, the union's fortunes might be turning. Since 1993, just as the company was on the cusp of becoming totally union-free, three significant sites have certified and a number of other sites are considered vulnerable. Its billion-dollar Norman Wells refinery in the Northwest Territories certified in 1993, followed shortly thereafter by its Edmonton Strathcona refinery, and its Nanticoke refinery in Ontario. (Reasons for the union victories are explored in Taras and Copping 1998). The Communication, Energy and Paperworkers (CEP) union, one of the largest Canadian private-sector unions, is ever ready to answer the call of Imperial employees, and remains anxious to add the relatively glamorous Imperial bargaining units to its roster of union locals.

Employee Representation at Imperial Oil—
The Joint Industrial Council and Forum

Union density in the Canadian petroleum industry appears low on the surface, partly due to an unusually small proportion of hourly workers relative to salaried employees (Statistics Canada 1994). When the potentially "unionizable" segment of the workforce is considered—that is, those workers who are the traditional targets of union organizing efforts—about 35 percent are certified, and almost 40 percent of hourly and field employees are covered by collective agree-

ments (Taras and Ponak 1999). Almost 30 percent of hourly workers belong to the CEP.

Imperial Oil has much lower union penetration (at under 5 percent) than the industry average. It operates an amalgam of industrial relations forms. Unlike its principal owner, Exxon, however, Imperial has no independent local unions. The Canadian petroleum industry does contain a number of ILU bargaining units (comprising just over 5 percent of hourly employees in the industry), but they are much less common than the certified bargaining units of the CEP.

At Imperial there is a clear separation of union from nonunion representation systems. This case study is confined to the upstream arm of Imperial, formerly known as Esso Resources and currently called Production Operations. Within Production Operations are three forms of employee representation: the JIC system, which in 1995 included 541 wage earners; the Forum system, in which all 260 employees at Cold Lake participated; and a union site at Norman Wells in the Northwest Territories (CEP Local 777), which represented 65 wage earners. Norman Wells employees were visible and active participants in the JIC until they joined the union and were expelled from the JIC by a formal vote of other plants' JIC worker representatives. (For a graphical presentation of employee representation systems at Production Operations, refer to Figure 1, Taras and Copping 1998, p. 29.)

The Inner Workings of the Contemporary JIC

In 1945 Imperial Oil's JICs expanded with the creation of Esso Resources as the company's exploration and extraction arm. Esso Resources (now called Production Operations) recently celebrated fifty years of JIC operation. Currently, five of the seven operation areas have local JICs that include elected delegates from that area, supervisors, and the area manager. There are between three and six elected delegates and alternates depending upon the number of business units within each operational area. On average, there are fifteen workers per elected delegate. The operations of the JIC are remarkably true to the thoughts first articulated by Mackenzie King in Figure 11.1. The separation between wage earners and managers is rigorously upheld, and Mackenzie King's label "wage earner" continues to be used in the contemporary JIC.

Table 11.1 describes the various levels of representation in Imperial Oil. For each level, the responsibilities and the nature of representation are described. The JIC is a two-tiered structure that exists below the corporate level. Each JIC level has a particular scope of issues that it has the autonomy to resolve without further consultation. Local-level issues tend to encompass area-sensitive needs, such as callouts or travel allowances for remote sites. The second tier is the district level. It deals with issues that affect all operating areas including shift differentials and scheduling of work in relation to compensation entitlements. The district JIC brings together between sixty-five and eighty delegates for a full-day conference at a private hotel in Edmonton. Because of the distances involved in coming to Edmonton, most of the delegates sleep over for at least the night prior to the meeting.

The corporate level exists above the JIC, and at that high level are developed the companywide policies on such vital concerns as wages and benefits. The JIC can comment, advise, protest, or praise, but it has no direct power to initiate or reverse corporate decisions.

Local committees generally meet once per month. District meetings are held approximately six to eight times per year. District meetings are attended by worker and management delegates from all of the operational areas as well as the district manager.[4] Worker delegates are elected by wage earner employees in their respective business units every two years. At the district level, both worker and management delegates elect two wage earners and one manager as district co-chairs. The other management co-chair position is filled by the regional operations manager. Alternate meetings are chaired by worker co-chairs and management co-chairs. Although there are occasions when non-JIC delegates may attend meetings, generally the meetings are restricted to delegates only. Before the meetings, worker delegates may consult with their constituents, and after the meetings delegates are expected to report the outcomes.

Elected JIC worker delegates are paid for the time they spend engaged in JIC activities, but they continue to perform their primary jobs. The busiest of the worker delegates, the co-chairs, estimate that about one-third of their working time is devoted to the JIC. The JIC has no full-time positions (an option that was discretionary in Mackenzie King's letter). The JIC structure is supported by a team of HRM staff positions at both local and district levels.

Almost half the agenda at district JIC meetings consists of information items. This agenda gives management delegates and HRM staff the opportunity to provide the rationale(s) and benefits of change. It also gives workers a chance to raise concerns about any negative impact that might arise from new policies. Throughout 1995 there were numerous presentations involving alteration to the benefits packages that were informative and thorough. Worker delegates were fully briefed and returned to their constituents with concrete knowledge.

Table 11.1

Structures and Functions of Resources Division JIC

Level	Responsibilities	Representation
Corporate level (exists above JIC structure)	Companywide policies on wages, benefits and pensions. Engaged in issues involving impact of restructuring and centralization.	Corporate executives, usually from Toronto. No formal JIC representation, although JICs are asked for feedback on decisions.
District JIC level	Issues that affect all operating areas including shift differentials, scheduling of work, handling hot rumors, hosting JIC golf tournaments and annual Christmas party. Empowered to create subcommittees.	65 to 80 delegates in total. Elected and selected delegates from all local JICs, plus district manager for Resources Division and all Human Resource Management (HRM) staff from Resources Division. District JIC is managed by four co-chairs: two elected delegates and two selected (including district manager), with senior HRM assistance. Agenda is set at co-chair meetings. Minutes are taken and distributed throughout Resources Division. Meets for full days six to eight times a year at an Edmonton hotel.
District JIC committees (answerable to district JIC)	Two most powerful ongoing committees are (1) Job Evaluation Team (JET), which evaluates wage positions to determine level of pay classification; and (2) External Wage Team (EWT), which gathers and analyzes information concerning the competitiveness of Imperial's wages and working conditions.	Equal number of elected and selected delegates with one or two representatives from all five local JICs and HRM assistance. Can make nonbinding recommendations to the District JIC. Meets at various sites on ad hoc basis.
Local JICs	Locally sensitive issues such as callouts or travel allowances for remote sites, recognition awards for employees. At Norman Wells, dealt with the provision of special clothing where winter wind chill temperatures fall below minus 60 degrees celsius.	Equal number of elected and selected delegates with local area HRM assistance. Usually three to six elected delegates and alternates depending upon the number of business units within each operational area. On average, there is one elected delegate per fifteen workers. Meetings occur on site, usually for a half day once per month. Minutes are taken and distributed throughout local area plus to district JIC level.

The JIC is empowered to create subcommittees to study and report on significant issues. The two most powerful ongoing committees are the Job Evaluation Team (JET), which evaluates positions, and the External Wage Team (EWT), which provides information concerning the competitiveness of Imperial's compensation package. A cross-section of worker and manager delegates are chosen for each committee. Delegates are encouraged to create and attend skills-development courses and new delegate training seminars, which take place at least once a year and are heavily subscribed. The February 1995 session spanned a two-day period and reviewed the expected roles of delegates, their key capabilities, suggested improvements in communication and meeting management skills, and, at the request of wage earners, included a session on negotiation skills.

A few years ago, the district JIC created its own mission statement, which is reproduced in the JIC Agreements. It also appears at every meeting on an enormous banner and is read aloud at the start of each meeting:

> Our Joint Industrial Council is committed to working together in an open and honest dialogue on any subject of importance to the Employees and the Company. Through trust and cooperation we can all achieve excellence.

During the past decade, the practice of worker delegates calling a meeting the night before the district JIC has become well established. Workers have a full and frank discussion of the upcoming agenda and brief each other on issues arising from each local, which are to be resolved at the district level.

A permutation of the JIC, the Forum system, was launched at the Cold Lake operating area in 1985 in hopes of addressing the perceived confrontational and closed nature of the JIC system at that time. The objective was to create an open and participative system of employee representation, communication, and problem solving where all employees—not just wage earners—could be involved in a cooperative environment.

The Forum is loosely modeled after the JIC, and Forum delegates participate in the district JIC and its committees.[5]

Case Study: Findings and Implications

In this section, the findings from the primary field research into the Imperial upstream nonunion systems are analyzed.

Case Study Research Methodology

This study drew upon three primary sources for research data: (1) observation of meetings; (2) reviewing corporate minutes and other written records, as well as searching the Energy and Chemical Workers Union (ECWU) archives (housed in the Alberta Provincial Archives, Edmonton); and (3) interviewing participants. With the consent of Imperial Oil, I was allowed complete access to Production Operations' industrial relations and human resource management (HRM) functions and eventually came to be treated as an "insider" by both workers and managers. While I have considerable latitude in describing in some detail the structure and functioning of its nonunion plans, I am required to respect the confidentiality of my sources and any proprietary information.

The data were gathered through an intensive immersion into Production Operations throughout 1995, with periodic follow-up through to February 1999. All seven operating areas were visited (six in Alberta and one in the Northwest Territories). Fourteen meetings were observed, ranging from the lowest to the highest level of the JIC structure, and including meetings of workers only (without managers) and smaller meetings between workers and managers for the purpose of planning the JIC agenda. The minutes of the previous two years of employee-management meetings from each operating area were examined. In 1999, I was the guest of the company's senior management team while it discussed its industrial relations challenges.

Over eighty-five people were interviewed at least once and up to three times, yielding over 155 interviews in all. Respondents were drawn from all seven areas and included a cross-section of managers and workers directly participating in, or affected by, the JIC process: Managerial, Professional, Technical and Administration Staff (MPT/Admin), HRM Personnel, Corporate Executives, Operations Managers and Union Officers of the CEP.

The study design was exploratory and inductive. To add rigor to the qualitative methods, I applied a well-known research technique used outside industrial relations, the critical incident method (Flanagan 1954). For example, when probing respondents about their relationship with management, I asked them to provide specific examples: "Can you recall and describe an event that led you to believe that the JIC was at the height of its effectiveness/was least effective?" Not only was I collecting and sorting the feelings and perceptions of employees, but I was able to put a great deal of emphasis on concrete events. By analyzing these critical incidents, I was able to avoid getting embroiled in respondents' (mis)perceptions, and instead, identify emergent themes or underlying constructs that help explain the JIC. Often, respondents were articulate in either favoring or criticizing the JIC and when probed for critical incidents, their current beliefs were built on deeply embedded responses to specific events.

Findings are divided into three main categories: (1) the nature of the relationship between employees and managers in the systems; (2) the advantages and disadvantages associated with both JIC and Forum in meeting the needs of workers and managers; (3) the adaptability of nonunion plans, specifically addressing the current strains that threaten JIC longevity.

The Nature of the Relationship

Opponents of nonunion representation argue that companies use the illusion of participation as a subterfuge to pacify and deceive workers. Proponents see these plans as a mechanism to foster genuine labor-management harmony. The more nuanced truth lies somewhere between these extreme views.

Is It a "Bargaining" Relationship?

Despite the superficial public appearance of complete cooperation, I found some important discrepancies existed between the private sentiments of wage earners and the face they were willing to display to managers, a finding that has dramatic implications for understanding the operation of nonunion forums. While manager delegates genuinely believe both publicly and privately that the JIC and the Forum are integrative systems capable of delivering "win-win" solutions, most workers do not share this belief beyond a surface appreciation that the integrative approach to problem solving avoids overt conflict. Workers are skilled at verbally framing issues within the rhetoric of the mutual gains approach *during* JIC meetings, but in their own premeetings they are more apt to adopt positions and then strategize about the approach that might be most persuasive to managers. Most worker delegates and substantial numbers of their constituents believe they are engaged in a traditional bargaining relationship with management. It is significant that a session on negotiation skills was included (at the request of worker delegates) in the 1995 JIC training session. Workers carefully tally management responses to worker requests in terms of wins and losses. Workers were unequivocal in their expectation that the JIC must deliver periodic wins, and that without these wins their sense of the efficacy of the JIC drops dramatically: they know the JIC easily can become a "toothless dog" (a phrase raised many times in interviews). There is a covert element in the relationship, where calculative worker delegates hope to manipulate their managers.

Bargaining Through "Vertical Linkages"

Managers are not without their own powers. Though they might hope that the JIC is truly a mutual gains mechanism, there is a great deal of socialization of workers to ensure that the management perspective prevails. There are two important differences between the bargaining that occurs in the JIC and what characterizes a unionized setting. First, each issue raised by workers is treated separately from all other issues, so that there are few "horizontal linkages." Clusters of unrelated issues are not linked into a single bargaining package—for example, wages and shift differentials and severance packages—as they might be in developing a collective agreement. Instead, each issue is assessed according to the business interests of Imperial Oil. For example, the workers' request in 1994 for a computer allowance was not tied to the other remuneration issues. Similarly, in 1995 their request for compensation to attend their regularly scheduled premeetings, which occur the night before the district JIC, was treated in isolation from other issues. In both cases, cost consciousness by the company led to denial of the requests.

Thus, in presenting each proposal, worker delegates are encouraged to frame their initiative according to its own costs and benefits. The strong presence of managers at the JIC and Forum reinforces this tendency, as managers often take on a coaching role to promote this method of assessing issues. Even in the absence of managers, however, workers continue to use business interest criteria to evaluate their proposals.

Structural Changes to Support Bargaining

The assertion that workers are engaged in a bargaining relationship is supported by their efforts to increase their bargaining power. In the past five years, worker delegates from all operation areas have held premeetings prior to district JIC meetings. These premeetings provide opportunities not only to raise wage-earner issues and have them inserted in the next day's district meetings but also to review issues collectively and develop a common stance. Worker delegates are aware that they are preventing management from adopting a "divide and conquer" tactic at the district level (1995 Interviews). The premeetings are also used by workers to prevent disarray and enhance their appearance of competence at the main meetings.

Bargaining Power and Use of the Union Threat

Occasionally, worker delegates use the union threat in a subtle but pointed manner. The union threat is a real one, as about one-third of all petroleum industry wage earners are unionized (Taras and Ponak 1999). Further, and more salient currently, Imperial Oil has been defeated in a series of union certifications, including the upstream-operated Norman Wells multibillion-dollar site and the Strathcona refinery in Alberta, as well as the Nanticoke refinery in Ontario. Conditions and bargaining outcomes at Norman Wells are raised at JIC district meetings, to the clear discomfort of some managers, and Norman Wells is a topic of informal conversation in the hallway during breaks. I probed the workers who raised the specter of Norman Wells about their intentions and was told that the company was being reminded that unionization at other sites was not outside the realm of possibility. One worker recounted that "When Norman Wells and Strathcona went union, the old toothless dog got a couple of molars."

These findings call into question the argument that nonunion forms are necessarily employer dominated and consequently are "cheap so-called forms of employee representation" and "unable to provide a legitimate voice for employees." (This was a common theme in the arguments to ban company unions in the United States.) Clearly, workers have developed their own arsenal of weapons, despite their procorporate socialization. The exercise of worker power is far more subtle than would be observed in a unionized setting, but not so subtle that it cannot be detected by managers. Second, these findings suggest that a union threat enhances the balance of power between workers and managers within a nonunion system.

Effectiveness of JIC and Forum for Employees/Managers

Employees' Perspective: Advantages

From the point of view of the wage earners, advantages associated with the JIC and Forum include having the opportunity to voice concerns regarding company policy, to work closely with management on various committees on issues of interest, to meet with workers from other operation areas, and to enjoy various perks associated with belonging to the JIC. I do not believe that Imperial's high compensation packages—at least comparable to those at unionized plants, without paying union dues—can be linked to the JIC structure.[6] Each point is discussed in turn.

Employee Voice. Both the JIC and Forum work effectively as bottom-up channels of communication. Employees are able to raise concerns, flag issues, and develop policies. For example, workers' complaints about corporate head office's lack of response to inquiries about a taxation issue were resolved relatively quickly as a result of the action of the JIC. As well, through the Forum, Cold Lake employees developed a "rebalancing" policy regarding downsizing that was later adopted throughout the Imperial organization. Wage earners play a prominent role in several HRM functions and worker delegates form half the membership on the vitally important JET and EWT committees. It is the role of HR departments in Imperial and in other petroleum firms to monitor compensation adjustments closely throughout the industry (using industry-commissioned wage surveys) and make adjustments to keep their companies in line with competitive wages. Currently, the JIC allows workers to verify information more generally available only to HR staff, and substantial ability to fine-tune the rather blunt application of corporate benefits policies. The degree to which hourly workers are given access to confidential information, particularly the specifics of competitor companies' compensation structures, is quite extraordinary when compared to the guardedness that characterizes even the best labor relations in both the unionized and nonrepresented components of competitor firms in this industry.

Multisite Information Sharing. The district JIC allows wage earners from different operation areas to meet collectively to discuss concerns. This is beneficial in that it gives wage earners an opportunity not only to present a unified front in dealing with management (as already discussed) but also to compare policies from different areas. Over the past five years, worker delegates have been able to ratchet up their benefits to the highest level attained within Production Operations sites. JIC worker delegates are vigilant in ensuring that when standardization occurs, it does so to the highest level attained, rather than at an average across sites.

Perquisites. The JIC and Forum provide tangible perquisites for workers. Not only do they meet with senior managers in a pleasant environment away from their worksites, they also participate in golf tournaments, Christmas parties, and other social events.

In certain cases, wage earners agreed to stand for election with the ultimate self-serving goal of attracting the notice of managers and increasing their opportunities for promotion. Many managers within Imperial Oil once were wage-earner delegates, and some admit that they were able to "catch the eye" of management through their exemplary participation in the JIC. On the other hand, this is not unusual even in unionized environments in this industry, and I have ample examples in other companies where promising candidates for management have been identified within the local union executive.

Impact on Wages and Benefits Is Questionable. The ability of the JIC to deliver enhancements to the actual wage and benefit structure is debatable. Within Production Operations, there is little difference in terms of wages and benefits between unionized employees at Norman Wells and nonunion employees at other sites. The official Imperial wage determination formula is that all Imperial workers are offered wages at the 75th percentile of the industry, which always meets or exceeds the union pattern. Admittedly, one could argue that Imperial's hourly workers are offered competitive wages and benefits to "bullet-proof" employees against unions, and there is some support for this perspective from our interviews. But these premium compensation packages are not the result of any overt bargaining within the JIC or Forum. Imperial does not explicitly bargain wages with the nonunion plans, and none of the companies in the oil industry bargain over benefits. An unusual feature of the petroleum industry is that the firms have banded together and agreed that benefits never will be bargained. The reason is that benefit plans are offered to all employees throughout the company, and management refuses to allow the union to negotiate changes to benefits that would echo into the nonunion hourly and salaried workforces. Given my knowledge of other companies in the industry, I believe that it is likely that Imperial would have exactly the same wage strategy in the absence of a JIC.

The manner in which the company decided to match the bonus schemes of its major competitors is illustrative of this point. Despite the existence of an active JIC system, Imperial lagged behind its competitors in the implementation of variable compensation plans. (For example, Petro-Canada, which is highly unionized, offered its employees a value-sharing scheme and a number of other companies without representation plans are bonusing their employees based either on productivity improvements or corporate profitability.) This gap was to the clear disadvantage of Imperial wage earners. Yet, throughout 1995, the gap was raised and discussed more by concerned managers than by the worker delegates. Finally, after meetings between top Production Operations managers and the corporate head office, a decision was made to equalize the compensation package to the 75th percentile of competitors, taking into account the amounts companies were paying to top-up base wages. This decision was announced at the JIC and the Forum, to a relatively muted reception that puzzled management. The feeling among worker delegates was that "of course they matched. They always do." The JIC was not credited with this change, and it was not considered a "win" for the JIC. It seemed instead to be business as usual.

The JIC currently is springing into action with regard to the actual implementation of the compensation adjustment. It seems likely that the EWT will take on the task of gathering and analyzing information gleaned from competitor companies. The team will make recommendations to the JIC, and the JIC will likely advise management as to its preferences. Thus, the JIC will help with implementation rather than initiation.

Employees' Perspective: Disadvantages

From the wage-earners' perspective, the greatest disadvantages associated with the JIC and Forum are the limited power of wage earners, their insufficient knowledge of the system, fear of reprisal, lack of legal recognition, and in the case of the JIC (but not the Forum), limited representation.

One of the strongest criticisms of company unions, and a perspective strenuously argued by Senator Wagner, was that they prevented workers from exerting real influence over industrywide conditions and allowed corporations to compete with each other by treating workers as mere factors of production, or commodities whose costs could be reduced. Wagner described this as the "nibbling of competition" and Douglas (1921, p. 97) as the "underbidding of the meanest man." Because of the tendency of the Canadian petroleum firms to share information carefully and match wages and compensation levels (Taras 1997a), even before unionization was a threat (Taras 1994, p. 214), this fundamental disadvantage is not in play in this case study.

Unilateral Management Authority. As already noted, although the JIC and Forum can make representations to the corporate head office, there is no employee representation at that level. Over the past five years, the head office has been reluctant to agree to any proposals that might increase costs. Both JIC wage earners and managers are in complete agreement these days that "if a proposal goes to corporate and costs money, it is a nonstarter." Moreover, the head office has begun centralizing a number of functions, which has had the effect of reducing the scope of issues that can be successfully bargained. For example, in the past, customizing some aspects of benefits plans were within the purview of the JIC and Forum at the local level. However, the corporate office has begun rationalizing and standardizing benefits across the company. On certain issues, such as savings plans, changes were made without any consultation and on other issues, such as the new health and dental plan, wage-earner input was minimal. (It should be noted, however, that as a result of worker delegates' sustained complaints concerning the closed nature of the process, wage earners will be involved in the revision of the pension plan.)

In attempts to assert greater impact on corporate-level issues, one of the interesting recent developments is the JIC's use of letters to the corporate head office, conveying the unified sentiments of the JIC and Forum members. The letters are sent directly to the chief executive officer of Imperial Oil, and they are intended to bypass the multiple levels of management between the JIC and the CEO. Although initially successful in getting attention, worker delegates noted with a degree of cynicism that two proposals they made to Imperial via letters yielded only "denials" in identically worded form letters. At present, the letters are losing their impact as venting mechanisms. This point is best illustrated by the September 1995 district JIC meeting at which a number of management delegates strongly coached the workers to send a letter critical of changes to the benefit package. This incident might indicate that corporate centralization is inadvertently creating a banding together of both worker and management delegates. Certainly, a common front might increase JIC power, or pending a negative outcome, JIC frustration, but it may do so at the expense of diluting the pure wage-earner voice.

Insufficient Knowledge. One of the basic requirements of the company union movement at the turn of the century until the Wagner Act ban was that employers must meet with their own employees and reject any "third-party" (a benign euphemism for union) involvement in the nonunion forum. Thus, as Douglas concluded in 1921,

> workmen are deprived of expert outside advice in putting their case and conducting their negotiations. The modern wage contract needs a great deal of skill in negotiating. The owners of a concern hire skilled experts to represent them. . . . It is only fair therefore that the workers should be allowed outside representatives as well. Men who work with their hands all day are seldom capable of driving as good a bargain as a skilled and shrewd negotiator. . . . Indeed it might be said that the union is in part a device whereby individual

> workmen are able to pool small amounts and hire a professional expert to represent them. This opportunity the shop committee virtually denies them. (Douglas 1921, pp. 98–99)

There is some trepidation among wage earners in facing management as "selected delegates are there forever and really know how to work the system, and can meet whenever they want" (Interview, 1995). By contrast, worker delegates, many of whom change office every two years, feel that they are relatively inexperienced, have few opportunities to share notes, and lack any deep understanding of Imperial's corporate strategy. Production Operations has attempted to address this issue by providing training not only in corporate matters but, more particularly, in issue analysis and delivering effective presentations. Wage earners also have used their JIC committees to increase access and knowledge about industry wages and benefits, but still, wage earners lack any independent budget to hire independent experts to gather information and further the prospect of employee "wins."

Weakness and Reprisal. In 1921 Douglas wrote that even in the most enlightened nonunion plans, the fear of reprisal exists: "the workmen . . . consequently moderate their claims and their method of presentation, because of their fear that they may be covertly punished if they are too active or question the employers too closely" (Douglas 1921, p. 96). Despite Imperial management's efforts to curb this perception by running an open and honest forum, reprisal remains a recurring theme. Not only have a number of workers indicated that they fear reprisal for speaking out at JIC meetings, but they are also able to cite examples. Whether or not these examples actually took place is immaterial. The critical fact is that the perception exists, and this impedes the effectiveness of the JIC as an avenue for bottom-up communication.

The structure of the JIC as it is constituted currently has ameliorated the more overt potential for reprisal. "Yes," describes one worker co-chair, "sure some guys are afraid to speak up, since the boss is sitting there," but the role of the worker co-chairs is to "surface issues" on behalf of other worker delegates. Because the worker co-chairs have control over setting the agenda for meetings, and frequently chair the meetings (alternating with management), they can ensure that issues are raised and dealt with, even as they keep the source of the issues confidential from management. Further, as co-chairs are elected from among the workers, workers are able to select co-chairs that they perceive are courageous, articulate, and trustworthy. Though more vulnerable to reprisal than they would be in a unionized setting, wage earners have much greater capacity to voice their interests through the JIC system than they would if they had no form of collective representation.

Legal Status of JIC. As the JIC employment contract lacks the status of a true collective agreement, it can be changed unilaterally by management. This was one of the primary reasons that the wage earners in Norman Wells certified. They were unhappy with the constant unilateral changes and threat of changes made by management concerning benefits. As well, because nonunion representation is not recognized under the law, management can cancel a particularly belligerent worker forum at its pleasure. Although this has not occurred at Production Operations, it has been done in one important refinery in Imperial's downstream operation.

Because nonunion representation forums are not subject to the labor code, there is no require-

ment for third-party arbitration. In the downstream Strathcona refinery, provision was put into place for binding third-party arbitration shortly before the refinery voted to become unionized, and one case was heard through this procedure. Third-party grievance arbitration has not spread. Although there is an elaborate and clearly specified grievance process, the final step resides within the company. Very few employees launch official grievances, and none have proceeded past the local JIC stage. While grievance arbitrations in the unionized sector of the industry are relatively rare, it is noteworthy that the CEP union has expended considerable resources fighting two human rights complaints against the company's stringent drug and alcohol policy. By contrast, absent resources and expertise, the only weapon against the company's application of the drug and alcohol policy was the irate downstream (Sarnia) JIC's threat to disband itself and refuse to meet with management.

Proscribed Membership. Finally, in the JIC system, formal representation is for wage earners only. Other groups of employees, including MPT/Admin personnel, do not have any formal representation system (except in the Forum). This is not perceived as a disadvantage by wage earners, as the majority of worker delegates do not want the inclusion of other classes of employees, fearing that they would reduce the amount of time to deal with wage-earner issues. It is, however, a disadvantage for those employees not represented.

At their own initiative MPT/Admin employees tried in the 1970s to create their own JIC, known at one time as a "JAC" (Joint Administrative Council), but the effort fizzled for lack of management support. I can speculate about a number of explanations for the poor launch of the JAC, including the lack of viable union threat, the complexity of running multiple overlapping forums based on different communities of interest within Imperial, the cost and time commitment required to operate yet another nonunion forum, the lack of embeddedness of the JAC into Imperial mythology, possible gender issues related to the majority female representation in the JAC ranks, the ability of Admin employees to resolve issues directly with their supervisors, and so on. All these explanations were raised by the MPT/Admin staff I interviewed who were knowledgeable about the history and fate of the JAC. Some MPT Admin believe they achieve spillover benefits from the JIC, but others feel inequitably treated and resent their exclusion from worksite voice mechanisms.

Managers' Perspective: Advantages

From the point of view of Imperial managers, four primary advantages associated with the nonunion representation include providing a mechanism for top-down communication of corporate initiatives, improving management policies by allowing periodic "reality checks" against employee expectations, facilitating the integration of workforces following the spectacular Esso-Texaco merger, and union avoidance.

Communication. As a form of top-down communication, the JIC and Forum systems enable managers to inform Production Operations' workers of Imperial corporate decisions. Although this type of communication has been fairly successful, if it becomes overwhelming it may squeeze out the opportunity of workers to express their positions. Certainly, management's information items create an atmosphere of passivity, since the "expert" makes the presentation and the wage earners simply assimilate new information. Without more participation from worker delegates, the JIC may become viewed simply as a tool of management.

The JIC and Forum also allow rapid communication of management decisions in response to worker delegate requests. On issues of a local nature, the area managers are able to make decisions virtually on the spot during local JICs. As well, the systems also provide a mechanism for area managers to promote worker involvement in corporate initiatives. For example, worker representatives in nearly all areas have participated in all aspects of a Supportive Work Environment survey in response to a program sponsored by the head office.

Fine-Tuning Employer Initiatives. The JIC allows for greater employee input into the formation and implementation of Human Resource Management policies. Worker delegates are harnessed as substitutes for, or complements to, HR advisers, facilitating the diffusion of HR initiatives within the company. In addition to their impact on the Supportive Work Environment program, worker delegates monitor and comment, often unfavorably, on alterations to existing benefits programs.

Postmerger Integration. The JIC system was quite effective in the aftermath of the Imperial-Texaco merger in amalgamating the Texaco employees into the Imperial Oil culture. Former Texaco employees were a significant presence within the JIC (even achieving the rank of worker delegate district JIC co-chair). The information provided from management in the JIC about Imperial Oil sites, initiatives, policies and HR practices helped integrate the two workforces.

Union Avoidance. Despite the recent CEP certifications of Norman Wells and the Strathcona and Nanticoke refineries, I believe that the JIC and the Forum are highly effective as part of a union-avoidance strategy. There are three aspects to this finding.

First, the JIC and Forum serve a vital early warning function of incipient discontent. Worker delegates provide management with all the clues, broad hints, and at times overt assessments of the union-proneness of various sites. Three times in 1995 I was present when management was informally advised by worker delegates (though not during the formal JIC local or district meetings) that "the union organizer is sniffing around . . . like a vacuum cleaner salesman," that "we've got some serious problems in [certain sites]" and that "wage earners are thinking about the advantages of a union" (quotes from 1995). There is enough trust in the relationship that wage earners will attempt to give the Forum/JIC managers "a chance" before deciding whether or not to become involved in union organizing. Not only are wage earners likely to advise management of union organizing activities, but management is kept informed of the issues that would likely to lead to an area being union-prone.

Specific incidents provide evidence of the early warning function. In 1990 Cold Lake wage earners contacted the CEP and began to hold meetings to discuss certification, keeping management informed of all activities. A rankling issue was the area manager's style. Wage earners concerns were addressed by top management, and the area manager was replaced by a new manager with strong interpersonal skills. Forum representatives subsequently withdrew support from the certification drive, and it failed. Similarly, in Norman Wells, JIC delegates frustrated with the lack of management responsiveness to their concerns contacted the CEP and began a certification drive, again ensuring that both management and JIC delegates at the district level were kept abreast of activities. When the Western Canada operational manager visited the site and promised changes, the delegates withdrew support, ensuring that the

drive would fail. When it was discovered that the promised changes were not forthcoming, however, a second drive, also led by the JIC worker delegates, was held, and the site was certified (Taras and Copping 1998). Managers at Imperial clearly admit that at Norman Wells, Cold Lake, and Strathcona they were made aware of union organizing and were given long periods of time to take corrective action. My point here is that management is advised about the actions it must take to forestall unionization; whether management complies is another matter. Management's failure to respond in Norman Wells and Strathcona was due partly to a misestimation of the likelihood of union certification. Today, with new sites unionized, top management at Imperial is shaken and is rapidly changing its estimation of the importance of industrial relations to the strategic interests of the firm.

The second aspect is the socialization function of the JIC and Forum. Both systems allow workers a considerable voice in the worksite and cultivate the capabilities and talents of some of the strongest natural leaders among the employees. Their efforts are channeled into the Forum or JIC rather than toward a union. One of the measures of the effectiveness of the JIC socialization process is that in Norman Wells, the JIC method of doing business continues to have considerable impact on the operation of the bargaining unit. The union executive remains committed to the JIC's JET system and continues to bargain a collective agreement that ties wage adjustments to the JIC rather than to the CEP's National Bargaining Program. Even with a transition to a union, and the expulsion of Norman Wells from the JIC, the JIC exerts strong residual effects. Generally speaking, workers are reluctant to abandon the JIC or Forum to support a union unless they perceive that they are "backed into a corner" by management (1995 Interview). Thus, from the corporate perspective, in the worst-case scenario of a successful union certification, the company decreases its prospects of facing an adversarial relationship because it has developed strong interpersonal affinities with the natural leaders within the workforce.

The third point regarding union avoidance is that the JICs do work to forestall union organizing. As noted by one CEP organizer, "The JIC is very effective as a union-avoidance strategy. It kept the union out for 40 years!" (1995 Interview). Why is the company so concerned with unionization? There are a variety of answers. Imperial, like most other integrated oil companies, has a dread of strikes. In this continuous process industry, workers are technically proficient at operating millions of dollars of equipment, and often these workers cannot be replaced legally (because compliance with government safety standards requires "certified" workers, and because of antireplacement worker legislation in a number of important jurisdictions). The most significant strike in this industry occurred in the late 1960s, and generally speaking, the labor-management climate is peaceful. Nonetheless, managers do fear powerful unions. When Imperial was having difficulty reaching a second collective agreement with the CEP union in Norman Wells, the company began training striker replacements, at a high cost in both financial terms and as measured by the disruption and sense of crisis. Although settlement was reached without a strike, the stereotype of adversarial union-management relations was reinforced.

Most managers tended to equate unionized worksites with industrial strife (giving examples of railway and postal unions) and restrictive work rules (erroneously believing that the CEP collective agreements give paramount consideration to

seniority over ability). Unions are thought to bring with them a fundamental anticapitalist ideology that necessarily fosters adversarialism. Managers tended to know very little about unions, and even less about the particular union, the CEP, which has the greatest penetration into the industry.

Another factor is the embeddedness of the JIC into Imperial Oil culture. Managers seem to be enamored of the JIC as a feature of industrial relations that makes Imperial distinct among the majority of its competitors. Although the JIC is not used to recruit and select employees, it is used to make conditions more attractive for retaining and satisfying the wage earners. Finally, managers resist having a "third party" scrutinizing decisions and fostering an overt bargaining relationship.

It would be extremely misleading to attribute Imperial's repulsion of unions exclusively to the JIC. Indeed, throughout its post–World War II history, Imperial has pursued both progressive HRM practices and an aggressive high-wage strategy that has always matched or exceeded the union wage pattern in the industry (Taras 1997a). From the union's perspective, Imperial's nonunion workers formed the largest free-rider group in the country, having achieved all the benefits of collective bargaining with none of the associated costs in the form of dues or strike action.

When Imperial sites have been union certified, the company has reacted with grace and cooperation. The union has had far worse companies to deal with than Imperial (ECWU interviews, 1991–92). Imperial managers admit that they are "not so much anti-union as pro-JIC. We just don't see why it is necessary for a third party [the union] to enter our relations with our employees." Support for the JIC approach is deeply embedded in Imperial's culture, and a number of senior managers react with horror whenever proposals are floated by less seasoned managers to alter or replace the JIC system (1995 interviews).

Managers' Perspective: Disadvantages

For managers, the primary disadvantages associated with the JIC systems are their costs both in terms of time and resources, the difficulty in managing the continuous nature of the covert bargaining relationship, the ever-present threat that a failure to meet employee expectations may lead to certification, and the stifling of the voice of lower and middle management within the JIC.

Costs. Unlike a union, which collects dues, the cost of the JIC and the Forum systems are borne entirely by the company. The direct cost of one district JIC meeting is estimated at $20,000 (constituting the travel, hotel, and meal costs but not including the wages and benefits of the attendees). Each year, six or seven district meetings are conducted, approximately sixty local JIC meetings, four district Forum meetings, and sixty local Forum meetings. The training bill for new delegate seminars and skill-development sessions for all delegates is in itself considerable. Although there is no central budget, we estimate that the direct cost of running the two representation systems annually exceeds $200,000, without even a consideration of the paid hours. This does not include the costs associated with the work of the various standing and ad hoc committees (i.e., JET, EWT); the preparation of the minutes for local meetings; and the various social events organized through JIC and the Forum, including a lavish Christmas dance and the many golf tournaments appended to JIC meetings. Although these costs are easily

absorbed by a company as large as Imperial, they might be prohibitive for a smaller corporation considering the JIC form of representation. On the other hand, I was recently assured by a senior executive at Imperial that the cost of training replacement workers in anticipation of a strike at Norman Wells far exceeded the costs of running the JIC.

Management Effort and Style. Bargaining is continuous, and the boundaries that separate issues exclusively within the purview of management from wage-earner discussion are permeable. If an issue is not resolved to the satisfaction of wage earners, it is not uncommon that it will be raised again in subsequent meetings. In this way, discussions concerning allowances for work boots lasted over fifteen years and even the word "boots" is a raucous in-joke as it has come to signify lack of closure. Also, workers will debate the contents of benefits packages tirelessly, even though benefit plans have never been on the bargaining table. This differs markedly from traditional union bargaining relationships when the majority of issues are settled in a relatively short time frame and bargaining ceases once the collective agreement is signed.

Continuous bargaining can also hamper management from introducing unpopular policies. For example, at the remote Norman Wells site, managers had wanted to transform their worksite from a permanent live-in/live-out arrangement to an exclusively live-in policy for a number of years. Because of the JIC, however, the area manager had budgeted a long period of time to foster the necessary conditions to proceed without aggravating JIC relations. Once the site was certified, however, the terms and conditions of the live-in policy were discussed and agreed upon within several months, and the area manager quickly imposed the policy. Production Operations managers admit that the transition to a live-in workforce was far easier with the union, since the management rights clause that permits this decision is clear and unambiguous.

Management style is a new issue. Until a few years ago, plant and area managers were more valued for their technical skills than their interpersonal strengths. Only an engineer could progress through the ranks to the senior line positions. According to top corporate managers, the union victories have brought home to Imperial the need for management at all levels to have greater "people skills," and a different kind of manager is valued: workers and managers both agree that the new breed is "more sensitive," "more honest," "reliable," "trustworthy," and so on. He need not be an engineer, though an engineer with people skills is the ideal combination.

Worker Resistance and Incipient Unionism. Although the JIC and Forum are successful union-avoidance strategies, there is a risk associated with these plans. Improperly managed, there are a number of factors that may influence wage earners to elect a union. First and foremost, the JIC may provide an organizational base to begin certification. At Norman Wells, the JIC worker delegates proved to be a useful contact point for the union organizer, and the former JIC leaders spearheaded the certification drive. Second, it provides workers with leadership skills that can be used in union or nonunion forums. Not only do JIC representatives receive training courses on presentation and communication skills, they also have an opportunity to use and develop those skills in the JIC structure. No impediment prevents workers from

exercising these talents to the detriment of management. Finally, the JIC exposes wage earners to collective action and raises expectations concerning the outcomes of this approach. Nonunion participation begot further union participation in the case of Norman Wells.

Role Ambiguity for Managers. A final disadvantage for managers is the ambiguity of the role of selected delegates within the JIC. They are not expected to "brainstorm" or to take strong roles in the meetings. With the exception of the top Production Operations management, who have some decision-making authority for district-level issues, other manager delegates find themselves dangling. "The purpose of the JIC is to hear from *wage earners*, not from supervisors, and not from human resources people," said one top manager. Some middle managers recall being silenced during meetings, quite overtly, while others who were too active in meetings were gently reprimanded afterward.

Via the JIC, workers are able to bypass at least two levels of management hierarchy in order to have wage-earner concerns heard directly. Workers develop personal relations with top managers, on a first-name basis, as golf partners, or as table mates at meetings. Foremen and supervisors are particularly vulnerable to being cut out of the loop entirely. Thus, the system of an equal number of worker and manager delegates masks status disparities within management ranks.

Future Role of the JIC

The primary reason for the JIC's survival over the years has been Imperial's ability to provide for its workers. Until the early to mid-1980s Imperial Oil led the industry in wage and benefits levels and innovative human resources practices (a conclusion based on my interviews with managers at other oil companies undertaken from 1991 to 1995). Imperial had one of the highest HR staff-to-employee ratios of the major oil companies. Given its tremendous profits over the years, the company was able to acquiesce to a large number of JIC demands. As a result of its munificence, Imperial fostered a strong loyalty among its employees, who believed that "Mother Esso" would provide "cradle to grave" protection. There was no reason to consider alternative forms of representation. Employees received the same, if not better, treatment at Imperial Oil than other employees in a unionized setting.

But the rationalization of benefits and the workforce reductions over the past seven years, and the increasing centralization of company functions, have created strains on the JIC and Forum. Rationalization has created concerns with job security, particularly in areas in the JIC system whose gas fields are nearing the end of their operational lives. When a site shuts down, the assumption no longer is that job transfer to another area is automatic. Corporate cost consciousness has steadily eroded benefits and viscerally threatened the "entitlement mentality" that had developed within the workforce. Issues that at one time were resolved at the district level now go to the corporate level. As a result, there is a decreasing efficacy of nonunion collective representation and declining loyalty to the company (1995 Interviews).

Centralization and rationalization have created a view that the JIC and Forum's grassroots communication are no longer as valued as they once were. Certainly, these nonunion plans have not "scored" any memorable wins lately. This perception is compounded by frustration with the

fact that the JIC is unable to address in any meaningful way an issue of great importance to the majority of wage earners in the JIC system: job security. Based on the description of several involuntary layoffs, it is also widely held that the JIC is ineffective in ensuring that the criteria used to determine which employees leave is fair and equitable. These decisions remain with management. The lack of formal grievances should not be misinterpreted as indicating an absence of dissatisfaction.

In the past, one of the pillars of the JIC system was the expectation that senior management within the top echelons of the JIC were capable of independent decision making. As late as 1994, the Cold Lake area manager was able to declare to Imperial that all employees in that region would receive time off in recognition of their efforts. The management co-chair of the JIC introduced second Fridays off. These deliverables went beyond the expectations of wage earners. Greater centralization has removed such discretionary decisions, and local managers' power has decreased. Worker and manager delegates find themselves forming natural lobbying coalitions to approach corporate offices, which has raised the popularity of some managers but has done nothing to defeat the notion that JIC power is declining.

Loyalty to the company is eroding. Up until the late 1980s, there seemed to be a perception among employees in general that "Mother Esso" was a benevolent custodian of her workers. This level of compensation and cradle-to-grave coverage is no longer taken for granted. Workers now speak disparagingly of the company (1995 Interviews). They like their jobs, but no longer trust their employer. Employees are taking a critical look at the company, and particularly rankling appears to be the simultaneity of benefits "take-backs" with the multibillion-dollar declared profits in recent years. Some employees who were indifferent to the union in the past are expressing (to me, at least) a greater willingness to consider other forms of employee representation.

As a result of the new realities, JIC and Forum are devising new strategies. Underlying many of the initiatives is the search for purpose. Nonunion plans at Imperial are complex and deeply embedded, and both managers and wage earners seem to be scrambling to infuse the experience with renewed vitality. At the JIC local level, greater consideration is being given to the concerns of MPT/Admin employees. This is particularly evident in the participation of local JIC in the design and administration of the Supportive Work Environment survey that was sent to all employees. The JIC can unify wage earners and Production Operations managers in a coordinated stance against corporate control.

The danger for the JIC in becoming a vehicle for voicing and resolving the concerns of MPT/Admin employees and Esso Resources as a whole is twofold. First, unlike Cold Lake, most JIC sites are against the inclusion of MPT/Admin. There is little community of interest between the wage earners and MPT/Admin. If JIC delegates choose to champion MPT/Admin issues, there is a potential that the system could further alienate wage earners, who already view the system as weakening. Second, by pursuing issues that are viewed by corporate managers to be outside the realm of wage-earner powers, there will be even less of an opportunity to achieve "wins." The Forum, in its search for purpose, is attempting a different approach. At site-level meetings, discussions also involve ways in which production processes can be improved, although district Forum meetings still focus on human resources issues.

Low energy in the JIC is not new. Interest in the system has waned in other periods in the past, notably the mid-1970s and the late 1980s. Nonetheless, the combination of decreasing efficacy and decreasing loyalty is a new phenomenon. Given these factors, there is a strong risk of union certification in multiple sites, especially at those sites where it appears that the employee representation system is ineffective, not only at the corporate and district levels, but at the local level as well. Employees in both the JIC and Forum systems are considering union benefits and costs, and are speaking surprisingly knowledgeably about the union (e.g., that it provides professional negotiators with knowledge about other companies, is capable of exerting "real bargaining power," and provides a third-party grievance procedure).

The current strains on the Forum and the JIC demonstrate the difficulty of managing these forms of employee representation when "times are tough." It also suggests that loyalty to the corporation is a fundamental ingredient of long-term nonunion representation. Without a basic trust in the employer, workers become pragmatic shoppers, prepared to choose the forum that they believe best represents their interests. It takes huge levels of management determination to maintain a system in the absence of genuine worker buy-in.

Conclusion

My findings should be interpreted with caution, for a variety of reasons. First, the Imperial plan may be an exemplar rather than the norm, and even so, I am providing only a perhaps atypical snapshot of its operations in the past few years. The JIC is an extraordinary commitment to a plan of worksite governance that few other corporations would countenance. Imperial Oil has a genuine pride in its record of accomplishment in HR practice, and the JIC is emblematic of its decades of effort to build an excellent worksite. This is no simple slapped-together plan designed to avoid unionization, but an integral component of a larger system of human relations. Second, unique characteristics of the petroleum industry further limit the study's generalizability. The industry is a leader in compensation levels. A typical gas plant operator can earn a gross wage of well over $60,000 a year, and it is not unusual that the total compensation package (including all benefits) might exceed $100,000. Imperial's wage earners are highly trained, articulate in expressing and pursuing their own interests, and have a great deal of personal efficacy (notwithstanding their current powerless in the face of corporate restructuring). In the continuous process petroleum industry, they are integral to the flow of the product through vast investments in capital equipment. Well paid as they are, the total cost of these workers to the corporations is a minuscule fraction of the final product pricing. Further, there is no economic incentive to join a union in this industry because there is no union-nonunion wage disparity. Despite these limitations, the study is valuable because it highlights the contemporary features and strains of a historically significant and complex multisite system of representation.

Earlier I reviewed a number of advantages and disadvantages associated with the JIC and the Forum for both managers and employees. Although employees work very closely with management, worker power concerning a number of issues is very limited and is diluted by considerable cooptation by the corporation. The JIC is a costly approach and often is more unwieldy than a union. The basic advantage of the JIC is that it "fine-tunes" the application of corporate policies, alerts the company to irritants, and allows the employees an ongoing and routinized mechanism of collective expression. Unlike many types of

employee involvement that focus on productivity gains, the JIC is devoted entirely to reviewing terms and conditions of employment. The JIC occupies the heart of the employment relationship.

After decades of participation in the JIC, workers have not abandoned the presumption that they are engaged in collective bargaining with management. In this sense, Mackenzie King's 1914 premise that nonunion forums are a form of collective bargaining is a more enduring vision than the idealistic Welfare Capitalism belief that through nonunion participation, employees and managers can achieve a complete unity of purpose. But bargaining is done on management terrain, evoking management language and using management criteria. It is bargaining without enmity.

Wage earners derive some benefits that are hard for a union to match. They are treated as partners, rather than adversaries, by management. The JIC and Forum deal with a number of HRM issues that at other companies would be the exclusive terrain of the HR department. While employees have little actual bargaining strength, they have a great deal more voice as a result of their participation and pay no union dues for this privilege. This enhanced voice permits management greater knowledge of worksite concerns, and therefore a better potential to meet the needs of the workforce effectively. The voice aspects are stronger in the JIC system than those I have witnessed in my various studies of both unionized sites and nonrepresented sites in other petroleum companies. But if they unionized, they almost certainly would lose their excellent relations with management. These workers tell me they do not want to unionize unless backed into a corner, and without the JIC, they would be unrepresented and lose many of the valuable benefits provided by the JIC. Clearly they are better off with the JIC than with no representation at all, and as long as the company is responsive to their needs, they are better off in the JIC than in a union.

While wage earners have enhanced voice, it is achieved at the expense of indigenous power. The JIC is not a vehicle that has the capacity to deliver victories except at the sufferance of management. The JIC's power waxes and wanes in relation to two vital elements: (1) the viability of the union threat, and (2) management's commitment and talent in infusing the JIC system with energy and purpose. And underlying all the complexities of the system that have been described throughout this chapter is a single essential truth: the JIC system is predicated on matching or exceeding compensation levels achieved by unions within the industry. It is imperative that the company remove any economic incentive for workers to join unions before it can share information, foster cooperative relationships, and achieve genuine harmony.

From a macroeconomic perspective, as long as the company matches the union pattern, wages are taken out of competition in the industry, and all petroleum employees benefit. There is little public policy rationale in Canada, in which unions pose a realistic and easily selected alternative for workers, for impeding the ability of firms to promote nonunion representation over no form of representation at all. In the long term, only those nonunion forums that match the union will survive. The alternative position is that JICs, because they are enterprise based, cannot act as watchdogs to prevent the deterioration of other companies' compensation levels and worksite conditions. For those who believe that only multienterprise unions can play a vital role in protecting workers, policies that allow workers to participate in alternative forms of collective representation would be seen as contrary to the social interest.

Acknowledgments

An earlier version of this chapter was published in *Employee Representation in the Emerging Workplace: Alternatives/Supplements to Collective Bargaining*, ed. Samuel Estreicher (Boston: Kluwer Law International, 1998). I would like to express my appreciation for the generous financial support from the Alberta Energy Company's Research Grant program. Excellent research assistance by Jason Copping and Janet Alford, and the helpful comments on earlier drafts by Allen Ponak, are gratefully acknowledged. The depth of the field research was due entirely to the cooperation of Imperial Oil. The company was extraordinary in valuing my desire to remain objective about the industrial relations systems I observed in practice. While I am indebted to many people at Imperial Oil, there are five people whose ongoing cooperation made this research possible: J. R. (Bob) Dixon (human resources manager), Robert G. Wilson (formerly manager, Production Operations and management co-chair of the district JIC), Rod Chiesa and Russ Radke (elected delegate co-chairs of the district JIC), and David Boone (manager, Production Operations and Management co-chair of the district JIC).

Notes

1. Section 2 of the NLRA, used in tandem with Section 8(a)(2), has the intent of eliminating most forms of nonunion employee representation. Section 2(5) of the NLRA defines "labor organization" as "any organization of any kind, or any agency or employee representation committee or plan, in which employees participate and which exists for the purpose, in whole or in part, of dealing with employers concerning grievances, labor disputes, wages, rates of pay, hours of employment, or conditions of work." Section 8(a)(2) makes it an unfair labor practice for an employer to "dominate or interfere with the forma-

tion or administration of any labor organization or to contribute financial or other support to it." In 1938, a Supreme Court decision effectively quashed any further hopes by companies for formal nonunion representation *(NLRB* v. *Pennsylvania Greyhound Lines*, 303 US 261).

2. Though a burgeoning literature on mutual gains enterprises suggests the need for nonunion mechanisms to foster industrial democracy, based primarily on German works councils or a strong sense of concern for the welfare of employees (Weiler 1990; Kochan and Osterman 1994; Pfeffer 1998), the authors generally remain vague as to the precise details or ramifications of their recommendation in the North American context. Since the American law forbids most nonunion representational-type systems, it is difficult for American authors to recommend them without offering a disclaimer as to their dubious status under the law, and a painstaking recounting of which characteristics might be permitted and which might cross the line.

3. See Imperial Oil's "Joint Agreement Between Imperial Oil Resources Limited and Monthly Wage Employees of Production Operations," January 1995, and all the preceding Imperial Oil agreements housed in the Alberta Provincial Archives, Edmonton, in the Energy and Chemical Workers Union (ECWU) collection. These agreements describe the plans' mission, rates of pay, hours of work, overtime and premium pay, vacations, promotions, transfers, layoffs, detail the impact of seniority, and offer an in-house formal grievance procedure. Imperial Oil's Sarnia JIC agreements are almost indistinguishable from union-management collective agreements. The second largest oil and gas company in Canada, Petro-Canada, also has nonunion agreements covering employees in some of its gas plants (Taras and Ponak 1999).

4. In the Rockefeller JIC, wage earner, or worker, delegates are officially called "elected delegates," while managers are officially called "selected delegates." Imperial Oil upholds this tradition, and workers refer to themselves as elected delegates. For the sake of convenience and greater clarity to the reader, I substitute the terms worker and manager delegates.

5. The Forum is a unique form of representation at Esso Resources (although there are sites in Imperial's downstream subsidiary that use a variant of the Forum). There are two levels in the Forum system. Site-level meetings are held at three different operational sites contained within the Cold Lake area on a monthly basis. All employees are also invited to attend. District Forum meetings are held approximately four to five times per year where all worker and manager delegates discuss issues of concern

to all sites. The Forum differs from the JIC. First, it is more inclusive, as MPT/Admin personnel participate with wage earners. Second, employee Forum delegates are elected by their particular business unit annually. Finally, there is only one elected co-chair at the district Forum, selected by all employees. The other co-chair is the area manager. Over the past four years, the Forum has developed close ties with the JIC system. Forum Representatives now attend district JIC meetings, skill-development courses, and join JIC committees, but cannot raise MPT/Admin issues at the district JIC meetings.

6. In their study of employee representation at Standard Oil of New Jersey, Gray and Gullet (1973, pp. 26–29) also had a difficult time determining whether the JIC had delivered tangible increases in wages and benefits. Of the eight individuals they interviewed in their study, six "expressed the belief that many of the economic concessions made during the plan's existence would have eventually been granted by the company even without the representation plan." These respondents indicated that company policy always had been to meet or exceed wage rates at other firms. The authors concluded that the JIC had a minor influence on the timing of wage increases and the design of the total compensation package, but had little impact on remuneration over the long term.

References

Brandes, Stuart. 1976. *American Welfare Capitalism, 1880–1940.* Chicago: University of Chicago Press.

Brody, David. 1989. "Labor History, Industrial Relations, and the Crisis of American Labor." *Industrial and Labor Relations Review* 43, no. 1: 7–18.

Canada. 1943. *National War Labour Board Proceedings.* No. 1–13. Ottawa: King's Printer, Edmond Cloutier.

Chase, Stuart. 1947. *A Generation of Industrial Peace: Thirty Years of Labor Relations at Standard Oil Company (N.J.).* New Jersey: Standard Oil Company.

Colorado Plan. 1916. "Industrial Representation Plan . . . of the Colorado Fuel and Iron Company," Public Archives of Canada, King papers, vol. C34, no. c24129.

Craven, Paul. 1980. *"An Impartial Umpire": Industrial Relations and the Canadian State 1900–1911.* Toronto: University of Toronto Press.

Douglas, Paul H. 1921. "Shop Committees: Substitute For, or Supplement To, Trades-Unions?" *Journal of Political Economy* 29, no. 2: 89–107.

Flanagan, John. 1954. "The Critical Incident Technique." *Psychological Bulletin* 51, no. 4: 327–358.

Freeman, R.B., and J.L. Medoff. 1984. *What Do Unions Do?* New York: Basic Books.

Gibbs, George Sweet, and Evelyn H. Knowlton. 1956. *History of Standard Oil Company (New Jersey): The Resurgent Years, 1911–1927.* New York: Harper.

Gitelman, Harold M. 1988. *Legacy of the Ludlow Massacre.* Philadelphia: University of Pennsylvania Press.

Grant, Hugh M. 1998. "Solving the Labour Problem at Imperial Oil: Welfare Capitalism in the Canadian Petroleum Industry, 1919–1929." *Labour/Le Travail* 41 (Spring): 69–95.

Gray, Edmund R., and C. Ray Gullett. 1973. "Employee Representation at Standard Oil Company of New Jersey: A Case Study." Occasional Paper Number 11, College of Business Administration, Louisiana State University.

Hogler, Raymond L., and Guillermo J. Grenier. 1992. *Employee Participation and Labor Law in the American Workplace.* New York: Quorum Books.

Imperial Oil. 1999. "Imperial Oil Limited" Corporate website: http://www.imperialoil.ca (02/17/99)

———. 1991. *Story of Imperial Oil.* Toronto: Author.

Jacoby, Sanford. 1989. "Reckoning with Company Unions: The Case of Thompson Products, 1934–1964." *Industrial and Labor Relations Review* 43, no.1: 19–40.

———. 1998. *Modern Manors: Welfare Capitalism Since the New Deal.* Princeton: Princeton University Press.

King, William Lyon Mackenzie. [1918] 1973. *Industry and Humanity.* Toronto: University of Toronto Press.

Kline, Burton. 1920. "Employee Representation in Standard Oil." *Factory and Industrial Management,* May, pp. 355–360.

Kochan, Thomas, and Paul Osterman. 1994. *The Mutual Gains Enterprise.* Cambridge: Harvard Business School Press.

Nelson, Daniel. 1982. "The Company Union Movement, 1900–1937: A Reexamination." *Business History Review* 56, no. 3: 335–357.

———. 1989. "Managers and Nonunion Workers in the Rubber Industry: Union Avoidance Strategies in the 1930s." *Industrial and Labor Relations Review* 43, no. 1: 41–52.

———. 1993. "Employee Representation in Historical Perspective." In *Employee Representation,* ed. Bruce E. Kaufman and Morris Kleiner. Madison: Industrial Relations Research Association.

Pfeffer, Jeffrey. 1998. *The Human Equation: Building Profits by Putting People First.* Boston: Harvard Business School Press.

Roberts, Walter. 1990. *Cracking the Canadian Formula: The Making of the Energy and Chemical Workers Union.* Toronto: Between the Lines.

Rockefeller, John D. Jr. 1916. *The Colorado Industrial Plan.* New York: n.p.

Statistics Canada. 1994. *Employment, Earnings and Hours.* No. 72–002.

Taras, Daphne Gottlieb. 1994. *Impact of Industrial Relations Strategies on Selected Human Resources Practices in a Partially Unionized Industry.* Ph.D. diss, University of Calgary.

———. 1997a. "Managerial Objectives and Wage Determination in the Canadian Petroleum Industry." *Industrial Relations* 36, no. 2: 178–205.

———. 1997b. "Why Nonunion Employee Representation Is Legal in Canada." *Relations Industrielles/Industrial Relations* 52, no. 4: 761–780.

———. 2000. "Portrait of Nonunion Employee Representation in Canada: History, Law, and Contemporary Plans." In *Nonunion Employee Representation,* ed. Bruce E. Kaufman and Daphne Gottlieb Taras. Armonk, N.Y.: M.E. Sharpe. In this volume.

Taras, Daphne Gottlieb, and Jason Copping. 1998. "Transition from Nonunion Employee Representation to Unionization: A Contemporary Case." *Industrial and Labor Relations Review* 52, no. 1: 22–44.

Taras, Daphne Gottlieb, and Allen Ponak. 1999. "Petro-Canada: A Model of a Union Acceptance Strategy with the Canadian Petroleum Industry." In *Contract and Commitment.* Kingston, Ont.: Queen's University Press.

Weiler, Paul. 1990. *Governing the Workplace.* Cambridge: Harvard University Press.

12

Nonunion Employee Involvement and Participation Programs: The Role of Employee Representation and the Impact of the NLRA

Bruce E. Kaufman, David Lewin, and John A. Fossum

Employer-sponsored employee involvement and participation (EIP) programs have proliferated over the past two decades among American companies (Lewin, Delaney, and Ichniowski 1989; Lawler, Albers, and Ledford 1992; Commission on the Future of Worker-Management Relations 1994a). The impetus behind these programs is the desire of companies to improve productivity and lower cost in response to greater competitive pressure, coupled with evidence from academic research and two decades of experimentation in industry that these programs can indeed deliver higher performance and increased employee job satisfaction (Cotton 1993; Kaufman 1997b; Applebaum, Bailey, Berg, and Kalleberg, 2000)

Given the widespread popularity of EIP programs, and their apparent success in boosting firm performance and employee job satisfaction, it is not surprising that recent rulings by the National Labor Relations Board (NLRB, or Board)—most notably *Electromation, Inc.* (1992)—have set off considerable controversy and debate (Nunn 1995; Morris 1996; Gely 1997). The *Electromation* ruling involved Sections 8(a)(2) and 2(5) of the National Labor Relations Act (NLRA). As described

in earlier chapters of this volume (Kaufman, Estreicher), Section 8(a)(2) prohibits employer domination, interference, administration, or financial support of a labor organization; and Section 2(5) defines a labor organization very broadly to include any kind of employee group that exists at least in part for the purpose of dealing with employers over one or more terms and conditions of employment.

The purpose of Sections 8(a)(2) and 2(5) is to prevent employers from establishing and operating so-called company unions, which, at the time of the enactment of the NLRA, were widely seen as a sham form of employee organization largely established by employers as a union-avoidance device (Brody 1994; Kaufman 1996, 1997a). A number of observers are concerned, however, that Sections 8(a)(2) and 2(5) substantially stifle and restrict legitimate employee involvement and participation programs. Many others, though, believe these provisions remain a necessary bulwark in the protection of workers' rights to organize free of employer interference. The *Electromation* case brought these conflicting viewpoints into stark relief.

The company, nonunion at the time, had established five employee "action committees" to obtain feedback and proposals for change on various company employment policies, such as attendance, pay progression, and smoking, that were a source of dissatisfaction to many employees (Nunn 1995). The Teamster's Union believed, however, that these committees were erected by the employer to thwart its efforts to organize the company and petitioned the NLRB to declare the committees a prohibited unfair labor practice. After extensive hearings and deliberations, the board agreed with the union and ordered the committees disbanded.

As previously noted, many representatives of management, and a number of legislators in Congress, reacted with shock and cries of alarm to the board's decision. They contend the *Electromation* ruling has the potential to seriously crimp the ability of nonunion companies to operate EIP programs, as these programs make extensive use of employee teams, councils, and committees, and many of the issues they consider inevitably involve some aspect of company employment policy, such as work-scheduling, safety, and incentive pay rates. Illustrative is the comment of Congressman Steve Gunderson (quoted in Devaney 1993) that the board's ruling, "called into question the legality of virtually every currently operating [employee participation] program in the nation." Gunderson subsequently co-sponsored legislation with Senator Nancy Kassebaum called the Teamwork for Employees and Managers Act (TEAM Act) that would allow EIP committees to discuss "matters of mutual interest" as long as the committees do not take on the role of bargaining agent for employees. President Clinton vetoed the TEAM Act in 1996 (Maryott 1997).

Representatives of organized labor and a number of policymakers in Congress and members of the academic community applauded the board's

decision, however, and staunchly deny that the NLRA needs revision (Devaney 1993; Morris 1994). They maintain that the ban on company unions does not significantly impede the ability of nonunion companies to operate legitimate EIP programs for purposes of enhancing productivity and efficiency, and that enactment of the TEAM Act would only give employers one more weapon in their drive to thwart unionization. Indicative of this sentiment is the statement of trade unionist Owen Herrnstadt (1997, p.108) that "although it is an understatement to say that the world has changed since passage of the NLRA, the need to ensure that workers' voices are heard through participation in legitimate unions and not muted by sham unions has not changed."

Given the sharp cleavage in opinion on the merits and impact of Sections 8(a)(2) and 2(5) on nonunion EIP programs, and the growing proliferation of such programs in American industry, it is surprising and disconcerting how little direct empirical evidence is available on this issue. The research literature on employee involvement and participation is extensive (see Cotton 1993; Levine 1995; McLagan and Christo 1995), but very little of it has explored the role of employee representational bodies as a delivery vehicle for EIP (see, however, LeRoy 1996, 1997), and no studies we are aware of have conducted field level, case study research to document the extent of representational bodies in American industry and the impact of the NLRA on their structure and operation.

To partially this gap, this chapter reports detailed case studies of EIP programs at eight American companies and the role of employee representational teams, councils, and committees therein. The object of these case studies is to provide factual evidence on the range and type of EIP programs extant in the American workplace and the degree to which these programs are constrained (if at all) by the provisions of the NLRA. Before presenting the case studies, however, we first examine the nature and structure of EIP programs and the EIP representational bodies that are legal and illegal under current and past NLRB rulings. The chapter concludes with an analysis of the case study evidence—supplemented by material obtained from personal interviews with managers, labor attorneys, and consultants—and a discussion of the implications for both current EIP practice in industry and the public policy debate regarding revision of the NLRA.

Structure of EIP Programs

A legal compliance analysis of nonunion employee involvement and participation programs first requires a careful definition of EIP and delineation of different types of EIP groups and organizational structures.

Cotton (1993), drawing on earlier work by Dachler and Wilpert (1978), suggests that EIP programs can be distinguished along five distinct dimensions. Modestly paraphrased, these are as follows:

Formal-Informal. Some EIP programs are formal in the sense of having a written constitution, bylaws, or governing rules and regulations, such as contained in an employee handbook or a company policy statement. Other EIP programs are informal with no written policy guidelines or defined structure. An example of the former might be a peer-review system of dispute resolution. An example of the latter might be a weekly breakfast meeting between the human resource director and a rotating group of employees.

Direct-Indirect. Some EIP programs provide direct, or "face-to-face," involvement for organizational members; others are indirect in that a subgroup of employees represents the entire workforce through participation in some type of committee or team. An example of the former is a system of management by objectives in which the individual employee and manager jointly determine the employee's goals for the coming year. An example of the latter is a plant-level committee composed of one employee representative from each department.

Influence in Decision Making. A key attribute of EIP is the extent of influence given employees in decision making. At one extreme, management provides no information to employees and makes all decisions beyond narrow task completion. In the middle range, management provides employees with information on a subject hitherto reserved to management and solicits their opinions. At the other extreme, employees may be given veto power over a decision and may in some cases even be delegated complete authority to choose. An example of the former extreme is a unilaterally announced change in work hours; an example of the latter extreme is complete delegation of inventory control to a self-managed work team.

Range of Issues. The range of issues considered in EIP programs can be distinguished by both breadth and depth. Breadth signifies the extent to which issues from different functional areas are considered, with production-related matters representing "narrow" EIP. Thus, a narrowly construed EIP program might deal only with product quality, such as in a quality circle, while a "broad" EIP program might deal with not only production matters but also a wide array of other subjects, such as customer relations, management succession, and employment policy. An example of the latter might be a European-style works council. Range of issues also has a depth (or high-low) dimension, where depth signifies the level of impact in the organization. Thus, low-level EIP might pertain to issues affecting only the individual worker or work team, while high-level EIP considers strategic matters that affect the long-run direction of the organization. An example of the latter is a German codetermination plan in which worker representatives serve on the board of directors.

Membership. The fifth dimension of EIP is membership—which persons from the organization are included in the EIP group. This dimension also has a breadth-depth duality. Greater breadth signifies that the EIP group draws persons from a successively wider range of work units, occupations, functions, or departments (a horizontal measure); while greater depth signifies that the EIP group includes people from a successively wider range of positions in terms of organizational hierarchy and authority (a vertical measure). A six-person team of production workers employed in one area of the paint department is "low" in terms of both the breadth and depth measures of membership, while a plantwide council composed of shopfloor workers and the plant manager is "high" on both measures.

Restrictions in the NLRA

Given these various dimensions of EIP programs, we now carefully delineate the prohibited types of EIP structures and practices in the NLRA. As previously described, Section 8(a)(2) of the NLRA makes it an unfair labor practice for an employer to dominate or interfere with the formation or administration of a labor organization or contribute financial or other support to it. Section 2(5), as previously stated, defines a labor organization very broadly as any organization or agency or employee representation committee in which employees participate and which exists for the purpose, in whole or in part, of dealing with

employers concerning grievances, labor disputes, wages, rate of pay, hours of employment, or conditions of work. [As described in the Estreicher chapter in this volume, the Railway Labor Act (RLA) of 1926, as amended, also prohibits companies from financially supporting labor organizations, but the specific language of the act and the different enforcement procedures within it provide employers covered under it with modestly greater room to operate nonunion employee committees.]

The impact of the NLRA on EIP programs depends, then, on the interpretation and application of these two sections of the law. This is a complex subject, given the six decades of litigation and NLRB and court rulings on the subject, the diversity of interpretations reached by the board and several of the federal courts, and the huge amount of extant commentary and analysis in the labor law literature. The key points, however, are these:

- The analysis of *Electromation, Inc.*-type cases proceeds in two steps (Devaney 1994; LeRoy 1996; Kaufman 1999). The first is to determine whether the EIP program falls within the Section 2(5) definition of a labor organization. If this is determined in the affirmative, then the analysis proceeds to consider if the program then violates the Section 8(a)(2) strictures regarding employer "domination."
- In the *Electromation Inc.* decision, the NLRB applied a three-part test to determine whether the EIP committee was indeed a labor organization as defined in Section 2(5). The three elements are (Devaney 1994) (1) that the organization is one in which employees participate; (2) that it exists, at least in part, for purposes of "dealing with" the employer; and (3) that these dealings involve the prohibited

subject areas of "grievances, labor disputes, wages," and the like.

- Any EIP committee or group that is representational in nature clearly meets the criterion of "employees participate in." Whether a committee or group that is nonrepresentational (e.g., a committee of the whole) is also illegal has not yet received a definitive ruling, but some form of agency function seems to be crucial in drawing the line.

- An EIP committee need not be formally constituted to be considered a labor organization. The board stated in *Electromation, Inc.* (309 NLRB 990, 1992): "Any group, including an employee representation committee, may meet the statutory definition of a 'labor organization' even if it lacks a formal structure, has no elected officers, constitution or bylaws, does not meet regularly, and does not require the payment of initiation fees or dues."

- EIP groups are illegal if they "deal with" the employer with respect to certain prohibited subjects. The phrase "deal with" has been interpreted broadly to cover not only bargaining and negotiation between employees and management, but a wide variety of bilateral interactions. In this vein, the board stated in *Electromation, Inc.*, "We view 'dealing with' as a bilateral mechanism involving proposals from the employee committee concerning the subjects listed in Section 2(5), coupled with real or apparent consideration of these proposals by management. A unilateral mechanism, such as a 'suggestion box,' or 'brainstorming' groups or meetings, or analogous information exchanges, does not constitute 'dealing with.'" Thus, in the earlier *Thompson Ramo Woolridge, Inc.* case (320 NLRB 993, 995, 1961) the board found that

an EIP committee that made presentations to management of employees' views but offered no recommendations still fell within the meaning of "dealing with," but in another case, *Spark's Nuggett, Inc.* (230 NLRB 275, 276, 1977), the board found that an employee group established for purposes of resolving grievances did not transgress the "dealing with" concept since this was a delegation of management authority, rather than a bilateral interaction.

- EIP committees may lawfully discuss matters related to production, quality, company business decisions, customer relations, and so on. Even so, the committees will be found illegal as an unfair labor practice if there is sufficient evidence to show that they are part of an employer's efforts to coerce or influence employees in choosing outside union representation (Devaney 1994). Any issue, on the other hand, related broadly to terms and conditions of employment, such as work scheduling, safety, or grievances, is illegal. In practice, a rule of reason has been applied that exempts from the strictures of Section 2(5) EIP committees that discuss these matters but where it is clear that the illegal activity was inadvertent and very infrequently done.

- Once these issues are settled, and assuming the EIP group falls within the definition of a labor organization, the analysis then proceeds to the second step—whether Section 8(a)(2) is violated. The basic issue here is whether the employer "dominates," "interferes with," or "supports" a labor organization. In the *Electromation, Inc.* decision, the board stated on this issue, ". . . when the impetus behind the formation of an organization of employees emanates from an employer and the organization has no effective existence independent of the employer's active involvement, a finding of domination is appropriate if the purpose of the organization is to deal with the employer concerning conditions of employment." Following this logic, in the past both the board and the courts have found evidence of domination, interference, and/or support when an employer financially or otherwise assists in the process of selecting employee representatives, helps draw up a charter for the group, provides any kind of ongoing financial support, provides meeting rooms, or pays employees for missed work time at council meetings. Although several federal circuit courts have attempted to relax the definition of "domination" by taking into account the employer's motive in setting up the EIP program—whether it was for the purpose of better communication or increased productivity, or union avoidance—the NLRB has so far ruled that Section 8(a)(2) constitutes a per se ban and thus employer motive is irrelevant (Nunn 1995).

Legal and Illegal Forms of EIP

We now come to the crucial question: which types of employee involvement and participation programs are legal under the NLRA, and which types are not? Two methods are used to determine the answer. The first is to return to the five dimensions of EIP programs previously discussed and see which ones are likely to run afoul of the law.

Formal-Informal. The formal-informal dimension is not determinative on the issue of legality. Either type may be legal or illegal, depending on other criteria.

Direct-Indirect. Subject to having violated at least one other prohibited criterion (e.g., discussing wages), an EIP program that provides some form of indirect representational or agency function will be ruled illegal. A group that provides "direct" participation, such as a committee of the whole or a production team, will typically not be found to violate the law.

Influence in Decision Making. The amount of influence or power exercised by the EIP group is not determinative of its legal status. Instead, the crucial issue is the structure of its authority and manner of interaction with management. As long as the authority to make decisions is clearly delegated to employees and they utilize it in an independent manner to reach decisions (e.g., in deciding grievance appeals), the EIP group is legal. Influence, no matter how small, that is exercised by an EIP group via bilateral interaction with management (e.g., discussing employee concerns) is likely to be ruled illegal.

Range of Issues. EIP groups that discuss any topic related to terms and conditions of employment are illegal. Literally interpreted, this includes such things as safety, work schedules, gain sharing, sexual harassment, and workplace violence.

Range of Membership. The membership composition of an EIP group is also not a determinative factor in judging its legality or illegality, as long as it includes at least some employees below the rank of first-level management. The committee may be limited solely to nonmanagerial employees, or it may be jointly constituted with representatives from both employees and management. Likewise, the representatives may be elected or selected in some other way (e.g., on a rotating basis). The crucial factors lie elsewhere—is the group representational in nature and does it deal in a bilateral manner with the company management?

These criteria should be able to distinguish the legal versus illegal nature of various types of EIP programs commonly found in American workplaces. Consider, for example, the following (Kaufman 1999):

Self-directed Work Teams. These are legal, since the participation is typically "direct" rather than representational in nature.

Quality Circles. These are also legal, since the issues considered are typically production-related.

Safety Committees. Although thirteen states have passed legislation mandating that companies establish some form of joint employee-management safety committee, these committees nonetheless are often illegal. This conflict is evidenced by recent proposed legislation, the Comprehensive Occupational Safety and Health Reform Act, which included a provision specifically exempting safety committees from the strictures of the NLRA (Watchman 1994).

Grievance Committees. These groups typically contain several management and employee members who hear disputes and render decisions on matters of discipline, discharge, and so on. If the grievance committee is delegated final authority to make decisions, it will pass the legality test. If its decisions are in some sense recommendations to management, or are reached only conditional on management approval, it runs the risk of being found illegal.

Ombudsperson. An ombudsperson is an individual designated by the employer to serve as a combination counselor, mediator, and problem solver with respect to workplace disputes. Although an ombudsperson is almost by definition not a collective entity, the person nevertheless often serves in an agency capacity for an employee grievant vis-à-vis the employer. Thus, an ombuds plan will be an illegal "dominated" labor organization if the ombudsperson represents an employee in a dispute over terms and conditions of employment (Morris 1994).

Employee Councils. Another form of EIP is an employee committee or joint employer-employee council, formed either on a department or plantwide basis, that meets with management on an ongoing basis to discuss matters of mutual interest. It is legal only as long as it avoids issues concerning terms and conditions of employment.

Focus or "Brainstorming" Groups. Some companies ask selected employees to meet with management as a focus or "brainstorming" group for purposes of offering suggestions and comments on some change in company policy or opinions on topics of concern to employees. These groups are legal as long as they are ad hoc, temporary, and for purposes of communication.

Scanlon Plans. A Scanlon Plan is a form of gain-sharing compensation system in which employees submit cost-saving suggestions to a joint employee-employer committee. The committee decides which ideas have merit and should be implemented. Employees then share in some portion of the savings. These committees are legal as long as management determines the payout formula and timing and size of any bonuses; they are illegal, however, if employee members of the committee participate in the pay determination process (Murrmann 1980).

Employee Representatives on the Board of Directors. One or more employees are sometimes chosen either by management or fellow employees to serve as members (voting or nonvoting) on the company's board of directors. This arrangement is legal only if the employee representatives either take part in the deliberations and decision making on issues unrelated to terms and conditions of employment or, if terms and conditions of employment are on the table, they participate only to the extent of communicating employee views and opinions or passing on relevant information to the other board members.

Nonunion Professional Employee Associations. Professional employees, such as nurses, engineers, and teachers, sometimes form an association to promote their employment interests. These interests often include a mix of professional issues, such as accreditation standards and training requirements, and issues related to the terms and conditions of employment, such as salary levels and work scheduling. These associations may cover only employees in one company, or they may represent employees across several companies or states. They are nonunion in that they have no formal certification from the National Labor Relations Board as an agency of collective bargaining. These nonunion employee associations are legal as long as they are not employer dominated, which is to say they are independently initiated by employees and do not rely on employee financial or administrative support for their continued existence.

The second method that sheds light on what types of EIP programs are legal under the NLRA is to examine guidelines given to companies on this matter by their corporate legal counsel. An illustrative example, cited with apparent approval by former board member and *Electromation, Inc.* co-author Dennis Devaney (1994), is the following. He states that in order to remain within the legal ambit of Section 8(a)(2), such plans should:

> 1. avoid structured groups in favor of ongoing employee involvement on an individual or unstructured group basis;
> 2. establish task-specific ad hoc groups that focus on a particular communications, efficiency, or productivity issue (as opposed to wages, hours....) on a short term basis and then go out of existence;
> 3. use irregular groupings of employees, such as occur during retreats and the like, to address communications, efficiency, or productivity issues; and

> 4. use staff meetings to address communications, efficiency and productivity issues. Such meetings should be attended by all staff, rather than a representative number, in order to avoid the problem of employees representing other employees.

EIP Programs in Nonunion Companies: Eight Case Studies

We next present minicase studies of EIP programs currently in operation at eight American companies. These companies, as indicated below, come from a variety of lines of business, are located in several areas of the country, and range in size from approximately 100 employees to over 100,000. They were selected largely on the basis that: (1) the unit (plant, division, company) is mostly or completely nonunion; (2) the plant or company has a well-developed EIP program, or is moving in that direction; (3) the companies represent different industries, including manufacturing, transportation, and services; and (4) the senior management was willing to be interviewed and allow us to publish a summary of what we found. High-level managers from three other companies with well-established EIP programs were also interviewed, but they requested that their companies not be featured in this study.

In selecting the companies, we relied largely on the advice of management consultants and attorneys as to which companies have advanced EIP programs. No effort was made to pre-screen the companies in order to find ones having a particular type of EIP structure or activity, nor were any companies interviewed subsequently excluded from this article because they did not in some way provide support for the policy positions we advance later in this article. All case studies reported here were reviewed by the companies for factual accuracy.

Company A

Unit: Individual Plant
Line of Business: Manufactures Soaps
and Detergents
Employment: 270

Structure of EIP

Self-Managed Work Teams. The plant runs on
two twelve-hour shifts, and each shift has two
production teams, one in the process (manufacturing) area and the other in the packaging
area. Duties of supervisors covering five functional areas have been delegated to the production teams: safety, production, training, administrative, and counseling. Various team
members ("technicians") assume responsibility for managing each of these functions as a
"second hat." This requires extensive, ongoing, cross-functional training, roughly estimated to be five to ten times the amount provided in a traditional plant. The most important of these areas is production coordinator,
and this job is elevated to a full-time position.
The production coordinator is a team member
selected by his or her peers on an annual basis. Teams are responsible for all aspects of
day-to-day operation, including ordering supplies, planning production runs, monitoring
quality, machine repair, and counseling peers
on performance or behavior problems. They
also interview new job candidates. When additional technical or management expertise is
needed, teams call on "resources" from a cadre
of nine people in a "leadership group," such
as the plant manager (who splits his time between this plant and another in a different
state), the human resource director, controller,

and so on. The least integrated and self-managed of the groups is the twenty-person administrative support group, composed of clerical and
administrative staff.

Packaging and Process Work Groups. The next
level of EIP in terms of organizational structure
is the Packaging Work Group and Process Work
Group. Each group meets once a week and has
twelve technicians and leaders. The group's mission is to review operating results; address problems or needs in production, quality, training, and
the like; perform medium- to long-range planning for their area; appoint special task forces to
work on some issue or problem (e.g., shift rotation, late delivery of supplies); and so on. Technicians rotate on and off each group as part of the
way they fulfill the "leadership" block in the pay-
for-knowledge compensation system. All technicians thus have an incentive and expectation to
develop leadership/management skills.

Plant Review Board. Problems or disputes related to job performance, interpersonal relations,
work assignment, and so forth are first dealt with
at the team level by the employee and one of the
several counselors. If not resolved at this level,
the HR director is called in as a "resource," and
as a final step the grievant can ask that the dispute be presented to a body known as the Plant
Review Board, a peer-review group composed
of both technicians and leaders. The board can
only make a recommendation; the plant manager
has final say-so. No employee can be discharged
without the Plant Review Board first examining
the case.

Special Project Teams/Committees. Ad hoc
committees and teams of technicians and leaders
are formed on an "as needed" basis to address a
particular problem or issue. They develop recommendations that are forwarded to the leader-

ship group, who then make the decision. The company would prefer to have greater joint decision making at this step, but has built a "wall" in the process to avoid a potential unfair labor practice charge of "dealing with" employees.

Compensation. The plant has a pay-for-knowledge system and an all-salaried workforce. A form of gain-sharing was recently introduced for all employees. Pay rates are pegged at the 95th percentile in the local labor market in order to attract and retain the cream of the local labor supply.

Information. Extensive information on all aspects of production, quality, cost, on-time-delivery, and so forth are provided to the technicians. "Nothing is hidden." Formal employee surveys are done, but relatively infrequently and largely in response to a perceived "need to know."

Company B

Unit: Individual Plant
Line of Business: Automobile Assembly
Employment: 2,400

Structure of EIP

Work Zone Teams. The plant is organized into "work zones" and each work zone typically has a "team" of ten to twenty employees, but these teams are not self-managed (an "area manager" oversees each team in a supervisory capacity). The teams meet at the start of each shift to review production issues, determine job rotation, and the like. They are also responsible for quality inspection, repairs, and so forth in their work zone. They do not interview job candidates or get involved in peer counseling.

IMPACT Groups. These evolved out of Qual-ity Circles, which proved to be ineffective. An employee may request of the area manager that an IMPACT group be formed to solve a problem or address an issue (e.g., a redesign of a work process to reduce heavy lifting). The manager forms a team of people with the relevant skills/knowledge (e.g., a safety engineer, an HR person) who develop a proposed solution. The area manager has the discretion to approve or disapprove the proposed solution, but usually approval is given (sometimes subject to modification).

Safety Committees. These are joint employee-management committees that meet periodically, investigate reports of unsafe conditions, sponsor training sessions, and consider new safety practices and policies. The safety committees are the most formal type of employee representation in the plant. They necessarily deal with subjects related to terms and conditions of employment, such as job rotation, work hours, and line speed.

Peer Review Panel. This is the most "empowered" committee in which employees participate. Employees who have reached the last step of the dispute resolution process, or who have been terminated for certain offenses, can request a hearing before a peer review panel. The panel is composed of five people, two from management and three from the employees. Employees who have received additional training in dispute resolution are drawn from a pool. Their decision is binding and results in reversal of a disciplinary decision in about 20 percent of the cases (a number that is relatively low, it is said, because the process is so carefully managed before cases get to this point).

Focus Groups. Management regularly convenes focus groups of employees to solicit opinions and suggestions on certain topics (e.g., change in vacation scheduling). Thirty to forty employees are selected from across the plant on a one-time basis and meet for an hour or so.

Breakfast and Lunch Meetings. The plant's vice president of human resources, as well as other executives, schedule regular breakfast and lunch meetings with employees for purposes of informal discussion and "taking the pulse."

Success Sharing Compensation. Part of the compensation system is a "success sharing" bonus, which makes payouts to employees based on plant level performance on several business plan objectives (e.g., defect rates).

Information Sharing. Periodic employee surveys are done. Video monitors are stationed in each work zone and are used for communicating with employees about new policies, upcoming events, etc. Weekly bulletins and monthly newsletters are also distributed.

Company C

Unit: Company
Line of Business: Airline Transportation
Employment: 68,000

Structure of EIP

Continuous Improvement Teams. Approximately 3,500 employees from across the company are organized into 300 continuous improvement teams (CIT). The teams are initiated by the management or employees of an individual work unit (e.g., a group of mechanics at a repair facility), usually include six to ten people, and focus on work process improvements. Team members volunteer and rotate on and off on an informal basis.

Personnel Meetings. Once every one or two years employees in each work unit participate in a "personnel meeting." The divisional vice president, or similar person, leads the meeting, ac-

companied by a representative of the personnel department. It is essentially a "town hall" event in which the executive first provides an overview of recent business developments, performance issues in the division/work unit, and the like, and then solicits questions and discussion from the audience on any and all issues. Suggestions/complaints are recorded for later management review and action.

Inflight Forum. One of the divisions of the company is "Inflight Service." It has 18,000 employees, most of whom are flight attendants. The senior vice president in charge of the division organized an employee representational group called the "Inflight Forum" composed of one representative from each of the company's twenty-six bases. Each representative is elected. The Forum, which meets three or four times a year at the company's headquarters, promotes improved communication and exchange of ideas between employees and senior management. Each base has its own "miniforum" with elected employee representatives who meet with base management. Issues are solicited from all the bases, and the two that are both systemwide in nature and of highest priority are put on the agenda of the Forum. Any subject can be discussed, but guidelines established by management stipulate that certain things are "off the table"—mainly subjects that are of a companywide nature, such as number of vacation days. Besides promoting dialogue, the Forum can form teams to investigate a particular topic, benchmark competitors' practices, and then develop a proposal to be presented to senior management. Management may accept or reject the proposal, or suggest the need for modifications or further deliberation by the Forum.

Personnel Board Council. Approximately two years ago a companywide body called the Personnel Board Council was established. In the last contract negotiations the company's pilots, who are unionized, successfully negotiated to get one nonvoting seat on the company's board of directors. The company decided also to provide the nonrepresented employees with nonvoting board seats. Toward that end, a representational group was formed, called the Personnel Board Council (PBC), which is composed of one person from each of seven divisions. One division covers management employees up to the senior executive level. The purpose of the PBC, as stated in a written charter, is to provide a two-way communication channel between the board of directors and the employees. The employees in each division establish the procedure for choosing their representative. None is elected; rather, the representatives are chosen through a process of nomination and personal interview conducted by employee peers. The PBC members serve for two-year terms. They solicit opinions, ideas, and complaints from fellow division employees, and also travel as a group to various company facilities to conduct focus groups and personal interviews with employees. They then decide among themselves which is the most important companywide issue and are given fifteen minutes at the next board of director's meeting to discuss it and present recommendations and proposals. Management does not participate in choosing the topics to be presented to the board or in developing the proposals, other than to provide information or resources if requested. A summary of the topics presented and the discussion thereof at the board meeting is distributed to employees through several methods, such as newsletters and an electronic intranet system.

Profit-Sharing. The company recently established a profit-sharing program for all employees. No other form of gain-sharing or incentive pay is provided.

Information Sharing. Periodic employee surveys are conducted. The results of the most recent one were made available to all employees. A once-a-month "phone-in" is held in which employees anywhere in the world can call in and ask a question of a designated senior executive.

Company D

Unit: Mill
Line of Business: Paper Manufacture
Employment: 700

Structure of EIP

Production Teams. Production employees are organized into teams built around distinct work processes (e.g., operation of a paper machine). The teams are responsible for day-to-day management of operations and administrative tasks (e.g., safety). Team members rotate jobs, so extensive cross-functional training is done. Each employee has a matrix of required and elective "skill blocks" to complete as part of the skill-based pay system. Successful completion of each skill block is determined by a panel of employee peers.

Dispute Resolution. The first step in dispute resolution is counseling with peer team members. If the problem is not satisfactorily resolved, the grievant can ask that a peer review panel be established. The panel's charge is to develop two or three possible courses of action, state as a recommendation which one the panel favors, and turn these over to the plant manager, who makes the decision. A discharged employee can also request arbitration if the person's team members disagree with the decision.

Department and Mill Core Teams. Every department has a "core team" composed of employee representatives and department management representatives that meets periodically to discuss department-level issues. These are generally related to production, quality, on-time delivery, and other such matters, but employment issues such as relief time and safety come up. There is also a "mill core team," composed of ten employees and six "leaders" (management), that meets regularly to discuss millwide issues. Both department and mill core teams have written charters. These charters explicitly state that the teams are not to consider personnel issues such as wages, vacations, and hours. The person interviewed felt this requirement "chilled" the effectiveness of the EIP process. The mill core team meetings tend to be bland, and the mill manager usually does not attend because employees tend instinctively to defer to his authority. The employee representatives on the mill core team select the employees to serve on the department core team, making it a "feeder" system for the former. Service on these teams is required for successful completion of certain skill blocks.

Listening Groups and Project Teams. Once a year the mill's human resource director forms a "listening group" of employees and solicits their opinion on a set of issues. The mill also puts employees on special project teams to investigate specific issues and make recommendations. Each year, for example, several employees and the human resource director serve on a compensation committee that surveys pay rates at other mills. The HR director then develops recommendations for senior mill management.

Employee Surveys. Done every two years.

Company E

Unit: State-level Unit of the Service Division of an 110,000-employee company

Line of Business: Service and Repair of Photocopiers

Employees: 450

Structure of EIP

Self-Managed Teams. The employees in this unit of the company are primarily service technicians who repair and service the company's brand of photocopiers. Up to the late 1980s, a manager would be assigned to coordinate and monitor approximately twelve technicians. It was the manager's job to act as a clearinghouse for customer calls, assign calls to individual technicians, take customer complaints, and monitor the work and performance of each technician. Technicians provided the manager with daily and weekly reports of their activities, the types of repairs done at each site, and the cost of parts used. A significant redesign of the traditional organizational structure and underlying work processes was done in the late 1980s as part of a companywide TQM program. Technicians were formed into work groups (teams) of six to seven members, and the group was made responsible for many of the tasks formerly done by the manager (but only after very extensive training). Thus, the work group is empowered to decide how the calls will be handled, who will be assigned to each, and how the work is to be done. Managers now have a span of control of thirty-to-one (approximately five work groups).

Information. Part of what allowed the large increase in span of control is new technology. Each technician has a laptop computer and, instead of giving the manager a written report, downloads the data to corporate headquarters, which can, in turn, be immediately accessed by all work group members, the manager, and work groups in other states. Technicians also have electronic access to extensive data on all aspects of the company's business performance. Intra-team coordination has also been facilitated by giving each technician a portable telephone in order to be in continual communication with each and can do field level group brainstorming sessions.

Compensation. Individual performance evaluation now has a large component related to performance of the work group. A gain-sharing program was also installed, which makes a part of individual pay depend on the team's performance vis-à-vis the annual expense budget and surveys of customer satisfaction.

Councils, Committees. The work groups are the only formal EIP structure in this state unit.

Company F

Unit: Plant
Line of Business: Manufactures Missiles
Employment: 1,000

EIP Structure

Self-Managed Work Teams. This plant converted to self-managed work teams over a twelve-month period in the late 1980s as part of a comprehensive transformation to a high-performance, total quality management (TQM) work system. Teams range in size up to twenty people, but eight to twelve is the preferred size. The teams are given monthly and annual production targets and expense budgets and are responsible for deciding how these are met. Thus, the teams determine the production schedule, assignment of tasks, extent of job rotation, and perform their own quality inspections. The teams also schedule vacations and can elect to take a temporary "layoff" if production is slow.

Plantwide Committees. Three plantwide joint employee-management committees are in operation. The first is the "workplace action team," which deals with issues such as work schedules and security (a large concern at this facility); the second is the "environment and safety team," which deals with occupational safety and health issues; and the third is the "gain-sharing team," which is responsible for managing the gain-sharing program. Each committee has a "diagonal slice" of employees, including senior plant management, persons from the engineering and administrative staffs, and shopfloor employees. The gain-sharing team is the one that elicits the most employee interest and is viewed as being the most prestigious. The gain-sharing program provides employees with a bonus payment based on their ability to reduce production costs below a target figure. The committee thus monitors expenses (including management expenses on furniture and travel); periodically adds, deletes, or modifies performance targets; and issues regular reports to the plant employees on the status of that period's gain-sharing pool.

People Council. This plant is one of five in its division. Three councils have been established that cover all five plants: a Production Council, a Growth Council, and a People Council (PC). The PC deals with all personnel-related processes and problems, including but not limited to traditional human resource issues. Twelve people serve on the PC, drawn from the five plants and from the ranks of management, the professional staff (engineering), and production employees. The PC meets once a week (via teleconferencing) and is very informally structured and run. Its members have no tenure and are selected by management on a consultative basis with key stakeholders. The People Council charters a variety of project teams that are charged with investigating specific issues (e.g., a new performance management system). These teams are also joint employee-management groups. They periodically update the PC with a progress report and in turn receive "mid-course" feedback. Eventually they present a report or set of recommendations to the PC, which through a process of informal consensus building decides to either accept, modify, or send back the proposal for further work. An accepted proposal is then submitted by the PC to the division's all-management "executive council," which makes the final decision.

Town Hall Meeting. Every year all employees attend a town hall meeting offsite where plant management and teams report on various aspects of plant performance, including profit and loss, followed by an open question-and-answer period.

Peer Review. A half dozen channels exist for resolution of workplace problems, but one option is to bring the matter before a plant-level peer review panel.

Employee Survey. A survey of employees is done regularly.

Company G

Unit: Plant
Line of Business: Powered Janitorial Maintenance Equipment
Employment: 100

Structure of EIP

Self-Managed Work Teams. The plant runs on two eight-hour shifts with six self-managed work teams, varying in size from two to twelve people. Each of the teams is responsible for final assembly of a particular product line. Five supervisors

(reduced from twelve in the traditional system) perform roles of coaching, mentoring, problem solving, communicating goals and feedback from higher management, and assisting in disciplinary/performance problems. Teams work with industrial and product engineers to design work areas and assembly procedures as new product prototypes are developed. Each team is responsible for its production planning consistent with output goals of the firm. Teams interview employees or job applicants who are interested in becoming team members and discuss with them team expectations and performance criteria. The teams provide the HR manager with feedback and recommendations but do not have final authority to select among applicants. Teams do have the authority to allocate overtime hours among members and were at one time given authority to allocate vacation days. They did an ineffective job with the latter, and this task was transferred back to management.

Team Leader Council. Each self-managed workteam elects a leader who serves on the Team Leader Council. The position rotates among team members. The mission of the council is to discuss issues that are general across work groups. The council has fallen into disuse, primarily because of the team-specific nature of many production problems and the temporary nature of the groups' incumbents (due to the rotation of team leaders).

Plant Advisory Board. The Plant Advisory Board (PAB) is an elected group among assembly workers. It meets periodically with top management and receives information about future production plans and wage survey data. The PAB also provides top management with information about employee concerns in these and other areas.

CEO Meeting. The company's chief executive officer (CEO) holds semiannual meetings with all employees to update them on sales, business developments, and other pertinent information.

Compensation. A pay-for-knowledge compensation system was installed when the company adopted self-managed work teams. The company has also had a profit-sharing plan for many years.

Company H

Unit: Company
Line of Business: Express Mail and Package Delivery Service
Employment: 121,000

Structure of EIP

Survey-Feedback-Action Process. A long-standing human resource practice of this company is its Survey-Feedback-Action (SFA) process. The SFA is a 29-item structured computerized survey that is administered on-line annually to a 10 percent sample of the company's U.S. and Canadian workforce. The human resource department analyzes the responses and distributes a summary report to all managers and supervisors, who, in turn, share the report with their employees (the feedback portion of the process). The HR department also uses the responses to develop suggested action items for managers and supervisors. Upon mutual agreement that these action items are appropriate, the line managers are required to inform employees of the actions they plan to take and to monitor their effectiveness. To reinforce use of the SFA, superiors regularly rate the performance of managerial/supervisory personnel in providing SFA feedback to employees.

Supervisor-Management Board. A standing committee, the Supervisor-Management Board (SMB), was established to facilitate communication and exchange of information between senior management and supervisors and lower/ middle managers in the various units/departments/ facilities. The supervisory members of the SMB are appointed by senior management. The board considers a wide range of issues but gives particular emphasis to company level matters. The board also serves as an "appeals" channel for supervisors and managers—for example, on issues such as promotion, relocation to other company facilities, and proposed areas of action based on SFA reports.

Employee Committees. The company often uses employee committees to deal with specific business and workplace issues. These are generally ad hoc committees of a "project" nature with the members recommended/appointed by management or solicited on a voluntary basis. Many of the issues examined are business related, such as tracking packages and the design of a new Web page, but some employment issues are also considered. Examples include revisions to the company's compensation plan, training and career development programs, job assignments, and an employee recognition and reward program. General managers of units/departments/facilities may establish their own ad hoc committees to deal with business and/or workplace issues, but must receive permission from the vice president for human resources before doing so. One such "local" ad hoc committee was formed to deal with the issue of relocating company facilities/depots from higher cost to lower cost locations; another was formed to deal with workplace safety issues for employees working the night shift in high-crime areas.

Employee Suggestion Program. A formal suggestion program is in place to encourage employees to submit ideas on how the company can reduce costs, improve quality, and so on. Employee suggestions are made at local facilities, and the most promising are forwarded to company headquarters for assessment and action. Over 3,000 suggestions are received annually. Monetary rewards of up to $25,000 are made, along with a variety of nonmonetary rewards and recognition.

Guaranteed Fair Treatment Program. Grievances that cannot be settled informally between the employee and first-line supervisor can be appealed through three levels of review: management review, office review, and executive review. This procedure is known as the Guaranteed Fair Treatment (GFT) program and is available to all employees up to the level of middle manager. About 5 written grievances per 100 employees are filed annually. A maximum of seven days is allowed for settlement at the first two steps and twenty-one days at the final step.

Profit-Sharing. The company's compensation program calls for 75 percent of an employee's pay to be in the form of a base wage or salary, and 25 percent to be in the form of "pay at risk." The latter component takes the form of profit-sharing. In addition, certain employees receive bonus payments based on achievement of individual, team, or department goals.

Information Sharing. In addition to information provided to employees through the SFA process, the company uses a printed newsletter and e-mail communications to inform employees about business developments. Also in place is a designated telephone "hot-line," which any employee in the company worldwide can use to pose a question or to raise an issue with a senior executive.

Compliance Analysis: The Case Studies

We believe that the breadth and depth of employee involvement and participation activities undertaken by these eight companies is quite striking. We also perceive a significant incongruence or gap between what a strict reading of the labor law says is permissible and what several of these companies are doing in their EIP programs.

Most noteworthy in this regard are Company C (airline transportation) and Company F (missile manufacture). Both companies have employee representational bodies that are in a number of respects closely akin to the 1920s-era employee representation plans. In the former case, the Inflight Forum and the Personnel Board Council are divisionwide or companywide representational bodies financed by the employer. They have written charters, elected or selected employee delegates, regular meetings with management, and agendas that include issues related to the terms and conditions of employment. In the case of Company F, the People Council spans five plants, has selected employee representatives who meet with management, and considers various aspects of the terms and conditions of employment. It should be noted that executives at both companies are well aware of the law regarding nonunion employee committees, have consulted labor attorneys on the matter, and have proceeded with their representation plans in the belief they meet all legal requirements of the relevant labor law (the Railway Labor Act in the case of Company C and the NLRA in the case of Company F). It can fairly be said, however, that parts of the EIP programs at these two companies appear to push against the boundary of what is permissible under the NLRA.

Five of the other companies—Company A (detergent manufacture), Company B (auto assembly), Company D (paper manufacture), Company G (janitorial equipment) and Company H (package delivery)—also have employee representational bodies that in some respects raise Section

8(a)(2) compliance issues, but not to the same degree as in Companies C and F.

In Company A, for example, the Packaging and Work Process groups are composed of employee representatives and selected managers, focus predominantly on production and quality issues but also on employment matters related to scheduling and safety, have authority to deliberate and make decisions, and are company financed and controlled. In Company B, the joint safety committees appear to be the part of the EIP program that comes closest to infringing on Section 8(a)(2), given that the committees are composed of employee representatives and selected management personnel and are empowered to make decisions jointly on safety matters. In Company D, the department and mill core teams appear to most closely infringe on Section 8(a)(2)'s prohibitions, for even though the focus of the groups is on production issues, the employee and management representatives on each team must occasionally consider employment subjects, such as work scheduling, job rotation, and safety, in the course of their deliberations. The EIP body in Company G that appears most questionable from a legal point of view is the Plant Advisory Board, since it is an elected representative group and confers with management over some issues that are related to terms and conditions of employment. The employee committees at Company H also sometimes deal with management on issues related to terms and conditions of employment, although, unlike the PAB at Company G, these employee committees tend to be one-time, more informally constituted project teams and thus less likely subject to legal challenge.

The only company of the eight considered here that appears clearly to fall within the permissible boundaries established by the NLRA is Company E (photocopier service). The work groups are composed of all technicians assigned to that unit and thus are not representational in nature. These work groups correspond most closely to the small, production-oriented "teams" that Estreicher (1994) calls "on-line" systems (as opposed to "off-line" systems that are more often representational and deal with issues beyond production and quality) and that are focused on in much of the contemporary management literature on high performance workplaces (Katzenbach and Smith 1993).

Another indication of the gap between actual practice among these eight companies and what is permissible under the NLRA is to compare their EIP programs with the practices cited by former NLRB member and *Electromation, Inc.* co-author Dennis Devaney (1994) as legally permissible. Briefly, they are: to avoid structured groups in favor of EIP conducted on an individual or unstructured group level; establish task-specific ad hoc groups focused on productivity, efficiency, and communication; use irregular groupings of employees, such as at retreats; and use staff meetings to address communications issues where all staff are present (to avoid representational issues). It is evident that only the EIP program at Company E, the photocopier service provider, comes reasonably close to meeting these criteria. The EIP programs at the other seven companies would all have to be modified, modestly at Companies A, B, D, G, and H and substantially at Companies C and F.

Comments of Managers, Attorneys, and Consultants

To gain further insight on the constraining effect of the NLRA on employee involvement programs in nonunion companies, in each interview at these eight companies we asked the management executive a series of open-ended questions about his or her opinion regarding the impact of the law on the company's EIP activities and whether the company would use more employee representational EIP structures if allowed. These matters were also explored in interviews with managers at three other companies who chose not have their EIP activities featured in this chapter. We also interviewed four labor attorneys on the management side who are familiar with EIP programs and Section 8(a)(2), and two management consultants who specialize in the design and implementation of high-performance workplace systems. Their comments and observations are summarized and synthesized below. Obviously, they are anecdotal, in some cases speculative, and based on a small number of cases, so caution is required in generalizing from them.

We queried the managers regarding the extent to which they think their EIP programs are within the legal constraints of the NLRA (or RLA). Reactions tended to fall into three groups. The first consists of several managers whose EIP programs were clearly within the law, or close to it (e.g., the photocopier service unit). Their perspective is that while the restrictions imposed by the NLRA may be counterproductive and out-of-date, this is of little practical concern since they do not have, and do not desire to have, the more formal systems of employee representation that might pose a significant legal problem.

The second response pattern was from managers whose EIP programs come closer to the legal boundary established by the NLRA but who have taken pains to make sure the programs meet not only the spirit but also the letter of the law, such as those at Company A. Typically, they were more likely to follow the counsel of a management labor attorney in setting up the EIP program and to structure it in ways that would pass muster with the NLRB. In this regard, the man-

agers uniformly saw attorneys as a conservative and restraining influence on their initiatives in the EIP area.

The commitment of these managers to a strict "better safe than sorry" approach to EIP forces them to make certain compromises or changes in the program that are typically viewed as awkward or counterproductive. To avoid a charge of "dealing with" employees in a manner that would violate the NLRA, companies resort to several stratagems. They may announce, for example, that all employment-related issues are "off-limits." Doing so, however, is seen by the managers as counterproductive on two counts: first, because many aspects of efficiency enhancement and quality improvement inevitably require detailed, indepth discussions with workers of various employment issues, such as work schedules, cross-functional training programs, and pay-for-knowledge incentive wage systems; and, second, because many employees see EIP programs devoted only to productivity and quality issues as serving largely management's interests and thus desire as a quid pro quo that issues central to them, such as pay, benefits, and vacation time, also be put on the table for discussion. Paradoxically, say these management executives, Section 8(a)(2) actually works *against* employee interests in this regard since it provides nonunion companies with a convenient excuse to avoid dealing with issues that primarily affect the well-being and livelihoods of workers.

Alternatively, the companies may completely delegate authority to the employee committees so that there is no bilateral interaction between management and labor, such as making the decisions of a peer review panel final and binding. From a management perspective, this approach both satisfies the law and increases the credibility and legitimacy of the decisions made by the employee representational committee, but on the other hand it makes the committees sometimes unpredictable and opens up the possibility that without upper-management review a committee's decisions may substantially change company employment policy (an "unholy precedent") or contravene employment law. Or, finally, to resolve the "dealing with" problem the companies may limit the employee committee's role to communication and information exchange, reserving to management the process of deliberation and final decision. As an example, one manager said the employee committee investigated the feasibility of alternative shift schedules, developed a list of pros and cons, and then "heaved the information over the wall" to management, who made the final decision. This approach reportedly satisfied neither management nor the employees, but was viewed as the price that had to be paid to stay within the law.

The third response pattern among the companies interviewed is to be cognizant of Sections 8(a)(2) and 2(5) but nonetheless make a tradeoff in favor of more effective EIP programs at the risk of crossing the line and doing something that may be determined to violate the NLRA. Thus, the attitude in these companies is to avoid clear violations but otherwise proceed with their EIP programs unless told to cease and desist. This attitude is the product of three convictions: that what they are doing is a win-win for the company *and* employees; that the restrictions imposed by Sections 8(a)(2) and 2(5) are out-of-date and counterproductive and, thus, if a legal problem exists, it is much more a negative statement about the law than their EIP practices; and that the penalties in the NLRA for violating Section 8(a)(2) are quite small (typically, a "cease and desist" order), as are the chances of being charged with a violation (Rundle 1994, reports that between 1973

and 1993 the NLRB ordered disestablished less than two employee committees per year).

As previously indicated, we also interviewed two management consultants who specialize in designing high-performance work systems and four management attorneys who specialize in EIP programs and Section 8(a)(2) cases. Both groups were unanimous in their opinion that the *Electromation, Inc.* decision initially cast a significant chill on EIP programs, but that over approximately the past five years these fears have eased considerably but not completely (also see the LeRoy chapter in this volume; and LeRoy 1997).

We were told that two factors contributed to the easing of concern over *Electromation, Inc.* One is a growing perception that the law still provides enough "wiggle room" to do EIP and remain within the bounds of the law or not far beyond, albeit subject to some of the awkward or counterproductive constraints noted above. The second, and the more important according to the people interviewed, is that companies increasingly realize that the probability of being charged with a Section 8(a)(2) violation is very small. According to the attorneys, usually the only time a nonunion company gets into legal trouble with its EIP program is when a union begins an organizing campaign, discovers an in-house employee committee, and files a Section 8(a)(2) charge. But most companies, we were told, view the probability of being a target of a union organizing campaign as quite small, and, indeed, several managers in high-performance plants told us they had experienced no union activity in a decade or more. Furthermore, several attorneys ventured the opinion that the NLRB under Chairman Gould has deliberately backed away from prosecuting Section 8(a)(2) cases in an attempt to forestall passage of the TEAM Act or other such legislation. And, finally, even if a company is ultimately found guilty of a Section 8(a)(2) unfair labor practice, the typical penalty, as previously noted, is quite modest.

For these reasons, the managers, attorneys, and consultants interviewed for this study believed that the restrictions contained in the NLRA on company unions are having a less adverse impact on legitimate EIP programs than was initially feared after the *Electromation, Inc.* decision in 1992. In effect, some companies have found ways, not always welcome or efficient but nonetheless serviceable, to live with the law, while others have chosen to go quietly beyond it, operating what one person described as "stealth" employee involvement committees.

It would, on the other hand, be incorrect to say that *Electromation, Inc.* is having *no* effect on nonunion EIP programs, based on the information gathered from our field work. Both managers and attorneys stressed that despite the small probability of being charged with a Section 8(a)(2) violation and the small penalties assessed if found guilty, most companies want to stay within the boundaries of the law as a matter of business ethics. Furthermore, most companies understandably want to avoid both the large financial costs and public embarrassment associated with litigation before the NLRB and courts. It was also noted that litigation of Section 8(a)(2) cases can drag out for years, should the company appeal an unfair labor practice charge, with significant costs of diverted management attention, organizational turmoil, and employee demoralization (see the Fuldner chapter in this volume). Finally, some managers said they also did not want to provide unions with a pretext for filing an unfair labor practice charge, or for otherwise harassing the company, and thus they deliberately restrict the expansiveness and scope of their EIP efforts.

We then asked how the EIP practices in non-union companies would change if unencumbered by legal considerations. The majority of managers, consultants, and attorneys interviewed for this study believed that a fairly large number of companies would modestly expand their EIP programs in terms of the breadth and depth of activities delegated to employee representation committees. One manager, for example, said if the law allowed he would empower the employee and management representatives on the plant compensation committee to determine, subject to certain policy guidelines established by top management, the size of the quarterly gain-sharing bonus for production employees. Another said she had formed a joint employee-management team to investigate employee complaints about the plant's vacation schedule, had the team research the issues and alternatives, and then present the information to her for her final decision. Had the law allowed, she said, she would have chosen to interact with the team in the decision-making process so there was a greater element of mutuality in the final product. These kinds of restrictions, it was felt by the people interviewed, are fairly common in advanced EIP programs and have a detrimental effect, albeit not overwhelmingly in most cases, on what can be accomplished.

While most nonunion companies would probably expand their EIP programs "on the margin," a smaller number, it was felt, would probably go further. Accordingly, we queried all the people interviewed whether in their opinion companies would, if unconstrained by the NLRA, desire to put in place some equivalent of the formal, company union-like representational structures found in the 1920s-1930s, per the fears of the opponents of the TEAM Act. The common response was that most companies would not go this far, for four reasons. One is that these types of formal plant- or companywide structures are too cumbersome, costly, and time-consuming, particularly in today's environment where operational flexibility and decentralization of decision making is increasingly emphasized. Second, many respondents doubted that these company union-like bodies provide much additional benefit, either in improved efficiency and customer service or improved employee morale, over and above what can be attained from smaller-scale, more-focused EIP activities (e.g., special project teams, safety committees, etc.). Third, many companies like to foster an organizational culture that emphasizes individual treatment and respect and thus shy away from formal systems of employee representation, which tend to create a sense of collective identity among employees and a collective approach to problem solving. Fourth, managers worry that in-house employee committees may become the launching pad for union organization of the company. One manager described in-house committees as "pet bears" and said that if not treated well they can quickly turn on the company and get out of control (the "pet bear" analogy is also reported in Taras and Copping 1996).

These negative features notwithstanding, the people interviewed believed that a small minority of firms would nevertheless choose to operate formal plant- or companywide employee committees and councils if permitted by the law. Examples cited were the formal employee representation plans at the Polaroid Corporation and Donnelly Corporation, both recently ordered disestablished by the NLRB (Commission on the Future of Worker-Management Relations 1994a; Kaufman 1999). Partly, it was felt, companies such as these adopt formal systems of employee representation due to the overriding importance attached by their founders or top executives to fair dealing with employees or the fostering of a "family" corporate culture. Also important, we were told, is that in very large companies, especially those experiencing organizational stress, a formal system of employee representation can be an effective method to promote improved communication between top executives and shopfloor workers, separated as they often are by many layers of corporate bureaucracy and thousands of miles of travel distance, and to foster a win-win approach to resolving potentially divisive issues, such as the structure of layoffs in a downsizing or a change in the work schedules of flight attendants.

A final issue discussed with the people interviewed was the role of employee committees and councils as a union-avoidance device (also see Taras 1998; Summers 1997). All managers interviewed stated a desire to avoid unionization of their facilities and said their human resource programs, including EIP activities, were operated with this goal (as well as numerous others) in mind. They did not see anything antisocial or illegal about this, as in their view their companies are avoiding unions by promoting win-win employment practices that yield additional productivity and quality for the company and more satisfying, highly compensated jobs for workers. Several noted, in this regard, that their facilities had not experienced a union organizing drive for many years, if ever, and were in general seen in the local community as highly desirable places to work.

Another point made by a number of the people interviewed is that there are other cheaper and oftentimes equally effective ways, at least in the short run, to avoid unions—such as targeting hiring and firing decisions to weed out people more likely to favor unions and use of "hardball" attorneys and consultants at the first sign of union activity—than employee representation committees and the other high-involvement practices utilized by companies, such as those interviewed for this study. They also noted that the companies most at risk of unionization are often also most likely to avoid establishing ongoing employee committees and councils, except perhaps as a stopgap device, because they do not wish to share power with employees nor give them an opportunity to develop a collective sense of grievance or forum for collective action. Even a number of progressive "high road" employers shy away from employee representation plans, it was stated, because the companies fear that the committees and councils can easily "backfire" and turn into an entry point for outside unions, in addition to the considerable management time and expense required to operate them successfully.

Conclusions and Policy Implications

This study provides what we believe to be the first case evidence of the composition and structure of individual employee involvement and participation programs in a set of advanced, "high-involvement" nonunion companies (also see Kaufman 1999). The specific components of these EIP programs differ markedly from one company to another, but common to all is an effort to share or delegate considerable information, decision making, and financial rewards to workplace-level employees that have heretofore been traditionally reserved to management. This process of sharing and delegating is achieved through a variety of means, but one important organizational vehicle is committees, councils, and panels composed of employee representatives who meet with selected management personnel to discuss and resolve a wide range of workplace issues. Often these issues pertain solely to production and quality matters, but inevitably subjects related to the terms and conditions of employment also arise—sometimes ancillary to a production or quality issue (e.g., a work-scheduling problem that has interfered with reaching a production target) but oftentimes because the employment issue is of direct importance to workers, management, or both.

As described in this chapter, the National Labor Relations Act, through Sections 8(a)(2) and 2(5), places significant constraints on the structure and operation of employee representation committees in nonunion companies. In particular, the law makes it an unfair labor practice for a company to operate a dominated labor organization, where "dominated" means that the labor organization is in some way created, supported, or administered by management. The act defines a "labor organization," in turn, quite broadly to include any kind of employee representation group that deals with the employer over a term or condition of employment. Considerable debate and controversy has ensued in recent years over whether these strictures in the NLRA impede and constrain the operation of legitimate, productivity-enhancing EIP programs in nonunion companies. This concern was heightened by the NLRB's decision in the *Electromation, Inc.* case in 1992 in which it ruled the company had violated the NLRA when it established five employee action committees to work with management on identifying and resolving sources of employee dissatisfaction with various aspects of pay and working conditions.

Although a welter of articles in the academic literature and practitioner press have debated the degree to which the NLRA—and the *Electromation* decision—constrain EIP programs, surprisingly little direct empirical evidence has been presented on the matter. This chapter, and the following one by LeRoy, are among the first to address this lacuna. The evidence obtained here from the minicase studies of advanced EIP programs in eight nonunion companies clearly suggests that the NLRA is a potentially significant constraint on what nonunion companies can legally do in this area. In particular, the large majority of the eight companies examined in this study use some type of employee representation committee, council, or board as part of their EIP programs that in some respect raises significant compliance issues with regard to Section 8(a)(2) of the NLRA (or similar provisions of the Railway Labor Act). A number of these potential violations arise from small-scale committees or panels that deal with issues such as safety, grievances, and production coordination, but in other cases companies have established plantwide or companywide representational bodies that explicitly investigate, discuss, or make recommendations to management on subjects related to the terms and conditions of employment.

The potential constraining effect of the NLRA on nonunion EIP programs is mitigated, in practice, by the small number of Section 8(a)(2) cases filed each year, the weak penalties for a Section 8(a)(2) violation, the uncertain legal boundary between legal and illegal practices, and the decision of some companies to move beyond what a strict reading of the law seems to permit with respect to employee committees. We find, as does LeRoy in the next chapter, that the initial alarm over the adverse impact of the *Electromation* decision has dissipated to some extent over time as companies have adjusted their EIP practices to conform with the law or chosen to practice "business as usual" on the expectation/hope that either their programs will escape legal scrutiny or, if challenged, pass such scrutiny. On the other hand, the evidence accumulated from the interviews with managers, attorneys, and consultants indicates that companies typically do not venture far outside the limits of the law for both ethical and practical reasons and, thus, the *Electromation* ruling and Section 8(a)(2) are meaningful constraints for companies that choose to have extensive, advanced EIP programs. A number are constrained only on the margin, but others would implement larger, more formal employee representation committees and councils if permitted, and would choose to deal with employees on a wide range of issues related to terms and conditions of employment.

These findings and conclusions suggest the following position on policy regarding revisions to the NLRA (Kaufman 1999). We believe public policy should promote two goals. The first is to permit and even encourage companies to implement programs for employee involvement and participation and to allow them considerable discretion with respect to the role and operation of employee representation committees therein. We take this stance given the widespread evidence that EIP programs not only promote increased productivity and competitiveness in industry, but also enhance employee job satisfaction and quality of worklife. The second goal we subscribe to is that public policy should fully protect the right of employees to join unions and collectively bargain and that employer practices of a coercive or punitive nature that infringe on this right should be prohibited. We hold this position given widespread evidence that some companies engage in exploitative, opportunistic, and/or inequitable practices vis-à-vis treatment of their employees (Friedman, Hurd, Oswald, and Seeber 1994) and that trade unions and collective bargaining are important and socially beneficial means employees have to rectify these conditions. But without strong legal protections, workers are too often prevented by employer acts of antiunion discrimination from obtaining independent representation.

The challenge for public policy is thus to provide as much latitude as possible for nonunion companies to use employee representation committees as part of legitimate, win-win EIP programs, but at the same time prevent companies from using them as illegitimate tools of union avoidance. We recognize that well-run, successful EIP programs tend to reduce employee interest in independent representation substantially, and are thus useful to employers as a union-avoidance device, but this practice seems largely benign and even beneficial to the extent the employer provides wages and conditions of work that meet or exceed what a union can deliver. The practices we wish to prevent are the use of "sham" employee committees that employers hastily put in place to short-circuit union organizing drives and that have no greater purpose than short-run union avoidance and protection of the employer's dominant position.

As one of the authors has argued elsewhere (Kaufman 1999), both policy goals can be accomplished by a two-pronged change in the NLRA. The first is to narrow the definition of a labor organization in Section 2(5) so that it applies only to independent employee organizations established for purposes of collective bargaining. This change effectively exempts from the coverage of the NLRA all nonunion employee committees that are company created and operated for EIP purposes. At the same time, Section 8(a)(2) should remain unchanged so that bona fide agencies of collective bargaining remain free of employer interference and domination. The other prong of the legislative change effort should be to both strengthen the penalties against employers for acts of antiunion discrimination and streamline the representation election process. Thus, financial penalties for employee discharge and discrimi-

nation for union activity should be substantially increased, and the NLRB should be given expanded authority to seek immediate injunctive relief to remedy illegal employer acts. Likewise, NLRB administrative procedures should be streamlined in order to expedite the holding of representation elections so that elapsed time from petition to election is reduced from a median of six weeks to, say, four weeks. Finally, a new unfair labor practice provision should be written into the law that declares it illegal for an employer to create or establish any employee representation committee or plan once a union has filed for a representation election. All these revisions parallel in broad outline Canadian law, as summarized in the two chapters in this volume by Taras.

The animating idea behind this proposal is that if employees have a relatively unrestricted, low-cost means to obtain union representation, then nonunion companies are effectively constrained to form and operate employee representation committees only in ways that promote mutual gain. Should the programs promote only management's interests, or be operated in a manner that is unfair or otherwise unsatisfactory, employees can readily voice their unhappiness and replace the company's representation plan with an independent union. The existence of a credible union threat thus serves as an effective competitive check on the uses and purposes of nonunion EIP employee committees. This check is then augmented, in our proposal, by an explicit ban on creation of employee committees during an organizing drive—the time "low road" employers are most likely to form an employee committee for illegitimate purposes of union avoidance. At the same time, as law provides employees relatively free access to independent representation, our proposal also frees nonunion employers to establish and operate whatever form of employee representation council or committee (if any) they desire, and to discuss with these groups as wide or narrow a range of topics as deemed appropriate. Those employers that are interested in long-run, constructive "high-involvement" employment practices are thus given maximum opportunity to use employee representation groups as part of their EIP programs.

These revisions to the NLRA are superior, we believe, to those in two other recent proposals. The first is the recommendations contained in the *Report and Recommendations* of the Commission on the Future of Worker-Management Relations ("Dunlop Commission"). These recommendations include the following (Commission on the Future of Worker-Management Relations, 1994b):

- The broad definition of a "labor organization" in Section 2(5) should be maintained.
- The language of Section 8(a)(2) should also be maintained in order to prevent the reemergence of management-dominated "company unions," but a qualifying statement should be appended that permits nonunion employee representation groups to deal with employers over terms and conditions of employment as long as these discussions are incidental to issues related to productivity and quality.
- The financial penalties for employer unfair labor practices should be strengthened, the time between petition and conducting representation elections should be shortened, and the NLRB should be given greater authority to issue injunctive relief in cases of employer acts of antiunion discrimination.

The second reform proposal is the TEAM Act legislation approved by both houses of Congress in 1996 but vetoed by President Clinton (Maryott

1997). It proposes the following changes in the NLRA:

- The Section 2(5) definition of a labor organization should be maintained.
- Section 8(a)(2) should be modified so that employers and employees can "address matters of mutual interest," including terms and conditions of employment.
- The prohibition of employer domination of labor organizations should be maintained for employee groups that seek certification as exclusive bargaining agents or to enter into collective bargaining.
- The union representation election process, penalties for unfair labor practices, and NLRB administrative procedures should remain unchanged.

Relative to the recommendations advanced in this chapter, it is apparent that both the Dunlop Commission proposal and the TEAM Act legislation are one-sided and unbalanced with respect to promoting competition and free choice in employee representation. The Dunlop Commission's proposals are one-sided because they strengthen the protections given to workers to obtain independent union representation but then, having established conditions for fair and effective competition between union and nonunion representational forms, fail to go the next step and remove the tight constraints imposed by Sections 2(5) and 8(a)(2) on nonunion employers. The net effect is to promote union representation while continuing to restrict nonunion representation. The TEAM Act proposal is also one-sided but in the opposite direction. The legislation largely frees nonunion companies to form and operate whatever type of employee representation plan is desired, but it does nothing to strengthen the

NLRA's protection of the right to organize. The net effect is to allow employers to establish dominated labor organizations without at the same time creating the conditions (i.e., low cost, relatively unobstructed access to independent representation) necessary to ensure that companies operate these groups only for mutual gain. Furthermore, the TEAM Act legislation (and Dunlop Commission recommendations) leaves untouched the root cause of the problem with the NLRA—the overly expansive definition of a labor organization in Section 2(5).

Our proposal combines in broad outline the recommendations of the Dunlop Commission and the provisions of the TEAM Act and, in so doing, achieves a compromise solution to reform of the NLRA that serves the interests of all parties to the employment relationship.

References

Appelbaum, Eileen, Thomas Bailey, Peter Berg, and Arne Kalleberg. 2000. *Manufacturing Advantage: Why High-Performance Work Systems Pay Off.* Ithaca, N.Y.: Cornell University Press.

Brody, David. 1994. "Section 8(a)(2) and the Origins of the Wagner Act." In *Restoring the Promise of American Labor Law,* ed. Sheldon Friedman, Richard Hurd, Rudolph Oswald, and Ronald Seeber, pp. 29–44. Ithaca, N.Y.: ILR Press.

Commission on the Future of Worker-Management Relations. 1994a. *Fact-finding Report.* Washington, D.C.: U.S. Department of Labor and U.S. Department of Commerce.

———. 1994b. *Report and Recommendations.* Washington, D.C.: U.S. Department of Labor and U.S. Department of Commerce.

Cotton, John. 1993. *Employee Involvement.* Newbury Park, Calif.: Sage.

Dachler, H., and B. Wilpert. 1978. "Conceptual Dimensions and Boundaries of Participation in Organizations." *Administrative Science Quarterly* 23, no. 1: 1–39.

Devaney, Dennis. 1993. "Much Ado about Section 8(a)(2): The NLRB and Workplace Cooperation after Electromation and Du Pont." *Stetson Law Review* 23 (Fall): 39–54.

———. 1994. "Electromation and Du Pont: The Next Generation." *Cornell Journal of Law and Public Policy* 4, no. 1: 3–24.

Estreicher, Samuel. 1994. "Employee Involvement and the 'Company Union' Prohibition: The Case for Partial Repeal of Section 8(a)(2) of the NLRA." *New York University Law Review* 69, no. 1: 125–189.

Friedman, Sheldon, Richard Hurd, Rudolph Oswald, and Ronald Seeber. 1994. *Restoring the Promise of American Labor Law.* Ithaca, N.Y.: ILR Press.

Gely, Rafael. 1997. "Whose Team Are You On? My Team or Your Team? The NLRA's Section 8(a)(2) and the TEAM Act." *Rutgers Law Review* 49, no. 2: 323–401.

Herrnstadt, Owen. 1997. "Section 8(a)(2) of the NLRA: The Debate." *Labor Law Journal* 48, no. 2: 98–112.

Katzenbach, Jon, and Douglas Smith. 1993. *The Wisdom of Teams.* Cambridge: Harvard University Business Press.

Kaufman, Bruce E. 1996. "Why the Wagner Act?" Reestablishing Contact with Its Original Purpose. In *Advances in Industrial and Labor Relations*, vol. 7, ed. David Lewin, Bruce Kaufman, and Donna Sockell, pp. 15–68. Greenwich, Conn.: JAI Press.

———. 1997a. "Company Unions: Sham Organizations or Victims of the New Deal?" In *Proceedings of the Forty-ninth Annual Meeting*, pp. 166–180. Madison: Industrial Relations Research Association.

———. 1997b. "The Growth and Development of a Non-union Sector in the Southern Paper Industry." In *Southern Labor in Transition, 1945–1995*, ed. Robert Zieger, pp. 295–329. Knoxville: University of Tennessee Press.

———. 1999. "Does the NLRA Constrain Employee Involvement and Participation Programs in Nonunion Companies?: A Reassessment." *Yale Law and Policy Review* 17, no. 2: 729–811.

Lawler, Edward, Susan Albers, and Gerald Ledford. 1992. *Employee Involvement and Total Quality Management: Practices and Results in Fortune 1000 Companies.* San Francisco: Jossey-Bass.

LeRoy, Michael. 1996. "Can TEAM Work? Implications of an Electromation and Du Pont Compliance Analysis for the TEAM Act." *Notre Dame Law Review* 71, no. 2: 215–266.

———. 1997. " 'Dealing With' Employee Involvement in Nonunion Workplaces: Empirical Research Implications for the TEAM Act." *Notre Dame Law Review* 72, no. 1: 31–82.

Levine, David. 1995. *Reinventing the Workplace.* Washington, D.C.: Brookings Institution.

Lewin, David, John Delaney, and Casey Ichniowski. 1989. *Human Resource Policies and Practices in American Firms.* Report 317. Washington, D.C.: U.S. Department of Labor.

Maryott, Michele. 1997. "Participate at Your Peril: The Need for Resolution of the Conflict Surrounding Employee Participation Programs by the TEAM Act of 1997." *Pepperdine Law Review* 24, no. 4: 1291–1326.

McLagan, Patricia, and Nel Christo. 1995. *The Age of Participation.* San Francisco: Berrett-Koehler.

Morris, Charles. 1994. "Déjà vu and Section 8(a)(2): What's Really Being Chilled by Electromation?," *Cornell Journal of Law and Public Policy* 4, no. 3: 25–32.

———. 1996. "Will There Be a New Direction for American Industrial Relations? A Hard Look at the TEAM Bill, the Sawyer Substitute Bill and the Employee Involvement Bill." *Labor Law Journal* 47, no. 2: 89–107.

Murrmann, Kent. 1980. "The Scanlon Plan Committee and Section 8(a)(2)." *Labor Law Journal* 31 (May): 299–304.

Nunn, Sandra. 1995. "Are American Businesses Operating within the Law? The Legality of Employee Action Committees and Other Worker Participation Plans." *Cincinnati Law Review* 63 (Spring): 1379–1445.

Rundle, James. 1994. "The Debate Over the Ban on Employer-Dominated Labor Organizations: What Is the Evidence?" In *Restoring the Promise of American Labor Law*, ed. Sheldon Friedman, Richard Hurd, Rudolph Oswald, and Ronald Seeber, pp. 161–176. Ithaca, N.Y.: ILR Press.

Summers, Clyde. 1997. "Works Councils in the American System." In *Proceedings of the Forty-ninth Annual Meeting*, pp. 106–112. Madison: Industrial Relations Research Association.

Taras, Daphne. 1998. "Nonunion Representation: Complement or Threat to Unions?" In *Proceedings of the Fiftieth Annual Meeting*, pp. 281–290. Madison: Industrial Relations Research Association.

Taras, Daphne, and Jason Copping. 1996. "When Pet Bears Go Wild: Triggering Union Certifications from Joint Industrial Councils." Paper presented at the Canadian Industrial Relations Conference.

Watchman, Gregory. 1994. "Safe and Sound: The Case for Safety and Health Committees under OSHA and the NLRA." *Cornell Journal of Law and Public Policy* 4, no. 3: 65–125.

13

Do Employee Participation Groups Violate Section 8(a)(2) of the National Labor Relations Act? An Empirical Analysis

Michael H. LeRoy

American employers increasingly use employee participation groups (Eaton 1994; Finding 3 of S. 295 [TEAM Act 1997]). Some groups have a specific and narrow purpose, such as continuous improvement of product quality. Others are broader and less defined. These are often found in firms that have trimmed management jobs, flattened their organizational structure, and embraced employee empowerment. The increased use of participation groups over the past twenty years also coincides with the American labor movement's membership decline.

Employer use of these groups has grown more controversial. While many unions are involved in labor-management cooperation programs with particular employers and locals, they are strongly suspicious of nonunion participation groups. Meanwhile, many employers embrace these organizations for reasons that have no ostensible connection to union avoidance. They see participation groups as organizational vehicles for being competitive in global markets. Many also link rapid change in information technologies with more decentralized groups that are premised on employee involvement and empowerment.

This chapter examines participation group compliance in nonunion settings with Section 8(a)(2) of the National Labor Relations Act (NLRA). This inquiry is important because the NLRA applies to most private-sector employers, whether or not their employees are represented by a union. Even though nearly 90 percent of these employees lack union representation, Section 8(a)(2) was conceived with them in mind. Congress, in 1935, was greatly concerned about employers who implemented sham forms of employee representation to avoid bargaining with unions. Thus, it devised a very broad definition of a "labor organization" in Section 2(5), to cover nearly every type of employee participation group. In Section 8(a)(2), it prohibited employer domination of these organizations. Since then, this prohibition has applied in nonunion, as well as union, workplaces.

This chapter addresses an informational void about this law's effects on nonunion participation groups. Employers believe that the law unfairly or inappropriately constrains these groups. They say its overbreadth curbs legitimate employee interaction with management. Thus, they have proposed legislation to loosen Section

8(a)(2)'s restrictions on participation group structure and governance.

However, employers have been unable to bolster this position by pointing to a large number of cases where Section 8(a)(2) was enforced to the detriment of nonunion employee groups. Only a handful of these cases have been litigated before the NLRB in the past decade. Employers make their case partly on the law's hypothetical effect, and partly by anecdotes that highlight beneficial aspects of employee groups.

This chapter analyzes the strength of these claims in more empirical terms. In 1997, I surveyed 131 participation groups in thirteen states. I found a very ambiguous picture of employee group compliance with the law.

Most of these participation groups appear to meet the statutory definition of a labor organization and thus are subject to NLRB scrutiny under leading precedents, *Electromation* (1992) and *Du Pont* (1993). About half the groups seem to run afoul of the law's prohibition against employer domination, even though many have participatory characteristics. On the other hand, I found little or no survey evidence of 1930s-style company unions (large-scale organization, minimal employee participation, strict employer control of group decision making). I also found, however, that employers exert a substantial degree of influence over these groups. This evidence is consistent with union concerns that these groups effectively control employee participation.

The Section 8(a)(2) Controversy

The National Labor Relations Act Is Restrictive for Employers and Ineffective for Unions

American employers often seek to avoid unionization. The shopfloor occasionally becomes a battleground for employees' loyalties (Freeman and Kleiner 1990). Some employers unlawfully dismiss union organizers (e.g., *NLRB* v. *Town and Country Electric* 1995), avoid bargaining after unions win a representation election (*NLRB* v. *Thill* 1992; *Calex Corp.* 1997; Zachary 1995), or close facilities in response to union organizing (*LCF, Inc.* 1996). Employer noncompliance with the NLRA is rational because of the law's weak remedies (Flanagan 1989).

Unions believe that Section 8(a)(2) suffers from underenforcement. Supporters point to the fact that Section 8(a)(2) cases constitute a tiny percentage of NLRB decisions (Kennedy 1997). They note that the law usually is enforced when they attempt to organize a workplace. The typical employee is too uninformed about collective bargaining laws to know when a Section 8(a)(2) violation occurs. Compounding this problem, union representation elections occur much less frequently, falling from about 8,000 in the late 1970s to about 3,500 a decade later (Chaison and Dhavale 1990, table 1). Thus, the probability of a nonunion workplace being organized has fallen sharply, from 0.61 percent in 1966 to .09 percent in 1986 (Freeman and Ribick 1989). From a union perspective, participation groups present a chicken-and-egg problem. Unions cannot organize more workplaces without Section 8(a)(2), but they cannot improve enforcement of this law because their organizing resources are relatively scarce.

Employers view Section 8(a)(2) as outdated and anticompetitive (Cohen 1997). They want to be law-abiding, but find that compliance imposes high opportunity costs (Budinger 1997). The law is so restrictive that it constrains even participation groups that promote genuine workplace democracy.

Section 8(a)(2) Applies to Most Types of Participation Groups

Section 8(a)(2)'s breadth is at the root of employer complaints. The law makes it an unfair labor practice for an employer "to dominate or interfere with the formation or administration of any labor organization or contribute financial or other support to it. . . ." Section 2(5) very broadly defines a labor organization as "any organization of any kind, or any agency or employee representation committee or plan in which employees participate and which exists for the purpose, in whole or in part, of dealing with employers concerning grievances, labor disputes, wages, rates of pay, hours of employment, or conditions of work."

This definition makes it difficult for employers to devise employee groups that are not statutory labor organizations. To avoid this classification, groups cannot handle common workplace matters (i.e., "grievances, labor disputes, wages, rates of pay, hours of employment, or conditions of work"). This still leaves some important topics, according to *Electromation*. Employee groups that deal with work process, efficiency, or product or service quality are not labor organizations. Employers decry this conception as too restrictive for the demands of a global economy (Perl 1993).

Conceivably, a participation group may handle a statutory subject such as discipline and avoid Section 8(a)(2) liability, but the price may be too high for many employers: total relinquishment of managerial input into a vital workplace decision. Employers rarely delegate key managerial functions, such as job design (*General Foods Corp.* 1977) and employee discipline *(John Ascuaga's Nugget* 1977; *Mercy Memorial Hospital* 1977).

In a more common delegation of managerial authority, employers retain some control over group decision making. Under Section 2(5), however, this participation group is likely to qualify as a labor organization. The touchstone is whether the employer "deal(s) with" this employee group over any of the aforementioned workplace subjects. In *Du Pont*, the board broadly interpreted "dealing with" to mean a bilateral exchange between an employee group and management.

To the dismay of employers, *Du Pont* ambiguously interpreted "dealing with." Group composition is not solely determinative, according to the board. The question is how much control employers exert in this bilateral relationship:

> In our view, the fact that the management persons are on the committee is only a difference of form; it is not a difference of substance. As a practical matter, if management representatives can reject employee proposals, it makes no real difference whether they do so from inside or outside the committee. In circumstances where management members of the committee discuss proposals with employee members and have the power to reject any proposal, we find that there is "dealing" within the meaning of Section 2(5). (p. 895)

The board tempered this view by stating:

> The mere presence, however, of management members on a committee would not necessarily result in a finding that the committee deals with the employer within the meaning of Section 2(5). For example, there would be no "dealing with" management if the committee were governed by majority decision-making, management representatives were in the minority, and the committee had the power to decide matters for itself, rather than simply make proposals to management. Similarly, there would be no "dealing" if management representatives participated on the committee as observers or facilitators without the right to vote on committee proposals. (p. 895)

From the perspective of employers, this framework is too neat for the real world. Many participation groups are now designed to operate by consensus. This decision-making mode is not squarely captured by the *Du Pont* analysis. Employers want managers to play influential roles on participation groups; but they also believe that employees contribute valuable know-how and insight. They recognize, therefore, that workers must have some latitude to question and challenge a manager. Apart from who is right at a given moment, there is a notion that give-and-take between employees and managers is good in its own right. Employers believe that *Du Pont*'s standard of "bilateral interaction" to detect "dealing with" imperils this free play. If this view is strictly enforced, old-style personnel hierarchies may return. In their view, it is only a short walk from the "dealing with" test to unlawful domination under Section 8(a)(2). Employer creation of a participation group, assignment of employees or managers to a group, and delegation of subjects to a group are all indicators of unlawful domination.

Consistent with this doctrinal analysis, emerging empirical studies suggest that many participation groups violate Section 8(a)(2)'s strictures. The first of these studies reached a contrary conclusion. My preliminary study of employee group compliance with the NLRA—based on data collected in 1994 and 1995—concluded that "three-fourths of the teams appear to comply with *Electromation* and *Du Pont*. The others, in varying degrees, seemed to have one or more features that conflicted with the guidance principles stated in *Electromation* and *Du Pont*" (LeRoy 1996, p. 218).

However, in a follow-up survey involving 78 different work groups, I found that a larger percentage appeared to violate Section 8(a)(2). This study concluded that "numerous teams . . . appear to meet all the definitional requirements of a Section 2(5) labor organization" (LeRoy 1997, p. 81). A contemporaneous study involving six

different and large employers reached a similar conclusion: "The majority of these companies make use of employee representation committees and . . . these committees often deal with management over terms and conditions of employment" (Kaufman 1999).

An Assessment of Employer Compliance with Section 8(a)(2)

Application of Case Law Doctrines to Participation Groups

This general policy framework can be used to determine whether or not Section 8(a)(2) constrains how participation groups are structured and how they function. First, questions should be asked to determine whether or not a group is a Section 2(5) labor organization. What subjects or assignments are delegated to them? If these include one or more statutory subjects, is there "dealing with" between employees and management? To assess this point, a group should be examined to determine the amount and quality of management participation in participation groups. At one extreme, a group may have no management representatives and have a delegation of authority to make workplace decisions without further review by management. Near the other extreme, the participation group may be structured like one of the *Du Pont* committees. A management representative might be a fully participating member. Even though the group is designed to act on consensus between nonsupervisory employees and the management representative, "dealing with" may exist if a manager can "reject employee proposals" (*Du Pont*, p. 894).

In a related vein, the participation group's reporting relationship to management should be assessed. To avoid the legal inference that a group is "dealing with" management, *Du Pont* suggests that virtually no bilateral interactions should occur. The decision particularly emphasizes suggestion making as a form of communication that falls short of bilateral interaction. Thus, groups should be analyzed to see whether or not they merely provide suggestions or advice or, in the alternative, whether they do more, such as make proposals to management or take a vote among nonsupervisory employees and management representatives. *Du Pont* strongly suggests that the latter activities bring a group within Section 2(5)'s very broad definition of "dealing with."

Even if a group meets the statutory definition of a labor organization, there is no legal presumption that employers unlawfully dominate them. How it is created and by whom, and its actual purpose, should be considered in analyzing for unlawful domination (*Ryder Distribution Resources* 1993; *Waste Management of Utah* 1993; *Research Federal Credit Union* 1993). Its freedom to act without management veto, permission, interference, or other intervention should also be considered *(Peninsula General Hospital* 1993). There is no domination where it is fully empowered; but domination occurs when its decision-making processes trivialize employee input. Harder cases involve a degree of group autonomy that is subject to limited forms of management control *(Dillon Stores* 1995, finding a group unlawful).

The board also considers how nonsupervisory employees are recruited to groups in determining unlawful domination. In *Electromation*'s finding of unlawful domination, the board noted that the employer "determined how many members would compose a committee and that an employee could serve on only one committee" (p. 998). To avoid unlawful domination, employers should relinquish control or influence over a group's recruitment process. Interviews with management attorneys (see below) disclosed that two common approaches for complying with this part of the law are to have nonsupervisory employees volunteer or be selected by peers. This is in contrast to management appointment of employees to participation groups.

This discussion would not be complete without considering Section 8(a)(2)'s clarity. In general, a clearly stated public policy is more likely than a vague one to constrain conduct. Since a vague law may have more than one plausible interpretation, it should generate a wider range of compliance responses.

Section 8(a)(2) has difficult ambiguities. This problem was evident in disagreements among board members who decided *Electromation*. In his scholarly concurrence, Member Raudabaugh observed that only one Supreme Court decision ever construed the unlawful domination element of Section 8(a)(2)(*NLRB* v. *Newport News Shipbuilding Co.* 1939). That decision, occurring in the shadows of prolonged congressional hearings that detailed the abuses of company unions, was premised on an adversarial model of industrial relations. Member Raudabaugh noted that since then "the labor-management world has changed" (p. 1011) and contemporary employee participation plans (EPPs) "are often set up by employers with the lawful motives of enhancing morale, communication, product quality, and increasing productivity. To achieve these goals, the employers usually retain some degree of control over the EPPs" (p. 1010). This led him to conceive a four-factor test of unlawful domination, a test that his colleagues did not adopt:

> In my view, the answer to the question turns on the following factors: (1) the extent of the employer's involvement in the structure and operation of the committees; (2) whether the employ-

ees, from an objective standpoint, reasonably perceive the EPP as a substitute for full collective bargaining through a traditional union; (3) whether employees have been assured of their Section 7 right to choose to be represented by a traditional union under a system of full collective bargaining; and (4) the employer's motives in establishing the EPP. I would consider all four factors in any given case. No single factor would necessarily be dispositive. (p. 1013)

Electromation's facile distinction between work process and quality—which are unregulated by Sections 2(5) and 8(a)(2)—and rates of pay or conditions of work—which are expressly regulated—leads to another ambiguity. Member Raudabaugh noted this when he observed that "it is hard to imagine an employee committee that would be able to avoid these matters completely. Even if the committee's stated purpose is to deal only with such entrepreneurial concerns as product quality or workplace efficiency, it seems clear that the committee, in order to achieve its purpose, would have to consider one or more of the subjects listed in Section 2(5)" (p. 1008).

Section 8(a)(2)'s ambiguity is further revealed in litigation. The board, in deciding *Peninsula General Hospital* (1993), had no doubt that the employer's restructuring of the Nurses Service Organization (NSO), and subsequent domination of it, violated Section 8(a)(2). The Fourth Circuit Court of Appeals, however, took a completely contrary view of the facts (*NLRB* v. *Peninsula General Hospital Medical Center* 1994). As if to illustrate that *Du Pont*'s bilateral mechanism test is vague, the court overruled two critical board fact-findings, stating "it is clear that the purpose of the NSO has remained constant throughout the relevant period of time and that purpose has not included dealing with Peninsula over matters affecting employment, and further that the NSO did not actually engage in a 'pattern or practice'

of making proposals to which Peninsula responded (i.e., 'dealing with')" (p. 1272).

When a public policy evinces such noticeable disagreement among policy experts and federal judges, it cannot be expected to command uniform compliance. Employers within the Fourth Circuit Court of Appeals' jurisdiction (e.g., in Maryland, Virginia, and North Carolina) should be less risk-averse in establishing and administering participation groups than employers in the seventh circuit (e.g., in Illinois, Indiana, and Wisconsin), or the sixth circuit (e.g., in Ohio, Michigan, and Kentucky). This is because appeals courts in the latter group have upheld the board's more stringent view of Section 8(a)(2) (*Electromation, Inc.* v. *NLRB* 1994; *NLRB* v. *Webcor Packaging, Inc.* 1997).

Development of Compliance Survey

A national survey would help to determine whether participation groups comply with and are constrained by Section 8(a)(2). The Bureau of Labor Statistics conducted a similar study on this scale soon after Section 8(a)(2) became law (U.S. Department of Labor 1937, surveying employee groups in 14,725 "establishments"). A study this large does not appear to be feasible today. My research uses three more limited methods to develop an empirical compliance picture.

1. Post-*Electromation* NLRB decisions involving Section 8(a)(2) issues offer some indication of employer compliance. Overlooking contextual data in these cases would be wasteful; after all, these cases reflect enforcement of this public policy. Nevertheless, there are several serious problems in relying solely on these data. One problem, as previously discussed, is enforcement bias that results from the need to have a knowl-

edgable and motivated party present to allege violations.

Lawyers surveyed for this research also noted a second problem: the NLRB does its enforcement work through regional offices. Occasionally, according to experienced lawyers, regional directors threaten unfair labor practice proceedings against participation groups. Attorneys point out that this kind of enforcement activity never shows up in published NLRB decisions or annual reports. Standing alone, therefore, NLRB decisions are likely to give a skewed picture of the policy's constraining effects.

2. I modified my earlier Section 8(a)(2) compliance survey. I asked employee groups to report subjects they handled. I also asked respondents to rank multiple tasks in order of importance. These subjects were partly derived from subjects enumerated and closely implied in Section 2(5)(e.g., pay, insurance, grievances, discipline, vacation, employee leave, tardy/absence policy, fitness and health, and scheduling). I also asked questions pertaining to safe-harbor subjects in *Electromation* (e.g., work process, product or service quality, efficiency).

Another set of questions aimed to assess management's interactions with a group. These were derived from *Du Pont*'s lengthy discussion concerning the "dealing with" element in Section 2(5). Thus, participation groups were assessed to see if they had only discussions, with no resulting decisions or suggestions to management; if they made suggestions; if they made proposals for management to consider; or if they reached decisions by voting or consensus.

Other questions derived from *Du Pont* focused on the group's decision-making processes. A key feature in that case was the presence of managers who vetoed decisions. Thus, respondents were asked to consider management's part in directing an employee group ("always directs," "usually directs," "occasionally directs," "rarely directs," "never directs," or "vetoes"); nonsupervisory employees' part in directing a group (same choices). Another survey item measured the presence of a joint decision-making process between employees and managers.

I tested domination or interference under Section 8(a)(2) by asking who created the participation group. I also asked how nonsupervisory employees became members ("volunteer," "peers select," "manager appoints," "part of job,"or "other"). A similar question was asked about manager recruitment to participation groups. Recognizing that some groups function with no management representatives (e.g., *General Foods Corp.* 1977), I asked whether a group had only nonsupervisory employees. I also evaluated a group's governance structure in light of the board's recent analysis of this issue in *Dillon Stores* (1995). Thus, an item asked whether employees served rotating, indefinite, or fixed-term assignments.

The surveys were administered in 1997 to employer-members of the Labor Policy Association (LPA). LPA agreed to announce the survey at its March meeting. They put interested employers in touch with this project. The association did not fund any part of this research, nor did it alter any part of this survey.

Six Fortune 500 employers participated in the survey. I asked their senior HRM executives to identify one or more locations with nonunion participation groups. Surveys were then provided for each specific group at a given location. The top of the survey clearly indicated that either a manager or a nonsupervisory employee could answer questions. The first page of the survey was printed on University of Illinois stationery, with my phone number and address clearly printed. Respondents were instructed to answer surveys truthfully and completely, and to mail the survey directly to me or to place the survey in a sealed envelope and return it to a central collection point for the participating firm. All respondents and participating firms were expressly told that a survey delivered to me with a broken seal would not be counted.

3. The third leg of this study involved a nationwide survey of highly experienced management attorneys. Kaufman and Stephan's (1995) in-depth interview of management attorneys concerning union-avoidance strategies suggested that this method would provide another layer of useful information. I identified 163 attorneys by researching Martindale and Hubbell's directory. This directory lists an attorney's specialties and professional history. I selected only attorneys who practiced at least ten years in behalf of employers. To be selected, an attorney had to specialize in labor law issues (e.g., experience as an NLRB attorney or membership in the American Bar Association's labor law section).

I contacted attorneys from September 1996 through February 1997 by faxing their offices with a request for their participation in this study. I followed up with a phone call to their voice mail or secretaries, and then a second follow-up call. Fifteen attorneys answered a one-page survey that I faxed, and six submitted to in-depth phone interviews.

Limitations of This Survey

Although my methodology tried to elicit factual and full accurate information, it was nevertheless vulnerable to significant sources of bias. As Kaufman observes, my reliance on mailed surveys rather than in-person or phone interviews was "apt to miss important qualitative evidence on the structure and operation of EIP (employee involvement) programs (Kaufman 1999). He also notes a related problem. Respondents will hesitate to disclose incriminating information about these groups. This flaw is amplified by the fact that respondent firms are active members of the Labor Policy Association, an employer interest group that lobbies for passage of the TEAM Act. Thus, selection bias is a problem with my survey.

In addition, the small number of participating employers also means that the survey results are not generalizable. Since my survey questions provide only partially useful information to make a compliance assessment, my study lacks the specificity of a typical Section 8(a)(2) analysis.

This scale problem was even greater in my attorney interviews. My very small response rate means, of course, that my results cannot be generalized. Still, it should be noted that the attorneys who responded were very experienced, averaging over twenty-five years in advising employers in labor-management relations, and practiced law in diverse jurisdictions (California, Maryland, Kentucky, Tennessee, and Pennsylvania).

These problems aside, Kaufman (1999) identified a more troubling problem. I asked respondents to categorize whether their group was (1) an employee involvement group, (2) a team, (3) quality-of-work life program, (4) employee committee, or (5) some other group. Kaufman correctly notes that these choices conflate a wide variety of participation groups, such as self-directed work teams, safety committees, grievance committees, employee councils, focus groups, and Scanlon Plans. This is a serious problem because my use of the term "team" may have resulted in sampling of a narrow spectrum of employee groups that focus on lawful sub-

---

Figure 13.1 **Section 8(a)(2) Cases Following** *Electromation* **and** *Du Pont*

NLRB Ruling on Participation Groups

Lawful	Unlawful
Stoody Co., 320 NLRB 18, (1995)	*EFCO Corp.*, 327 NLRB No. 71 (1998)[*]
Vons Grocery, 320 NLRB 53 (1995)[*]	*V & S Progalv, Inc.*, 323 NLRB No. 144 (1997)
Hamilton, 313 NLRB 1303 (1993)	*Simmons Industries*, 321 NLRB No. 32 (1996)[*]
	Aero Detroit, Inc., 321 NLRB No. 136 (1996)[*]
	Autodie Int'l, Inc., 321 NLRB No. 98 (1996)
	Vic Koenig Chev. 321 NLRB No. 168 (1996)
	Webcor Packaging, Inc., 319 NLRB 1203 (1995)[*]
	Reno Hilton, 321 NLRB 1154 (1995)[*]
	Keeler Brass, 317 NLRB 1110 (1995)[*]
	Dillon Stores, 319 NLRB 1245 (1995)
	Magan Medical Clinic, 314 NLRB 1083 (1994)[*]
	Garney Morris, Inc., 313 NLRB 101 (1993)[*]
	Ryder Dist. Resources, 311 NLRB 814 (1993)[*]
	Waste Mgt. of Utah, 310 NLRB 883 (1993)[*]
	Research Fed. Credit U., 321 NLRB 56 (1993)[*]
	Peninsula Gen. Hosp., 312 NLRB 582 (1993)[*]

*Case arose in nonunion workplace.

---

jects under *Electromation*. Thus, my "undue focus on employee 'teams' may quite possibly explain why (my first survey) found little evidence of more formal company union-like structures" (Kaufman 1999).

Research Findings: Survey of Participation Group Compliance with Section 8(a)(2)

Survey Results

Figure 13.1 shows that the NLRB has decided only nineteen cases involving Section 8(a)(2) issues since *Electromation*. Technically, one case did not involve a Section 8(a)(2) issue. In *Hamilton* (1993), an employer instituted continuous improvement teams over a union's strong objections. This case involved a Section 8(a)(1) complaint that the employer interfered with the employees' collective bargaining rights by sending them a detailed letter that explained why the teams were good for their workplace. The case is included here because its facts closely parallel the others.

Figure 13.1 provides limited information, but has some interesting findings. Most participation groups that are scrutinized for Section 8(a)(2) violations were found to be unlawful. Most were also nonunion. Finally, most unlawful participation groups arose either after a union organizing drive was imminent or under way, or as part of a decertification campaign. Some of the cases that appear in Figure 13.1 involve employers setting up 1930s-style company unions under the guise

Table 13.1

Employee Participation Groups and Coverage of Section 2(5) Subjects (in percentages)

	All groups (N = 131)	Teams (N = 90)	EI groups (N = 17)
Types of groups			
Team	77		
Employee involve- ment	14		
Quality circle	3		
Quality of work life	1		
Employee committee	3		
Other	2		
Subjects covered by groups			
Lawful subjects			
Product quality	75	80	71
Work process	82	87	77
Unlawful subjects			
Attendance	15	18	12
Discipline	12	14	12
Diversity	15	15	6
Grievance	17	19	18
Handbook	9	12	6
Health	11	12	12
Insurance	4	4	6
Leave	12	13	12
Other	21	22	24
Pay	11	14	0
Safety	47	51	65
Scheduling	58	66	29
Vacation	25	29	18

of empowerment. These unlawful cases involved sham employee representation with a transparent antiunion pretext (e.g., *Aero Detroit*).

Tables 13.1 and 13.2 summarize survey results from 131 participation groups in Iowa, Texas, Mississippi, California, Missouri, North Carolina, Michigan, Oklahoma, Utah, Illinois, Colorado, Ohio, and Pennsylvania. These were in existence

3.6 years (mean); nearly 73 percent were established after the NLRB decided *Electromation*. They averaged nearly fourteen members; only 9 percent had more than thirty members. Employees created very few groups (about 4 percent). Nearly 50 percent of these groups were unilaterally created by management. A combination of employees and management created the remaining 41 percent.

In about 12 percent of the groups, nonsupervisory employees selected the managers who participated. Managers volunteered to participate in about 16 percent of these groups. In 32 percent of the groups managers were assigned to participate; in 24 percent they participated as part of their job; and in 16 percent they did not participate at all.

Table 13.1 shows the types of groups that were sampled. A clear majority classified themselves as a team (77 percent). The next largest category, EI group, comprised only 14 percent of the sample. Quality Circles, QWL groups, employee committees, and others made up the remaining 9 percent.

Since teams and EI groups were so predominant in the sample, and because these groups may have different compliance characteristics, results for these groups are presented next to findings for all groups.

The data for all groups show that most handle subjects permitted by *Electromation* (work process, 82 percent; quality, 75 percent). About half also handle subjects that do not fall within a safe-harbor category (scheduling, 58 percent; safety, 47 percent). Some groups (ranging from 4 percent to 25 percent) handle a wide mix of subjects (attendance, discipline, diversity management, employee handbook, health insurance, employee leave, pay, and vacations).

A comparison between teams and EI groups

Table 13.2

Employee Participation Groups: Recruitment of Employees, Interaction with Management, and Direction of Group (in percentages)

	All groups (N = 131)	Teams (N = 90)	EI groups (N = 17)
How employees join groups			
Employees volunteer	39	43	47
Peers select employee	36	37	24
Manager appoints employee	50	48	30
Employee participates as part of job	39	35	41
Other	4	2	6
Manager-employee interactions in groups			
Groups only discuss Section 2(5) subjects	2	2	0
Groups make suggestions on Section 2(5) subjects	35	35	70
Groups make proposals on Section 2(5) subjects	47	50	56
Groups vote on Section 2(5) subjects	18	19	19
Groups form consensus on Section 2(5) subjects	51	50	56
Employee and managerial direction of groups			
Management always directs group activities	7	7	6
Management usually directs group activities	27	33	18
Management occasionally directs group activities	41	36	59
Management rarely directs group activities	8	6	0
Management vetoes group activities	8	10	0
Employees always direct group activities	8	8	0
Employees usually direct group activities	43	42	47
Employees occasionally direct group activities	40	42	33
Employees rarely direct group activities	6	6	13
Employees veto group activities	4	4	7

shows some important differences. In this sample, EI groups tended to cover fewer Section 2(5) subjects than teams. Safety was the only Section 2(5) subject that most EI groups covered (65 percent). As *EFCO Corp.* notes, however, safety committees may fall outside Section 2(5)'s definition of a labor organization. In sum, the fact that more EI groups than teams covered safety does not necessarily mean that these EI groups are more prone to violate Section 8(a)(2).

In fact, the limited evidence here suggests that teams have more potential for compliance problems with Section 8(a)(2). This is because a much greater percentage of teams handled scheduling, a matter that clearly falls within the ambit of Section 2(5) (66 percent of teams, but only 29 percent of EI groups). Consistent with this difference, none of the EI groups covered pay; in sharp contrast, 14 percent of the sampled teams did.

Table 13.2 summarizes essential group behaviors that are connected to Section 8(a)(2) compliance. Since the NLRB examines how nonsupervisory employees become members of participation groups, the survey asked questions about employee recruitment. Two items would tend to insulate an employer from an adverse Section 8(a)(2) ruling: employees volunteer and peers select employees to participate. About one-third of the total sample employed these recruitment methods (39 percent for voluntary joining; 36 percent for peer selection). Teams and EI groups had higher levels for voluntary association (43 percent for teams; 47 percent for EI groups).

The NLRB tends to view managerial appointment of nonsupervisory employees to groups as evidence of employer domination. On this dimension, half of the sample was in potential violation of Section 8(a)(2). Teams mirrored this tendency (48 percent), but notably, a greater percentage of EI groups appeared to comply with this aspect of the law (only 30 percent had managers appoint group members).

In theory, employers who require employees to participate by writing this into a job description can be found in violation of Section 8(a)(2). There is no definitive NLRB doctrine to this effect, but this kind of conduct has implications for employer domination of groups. Data on this aspect of recruitment was very similar to the findings for voluntary participation (39 percent of all groups, with no meaningful differences observed for teams and EI groups).

The NLRB also examines a group's decision-making interactions between management and nonsupervisory employees. This falls under Section 2(5)'s definitional element of "dealing" between employees and their employer.

If participation groups behaved so as to strictly conform to the law, observations would heavily cluster in the "discuss" and "suggest" categories. The findings were contrary to this, however. Only an extremely small number of groups conformed to the safest legal option of limiting themselves only to discussing matters between employees and management (2 percent for all groups). Much more often, groups made proposals to management (50 percent for teams, and 56 percent for EI groups) and made decisions by reaching a consensus between employee and manager members (50 percent for teams, and 56 percent for EI groups). The results for voting have potential implications for group compliance because this conduct typifies a group's representational function. In this sample, nearly one-fifth of the groups used this potentially unlawful method (19 percent for teams, and 19 percent for EI groups).

The survey also attempted to assess whether managers or nonsupervisory employees directed participation groups. Certainly, this measurement has limited value because this assessment was subjective (82 percent of the respondents were management members of these groups).

The modal response for management control was that these members "occasionally" directed group activities (41 percent for all groups). Teams and EI groups differed on this dimension, however (36 percent for teams, and 59 percent for EI groups). In a consistent vein, teams were more likely than EI groups to have managers usually direct activities than EI groups (33 percent for teams, and 18 percent for EI groups). Also, this pattern was reflected in managerial veto of group activities. Ten percent of teams experienced managerial vetoes, compared to none for EI groups.

The modal response for employee control was that they "usually" directed group activities (42 percent for teams, and 47 percent for EI groups). "Employees occasionally direct group activities" followed closely (42 percent for teams, and 33 percent for EI groups). No EI groups had employees always direct their activities, although this was observed in 8 percent of the teams.

Preliminary Conclusions from Survey

Most of the surveyed groups do not strictly conform to the safe-harbor dictates of *Electromation.* That 58 percent of teams handle scheduling and 47 percent handle safety issues implies that a majority of participation groups meet the NLRA's subject-matter test of a labor organization.

In *EFCO Corp.* the board provided an extended discussion of when safety committees are Section 2(5) labor organizations. If such a committee merely reports and corrects safety problems, or imparts safety information or plans educational programs, it falls outside this highly regulated category. If, however, the committee reviews safety rules and policies, or develops safety incentive programs, and in connection with either that committee makes policy proposals to management, it is a Section 2(5) labor organization. Since this survey did not go into detail about the functions of safety groups, the finding on this dimension has no definitive interpretation. It suggests, however, that many of these groups may be expanding beyond the safe-harbor limits in *Electromation.*

The finding for groups that handle scheduling is less ambiguous. Since this subject clearly falls under Section 2(5)'s "hours of employment" element, groups that handle scheduling are likely to be found as labor organizations. While the NLRB would likely make this ruling, this outcome is not absolutely certain. If these groups were scrutinized by the NLRB, employers could present evidence tending to show that a group's dominant purpose was lawful under *Electromation.* Presumably, these employers would argue any

departure from *Electromation* is a *de minimus* violation, consistent with *Stoody Co.* (1995).

Since the board has had so few Section 8(a)(2) cases following *Electromation* and *Du Pont*, no one can predict with confidence whether the board will significantly expand its *de minimus* violation doctrine. It appears that many of the groups surveyed here could present this issue in litigation. If present case law indicates future tendencies, the board will likely construe this doctrine narrowly. So, for example, a group that predominantly handles work-process issues, but also schedules vacations once a year, is likely to be found a labor organization.

In cases where the board finds that a group handled a Section 2(5) subject, the board's analysis would continue by examining evidence that the group was "dealing with" an employer. This survey suggests that the board will find that many participation groups meet this standard. About half of all sampled groups (47 percent) made proposals to management (50 percent for teams and 56 percent for EI groups). And since only a few groups had no management representative (13 percent), the presence of managers in a group would be more evidence of "dealing."

The method by which groups made decisions reinforces this conclusion. In evaluating the 51 percent of groups (50 percent for teams; 56 percent for EI groups) that were directed by consensus, the board would likely find some amount of "dealing with." Given that only 2 percent of participation groups only discuss matters with management, it seems clear that many of these groups "deal with" employers.

A majority of groups appear, therefore, to be Section 2(5) labor organizations. Section 8(a)(2) applies to them. The board would then examine these groups to see whether employers unlawfully dominated them. On this dimension, the survey evidence is highly ambiguous.

Managers appoint employees in half of the groups. This mode of placing employees on a participation group is presumptive evidence of employer control (see *Electromation*).

Still, a sizable percentage of participation groups (about 40 percent) mitigate such a presumption by having employees volunteer or select peers. Also, the finding that just over half the groups operate by employee-managerial consensus, while only a handful permit management veto of a group decision or activity, has no clear implication for determining whether employers unlawfully dominate these groups. Given the board's case-by-case approach, and lack of clear rules to find domination, the survey results for indicators of employer domination have no clear implication.

Research Findings: Attorney Interviews on Section 8(a)(2) Compliance

I augmented my analysis of participation-group compliance with the NLRA to that law's constraining effect by interviewing management attorneys who have significant experience with employer responses to Section 8(a)(2). These in-depth interviews provide a fuller context for interpreting my survey data. Nevertheless, these interviews do not overcome my survey's limitations. Therefore, the following must be viewed as impressions grounded in a limited range of experience rather than conclusions based on data.

Employers Appear to Be Experimenting with Participation Groups

Electromation and the ensuing policy debate may be causing employers to experiment with partici-

pation groups by pushing the boundaries of Section 8(a)(2). My study suggests that employers are constantly creating or re-creating these groups. Large workplace surveys in the late 1980s and early 1990s showed that about 40 percent of American workplaces already had participation groups (Delaney et al. 1989 [survey of 495 respondents found 43 percent had these participation groups]; LeRoy 1993 [survey of 558 respondents found 38 percent had employee groups]; Osterman 1994 [survey of 694 respondents found that 37 percent had employee groups]). Most large employers use some form of these groups (about 80 percent according to Finding 3 of S. 295 [TEAM Act 1997]).

Thus, the Fortune 500 employers in my survey would be expected to have long-standing participation groups. Interestingly, however, this study's finding that more than 70 percent of the surveyed groups were created after *Electromation* and the first TEAM Act was proposed suggests that these public policy watersheds are spurring employer experimentation.

The fact that about 80 percent of the surveyed groups handle work-process and quality issues implies that the NLRB's formulation of these safe havens was attuned to current workplace realities. By explicitly defining safe-harbor subjects for employee groups, *Electromation* signaled greater policy toleration of nonunion employee groups. The board defined these safe havens to remove at least some policy ambiguity and thereby improve compliance with Section 8(a)(2).

Despite these good intentions, the board may have promoted an unintended effect. In trying to draw a policy line, it may have invited employers to experiment more with participation groups.

The lawyers I interviewed at length are divided about this. One group says that over the past four years employers have come to regard *Electromation* as irrelevant. Harry Reagan (Morgan, Lewis, & Bockius, LLP, Philadelphia, Pennsylvania) observed:

> Among my nonunion clients, once a committee is formed and operates, there is a tendency for other committees to be formed. It's like a multiplier effect. Typically, an employer begins with a safety committee. Other typical starting committees handle productivity issues, production standards, and changes in work methods.
>
> Initially, employers encounter problems in starting-up employee committees. Typically, employees mistrust management. Supervisors, in particular, are a source of friction because their authority is nicked as a result of these committees. Generally, employees grow to trust and like their committee experiences, and managers get used to the fact that they must share some authority and decision making.
>
> As long as there is no union on the scene, employers usually let these committees multiply and evolve in function, often taking on new problem-solving areas.

Stephen Shawe (Shawe & Rosenthal, Baltimore, Maryland) offered a similar view of how nonunion participation groups are created:

> Many nonunion employers set up teams or committees on an as-needed basis. Most are ad hoc rather than permanent, typically directed to solve a specific problem. Recent committees have been established to address production concerns and employee productivity, health insurance, other benefits, attendance, and working conditions (for example, controlling temperature in a manufacturing plant). A fairly loose employer methodology is the norm for forming a committee. A plant manager or owner gathers supervisors and nonsupervisors who have an interest and skill or expertise in solving a particular problem. These people then sit down and try to figure out what can be done to address the matter.

Thomas Burke's (Brobeck, Phleger & Harrison, Los Angeles, California) perspective on the new generation of participation groups was similar:

> For those employers who want to set up participatory teams, few want to or actually do comply with current NLRB doctrines. They set up forms of teams against my advice. The purpose is not necessarily to frustrate union organizing. For some employers, it becomes a philosophical issue.

But Stephen Cabot (Harvey, Pennington, Herting, & Renneisen, Ltd., Philadelphia, Pennsylvania) had a different emphasis. Acknowledging the noncompliance intentions of some of his clients, he also noted that "about 80 percent of my nonunion clients who have some form of employee participation adhere to the guidance principles of *Electromation*. The other 20 percent openly and knowingly disregard *Electromation*."

Many Participation Groups Appear to Be in "Fuzzy" Compliance

Even if many employers do not openly defy *Electromation* and Section 8(a)(2), most do not strictly comply with these policy restrictions and appear to operate in a zone of fuzzy compliance.

According to in-depth interviews with management attorneys, most employers start from the point of seeking to comply with Section 8(a)(2); however, their motivation may simply be pragmatic. Harry Reagan best summarized this view:

> I counsel employers against dominating committees once they are established. First, a clear majority of committee members are, or should be, nonsupervisory. Decisions are, or should be, made by consensus, without a management veto. When management vetoes committee decisions, these committees die on the vine. In short, if employee participation is to be meaningful, their decisions must count.

By itself, attorney advice tends to constrain employer use of these groups. All the attorneys said that they advise nonunion clients to mute the overtly representational functions and characteristics of newly formed employee groups. Stephen Shawe said:

> Some nonunion employers have standing committees. These groups tend to meet regularly, on a monthly or bi-monthly basis. Note-taking occurs at these meetings. I suggest that the groups take actions that are later subject to management review; but I also strongly advise that nonsupervisory employees rotate in and out of assignments to minimize the prospect of a finding of employer domination.

Harry Reagan's advice had a similar objective, although his method for avoiding a finding of employer domination under Section 8(a)(2) was somewhat different:

> I advise employers to have all employees serve on the committee on the theory that it does not constitute a representational group, but merely is a venue for individual employee concerns to be raised and addressed. In my view, the NLRB does not prohibit this kind of dialogue between individual employees and an employer.

Fletcher Hudson (McKnight, Hudson, Lewis & Henderson, PLLC, Memphis, Tennessee) offered a third variation with the same compliance objective:

> When nonunion employers state that they want to institute some form of a standing employee committee, I advise that such an organization be formed according to these guidelines: Make it informal but functional; have no charter, no formal structure, no rules, no bylaws, no set timetable; in short, no formal organizational structure. By following this advice, employers are likely to avoid liability under the employer domination provision in Section 8(a)(2).

Some Participation Groups Appear to Facilitate Union Organizing

Employer creation and administration of participatory groups may have the unintended effect of facilitating union organizing. Some management attorneys who advise employers about Section 8(a)(2) said they caution employers that forming participation groups can facilitate union organizing.

Their experience and advice are ironic in light of Section 8(a)(2)'s legislative history. The law's prohibition against sham unions was meant to protect employees' right to organize their own unions (Jacoby 1997; Kaufman 1997). In the current debate over the TEAM Act, unions emphasize the relevance of this historical experience. Robert Muehlenkamp (1997), director of organizing for the Teamsters, summarized this view when he testified before Congress that "this change in the law would deny employees the right to be represented by someone independent from the employer, as currently guaranteed by Section 8(a)(2)."

At least one study lends support to this view. Jim Rundle's (1996) research of 165 NLRB representation elections showed that unions encountered an employee involvement program in 38 percent of their campaigns, up from 7 percent since 1988. Moreover, he found that unions won 48 percent of the elections where no employee involvement program existed, but only 32 percent where such a program was in place.

In-depth interviews with some management attorneys disclosed a different view. When advising employers who form new employee groups, they give thought to the dual risks of adverse enforcement under the NLRB and union organizing that could spring from a newly formed participation group. Michael Luvisi (Woodson,

Hobson & Fulton, Louisville, Kentucky) shared this experience:

> On my advice, employers who do not already have participatory programs usually avoid establishing them if a union is organizing that workplace. Nonunion employers are reluctant to start teams even when a union is organizing other employers in the community or area.

Fletcher Hudson echoed a similar experience. He noted several instances where employer attempts to establish participation groups led to successful unionization.

> I advise my nonunion clients *not* to set up any kind of employee committee because in several instances I've seen these committees take on a life of their own. They became vehicles for organizing employee dissatisfaction. When my clients inadequately addressed employee concerns, these committees evolved into explicit union organizing committees, and ultimately resulted in union representation.

Thomas Burke noted that some employers feel threatened by employee empowerment:

> Another segment of my clients is fearful of empowering employees. Their real concern is that, even in the absence of a union organizing campaign, a team approach will embolden employees to speak up more. In short, these employers are fearful of creating their own representational structures for employees. These employers do not really want to hear from their employees.

These interviews do not controvert union claims that participation groups diminish the attraction of forming a union, but they suggest a more complex reality. Sandy Jacoby's (1997) historical analysis of independent local unions that evolved from disbanded company unions offers insight:

> (A) growing number of company unions were taken over by national affiliates, as in the automotive, steel, and agricultural equipment industries. Company unions made tantalizing targets for national unions because it was easier to take over a company union than to organize a group of nonunion employees. (p. 3)

Daphne Taras (1997) offers a similar view of the Canadian experience:

> Nonunion forms of representation exist in the realm of individual contracts of employment. Unions are free to raid nonunion plants at any time, as any agreements reached between management and its nonunion workers cannot be used as a shield against union organizing. Many Canadian unions (e.g., Steelworkers, Communication, Energy and Paperworkers) have been successful in courting nonunion plans and winning union certifications. (p. 25)

To be clear, these attorneys do not view Section 8(a)(2) as a good stimulus for union organizing. Burke's comment suggests that some employers view employee empowerment as a Pandora's box, regardless of Section 8(a)(2). The main point is that these lawyers believe that formation of a participation group tends to raise employee expectations, and if those expectations are unfulfilled, an employer is more vulnerable to union organizing.

Their view has an ironic validation. This happened to *Electromation* after the Teamsters prevailed in a rerun election. Commenting on this development, attorneys remarked that because Section 8(a)(2) limits subjects that groups can address, employers lack flexibility to make these groups fully responsive and representational. Thus, they implied that Section 8(a)(2) fosters some organizing because unions can address bread-and-butter employment issues that are off-limits to nonunion groups.

Conclusion: Section 8(a)(2) Should Be Amended

This question is asked with more urgency than in the past. Opponents to modification of this law stress that Congress viewed Section 8(a)(2) as a key policy for promoting workplace democracy through genuine collective bargaining (Gely 1997). Kaufman (1997) effectively argues, however, that this reading of legislative history is too narrow, and misses crucial historical evidence of the positive aspects of participation groups in the 1920s. In addition, proponents for loosening Section 8(a)(2)'s strictures believe that circumstances have fundamentally changed since 1935 (Estreicher 1994). This group, it must be emphasized, advocates limited modification of the law. No one advocates repeal.

My study falls into this second group. Cases in Figure 13.1 offer convincing evidence that company unions still exist (e.g., *Aero Detroit*; *Ryder Distribution Resources*). Repeal of Section 8(a)(2) would invite more abuses of nonunion employee representation. The small number of these cases also suggests, however, that these abuses are fairly uncommon.

On the other hand, this study uncovered much evidence of genuine employee participation in nonunion groups. Adding to the statistical findings presented here, open-ended survey responses suggested that these groups are energized by a healthy dose of workplace democracy.

One nonsupervisory respondent said: "We are a multi-functional team. Our objective is to perform . . . using our common values! Each member respects the thoughts and opinions of the other members. Customer satisfaction is our primary goal while continuous improvement is our theme. . . . Our team is highly motivated to deliver high quality products and services to our customers and be timely with information to our suppliers."

These employees also believed that participation groups improved communication. One said that his "team supports three separate cells in small teams and meets once a week to coordinate activity and share information." In another setting, an employee reported that "meetings are very open, informal, with all members participating equally." A different employee reported that "ongoing program status (is) discussed—problem areas surfaced and suggested solutions sought. . . . All members contribute; no ideas (are) unwelcome." Some nonsupervisory employees also found that their groups unleashed and harnessed creativity. One respondent wrote that her group "uses facilitators, flipcharts, brainstorming tools to come to a team consensus."

These observations, as well as the statistical findings presented here, have potential relevance to public policy. Section 8(a)(2) was conceived in response to employee participation plans that were intended to mute employees and deny them self-governance. In contrast, many of the surveyed groups appear to promote these fundamental democratic values.

Current law unduly prevents participation groups from experimenting and evolving in healthy ways. Scheduling of work, for example, is important to many employees; but since this is a Section 2(5) subject, nonunion groups that propose work schedules to their employers are probably unlawful. In short, the law should be modified to permit these groups to handle more workplace subjects with their employers.

The law is also too restrictive in its tendency to curb consensus decision making between managers and employees. A middle ground is possible and desirable. The law can be amended to prohibit employer domination of groups by defining employee participation standards. The most recent version of the TEAM Act addressed this by requiring that "employees . . . participate to at least the same extent practicable as representatives of management," if participation groups are to be free from unlawful domination. This standard is sensible and enforceable.

Unless the law changes, legitimate interactions between employees and employers will continue to be prohibited. This, in turn, will tend to minimize the NLRA's relevance as participatory forms of employment continue to evolve. Congress, therefore, should articulate a policy that better separates legitimate and illegitimate uses of participation groups.

References

Aero Detroit, Inc. 1996. 321 N.L.R.B. No. 1101.

Autodie International, Inc. 1996. 321 N.L.R.B. 688.

Budinger, William. 1997. *Hearings Before the U.S. Senate Labor and Human Resources Committee*, February 12, available in WESTLAW, 1997 WL 60501.

Calex Corp. 1997. 322 N.L.R.B. 977.

Chaison, Gary N., and Dileep G. Dhavale. 1990. "A Note on the Severity of the Decline in Union Organizing Activity." *Industrial and Labor Relations Review* 43 (April): 366–381.

Cohen, Charles. 1997. *Hearings Before the U.S. Senate Labor and Human Resources Committee*, February 12, available in WESTLAW, 1997 WL 60517.

Delaney, John Thomas, David Lewin, and Casey Ichniowski. 1989. *Human Resource Policies and Practices in American Firms*. Washington, D.C.: U.S. Department of Labor.

Dillon Stores. 1995. 319 N.L.R.B. 1245.

Eaton, Adrienne E. 1994. "Factors Contributing to the Survival of Employee Participation Programs in Unionized Settings." *Industrial and Labor Relations Review* 47 (April): 371–389.

EFCO Corp. 1998. 327 N.L.R.B. No. 71.

E.I. Du Pont. 1993. 311 N.L.R.B. 893.

Electromation. 1992. 309 N.L.R.B. 990.

Electromation, Inc. v. NLRB. 35 F.3d 1148 (7th Cir). 1994.

Estreicher, Samuel. 1994. "Employee Involvement and the 'Company Union' Prohibition: The Case for Partial Repeal of Section 8(a)(2) of the NLRB." *New York University Law Review* 69, no. 1: 125–189.

Flanagan, Robert J. 1989. "Compliance and Enforcement

Decisions under the National Labor Relations Act." *Journal of Labor Economics* 7, no. 1: 257–281.

Freeman, Richard B., and Morris M. Kleiner. 1990. "Employer Behavior in the Face of Union Organizing Drives." *Industrial and Labor Relations Review* 43 (April): 351–369.

Freeman, Richard B., and Marcus E. Ribick. 1986. *Crumbling Pillar? Declining Union Density in Japan*, Working Paper No. 2693. Cambridge, Mass.: National Bureau of Economic Research.

Freeman, Richard B., and Joel Rogers. 1993. "Who Speaks for Us? Employee Representation in a Nonunion Labor Market." In *Employee Representation: Alternatives and Future Directions*, ed. Bruce E. Kaufman and Morris M. Kleiner. Madison: IRRA Press.

Garney Morris, Inc. 1993. 313 N.L.R.B. 101.

Gely, Rafael. 1997. "Whose Team Are You On? My Team or My Team?" *Rutgers Law Review* 49: 323–388.

General Foods Corp. 1977. 231 N.L.R.B. 1232.

Hamilton Standard Division. 1993. 313 N.L.R.B. 1303.

Jacoby, Sanford M. 1997. "Unnatural Extinction: The Rise and Fall of the Local Independent Union, 1935–1970." Paper read at the Conference on Alternative Forms of Employee Representation, Banff, Canada, September.

John Ascuaga's Nugget. 1977. 230 N.L.R.B. 275.

Kaufman, Bruce E. 1997. "Company Unions: Sham Organizations or Victims of the New Deal?" *Proceedings of the Forty-ninth Annual Meeting of the Industrial Relations Research Association* 49: 166–180.

———. 1999. "Does the NLRA Constrain Employee Involvement and Participation Programs in Nonunion Companies: A Reassessment." *Yale Law and Policy Review* 17: 729–811.

Kaufman, Bruce F., and Paula E. Stephan. 1995. "The Role of Management Attorneys in Union Organizing Campaigns." *Journal of Labor Research* 16, no. 4: 439–451.

Keeler Brass. 1995. 317 N.L.R.B. 1110.

Kennedy, Edward. 1997. *Hearings Before the U.S. Senate Labor and Human Resources Committee.* February 12, available in WESTLAW, 1997 WL 70683.

LeRoy, Michael H. 1993. "Employer Domination of Labor Organizations and the *Electromation* Case: An Empirical Public Policy Analysis." *George Washington Law Review* 61, no. 6: 301–344.

———. 1996. "Can TEAM Work? Implications of an *Electromation* and *Du Pont* Compliance Analysis for the TEAM Act." *Notre Dame Law Review* 71, no. 2: 215–266.

———. 1997. " 'Dealing With' Employee Involvement in Nonunion Workplaces: Empirical Research Implications for the TEAM Act and *Electromation*." *Notre Dame Law Review* 72, no. 1: 31–82.

LCF, Inc., d/b/a La Conexion Familiar and Sprint Corp. 1996. 322 N.L.R.B. No. 137.

Magan Medical Clinic. 1994. 314 N.L.R.B. 774.

Mercy Memorial Hospital. 1977. 231 N.L.R.B. 1108.

Muehlenkamp, Robert. 1997. *Hearings before the U.S. Senate Labor and Human Resources Committee*, February 12, available in WESTLAW, 1997 WL 60522.

NLRB v. *Newport News Shipbuilding Co.* 1939. 308 U.S. 241.

N.L.R.B. v. *Peninsula General Hospital Medical Center.* 1994. 36 F.3d 1262 (4th Cir).

NLRB v. *Thill, Inc.* 1992. 980 F.2d 1137 (7th Cir).

NLRB v. *Town and Country Electric.* 1995. 516 U.S. 85.

NLRB. v. *Webcor Packaging, Inc.* 1997. 118 F.3d 1115 (6th Cir).

Osterman, Paul. 1994. "How Common Is Workplace Transformation and How Can We Explain Who Adopts It?" *Industrial and Labor Relations Review* 47 (January): 173–188.

Peninsula General Hospital. 1993. 312 N.L.R.B. 582.

Perl, Arnold E. 1993. "Employee Involvement Groups: The Outcry Over the NLRB's *Electromation* Decision." *Labor Law Journal* 44, no. 4: 195–206.

Reno Hilton. 1995. 321 N.L.R.B. 1154.

Research Federal Credit Union. 1993. 321 N.L.R.B. 56.

Rundle, Jim. 1996. "Winning Hearts and Minds: Union Organizing in the Era of Employee Involvement Programs." Paper read at the Cornell University and AFL-CIO Conference on Labor, Washington, D.C., April.

Ryder Distribution Resources. 1993. 311 N.L.R.B. 814.

S. 295. 1997. *The Teamwork for Employees and Managers Act* (also, *TEAM Act*) 105th Cong., 1st sess.

Simmons Industries. 1996. 321 N.L.R.B. 228.

Stoody Co. 1995. 320 N.L.R.B. 18.

Taras, Daphne Gottlieb. 1997. "Why Nonunion Representation Is Legal in Canada." Paper read at the Conference on Alternative Forms of Employee Representation, Banff, Canada, September.

U.S. Department of Labor. 1937. *Characteristics of Company Unions.* Bull. 634.

V & S Progalv, Inc. 1997. 323 N.L.R.B. No. 144.

Vic Koenig Chevrolet, Inc. 1996. 321 N.L.R.B. 1255.

Vons Grocery. 1995. 320 N.L.R.B. 53.

Waste Management of Utah. 1993. 310 N.L.R.B. 883.

Webcor Packaging, Inc. 1995. 319 N.L.R.B. 1203.

Zachary, G. Paschal. 1995. "Labor: Long Litigation Often Holds Up Union Victories." *Wall Street Journal*, November 17, p. B1.

14

Employee Involvement and Representation in Nonunion Firms: What Canadian Employers Do and Why?

Anil Verma

Over the course of this century, nonunion employers in Canada have experimented with a variety of ways to involve their employees in work- and workplace-related issues. Their efforts have been shaped by social, legal, and economic constraints. In the 1920s the rise of the *human relations* school saw a variety of plans to involve workers in work-related concerns. In later years similar plans evolved into quality circles and work teams to seek worker input into work-related concerns such as quality and productivity. Other firms went on to create formal employee organizations such as Joint Industrial Councils (JICs)[1] to solicit employee input into decisions ranging from wages and benefits to grievances and job classifications. While some of these plans seek workers' participation in *integrative* issues such as quality and productivity, other initiatives seek employee input on *distributive* issues such as wages, benefits, and grievances. Direct input from the rank and file is often labeled as *participation*, while indirect input from employees' representatives is seen as *representational* input. Both *participative* and *representational* forms have waxed and waned in popularity over the years. As out-

lined in the earlier chapters, their evolution in the United States has been shaped, at least in part, by legal strictures, such as Section 8(a)(2) in the National Labor Relations Act, which prohibit the employer from creating or dominating labor organizations that deal with issues of wages, benefits, and working conditions. Such restrictions on employer-sponsored employee involvement (EI) plans have never been enacted into law in Canada. Thus, if legal provisions were the defining constraint on EI forms, we may expect a different outcome for employee participation and representation in Canada relative to the United States. The lack of empirical research on this issue makes it difficult to address this hypothesis.

Notwithstanding legal constraints such as Section 8(a)(2), other economic and sociological factors may explain the observed patterns of EI. Systems of employee voice may be adopted because managers may believe that this is a "better way to manage" (i.e., that EI brings greater efficiency). Alternately, employers may also be motivated by a desire to avoid unions, believing that EI systems reduce demand for unionization by meeting employee needs for voice. It can also be argued that adoption of EI is an efficiency response to the increasing size and complexity of organizations. Size and complexity increase transaction costs, while EI reduces these costs through better communication and coordination. Lastly, adoption of EI can also be viewed as a spillover from high unionization areas to nonunion sectors as employers simply extend practices that become dominant in a given firm or industry.

More systematic investigation of the emergent forms of EI and the factors that have influenced their evolution is warranted for several reasons. The treatment of participative and representational forms in the literature has occurred somewhat independent of each other. The industrial relations literature has concentrated mainly on representational issues. In contrast, issues of direct employee participation have been studied more extensively by management and organizational behavior researchers. Similarly, defining the scope of employee involvement has suffered from a lack of clarity in a way that would encompass both participative and representational issues. Further, the term EI has been used in the literature frequently without making clear the specific form being addressed and without addressing the implications of one form for other EI forms. This chapter builds on the premise that unless greater conceptual clarity and integration are brought to various forms of EI, we will find it frustrating to explain observed patterns of EI.

Accordingly, this chapter first clarifies the terminology used to describe various forms of EI. This is followed by an empirical examination of the practices of eight Canadian nonunion firms in the area of employee participation and representation. This evidence is then used to derive inductively a framework in which the evolution of these programs and the policy dilemmas they pose may be understood for both theory and prac-tice. This chapter has two objectives, one specific and another more general. The specific objective is to investigate if Canadian nonunion employers consult their employees on issues of wages and benefits, a practice denied to American nonunion employers by the NLRA. If indeed the Canadian employers do discuss wage and benefits issues with their employees, what forums, formal or informal, are used to solicit this input? The general objective of the chapter is to move toward a theory that would explain employer behavior with respect to three important choices that employers face:

- Should the employer seek employee input ?
- If yes, into what types of workplace decisions?
- What are the most appropriate forums for seeking that input?

Concepts and Definitions

Employee involvement practices in North American organizations are not new phenomena. They date back to the 1910s as formalized activities and perhaps to even earlier times as informal practices (Jacoby 1985).[2] Similarly, employer-employee dialogue over terms and conditions of work in the absence of a union is also as old as industrialization itself. A quick survey of the literature reveals that there have been a wide variety of policies and practices used by employers to solicit the involvement of their employees. It is important, therefore, to develop a typology of these practices in order to bring greater conceptual clarity necessary for research and practice. As noted by many writers on this subject, there are several key dimensions to EI practices (Dachler and Wilpert 1978). For the purpose of this chapter, two dimensions are most pertinent: the scope of decisions in which employee input is sought; and the format, direct or indirect, in which

Figure 14.1 **Dimensions of Employee Involvement**

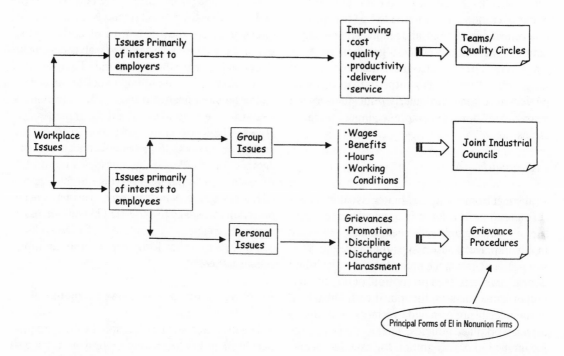

such input is solicited. First, I describe the *scope* of employee involvement, that is, the range of issues in which employees' input may be sought.

To delineate various areas of workplace issues in which employees may be involved, the following broad categories may be used (see Figure 14.1). Each area is associated with developments at different points in history. For a more detailed discussion of the history associated with various forms of EI, please refer to Kaufman, Fossum, and Lewin in this volume.

Cost, Quality, and Productivity Issues

Employers frequently seek employee involvement in activities that improve organizational outcomes. These are generally issues of efficiency that are of primary interest to managers. Nevertheless, economic, social, and psychological factors can increase employee interest in these issues. For example, the threat of job loss can pique employee interest in improving product quality. For these reasons, these issues have been referred to as *integrative* issues. The most common forms of employee involvement in these issues are forms of *direct* participation in decision making in such forums as teams and quality circles.

Bread-and-Butter Issues

This term has been used in the past to refer to basic issues such as wages, benefits, and working conditions. These issues formed the basis for early collective bargaining and with some refinements over the years continue to be the principal preoccupations of most labor-management negotiations. These issues concern group interests of employees. They are also more distributive than integrative in nature. No surprise then that employers have been particularly reluctant over the years to seek or permit employee input into these issues.

Individual Issues

As distinct from bread-and-butter issues that concern group issues, there is a set of personal issues on which employees need to have some say in a workplace. These issues may take the form of a personal grievance in the case of a discipline or discharge, a missed promotion, or discrimination or harassment on the job. It could also be a desire to be heard on a wide variety of employer-driven workplace policies, such as drinking coffee on the job or recognition for excellent work. The attempt to be heard is normally initiated by the individual employee, but it may involve a strictly personal issue that, by extension, also becomes a group issue. The line between a personal complaint, a generic complaint, and a simple desire to be able to speak up on any workplace matter frequently blurs in practice. Some forms of EI discussed in the next section have evolved to capture employee concerns that cross the boundaries between *participation* in workplace decisions and *representation* of personal and group grievances.

Each of these three areas for employee involvement became associated with certain forms of EI. As shown at the far right of Figure 14.1, teams and quality circles have emerged as principal vehicles of EI in quality and productivity issues. JICs have been associated with employee voice

in wages, benefits, and working conditions. Similarly, grievance procedures have become identified as one of the typical methods for individual issues. Despite the popularity of these forms, newer forms of EI have emerged that do not neatly fit into one of these three categories. For example, focus groups, in which employees are asked to address their concerns in small groups, provide a forum for venting ideas on all the three sets of issues. The same is true of phone-in lines that employees can use to provide feedback to management on a wide variety of issues. Figure 14.2 shows a conceptual map of voice in the equity-efficiency space. Various forms of EI have been placed in this space to show that in addition to EI forms that capture a single set of issues, there can be several other forms that capture multiple sets of issues.

Employee Input on Wages and Benefits

Since strictures such as Section 8 (a)(2) are primarily intended to prevent employers from engaging employees on wages, benefits, and working conditions, it is important to examine ways in which employers may deal with these issues in the absence of such prohibitions. As stated earlier, employee input on issues such as wages, benefits, and grievances have been sought by many employers within JIC-type structures. JICs are ongoing formal structures even though the degree of their independence from management may vary from workplace to workplace. Other employers may simply rely on less formal structures such as focus groups to solicit such input directly from rank-and-file workers. Compensation and benefits issues can also be addressed through employee surveys. Both focus groups and annual surveys are not necessarily ongoing activities. Management may constitute and disband these groups as and when the need to consult is

Figure 14.2 **Forms of Employee Involvement: Voice in Equity Versus Efficiency Issues**

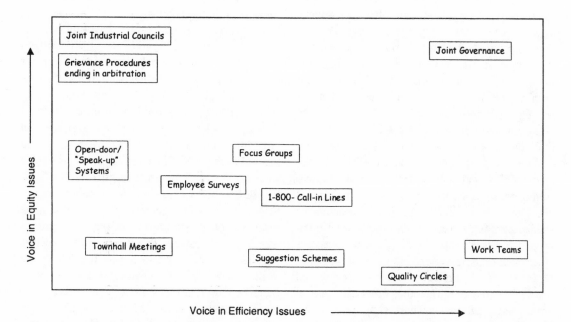

felt. It is also possible for management to create semiformal or limited-term structures such as a task force on wages and benefits that meets and reports in, say, three months, after which it disbands. Another task force may follow the following year, or it may not be formed for years to come. For these reasons, it is tempting to hypothesize that the degree of formalization of a structure is positively associated with the degree of independence from management. The less formal the structure, the less likely that it is independent of management. This discussion suggests three dimensions that characterize EI forums: formality, continuity, and independence (from management).

Empirical Evidence from Canadian Firms

With the scope of EI defined in the previous section, a brief study was undertaken across several prominent Canadian firms to assess their practice of EI both in terms of scope and adopted forms. The firms were selected to represent a variety of industries, size groups, and union density[3] both within their industry and within the firm. These firms are all quite visible as Canadian organizations or multinational corporations. It is also assumed that they are likely to represent leading-edge practice in EI given their prominence in national and international settings.

As shown in Table 14.1, the reference group of employees in the first four firms were all quite small, ranging from 100 to 300 employees. Despite being part of some very large corporations, the small size of these units reflects, in part, the restructuring that took place in the post-1980 period to create smaller business units. The only very large unit in the sample is a bank, Firm E, which is one of the five biggest banks in the country with thousands of locations. Two organizations, Firm F and Firm G, were medium sized. In terms of industry, four came from secondary manufacturing, another two from process manufacturing, and the last two from services. In terms of occupation, the groups ranged from blue collar to clerical and professional. Unionization within the industry was high in four cases, moderate in one case, and low in the other three. Unionization within the firm was high in one case, moderate in another, and low in the others.

Table 14.2 provides a summary of the various forms of EI found in these firms. Brief descriptive summaries of each case are enclosed in the Appendix. The first column summarizes EI mechanisms used in these firms to engage the employees in quality and productivity issues. All firms reported extensive use of these forums. In four firms, Firms C, D, G, and H, all production work was organized primarily into teams. The other firms made use of project and quality teams. These teams were formed for specific tasks and were frequently dissolved when the task was completed and reconstituted when new problems arose.

In the area of employee input into wages, benefits, and other working conditions, only Firm F reported an independent employee association. None of the others appeared to have a formal, ongoing, and independent forum for systematic input. Most others, with the exceptions of Firms A and B, reported use of ad hoc committees, focus groups, employee surveys, and task forces composed from time to time to make inputs on issues such as wages and benefits. These committees and teams were constituted at management initiative. Their membership was almost always assigned by management with minimal input from the employees. Thus, employee consultations appear to be widely practiced on such distributive issues, but they appear to be less formal, less ongoing, and less independent of management compared to the employee association for nurses found in Firm F.

Grievance procedures for individual complaints were informal in six firms and formalized as four-step processes at Firm A and Firm F. At Firm E, a phone-in line took both anonymous and self-identified calls. This line appeared to serve dual needs of receiving complaints as well as suggestions for improvements. The distinction between complaints and suggestions is also blurred in the use of focus groups and employee surveys. The last column shows that all the firms made some use of surveys and focus groups. At Firm E their use was reported to be extensive. At Firm A surveys were not used, but focus groups were used extensively. Small size of the unit was cited as the reason for this choice. It is interesting to note that despite their widespread usage, with the exception of Firm E none of the other firms reported regularly scheduled surveys. Both surveys and focus groups were used when "deemed necessary" by management. At Firm H, management introduced instantaneous electronic polling to facilitate focus-group discussions. When a question is put to the employees, everyone responds, using a hand-held remote switch. The results are flashed within moments on a screen. These results are then discussed by the group to explore the underlying reasons for the answers.

The foregoing review shows that while all the employers surveyed were engaged extensively in EI activities that solicited employee input into quality and productivity issues in a more formal and structured way, their approach to seeking employee input into bread-and-butter and personal issues was much less structured. Two of the firms had no forums for EI in bread-and-butter areas. The other five firms sought some input in ad hoc forums, but in all these cases the process was less transparent

Table 14.1

Comparative Profile of Firms

Firm	Products/industry	Employment		Employment category	Unionization rate	
		Firm worldwide/ Canada	Reference group		Firm	Industry
A	Pharmaceuticals/ personal products/ confectionery	38,000/1,500	300	Blue collar, production workers	Low	Low
B	Pulp and paper	6,800/5,000	160	Clerical, office staff	High	High
C	Petrochemicals	11,700/1,000	100	Blue collar, production workers	Low	Moderate
D	Electrical controls	239,000/2,000	200	Blue collar, production workers	Low	High
E	Banking	32,000/30,000	20,000	Clerical	Low	Low
F	Hospital	2,000	800	Nurses	Moderate	High
G	Pharmaceutical	53,500/1,200	950	Mixed: blue and white collar	Low	Low
H	Steel	6,000	5,000	Blue collar	Low	High

Table 14.2

Comparative Employee Involvement Practices

Firm	EI in quality/productivity issues	EI in wages/benefits/hours	EI in personal issues	EI through surveys/focus groups
A	Mostly project teams; one-third employees covered last year.	No formal employee forum for systematic and representative input.	Four-step grievance process ending with site manager.	No surveys. Focus groups: occasionally. Sitewide communication meetings quarterly.
B	Volunteer committees for projects such as orientation, site visits, and so on. Suggestion Box for individual input. Limited use of project teams.	No formal employee forum for systematic and representative input.	Informal open-door policy.	Surveys: occasionally. Focus groups: occasionally.
C	All workers are in work teams. Project teams used extensively.	No formal employee forum such as a JIC. Task-specific project teams used for input on compensation and hiring.	Informal open-door policy.	Surveys: periodically. Focus groups: not used.
D	All workers are in highly autonomous work cells.	No formal employee forum for systematic and representative input. Employees are surveyed for their reaction to management proposals on wages, benefits.	Informal open-door policy.	Surveys: sporadically. Focus groups: used to gauge reactions to management proposals.
E	Work teams: none. Project teams: few. Suggestion program.	Numerous standing committees made up of all levels of employees on topics such as employment equity, safety, work and family, careers, work environment. Membership is by management nomination.	"Between Us" is an ombuds-style program for anonymous and self-identified complaints. Up to 4,000 calls are fielded annually.	Surveys: used extensively. Focus groups: used extensively.

F	Ad hoc committees consider problem areas. Quality teams in all departments and areas.	Nursing Staff Association: independent; management deals extensively with the NSA on a wide range of workplace issues. Wages and benefits are almost the same as those paid in the unionized sector. Ad hoc committees consider issues such as job sharing.	Four-step grievance procedure ending in a final decision by the CEO. Roughly 25 written complaints a year with 2–3 going to the final step. Confidential phone line for calln on all issues.	Surveys: periodically. Focus groups: occasionally.
G	Teams are used extensively: Work teams Quality teams Project teams Cross-functional teams	No formal structure but an annual survey and many focus groups consult workers on compensation and benefits.	Formal guidelines but no formal procedure. Informal resolution of most complaints. Formal investigation in serious cases.	Annual survey of employees is undertaken. Focus groups used often.
H	Roughly 70% of all production workers have team experience: Work teams Quality teams Issue specific, cross-functional teams	No formal structure but focus groups used extensively to consult workers on compensation, benefits, and working conditions.	Informal "open-door" policy.	Focus groups used frequently. Communication meetings. Instantaneous electronic polling of employee views followed by discussions.

to the employees, less likely to be ongoing, and less independent of management control. This meant that the timing, scope, and membership of these forums were decided unilaterally by employers. Where the employer did consult employees on such issues, the process was "soft" in that it was not formalized and the employees could not act on the basis of a set of previously established rules or policies to govern these procedures. None of these firms, with the exception of the nurses' association, had any forum that was ongoing, formal, and independent (of management) to make decisions or even to advise management on distributive issues.

Only one firm in this sample reported an independent employee organization. When Firm F, a hospital, was founded in the late 1970s, the nurses decided, by a vote, not to join the province-wide nurses' union. Instead, they voted to form an in-house, independent, and unaffiliated staff association. The employer had no role in its formation and currently plays no role in its internal governance. The nurses' association runs its affairs at arms' length from the employer. However, the employer supports the association by engaging in an active dialogue with it and by not taking an adversarial position, at least at the process level. The management views the association with a degree of respect and accords it a union-like status. The association is regularly consulted on all matters of policy and invited to attend most committee meetings. Whether this is born out of a belief that employee consultation is a better way to manage or whether the favors are granted under the ever-present threat of unionization is hard to discern. Since almost all nurses in the province are unionized, it would be relatively easy for this group to join a certified trade union. Perhaps for this reason, wages and major benefits are seldom the topic of consultations. Since the employer pays union wages and benefits so that this has never been an issue on the table.

In the area of employee input into personal issues, five firms had no formal procedures, two had four-step grievance procedures, and another employed an ombudsperson-type program mostly to counsel employees but sometimes to investigate serious complaints of ill treatment or unfairness in company policy. Similarly, only half the firms in our sample used surveys and focus groups on a regular basis.

With the caveat that this small sample of firms may not be representative of the typical Canadian nonunion employer, we may make the following generalizations. First, nonunion employers appear to seek employee input into a wide variety of workplace issues that deal with quality and productivity on the job. These forums are extensive, formalized, and well-resourced in terms of training and time off the job for meetings. Second, most employers do appear to take advantage of the absence of Section 8(a)(2) prohibitions to seek employee input into bread-and-butter and personal issues. Nevertheless, the use of formal structures such as JICs or employee associations did not appear to be popular. More widely used forums are ad hoc committees, limited-term project teams or task forces, focus groups, and employee surveys. The use of grievance procedures is not always formalized, but the concept appears to have diffused through most nonunion organizations. Similarly, the formal and regular use of employee surveys and focus groups has not been adopted by all employers, but most appear to use them sporadically depending on perceived need.

Analysis and Explanations

In light of the evidence from a small sample of firms presented above it is now possible to consider a number of alternate explanations for the observed patterns of EI. I briefly consider the legal argument followed by some traditional economic arguments. These two explanations are supplemented with perspectives from decision theory that offers explanations for departures from "rational" behavior.

The Legal Argument

The Kaufman et al. chapter in this volume hypothesizes that prohibitions such as Section 8(a)(2) have chilled employer interest in fostering ongoing, formal employee forums for involvement in decision making. It implies, conversely, that if such restrictions in the law were not to tie up employers' hands, firms would indeed be more prone to establish forums for employee input into a wide variety of issues. Accordingly, the Canadian sample was chosen for comparison because Canadian law does not include such prohibitions. The limited evidence suggests that most employers have used a variety of forums for employee involvement. What we observe is a trend similar to that in the United States of participative forums in the area of quality and productivity programs and some limited use of formal grievance procedures and use of employee surveys and focus groups. What we did not observe was any significant adoption of formal structures such as the joint industrial councils (JICs), which provide the employees with a formal, ongoing, and independent forum to make inputs into a wide variety of workplace issues including wages, benefits, and working conditions. Most of the firms in the sample did report consulting employees on wage and benefits issues, just as predicted by Kaufman et al., but they did so using less formal or ad hoc structures such as committees, task forces, and focus groups. These initiatives tend

to be episodic rather than continuous; and they are mostly controlled by the employer in terms of timing, scope, membership, and follow-up.

If the evidence in this chapter were proved to be representative of the general Canadian context, it would suggest acceptance of the hypothesis that legal prohibitions such as Section 8(a)(2) have played a defining role in discouraging U.S. employers from using EI forums to consult employees on distributive issues. But the legal restrictions do not explain why Canadian employers have not embraced the JIC-type of employee involvement. For this we have to look to other explanations.

Threat Effect

The threat effect suggests that when employers are faced with the threat of unionization, they will be more willing to adopt formal, ongoing, independent forums for EI. The motive here is to preempt unionization by meeting employee needs for voice. The threat hypothesis would suggest EI forums such as JICs in nonunion firms within highly unionized industries. Four of the firms came from highly unionized industries: Firm B from pulp and paper, Firm D from electrical manufacturing, Firm F from health care, and Firm H from steel. At Firm B, neither the high unionization rate in the industry nor within the firm prompted the employer to provide such EI forums. The same is true of Firms D and H. Only at Firm F, a formal structure in the form of an independent employee organization did exist at arms' length from the employer who was not involved in its formation but was actively supporting it by engaging in dialogue and consultation. Given the small sample size, it is difficult to come to a conclusion with any confidence; however, the evidence from Firm F suggests some support for the threat effect.

Spillover Effect

The spillover effect suggests that employers who have some experience with EI forums in parts of their company would be more likely to adopt it for other segments of their nonunion employees. This argument builds on the hypothesis that employers would be generally apprehensive of any formalization of EI for fear that they may lose control of work processes and costs. If they have learned to live and work with unions in other parts of their firm, however, they would be more prone to adopt EI forums, for at least two reasons. First, they would have a more realistic assessment of the efficacy of EI forums in staving off unionization. Second, the employers would know more about the true benefits and costs of EI forums. Such knowledge would make it more likely for such employers to adopt EI.

In our sample, only one firm, Firm B, fits this category. Data were collected in respect of the non-union office staff of a large pulp and paper firm whose production workers are unionized. No formal EI forum along the lines of a JIC was reported. Thus, the support for a spillover effect is weak. Alternately, it is likely that despite high unionization in the firm and the industry, the threat of the office staff forming a union may be low because of occupational norms (office staff, generally females in clerical occupations, have a low unionization rate in Canada). In that case, this is not a good test of the spillover effect. Instead, what is observed is a result of the threat effect, that is, low threat of unionization within the office occupations.

Size/Formalization Arguments

Yet another argument in favor of adopting JIC-type forums comes from a consideration of transaction costs. In small organizations, employer-employee communications are informal because of the low cost of making these "transactions." As the organization grows in size and complexity, transaction costs of employer-employee communications rise, forcing the employer to adopt EI forums which can reduce transaction costs. Both in the industry in general and in our sample there was a marked trend toward creating smaller business units with sufficient autonomy to manage their own EI practices. In only one case of a large bank, Firm E, did there appear to be a large group of employees for whom EI appeared to be managed centrally. In four other cases, the reference group ranged from 100 to 300 workers. Thus, if size were a determining factor, our sample is biased to show fewer examples of JIC-type EI forums than might be the case in the industry at large. In two cases, Firm C and Firm D, informants suggested that if the plant were to get much bigger they might consider formal EI forums for wider employee input consultation.

These considerations suggest a larger view of why employers have not adopted more JIC-type forums despite the absence of Section 8(a)(2) restriction. Large-scale restructuring of industry in the 1980s and the 1990s have created smaller business units. Such units may offer better accountability, more entrepreneurial behavior, and lower transaction costs in communicating with employees. In that case, we would see a proliferation of informal, ad hoc, and employer-directed EI forums, rather than formal, ongoing, independent forums such as JICs. This explanation certainly fits the data collected here quite well.

Framing

I now turn to a possible explanation offered by developments in the decision-theory literature. A number of scholars have explored factors responsible for "irrational" decision making. For example, Kahneman and Tversky (1979) reported a number of cognitive biases in decision making that keep people from making "rational" decisions to maximize their utility. Others have reported biases that originate in the way a decision is framed (Whyte 1993). In the case of employers' adoption of formal JIC structures it is important to examine the reference frame within which employers make such decisions. For example, if avoidance of unionization is a primary goal for employers, their reference frame may have shifted several times over the course of this century. During the first half of this century the threat of a militant union organizing their workers may have been real, prompting many employers to adopt a variety of forums for employee input. Later, in the 1960s and the 1970s, as employers developed a set of employee communication and voice mechanisms, their ability to stay nonunion increased. With this newfound ability to neutralize the unionization threat, the inclination to create formal EI forums for employee input may have decreased.

Thus, a formal JIC structure may look like a gain to an employer facing a real threat of being organized by a militant international union. If that threat recedes, however, because of shifts in the external political, economic, social, and legal environment, the JIC structure may look like a loss when compared with the choice of staying nonunion.

This line of thinking suggests that employers may have an ordered set of priorities in the way they wish to approach EI. The choice of an EI system would be determined by the reference frame within which employers view their choices. One possible ordering of these choices may look as follows:

- First preference: nonunion with informal EI forums
- Second preference: nonunion with more formal EI forums
- Third preference: in-house unions
- Fourth preference: national or international unions

Thus, when employers faced the prospect of being organized by independent national unions such as the USWA or the IAM, many chose to adopt JICs and even promote in-house unions. But if the choice is between staying nonunion with less formal as opposed to more formal EI forums, employers appear to opt for the informal systems. In this sense, framing offers a more sophisticated view of the older unionization threat argument. It is not unionization per se but the perceived available alternatives that offer a more powerful explanation for understanding employer behavior.

Conclusions

In conclusion, two perspectives for policy and research emerge from this exercise. First, the data collected for this chapter strongly suggest that the somewhat artificial separation of employee *participation* and *representation* in the literature must yield to a more integrative treatment. For employers and employees, the dividing line is frequently blurred. In forums such as quality circles and work teams, employees frequently raise issues of compensation despite strong discouraging signals from the employers. Phone-in lines, focus groups, and employee surveys also address issues across a broad range. Employers also need to develop better ways to sift through the information they receive from such forums. Given the separation between work-related and people-related issues, there is some confusion about the best way to handle the volley of employee input generated every time employers seek employee input. In many firms, EI remains episodic because employers are "afraid" of getting too much information and of "unduly raising expectations."

Second, evidence presented in this chapter also points strongly to employer ambivalence toward various forms of EI. While they may be in relative agreement over the need to introduce EI, employers appear highly ambivalent in their assessment of forums such as JICs. A key question is whether JICs act as a substitute for unionization or whether they spur unionization by giving workers a taste for independent voice (Taras and Copping 1998). This question also poses an important challenge to theorists because the state of received theory has no clear predictions. The evidence from research on independent labor unions (ILUs) is somewhat mixed (Jacoby 1985; Jacoby and Verma 1992). Some ILUs went on to affiliate with national and international unions over time while others retained their in-house status for decades after formation. If we were to extend this pattern to JICs, it would suggest that employers take a finite risk when they promote such EI forums. Some of them may stave off unionization while others may encourage employees to go further in the direction of seeking independent voice. The task of specifying a complete model that would predict the conditions under which each course is likely to occur, remains a challenge to scholars.

Appendix
Profile of Cases

Firm A

Profile

Principal Products: Confectionery, over-the-counter drugs, cosmetics, and toiletries
Number of Production Workers: 300
Demographics: 55 percent female; average age 40 years; typical education level: Grade 10

Continuous Improvement Teams. The plant uses a variety of teams. Project teams are constituted around a specific problem. The team is frequently multidisciplinary and cross-functional, which means that employees from various departments and levels may be included. Thus, employees serve on these teams along with managers and professionals. Other teams include "natural work groups," which consist of employees engaged in similar or complementary tasks in close proximity of each other. Teams are also constituted for implementing new technology. Participation in any team is voluntary. In most cases, they are selected by management, and it is generally considered a privilege to be picked for most teams. Roughly one-third of the employees would have been involved in a team in the past year.

Grievance Procedures. There is a formal grievance procedure consisting of four steps. The final step involves a decision by the top site manager, roughly equivalent to a plant manager or a general manager. Typical incidence is two or three grievances at the second stage of which one has gone to the final step in the past year. A similar but separate procedure is in effect for complaints of sexual harassment. In general, the latter procedure expedites and cuts short the more elaborate and the relatively slower procedure for other complaints.

Surveys, Focus Groups, and the Like. The plant does not use surveys given the small size. Focus groups have been used to solicit employee input into a variety of topics such as teams, work groups, and working conditions. Virtually no input has been sought on wages and major benefit issues. This is not considered important because the employer pays well above wages in the industry and geographical area.

Communication Meetings. The management team holds sitewide meetings once a quarter at which strategic plans for the plant are presented to all employees. Employees then have an opportunity to have their questions answered on a variety of topics.

Postscript. The plant has faced no unionization drives in the past five or seven years. Although many such plants in the area and industry are unionized, workers at this plant appear to be quite satisfied with their nonunion status.

Firm B

Profile

Principal Products: Pulp and paper
Number of Clerical Workers: 160; office staff of a larger manufacturing firm in which production workers are unionized

Demographics: 85 percent female; average age 40 years; typical education level: Grade 12 + vocational training

Monthly Meetings. Employees meet monthly of their own accord. Attendance is voluntary and has waned since these meetings were first initiated. Employees establish and control the agenda. Some typical activities include a Welcome Committee, invited presentations from senior management, and arranging visits to interesting sites of professional interest. The Welcome Committee was a volunteer committee that put together a package of materials for new hires. Invited presentations were on topics such as how to read and understand financial reports, history of the firm, and emerging markets and technology in the pulp and paper business. Visits for employees were arranged to an Internet demonstration, a pulp and paper mill, and a forestry information center. These activities are completely voluntary, and employee interest in them appears to be somewhat uneven.

Suggestion Box. Employees are encouraged to put forth suggestions, many of which have resulted in changes in workplace policy. Issues covered may be work related or they may be people related. For example, a suggestion for flexible hours during the summer was followed through, resulting in new hours for the summer. Another tip in the box complained of unfair or uneven treatment in one of the staff departments. This complaint led to an investigation by management followed by remedial steps.

Surveys, Focus Groups. Employees were surveyed once in the past twelve months although there is no fixed policy of conducting them periodically. Focus groups have also been used to obtain feedback from the employees on a range of workplace and personal issues.

Teams. A variety of teams have been formed to tackle specific workplace issues. These teams are formed for a limited term to solve specific problems. They are dissolved after the task is accomplished.

Postscript. This is a heavily unionized industry in Canada in which most production and maintenance workers are unionized, as they are in this firm as well. White-collar office staff, however, is not as heavily unionized. This case illustrates potential spillover of employee involvement practices from the unionized sector.

Firm C

Profile

Principal Products: Petrochemicals
Number of Clerical Workers: 100 hourly; 165 total
Demographics: 85 percent male; average age 37 years; typical education level: Grade 12 + vocational training

Teams. The dominant method for identifying and solving workplace problems is to create project- and task-specific teams primarily made up of employees. There are no first-line supervisors in the plant. All teams are self-managing. One worker serves as the group leader by rotation. Several major problems were given to teams in the past year: safety, a quality problem within the chemical process, and a distribution problem. In each case, the teams studied the problem, devised solutions, and implemented them successfully.

Apart from issues related to work methods and processes, teams get involved in a wide range of other issues, such as compensation and hiring. One team examined the issue of compensation for team achievement and submitted a set of recommendations. As a result, a bonus pool of $30,000 was created to reward team achievements. The recognition plan was initiated by management, but it is now run completely by employees. Teams are also involved in the hiring process. A hiring team is constituted for every new hire. It consists of employees and managers and some staff specialists. Another team was involved in developing benchmarks for and recommending wage increases. This team also communicated the rationale behind the increase to all employees. Other areas of team involvement: policy reviews, employee savings plan, and the benefits package.

Management seeks volunteers for all team assignments and selects individuals based on expertise from among them. It is not customary to have elections to fill the slots when volunteers exceed the number of slots available. Sometimes, management would ask the team to pick one person from the team. Occasionally, a team may decide to elect its representative.

Grievance Procedure. No formal appeal process exists. Employees are encouraged to bring their problems to any level of management. Employees do complain but there are no estimates of how often this may happen and at which levels. There are "facilitators" who may be assigned to mediate conflicts within or across teams.

Surveys, Focus Groups. Employee surveys are conducted periodically, although focus groups have not been used to obtain employee feedback.

Employee Council. There is no employee council or similar organization in which employees could participate. Plant management is of the view that the small size of the plant allows them not to formalize employee involvement any further. Should the size double as per the most recent expansion plan, however, they would be inclined to consider a more formal and ongoing structure for employee input into all issues.

Firm D

Profile

Principal Products: Power Relays and Controls
Number of Production Workers: 200 hourly
Demographics: 65 percent male; average age 32 years; typical education level: Some college + vocational training

Teams. This is a team concept plant in which all work is performed in work cells. The underlying principle is that of a focus factory. There are no first-line supervisors. The work cell retains complete autonomy within the group to perform its work. It can also redesign its work processes and resource allocations. There is a work-cell leader chosen from among its members.

Project Teams. In addition to the work cells, specific task-oriented teams are often constituted to tackle certain problems. Such project teams have studied quality and health problems in the recent past.

Quality Assurance. The plant participates in a corporationwide quality management program that requires a high degree of quality assurance. As part of this program, work cells and employees have acquired higher levels of autonomy in their work.

Grievance Process. There is no formal grievance procedure. The informal procedure is called the "open-door" policy. All employees have been trained in conflict resolution. People experiencing conflict may enter a "happy room" for reflection and introspection. The plant manager frequently arbitrates disputes across work cells.

Wages and Working Conditions. A consultative process is used to get employee reactions to changes contemplated by management. Proposals are passed from cell to cell to obtain employee reactions. At the end, management will often "tweak" the proposals to make them fit better with employee expectations.

Focus Groups. Focus groups used often for obtaining feedback about a new manager. Soon after a new manager takes up a position, employees are asked to express their reactions toward the manager in small focus groups. The manager receiving this feedback is expected to address employees' concerns.

Surveys. No periodic surveys are conducted. There was no survey done in the past twelve months although they have been conducted sporadically in the past.

Firm E

Profile

Principal Products: Banking, national and international

Number of Employees: 30,000 total; clerical 20,000

Demographics of Clerical Employees: 70 percent female; average age 34 years; typical education level: Grade 12 + some college

This is a large, full-service bank with branches across Canada that has expanded into brokerage and other financial services in recent years. Despite some union organizing in the 1970s, the banking industry has remained largely nonunion. The unionization threat has been minimal in the 1980s and the 1990s. The policies below are in respect of nonmanagerial white-collar staff.

Teams. There are no work teams. Project teams have been used on a few occasions but are not widespread. Most employee input on work-related issues comes through standing committees described below.

EI in Wages, Working Conditions. The bank uses numerous standing committees to solicit employee input on matters of workplace policy. Some recent examples include work and family issues, employment and gender equity, career advancement, and work environment. The committees are composed of all levels of employees including managers. Employees are typically nominated by management to serve on the committees, which can occur at firm level, divisional level, or branch level.

Surveys, Focus Groups. Employee surveys are done regularly at all levels within the bank. This is a principal method used in assessing employees' views on all aspects of employment and working conditions. There is also a standing focus group of 175 employees, who are brought in to discuss employment conditions on a regular basis.

Grievance Procedure. A high-profile ombudstype program, "Between Us," is used to encourage "two-way" communication with employees. Roughly 4,000 employee complaints were received last year. Employees can register their concerns either anonymously or by identifying themselves. Every complaint or concern is investigated. In most cases, the employee is counseled on how best to get the situation resolved. A smaller number of cases are referred to other departments for specialist attention. These referrals may go to the human resource department, another staff department, or to a line department.

Firm F

Profile

Principal Products: Health care

Number of Employees: 2,000 total; 800 nurses
Demographics: 99 percent female; average age 40 years; typical education level: College + professional certification

Teams. There are no work teams among the nurses, but they may be part of a work team with other types of employees in some areas. Quality teams are used for the nursing staff, whose mandate it is to develop and maintain standards of professional conduct.

Wages, Benefits. The wages and benefits at this hospital are virtually identical to those paid by the unionized sector. Hence, there is little attempt to seek employee input into such areas.

Working Conditions and Other Workplace Issues. The nurses at this hospital belong to the Nurses' Staff Association (NSA) that has no organizational ties with either the hospital or any union central. It is not certified as a trade union. The NSA meets monthly to discuss and develop policies on all work- and workplace-related matters. The management frequently deals with the NSA in a variety of ways. Sometimes it goes to the NSA to name representatives who may sit on a variety of hospital committees. At other times it will communicate policy matters with the NSA and seek its help in communicating it to the rest of the nurses. The management also invites the NSA to send representatives to most policy meetings at the hospital. According to our informant, the hospital makes an effort to "cooperate" with the NSA. It does not see the NSA as an adversary but as a legitimate organization of nurses that can be helpful to the management in many of its objectives. The hospital is willing to share information and discuss matters of policy with the NSA.

The NSA operates less formally than a certified union but more formally than an ad hoc group of nurses meeting to discuss work and employment issues. It elects its officers according to a set of bylaws. Membership and dues collection are not as formalized as they would be in a certified union, however.

Ad hoc committees consisting of employees from a single group or from diverse groups are used to garner employee input. A nurses' committee recently investigated and recommended policies for job sharing.

Grievance Procedure. A formal four-step grievance procedure is in place. The final step is a decision by the president of the hospital. Roughly twenty-five grievances in the past year went to the written stage. Typically, two or three make it to the final step.

Surveys, Focus Groups. Both surveys and focus groups have been used only sporadically. A survey was last conducted three years ago. Focus groups have been used to supplement the work of committees.

Firm G

Profile

Principle Products: Pharmaceuticals
Number of Employees: approximately 1,200; manufacturing (250), research and development (250), commercial (450), information technology, distribution & administration (250)
Demographics: 55 percent female; average age 37 years; typical education level: university graduates

People Strategy. Firm G's human resource vision is called the "People Strategy." It consists of three interconnecting components: rewards and recognition, selection and development, and the environment. This human resource system is designed to be aligned with the organization's overall business strategy.

Personal Development Plan (PDP). Firm G considers the PDP to be a powerful involvement tool. Each employee meets with a coach on a quarterly basis to establish his or her career objectives, create an action plan, and discuss and evaluate their progress. The coach is usually the individual who supervises the employee's daily activities.

Teams. Teams are ad hoc groups created to discuss a certain matter or work on a specific project. They may also exist on a more permanent basis, in the form of work teams. Teams may consist of a cross-section of employees from various departments or may be pulled from one specific area.

Surveys, Focus Groups. An annual survey is conducted to obtain employee input on various aspects of the workplace, including salaries and benefits. Focus groups may be initiated by management or employees to consider a specific issue. Some of these issues may be those concerning compensation, benefits, and working conditions, in addition to issues of quality and costs.

Communication Meetings. Meetings provide a forum for employees to express their concerns, raise questions, or make suggestions. They are also used by management to inform employees of new initiatives. The annual "All Employee Meeting" is a formal group event. Informal group meetings, such as "Coffee with the President," also take place. In addition, input is obtained on an individual basis, for example, in the form of an exit interview.

Grievance Procedures. Employees are provided with guidelines regarding the steps they should take to voice a concern. These guidelines describe an informal chain of command that can be approached for assistance. For more "serious"

conflicts, the organization conducts a full investigation, including interviews, to reach a resolution.

Firm: H

Profile

Principal Products: Integrated steel manufacturer
Number of Production Workers: 5,000 (1,500 primary manufacturing; 1,500 secondary manufacturing; 2,000 product finishing)
Demographics: 95 percent male; average age 45 years; typical education level: high school diploma

Teams. The plant uses three major types of teams. Seventy percent of the production employees participate in cross-functional Work Area Teams, which are the basic unit of the workplace. Team size varies, consisting of six to twenty-four persons. Workers are cross-trained to perform a variety of tasks related to production, safety, training, and administrative work.

Quality Improvement Teams (QITs) are integral to the overall "quality effort." These groups are set up on an ad hoc basis to address an issue prescribed by management. In addition, QITs may be established to undertake a particular project.

Involvement Teams work together to identify problems and generate ideas. Unlike the QITs, these teams provide a bottom-up, worker-controlled forum for promoting communication and involvement in the workplace.

In addition to these three teams, ad hoc or formally assembled groups meet to create policies, share information, or monitor workplace health and safety standards. These issues may include matters of compensation, benefits, and working conditions, in addition to quality and cost issues.

Grievance Procedure. There is no formal, documented procedure for managing worker grievances. Instead, Firm H promotes an "open-door policy" to encourage employees to present their concerns to any member of management. Typically, individuals speak to their immediate supervisor or local human resource representative before approaching higher levels of management.

Surveys, Focus Groups. Focus groups occur on a regular basis for the purposes of "pulse taking," decision making, and the introduction of new initiatives. These discussions are facilitated by the use of electronic polling[4] so that management may gauge and investigate the reasons behind specific responses. Focus groups are used to consult employees on a full range of issues including wages, benefits, quality, cost, and other issues.

Surveys are not conducted regularly. The most recent survey was carried in 1994 on a range of workplace issues. A new survey to measure employee satisfaction will be implemented in 1998.

Communication Meetings. Communication meetings take place at the discretion of the employees. Although these meetings may be sitewide, they usually occur in smaller groups. Participants may include members of Work Area Teams, shopfloor employees, and team leaders.

Acknowledgments

The author is grateful to many individuals in the participating organizations who shall remain anonymous by choice. Excellent research assistance was provided by Manisha Burman and Aileen Cassells.

Notes

1. The term JIC is used here to refer to a genre of employee representation schemes in which a formal representative council is elected by employees. Such forums are not certified as bargaining agents under the law. With only rare exceptions, employers generally play an active role in organizing and supporting these councils. For an example of a long-standing JIC in the petrochemical industry, see the chapter by Taras in this volume.

2. See discussion of NERPs in Kaufman et al. in this volume.

3. All employee groups examined in this chapter were nonunion, and most organizations were mostly nonunion. The exceptions are Firm B, in which I picked a nonunion employee group from a predominantly unionized company, and Firm F, a hospital, in which most employees are unionized with the exception of the reference group, the nursing staff. In both cases, the level of unionization within their industries is very high.

4. Employees in small groups (25–30 each) are brought in for discussion and feedback. Questions are posed to which employees respond with a hand-held wireless remote control switch. The responses are tabulated instantaneously by a computer and flashed on a screen. The results are then discussed by the group. This technique is particularly effective in using the bulk of the time on "why" employees feel the way they do, rather than on the issue of "what" they think, which is done quickly and efficiently with the help of technology.

References

Dachler, Peter H., and Bernard Wilpert. 1978. "Conceptual Dimensions and Boundaries of Participation in Organizations: A Critical Evaluation." *Administrative Science Quarterly* 23, no.1 (March): 1–39.

Jacoby, Sanford. 1985. *Employing Bureaucracy: Managers, Unions and the Transformation of Work in American Industry: 1900–1945.* New York: Columbia University Press.

Jacoby, Sanford, and Anil Verma. 1992. "Enterprise Unions in the Modern Era: A Case Study of Corporate Compensation and Industrial Relations Strategies." *Industrial Relations* 31, no. 1: 137–158.

Kahneman, Daniel, and Amos Tversky. 1979. "Prospect Theory: An Analysis of Decisions Under Risk." *Econometrica* 47: 263–291.

Taras, Daphne Gottlieb, and Jason Copping. 1998. "The Transition from Formal Nonunion Representation to Unionization: A Contemporary Case." *Industrial and Labor Relations Review* 52, no. 1: 22–44.

Whyte, Glen. 1993. "Escalating Commitment in Individual and Group Decision-making: A Prospect Theory Approach." *Organization Behavior and Human Decision Processes* 54: 430–455.

15

Advancing Public-Sector Labor-Management Relations Through Consultation: The Role of the National Joint Council of the Public Service of Canada

Richard P. Chaykowski

The conduct of labor relations in Canada and the United States is typically most closely identified with the contemporary system of collective bargaining. Indeed, in the Canadian federal public service, the right of employees to form unions and engage in collective bargaining originated with the passage of the Public Service Staff Relations Act in 1967. While this represented a major turning point in federal public-service labor relations, it was, in fact, not the beginning of the formal system of industrial relations. Instead, it was a natural extension of what was then a nonunion system of labor and employment relations in the federal public service that had been in existence since the end of World War II and that had a formal arrangement for joint labor-management consultation as its centerpiece. This chapter examines the origins and development of the joint employee-employer council that afforded employees of the Canadian federal government a formal forum for joint consultation with their employer prior to the advent of unionism.

Before the granting of collective bargaining

rights, well-organized staff associations and representatives of the government "as employer" engaged in joint consultations over a wide range of employment and working conditions. Up until World War II, however, this process was somewhat informal. The employee associations typically approached the government "cap in hand" with a view to obtaining whatever improvements the government was disposed to provide. This early form of nonunion representation of federal government employees was therefore relatively ineffective, certainly by contemporary standards, since the government had little incentive to work with the staff associations over difficult (typically distributive) issues.

With some disunity among the ranks of the employee associations regarding the issue of whether to establish an all-inclusive council of associations or separate councils for the larger associations, successive governments were more readily able to put off the idea. Yet, as early as 1926, while briefly in government opposition, Mackenzie King had indicated that he was supportive of the concept of joint councils in the federal civil service—a view that was probably consistent with his broader views on employee representation in labor relations (Barnes 1974, p. 19; Rump 1972, p. 6; Chernow 1998, pp. 581–590). The process of consultation was finally given both form and substance with the establishment of the National Joint Council of the Public Service of Canada (NJC) under a Liberal government led by Mackenzie King. This joint employee-employer council was a bipartite mechanism that was constituted in May 1944 through federal Order-in-Council PC3676, and the NJC has remained active throughout its more than fifty-year history (Rump 1972, p. 8). It has undergone a series of major organizational and operational adjustments during this period, however, partly in response to environmental pressures, and partly in response to many of the perceived shortcomings of the original mechanism. In this regard, the advent of formal unionism and collective bargaining in the federal public service in 1967 was perhaps a watershed event in that it altered the established system of nonunion employment relations, thereby creating a closer correspondence with the broader industrial relations system in place in the private sector. But by then, the joint council had established itself over the period of a quarter century as a viable forum of consultation between employee associations and the government.

Consequently, the development of industrial relations in the Canadian federal public service may usefully be characterized as having evolved through three distinct stages. The first stage spans the period prior to the founding of the NJC in 1944, during which time it was essentially employee associations that took root and began various degrees of consultation with the federal government over employment issues. But at this stage the extent of consultation was limited with

respect to both the scope of issues and degree of influence that the associations actually had on employment outcomes.

The second stage included the period from 1944 through the introduction of collective bargaining rights in 1967. This was a period of consultation that took on several forms, including informal consultations (which had been the case since the turn of the twentieth century), joint committees established by the government and with an advisory role, and the bipartite NJC itself. Clearly, during this period in the development of labor-management relations, the NJC became the centerpiece of an industrial relations system in which associations were the primary (nonunion) form of employee representation and in which the principal focus was consultation. During this second stage in employment relations, the NJC consolidated its position as a formal institutional mechanism and was able to produce tangible improvements in a wide range of terms and conditions of employment. Ironically, the beginning of the NJC era in 1944 also coincided with the introduction of unionism and collective bargaining rights into the Canadian private sector. Thus, at the very time that collective bargaining had become the primary means by which labor relations would be conducted in the private sector, a nonunion joint consultative mechanism became central to the system in the federal public service.

Was the government's interest in joint councils for the federal civil service simply a means for it to mitigate any employee aspirations for unionization? It appears that the government, while perhaps not outwardly resistant to establishing councils during the 1930s, recognized that differences among the associations on the issue of councils allowed it to delay acting more proactively to establish them in the federal civil service, thereby continuing to provide it with a free hand in deciding employment matters

(Chaykowski 1999). However, the timing of the passage of the Order-in-Council establishing the NJC in 1944 suggests that, although the government was in the process of providing the private sector with full collective bargaining rights, the federal civil service was afforded only a half-measure. Even if this "resistance" explanation for the federal government's decision to establish the NJC is accepted, however, it is not inconsistent with a desire to advance genuine cooperation and consultation in the context of the public service.

The third era in industrial relations commenced in 1967 with the beginning of collective bargaining rights in the federal public service. Yet, ultimately, this important development did not completely obviate the need for the NJC. At first, the parties did indeed believe that the NJC would no longer be required—particularly in view of its limitations, relative to collective bargaining, as a means of furthering the terms and conditions of employment. Perhaps the primary drawback of the NJC was that the Treasury Board of Canada, acting for the government as employer, reserved final decision-making power over employment matters. That is, the bipartite agreements reached through consultation at the NJC were not binding on the parties. In addition, the subject matter of consultation through the NJC was circumscribed in important ways; perhaps most critical to the associations was that compensation matters were not subject to joint consultation. In the end, the fundamental power imbalance between the associations and the government "as employer" was underscored by the decision-making authority that the employer reserved unto itself.

Indeed, these limitations had become major issues that reinforced the desire of the staff associations to obtain certification and collective bargaining rights in an effort to obtain outcomes in areas that were previously denied them and to gain greater improvements in areas that were not. In the end, it was clear to the unions that a joint consultative mechanism with these types of limitations was not a sufficiently advantageous substitute for formal unionization and collective bargaining rights. Nevertheless, while collective bargaining did replace the NJC as the centerpiece of the post-1967 system of industrial relations, the NJC ultimately adapted to the new environment and recovered to the point where it served as an important complement to the collective bargaining system. Why was the NJC able to survive?

After 1967, employee associations were converted into formal unions, so they naturally looked to collective bargaining as the primary vehicle for advancing the terms and conditions of employment. While some of the new unions probably flirted with the idea of abandoning their participation in the joint council, they came to realize that collective bargaining had its limitations as well: foremost among these limitations was the government's continued ability, either directly or indirectly, to achieve their desired outcomes by means of "legislative fiat." That is, over time the new unions discovered that collective bargaining rights were not unrestricted (e.g., they could be suspended), were not immune to political considerations (e.g., public perceptions of public-sector earnings levels), and the government stance at the negotiating table could not always be simply disengaged from broader public policy positions (e.g., concern with inflation and accelerating wage demands). In effect, collective bargaining also demonstrated its own limitations as a vehicle for advancing employee interests.

On the other hand, obtaining a resolution to issues that applied across the civil service (i.e., across diverse departments or regions of the country) through joint consultation would be preferable, from the standpoint of both sides, to attempting to negotiate these issues at each of numerous bargaining tables, possibly over successive bargaining rounds. In addition, the NJC afforded the parties an opportunity to consider many issues on an ongoing basis outside of periodic bargaining rounds. In this regard, the value of cooperation itself, fostered through an established and trusted institution, proved of considerable value to both unions and management in achieving mutually advantageous outcomes. The ability of the NJC forum to continue to add value to labor relations was likely dependent upon the fact that the employee side became the "bargaining agent" side, so that unions were involved in both the consultative and collective bargaining dimensions of labor relations and that there was no ongoing form of consultation outside of the unions. In this way, the NJC and collective bargaining emerged more as complements than substitutes.

Clearly, the conduct of industrial relations in the public sector is distinct because of the public good nature of the outputs, the "essential service" aspect of many of the activities and, importantly, the fact that the government assumes the dual roles of conventional management and employer as well as that of a policymaker that can determine both the broader legal framework and the more specific constraints on the system (Swimmer and Thompson 1995, pp. 1–3). Even today, within the Canadian public sector and, in fact, across sectors of the Canadian economy, the extent to which industrial relations is conducted through a combination of a formal sectoral joint council that operates "in parallel" with the conventional system of collective bargaining is unique to the federal public service.[1]

In order to situate the establishment of the NJC in the context of the evolution of federal public-sector employment relations, the chapter continues in the next section with a discussion of the

development of employment relations and representation prior to the founding of the NJC. The third section focuses on the second stage in the development of industrial relations in the Canadian federal public service, including the origins and development of the National Joint Council prior to the establishment of collective bargaining. In the fourth section, I examine the broader development of the relationship between the NJC and collective bargaining as parallel, but related, aspects of labor relations, in order to highlight the recent adaptation of the NJC as a consultative mechanism. In the fifth section, I consider the contemporary industrial relations challenges to the federal public service and the NJC, including the main actors in the system, the conduct of collective bargaining, and public-sector restraint. The final section considers the strengths and value of the NJC as an enduring institutional arrangement for consultation and cooperation in federal public service industrial relations.

Federal Public-Sector Employment Relations Prior to World War II

The Early Progress of Employment Relations and Employee Representation

Interest in collective representation among Canadian federal government employees dates back to the late 1800s. Indeed, some of the earliest public-sector interest in unions developed among postal employees, who were akin to rail employees in their activity in collective action. Early focal points of interest that were specific to federal civil servants included such monetary issues as superannuation and survivor death benefits (Rump 1939a; 1939b; 1939c).

The first major civil service umbrella organizations had formed by the early 1900s and included the Civil Service Association of Canada and the Civil Service Association of Ottawa. These two major organizations joined with some twenty-one others (e.g., customs and excise employees) in 1909 to form a broader umbrella organization named the Civil Service Federation of Canada (Johnston 1953; Rump 1939c). In 1920, the Professional Institute of the Public Service of Canada (PIPSC) was formed among scientific and professional employees, followed in 1921 by the formation of the Amalgamated Civil Servants of Canada, which was originally formed around a core of postal employees.[2]

From the outset, these associations began to evolve along both "industrial" and "regional/craft" lines. In the former situation, associations would organize workers in a particular department (such as postal workers or customs and excise workers, respectively) but who were employed across Canada. In the latter case, in an association such as the Civil Service Association of Ottawa, workers tended to be employed across departments, but membership was limited to the Ottawa region, while the PIPSC confined itself to organizing professionals and scientists. As the associations grew alongside the expansion of the civil service, they vied for members and eventually for jurisdiction, particularly in the core area of Ottawa. This contributed to a degree of disunity among the associations that, at times, hindered them in their submissions to the government.

Thus, prior to the establishment of the NJC in 1944, employees in the Canadian civil service were typically represented by a growing number of associations. While these associations were not certified as bargaining agents and had no formal bargaining rights, they nonetheless represented their members through consultations with the government over employment matters.

On the employer side, during this period the personnel management of the federal civil service was conducted through the Civil Service Commission (CSC). The CSC was established in 1908 under the Civil Service Amendment Act, following the recommendation of a Royal Commission on the matter (Hodgets et al. 1972, p. 26). The central element of management practice at this time was the administration of a "merit system" for the management of the civil service.[3] The CSC had a broad range of responsibilities, including the organization of the civil service, classification, and recruitment and selection (Hodgets et al. 1972, pp. 56–57). In other matters related, for example, to compensation, the government of the day could direct the CSC to proceed on a matter.

During this period, the associations made representations to the government, primarily on an issue-by-issue, ad hoc basis. During these early years, salary increases were naturally a major issue for the associations. For example, in 1924 the associations demanded that civil service salaries be adjusted; among the most militant were the postal union associations, which ultimately engaged in a strike to back their demands (Hodgets et al. 1972, pp. 121–127). In general, however, the positions of the associations were weakly represented to the government, for several reasons: first, the associations represented only roughly 50 percent of all employees; and second, the lack of organizational unity in their representations to the government was exacerbated by ongoing interorganizational rivalries (Hodgets et al. 1972, pp. 174–175, 195). Moreover, throughout the period up to World War II, at the level of individual employees there was essentially no viable formal appeal mechanism (e.g., boards) available (Hodgets et al. 1972, pp. 172–174, 178–180). In this context, the associations began to observe the tangible progress in labor relations that was occurring elsewhere (especially in the British civil service) and appreciate the value of a formal consultative mechanism.

Evolution Toward a Joint Council in the Federal Civil Service

The concept of an industrial council in the public service originated in Britain around World War I with the efforts of John Whitley, who chaired a government-appointed industrial relations committee (the Committee on Relations between Employers and Employed, or "Whitley Committee") that had recommended that industrial councils be established across industries (Barnes 1974, pp. 7–8). Although the government originally resisted this idea for the public service, in 1919 it finally yielded:

> The staff associations maintained their pressure on the government and in March 1919 the Cabinet gave its approval to a plan for a National Joint Council for the non-industrial civil service with associated departmental and local councils but again as consultative bodies only. (Barnes 1974, p. 12)

Importantly, these Whitley Councils, as they came to be known, were vested with executive powers. This was an exceptional development then and remained so because it conferred on Whitley Councils a degree of independent authority; that is, decisions jointly agreed to by both sides of the Whitley Council were meant to be binding on the government of the day (Hodgets et al. 1972, p. 194).

In Canada, industrial councils emerged by the end of World War I in such industries as clothing, construction, railways, and autos (ILR 1921, p. 57). The first industrial council in a Canadian public service was created in Saskatchewan in 1920, but its role was limited to that of a consultative body that made recommendations to the government (ILR 1921, p. 60). Despite a growing interest in councils among the associations in the Canadian civil service, the federal government continued to resist the idea of a Whitley Council, with their position being facilitated by conflicting positions among the associations themselves. In particular, the PIPSC initially failed to support the idea of a joint council with broad association membership in favor its own separate council with the government.[4] But by 1928, the idea finally surfaced in Parliament in the form of a (private member) bill that favored the idea of a National Joint Council for the public service; although a joint labor-management drafting committee was subsequently struck in 1930 to develop a constitution, its mandate ended when the King government of the day fell (Barnes 1974, pp. 19–23; Rump 1972, p. 8; Frankel 1956, p. 509; Knowles 1955b, p. 6).

While in the following years the idea of a National Joint Council languished somewhat on the agenda of policymakers, a major development occurred when a unified position among the staff associations in favor of a National Joint Council finally emerged. Whereas in earlier years the Professional Institute of the Public Service of Canada had formally expressed reservations about the concept, by the end of the 1930s the PIPSC was firmly in support of it (Chaykowski 1999).

In addition, by wartime, pressures on the economy led the government to adopt a policy of support for labor-management negotiations and cooperation in the private sector in order to avoid costly disputes (Rump 1972, p. 8). An active government policy on labor relations was clearly required in the wartime circumstances, just as it was in the United States. In this context, the government increasingly felt that requests by its own employees for a joint council could less readily be set aside—and the government essentially found itself drawn along in the same direction as the policy it advocated for the private sector (Barnes 1974, p. 27). Finally, after successive attempts by the staff associations to convince the governments of the day that it was a desirable advancement of labor relations, a joint labor-management council was finally founded in 1944:

> The general purpose of the national joint council will be to secure a greater measure of cooperation between the state in its capacity as employer and the general body of the civil servants in matters affecting the civil service. (Ilsley 1944b, p. 779)

The specific purposes of the council were to improve efficiency, improve employee welfare, provide a means for addressing grievances, and facilitate the exchange of views (Ilsley 1944b, p. 779). The Canadian NJC differed from the British model in several important ways, however. First, it had no executive decision-making powers; instead, its mandate was to advise (Ilsley 1944b, p. 779). That is, the NJC was to function by consulting on matters in order to make recommendations to the government, but which the government was not bound to follow.

Second, the Canadian NJC was structured as a national council only, whereas in the British system complementary councils had been established at the local and establishment levels (Barnes 1974, p. 9). From an institutional standpoint, the Canadian model limited the extent of consultation and cooperation in the industrial relations system to matters that were themselves national in scope.

Third, whereas the Canadian council could not consult over matters related to compensation, the British council could (Barnes 1974). In fact, in setting up the NJC, the government was clear in its intention not to confer any powers on the NJC that could in any way limit the authority of the

government or of Parliament (Hodgets et al. 1972, p. 194). This was especially evident in the domain of compensation. In this area, the government steadfastly retained all authority until collective bargaining was introduced. In turn, this policy increasingly led to frustration among the associations and eventually became a major factor in motivating the associations to obtain bargaining rights.

The Development of the NJC as the Centerpiece of Employment Relations, 1944–1966

Membership Developments in the NJC Prior to Collective Bargaining

The original NJC consisted of eight representatives from both the "official" and "staff" sides (Ilsley 1944a; 1944b). In the 1944–67 period, the most significant changes in the composition of the NJC arose on the employee side, particularly in the years leading just up to 1967. The story of the evolution of the employee-side members is rooted in the development of the labor movement itself. On the staff side, among the original founding members, the largest staff associations were the Civil Service Federation (around 40,000 members) and the Amalgamated Civil Servants of Canada (roughly 6,000 members). Taken together, the original staff associations accounted for roughly 55,000 employees (Chaykowski 1999). Among the major original NJC members, the Civil Service Federation (founded in 1909) and the Amalgamated Civil Servants of Canada (founded later in 1921) had begun overtures to consider unity by the early 1940s.[5] But the merger floundered in part because the former was largely organized along departmental lines, while the Amalgamated Civil Servants was organized within occupations—and both declined to defer to the structure of the other in forming a combined organization.[6]

Through the 1950s, the Civil Service Federation (CSFC) experienced its own internal problems. One of its key members, the Civil Service Federation of Ottawa (CSAO), was actually organized along occupational lines with its membership concentrated in the Ottawa region. However, considerable growth in the member units of the federation had begun to occur outside Ottawa and throughout Canada, but this growth was organized along departmental lines. Following a jurisdictional dispute between the CSAO and the CSFC, the former was eventually ejected from the CSFC.[7] Meanwhile, the Civil Service Federation of Ottawa and the Amalgamated Civil Servants of Canada had begun to explore merger possibilities, which eventually resulted in a successful merger in 1956 that created the Civil Service Association of Canada.[8]

Ultimately, the prospect of collective bargaining in 1967 impelled the larger staff organizations to consider further consolidation. In this way, the Public Service Alliance of Canada was created in 1966 from the merger, in part, of the Civil Service Association of Canada and the Civil Service Federation (Chaykowski 1999). Thus there was considerable change in the makeup of the staff association membership of the NJC. Interestingly, although the PSAC ultimately became the overwhelmingly largest union member on the NJC, it maintained only one seat on the council at par with the other, much smaller, unions.

The evolution of the employer side was somewhat different. Although the official-side members were drawn from various government departments, the real power was concentrated at the Treasury Board.

The NJC's Early Achievements Amid Unmet Expectations

The NJC functioned as a consultative forum, in which the associations typically brought issues to the table to discuss with government representatives. The NJC essentially operated by consensus, so that joint recommendations were then forwarded to the government for consideration. However, since most employment issues discussed had some fiscal dimension (e.g., length of the workweek, benefit plans, health and safety issues), in practice all recommendations ultimately had to be approved by the Treasury Board before they could subsequently be implemented by the Civil Service Commission, Treasury Board, or Governor General in Council—each of which had different administrative responsibilities (Frankel 1956, p. 514).[9] In effect, this made the Treasury Board the most powerful employer-side representative on the NJC.

Since the NJC operated by consensus, difficult issues could take considerable time to resolve. Once achieved, NJC recommendations were nonbinding on the government. In practice, as the work of the NJC proceeded and it matured as an institutional arrangement, the government tended to regard these recommendations seriously, particularly since they were the outcome of a joint process. Moreover, the government itself typically had a stake in fostering effective consultation with a view to enhancing labor relations and the effective operation of the civil service. Even so, the government often favored proceeding incrementally on recommendations that involved substantive change.

Depending on the particular issue at hand, the government of the day generally considered several key (and sometimes interrelated) elements in considering whether or not to accept NJC recommendations:[10] first, the government sometimes considered current employment norms in the private sector, with a view to providing comparable employment conditions (however, the governments preference was to "follow" developments in the private sector and to avoid "leading"); second, the government would consider the efficiency of operations and the direct costs of the proposals; and third, the government always attempted to assess the potential for any public inconvenience and, more generally, to gauge public opinion in the matter.

Throughout the 1944 to 1967 period, the NJC considered a range of issues, for the most part quite successfully. The issues addressed spanned the spectrum from health and safety issues (e.g., office working conditions, electrical safety, construction safety), to technological change, to the establishment of medical plans, to the introduction of cafeterias. Two of the most contentious issues before the NJC during this period included the attempt to move from a five-and-a-half-day workweek (of forty-four hours) to a five-day week (of forty hours) and the introduction of premiums for overtime pay, both in the 1950s (Barnes 1974, pp. 64–66, 85). Another major achievement for the staff associations occurred in 1953 when, through the NJC, they won the right to ("voluntary revocable") membership dues deduction, which in turn secured the financial strength of these organizations (Barnes 1974, p. 60).

As the first era of the NJC drew to a close, several fundamental institutional limitations of the NJC became apparent (Frankel 1956; Edwards 1974; Barnes 1974). Within the NJC, there was an ongoing risk of interorganizational differences that made the work of the NJC and the operationalization of its recommendations a challenge. The associations themselves often represented a diverse set of constituents with different objectives; while on the employer side, the Civil Service Commission, Treasury Board, and Governor General in Council each had administrative roles. While the issue of organizational diversity on the joint council is somewhat particular to the NJC, several other limitations are more prevalent among nonunion forms of employee representation. First, the associations had often observed lengthy periods of time (often marked by delays or, in the limit, by a temporary rejection) between the submission of a recommendation to the government and the time at which it was finally implemented. Importantly, in the case of an impasse within the NJC, there was no dispute-resolution mechanism and NJC recommendations, once achieved, were not binding on the government. Finally, once implemented in the civil service, there existed no formal grievance mechanism. Thus, employees could not seek redress when NJC policies accepted by the government failed to be implemented at the workplace level. Another major limitation of the NJC was the complete exclusion of areas related to compensation from its purview.

As the 1960s began, the pressure for the introduction of collective representation and bargaining rights in provincial civil services and broader public sectors had gained considerable momentum and substance. In this context, the federal civil service associations began to look to collective bargaining as the avenue by which the limitations imposed by the NJC mechanism could finally be eliminated.

The Advent of Collective Bargaining and the Evolution of Complementarity with the NJC

The Introduction of Collective Bargaining in the Federal Civil Service: The New Context for the NJC

During the 1950s and early 1960s, the employee associations had become increasingly dissatisfied with the limitations of consultation in improving the terms and conditions of employment. At the same time, labor policy toward the issue of granting collective bargaining had shifted across the public and quasi-public sectors, so that these rights were being considered for employees of the government administration in the provincial jurisdictions as well as for employees of the growing health and education sectors.

Set against this backdrop, in 1965 the federal government struck the influential Heeney Committee with a view to preparing the public service for the right of employees to form unions and bargain collectively with the government. Employees in the federal public service were granted the right to form unions and to bargain collectively in 1967 under the Public Service Staff Relations Act. As a result, employees who had previously been represented by staff associations were essentially converted into formal unions, while employees who had not previously been members of associations were almost immediately organized, typically by the largest of the newly formed unions (i.e.,

Public Service Alliance of Canada). Some certification applications did require extended board hearings; however, in other cases, smaller unions (e.g., Merchant Service Guild) vied for members with the Public Service Alliance of Canada. The act provided for the creation of the Public Service Staff Relations Board to oversee the establishment of bargaining units along occupational lines and the conduct of collective bargaining (Finkelman and Goldenberg 1983; Finkelman 1974).

Several areas of the terms and conditions of employment were not subject to collective bargaining (i.e., are excluded areas), such as matters relating to layoffs, promotions, or job classifications (see Ponak and Thompson 1995, p. 431). Outside of collective bargaining, there are also a range of issues that may be subject to formal labor-management consultation through the NJC.

At the time of the original act, the Treasury Board was designated as the "virtual employer" for purposes of collective bargaining. Since then, several other separate employers have been designated although, taken together, their bargaining unit employment remained quite small (at 7,200 in 1996) relative to that of the Treasury Board (at 191,000 in 1996). Separate employer designation only began to occur following the introduction of collective bargaining rights so that, although the Treasury Board clearly dominated, the number of employers on the NJC still increased. By 1984, the number of employers totaled four, and by 1994 it had increased to six, although the composition changed in the intervening years. Even so, over the years the number of individual unions typically greatly exceeded the number of individual employers. Indeed, the number of staff associations (and later unions) changed substantially over time (Chaykowski 1999).

The Functioning of the NJC in the Era of Collective Bargaining

Up to 1967, with the advancement of employment relations focused on consultation, the NJC had considered an impressive range of employment matters and gradually built a track record of achievement that included a regular means of formal (and informal) consultation that, for the most part, resulted in higher levels of communication and trust than would otherwise have evolved. While the staff associations were clearly frustrated by the limitations of the consultative process (e.g., the nonbinding nature of agreements; the exclusion of pay as a subject for the NJC), it nonetheless served to build a series of what were essentially nonadversarial labor-management relationships. Thus the conduct of labor relations may be characterized as one of "restrained accommodation."

Nevertheless, policymakers and associations alike appeared to have expected the role of the NJC to become much more circumscribed in the new era of collective bargaining, but that the NJC would continue to be of value in assisting with servicewide issues (Heeney Committee 1965, p. 40). In the mid-1960s, association (and subsequently union) expectations surrounding the introduction of collective bargaining were high. Partly this was due to the formation of the large and potentially very powerful Public Service Alliance of Canada, but also because the scope of—and prospect for gains in—employment outcomes under a system of collective bargaining appeared to be substantially greater. Moreover, this view appeared to rest largely on the belief that the government's power to decide the terms and conditions of employment unilaterally would finally be limited (Edwards 1966).[11]

Since 1967, the unions and designated employers engaged in numerous rounds of collective bargaining. The conduct of collective bargaining in the federal public service has clearly been "traditional" (Cappelli et al. 1997; Chaykowski and Verma 1992; Kochan, Katz, and McKersie 1986): the parties have typically been adversarial in their approaches; the focus has been on traditional objectives associated with job control unionism (e.g., a focus on wages and job-security issues); and there have been clearly separated roles for management and labor along with complex, yet standardized, rules for workplace governance. The adversarialism has been manifested in conflict through strike action on the union side as well as by legislatively imposed restraints on the employer side. The results of these particular actions have often been further animosity and mistrust.

Given this type of collective bargaining experience, and in view of the centrality of collective bargaining to the industrial relations system in the post-1967 period, it is perhaps not surprising, then, that "spillover" developed between collective bargaining and the consultative process of the NJC. Aside from any effects of formal bargaining on the degree of formality and accommodation in the conduct of consultation at the NJC, by the 1980s the union had also resorted to taking some issues, on which little progress had been achieved at the NJC, over to the bargaining table in order to leverage better outcomes (Chaykowski 1999). This clearly had the effect of straining the NJC as an institution. Despite these challenges to the NJC, the institution survived and adapted, so that labor relations was conducted through the parallel avenues of collective bargaining, on the one hand, and consultation through the NJC, on the other hand.

Building from its base of achievement in the 1944–67 period, the NJC further advanced the employment relations agendas of the parties during the period that began with the introduction of collective bargaining rights. Examples of some of the major achievements during this period included:

- The establishment of comprehensive health care plans (e.g., dental plans); and improvements in group hospital insurance plans.
- Progressive improvements in the cost-sharing arrangements for the premiums associated with the various plans.
- The expansion of the coverage of these plans to nonstandard employees (e.g., extension of the Disability Insurance Plan to part-time employees in 1981; extension of the Dental Care Plan to seasonal employees in 1987).
- Introduction of new allowances (e.g., for provision of first aid to the public).

Other workplace issues that emerged in the 1980s and were considered at the NJC included the impacts of technological change (e.g., health and safety effects of VDTs) and AIDS in the workplace, the provision of day care, and the reintegration of disabled workers into the workforce (Chaykowski 1999). The achievements therefore encompassed most nonwage aspects of the employment relationship. The cumulative improvements in working conditions and in the monetary value of various benefits were substantial and, taken together, illustrate the significant gains that were achievable outside the collective bargaining sphere.

Stresses Leading to a Growing Interface Between the NJC and Collective Bargaining Process

Despite these achievements, several major shortcomings of the NJC persisted, including the oftentimes long delays in achieving the outcomes desired by the unions, the lack of a binding dispute-resolution process in cases where an agreement between labor and management could not be achieved through consultation, and the limited scope for the purview of the NJC (Chaykowski 1999; Barnes 1974; Frankel 1956). These shortcomings were to surface in a concrete manner around consultations over several specific issues. More importantly, the resolution of these issues served as catalysts for institutional reform of the NJC and to better define the interrelationship between the process of consultation through the NJC and the conduct of collective bargaining.

The first of these issues related to language policy. Both parties had worked hard in the early 1970s to provide a framework within which government departments could implement the new official policy on (French and English) bilingualism in the public service. This new policy, which was contained in NJC Directives, provided for what was essentially a language-skill bonus for employees (referred to as a "bilingualism bonus"). When the government unilaterally announced in August of 1978 that it intended to cancel the bonus, however, it provoked a major crisis in confidence in the NJC, since the union side immediately understood that NJC Directives were not legally enforceable and that this action could lead to further arbitrary government action (Chaykowski 1999).

Clearly, it would be in the best interests of the unions to consider the use of collective bargaining over all issues if agreements achieved through consultation were subject to unilateral cancellation. However, this crisis had the benefit of reinforcing the determination of the union side to introduce NJC bylaws that included a grievance procedure over NJC directives as well as a process for referring items on the NJC table over to collective bargaining.[12] The parties agreed, by a Memorandum of Understanding, that an agreed-upon list of NJC directives were to be "considered" as part of the collective agreements; contracts would be amended to include a clause that recognized this status. The result was that these items gained the force and protection of a contract clause.[13]

Several other issues led to further changes in the NJC. First, a protracted dispute over parking policies in the late 1970s, essentially over what amounted to the provision of space to employees in one area of the capitol, was finally resolved when the parties agreed to break the impasse in consultation over the issue by submitting it to a third party for mediation. This marked a turning point in the way that such impasses were handled at the NJC.

Subsequently, during the late 1980s, the issue of allowances for uniform cleaning came before the NJC for consideration. Part of the agreed-upon process was to have surveys of employer practices, in this regard, conducted. After several years of consideration, however, in which the employer effectively "stonewalled" on the issue by requesting further surveys (largely on technical grounds), the union side had decided that the existing impasse resolution machinery was clearly inadequate. Largely as a result of this experience, the NJC developed a process by which the parties could agree, in advance, on binding arbitration in the event of an impasse on new NJC issues that came before the council. But this still left open the door to opting out of the arbitration alternative.

Indeed, throughout the post-1967 period, the NJC continued to demonstrate several strengths. First, its national coverage afforded it the ability to address servicewide issues successfully; for the employer, this avoided the prospect of bargaining separately over issues that would otherwise have been prone to whipsawing across bargaining tables; on their part, the unions saw added advantage in being able to standardize a variety of employment conditions through consultations at one table. Second, the agreements achieved through consultation carried with them a high degree of credibility for both parties. In the long run, this proved to be one of the most enduring, if not the most significant, advantages of the NJC (Chaykowski 1999).

The NJC in the 1990s

The Contemporary Structure and Operation of the NJC

The National Joint Council continues to consist of representatives from the union and employer sides. The council itself has an employer-side chair and two vice chairs, while the bargaining agent side has one co-chair and two vice co-chairs. The council members are drawn from the respective designated employers from the government and the unions. The ongoing decision-making authority of the NJC is effected through a joint Executive Committee that was formed in 1970 and subsequently given the authority to resolve impasses in 1987.[14] Eventually, impasses could be sent to a third party for mediation.

The ongoing work of the NJC is regularly conducted through a large number of joint working committees (e.g., Office Technology; Union-Management Relations; Employment Equity; Health Insurance Programs; Occupational Safety and Health; Government Travel; Employee Assistance Program; Official Languages; and Work Force Adjustment). The number and scope of these activities has increased over time as new issues have emerged and as the breadth of NJC activities has expanded. These working committees convey formal reports and decisions reached by consensus, or the nature of impasses, back to the NJC Executive Committee/Council. The actual operation of the NJC and coordination of its activities are conducted through the office of a general secretary, which was made full-time in 1979 in order to deal with the increasing activity of the NJC.[15]

One of the most important aspects of the NJC is that agreements reached are given effect through "directives" that form regulations that govern the workplace. Misapplications of these directives are grievable under an NJC grievance procedure that is separate and distinct from the grievance procedure established through a collective agreement. The NJC grievance procedure essentially follows a standard three-stage sequential process, but with several important differences (Chaykowski 1999).

First, the highest step at the unit level (e.g., within a government department) is a Departmental Liaison Officer (DLO), after which the grievance is typically referred by the general secretary to a standing (working) committee of the NJC for their consideration (e.g., a health issue would be referred to the Occupational Safety and Health Committee of the NJC). Once the committee forms a report, the grievance is forwarded to the Executive Committee of the NJC for consideration. The grievance may be sent directly to the Executive Committee in cases where a resolution may be readily obtained (essentially on the basis of past case decisions).

Once a decision is rendered through the NJC machinery it must then be conveyed back to the unit-level DLO, who in turn informs the grievor; this last procedure is required because the NJC executive is not considered an employer for purposes of the PSSRA. Of course, all unfavorable decisions are subject to binding third-party adjudication. Importantly, the NJC grievance procedure specifically allows for consideration of policy "intent," which opens up considerable latitude in scope for resolving a grievance (Chaykowski 1999).

The Actors and Scope of the Employers and Unions in the Federal Public Service[16]

Within the federal public service, the Treasury Board of Canada is the largest single employer. In 1996, total employment (including full-time and all nonstandard employees) was just over 200,000, of which roughly 190,000 were included in bargaining units. In fact, from 1985 through the 1990s, the proportion of employees with Treasury Board as employer who were also covered under a collective agreement has remained at about 90 percent. In 1996, Treasury Board alone bargained with fourteen major unions in seventy-eight bargaining units. There are also several other smaller designated employers in the federal public service so that taken together (in 1996), there were a total of ninety-nine bargaining units covering just over 190,000 employees in the public service.[17] Clearly, the Treasury Board is the dominant employer and negotiations with the Treasury Board sets the pattern in the federal public service. These employers all have a seat on the NJC.

On the union side, there are fourteen members of the NJC. By far, the largest union is the Public Service Alliance of Canada (PSAC). The PSAC was formed in 1966 in anticipation of the establishment of collective bargaining in 1967. By the 1990s, its membership was roughly 160,000. The PSSRA had essentially mandated that the new bargaining units in the public service were to be organized along (approximately eighty) occupational lines (Connell 1973, p. 48; Finkelman 1974, p. 4). Thus, while the PSAC is administratively organized along departmental lines, the bargaining units for the workers that it represents are organized along occupational lines.[18] The organization of employees under the PSAC has been confined exclusively to the federal public service, and it remains one of the top ten unions in Canada in terms of size.

The second largest union is the Professional Institute of the Public Service of Canada (PIPSC), whose membership in the 1990s was around 33,000. While the membership of the PIPSC has remained focused on professional and scientific employees of the federal government since it was founded in 1920, in 1982 the PIPSC began to organize workers outside the federal public service.[19]

Therefore, the members of the two largest unions (the PSAC and PIPSC), which taken together account for roughly three-quarters of total employment in the public service, are covered by the NJC. The remaining unions tend to be much smaller in membership. There are around a dozen other unions active in the federal public service and that have membership in the NJC. They have typically organized employees across a range of more specific occupational groups that reflects particular activities of the federal government, although the public service membership levels are small relative to the PSAC and PIPSC. For example, two private-sector unions, the Canadian Merchant Service Guild and the IBEW, have both organized public-service employees, each with around 2,500 members, under the Treasury Board as employer.[20]

Key Developments and the Challenges of the 1990s

The federal public service of Canada represents the largest individual component of federal government employment—as well as the single largest source of civilian employment in Canada. Considering the period from 1976 through 1996, bargaining unit employment as a whole increased from around 230,000 to a peak of just over 250,000 in 1981; bargaining unit employment then declined sharply to just over 200,000 in 1982, after which it fluctuated in the range of 200,000 to 217,000 until 1995; after 1995, bargaining unit employment levels again declined to just under 200,000.[21] This recent decline was the result of a concerted government effort to reduce the size of the public service.

Indeed, by the 1970s, the federal government had recognized that restraint in the public service (e.g., wage and employment restraints) was, at least politically, an important element of the government's strategy in an era of public-sector retrenchment. This set the context for changes in broader employment levels and, particularly, later attempts to reduce the size of the federal public service (Swimmer 1995).

The employment developments of the past several decades have been reflected in the membership levels of the major unions—particularly the significant program to cut employment that occurred in the early 1990s. For example, membership in the PSAC increased from just over 150,000 in 1977 to a peak of around 180,000 in the mid-1980s before declining to the 160,000 range thereafter. Similarly, membership in the PIPSC increased steadily from just over 15,000 in the late 1970s to a peak of just under 35,000 in 1993 before declining modestly through 1996.

Not surprisingly then, one of the longer-run issues that began to receive greater attention at the NJC was the issue of job security. As early as 1975, the announcement of government cutbacks gave rise to the formation of an NJC committee that began to consult over the job-security issue.[22]

Thus, by the end of the 1970s, the key issues of advance notice, retraining, and employment security had already emerged (Chaykowski 1999). By the 1980s, a comprehensive Workforce Adjustment Directive had been established through the NJC that addressed many of these concerns. However, in the context of significant government cutbacks in the 1990s, union concerns over job security became a key issue in the federal public-service strike of 1991.

By the 1990s, the issue of the unions taking issues over to the bargaining table remained unresolved. While the PSAC had essentially done this in the 1980s in order to obtain improvements in their dental plan, the key issue in the 1990s was job security. Although some agreement over a revised Workforce Adjustment Directive had been obtained at the NJC prior to the end of the 1991 round of collective bargaining, the PSAC found this agreement unacceptable. Instead, the PSAC moved the issue of job security over to the bargaining table —where it remained as a central issue through the course of a twenty-five-day strike. Importantly, the PSAC had initially included the PIPSC in these discussions over job security, but at the final stages of the negotiations the PIPSC was excluded and the PSAC obtained a final agreement on job security on its own. The fallout was increased strain on the relationship between these two unions, and further revisions to the structure of the NJC that ensured that all decision-making bodies (e.g., the Executive Committee) would have more than one union representative on them to ensure that no one union could make agreements on behalf of all others (Chaykowski 1999).

The 1991 strike ended with the employees legislated back to work and the PSAC successfully negotiating a series of improvements around job security that, taken together, virtually provided full employment security for permanent employees (e.g., guaranteed offer of alternative employment in the public service; enhanced advance notice; and salary protection if moved to a lower-paying job). But the PSAC did not include this agreement in the new contract. Instead, they "moved" it back to the NJC, where it was jointly approved by the council (Chaykowski 1999). Apparently, the link between the NJC and collective bargaining could flow both ways.

Several outstanding challenges continued to confront the parties as well as the viability of the NJC as a consultative mechanism. First, there continued to be some interorganization strain among the unions. Clearly, one recent source of this tension was the action of the PSAC vis-à-vis the PIPSC in excluding them over the job-security negotiations in 1991. A longer-run issue for the PSAC is raiding; they have already lost some employee groups. The PSAC believes that it could avoid the free-riding of other, smaller, breakaway unions (that subsequently gain an NJC seat) by withdrawing from the NJC and possibly consulting with the employer side on their own. Whether or not this occurs in the future will depend to a large extent on whether the various unions can adhere to a no-raid agreement.

Concluding Remarks

The NJC emerged at around the time that the government created a comprehensive framework for establishing collective bargaining rights for private-sector employees in Canada. In the private sector, the Canadian federal legislation that established the pattern for industrial relations was directly inspired by the American Wagner Act. At about the same time as this was occurring, however, the consultative mechanism of the NJC, which was to come to form the centerpiece of industrial relations in the federal civil service, was the offspring of quite a different institutional arrangement generated by the British industrial relations system. Indeed, Canadian industrial relations have historically been influenced by industrial relations developments in both the United States and Great Britain, and arguably, along some dimensions, the Canadian system is a hybrid of both countries' experiences.

Initially, the NJC afforded the government the opportunity to facilitate increased cooperation with employees and good relations regarding matters of employment, while avoiding the extension of full bargaining rights. For employees and their associations, it formalized joint consultation and provided a concrete, albeit imperfect, mechanism to seek improvements in their terms and conditions of employment. But over time, as an industrial relations institution that was constrained to its original advisory role, the NJC appeared increasingly limited in its capacity to deliver outcomes that met the full expectations of the employee side, especially as the associations and their members saw collective bargaining rights expanded over time in the broader public sector.

Would the employee associations have pressed for bargaining rights had the authority of the NJC been extended beyond its original mandate (to serve in an advisory capacity) to include decision-making powers? This issue of the extent of decision-making authority remains at the heart of the success or failure of most forms of nonunion employee consultation mechanisms. In the private sector, firms are reluctant to relinquish managerial authority to joint labor-management bodies, but sometimes do so in limited ways (e.g., to joint health and safety committees). But in the public government sector, vesting a joint council with executive powers over matters with budget-

ary implications could infringe on basic government authority—something the minister of finance responsible for the formation of the NJC noted early on that the government would never permit (Ilsley 1944b, p. 779). Apparently, there was no prospect of extending the authority of the NJC.

With the arrival of collective bargaining in the federal public service in 1967, the NJC's future naturally appeared to be in jeopardy, even though the employee side of the NJC was now composed of unions instead of what were once employee associations. The new unions perceived the collective bargaining framework as having an absolute advantage over a consultative mechanism that was limited to an advisory capacity. Yet, since the establishment of collective bargaining rights in the federal public sector, its limitations have also emerged and become quite apparent to the unions. Perhaps the most important of these is the tendency of the government to either suspend collective bargaining altogether (as it did from 1982 to 1984 through the Public Sector Compensation Restraint Act) or to impose settlements (as it did in 1991 with wages) (Swimmer 1995). Gaining the right to bargain collectively was a considerable advance, but collective bargaining in the federal civil service was limited in ways similar to public-sector bargaining elsewhere.

The NJC appears to have endured as a viable form of nonunion employee representation precisely because it has demonstrated some comparative advantages, relative to collective bargaining, in achieving certain employment outcomes. It has provided a constructive forum for consultation that yielded both substantive and process outcomes. In the area of substantive outcomes, joint consultation through the NJC has yielded gains in both working conditions and benefits and has proven to be an useful forum to address issues that apply across the civil service for which obtaining agreement through joint consultation is preferable, from the standpoint of both sides, to negotiating such issues at each of numerous individual bargaining tables. But perhaps most impressive has been the value of joint consultation in the broader sense of advancing cooperative relations, which the parties value as an important process outcome. By focussing on the shared interests of the parties, the consultation process at the NJC has essentially operated on many of the same principles as interest-based bargaining.[23] In contrast, the collective bargaining process remains adversarial and mired in traditional positional approaches to the issues on the table. While the NJC provided a valuable consultative forum for associations and subsequently for unions, it also did so for the employer. Ultimately, the success of the NJC has depended upon the desire and efforts of both sides, and the strengths of the NJC have matured as the mechanism has evolved and been adapted by the parties.

One of the major impediments to the coexistence of consultation and collective bargaining turned on defining the institutional inter-relationships between the two systems. Over time, various critical issues arose that forced the parties to either define, and then often later redefine, the rules and regulations that govern their inter-relationship. It is because the two parties have, so far, been able to accomplish this successfully that the two systems appear to have emerged as complements to each other. Plausibly, together they provide a more comprehensive system for the conduct of labor relations in the federal public service. Functionally reconciling the operation of cooperative mechanisms with formal collective bargaining is likely to be an important consideration in private-sector attempts to introduce cooperative arrangements into a unionized setting.

Acknowledgments

This chapter is based on research conducted as part of a larger project on the development of the National Joint Council. The author gratefully acknowledges the support of the National Joint Council of the Public Service of Canada for facilitating the archival research in this project. The author also acknowledges the benefit of helpful comments and suggestions from Des Davidge and Bruce Kaufman.

Notes

1. The federal government has sponsored numerous human resource sectoral councils. In unionized private-sector industries, the councils bring together management and unions to consult over issues such as the provision of training or employee dislocation (Gunderson and Sharpe 1998). The parties do not negotiate over issues, however, and where joint activities are undertaken, they typically function at the industry level and apart from the firm level and associated collective agreements. In some industries (e.g., mining), the activities of the sectoral council are linked to the workplace level (Chaykowski 1999).

2. See F. Knowles (1955a, 1958).

3. In establishing a "merit system" the government (as employer) had been concerned with the elimination of patronage, unbiased selection, and the application of "scientific management" methods (see Hodgets et al. 1972, pp. 56–57).

4. See *Journal of the Professional Institute of the Civil Service of Canada* 22 (March 1943): 56.

5. Ibid., p. 58. See also Johnston (1953).

6. See F. Knowles (1956b).

7. See *Civil Service News*, December 1954, p. 5.

8. See *Canadian Civil Servant*, December 1956, p. 2; April 1958, p. 6.

9. Of these three bodies, it was the Civil Service Commission that was responsible for operationalizing most issues because of its personnel management function.

10. See *Journal of the Professional Institute of the Civil Service of Canada* 31 (June 1952): 129–131.

11. However, what was not foreseen was the potential for and, in time the willingness of, future governments essentially to legislate the outcomes it desired.

12. Prior to the bilingualism bonus crisis, the parties had already been consulting with a view to creating such bylaws.

13. The Memorandum of Understanding also provided a means for the resolution of impasses over which particular NJC items should actually be "referred" to the collective agreement.

14. See National Joint Council 1981. See also *Minutes of the 175th Meeting of the Administrative Committee of the NJC*, February 19, 1987.

15. See National Joint Council. See also *Minutes of the 230th Meeting of the NJC*, September 8, 1977.

16. See *Employment Statistics for the Federal Public Service* (various years); see also *Public Service Staff Relations Board Annual Report* (various years). See also Chaykowski (1999).

17. In 1996 these smaller designated employers included the Medical Research Council (with 1 bargaining unit of 22 employees), the National Research Council (with 12 bargaining units covering 2,758 employees), the Office of the Auditor General (with 4 bargaining units covering 254 employees), and the Office of the Superintendent of Financial Institutions (with 4 bargaining units covering 336 employees).

18. When the PSAC was formed in July of 1966, in anticipation of the imminent establishment of collective bargaining rights, it was essentially formed by the unification of two major staff associations. One of the two associations (the Civil Service Federation of Canada) had organized employees across occupations within a department, so its components were essentially departmental. In contrast, the second founding member of the PSAC—and a previous rival of the Federation—the Civil Service Association of Canada, was organized along occupational lines, as its membership was concentrated primarily in the capitol region of Ottawa (Finkelman and Goldenberg 1983, p. 18, fn 10).

19. These workers are found primarily among provincial government employees in several jurisdictions (e.g., Manitoba; New Brunswick) as well as in the quasi-public sector (e.g., health care in Manitoba) Source: Personal Correspondence, November 24, 1994.

20. Other unions organized primarily in the federal public service and that bargain with the Treasury Board include (at 1994 membership levels) the Aircraft Operations Group Associations (532); the Canadian Association of Professional Radio Operators (1,158); Council of Graphic Arts Unions (2,257); Canadian Military Colleges Faculty Association (34); Canadian Union of Professional and Technical Employees (820); Federal Government Dockyard Trades and Labor Council (1991); Economists', Sociologists' and Statisticians' Association (5,234); and the Professional Association of Foreign Service Officers (1,078). Taken together, these unions represent employees across the spectrum of federal government activities.

21. See *Public Service Staff Relations Board Annual Report* (various years).

22. *Minutes of Special Meeting of the NJC*, December 19, 1975, and *Minutes of NJC Meeting*, January 16, 1976.

23. Refer to Fisher and Ury (1983).

References

Barnes, L. 1974. *Consult and Advise: A History of the National Joint Council of the Public Service of Canada 1944–1974*. Kingston, Ont.: Industrial Relations Centre, Queen's University.

Canada. *Report of the Preparatory Committee on Collective Bargaining in the Public Service*. Heeney Report 1965. Ottawa: Queen's Printer.

Cappelli, P., L. Bassi, H. Katz, D. Knoke, P. Osterman, and M. Useem. 1997. *Change At Work*. New York: Oxford University Press.

Chaykowski, R. 1999. "A Legacy of Labour-Management Cooperation in the Federal Public Service: The National Joint Council of the Public Service of Canada." Manuscript.

Chaykowski, R., and A. Verma, eds. 1992. *Industrial Relations in Canadian Industry*. Toronto: Holt, Rinehart, and Winston.

Chernow, R. 1998. *Titan: The Life of John D. Rockefeller, Sr.* New York: Random House.

Connell, J.P. 1973. "Collective Bargaining in the Public Service of Canada." In *Collective Bargaining in the Public Services*. The Institute of the Public Administration of Canada, pp. 45–55. Toronto: The Institute of the Public Administration of Canada.

Edwards, Claude A. 1966. "Address to the Founding Convention of the Public Service Alliance of Canada." *Civil Service Review*, December, pp. 2, 4, 6, 40.

———. 1970. "Collective Bargaining in Canada Between the Federal Government and Its Employees." *Civil Service Review* 43, no. 2 (June): 2–12.

———. 1974. "The Future of Public Service Unionism." *Civil Service Review* 47, no. 3 (September): 6–10.

Finkelman, Jacob. 1974. *The Rationale in Establishing Bargaining Units in the Federal Public Service of Canada*. Reprint Series, no. 25. Kingston, Ont.: Industrial Relations Centre, Queen's University.

Finkelman, Jacob, and Shirley Goldenberg. 1983. *Collective Bargaining in the Public Service: The Federal Experience in Canada*. Vol. 1 Montréal: Institute for Research on Public Policy.

Fisher, R. and W. Ury. 1983. *Getting to Yes: Negotiating Agreement Without Giving In.* New York: Penguin Books.

Frankel, S.J. 1956. "Staff Relations in the Canadian Federal Public Service: Experience with Joint Consultation." *Canadian Journal of Economics and Political Science* 22, no. 4 (November): 509–522.

Gunderson, M., and A. Sharpe. 1998. *Forging Business-Labour Partnerships: The Emergence of Sector Councils in Canada.* Toronto: University of Toronto Press.

Hodgets, J.E., W. McCloskey, R. Whitaker, and V.S. Wilson. 1972. *The Biography of an Institution: The Civil Service Commission of Canada 1908–1967.* Montreal: McGill-Queen's University Press.

International Labour Review (ILR). 1921. "Control of Industry: Joint Councils in Canadian Industry." *International Labour Review* 3, no. 3 (September): 56–63.

Ilsley, J.L. 1944a. *Dominion of Canada Official Report of Debates House of Commons.* Vol. 3, pp. 2945–2946. Ottawa: King's Printer.

———. 1944b. *Dominion of Canada Official Report of Debates House of Commons.* Vol. 1, pp. 778–779. Ottawa: King's Printer.

Johnston, V. 1953. "The CSAO and the Federation." *Civil Service News*, March, pp. 2–3.

Knowles, F. 1955a. "History of the Amalgamated Civil Servants of Canada." *Canadian Civil Servant*, June, pp. 2–6.

———. 1955b. "History of the Amalgamated Civil Servants of Canada." *Canadian Civil Servant*, September, pp. 6–7.

———. 1956. "History of the Amalgamated Civil Servants of Canada." *Canadian Civil Servant*, December, pp. 9–10.

———. 1958. "Not to Be Forgotten." *Canadian Civil Servant*, April, pp. 2–6.

Kochan, T., T.H. Katz, and R. McKersie. 1986. *The Transformation of American Industrial Relations.* New York: Basic Books.

National Joint Council. 1980. *Third Annual Report of the National Joint Council: 1979–80.* Ottawa, Ont.: Minister of Supply and Services Canada.

———. 1981. *Fourth Annual Report of the National Joint Council: 1980–81.* Ottawa, Ont.: Minister of Supply and Services Canada.

Ponak, A., and M. Thompson. 1995. "Public Sector Collective Bargaining." In *Union-Management Relations in Canada*, ed. M. Gunderson and A. Ponak, 3rd ed., pp. 415–454. Don Mills, Ont.: Addison-Wesley.

Rump, C.W. 1939a. "A History of the Civil Service Association and Reasons Why You Should Be a Member." *Civil Service News* 17, no. 2 (February): 33–36.

———. 1939b. "A History of Civil Service Association and Reasons Why You Should Be a Member." *Civil Service News* 17, no. 3 (March): 65–70.

———. 1939c. "A History of Civil Service Association and Reasons Why You Should Be a Member." *Civil Service News* 17, no. 4 (April): 97–104.

———. 1963. "The National Joint Council of the Public Service of Canada." *Civil Service Review*, March, pp. 41–43, 45–47.

———. 1972. "Employer-Employee Consultation in the Public Service: 1944–1972. A Review of the History, Functions and Achievements of the National Joint Council of the Public Service of Canada." *Civil Service Review* 45, no. 2 (June): 6–16, 48.

Swimmer, Gene. 1995. "Collective Bargaining in the Federal Public Service of Canada: The Last Twenty Years." In *Public Sector Collective Bargaining in Canada*, ed. G. Swimmer and M. Thompson, pp. 368–407. Kingston, Ont.: Queen's University IRC Press.

Swimmer, Gene, and M. Thompson. 1995. "Collective Bargaining in the Public Sector: An Introduction." In *Public Sector Collective Bargaining in Canada*, ed. G. Swimmer and M. Thompson, pp. 1–19. Kingston, Ont.: Queen's University IRC Press.

16

The Effectiveness of Diversity Networks in Providing Collective Voice for Employees

Roy B. Helfgott

The claim that trade unions provide employees with "collective voice" has become the leading intellectual justification for unionization. Labor leaders and the advocates of unionism in academia, therefore, contend that the decline in unionization and collective bargaining in recent years has left American workers without voice, while concern about job security has curtailed their ability to exercise the exit option. Not all industrial relations scholars, however, agree that employees lack voice in the workplace. Many argue that employees can and do have voice, albeit outside the areas covered by collective bargaining. (Providing voice with respect to wages, hours, and other terms and conditions of employment is reserved to unions by the National Labor Relations Act.)

Attempts to provide voice include forms of alternative dispute-resolution procedures, committees dealing with specific problems of the workplace, such as safety and health, and programs of employee involvement. Another vehicle for employee voice might be the "diversity network" or "minority caucus," which is an organization composed of members of an identity group, as for example, women, African Americans, and Hispanics. Being based on identity, it addresses issues that employees from the minority in a company see as peculiar to them.

This study examined diversity networks in four companies. Its aim was not to judge the success of a company's equal employment or diversity efforts, but to appraise the effectiveness of these groups in securing a collective voice in the workplace for their members. The conclusion, as we later see, is that they have not been very effective.

The Concept of Collective Voice

Albert O. Hirschman coined the terms *exit* and *voice* in describing consumer behavior in a situation in which the quality of a product deteriorates (Hirschman 1970). Consumers could simply stop buying the product, which Hirschman calls "exiting" the market. They do have an alternative, however, which is to exercise "voice," that is, to express their opposition and fight deterioration, trying to force the producer to restore the quality of the good.

The exit-voice concept was later applied by Richard B. Freeman to the labor market and employer-employee relations (Freeman 1989a). Freeman said that if workers were unhappy on the job, they could exercise their exit option and quit. (There are other forms of exit behavior, including rejecting a job offer, absenteeism, partial withdrawal of labor time, reduction of work effort, and even sabotage.) He claimed, however, that the presence of a union offered workers the alternative of a collective voice, through which they could seek to alter the conditions that displeased them. Union leaders negotiated collective bargaining agreements with management that at least partially brought about a situation on the job that was more to the workers' liking. Once an agreement was reached, moreover, the union would police it to ensure that management adhered to its terms, and the grievance procedure provided the individual worker with the right to challenge management when he thought that it had not abided by the contract.

According to Freeman, unionization provides a direct channel of communication between workers and management, an alternative mode of expressing discontent than quitting, and social relations of production that can mitigate the problems associated with the authority relations in firms. He views the union-management relationship as a win-win situation—collective voice benefits not only the workers but also management, because the enhanced communication makes it aware of, and thus able to address, employee relations problems. An advantage of collective voice is that it reflects the demands of average workers, while quits express the desires of marginal workers.

By treating unions as instruments of collective voice, Freeman seeks to counter the neoclassical economic view of unions as monopolies that raise wages and create inefficiencies in resource allocation. He has presented statistical data showing that, by serving the role of collective voice of workers, unions have reduced quits and absenteeism and encouraged firm-specific training (Freeman 1989b). By doing so, they may have increased labor productivity enough to offset the higher compensation for their members that they have extracted from employers (Freeman and Medoff 1984).

The Diversity Network

One possible nonunion vehicle for employee voice goes by a variety of names: diversity network, minority or identity caucus, and affinity group. They arose three decades ago and have existed for quite a while at companies such as Xerox, Corning, AT&T, and DEC. Ray Friedman surveyed the human resource managers of all Fortune 500 and Service 500 companies, members of the National Black MBA Association, and members of the Executive Leadership Council (Friedman 1996). Among the Fortune and Service 500 companies that responded, 29 percent reported having networks; among ELC respondents, 43 percent; and among NBMBAA respondents, 34 percent. Friedman concluded that network groups were expanding rapidly among large American corporations.

Such network groups are not comparable to and cannot be considered alternatives to unions. They are not established by law and do not negotiate with management over wages, hours, and other terms and conditions of work, but represent identity groups and seek to deal with issues such as acceptance and upward advancement that the group faces as a minority in a company. We know of groups covering African Americans, American Indians, Asian/Pacific Islanders (and components, e.g., Vietnamese), Disabled, Gays and Lesbians, Hispanics, and Older Employees. There are reported to be Christian fellowship and Jewish cultural groups operating at Apple Computer, but they are not affiliated with Apple's formal Multicultural Alliance. Other companies will not recognize groups based on a specific religion or political outlook. In a few cases, management had fostered networks, but in others, it had either actively discouraged their formation or ignored them. Networks have been firm based, but recently a National Hispanic Employee Association, linking networks from high-technology firms, was formed in the Bay Area of California (Hyde 1997). It seeks to further the upward mobility of Hispanics in the private and public sectors.

As identity rather than organization groups, all members of the particular group may join, so networks can encompass both exempt and nonexempt employees. Among African American groups, Friedman found that many were composed exclusively of professionals or of all nonexempt employees (Friedman and Carter 1993). We, too, discovered that many, if not most, networks originally had been professional employee organizations, but they now admit all workers. Even though their ranks have been opened, in most cases the groups have remained essentially professional/managerial organizations, with few nonexempt employee members.

Diversity networks might best be described as focus groups engaging in "brainstorming" and "roundtable discussion." They avoid confrontation with management, seeking to achieve results through influence rather than demonstrations of power. (As we later see, they possess little power to demonstrate.) Groups may receive company financing, in addition to dues from their members. Indeed, in one company that we examine, the diversity networks are part of Personnel Management's diversity efforts, rather than independent bodies. In fact, a recent issue of a publication oriented toward human resources managers carries the title "Well-Managed Employee Networks Add Business Value" (Digh 1997).

Friedman sees the diversity network as having an "ambiguous form," not fitting under the domains of personnel management or labor relations. He defines it as "a group of employees who get together to address the problems that they face as minorities in a company" and pursue their goals through a combination of self-help activities, for example, information, training, mentoring, and efforts to change the company; that is, influence it to adopt policies and programs to ensure that minorities are successfully recruited and advanced. (Friedman 1996) He sees a network as having three major functions: (1) to help management deal with issues related to diversity, (2) to use joint problem solving to address issues and seek to align employees with company goals, and (3) to provide a sense of community to its members. The overriding goal is to help members advance within the company by influencing them and the company. As Freeman asserts with respect to unions, so Friedman claims that network activities have reduced turnover among minority-group members.

We sought to determine if, in fact, networks have performed the functions attributed to them by Friedman, particularly the ability to alter company policy. If they were able to do so, then they would be providing collective voice for their members. Indeed, Friedman specifically claims that they often do serve as a means of voice but without the leverage of monopoly power that unions possess. Our aim, therefore, was to determine how effective networks are in providing collective voice. Furthermore, if they are effective in providing voice, we should then ask if this type of body might serve as a model for representation of employees on broader employment-related matters in nonunion situations.

Case Study Findings

We were afforded the opportunity by Organization Resources Counselors, Inc. to present our research project to a regularly scheduled regional meeting of an ORC Equal Opportunity Group (EOG). Such groups are composed of large companies seeking to advance equal employment opportunity within their organizations. Their meetings discuss new matters relating to equal employment opportunity and are attended by the people in charge of that function.

Despite the fact that these were companies that promoted equal employment opportunity and diversity within their organizations, we were surprised and disappointed to learn that of the ten present, only two (one in durable goods manufacturing and the other in transportation and public utilities, the latter unionized and the former not) reported that they had functioning networks. Other companies said that networks had arisen, but either were no longer functioning or their activities were so sporadic as not to qualify them for consideration. Thus, we were able to obtain information on minority networks from only two companies in this group, and with advice from the meeting group, from two others at a later time.

Our second surprise was that, where networks existed, only a small proportion of their constituencies had joined. In both firms, on average, about 20 percent belonged to the networks, and almost all blue-collar workers, unionized or not, eschewed membership due to a combination of a lack of interest and not wanting to spend extra time at the workplace. Also, some of the networks originally had been confined to professional employees and were still so regarded by production workers. Failure to participate among other employees represented a combination of a lack of interest and not wanting to be labeled a "militant," which they feared might hinder advancement. Moving up the ladder depends heavily on one's immediate supervisor or department head, who may be less supportive of network activities than are human resource people or top management. The gay and lesbian networks had seemingly high representation (though it is hard to determine if this is so, since there are no data on the universe), and their members appeared to be unafraid and, in some instances, even desirous, of being labeled "militants."

In both companies, the networks had been inaugurated by employees, and we interpreted management's attitudes to be generally unfavorable, but willing to deal with them. While the companies might be happier if the networks did not exist, they realize that some employees may feel a need for them and that they provide a safer channel for expression of employee concerns than would the festering of discontent. Management, moreover, recognizes that it can learn of unhappiness and deal with it a lot sooner when there is a group to express it openly.

Although seeking to keep networks at arm's length, one of the companies offers advice on constitutions and bylaws when a group is trying to form and, once its mission has been approved, it is formally recognized. The firm had given financial subsidies to networks on occasion, but that ended when one requested $500,000 to conduct a research project. Both companies provide meeting space, but all activities are on the employees' own time. Other forms of help are the use of copying machines and the ability to inform members of meetings, including through the use of company e-mail. Neither company accepts the networks as spokespersons for those groups of employees. Their low membership relative to the employment of those minorities helped to determine management's position with respect to their being spokespersons. Of course, the companies' attitudes, in turn, probably help to hold down network membership.

Companies with diversity networks and unionized production and maintenance workers have not, as far as we can determine, reported conflicts between the two. The company in transportation, communication, and utilities in our study ran into one problem when it recognized a gay and lesbian group and accorded it the privileges extended to other networks. Management suddenly was flooded with complaints from blue-collar workers, and the suspicion was that the union local had instigated and coordinated the protest.

Durable Goods Manufacturer

More detailed information was provided by the leaders of four networks (black, Hispanic, Asian/Pacific, and women) at the durable goods manufacturing firm. (See Appendix for a copy of the questionnaire.) All four were companywide, but the black and women's groups were active at only three locations, the Asian at four, and the Hispanic, which was the only one to claim to be very active, at eight. The following table, showing the percentage membership of each network by major job category, reveals the paucity of membership among the nonexempt employees and almost total absence among blue-collar workers:

Network	Managerial	Professional	Production	Clerical
Asian/Pacific	5	85	5	5
Black	10	60	(no breakdown)	
Hispanic	15	60	10	15
Women	20	60	0	20

With respect to the importance of network activities to their members, the Asian/Pacific group reported that training and development, adjustment to environment, and cultural awareness were of some importance, but advice and mentoring of little or none. The black network, on the other hand, claimed that advice, training and development, mentoring, and adjustment to environment were all very important, as did the women's network, except that training and development ac-

tivities were only of some importance for it. For the Hispanic group, advice, mentoring, and adjustment to environment were of some importance, but training and development of little or none. Interestingly, there was no correlation between how active each network claimed to be and the perceived importance of its activities to its members.

Looking at the degree of importance of the network as a source and channel of information for its members, the black network claimed "very" with respect to job/career opportunities and problem areas, and "some" relative to company goals, yet it answered only "somewhat" to the question "Does network act as a channel of information between its members and management?" The Hispanic network claimed to be of some importance in all three areas, but answered "definitely" with respect to being a channel of information. The women's network answered "very" for job/career opportunities and company goals, but "little or no" regarding problem areas and "somewhat" with respect to being a channel of information. The Asian/Pacific network said that it was of little or no importance in all categories, yet answered "somewhat" to the question of being a channel of information.

As to how important the network was as a channel of information to management, the black network said "very" with respect to both alerting management on problems and as a recruiting channel. The women's group reported "very" on alerting management to problems but "little or no" with respect to recruiting. The Hispanic caucus claimed "some" on alerting to problems, but "little or no" on recruiting, and the Asian group, "little or no" in both areas. None of the four claimed any importance in reducing either employee turnover or absenteeism, purported results of collective voice.

Of the four networks, the black believes its members see it as spokesperson, but management does not; the women's said that neither did; and the Hispanic and Asian reported that their members did not view them as spokespersons, but management did. "Do members see network as a source of help when they have problems on the job?" elicited "definitely" from the black caucus, "somewhat" from the Asian and women's, and "no" from the Hispanic. "Has network helped solved individual members' problems?" drew an "occasionally" response from the black network, but "rarely" from the others. All claimed a cooperative, nonconfrontational attitude toward management. Network-management interaction was reported to be formal by the black group, informal by the Asian and women's caucuses, and both by the Spanish network. As to frequency of interaction, the black group reported "seldom" and the others "occasional." All listed management's attitude toward them as "noncommittal," rather than "supportive" or "wary." On the crucial issue of having affected changes in company policy and procedures, all the responses were negative, demonstrating that the networks exercise little influence on management.

Nondurable Goods Manufacturer

Two other companies at which diversity network experience was reportedly more positive were contacted. Management at one, a nondurable goods manufacturer, employing large percentages of women and minorities, claimed to be very supportive of networks as part of overall diversity efforts. A diversity council, composed of representatives of the various groups, serves as an advisory body to top management on issues of concern to their members. Despite this apparently supportive management attitude, the answers of

the groups to our questions were not very different from those at the durable goods manufacturer. Again, relatively few potential members join the networks.

Three of the networks at this company completed our questionnaire: Women, Asian/Pacific, and gay/lesbian, but the African American and Hispanic ones did not. None of the three reporting groups claimed to be "very" active, only "somewhat." None would disclose its membership as a percentage of its potential, but we infer that, on average, it probably was not appreciably higher than the 20 percent at the other firms. The Asian/Pacific and gay/lesbian groups provided a breakdown of membership by job category, which also was quite similar to that of the other manufacturing firm, indicating that they are basically organizations of professional employees, with little membership among nonexempt employees. (The total absence of production workers in the gay/lesbian network probably also reflects the fact that attitudes toward homosexuality have changed less within the working class than in the middle classes, and so one should not expect "outing" to occur.) The distribution of membership among job categories was:

Group	Managerial	Professional	Production	Clerical
Asian/Pacific	20	45	5	30
Gay/Lesbian	10	70	0	20

With respect to the importance of group activities to their members, the Asian/Pacific network said "very" for advice, mentoring, and adjustment to environment, but only "some" for training and development. The women's and gay/lesbian groups see their advice activities as being of some importance, but the others of little or none. On the importance of the group as a source and channel of information for members, all reported "some" with respect to job/career opportunities; and regarding company goals, the Asian/Pacific and gay/lesbian groups answered "some," but the women's group "little or no."

As to the importance of their activities on problem areas, the Asian/Pacific group claimed "very," but the others "little or no." On solving individual members' problems, all answered "rarely," and the women's group went out of its way to state that that was not part of its charter. None of the groups reported that their existence had been of any consequence in reducing either employee turnover or absenteeism.

All groups claimed to be of some importance as a channel of communication between members and management. As to importance in alerting management to problems, the Asian/Pacific group said "very," but the others only "some." The Asian/Pacific and women's groups claimed to be of "some" importance as recruiting channels, but the gay/lesbian network of "little or none." The Asian/Pacific network said that both its members and management considered it their spokesperson, but the women's caucus answered that neither did, and the gay/lesbian group reported that its members did not, but management did. With regard to whether members see the group as a source of help when they have problems on the job, the first two groups answered "somewhat," but the gay/lesbian group "no."

All asserted that their attitudes toward management were cooperative, not confrontational. The Asian/Pacific and women's networks reported that group-management interaction was both formal and informal, but the gay/lesbian group said it was only informal. The Asian/Pacific and women's groups said that they interacted with management "occasionally," and the gay/lesbian

group "seldom." With respect to management's attitude toward them, the Asian/Pacific and women's groups listed it as "noncommittal," but the gay/lesbian group "supportive." Once more, the key issue of the groups having affected change in company procedures drew a unanimous "no."

Company in Finance, Insurance, and Real Estate

Diversity groups in the final company examined in the finance, insurance, and real estate industry (FIRE) are significantly different from the others in that they are not divided into specific minority groups, but composed of all employees interested in advancing diversity within the organization. Their genesis, however, was more typical, having arisen in the early 1980s in a company that later merged with the one under discussion as networks of specific minority groups—Asian, black, Hispanic—that were joined together in a network system. At that time, they were limited to managerial and professional personnel, both by their own desires and at the insistence of the company's legal department, and their stress was on career development and professional growth. The stated goal of the networks was to increase the representation of minorities in the company's higher ranks through a combination of mentoring activities and monitoring executive development programs to ensure significant minority representation.

In the merger, a decade later, of this company with the one we are examining, it was the junior partner. The parent company also was promoting diversity, but its philosophy was to emphasize inclusiveness, rather than separation. It moved, therefore, to expand the networks to the entire company, but to have them composed of all employees interested in promoting workplace diversity. Management believes that separate networks for specific minorities is less effective in advancing those groups' goals because it can lead to divisiveness and preaching to oneself, while inclusive networks permit employees with different backgrounds to interact and better understand each other's concerns. Recently, some gay and lesbian employees wanted to set up their own network, but management convinced them that, given societal attitudes, that would generate more hostility than understanding and that fighting for their positions within the overall diversity cause would be more successful.

Starting with seven networks inherited from the acquired firm, the company now has thirty-one in locations across the country. They are open to employees at all job levels, but still are primarily organizations of professional and managerial employees; personnel management, however, is prodding them to put greater emphasis on attracting nonexempts. They are employee-run volunteer organizations seeking to promote personal and professional development among all employee groups. A network meets regularly and conducts activities, such as seminars in marketing one's skills, and career fairs to acquaint employees at its location with the jobs and career paths available and the training needed to qualify for them. There also is a council of presidents, which meets monthly, and an annual conference of all networks.

Although a network is employee run, it is required to have a management adviser to ensure its smooth operation. The networks, which are akin to employee clubs, are but one component of the company's overall diversity program, and there is a specific budget item for their funding. Network activities take place on company premises during nonworking hours, mentors for network training and development activities usually come from higher managerial ranks, and meet-ings tend to feature speakers from upper management. The networks, however, determine their own activities; for example, a recent focus was on advancing women into top management.

Since networks operate under the aegis of management, employees are not likely to be deterred from membership because of fear of being considered militant. On the contrary, they may perceive the situation to be one in which they can earn brownie points by joining. Even so, participation rates were not particularly high. Although the networks, through the presidents' council, participate in an advisory group to top management, the networks are not seen as advisory groups per se, but are viewed as part of company communications, basically, as sources of information for employees. They are definitely not considered to be representational bodies speaking for employees.

Conclusions

The Legality Issue

Before drawing conclusions with respect to the effectiveness of diversity networks in providing employees with collective voice, we must deal with the issue of their susceptibility to running afoul of the National Labor Relations Act ban on employer-domination of labor organizations, Section 8 (a)(2). This issue was raised recently, and based on the case of a hypothetical network operating in a hypothetical situation (i.e., a group of black journalists at a newspaper forming a joint committee with management to improve the job status of the black journalists), the conclusion was that, under the *Electromation* decision, the network would be found to be illegal (Note 1994). Based on our research, we believe that the danger is far-fetched for most diversity networks.

The first question is, "Are the networks 'labor organizations,' as defined under the act?" The answer clearly is "no" for those at the last company examined and probably the same for the others. In all cases, the stated purposes of the networks revolve around personal advancement and not dealing with the employer. Unlike labor organizations, they do not deal with "grievances, labor disputes, wage rates, employment hours, or working conditions."

Even if some networks were to be defined as labor organizations, it is most unlikely that they would be deemed to be dominated by management. The only case in which the networks are management influenced, those at the company in FIRE, they are not labor organizations but part of the company's diversity program. In the others in which networks might be construed to be labor organizations, they are clearly of the employees' own choosing and, since management has as little to do with them as possible, they hardly could be considered to be management dominated.

Finally, one must ask who would raise the question of network legality. A union seeking to represent employees at a workplace could lodge a complaint against a network, but no such event has occurred to date. Indeed, unions themselves have internal minority caucuses. Networks present no challenge to unions—they have almost no membership among what would be considered "bargaining unit" employees and are not involved in activities that fall within the purview of collective bargaining. Indeed, networks coexist with unions in a number of companies. In the unionized situations that we examined, they were totally ignored by the unions (with the one exception of when a company recognized a gay and lesbian caucus, but that reflected working-class homophobia rather than having anything to do

with labor-management relations). It is conceivable, of course, that if diversity networks were effective in providing collective voice for their members, they would then become vulnerable to being charged with illegality under the National Labor Relations Act.

Diversity Networks and Collective Voice

Having dealt with the legal issue, let us return to our main concern, the effectiveness of diversity networks in providing collective voice. Given the fact that some networks are of long standing, they obviously have value to their members, and they do play a role in mentoring and acculturating employees to a company's environment. They offer some employees the opportunity to interact with others like themselves and a sort of safe haven within what may be perceived as a strange, if not hostile, environment. Such motivations were probably strong when networks first arose among African American professionals, but have become less important as their numbers have grown in companies and a degree of upward movement achieved. Today, these motivations seem to be strong among gays and lesbians, who only recently have asserted themselves. Networks tend to exist, moreover, in companies with very good records concerning equal employment opportunity, dampening their appeal to large numbers of employees, who find little personal need for a support group.

Friedman's survey on the extent of networks may have been accurate at that time, but many have ceased to function since then. Although he found this type of organization growing, we doubt that it has spread to many other companies and, in fact, it may be less important today. Furthermore, as the discussant of Friedman's IRRA paper pointed out, the number of network groups may not be a good measure of their popularity. The proportion of a firm's minority employees who join the network is more important because it determines if it can influence policy or be ignored as a "fringe" group (Chandler 1996). Although networks now accept nonexempts into membership, few have responded, and among what we would call traditional bargaining unit employees, the production and maintenance (P & M) group, almost none have. Even among professional and managerial personnel, only a small minority belongs to existing networks, and management does view them as "fringe" groups.

Networks, of course, may play more positive roles at other companies, and there are examples of such activities. They have been reported to have served as advisers to business units at 3M, helped in recruitment and retention efforts at AT&T, and aided Honeywell to understand better cultural differences in its expansion abroad (Digh 1997). Networks at the companies that we examined, however, played no such roles.

A somewhat more positive view of the identity network emerges from Hyde's research in Silicon Valley (Hyde 1997). This is an economic sector that has a very high percentage of professional and technical employment, the group that is most involved in networks everywhere. Hyde calls the identity network "the one institution of employee organization that has been distinctive in high technology employment," and he found one area in which networks had served as a collective voice for constituents—companies complied with requests from gay and lesbian caucuses to open benefit programs to nonmarried domestic partners. Once a company had granted the request, however, the caucuses returned to their self-help and social activities. Indeed, Hyde is critical of them for limiting themselves to indi-

vidual advancement within the firm and making no attempt to forge links across firm boundaries; he would like them to be something other than what they are.

The networks we examined continued to function, but their activities are highly circumscribed and they fulfill only one of the three major roles ascribed to them by Friedman, that of providing a sense of community to members. The other two functions—helping management deal with issues related to diversity and using joint problem solving to address issues and seeking to align employees with company goals—are only partially fulfilled, largely because management does not want their help or is not willing to engage in any joint problem solving. As Friedman contends, diversity networks avoid an adversarial stance and seek cooperation with management; even so, there is fear within management ranks that they could be harbingers of union organization or sow discord within the company.

On the crucial issue of networks acting in a representational role, our findings are decidedly negative. They serve somewhat as communication channels, but neither they nor management consider them spokespersons for those minorities. Networks rarely, if ever, have solved problems of individual members, have not affected changes in company policy, and have had no discernible influence on turnover or absenteeism rates. We must conclude, therefore, that diversity networks, whatever their other merits, have been poor vehicles through which to provide employees with collective voice.

Broader Implications of Findings

Implications for other forms of nonunion employee representation flow from our findings. We exclude programs of employee involvement (EI) as practiced in North America, since they do not involve representation, unlike what is called "worker participation" in Europe that takes place through unions and entails overall plant or company decision making (e.g., German codetermination). In North America, EI means workers having a say in decisions with respect to their own work through direct participation in a quality circle, autonomous team, or whatever, and no group speaks for them. Employee involvement provides workers with individual voice on how they perform their jobs, but that is different from having a collective voice to speak for a group of employees. Such employee involvement does not fall under the term nonunion employee representation and it can and does coexist with unionism.

A basic problem facing all forms of employee representation, including diversity networks and trade unionism, is that there appears to be little demand for it on the part of employees. As Verma and Kochan have stated, "Workers today have acquired a taste for a cooperative, productive, and informal workplace," rather than one "characterized by conflict, legalistic, and impersonal work rules" (Verma and Kochan 1985). Many nonunion plants opened in recent years provide such an informal atmosphere, using behavioral science techniques for involving employees in production matters. Thus, employees seem to be content with having individual voice with respect to their work and not particularly desirous of collective voice on broader workplace matters.

In the Princeton employee opinion survey, a majority favored some form of representation in dealing with management, even if it were not free of management control (Freeman and Rogers 1994). One wonders, however, that if such an organization existed, when it came time to sign up and pay dues, how many would be interested enough actually to do so. For others, even legal nonunion representation might not quell fears that membership and activity could hurt advancement. In the workaholic environment existing in some companies today, any time that employees would devote to "nonwork"-related activities might be seen as akin to sabotage by some managers.

If employees are not demanding representation, management certainly looks askance at it. According to Freeman, ". . . the essence of voice is to reduce managerial power and create a dual authority channel within the firm" (Freeman 1989b). He concludes that only an independent union or union-type organization, therefore, provides employees with voice. We disagree that only a union can provide collective voice, but concur that effective nonunion representation would require not only legalization but erecting for it the protections that surround worker membership and activity in trade unions.

The likelihood of such legislation in the United States at this time is slight. Organized labor is vehemently opposed to legalizing any nonunion form of representation. Management, in turn, views any form of employee organization with which it would have to negotiate on any subject as a threat to its decision making, which, it believes, could undercut a company's ability to maneuver in a highly competitive global economy.

We began our research with optimism concerning diversity networks providing employees with collective voice, but this has not been the case. Although the number of companies studied—four—is small, basically because the universe from which to choose is small, we believe that it presents a fairly accurate picture of the situation. Our conclusion, therefore, is that diversity networks are not effective in providing collective voice, and that finding, in turn, leads to skepticism that, in the absence of legislation, any form of nonunion representation would be able to do so.

References

Chandler, Timothy D. 1996. "Discussion, Refereed Papers: Labor-Management Relations." In *Proceedings of the Forty-Eighth Annual Meeting*, ed. Paula B. Voos, pp. 251–253. Madison: Industrial Relations Research Association.

Digh, Patricia. 1997. "Well-Managed Employee Networks Add Business Value" *HR Magazine*, August, pp. 67–72.

Freeman, Richard B. 1989a. "Individual Mobility and Union Voice in the Labor Market." In *Labor Markets in Action*, pp. 159–168. Cambridge: Harvard University Press. Originally published in *American Economic Review*, May 1976.

———. 1989b. "The Exit-Voice Trade-Off in the Labor Market: Unionism, Job Tenure, Quits and Separations." In *Labor Markets in Action*, pp. 169–196. Originally published in *Quarterly Journal of Economics*, June 1980.

Freeman, Richard B., and James L. Medoff. 1984. *What Do Unions Do?* New York: Basic Books.

Freeman, Richard B., and Joel Rogers. 1994. *Worker Representation and Participation Survey: First Report of Findings*. Princeton: Princeton Survey Research Associates. December. Mimeographed.

Friedman, Raymond. 1996. "Network Groups: An Emerging Form of Employee Representation." In *Procedures of the Forty-Eighth Annual Meeting*, ed. Paula B. Voos, pp. 241–250. Madison, Wis.: Industrial Relations Research Association.

Friedman, Raymond A., and Donna Carter. 1993. *African American Network Groups: Their Impact and Effectiveness*. Washington, D.C.: Executive Leadership Council.

Hirschman, Albert O. 1970. *Exit, Voice, and Loyalty*. Cambridge: Harvard University Press.

Hyde, Alan. 1997. "Employee Identity Caucuses in Silicon Valley: Can They Transcend the Boundaries of the Firm?" In *Proceedings of the 1997 Spring Meeting*, ed. Paula B. Voos, pp. 491–497. Madison: Industrial Relations Research Association. Reprinted from *Labor Law Journal*, August 1997.

Note. 1994. "Labor-Management Cooperation After Electromation: Implications for Workplace Diversity." *Harvard Law Review* 107, no. 3: 678–695.

Verma, Anil, and Thomas A. Kochan. 1985. "The Growth and Nature of the Nonunion Sector within a Firm." In *Challenges and Choices Facing American Labor*, ed. Thomas A. Kochan, pp. 89–117. Cambridge: MIT Press.

Appendix
Diversity Network Questionnaire

Company _____

Representative _____

Diversity Network:

Number of Members_____ At how many locations? _____

Type: Afro-American _____ Hispanic _____ Women _____ Other _____

Does the network have a company-wide organization? Yes _____ No _____

How active is network? Very _____ Somewhat _____ Barely _____

Network attitude toward management: Cooperative _____ Confrontational _____

Percent of potential membership affiliated with network: _____

Percent membership by job type: Mgrl._____ Prof. _____ Prod. _____ Cleric. _____

Importance of network activities to its members:

Advice : Very _____ Some _____ Little or no _____

Training and development: Very _____ Some _____ Little or no ____

Mentoring: Very _____ Some _____ Little or no _____

Adjustment to environment: Very _____ Some _____ Little or no _____

Other (specify): Very _____ Some _____ Little or no _____

Importance of network as a source and channel of information to members:

Job/career opportunities: Very _____ Some _____ Little or no _____

Company goals: Very _____ Some _____ Little or no _____

Problem areas: Very _____ Some _____ Little or no _____

Other (specify): Very _____ Some _____ Little or no _____

Does network act as a channel of communictions between its members and management?

Definitely _____ Somewhat _____ No _____

Do members see network as their spokesman vis-à-vis mgt? Yes ____ No ____

Does mgt. see network as spokesman for that group? Yes _____ No _____

Do members see network as a source of help when they have problems on the job?

Definitely _____ Somewhat _____ No _____

Importance of network as a source and channel of information to management:

Alert on problems: Very _____ Some _____ Little or no _____

Recruiting channel: Very _____ Some _____ Little or no _____

Other (specify): Very _____ Some _____ Little or no _____

Network/Management interaction: Regular _____ Occasional ____ Seldom ____

Network/Management interaction: Formal _____ Informal _____ Both _____

Mgt. attitude toward network: Supportive ____ Noncommittal _____ Wary ____

Where a union exists, its relationship with network: Good _____ Fair __ Bad ___
Has network affected changes in policy and procedures? Yes ___ No _____
Has network helped solve individual members' problems?
Often _____ Occasionally _____ Rarely _____
Has network's existence been of importance with respect to employee turnover?
Yes _____ No _____ If yes, degree of change _____
Has network's existence been of importance with respect to employee absenteeism? Yes _____
No _____ If yes, degree of change _____

International Perspectives

17

Nonunion Representation in Germany

John T. Addison, Claus Schnabel, and Joachim Wagner

The German works council, or *Betriebsrat*, continues to attract considerable attention in the United States because of the precipitous and ongoing decline in unionism in the private sector, where just 9.8 percent of the workforce is currently unionized. The works council is seen by many U.S. observers as offering an alternative form of worker representation that meets the requirements of equity (i.e., industrial democracy) and efficiency. Given these supposed attributes, it should come as no surprise to learn that some have seen it as forming the basis of a participation mandate.

Yet, paradoxically, rather little is known about the operation of the German institution on this side of the Atlantic. In the present treatment, therefore, we seek to establish whether German experience suggests that the *Betriebsrat* is a substitute for conventional representation (i.e., trade unionism), to consider its role as a vehicle of industrial democracy, and to examine its efficiency implications. Answers to these questions should assist in the explanation of what might happen were works councils to come to the United States.

The plan of the chapter is as follows. First, we provide a brief history of the *Betriebsrat*. Second, we identify the sense in which German works councils are mandatory, and chart their powers and responsibilities. Third, the coverage of works councils is discussed. Fourth, results of econometric (and other) studies of works council im-

pact are reviewed. Fifth, having contextualized the works council, we compare its properties with the Freeman-Lazear (1995) characterization. Finally, in returning to the question of what might happen if works councils were to come to the United States, we draw together the threads of our preceding analysis and in passing note some interesting findings from another literature.

A Brief History

The rights of the works council are laid down in the Works Constitution Act (*Betriebsverfassungsgesetz*) of 1972.[1] The act strengthened early postwar legislation dating from 1952 by extending the codetermination rights of the works council. (Codetermination is a translation of the German word *Mitbestimmung* and refers here to the right of the works council to codetermine certain kinds of decisions with management. The decisions in question are documented in the next section.)[2] The information and consultation rights of the works council were expanded at the same time, and the relation between the union movement and the works council made more explicit. It is conventional to describe the new law as a victory for organized labor, in contrast to its 1952 precursor, which is typically labeled a defeat (e.g., Thelen 1991).

As a matter of fact, works councils long predate World War II. They can be traced back to the workers' committees (*Arbeiterausschüsse*) set up during World War I in an attempt to mobilize union support for the war effort (*Vaterländischer Hilfsdienst*).[3] These committees were transformed into works councils (in establishments with at least twenty workers) under a 1920 law. The new bodies were to be distinctly subordinate to the unions, who were not only given the right to advise the councils but also the right to introduce collectively bargained alternatives.

The backdrop to this 1920 Works Councils Law (*Betriebsrätegesetz*) was threatened revolution in the aftermath of war. The political goal was to marginalize the splinter revolutionary works council movement of the communists and independent socialists. Legislation that strengthened the shopfloor power of mainstream unions but did not fundamentally challenge capital was initially accepted by employers, precisely because of the revolutionary alternative. To repeat, works councils at this time were little more than the representatives of the union at plant level, creatures of the "reformist" unions (Brigl-Matthiaß 1978).

But things were shortly to change. In the first place, the economic crisis of the 1920s systematically eroded works council influence as employers sought to restore management prerogative. Second, the National Socialist government dismantled the "divisive" industrial relations apparatus at a stroke. For their part, unions were simply absorbed within the Labor Front (*Deutsche Arbeitsfront*), a unitary organization embracing a "social community" of labor and capital. Works councils were in fact replaced by "committees of trusted men," to advise management on production and personnel matters, although Thimm (1980, p. 7) argues that in practice these committees were "closer to the works councils of the Weimar Republic than to the more paternalistic joint production and joint factory committees of Hohenzollern Germany."

Following World War II, works councils sprang up in an attempt to build unions "from the bottom up" (Thelen 1991, p. 72). Informal and sometimes far-reaching arrangements at plant level were subsequently formalized under various state laws, facilitated by the labor policy of the occupying powers that promoted strong ties between union and works council. Because the 1952 act ceded fewer rights than some of the (now superseded) state provisions, it is often represented as a defeat for labor.

The 1952 act still forms much of the basis of the information, consultation, and codetermination rights of the works council, described below. We focus here therefore on the autonomy and responsibility issues. First, the act emphasized the independence of the works council from the union, and recognized only limited rights for unions in the plant. Second, the works council was enjoined to work together with the employer in a "spirit of mutual trust." As part and parcel of their peace obligation, works councils were forbidden to strike. In each case, these terms represent important changes from the 1920 Works Council Law. A final point is that the 1952 act sought to protect the representation rights of minorities and salaried workers through specific election rules.

The initial reaction of the union movement to these setbacks, and the implicit threat to the recruitment of union members, was to seek to develop committees of shop stewards (*Vertrauensleutekörper*) as well as to "infiltrate" works councils directly. Works councils continued to be viewed with suspicion by the unions until the early 1960s. Interestingly, as the tendency toward centralization of collective bargaining proper gathered momentum, the works council was actually to become the unions' preferred means of deflecting a challenge to its authority from below (Thelen 1991, p. 81). The demand for decentralization was met by a combination of more aggressive wage bargaining at the national level and, at the local level, by increasing union support for a (reformed) works council apparatus. In other words, a reformed works council with increased powers was to substitute for a fundamental shift in power between the union and the shop floor.

The reform sought by organized labor came with the election in 1969 of a Social Democratic government (in coalition with the Free Democrats). The principal changes introduced under the new administration's 1972 Works Constitution Act were threefold. First, the information and consultation rights of the works council were materially extended in respect of management decisions that would involve changes in capacity, working operations, and production processes, inter alia. Second, the legislation strengthened the existing codetermination rights of the works council by providing for adjudication in the event of impasse. Third, although the formal independence of works councils was maintained, the access of unions to the workplace was improved (e.g., the right to attend meetings between management and the works council), and they could require the works council to call works meetings. More importantly, unions could now submit lists of candidates in works council elections without having to meet the minimum initial support levels set for other groups (see the following section), while works councillors could simultaneously hold union office (e.g., serve on bargaining committees) and attend union training courses (at the expense of the employer).

But note that no generalization can be made as to the works council's union-nonunion status. A number of typologies have been offered in the literature. Schmidt and Trinczek's (1991) case

study analysis, for example, differentiates between a number of works council types: those that have only an instrumental orientation toward the union; those for whom the interests of the workforce and the firm are perceived to be equally important to those of the union; and those works councils that are virtual union clones. Other analysts have drawn different distinctions between councils based on the rights of labor (board representation) and the level of union density at plant level (Thelen 1991). Yet others have downplayed the union connection, stressing instead the "insider" nature of works councils (Hohn 1988). We have more to say about the works council-union nexus in what follows next.

The Election of Works Councils and Their Functions

We first consider the sense in which works councils are mandatory. This is important because "mandatory" does not mean automatic. Section 1 of the German enabling legislation, the Works Constitution Act (*Betriebsverfassungsgesetz*) of 1972, states that "works councils shall be elected in all establishments that normally have five or more permanent employees with voting rights, including three who are eligible [to be works councillors]."[4] Voting rights accrue to all workers aged eighteen years and above—including regular part-timers—and eligible employees are all workers who have been employed by the firm for not less than six months. Thus, the size threshold requires a minimum of five permanent employees, all of whom must be at least eighteen years of age and three of whom must have at least six months' service.

The procedure for setting up a works council is straightforward: just three employees with voting rights, or a trade union represented in the establishment, are needed to call for a works meeting to elect an electoral board (*Wahlvorstand*), which is then responsible for holding the election. Alternatively, a labor court can set up an electoral board if the works meeting is not held or fails to elect a board, again on petition from three employees or the union.[5] Once elections for a works council are under way, the works council is a fait accompli. Nevertheless, a minority of firms have works councils even if they do account for the large majority of employees in employment (see the following section).

The works council is elected by the entire labor force with the exception of employers and senior executives (these so-called *Leitende Angestellte* make up 2 percent of all employees, and since 1989 have had their own executive committees, or *Sprecherausschüsse*). The law fixes the size of the works council, which ranges from one to thirty-one members for establishments with up to 9,000 employees. For larger establishments, two additional members are added for each increment of 3,000 employees. Note also that the legislation provides for "central works councils" (*Gesamtbetriebsräte*) for companies with more than one plant and for the election of "combine councils" (*Konzernbetriebsräte*) in groups of companies. These bodies deal respectively with issues that the individual works council and central works council are unable to settle in-house. Neither is deemed to be a higher organ than the individual plant works council.

Participation in works council elections has typically been around 80 percent, but fell to below 70 percent in the 1998 elections (see Niedenhoff 1998). The salient features of the electoral process are as follows: First, employees with voting rights, as well as trade unions represented in the establishment, are entitled to submit lists of candidates. Second, each list offered by employees must be supported by not less than 5 percent of employees with voting rights—with exceptions for very small firms—while each list of candidates from a trade union must be signed by two union representatives. Third, elections are direct and by secret ballot, with winners elected on the basis of proportional representation. (That is, workers vote for one of the lists, each of which typically contains a number of ranked candidates equal to the number of seats set for the council, and the share of votes garnered by a particular list in conjunction with the total number of seats available determine the number of councillors won by the list.) Fourth, wage earners and salaried employees may have separate or joint elections. In the latter case, which is increasingly the norm, elections are on the basis of joint lists of candidates. Finally, the law does not make formal provision for minority representation in the usual sense of that word. That said, younger workers (under eighteen years of age) may be represented indirectly through a youth delegation (*Jugendvertretung*), whose representative may attend any meeting of the council and vote on matters affecting youth.

Expenses of works council apparatus are borne by the employer. These costs include elections, facilities, and release time.[6] In the latter context, there are full-time as well as part-time works councillors, their number depending on the employment size of the plant. In establishments with between 300 and 600 employees, for example, one (of the nine) works councillors is released from any work duties, whereas in plants with, say, 9,000 employees ten (of the thirty-one) councillors are full-time.

The works council is made up exclusively of employees. There are therefore no external works councillors (e.g., union representatives) and no management members. Meetings are normally held within working hours and are not public. Their frequency is supposed to take account of the operational needs of the establishment. (The employer and the works council usually meet at least once a month in joint conferences to discuss matters at issue.) If the council consists of nine or more members, its day-to-day business is conducted by a works committee, elected by the works council and in accordance with the rules of proportional representation. The council can on a majority vote also delegate tasks to the works committee for independent action. Where the works council is less than nine members strong, it can delegate day-to-day business to its chairman or other of its members.

Returning to the theme of the union-works council nexus, most works councillors are union members (67 percent in 1998 at a time when union density is around one-third). Moreover, some 62 percent are elected on the lists of industrial unions affiliated to the *Deutscher Gewerkschaftsbund* (Niedenhoff 1998).

We next turn to the rules governing the information, consultation, and codetermination rights of works councils, which are perhaps better known than those determining their establishment and composition.[7] Beginning with the employer's duty to disclose information, the employer has to provide the works council with both timely and "comprehensive" information to enable it to discharge its general duties. These duties include proposing measures that further the interests of the enterprise and the employees, monitoring existing collective bargaining agreements (as well as internal works agreements, on which more below) and government regulations, and processing grievances. (Information disclosure is of course a prerequisite of the specific consultation rights next discussed.) Moreover, in plants with more than 100 permanent employees, the em-

ployer has also to inform a finance/economic committee (*Wirtschaftsausschuß*), appointed by the works council, "in full and good time," of the financial affairs of the establishment and supply the relevant documentation. This information covers the current and future economic situation of the company.

Consultation rights, for their part, cover all matters relating to manpower planning as well as planned changes in work processes, the working environment, and jobs. (Works council and employee rights in respect of the latter were expanded in 1989.) In these cases, employers have not merely to inform the works council but also consult it in good time so that its suggestions/objections can be taken into account. The works council must also be consulted on individual dismissals. Failure to consult renders the dismissal null and void.[8] Finally, in companies that have twenty-one or more employees with voting rights, the employer has to inform the works council of proposed "alterations" that may "entail substantial prejudice" to staff interests. In such circumstances, as we later see, the rights of the works council extend beyond consultation to encompass negotiation. In light of these remarks, it can be seen that works council powers are formally at least a function of establishment size. Alternatively put, the Works Constitution Act is not strictly a one-size-fits-all mandate.

What distinguishes the German works council from its counterparts in other countries is its codetermination powers. The *Betriebsrat* has a full right of codetermination with the employer on a set of issues strictly prescribed by legislation and termed "social matters." These include such things as the commencement and termination of working hours; the regulation of overtime and reduced working hours; leave arrangements; the introduction and use of technical devices to monitor employee performance; remuneration arrangements, including the fixing of job and bonus rates and other forms of performance-related pay; and, of course, health and safety measures. In all such matters, then, the employer cannot take action without the agreement of the works council, which can itself also take the initiative. Failure to reach agreement in any of these areas leads to their adjudication through a conciliation panel (*Einigungsstelle*). This panel comprises an equal number of employer and works council nominated members, plus an independent chairman.

In addition to this comanagement role, the works council has a somewhat weaker set of what are called "consent rights" in establishments normally employing twenty-one or more employees with voting rights. These cover the engagement, grading/regrading, and transfer of workers within the firm. Consent rights also obtain in the case of individual dismissals, noted earlier. If the works council withholds its consent, the employer can apply to the labor court for a decision in lieu of that consent.[9]

Finally, the works council can negotiate social compensation plans (*Sozialpläne*) and works agreements (*Betriebsvereinbarungen*). In all plants normally employing twenty-one or more employees, works councils have separate rights under the 1969 Dismissals Protection Act (*Kündigungsschutzgesetz*) to demand compensation for the dislocation caused by plant closings or partial closings, major changes in organization or equipment, and the introduction of new working methods or production techniques—changes involving "substantial prejudice" to the workforce referred to earlier. Where the parties cannot reach agreement on compensatory payments, retraining measures, and the like, either side can petition the conciliation board to formulate a compromise plan or decision.

Social plans may be regarded as a special case of works agreements. These set down the outcome of negotiations between the works council and management—as well as awards of the conciliation committee. Although the Works Constitution Act makes explicit provision for the execution of joint decisions through such agreements, it also rules out agreements relating to remuneration and other conditions of employment that "have been fixed or that are normally fixed by collective agreement." The proviso is that the latter have not expressly authorized the negotiation of supplementary works agreements.

As a matter of fact, framework agreements at industry level have increasingly made provision for their supplementation at local level. But beyond this, there is every indication that bilateral plant-level agreements have in practice ranged well beyond those prescribed by the law and, in particular, those areas where the works council has enforceable codetermination rights (Müller-Jentsch 1995, pp. 60–61). This proliferation of works agreements might therefore hint at distributive (as opposed to integrative) bargaining or rent-seeking behavior, although formal agreement is of course not strictly necessary for such behavior. Thus, for example, by threatening to be uncooperative in those areas where their consent is necessary, works councils could informally extend their authority to issues that are nowhere covered by the terms of the Works Constitution Act. We return to this theme below.

Works Council Coverage

There are no official data on works council coverage. Fortunately, a 1994 survey of approximately 1,000 manufacturing establishments in the state of Lower Saxony (*Niedersachsen*)—the dataset, the Hannover Firm Panel, is briefly described in the following section—allows us to address the coverage issue, as well as comment on the determinants of works council presence. The survey reveals that, in weighted terms, only 20.1 percent of firms (with five or more employees) had works councils. But these establishments accounted for no less than 73.4 percent of all employees. The low coverage of firms may strike the reader as surprising, given the rules for setting up a works council documented in the previous section, but the basic result is confirmed by the IAB (*Institut für Arbeitsmarkt- und Berufsforschung*) Establishment Panel, an annual representative survey of more than 7,000 establishments. This reveals that works council coverage in western and eastern Germany in 1996 was 17 and 15 percent, respectively (weighted data). The corresponding employment shares were 58 and 53 percent.[10]

Table 17.1 provides descriptive information on the distribution of works councils by firm size. It is readily apparent that coverage is more extensive in larger firms. The discussion in the previous section has already suggested one factor that might be expected to produce this outcome: the potential influence of the works council is increasing in firm size. A variety of other size-related factors may also be at work here, including the public goods aspects of many working conditions, monitoring considerations, internal labor market structuring, and, less positively, the dissatisfaction associated with routinized, regimented work settings.

Addison, Schnabel, and Wagner (1997, 1998) have recently investigated the determinants of works council coverage. In addition to firm size (and its square), the authors control for branch plant status (to capture any demonstration effect a mother plant might have on its affiliate) and plant age (to capture a tradition of collective bar-

gaining). Apart from these "structural" variables, the authors include several variables meant to pick up a taste for collective representation on the part of workers, namely, the percentage of blue-collar, female, and shift workers.[11] Moreover, to test for some associations suggested in an earlier econometric literature, the authors deploy a number of "participation" variables in the form of dummies for teamworking and profit sharing (for management and workers separately), as well as the percentage of workers covered by incentive pay. Finally, the authors' specification contains a set of (thirty) industry dummies.

Addison, Schnabel, and Wagner (1997) present probit results for their total sample of firms and for a subsample of firms in the size range 10–249 employees. Across both samples there is a consistent relationship between works council presence and the structural variables. That is, the probability of observing a works council increases with firm size (albeit at a decreasing rate) and with firm age, and is also greater if the establishment is a branch plant. As for the three taste-for-collective-representation variables, these all behave in the anticipated manner, but only the share of female workers is statistically significant across both samples.

The effect of the "participation" variables is rather interesting. There is, for example, the suggestion that teamwork is associated with a reduced probability of observing a works council. (The same is true for the employee profit sharing and payment by results variables but in neither case is the coefficient estimate statistically significant). Although this result is consistent with the argument of FitzRoy and Kraft (1985, 1987) that better managers can devise efficient communication and motivational alternatives to the *impedimenta* of the works council, there is no support for the other half of their argument to the effect that hard-

Table 17.1

Coverage and Participation Rights of Works Councils by Establishment Size

Establishment size (number of employees)	Hannover Firm Panel. Share of firms with a works council in 1994 (percent)	IAB Establishment Panel. Share of firms with a works council in 1996		Some important incremental participation rights
		Western Germany	Eastern Germany	
5–20	5	9	6	Establishment of works council
21–100	45	36	32	Detailed information on personnel movements (plus documentation) and notification of reductions in force
101–299	88	78	72	Establishment of an economics committee
300–1,000	97	90	85	Provision for full-time works councillors
1,001–2,000	100	96	96	Development of guidelines for criteria in personnel selection and movements
2,001 and above	100	98	100	Parity worker representation on company boards
Total	20	17	15	

Sources: Hannover Firm Panel. Wave 1, 1994; IAB Establishment Panel, Wave 4 (Western Germany)/Wave 1 (Eastern Germany); Niedenhoff (1997).
Note: The above calculations are based on weighted data.

pushing managers will be less pushy and therefore less likely to stimulate worker organization if they themselves have profit-sharing schemes. That is, the coefficient estimate for management profit sharing is positive (and statistically significant in the overall sample).

Addison, Schnabel, and Wagner (1997) also report that profits are negatively and union density positively associated with the probability of observing a works council. Each variable is strongly significant throughout. But simultaneity issues loom large in the former case (see below), while inspection of the raw data suggests that management responses to the union question are simply too inaccurate to give any confidence in the point estimates. Subject to this important caveat, however, the union results do accord with the thrust of the industrial relations literature and have not previously been reported in empirical work (cf. Frick and Sadowski 1995).

The bottom line of this inquiry is that variables consistent with organizational elements and factors associated with the specific functions of the works council dominate alternative arguments. And though the negative association between teamworking and presence of a works council might suggest the two are alternatives, this conclusion is necessarily tentative since it was not found in all configurations of the data (e.g. firms in the size range 21–100 employees), and because the industrial relations literature does seem to suggest that works councils have lost some of their earlier reluctance to embrace such schemes (Müller-Jentsch 1995, p. 69).

And frankly there remains a wider puzzle in the data. There is no indication that wages are higher in works council-free regimes. Indeed, the evidence is to the contrary (Addison, Schnabel, and Wagner, 1998). In other words, employees do not seem to "buy" their non-works council status through higher wages. The puzzle is why works council coverage is so thin in these circumstances.

Effects on Performance

There is a clear distinction in the works council literature between industrial relations and economic approaches. The former literature is richer, and has focused on the relations between works councils and employers, unions, and workers. (Political issues have also assumed importance in the industrial relations analysis.) In this qualitative literature, case studies have been the preferred method of inquiry. Economic analysis of the *Betriebsrat* is somewhat sparse and has focused squarely on firm performance under works councils. Frankly, at their points of contact, the two literatures have often clashed.

Economic treatments have tended to abstract from issues emphasized in the industrial relations literature. In particular, there has been little attempt to take account of the diversity of works council type/behavior suggested by industrial re-

lations studies. That is to say, works council impact has typically been captured via the use of dummy variables. This approach may be justified as a first step, although it runs into obvious difficulty where the firm sample is made up of large plants. As we have seen, the vast majority of firms with 300 or more employees will have works councils. In this connection, we note that case study work in the industrial relations mainstream has suggested that the impact of the *Betriebsrat* as an instrument of "effective independent voice" (on which more below) varies considerably across works councils (Wever 1994, 1995; Kotthoff 1981, 1994).

The econometric literature on works councils has generally been unable satisfactorily to incorporate unions into the analysis of outcomes. For its part, the industrial relations literature has emphasized the role of unions in supplying works councils with information, training, and advice, and has further suggested that they are critical to the ability of the works council to shape local outcomes strategically because of the support they offer to resource-strapped councils (Wever 1994). The union relation, and indeed the wider institutional influence, would also include worker representation on company boards. We are not aware of any economic work that has incorporated board representation directly into the analysis of works council impact, although this will in part be captured by the firm size covariate.[12]

The mainstream German industrial relations literature has tended to emphasize processes rather than outcomes. Workplace representation is not justified in economic terms largely because collective worker representation is taken to be "a basic political right" (Wever 1994, p. 469). To be sure, management perceptions of whether the works council is a positive production factor have been calibrated (Wever 1995). At this level, there are clear signs that management acceptance of the institution has grown. Kotthoff's (1994) follow-up study of fifty-five of the sixty-four firms in his earlier analysis (Kotthoff 1981) traces a sea-change in management attitudes. Whereas in 1975 two out of three works councils were adjudged to have an ineffective machinery, by 1990 fully two-thirds of the sample were engaged in a constructive dialogue with management (see also Niedenhoff 1990; Eberwein and Tholen 1990). The cooperation of the works council in unavoidable downsizing is often mentioned as contributing to this attitude change on the part of management (Müller-Jentsch 1995, pp. 67–68). A further aspect of this change in management perception is linked by Kotthoff to new attitudes among works councils toward quality circles and teamwork as vehicles of "work development." Nevertheless, the more general thrust and indeed presumption of the literature is that "social consensus," said to be both created and consolidated by the works council, is pro-productive. Standard additional arguments are of course that the works council cuts transaction costs, improves the works atmosphere, and is an ongoing source of organizational innovation. One also sees reference in the industrial relations literature to the role of the works council in forcing employers to follow a "high wage/high skill/labor-value-added competitive strategy" (Wever 1994, p. 478; Sorge and Streeck 1988; Thelen and Turner 1997), which argument also takes account of the works council role in training, also viewed as central to firm performance (Sadowski, Backes-Gellner, and Frick 1995).[13]

In the industrial relations literature there has also been considerable discussion of the relation between works councils and workers and between works councils and unions. Beginning with the former, German works councils appear to be a classic instrument of collective voice (Freeman and Medoff 1984), aggregating worker preferences and transmitting them to management which is in turn required to do more than consult. Our preceding discussion has suggested that works councils are representative institutions. That said, certain constituencies such as women and, most importantly, foreign/guest workers are underrepresented. In the most recent elections, the share of female members of works councils was 24 percent and that of foreign workers was roughly 4 percent (Niedenhoff 1998). Their respective employment shares in 1998 were 44 and 7 percent. Moreover, it has also been suggested that foreign workers have suffered disproportionately in mass layoffs in the auto, steel, and coal industries (see Müller-Jentsch 1995, p. 74), while in a generally dissenting treatment Thimm (1980, p. 44) notes that "large segments of the work force do not participate directly in works council activities" and that, despite the high turnout at works council elections noted earlier, "exhibit only moderate interest and approval of works-council codetermination."

More interesting is the evolving relation between unions and works councils traced earlier. These links will be further commented on below. One strand of the industrial relations literature sees the relation as central to a successful works council, where success is indexed by full-blown codetermination. Thus, Wever (1994) argues that the legal rights of works councils are insufficient to achieve this (necessary) end, so that success hinges on the ability of the institution to draw on external resources. The primary external resource which allows the works council to "plan, strategize, and anticipate" is of course the union. In view of the Freeman-Lazear model, reviewed in the following section, it is interesting that a number of German observers have sought to emphasize the limited legal rights and resources of the works council and the strategic importance of the union in this regard. A number of industrial relations studies have identified some of the more spectacular instances of labor-management innovation as being determined by the strategy and power of the unions (e.g., Thelen 1991). In any event, such analyses again underscore the point that the works council is not a datum. In this context, we should also note that Kotthoff's (1994) work confirms that, as compared with 1975, works councils are today better accepted and assisted by unions, but that due to their growing importance they have also become both more self-confident and autonomous.[14]

But for all its richness, the mainstream literature has tended either to ignore economic outcomes, largely taking it for granted that what is good for (certain identified aspects of) workplace relations is necessarily good for performance, or to regard performance outcomes as something of a black-box process in which valuable worker responses are mediated/obfuscated by all manner of other forces including managerial incompetence. Interestingly, in an otherwise careful and comprehensive analysis of the process of consultation, worker representation, and cooperation in industrial relations one can find almost no discussion of works councils and economic performance in the influential Rogers and Streeck (1995) volume.

Before turning to the economists' parsimonious representations of works council impact on firm performance, we should also note that some criticism (and support) for the works council machinery is to be found in a third body of research, namely, the management/human resource literature. The most accessible treatment is Wever (1995), whose (comparative) analysis characterizes human resource policies in German compa-

nies as targeting collective achievement, providing employment security, involving slow movement within the internal labor market, and emphasizing formal skills and functional specialization. German management structures are said to be hierarchical, generally offering low management responsibility. The shared organizational culture favors stability, consensus, and a process of slow, steady adaptation. German human resource departments, for their part, serve employees and provide liaison between management and labor. These characteristics are seen to be almost the exact opposite of those found in the "unilateral," as opposed to "negotiated," U.S. model.

Wever is concerned to point out that the German system has its advantages and its disadvantages. The strengths of the system reside in its inclusiveness and ability to enhance overall collective achievement, its acceptance of change when that change ultimately occurs, its predictability, and the high average degree of competence of its actors. The downside of this management system is that "it can stifle individual creativity and initiative, significantly slow the pace of change, and diminish the effectiveness of interdepartmental or cross-functional communication and collaboration" (Wever 1995, p. 140).

Wever does not of course single out the works council. It is but one element of a common cultural and institutional structure with offsetting advantages and disadvantages, no less than German hierarchical management. In addressing the deficiencies, however, she notes the limitations of an approach that channels the labor-management relation into contacts between the works council and the personnel/HR department. The diagnosis is that the process of enterprise-level negotiated adjustment may be dysfunctional or counterproductive. Her solution takes the form of a more direct and less formal mechanism for labor-management negotiation and labor participation in management. Specifically, she argues that every manager needs to be a HR manager. This fluidity is lacking in the highly institutionalized German system of industrial relations. For the future, the works council will have to cede its rights of information, consultation, and codetermination to smaller work groups. Works councils will have to become consultants to managers and workers on the line.

Wever's analysis, on the one hand, recognizes the deficiencies of works councils noted by many of their critics; in particular, the inflexibility, inertia, and slowed decision making. On the other, it both identifies the advantages and contextualizes the disadvantages within those of the overall system. It does not address management and the human resource function of works council-free regimes in Germany, leaving open the question of whether these units are at the vanguard in human resource management, as some economists have alleged.

With these preliminaries/caveats in mind, we next turn to econometric studies of works council impact on firm performance along the dimensions of productivity, profitability, investment in tangible and intangible capital, labor turnover, and wages. The key findings are reported in Table 17. 2. We choose to differentiate between the findings of the small-scale studies (rows 1 through 7) and results from larger and more representative data sets (rows 8 and 9).

The most econometrically sophisticated studies summarized in rows 1 through 3 of the table point to markedly unfavorable works council effects. The first two studies by FitzRoy and Kraft offer a management pressure/competence model that, if anything, sees unions in a more favorable light than works councils. The basic idea is that hard-driving managers elicit more effort from their workforces and are rewarded with higher salaries and profits. For their part, workers react by joining a union—hence the positive though indirect relation between unions and productivity and profits. The workers are also more likely in these circumstances to elect a works council both for reasons of protection and also to obtain a compensating differential for their greater effort. Independently, by limiting managerial discretion, works councils have an adverse effect on productivity and profits that better managers are able to avoid by offering better conditions and alternative channels of communication.

FitzRoy and Kraft also argue that the paraphernalia of the works council is inimical to the flexibility essential for innovation and modern technology. In their innovation study (row 3), they now interact union density in the plant with works council presence on the grounds that a works council will have more influence when density is high and also be more likely in these circumstances to take a hard line in conflict situations. This "composite" worker representation variable has a strongly negative effect on innovative activity. Note that in both this study and the productivity analysis (row 2) the authors model the determinants of worker representation rather than assume it to be exogenous.[15]

The largely single-equation studies shown in rows 4 through 6 of the table generally fail to tell as consistent a story of works council impact. But alone among the studies is Schnabel and Wagner's (row 4) finding of a positive association between works council presence and a measure of investment in intangible capital. (This result has of course to be contrasted with the finding of the study by Addison, Kraft, and Wagner in row 5, which points to a statistically significant negative association between works councils and investment in physical capital.) Interestingly, this beneficial effect hinges on the level of union density: once this exceeds 50 percent, works council impact turns negative.

The study in row 6 is notable insofar as it attempts to measure the degree of "involvement" of the works council is decision making. But although it uncovers a negative effect of works councils on a subjective, management self-reported measure of profits—"high profitability"—this does not carry over to the innovation performance indicator.

The issue of works council effect on labor turnover is examined in the study by Kraft in row 7. His attempt to peer inside the black box of works council effects uses a subjective measure of quits, namely, a "high quit rate" dummy variable defined on the basis of management responses, instead of the more familiar continuous measure, and seeks to distinguish between individual and collective voice. The former argument is constructed on the basis of management's assessment of the decision rights enjoyed by individual blue-collar workers, while the latter is simply proxied by the presence of a works council. As can be seen, it is reported that as high quit rates are strongly reduced, the greater the opportunities for the exercise of individual voice. By contrast, the indicator for collective voice is statistically insignificant.

There are a number of statistical problems attaching to all these studies. In the first place, there is the very real issue of their representativeness, given the very small sample sizes investigated (and revisited). Second, the sensitivity of the results is a cause for concern even if, as noted earlier, the major differences between the FitzRoy-Kraft studies and the rest may reflect certain changes in the works council behavior with the passage of time. Third, the likely nonrandom distribution of works councils is likely to pose special problems for estimates derived from such small samples. The

much larger firm samples investigated in the last two rows of Table 17.2 pose somewhat fewer problems in these respects, although the cross-sectional nature of the data means that causality remains an issue.

Turning therefore to the last two row entries in the table, it can be seen that the study by Frick and Sadowski (row 8) points to significantly lower labor turnover in works council regimes. The quits result contrasts with the findings of Kraft, reported in row 7, although the two models differ greatly. The argument that works councils lower quits is of course consistent with the collective voice model, and the dismissals result presumably in part reflects the somewhat greater difficulty of separating individuals in works council regimes (see also Frick 1997).

The final row summarizes results from two studies using the first wave of the Hannover Firm Panel (some other results from this database were reported in an earlier section). The interest of this material is that it is the first large-scale German database in which the works council is of other than peripheral interest; that is, the focus is on personnel issues rather than employment issues. The population covered by the survey generating the data is all manufacturing establishments within the state of Lower Saxony. The sample of establishments is stratified by firm size and industry, with oversampling of larger firms (hence the weighted data in Table 17.1). Of those firms approached, 51 percent agreed to participate in the survey, yielding a sample of 1,025 establishments.[16]

Addison, Schnabel, and Wagner's analyses of the Hannover Firm Panel provide a mixed bag of results that have been confirmed by Jirjahn (1998). Thus, for example, although works councils in the full sample are associated with higher value-added per worker, no such relation is observed among smaller firms. Innovation, as mea-

Table 17.2

The Effects of German Works Councils on Firm Performance

Study	Source	Methodology	Findings
1. FitzRoy and Kraft (1985)	Pooled data on 61/62 firms in the metalworking industry, 1977/79.	Four-equation system, estimated by 3SLS. Dependent variables: profitability, union density, wages, and salaries. Detailed firm controls. Works council presence not endogenized.	Union density has a positive and significant effect on profitability (and on wages and salaries). Coefficient estimate for works council dummy is negative and significant in the profit equation.
2. FitzRoy and Kraft (1987)	As above.	Two-equation system. Dependent variables: total factor productivity and presence of a works council.	Works council presence associated with significant reduction in productivity. Union density effects positive and significant throughout.
3. Fitzroy and Kraft (1990)	57 metalworking firms, 1979.	Two-equation system. Dependent variables: innovation, as proxied by the proportion of sales consisting of new products introduced in the preceding five years, and an "organized labor" measure derived from the interaction of the wage council dummy with union density.	Organized labor interaction variable is associated with a significant reduction in innovative activity.
4. Schnabel and Wagner (1994)	31 manufacturing industry firms in two German *Länder*, 1990.	Single-equation Tobit model. Dependent variable: proportion of revenues spent on R&D in 1979. Parsimonious specification.	Coefficient estimate on works council dummy is positive and marginally significant. Union density has strongly negative effect on R&D intensity.
5. Addison, Kraft, and Wagner (1993)	C. 50-firm sample from same dataset as row 4.	Single-equation specifications estimated by least median of squares/reweighted least squares. Dependent variables: profitability, value-added, and investment.	Mixed pattern of generally insignificant coefficient estimates for the works council dummy. But statistically significant negative effect of works councils on investment in physical capital.
6. Addison and Wagner (1997)	74 manufacturing firms in one German *Land*, 1993.	Probit models. Dependent variables: subjective measure of "high profitability," and an innovation measure (introduction of a new product in 1992). Three works council	Mixed pattern of generally insignificant coefficient estimates for all three works council variables. The exception is the degree of works council involvement measure which is

		indicators: works council presence, degree of participation or voice of works council, and instrument for presence of works council.	negatively associated with high profitability albeit only at the .10 level.
7. Kraft (1986)	As in rows 1 and 2.	Two-equation system. Dependent variables: a subjective measure of "high quits," and a synthetic measure of "individual voice" (see text).	Individual voice, and not collective voice (proxied by presence of a works council), significantly reduces high turnover.
8. Frick and Sadowski (1995)[a]	1,616 firms taken from a represen- tative survey of 2,392 private enterprises in the industrial and service sectors, 1987.	Single-equation log-odds model estimated by OLS. Dependent variables: quit and dismissal rates.	Works council presence associated with reduced quits and dismissals (2.4 and 2.9 percentage points, respec- tively).
9. Addison, Schnabel, and Wagner (1996, 1998)[b]	C. 1,000 establish- ments from a stratified sample of manufacturing firms in one Ger- man *Land*, 1994.	Single-equation plus instrumental variables approach. Dependent variables: value-added per worker; subjective measures of profitability, expressed as dummies or a five-element index; two measures of innovation (viz., introduction of new products or processes); wages and salaries per employee; and three turnover measures (hires, separations, and gross turnover). Various sample configurations used, and works council instrumented in some specifications.	Works council presence associated with higher labor productivity overall but not for firms employing 21–100 workers. Profits systematically lower in presence of works councils, with and without instrumentation. Innovation generally unaffected by presence of works council. Wages uniformly higher in works council regimes. Labor turnover measures lower in the presence of works councils for the overall sample but not for smaller firm subsample.

[a]See also Frick (1997).
[b]See also Jirjahn (1998).

---

sured, does not appear to be materially influenced by council presence, but across all sample con- figurations wages are higher and profitability is lower in works council regimes. The wage effect is of some interest precisely because of the mixed evidence in the earlier literature. That being said, the source of the *cet. par.* wage advantage asso- ciated with works councils—in particular, whether it stems from wage or grade drift—can- not be ascertained from this dataset. As for labor turnover, the results are generally consistent with those reported in row 8. But the data also indi- cate that establishments with works councils are more likely to complain (than establishments without them) that existing employment levels are excessive, that dismissal costs are too high,

and that workplace motivation is too low. The basic conclusion from this study would appear to be that smaller firms may be well advised to avoid works councils—though we have only hinted as to how they might do this (the teamwork result)— and that the benefits of collective voice, for want of a better term at this stage, are apparently ac- companied by costs to employers.

We enter some more general remarks of an interpretative nature in the following section. In the interim, we note that a number of potential problems attach to the results in row 9, inter alia, because of the cross-sectional nature of the data. The most important of these again stems from the nonrandom distribution of works councils. Although large-scale datasets often include a richer array of controls that may reduce the problem of works council endogeneity and allow more statistically reliable inferences, the negative effects of works councils, where observed, may still reflect reverse causation. That is, the least productive or profitable firms may turn to a works council as a solution to their predicament. Panel data may offer some assistance here.[17] But panel data are not a panacea. Thus, for example, if changes in the outcome indicator lead firms to introduce works councils, or if such firms simultaneously alter their management practices, estimates derived from panel data will still be subject to biases. This qualification and the bluntness of the works council variable reinforce the conclusion that economic analysis needs to be conducted alongside industrial relations studies of a case study nature and thence to incorporate insights from the latter. In the interim, we must observe the usual caution in attributing causality to the results provided in Table 17.2.

The Role of the Works Council Once More

It is useful to juxtapose the empirical evidence summarized in Table 17.2 against the recent applied theoretical analysis of works councils offered by Freeman and Lazear (1995). Their argument is an application and extension of the collective voice model. Specifically, Freeman and Lazear argue that the works council holds out the prospect of an improvement in the joint surplus of the enterprise as a result of information exchange, consultation, and participation/codetermination.

Consider each element in turn. First, management's use of a works council as a communicator to workers about the state of nature can generate an optimal provision of effort on the part of workers, leading them in particular to work harder in adverse states. Absent credible information, equated by the authors with a legal requirement to disclose profit information, inter alia, to the works council, workers may discount valid management claims about the precariousness of business—seeing them as opportunistic—and as a result be too aggressive in bad economic times. Such behavior by workers may prejudice the survival of the firm, and will in any event lower the joint surplus. (Similarly, the disclosure of private information by the worker side raises the joint surplus.) Second, consultation allows new solutions to production and other workplace problems, since the two sides have nonoverlapping information sets and because discussion is creative. Third, participation or codetermination provides workers with greater security, thereby encouraging them to take a longer-range view of the prospects of the firm, which again serves to increase the joint surplus.

In general, the joint surplus increases as one moves from information, through consultation, to participation. But the joint surplus does not continue to grow with the amount of power given to the works council. This is because there comes a point in the process when management no longer has sufficient control. There is another more basic problem: Freeman and Lazear argue that the workers' share in the surplus increases with that surplus and that profit declines both relatively and absolutely. The workers' share rises because knowledge and involvement are power. The same factors that cause the surplus to rise also cause profit to fall.[18]

The net result is that the powers of the works council will diverge from what is socially optimal. Firms will either oppose works councils or vest them with too little power because of the profit effect. And workers will always demand too much involvement/power, their share continuing to rise after the joint surplus has peaked. In this way, the authors make a general case for a participation mandate but one in which some limit has to be set on the power of the works council because after some point the joint surplus, and not merely firm profitability, will be dissipated by rent seeking.

The attraction of the German works council to Freeman and Lazear is twofold. First, its particular concatenation of information, consultation, and codetermination rights accord with their theoretical priors (e.g., in the presence of asymmetric information, the incentive of the worker side to disclose valuable information is heightened because of its partial control over how the information will be used). Second, the works council's rent-seeking powers are in practice circumscribed by the dual system in which it is embedded.

A natural question that arises therefore is this: Might not the widely observed negative effect of works councils on profitability reported in Table 17.2 be regarded as benign (i.e., neutral from an efficiency perspective) when taken in conjunction with positive productivity effects, a proxy for the joint surplus? Frankly, this interpretation is something of a stretch for a variety of reasons. One obvious response, of course, would be that positive productivity effects are not generally observed, while the suggestion in some of the studies that capital investment and innovation are impaired is not compatible with the model. But is not the Freeman-Lazear story more compelling if we focus instead on the results from the likely more representative results in row 9 of Table 17.2?

The issues that arise here are threefold. First, does the productivity effect dominate the profit effect? It may, although there is no way to scale the offsetting effects observed in this study. Second, abstracting from problems of statistical in-

ference, there is no suggestion that works councils increase the joint surplus of smaller firms; only that they are associated with lower profitability. Whatever the benefits to larger enterprises—works councils may indeed help overcome the problems stemming from the public goods nature of the workplace—these are distinctly secondary in smaller firms, not merely a priori, but also apparently empirically too. Accordingly, even if it is accepted that the German mandate might not disadvantage large firms, the powers set for the works council under German legislation may still be too intrusive for smaller firms. Third, and more generally, what assurance do we have that reduced profitability will not (indirectly) reduce investment in long-lived, relation-specific capital, as the U.S. evidence clearly and consistently suggests (e.g., Hirsch 1991)?

Some may choose to conclude from the more recent evidence reported here that the German legislation may not have been too far off the mark, perhaps adding Thimm's (1980) caveat that this applies more to the 1952 than the 1972 legislation. Such a conclusion is not inconsistent with the Freeman-Lazear model, but it does not establish the relevance of that model. For example, if works councils "work" in situations where the issues of the size of the surplus and its distribution are largely decoupled, what is the efficiency loss from not having a mandate? In such circumstances, firms will likely elect to introduce analogous forms of participation. Issues of the counterfactual aside, if the participation obligations fixed under a mandate are endogenous—reflecting, say, the interests of the parties—then the reach of the model is rather limited. *Vulgo:* what is to be gained from a mandate in decentralized bargaining regimes? In sum, any statement to the effect that the "Germans may not have got it far wrong," is best viewed as a simple argument against government failure; no more and no less.

Concluding Remarks

If it is appropriate to frame our concluding remarks in terms of "what if German works councils were to come to the United States?" the first observation should most probably be that works councils as they have developed in Germany are complements to, rather than substitutes for, conventional unions. On this basis, and given the decentralized collective bargaining tradition in the United States, works councils should be viewed as clearly benefiting workplace union organization. This may of course not be the intention of many of their proponents, who have perhaps rather misunderstood the history of the German *Betriebsrat* and its evolving place in the dual system. Second, the representative nature and functions of the works council would appear in principle to meet U.S. worker demands for increased representation (Freeman and Rogers 1995), so that the crux of the works council debate might then appear to devolve on issues of economic impact versus equity. But even if one takes a sanguine view of the German evidence, it is doubtful whether one would seek to transplant German institutions and risk tissue rejection. The question therefore becomes one of whether there are alternatives. The fact that mandates are effectively foreclosed in the post-Dunlop United States in no way detracts from the importance of this question (see Commission on the Future of Worker-Management Relations 1994).

Given the limited points of institutional contact between Germany and the United States, might not more be learned about the effects of and limits on participation from, say, the increasingly decentralized British collective bargaining regime with its plethora of employee involvement schemes and declining unionization? This is not the place to review the rather intriguing British evidence in any detail, but some conclusions from a study by Fernie and Metcalf (1995) might whet the appetite. The authors summarize their detailed analysis of the Workplace Industrial Relations Survey (WIRS) data by examining three synthetic benchmark workplaces—authoritarian (traditional nonunion), collective bargaining (traditional union), and employee involvement (nonunion) enterprises—in terms of economic impact (e.g., productivity change) and industrial relations outcome (e.g., climate of employee-management relations). It is reported that authoritarian workplaces surprisingly have good industrial relations performance but not economic performance, and conversely for employee involvement workplaces. It is also found that, apart from their beneficial effect on quits (though these may of course be artificially reduced), collective bargaining regimes score poorly on both economic and industrial relations indicators. Interestingly, both this and other WIRS-based research (e.g., Siebert and Wei 1997) shows that voluntary consultative mechanisms in nonunion but not union regimes are associated with improved outcomes. Methodologically, there are close points of contact between the British and U.S. literatures here (see, for example, Cooke 1994), and it would be interesting to evaluate the sources of difference between them.

But more important than the lessons of comparative exercises are the increasingly sophisticated analyses of the consequences of human resource management in the United States (for an interesting review, see Ichniowski et al. 1996). For its part, German research must now attempt to distinguish between types of works councils and examine the covariation of innovative work practices and works councils. In the process, closer links must be effected between the econometric and case study analyses.

Notes

1. The 1972 act was revised in 1989, at which time the general information and consultation (but not codetermination) rights of the works council were reinforced in respect of the introduction of new technology.

2. Strictly speaking, we are here describing codetermination at the workplace (*betriebliche Mitbestimmung*). There is also codetermination at the enterprise level (*Mitbestimmung auf Unternehmensebene*), whereby worker representatives sit on the supervisory boards of companies. Indeed, the 1952 Works Constitution Act also provided for such representation. It was preceded, however, by the Codetermination Act (*Mitbestimmungsgesetz*) of 1951, which gave workers in the coal, iron, and steel industries full parity representation on their company boards. This system of so-called *Montanmitbestimmung* was interestingly enough inherited from what was established practice in the British occupation zone under Allied Law (*Kontrollratsgesetz*) 45. For its part, the 1952 Works Constitution Act extended worker representation on company boards—this time one-third of the seats on company supervisory boards—to the generality of firms employing more than 500 workers. Subsequently, a further and highly controversial piece of legislation, the Codetermination Act of 1976, provided for quasi-parity representation on company boards in all firms employing over 2,000 workers.

3. The immediate precursors of these joint factory committees were the largely advisory worker councils set up under Bavarian and Prussian mining laws (*Bergwerkgesetze*) in 1900 and 1905, respectively, to administer safety rules and cooperate with management in improving productivity.

4. For an official English-language translation of the Works Constitution Act, see Federal Minister of Labor and Social Affairs (1990). And for more detailed legal information and interpretation, also see Stege and Weinspach (1999).

5. The union has only to claim that it has at least one member in the plant; no formal registration procedure is required, and the identity of the union member does not have to be disclosed.

6. The employer also bears the cost of the conciliation committee apparatus, briefly discussed below.

7. Case studies of the operation of the works council are provided by Thimm (1980, ch. 5), and Wever (1994).

8. Works councillors themselves are given special protection against dismissal. There is no indication that councillors or the works council as a body are in the U.S. sense "dominated" by the employer.

9. As a practical matter, any works council consent rights in the area of individual dismissals coexist with statutory regulation, which requires that job terminations be "socially justified" and the rulings of the labor court in this regard. (Yet it is interesting to note that legal protection against dismissal was first introduced under works council legislation, namely, the 1920 *Betriebsrätegesetz*.)

10. We thank Peter Ellguth and Lutz Bellmann of the IAB for providing us with this information. We further note that Frick and Sadowski (1995) in an analysis of a large-scale establishment database for 1987 report that works councils are found in just 24 percent of the sample, although they account for 60 percent of employment.

11. Although the shift-work variable might be justified on "defensive grounds," it is also mechanically linked to works council formation by virtue of that institution's codetermination powers with respect to the organization of working time.

12. For separate analyses of the effect of board representation on firm performance, see, inter alia, the events study of Baums and Frick (1997), and the references contained therein.

13. Streeck et al. (1987) investigate the works council and union role in training. For a revealing earnings function analysis of apprenticeship training in Germany, see also Harhoff and Kane (1996).

14. There is a general point to be made here. The shifting institutional order complicates the task of measurement and could conceivably explain why early econometric studies, reviewed below, produce results that are so much at odds with the qualitative findings of the industrial relations literature.

15. In a follow-up study, not shown in Table 17.2, FitzRoy and Kraft (1995) find a positive effect of works councils on productivity in a subsample of profit-sharing firms, whereas in nonprofit-sharing firms the works council effect is still negative.

16. In spite of this fairly high attrition rate, the deviation between actual and planned stratification in the net sample is relatively small, so that the data are representative of the population of manufacturing establishments. See Brand et al. (1996).

17. The row 9 dataset has a longitudinal capacity, and some modest changes in works council status are observed between the relevant (first and third) waves of the panel that the authors plan to exploit in future research.

18. The Freeman-Lazear model is thus couched in terms of potential rather than actual Pareto improvements (cf. Levine and Tyson 1990).

References

Addison, John T., Kornelius Kraft, and Joachim Wagner. 1993. "German Works Councils and Firm Performance." In *Employee Representation: Alternatives and Future Directions*, ed. Bruce E. Kaufman and Morris M. Kleiner, pp. 305–336. Madison: Industrial Relations Research Association.

Addison, John T., Claus Schnabel, and Joachim Wagner. 1995. "German Industrial Relations: An Elusive Exemplar." *Industrielle Beziehungen* 2, no. 7: 25–45.

———. 1996. "German Works Councils, Profits, and Innovation." *Kyklos* 49, no. 4: 555–582.

———. 1997. "On the Determinants of Mandatory Works Councils in Germany." *Industrial Relations* 36 (October): 419–445.

———. 1998. "Betriebsräte in der deutschen Industrie: Verbreitung, Bestimmungsgründe und Effekte." In *Ökonomische Analysen betrieblicher Strukturen und Entwicklungen-Das Hannoveraner Firmenpanel*, ed. Knut Gerlach, Olaf Hübler, and Wolfgang Meyer, pp. 59–87. Frankfurt/Main and New York: Campus Verlag.

Addison, John T., and Joachim Wagner. 1997. "The Impact of German Works Councils on Profitability and Innovation: New Evidence from Micro Data." *Jahrbücher für Nationalökonomie und Statistik* 216, no. 1: 1–20.

Baums, Theodor, and Bernd Frick. 1997. "Codetermination in Germany: The Impact on the Market Value of the Firm." Working Paper 1/97, Institut für Handels- und Wirtschaftsrecht, University of Osnabrück.

Brand, Ruth, Vivian Carstensen, Knut Gerlach, and Thomas Klodt. 1996. "The Hannover Panel." Discussion Paper No. 2, University of Hannover.

Brigl-Matthiaß, Kurt. 1978. "Das Betriebsräteproblem in der Weimarer Republik. In *Die Betriebsräte in der Weimarer Republik*, ed. Reinhard Crusius, Guenther Schiefelbein, and Manfred Wilke. Berlin: Olle & Wolter.

Commission on the Future of Worker-Management Relations. 1994. *Report and Recommendations*. Washington, D.C.: U.S. Department of Commerce and U.S. Department of Labor.

Cooke, William N. 1994. "Employee Participation Programs, Group-Based Incentives, and Company Performance: A Union-Nonunion Comparison." *Industrial and Labor Relations Review* 47 (July): 594–609.

Eberwein, Wilhelm, and Jochen Tholen. 1990. *Managermentalität*. Frankfurt/Main: Frankfurter Allgemeine Zeitung.

Federal Minister of Labor and Social Affairs. 1990. *Codetermination in the Federal Republic of Germany*. Bonn: Federal Minister of Labor and Social Affairs.

Fernie, Sue, and David Metcalf. 1995. "Participation, Contingent Pay, Representation, and Workplace Performance: Evidence from Great Britain." *British Journal of Industrial Relations* 33 (September): 379–415.

FitzRoy, Felix R., and Kornelius Kraft. 1985. "Unionization, Wages, and Efficiency—Theories and Evidence from the U.S. and West Germany." *Kyklos* 38, no. 4: 537–554.

———. 1987. "Efficiency and Internal Organization: Works Councils in West German Firms." *Economica* 54 (November): 493–504.

———. 1990. "Innovation, Rent-Sharing and the Organization of Labour in the Federal Republic of Germany." *Small Business Economics* 2, no. 1: 95–103.

———. 1995. "On the Choice of Incentives in Firms." *Journal of Economic Behavior and Organization* 26 (January): 145–160.

Freeman, Richard B., and Edward P. Lazear. 1995. "An Economic Analysis of Works Councils." In *Works Councils: Consultation, Representation, and Cooperation in Industrial Relations*, ed. Joel Rogers and Wolfgang Streeck, pp. 27–50. Chicago: University of Chicago Press.

Freeman, Richard B., and James L. Medoff. 1984. *What Do Unions Do?* New York: Basic Books.

Freeman, Richard B., and Joel Rogers. 1995. "Worker Representation and Participation Survey." Princeton: Princeton Survey Research Corporation.

Frick, Bernd. 1997. *Mitbestimmung und Personalfluktuation*. Munich: Rainer Hampp Verlag.

Frick, Bernd, and Dieter Sadowski. 1995. "Works Councils, Unions, and Firm Performance." In *Institutional Frameworks and Labor Market Performance—Comparative Views on the U.S. and German Economies*, ed. Friedrich Buttler, Wolfgang Franz, Ronald Schettkat, and David Soskice, pp. 46–81. London and New York: Routledge.

Harhoff, Dieter, and Thomas J. Kane. 1996. "Is the German Apprenticeship System a Panacea for the U.S. Labor Market?" Discussion Paper No. 1311. London: Centre for Economic Policy Research.

Hirsch, Barry T. 1991. *Labor Unions and the Economic Performance of Firms*. Kalamazoo: W.E. Upjohn Institute for Employment Research.

Hohn, Hans-Willy. 1988. *Von der Einheitsgewerkschaft zum Betriebssyndikalismus: Soziale Schließung im dualen System der Interessenvertretung*. Berlin: Edition Sigma.

Ichniowski, Casey, Thomas A. Kochan, David Levine, Craig Olson, and George Strauss. 1996. "What Works at Work: Overview and Assessment." *Industrial Relations* 35 (July): 299–333.

Jirjahn, Uwe. 1998. *Effizienzwirkungen von Erfolgsbeteiligung und Partizipation*. Frankfurt/Main and New York: Campus Verlag.

Kotthoff, Hermann. 1981. *Betriebsräte und betriebliche Herrschaft: Eine Typologie von Partizipationsmustern im Industriebetrieb.* Frankfurt and New York: Campus Verlag.

————. 1994. *Betriebsräte und Bürgerstatus: Wandel und Kontinuität betrieblicher Interessenvertretung.* Munich: Rainer Hampp Verlag.

Kraft, Kornelius. 1986. "Exit and Voice in the Labor Market: An Empirical Study of Quits." *Journal of Institutional and Theoretical Economics* 142 (December): 697–715.

Levine, David I., and Laura D'Andrea Tyson. 1990. "Participation, Productivity, and the Firm's Environment." In *Paying for Productivity: A Look at the Evidence*, ed. Alan S. Blinder, pp. 183–237. Washington, D.C.: Brookings Institution.

Müller-Jentsch, Walther. 1995. "Germany: From Collective Voice to Co-management." In Rogers and Streeck 1995, pp. 53–78.

Niedenhoff, Horst-Udo, ed. 1990. *Die Zusammenarbeit mit dem Betriebsrat.* Cologne: Deutscher Instituts-Verlag.

————. 1997. *Mitbestimmung in der Bundesrepublik Deutschland.* Cologne: Deutscher Instituts-Verlag.

————. 1998. "Schlappe für den DGB - Betriebsratswahlen 1998: Keine Lust auf Experimente." *IW-Gewerkschafts-Report* 32, no. 3: 3–13.

Rogers, Joel, and Wolfgang Streeck, eds. 1995. *Works Councils: Consultation, Representation, and Cooperation in Industrial Relations.* Chicago: University of Chicago Press.

Sadowski, Dieter, Uschi Backes-Gellner, and Bernd Frick. 1995. "Works Councils: Barriers or Boosts for the Competitiveness of German Firms?" *British Journal of Industrial Relations* 33 (September): 493–513.

Schmidt, Rudi, and Rainer Trinczek. 1991. "Duales System: Tarifliche und betriebliche Interessenvertretung." In *Konfliktpartnerschaft: Akteure und Institutionen der industrielle Beziehungen*, ed. Walther Müller-Jentsch, pp. 167–199. Munich: Rainer Hampp Verlag.

Schnabel, Claus, and Joachim Wagner. 1992. "Unions and Innovation. Evidence from German Micro Data." *Economics Letters* 39 (July): 369–373.

————. 1994. "Industrial Relations and Trade Union Effects on Innovation in Germany." *Labour* 8 (Autumn): 489–503.

Siebert, W. Stanley, and Xiangdong Wei. 1997. "Consultation, Communication and Firm Performance." University of Birmingham. Mimeographed.

Sorge, Arndt, and Wolfgang Streeck. 1988. "Industrial Relations and Technical Change: The Case for an Extended Perspective." In *New Technology and Industrial Relations*, ed. Richard Hyman and Wolfgang Streeck. London: Basil Blackwell.

Stege, Dieter, and Friedrich K. Weinspach. 1999. *Betriebsverfassungsgesetz: Handkommentar für die betriebliche Praxis.* Cologne: Deutscher Instituts-Verlag.

Streeck, Wolfgang. 1995. "Works Councils in Western Europe: From Consultation to Participation." In Rogers and Streeck 1995, pp. 313–347.

Streeck, Wolfgang, Josef Hilbert, Karl-Heinz van Kevelaer, Friedericke Maier, and Hajo Weber. 1987. *Steuerung und Regulierung der berufliche Bildung: Die Rolle der Sozialpartner in der Ausbildung und beruflichen Weiterbildung in der Bundesrepublik Deutschland.* Berlin: Edition Sigma.

Thelen, Kathleen. 1991. *Union of Parts—Labor Politics in Postwar Germany.* Ithaca, N.Y.: Cornell University Press.

Thelen, Kathleen, and Lowell Turner. 1997. *German Codetermination in Comparative Perspective.* Expertise für das Projekt "Mitbestimmung und neue Unternehmenskulturen" der Bertelsmann Stiftung und der Hans-Böckler Stiftung. Gütersloh: Verlag Bertelsmann Stiftung.

Thimm, Alfred L. 1980. *The False Promise of Codetermination—The Changing Nature of European Workers' Participation.* Lexington, Mass.: D.C. Heath.

Wever, Kirsten S. 1994. "Learning from Works Councils: Five Unspectacular Cases from Germany." *Industrial Relations* 33 (October): 467–481.

————. 1995. *Negotiating Competitiveness: Employment Relations and Organizational Innovation in Germany and the United States.* Boston: Harvard Business School Press.

18

Nonunion Employee Representation in Japan

Motohiro Morishima and Tsuyoshi Tsuru

In past studies, academic attention has focused on two aspects of Japanese industrial relations. The first is enterprise unionism, and the second is employee involvement and participation in management (Shirai 1983; Koike 1988; Nakamura and Nitta 1997). Both of these aspects, however, have been discussed with almost no reference to nonunion forms of employee representation.[1]

Yet nonunion employee representation is crucial to understanding industrial relations and human resource management (IR/HR) practices in contemporary Japan. First, the organization rate of unions has fallen steadily for over two decades. Hence, nonunion employee representation has come to provide an increasingly important alternative source of voice for workers. Further, Japanese firms have devoted great effort to developing participation in management, and there is reason to believe that they have used nonunion representation practices innovatively and effectively to structure and enlarge employee participation in decision making. Nevertheless, these aspects of nonunion employee representation have been largely ignored.

This chapter seeks to begin filling this void by providing the quantitative data necessary to understand the basic context of nonunion employee representation. Specifically, we attempt to provide the data necessary to grasp critical information such as the extent to which organized labor is in decline and nonunion employee representation is substituting for unions, and the extent to which nonunion employee representation promotes employee involvement in nonunion firms. This is done by using data from the extensive surveys conducted to gauge the impact of nonunion employee representation on key IR/HR factors including turnover, job satisfaction, and influence on managerial decision making.

The analysis proceeds as follows. The next section describes the institutional framework that structures nonunion employee representation. Then we analyze data compiled from surveys of employers in order to assess the extent to which various types of employee representation mechanisms are found in the Japanese economy, and to estimate the effect of those mechanisms on employee voice and exit. Following that section we use data collected from employees to examine whether their perceptions regarding the effectiveness of representation mechanisms correspond to evaluations by employers. The chapter concludes by comparing the two datasets and interpreting the main findings.

Institutional Framework for Employee Representation in Japan

Developments of Enterprise Unionism

Beginning in the late 1950s, a distinctive set of employment practices emerged in large enterprises in Japan. First, blue-collar workers came to enjoy job security and opportunities to pursue careers comparable to those of white-collar workers. Second, in order to raise the productivity of long-staying blue- and white-collar employees, major firms began to develop comprehensive in-house systems for training and skill formation. Third, corresponding to those two factors, a wage structure emphasizing both length of service and skill development became dominant. The wage system, in turn, complemented and reinforced the practices of long-term employment and intrafirm skill formation.

This set of employment practices has provided a solid basis for a particular form of labor organization, namely, unions that are organized at the enterprise level. Given the situation described above, it is natural for workers to bargain over major working conditions, such as wages and job security, at the level of the firm rather than at industry or regional levels. Also, workers entitled to such benefits tend to feel a strong sense of identity with their firms. These conditions encourage the formation and continued maintenance of an enterprise-centered system of industrial relations, hence, enterprise unionism (Shirai 1983; Gordon 1985).

Enterprise unionism implies at least three practices. First, employees of a single firm organize their own union, and all employees, excluding managers and temporary workers, can participate in this firm-level structure. Second, there is no segregation based on employees' occupational classification or job category. Third, collective bargaining takes place at the level of the firm, leading to a very decentralized bargaining structure. Consequently, at the firm level, Japanese enterprise unions have functioned both as labor unions for gaining higher wages and improving working conditions in negotiations with management and also as employee representative bodies to promote participation in and cooperation with management.

Enterprise unions have also developed webs of supraenterprise organizations in respective industries and industrial sectors to engage in industrywide coordination of negotiation and other activities. Particularly noteworthy are the nationwide synchronization and coordination of wage negotiations in *shunto* (spring wage offensive) and extensive union involvement in the government's policymaking processes. As many authors have noted (Tsuru 1992; Sako 1997), Japanese enterprise unions, through the institutionalization of *shunto*, have developed a relatively centralized coordination mechanism.

As a result, one important characteristic of *shunto* is that it serves as a pattern-setting device for the rest of the economy, influencing both union and nonunion sectors. Formally, *shunto* occurs within the unionized sector because coordination and synchronization of wage bargaining are conducted by industry-level federations composed of individual enterprise unions. Nonunion firms are not covered by *shunto* negotiations. Nevertheless, substantial evidence (see Tsuru 1997) suggests that nonunion firms often use *shunto* settlements as their "norms" for annual wage increases. In particular, smaller-size firms, which are often unorganized, tend to follow *shunto* wage increases with only minimal modifications.[2]

One of the problems Japanese enterprise unions face today is that they have not been able to offer these achievements as their "competitive advantage" vis-à-vis the nonunion sector. More specifically, when union-nonunion wage differentials are calculated, most studies do not find significant advantages in the union sector and some even find disadvantages (Tachibanaki and Noda 1993; Tsuru and Rebitzer 1995). Employment security, for which Japanese enterprise unions fought bitterly in the 1950s and 1960s, is also fairly strong in the union and nonunion sectors alike. This is due, in part, to the adoption of long-term employment practices by nonunion firms to attract qualified workers, and, in part, to the strong constraints that Japanese courts often impose on employers with regard to the termination and layoff of their regular-status workers.

One may interpret this lack of union-nonunion differentiation as an indication of either strength (i.e., unions have spillover effects to nonunion sectors) or weakness (i.e., unions have not been able to increase wage and employment security levels above market rates), but one thing is clear: Japanese enterprise unions have not been able to offer strong incentives to nonunion employees to form and join unions. From the workers' perspective, existing unions are not attractive since they can obtain union benefits without actually joining unions or establishing unions in nonunion workplaces. Some have argued that it is the unions' inability to offer strong advantages in the union sector, not employer opposition, that is a major factor in the decline of union density in Japan, as is the case in other industrialized countries (Tsuru and Rebitzer 1995). In Japan, since 1975, when the level of union density was 34.4 percent of the labor force, the organization rate has declined steadily to 22.2 percent in 1999. Among OECD countries, this rate of decline has been exceeded only by France and the United States.

Despite the declining union density, employees do seem to desire representation. The individual-level data to be used in the following sections (Data Appendix B) indicate that, in fact, the desire for representation is especially strong in the nonunion sector. In the sample of approximately 1,600 individuals, 53.9 percent of nonunion employees report that they would like to see their concerns and desires reflected in the management of their firms, and 50.2 percent report that they would like managers to share with

them more information on corporate performance. Equivalent figures for the employees in union firms are 37.0 percent and 32.6 percent, respectively.

The Legal Foundations

The Union Sector

In Japan, as in other democratic countries, workers' rights to collective bargaining and union representation are constitutionally guaranteed. Compared to the United States, it is also relatively easy for Japanese employees to establish trade unions. The Japanese Trade Union Law requires neither majority support for certification nor the recognition of exclusive bargaining rights. Instead, the Trade Union Law focuses on defining the nature and functions of unions. In the main text of Article 2 of the Trade Union Law, unions are defined as those organizations or federations thereof, formed autonomously and predominantly by the workers for the main purpose of maintaining and improving the conditions of work and for raising the economic status of the workers. A union is also required to have a character as an "organization" with an expectation of continued existence, a constitution, and a structure for its operation. Further, this definition is limited by provisos that exclude those organizations (1) that admit to membership workers at the supervisory post and other workers who represent the interest of the employer, (2) that receive financial support from the employer, (3) whose objectives are confined to mutual aid or other welfare work, or (4) that principally aim at engaging in political or social activities.

In Japan, when a group of workers wishes to form a "statutorily qualified union" and receive legal protection under the Trade Union Law, an application must be filed with the Labor Commission. The commission conducts a "qualification examination." The details of the procedures followed in a qualification examination are set forth in rules of the Labor Commission (see Sugeno 1992 for details). When these organizations are qualified as unions, employers are required by law to engage in collective bargaining even with unions that represent a very small proportion of employees.

According to the law, employers cannot interfere with the establishment of a union. In practice, however, management does play an important role. In most cases, at the beginning of union formation, union organizers, usually sent by an industry-level federation of enterprise unions, visit employers to obtain their consent. According to Fujimura (1997), it is important to secure employers' consent because many employees do not want to join unions that are opposed by the employer. It is rare that employers engage in active union opposition or suppression activity at this point.

The Nonunion Sector

In contrast to the union sector, the legal structure that regulates nonunion forms of employee representation is almost nonexistent. There is virtually no law regulating or governing the forms or functions of nonunion employee representation in Japan. Consequently, these organizations range greatly in function, from those that engage in discussions and negotiations on wages and other working conditions and even enter into written agreements with employers, to those whose purposes are primarily social or mutual friendship among workers. There is also a wide range in form. Some nonunion organizations take the form of committees composed of employee representatives, while others are structured similarly to trade unions. There is also no

requirement regarding the organizational character of these organizations.

The thrust of the legal framework governing employee organizations in Japan differs significantly from that of the United States. In the United States, NLRA Section 8(a)(2) mandates the exclusion of almost any organization other than unions from workplaces, in order to forestall employer use of such organizations to influence or control workers illegally. The main exceptions are organizations such as quality-control circles, which deal directly with production, and do not deal with wages or working conditions. In contrast, Japanese labor law specifies the characteristics and functions of unions, but does not prohibit the existence of other types of employee organizations. In the case of disputes between labor and management, the first task of the Labor Commission is often to determine whether a particular labor organization is, in fact, a union; if it is not, it may legally include managers as members and receive financial assistance from the enterprise. Under present U.S. labor law, the existence of many, if not most, Japanese employee organizations would be regarded as interfering with union organization or the conduct of union activities.

While there are many types of nonunion forms of employee representation in Japan, attention centers on two, the joint consultation system and employee associations, because these are most likely to allow workers some level of representation regarding their working conditions. The current decline of union density in Japan has prompted a debate on the desirability of mandating by law some form of nonunion representation schemes. Some observers advocate nonunion representation systems similar to the German works councils, with joint consultation and employee associations being the most likely candidates (Nakamura 1995; Sato 1997).

The joint consultation system is probably the best-known mechanism for protecting employee interests in nonunion firms. Joint consultation typically involves more or less formal committee meetings of labor and management representatives for extensive discussion of business conditions and production, working conditions, and fringe benefits. According to a survey conducted by the Labor Ministry Secretariat Policy Research Department (MOL), the issues discussed most frequently by joint consultation committees are: (1) job safety and health (83 percent of nonunion establishments with joint consultation committees); (2) working hours, holidays, and break time (82.5 percent); and (3) fringe benefits (80.3 percent). However, joint consultation is primarily a characteristic of union firms. More than 80 percent of union establishments have joint consultation committees, but the rate drops to the level of 30 percent for nonunion establishments, according to the MOL survey.

Although joint consultation is the best-known means of nonunion employee representation, in fact nonunion firms more often use employee associations to represent employee interests. An employee association is defined as an organization for a company's staff or employees. Employee associations are often called, for example, friendship societies (*shinbokukai*) or staff councils (*shainkai*). More than 50 percent of nonunion firms have such organizations (Tokyo Metropolitan Labor Research Institute 1990).

There are two types of employee associations. Two-thirds are oriented toward recreational activities, while the remaining third are voice-oriented organizations that discuss working conditions with management (Intrafirm Communication Research Group 1991). Voice-oriented employee associations often discuss working conditions and industrial planning with management, and managers have a high regard for their functions of aggregating and communicating employee views. Further, when joint consultations are conducted in nonunion firms, employee associations often serve as employee representatives (Sato 1997).

Nonunion Employee Representation Mechanisms: Adoption and Outcomes

The Diffusion of Various Practices

As described in the previous section, joint consultation systems and employee associations are the main means of nonunion employee representation in Japan. But they do not account for all forms of employee voice. Various representation practices are also used. Table 18.1 summarizes the basic structure of voice mechanisms in Japanese firms. (The data are derived from a survey of personnel managers on their own companies. For further details, see Data Appendix A.) We can identify four types of collective voice mechanisms used by over 20 percent of nonunion firms: (1) announcements of firm strategy to all employees (every year all employees attend a meeting at which management reports on firm performance, followed by an open question-and-answer period), (2) middle management and employee workplace discussions (supervisors and employees attend meetings in the workplace to discuss workplace issues), (3) group off-the-job training for communication (management and employees meet and communicate at a location where off-the-job training is conducted), and (4) joint consultation systems (mentioned earlier). Management evaluation of the effectiveness of these four mechanisms in communicating employees' opinions is fairly high.

Table 18.1

The Structure of Intrafirm Voice Mechanisms

Practices	Nonunion firms		Union firms	
	Adoption rate %	Effectiveness score[a]	Adoption rate %	Effectiveness score
A. Collective voice mechanisms				
1. Announcements of firm strategy to all employees	33.2	1.01	21.5	1.09
2. Middle management and employee workplace discussions	32.4	1.13	22.7	1.28
3. Group off-the-job training for communication	29.2	0.85	27.6	1.04
4. Joint consultation systems	25.3	0.99	83.1	1.51
5. Small-group activities	19.2	0.78	18.0	0.92
6. Voice-oriented employee associations	11.4	0.87	3.1	0.50
7. Discussions between top and middle management	11.2	1.13	5.7	1.40
8. Others	4.1	0.85	2.5	0.61
9. Collective bargaining	—	—	92.7	1.22
B. Individual voice mechanisms				
1. Means of individual expression (written reports)	47.0	0.81	53.8	1.03
2. Suggestion systems	34.2	0.68	36.1	0.48
3. Individual interviews conducted by personnel departments	26.1	1.04	17.5	1.23
4. Others	9.2	0.81	5.9	0.62
5. Opinion surveys of employees	8.9	0.84	6.5	0.89
6. Grievance procedures	6.6	0.58	12.0	0.91

[a]Figures are weighted averages, using the following values: 2 = very effective; 1 = effective; 0 = neither effective nor ineffective; −1 = not very effective; −2 = not effective at all—to reflect the employees' opinions.

There is a clear contrast in the mechanisms of collective labor-management communication between union and nonunion firms. While collective bargaining and joint consultation are central in union firms, announcements of firm strategy and workplace discussions are much more important in nonunion firms.

There are three main types of individual voice mechanisms, each of which is utilized in over 20 percent of nonunion firms: (1) means of individual expression (individual employees submit written reports on workplace issues), (2) suggestion systems (employees propose suggestions for improvements in work practices and related issues), and (3) individual interviews conducted by personnel departments (personnel staff conduct circuit interviews with individual employees). The individual interviews are the most effective of the three, according to evaluations by managers. In the case of individual voice mechanisms, there is no marked difference in practice between union and nonunion firms. In sum, many nonunion firms utilize various voice institutions simultaneously.

The Outcomes of Employee Representation Mechanisms

While several practices are utilized in nonunion firms, whether a system formally exists and whether workers can effectively exercise their voice are, of course, not at all the same thing. It is thus necessary to consider what effects labor unions and other means of employee representation mechanisms have on worker voice, separation rates, and other outcomes. This section highlights four key institutions of employee representation: (1) labor unions; (2) recreation-oriented employee associations in nonunion firms; (3) voice-oriented employee associations in non-

union firms; and (4) joint consultation conducted in firms with neither unions nor employee associations. We then analyze the extent to which these four voice structures influence worker voice and separation rates.

Effects on Voice

The analysis uses the framework of voice and exit, which assumes that unions or other employee representation mechanisms significantly strengthen employees' voice and reduce separation rates, even when major working conditions, firm characteristics, and employee attributes are controlled for (Freeman and Medoff 1984; Muramatsu 1984; Tomita 1993). We conducted an ordered probit analysis of the strength of employee voice. The dependent variables are the strength of worker voice on working conditions and management practices (workers "strongly stated their opinions" was coded as 1, and "did not voice opinions at all" was coded as 5). The independent variables were types of representation mechanisms, working conditions, firm characteristics, and employee attributes. The bases of the dummy for representation mechanisms were firms that did not have labor unions, employee associations, or joint consultation. It should be noted that the respondents who provided their opinions on the strength of worker voice were personnel managers, and therefore the data has a potential upward bias.

The results are presented in Table 18.2. Four conclusions are derived from the table. First, labor unions strengthen worker voice with regard to almost all aspects of working conditions and management practices, with the exception of employment adjustment (including downsizing). Second, recreation-oriented employee associations tend to suppress voice with regard to wage increases but strengthen voice with regard to working hours, holidays, break time, and fringe benefits. They have no effect on other management practices. Third, voice-oriented employee associations strengthen voice concerning fringe benefits as well as yearly business and production planning. Fourth, joint consultation systems strengthen voice in the areas of wages, working hours, holidays, and break time.

As the above paragraph indicates, labor unions serve to strengthen voice toward almost all aspects of working conditions and management practice, while the areas in which joint consultation systems and employee associations exert significant impact are quite limited. In brief, joint consultation may strengthen voice toward working conditions and employee associations may strengthen voice toward working conditions and toward some aspects of management practice. In any case, there is no doubt that labor unions exercise the superior voice-strengthening effect.

Effects on Exit

Should we expect the above representation mechanisms to suppress exit (lower the separation rate)? We employed the same equation to analyze separation rates that we used to examine the effects of voice on working conditions and management practices. This makes it possible directly to compare differences in the determinants of voice and exit. Separation rates are dependent variables, while the independent variables are employee representation mechanisms, working conditions, firm characteristics, and employee attributes. The equation of the separation rate is estimated using ordinary least squares.

The results are shown in Table 18.3.[3] They indicate that labor unions, voice-oriented employee associations, recreation-oriented employee associations, and joint consultation do not help to lower separation rates, either for regular employees in general or for regular male employees, even after controlling for the most important working conditions, for firm characteristics, and for employee attributes.[4]

Labor unions, even though they function to strengthen worker voice, do not have the effect of lowering separation rates. Neither do employee associations or joint consultation have a significant effect on separation rates. Some of the factors that do have a significant effect on separation rates are firm size, amount of annual cash earnings, and average annual straight-time hours. It should be concluded that employee representation mechanisms have considerably less effect than these factors.[5]

The preceding results indicate that labor unions, viewed with respect to economic outcomes, do more to strengthen worker voice than the practices used in nonunion firms. Nevertheless, the results also reveal that neither unions nor nonunion voice mechanisms affect separation rates in Japan.

Employee Perceptions of Voice Through Nonunion Representation Mechanisms

The preceding sections have established that while nonunion forms of employee representation are quite widespread in the Japanese economy and are gaining popularity as alternative avenues for employees to express voice, their effects on industrial relations outcomes measured at the firm level vary depending on the form of nonunion representation. One drawback of these analyses is that the data, including the judgment regarding the extent of voice that employees are able to exercise through the three representation mecha-

Table 18.2

Determinants of the Degree of Employee Voice Related to Working Conditions and Management Factors

	Wage level (1)	Working hours/ holidays/ break time (2)	Fringe benefits (3)	Employment adjustment (4)	Changes in staff (5)	Annual management/ production planning (6)	Long-term management/ production planning (7)	Management strategy (8)
Union dummy	-1.386** (-4.367)	-1.893** (-5.847)	-1.542** (-4.785)	-0.393 (-1.181)	-0.743** (-2.438)	-0.692** (-2.181)	-0.551* (-1.717)	-0.722** (-2.263)
Recreation-oriented employee association dummy	0.587** (2.035)	-0.604** (-2.104)	-0.613** (-2.084)	0.198 (0.632)	-0.281 (-0.993)	-0.383 (-1.298)	0.106 (0.362)	-0.055 (-0.185)
Voice-oriented employee association dummy	0.460 (0.837)	-0.660 (-1.138)	-1.018* (-1.857)	-0.062 (-0.103)	-0.924 (-1.622)	-1.035* (-1.802)	-0.260 (-0.398)	-0.678 (-1.043)
Joint consultation system dummy	-1.087** (-3.358)	-0.853** (-2.647)	-0.483 (-1.511)	-0.004 (-0.013)	-0.020 (-0.065)	0.060 (0.193)	-0.356 (-1.134)	-0.400 (-1.260)
Amount of average annual cash earnings	-1.087* (-1.692)	-1.470** (-2.283)	-1.218* (-1.830)	-2.227** (-3.112)	-1.331** (-2.100)	-0.020 (-0.031)	1.006 (1.538)	0.163 (0.247)
Amount of average annual fringe benefits	-0.540** (-2.140)	-0.349 (-1.427)	-0.226 (-0.975)	-0.670** (-2.383)	-0.429* (-1.742)	0.049 (0.192)	-0.036 (-0.140)	0.031 (0.121)
Amount of severance pay for university graduates	-0.001 (-0.005)	-0.086 (-0.318)	0.012 (0.047)	-0.061 (-0.218)	0.546** (2.128)	-0.186 (-0.706)	-0.658** (-2.462)	-0.656** (-2.465)

Average annual straight time hours	-0.0004 (-0.510)	-0.001 (-1.425)	-0.0003 (-0.440)	0.0003 (0.288)	0.0004 (0.479)	0.001 (0.616)	-0.0003 (-0.346)	-0.0002 (-0.264)
Average annual overtime hours	-0.002** (-3.084)	-0.0004 (-1.019)	-0.0001 (-0.249)	0.0004 (0.759)	0.0003 (0.565)	-0.0004 (-0.809)	-0.001** (-2.825)	-0.0003 (-0.533)
Firm size	-0.139 (-1.230)	-0.034 (-0.304)	-0.020 (-0.181)	-0.004 (-0.039)	0.012 (0.117)	0.239** (2.225)	0.199* (1.809)	0.217** (2.013)
Average age	-0.139 (-0.190)	1.336** (1.797)	1.738** (2.275)	-0.045 (-0.056)	-0.062 (-0.086)	1.374* (1.838)	-0.304 (-0.393)	0.183 (0.247)
University graduates	0.557 (1.124)	1.058** (2.108)	1.042** (2.108)	1.409** (2.598)	0.135 (0.276)	-0.533 (-1.087)	-1.593** (-3.130)	-0.736 (-1.472)
Proportion of women	0.957 (1.374)	1.544** (2.193)	1.149 (1.597)	-1.937** (-2.653)	-0.314 (-0.464)	-0.770 (-1.118)	-0.505 (-0.726)	-0.698 (-1.006)
Industry dummies	yes	yes	yes	yes	yes	yes	yes	yes
Sum of weights	7.2660e+03	7.2140e+03	7.1650e+03	6.4650e+03	6.9180e+03	6.7330e+03	6.4580e+03	6.7480e+03
Log likelihood	-166.937	-171.351	-178.014	-152.400	-195.677	-192.998	-179.605	-194.672

Notes: All estimates are ordered probits. Upper numbers denote coefficients and the numbers in parentheses denote asymptotic *t*-statistics. Estimates are derived from a sample selected so that its characteristics match those of the general population. The dependent variable for each column is derived by assigning values to answers to the question, "To what degree did employees voice their opinions during the last five years [1991–95]?" Responses were coded: 1 = strongly stated their opinions; 2 = voiced opinions to some degree; 3 = voiced opinions but neither strongly or weakly; 4 = did not voice opinions very much; 5 = did not voice opinions at all..
** = $p < 0.05$; * = $p < 0.1$.

Table 18.3

Determinants of Separation Rate

	Separation rate (regular employees) (1)	Separation rate (regular male employees) (2)
Union dummy	2.369	1.548
	(1.240)	(0.902)
Recreation-oriented employee association dummy	−1.673	−1.145
	(−0.921)	(−0.704)
Voice-oriented employee association dummy	0.445	−0.283
	(0.114)	(−0.084)
Joint consultation system dummy	−1.051	−0.890
	(−0.509)	(−0.488)
Amount of average annual cash earnings	−8.122**	−7.363**
	(−2.051)	(−2.156)
Amount of average annual fringe benefits	−0.387	0.033
	(−0.270)	(0.026)
Severance pay for university graduates	0.822	0.122
	(0.506)	(0.083)
Average annual straight time hours	0.020**	0.015**
	(3.549)	(2.969)
Average annual overtime hours	−0.0002	−0.0002
	(−0.081)	(−0.089)
Number of employees	−1.639**	−1.169**
	(−2.470)	(−1.986)
Average age	−13.321**	−8.282**
	(−2.911)	(−2.008)
Proportion of university graduates	3.723	1.113
	(1.206)	(0.403)
Proportion of women	3.636	
	(0.845)	
Industry dummies	yes	yes
Sum of weights	7.2220e+03	7.3890e+03
Adjusted R^2	0.303	0.230

Notes: All estimates are ordinary least squares. Upper numbers are coefficients and numbers in parentheses denote asymptotic t–statistics. Estimates are derived from a sample selected so that its characteristics match those of the general population.
** = $p < 0.05$; * = $p < 0.1$.

nisms, were obtained from the management side.

In this section, we examine employees' own perception regarding the effectiveness of nonunion forms of employee representation. More specifically, another dataset (see Data Appendix B), which was obtained separately from the one used in the preceding sections, is analyzed using a similar framework to the one used previously. This dataset contains employees' own responses regarding whether mechanisms such as joint consultation committees and employee associations have strengthened their voice.

Measuring Employee Voice

In this section, three classes of employee voice measures are used: (1) information sharing and employee influence on corporate management; (2) procedural justice practices in employee evaluations; and (3) perceived degrees of influence on work allocation and training schedules.

The first group of employee voice measures includes four items: whether management shares information on corporate strategies and management, whether employee concerns are reflected in corporate management, whether management shares information related to the determination of working conditions, and whether employee concerns are reflected in the determination of working conditions. These four are traditional industrial relation issues and are labeled as "information sharing and employee influence on corporate management." All of these items are measured on a three-point scale, with smaller values indicating stronger employee voice.

The second category of employee voice, procedural justice in employee evaluation, contains four items: disclosure of evaluation criteria and forms, disclosure of evaluation results to individuals, discussion of evaluation results with supervisors, and mechanisms for submitting grievances regarding evaluations. The scales used for these items are dummy coded with a 1 indicating the existence of a procedural justice practice (such as disclosure of evaluation criteria and forms).

The third category covers employee voice with regard to work allocation and training schedules. It refers to employees' perceptions of whether they have influence on three issues: work allocation and scheduling, assignment to new positions, and choice of training opportunities and content. These items are measured on a three-point scale with lower values indicating stronger employee voice.

In addition, as a counterpart to the firm-level analysis on the effects of employee voice on exits, the relationship between the existence of employee representation mechanisms and employees' overall satisfaction with the company was examined. As noted earlier, the analyses in this section are conducted using a framework similar to the one used in the previous section, namely, that based on the exit-voice model. It is not, however, entirely clear whether the lack of employee representation mechanisms at the firm level necessarily leads to a higher turnover rate of individual employees in Japan. This is due, in part, to the perceptions of Japanese employees that employment opportunities in the outside labor markets are very limited and, in part, to the fact that given the level of employment security, they may tend to be risk averse. Based on this argument, company satisfaction will be used as a measure of employee attitudes toward their employing organizations. The expectation is that union and nonunion representation mechanisms raise employees' satisfaction with the firm when they perceive little likelihood of improving their working conditions by changing employers.

Results of all the analyses are presented in Tables 18.4 and 18.5. The analytic methods are

Table 18.4

Determinants of Employee Perceptions of Voice Related to Working Conditions and Management Factors

	Information sharing and employee influence on corporate management			
	Information sharing on employment conditions[a] (1)	Reflection of employee concerns in the determination of working conditions[a] (2)	Information sharing on corporate management[a] (3)	Reflection of employee concerns on corporate management[a] (4)
Union dummy	−0.735** (−7.206)	−0.924** (−8.556)	−0.115 (−1.139)	−0.295** (−2.837)
Employee association dummy	−0.155** (−2.422)	−0.205** (−3.106)	−0.088 −(1.397)	−0.136** (−2.092)
Joint consultation system dummy	−0.164 (−0.901)	−0.377** (−1.995)	−0.272 (−1.486)	−0.045 (−0.238)
Amount of annual cash earnings	0.623** (5.024)	−0.756** (−5.860)	0.680** (5.484)	0.620** (4.921)
Average monthly overtime hours	−0.002 (−1.000)	0.001 (0.500)	−0.000 (−0.0001)	−0.003* (−1.500)
Number of employees	0.163** (5.821)	−0.144* (−4.966)	0.219** (7.821)	0.089** (3.069)
Age of the respondent	−0.081** (−2.893)	0.078** (2.690)	−0.121** (−4.321)	−0.140** (−4.828)
Age squared	0.001** (−0.0001)	−0.001** (−0.0001)	0.002** (−0.0001)	0.002** (−0.0001)
University graduate dummy	−0.171** (−2.631)	0.175** (2.574)	−0.254** (−3.908)	−0.139** (−2.106)
Sex of the respondent (1 = male)	−0.050 (−0.556)	−0.060 (−0.645)	0.083 (0.922)	0.054 (0.587)
Marital status dummy (1 = married)	0.147* (1.815)	−0.074 (−0.871)	0.027 (0.329)	0.046 (0.548)
Job change dummy (1 = changed)	−0.217** (−2.932)	0.105 (1.364)	−0.086 (−1.147)	−0.103 (−1.355)
Union member dummy (1 = union member)	0.249** (3.507)	−0.157** (−2.151)	0.223** (3.141)	0.162** (2.219
Occupation dummies	yes	yes	yes	yes
Manufacturing dummy	yes	yes	yes	yes
Number of observations	1,736	1,732	1,735	1,732
Log likelihood	−1,534.103	−1,421.302	−1,504.905	−1,430.023

Notes: All estimates except columns 5–8 are ordered probits. Columns 5–8 are estimated using a probit analysis. Upper numbers denote coefficients and the numbers in parentheses denote asymptotic *t*–statistics.

[a]The dependent variable is derived by assigning values coded: 1 = strongly voiced; 2 = voiced to some degree; 3 = not voiced at all.

Procedural justice practices in employee evaluation				Work allocation and training schedules		
Disclosure of evaluation forms and criteria[b] (5)	Disclosure of evaluation results to employees[b] (6)	Discussion of evaluation results with supervisors[b] (7)	Mechanisms for submitting grievances on evaluation results[b] (8)	Work allocation and scheduling[a] (9)	Assignment to new positions[a] (10)	Training opportunities and contents[a] (11)
0.517** (4.457)	0.197* (1.698)	0.267** (2.302)	0.064 (0.525)	−0.067 (−0.677)	−0.160 (−1.524)	−0.110 (−1.078)
0.226** (3.694)	0.402** (5.507)	0.307** (4.205)	0.229** (3.013)	−0.033 (−0.524)	−0.057 (−0.877)	−0.164** (−2.563)
0.449** (2.434)	0.897** (4.192)	0.678** (3.153)	0.278 (1.287)	0.048 (0.270)	−0.004 (−0.021)	−0.437** (−2.362)
−0.458** (−3.271)	−0.304** (−2.141)	−0.320** (−2.238)	−0.234 (−1.570)	0.817 (6.642)	0.538** (4.236)	0.433** (3.464)
−0.003 (1.500)	−0.004** (−2.000)	−0.006** (3.000)	−0.004** (2.000)	0.003 (1.500)	0.002 (1.000)	−0.002 (−1.000)
0.001 (0.031)	−0.168** (−5.091)	−0.087** (−2.636)	−0.043 (−1.265)	0.065 (2.321)	0.068** (2.345)	0.117** (4.179)
0.003 (0.094)	−0.034 (−1.030)	−0.004 (−0.121)	−0.009 (−0.265)	−0.011 (−0.393)	−0.030 (−1.034)	−0.041 (−1.464)
0.000 (0.0001)	0.001 (0.0001)	0.000 (0.0001)	0.000 (0.0001)	0.000 (−0.0001)	0.000 (−0.0001)	0.000 (−0.0001)
−0.130* (−1.757)	−0.237** (−3.160)	−0.097 (−1.293)	−0.070 (−0.886)	0.095 (1.484)	−0.72 (−1.075)	0.132** (2.031)
0.039 (0.379)	0.142 (1.379)	−0.151 (−1.452)	0.058 (0.532)	−0.116 (−1.303)	0.022 (0.232)	0.286** (3.109)
−0.047 (−0.505)	0.038 (0.409)	0.060 (0.638)	0.075 (0.765)	−0.046 (−0.575)	0.144* (1.674)	0.022 (0.265)
0.076 (0.884)	−0.041 (−0.477)	0.015 (0.172)	−0.010 (−0.111)	−0.080 (−1.081)	−0.093 (−1.208)	−0.118 (−1.573)
0.071 (0.877)	0.018 (0.220)	0.058 (0.707)	−0.105 (−1.221)	−0.001 (−0.014)	−0.177** (−2.425)	−0.112 (−1.577)
yes	yes	yes	yes	yes	yes	yes
yes	yes	yes	yes	yes	yes	yes
1,715	1,717	1,712	1,707	1,743	1,736	1,736
−1,062.305	−1,046.019	−1,029.090	−922.644	−1,598.190	−1,536.341	−1,643.754

[b]The dependent variable is set to 1 if the practice exists; otherwise to 0.
** = $p < 0.05$; * = $p < 0.1$.

either probit or ordered probit. In Tables 18.4 and 18.5, included in the equations are three main explanatory variables: existence of enterprise unions, existence of employee associations (in the absence of unions), and existence of joint consultation systems (in the absence of unions).[6] The reference category is employees in firms without unions, employee associations, or joint consultation systems. In addition, fourteen control variables are included: firm size, industry (1 = manufacturing, 0 = wholesale/retail), gender of the respondent, age and age squared of the respondent, whether the respondent has changed employers at least once, whether the respondent has a four-year college degree, whether the respondent is married, three job category dummies (clerical, sales, and engineering, with production workers being the reference category), whether the respondent is a union member, the respondent's monthly overtime hours, and the respondent's annual income.

Effects on Perceptions of Voice

Information Sharing and Employee Influence on Corporate Management

The results regarding traditional industrial relations outcomes, presented in columns 1 through 4 of Table 18.4, indicate that enterprise unions and employee associations appear to strengthen employees' perceptions of voice.[7] Unions and employee associations show significant correlations to the degrees to which management shared information (on matters related to working conditions), and their concerns are reflected in determining working conditions and corporate strategies. Regarding the extent to which employee concerns are reflected in the determination of working conditions, joint consultation

Table 18.5

Determinants of Company Satisfaction

	Company satisfaction
Union dummy	−0.0001
	(−0.0001)
Employee association dummy	−0.089
	(−1.508)
Joint consultation system dummy	−0.114
	(−0.675)
Amount of annual cash earnings	0.558**
	(5.158)
Average monthly overtime hours	−0.0001
	(−0.0001)
Number of employees	0.110**
	(4.231)
Age of the respondent	−0.033
	(−1.269)
Age squared	−0.0001
	(−0.0001)
University graduate dummy	−0.02
	(−0.333)
Gender of respondent (1 = male)	−0.068
	(−0.819)
Marial status dummy(1 = married)	−0.029
	(−0.386)
Job change dummy (1 = changed)	−0.017
	(−0.0001)
Union member dummy (1 = union member)	−0.059
	(−0.894)
Occupation dummies	yes
Manufacturing dummy	yes
Number of observations	1,717
Log likelihood	−2,295.079

Notes: All estimates are ordered probits. The dependent variable is measured on a five-point scale ranging from: 1 = very satisfied to 5 = not satisfied at all.
** = $p < 0.05$; * $p < 0.1$.

systems also have significant correlations to perceptions of employee voice.

One exception is the degree to which management shares information on corporate strategies and management (see column 3). It may be that since there is a wide range of items to be covered in "information on corporate strategies and management," and it is quite unlikely that employers share complete information in this area, employees may not be able to determine whether voice institutions had any inroads in opening management's books. Another notable finding is that joint consultation systems tend to have relatively weaker effects on employee voice. Nevertheless, the significant effect which the joint consultation variable has on employee voice in the determination of working conditions is consistent with findings in the previous section.

Procedural Justice Practices in Employee Evaluation

The items included in this category are relatively new industrial relations issues on which employees seek influence. In Japan, however, where both white-collar and blue-collar employees are evaluated even in the presence of enterprise unions (Koike 1988), increasing employee influence on these issues is a critical concern for the labor side.

Results are exhibited in columns 5 through 8 of Table 18.4 and indicate that union and nonunion voice institutions appear to have strong correlations to the likelihood that employers provide some type of procedural justice practices in employee evaluations. Regarding all four items, the presence of at least one of the nonunion voice institutions—either employee associations or joint consultations systems or both—has a positive significant correlation to employee reports of whether these practices are available to them.

In particular, employee associations have significant relationships to all the practices.

One notable finding is that the handling of grievances regarding evaluation outcomes is available only in the firms where employee associations exist. Enterprise unions do not appear to provide this form of employee voice with regard to evaluations. Whether or not employee associations themselves are used for such grievance handling is not clear. One possibility, however, is that precisely because they are not labor unions, employee associations might be able to bargain for a system that protects the individual interests of employees, as opposed to focusing mostly on collective interests.

Perceived Influence on Work Allocation and Training Schedules

Finally, the effects that nonunion voice institutions have on employee perceptions of voice in the area of work allocation and training schedules are examined. The results shown in columns 9 through 11 of Table 18.4 indicate that unions and nonunion institutions have no significant effects on employee voice on work allocation and scheduling, or on assignment to new positions. These human resource management practices are usually considered management prerogatives, and the present results indicate that employee-side institutions increase the level of employee voice only to a limited degree, if at all.

In contrast, both employee associations and joint consultation systems show a significant correlation to employee influence on the choice of training contents and scheduling. Decisions regarding the provision of training opportunities have long been considered to be a management prerogative because they are a critical factor in determining the value of human capital within firms. However, decisions regarding training are also important to employees, since their value in the labor market is largely determined by the type of training received. Thus, the labor side has strong stakes in increasing the level of employee voice in this category, and perhaps especially so in Japan, where so much training is conducted within firms.

Effects on Employee Satisfaction

Results on employee satisfaction with the current employer are reported in Table 18.5. None of the representation mechanisms show any significant correlations to employee satisfaction with their employing firms. Moreover, when other satisfaction measures (satisfaction with their lives in general, pay satisfaction, and satisfaction with career prospects) are used as the dependent variables, conclusions do not change (not reported in this chapter). Thus, these union and nonunion voice institutions appear to have no impact on employees' satisfaction with their work lives.

These results indicate that the increased level of influence that these nonunion institutions afford to workers is not enough to raise employee satisfaction with the company. One explanation for this may be that although workers perceive that they have more say through such mechanisms, they do not see any impact on the quality of their work lives. The relationship of these institutions to their overall welfare is so small that exercising voice through nonunion forms may not have significant effects on how workers feel about their jobs and companies. In other words, workers may perceive that they have increased voice in their workplaces, but do not view this increase as large enough to regard the company more favorably.

Unlike the United States and Canada, Japanese forms of nonunion employee representation are not intended to be mechanisms for boosting worker morale (and thus individual workers' performance). They are considered more as mechanisms for management and labor to share information and reduce transaction costs in the operation of the firm. In this sense, these institutions may have productivity effects that are not actualized through improved employee motivation. In contrast, employee morale and satisfaction in Japanese firms are likely to be maintained through practices other than nonunion employee representation. For example, Lincoln and Kalleberg's (1990) study shows that employment practices traditionally associated with large Japanese firms—long-term employment security, pay related to length of service, and intrafirm skill formation—are strongly related to employees' positive attitudes toward their employing organizations.

Summary of the Results on Employee Perceptions of Voice

Overall, the results presented in Tables 18.4 and 18.5 suggest the following conclusions. First, with regard to the traditional industrial relations issues such as information sharing and the determination of working conditions, both unions and employee associations appear to play similar roles in raising employee voice. Joint consultation systems do not appear to be as effective. In addition, unions and nonunion institutions appeared to strengthen employee voice in management's decisions regarding the provision of training.

Second, the likelihood of procedural equity practices seems to be enhanced by labor unions, employee associations, and, to a lesser extent, by joint consultation systems. Since these are issues that matter at the individual (as opposed to collective) level, the findings may indicate newer avenues for Japanese collective institutions to protect employee interests.

In contrast, the effectiveness of these collective institutions in strengthening employee voice in work allocation issues appears weak. Unions and nonunion voice institutions in Japan may not be very effective at the workplace level. Finally, workers' overall satisfaction with their employers was not related to the existence of union or nonunion representation mechanisms.

Conclusions and Policy Implications

The results presented in the previous sections lead us to conclude that nonunion employee representation mechanisms such as joint consultation systems and employee associations do strengthen employee voice. The existence of these mechanisms is related both to management's belief that the labor side can use them to express its opinions in the determination of important industrial relations outcomes and to employees' perceptions that they can influence management's actions. Thus, as far as employee voice is considered, these mechanisms appear to act as imperfect alternatives to enterprise unions and partially to fill the representation gap in Japan.

In addition, we found significant differences among enterprise unions, joint consultation systems, and employee associations. When employee voice is measured through management reports, the results indicate that nonunion employee representation mechanisms enhance employee voice, but not as much as enterprise unions. Joint consultation systems and employee associations are less effective than enterprise unions in strengthening employee voice, but are about equally effective. When employee voice is measured through employee perceptions, the results indicate that employee associations do enhance voice

as much as, and in a few cases more than, enterprise unions. With regard to such traditional industrial relations issues as information sharing and the reflection of employee concerns in the determination of working conditions, employee associations strengthen the belief among employees that they exercise voice. Employee associations are also correlated with the existence of procedural justice practices in employee evaluation. In contrast, joint consultation systems do not perform well in strengthening employee perceptions of their voice.

These differences between management reports and employee perceptions may result, in part, from the natures of the two representation mechanisms. Joint consultation mechanisms are indirect (representative) forms of employee participation, whereas employee associations involve more direct forms of participation.

But a more serious qualification to the initial conclusion comes from our empirical findings which show that these union and nonunion representation mechanisms are not related to outcome variables such as employee separation rates and satisfaction levels. Neither separation rates measured at the firm level nor individual employees' satisfaction with companies was significantly related to the existence of representation mechanisms, union or nonunion. Since these results indicate that voice attributable to union and nonunion representation mechanisms are not alternatives to exit, they put us in a bind. Theoretically, our results question the validity of the exit-voice model in the Japanese context.

More importantly, the results also make us question the role of representation mechanisms, union or nonunion, in Japanese labor-management relations. What are the values of representation institutions that strengthen employee voice but do not affect employee behavior (separation) or attitudes (satisfaction with the company)? Why do these institutions not affect employees' linkages to their employing organizations even though they enhance voice? We offer two possible explanations.

Our first explanation rests on the findings referred to earlier in this chapter: lack of union and nonunion differentials in objective working conditions such as wages and employment security. A similar lack of advantages is even more likely to be found for nonunion representation mechanisms since nonunion mechanisms usually do not allow workers recourse to strikes and are not related to industrywide coordination through *shunto*. If this is the case, institutions such as joint consultation systems and employee associations may not affect employee behavior and attitudes because, while strengthening employee voice, they do not affect critical working conditions that relate to employees' decisions to exit. Reasons for this lack of differentials may be found in such factors as widespread patterning of working conditions throughout the economy and weaker bargaining power due to the enterprise-based structure of these institutions.

The second explanation rests on the structure of labor markets in the Japanese economy. As has been noted by a number of scholars (Koike 1988), Japanese labor markets are characterized by very limited outside opportunities and high employment security for the core workers. Under these conditions, employees may tend to be risk averse and may not consider exit as one of the ways to improve their situations. Employees' attitudes toward their employing organizations may not be related to the level of voice since, regardless of the level of voice they have, they cannot improve their working conditions by changing employers.

Moreover, since, in a relatively closed internal market, two effective ways for employees to improve their working conditions are to advance in the hierarchy and for the firm to be prosperous, they may view such issues as participation in strategic decision making and procedural justice in evaluation as critically important to the quality of their work lives and as areas in which they would like to have more influence. If this argument holds, in an economy where relatively closed firm labor markets are the norm, enhancing employee voice in these areas fulfills the main function of both union and nonunion employee representation mechanisms.

At this moment, we cannot offer either of the explanations as final because very little empirical research exists. Both hypotheses, however, present a challenge to the ways in which union and nonunion representation mechanisms are viewed in Japan. As was noted earlier, union density is declining in Japan, but the workers' demand for representation persists, creating a representation gap. This situation has provoked a debate on the desirability of legally mandating some form of nonunion representation, of which joint consultation and employee associations are the most likely options.

Our chapter by no means puts a closure on this debate. But what it does suggest is that these two mechanisms strengthen the belief among managers and employers that workers exercise voice. In this limited sense, joint consultation systems and employee associations are effective substitutes for enterprise unions, and they merit close consideration in future debates of mandatory nonunion employee representation mechanisms in Japan.

Notes

The ordering of names is not intended to communicate the relative contributions of the authors.

1. Works presenting valuable perspectives and research findings on nonunion labor-management relations in Western firms include Kochan, Katz, and McKersie (1986), Freeman and Rogers (1993), Kaufman and Kleiner (1993), Commission on the Future of Worker-Management Relations (1994), and Freeman and Lazear (1995).

2. It appears that there is an interesting parallelism between the Japanese *shunto* system and the two-tier structure of German industrial relations. However, a critical difference between the two does exist. In Germany, works councils are establishment-level representational bodies that are complemented by labor unions, which are regional and national representational institutions. Works councils deal with nonwage issues, and by and large pursue a cooperative role, while unions negotiate wages and pursue the more distributive bargaining agenda. In Japan, despite the similar two-level system, both enterprise-based and industry-based organizations are labor unions, and can negotiate both wage and nonwage issues, although actual decision making usually takes place at the firm level. In this sense, the division of work between the two types of organizations is less clear in Japan than in the German case.

3. The variations in separation rates for union and nonunion firms are as follows (mean for regular employees in general, mean for regular, male employees; coefficient of variation for regular employees in general, coefficient of variation for regular, male employees): (1) union firms (7.64 percent, 5.20 percent; 1.42, 1.36), (2) nonunion firms with recreation-oriented employee associations (7.94 percent, 6.27 percent; 1.12, 1.37), (3) nonunion firms with voice-oriented employee associations (6.63 percent, 4.77 percent; 0.83, 1.11), (4) nonunion firms conducting joint consultation (8.20 percent, 5.62 percent; 0.77, 0.93), (5) nonunion firms without employee associations and not conducting joint consultation (9.78 percent, 8.26 percent; 0.92, 1.18). As observed, separation rates appear to vary according to the types of voice mechanisms used in the firms. After controlling for major characteristics of firms and employees, however, differences in separation rates among representation mechanisms disappear.

4. Persons reaching mandatory retirement age are not included in figures for separation rates, but no distinction can be made between separations occurring because of "management conditions" or "personal reasons." According to Labor Ministry Secretariat Policy Research Department (1994), *Survey on Employment Trends*, persons leaving firms because of management conditions accounted for 7.5 percent of separations, while those leaving for personal reasons accounted for 71.5 percent. The shares vary according to business cycles, but the former almost always account for 6–8 percent and the latter for 70–80 percent of separations.

5. Because the survey was conducted in July and August of 1995, it is possible that separation rates were affected by the recession. The job openings to applicants ratio in both months was 0.61.

6. Unlike the dataset used in the preceding section, the current dataset cannot separate recreation-oriented employee associations from voice-oriented ones.

7. It must be noted that since smaller values of the dependent variables indicate stronger voice in columns 1–4 and 9–11 of Table 18.4, negative relationships indicate positive relationships of voice institutions to employee perceptions.

References

English Literature

Commission on the Future of Worker-Management Relations. 1994. *Fact Finding Report.* Washington, D.C.: U.S. Department of Labor and U.S. Department of Commerce. May.

Freeman, Richard B., and Edward P. Lazear. 1995. "An Economic Analysis of Works Councils." In *Works Councils: Consultation, Representation, and Cooperation in Industrial Relations,* ed. Joel Rogers and Wolfgang Streeck, pp. 27–50. Chicago: University of Chicago Press.

Freeman, Richard B., and James L. Medoff. 1984. *What Do Unions Do?* New York: Basic Books.

Freeman, Richard B., and Joel Rogers. 1993. "Who Speaks for Us? Employee Representation in a Nonunion Labor Market." In *Employee Representation: Alternatives and Future Directions,* ed. Bruce E. Kaufman and Morris M. Kleiner, pp. 13–79. Madison: Industrial Relations Research Association.

Fujimura, Hiroyuki. 1997. "New Unionism: Beyond Enterprise Unionism?" In *Japanese Labour and Management in Transition: Diversity, Flexibility, and Participation,* ed. Mari Sako and Hiroki Sato, pp. 296–314. London: Routledge.

Gordon, Andrew. 1985. *The Evolution of Labor Relations in Japan: Heavy Industry, 1853–1955.* Cambridge: Harvard University Press.

Kaufman, Bruce E., and Morris M. Kleiner, eds. 1993. *Employee Representation: Alternatives and Future Directions.* Madison: Industrial Relations Research Association.

Kochan, Thomas E., Harry C. Katz, and Robert C. McKersie. 1986. *The Transformation of American Industrial Relations.* New York: Basic Books.

Koike, Kazuo. 1988. *Understanding Industrial Relations in Modern Japan.* London: Macmillan.

Lincoln, James, and Arne Kalleberg. 1990. *Culture, Commitment and Control.* Cambridge: Cambridge University Press.

Locke, Richard, Thomas Kochan, and Michael Piore, ed. 1997. *Employment Relations in a Changing World Economy.* Cambridge: MIT Press.

Morishima, Motohiro. 1995. "Embedding HRM in a Social Context." *British Journal of Industrial Relations* 33, no. 4 (December): 617–640.

Nakamura, Keisuke, and Michio Nitta. 1997. "Developments in Industrial Relations and Human Resource Practices in Japan." In *Employment Relations in a Changing World Economy*, ed. Richard Locke, Thomas Kochan, and Michael Piore, pp. 325–358. Cambridge: MIT Press.

Sako, Mari. 1997. "*Shunto:* The Role of Employer and Union Coordination at the Industry and Inter-Sectoral Levels." In *Japanese Labour and Management in Transition: Diversity, Flexibility, and Participation*, ed. Mari Sako and Hiroki Sato, pp. 236–264. London: Routledge.

Sato, Hiroki. 1997. "Labor-Management Relations in Small and Medium-Sized Enterprises: Collective Voice Mechanisms for Workers in Non-Unionised Companies." In *Japanese Labour and Management in Transition: Diversity, Flexibility, and Participation*, ed. Mari Sako and Hiroki Sato, pp. 315–331. London: Routledge.

Shirai, Taishiro. 1983. "A Theory of Enterprise Unionism." In *Contemporary Industrial Relations in Japan*, ed. Taishiro Shirai, pp. 117–143. Madison: University of Wisconsin Press.

Sugeno, Kazuo. 1992. *Japanese Labor Law.* Seattle and London: University of Washington Press.

Tsuru, Tsuyoshi. 1992. "Shunto: The Spillover Effect and the Wage-Setting Institution in Japan." International Institute of Labor Studies, International Labor Organization, DP/51/1992.

———. 1997. "Intrafirm Communication and Wage Determination in Japanese Nonunion Firms." The Institute of Economic Research, Hitotsubashi University. Discussion Paper A-327 (January).

Tsuru, Tsuyoshi, and James B. Rebitzer. 1995. "The Limits of Enterprise Unionism: Prospects for Continuing Union Decline in Japan." *British Journal of Industrial Relations* 33, no.3 (September): 459–492.

Japanese Literature

Kigyonai Komyunikeeshon Kenkyukai [Intrafirm Communication Research Group]. 1991. *Chusho Kigyo niokeru Kigyonai Komyunikeeshon no Jittai* [The Reality of Intrafirm Communication in Small- and Mid-Sized Firms]. Tokyo: Rodo Mondai Risaachi Sentaa.

Muramatsu, Kuramitsu. 1984. "Rishoku Kodo to Rodo Kumiai: `Hatsugen-Taishutsu Apuroochi' Yori" [Separations and Labor Unions: From a `Voice-Exit' Approach]. In *Gendai no Shitsugyo*, ed. Kazuo Koike, pp. 143–173. Tokyo: Dobunkan.

Nakamura, Keisuke. 1995. "Jugyoin Daihyousei Rongi de Wasure Rarete Irukoto" [What Is Often Forgotten in the Debates on Nonunion Employee Representation Systems]. *Jurisuto*, no. 1066 (May): 1–15.

Rodo Daijin Kanbo Seisaku Chosabu [Labor Ministry Secretariat Policy Research Department]. 1995. *Roshi Komyunikeeshon Chosa Hokoku* [Report on the Labor-Management Communication Survey].

Tokyo-Toritsu Rodo Kenkyusho [Tokyo Metropolitan Labor Research Institute]. 1990. *Chusho Kigyo ni okeru Jugyoin Soshiki no Yakuwari* [The Role of Employee Associations in Small- and Mid-Sized Firms].

Tachibanaki, Toshiaki, and Tomohiko Noda. 1993. "Chingin, Rodo Joken to Rodo Kumiai" [Wages, Working Conditions, and Labor Unions]. In *Rodo Kumiai no Keizaigaku: Kitai to Genjitsu* [Economics of Labor Unions: Expectations and Realities], ed. Tachibanaki and Rengo Sogo Seikatsu Kaihatsu Kenkyusho, pp. 195–216. Tokyo: Toyo Keizai Shimposha.

Tachibanaki, Toshiaki, and Rengo Sogo Seikatsu Kaihatsu Kenkyusho [Japanese Trade Union Confederation Research Institute for Advancement of Living Standards], ed. 1993. *Rodo Kumiai no Keizaigaku: Kitai to Genjitsu* [Economics of Labor Unions: Expectations and Realities]. Tokyo: Toyo Keizai Shimposha.

Tomita, Yasunobu. 1993. "Rishokuritsu to Rodo Kumiai no Hatsugen Koka" [The Separation Rate and the Voice Effect of Labor Unions]. In *Rodo Kumiai no Keizaigaku: Kitai to Genjitsu* [Economics of Labor Unions: Expectations and Realities], ed. Tachibanaki and Rengo Sogo Seikatsu Kaihatsu Kenkyusho, pp. 173–193. Tokyo: Toyo Keizai Shimposha.

Appendix

A. Data Used for Tables 18.1–18.3

The basic materials are responses to written questionnaires distributed to head managers of personnel departments or other comparable managers in private-sector firms. The survey was conducted in the area lying within a 30-kilometer radius of Tokyo Station, and the population was the 25,362 private firms within this area having at least fifty employees. The sample was 1,250 firms selected at random from the population. The sample frame was a list of private-sector firms with head offices located in the above area having fifty or more employees.

The survey methodology consisted of having professional opinion pollers personally distribute questionnaires to the personnel managers, and personally to collect the completed questionnaires as well. The period of the survey was in 1995, from July 26 to August 31. All respondents completing questionnaires were personnel department head managers or managers actually in charge of labor management at their firms.

The basic characteristics of the population and sample are shown in Table 18.A1. Responding were 516 firms, yielding a response rate of 41.3 percent. Unionization rate at the level of firms was 29 percent for the entire sample. A more detailed explanation of this dataset is found in Tsuru (1997).

B. Data Used for Tables 18.4 and 18.5

The data on which the analyses reported in Tables 18.4 and 18.5 are based come from a survey conducted by a private management consulting firm under contract from the Japanese Ministry of Labor. One of the authors (Morishima) participated as one of the project members. The survey was done in two stages. The first stage was the firm-level survey in which information on firms' human resource management practices was collected. The firms were restricted to two industries, manufacturing and wholesale/retail, since the purpose of the first-stage survey was to compare the HRM practices of these two sectors. Completed questionnaires were returned from 1,618 firms out of 3,788 distributed. A more complete description of this initial survey appears in Morishima (1995).

Then, in the second stage, each of these 1,618 firms was asked to provide a random sample of at least thirty individuals from their payroll list in order to allow project members to conduct a follow-up survey with individual employees. In some cases, researchers went to firms and conducted the sampling procedures; in others, firms provided what they claimed to be random samples. Because we insisted on having random samples, cooperation was obtained from only sixty-nine firms, which produced a dataset containing completed surveys from a total of 1,804 employees. The number of respondents per firm ranged from five to fifty-two. Employee-level questionnaires were distributed through employers and returned directly by regular mail.

Descriptive statistics shown in Table 18.A2 are calculated on the basis of individual responses. At the firm level, 66.7 percent of the sample firms were organized by labor unions, 58.1 percent had joint consultation systems, and 37.6 percent had nonunion employee associations. These statistics are higher than those reported in a nationally representative survey conducted by the Ministry of Labor in 1994 and the results obtained using the establishment-level survey in Appendix A. This may be due to the overrepresentation of larger firms (employment > 1,000) in the present sample.

Table 18.A1

Basic Characteristics of Population and Sample

Firm size (number of employees)	Number in population[a] (1)	Sampling rate[b] (2)	Number in samples (3)	Response[c] (4)	Unionization rate (5)
50–99	12,051	1/33	367	101 (27.5%)	21.8%
100–299	8,807	1/24	365	170 (46.6%)	26.5%
300–999	3,200	1/9	355	150 (42.3%)	46.1%
1,000 or more	1,304	1/8	163	95 (58.3%)	71.6%
Total	25,362	1/20	1,250	516 (41.3%)	29.0%

[a]This survey takes as its sample frame a list of private firms (compiled from Teikoku Databank COSMOS2) that are within a 30-km radius of Tokyo and have at least 50 employees.
[b]Within each firm size grouping, the number of sample firms was chosen to provide accuracy to within 7.2%.
[c]Number in parentheses is the response rate.

Table 18.A2

Variable Definitions and Descriptive Statistics

Individual-level variables

Union dummy	% of 1 = 65.1
Joint consultation system dummy[a]	% of 1 = 36.1
Employee association dummy	% of 1 = 34.8
Firm employment	4,448.1
Manufacturing dummy (0 = wholesale/retail)	% of 1 = 56.3
Gender of the respondent (1 = male)	% of 1 = 75.2
Age of the respondent	36.4
% of respondents who changed employers at least once	23.3
% of respondents who have at least university degree	59.8
% of respondents who are married	61.5
% in clerical job classification	55
% in sales job classification	21.5
% in engineering job classification	16.6
(reference category: production job classification)	
Union member dummy	% of 1 = 45.6
Average monthly overtime hours	21.5
Annual cash earnings in 1993	6.16 million Yen

Firm-level variables

Union dummy	% of 1 = 66.7
Joint consultation system dummy[a]	% of 1 = 35.3
Employee association dummy	% of 1 - 37.7
Subjective firm performance measure (1 = much better than competitors; 5 = much worse)	2.82 (SD = 1.06)
Capital-labor ratio	1.58 (SD = 7.21)
% of white-collar employees	24.10 (SD = 15.90)
Firms' HR strategy (1 = emphasize performance and ability levels; 4 = emphasize seniority)	3.17 (SD = 0.73)
Average age of employees in a firm	36.43 (SD = 3.53)

[a]These figures are much lower than those reported in the text because the dummy variable takes a value of 1 only when firms have joint consultation systems and no unions exist.

19

Nonunion Forms of Employee Representation in the United Kingdom and Australia

Paul J. Gollan

It is apparent from existing research in the United Kingdom (U.K.) and Australia that little is known about how forms of nonunion employee representation (NER) are composed, their independence from managerial influence, the "representativeness" of such bodies, and their accountability. In addition, little has been documented about the impact of such structures on either the managerial objective of securing consent to organizational change or the employee objective of influencing managerial decisions. This chapter attempts to address these issues by examining NER structures in Australia and the U.K.

Despite a common heritage, the U.K. and Australia have very different industrial relations systems. The U.K. has a "voluntarist" tradition with little regulation over the employment relationship. In contrast, Australia has a highly regulated structure based on compulsory arbitration and conciliation reinforced by a highly developed industrial "Award" contract system. In spite of these differences, a common feature in both countries is that forms of NER have tended to play a minimal role in each system, with no formal processes or legal requirements.[1] However, the lack of representative structures covering increasing numbers of nonunion employees due to declining levels of trade union density, and legislative changes banning closed shop or compulsory union arrangements, have prompted the current interest in NER structures.

Drawing on qualitative and quantitative evidence, the chapter examines recent developments in NER structures with a focus on six interconnected themes—their presence, level, structure, process, agenda and outcomes.[2] The chapter first highlights the definitional problems involved in researching NER structures. Second, the conceptual issues are examined, focusing on the objectives and outcomes of NER forms. Third, the environmental context is described, highlighting the institutional context, historical development, external influences, and legal developments in the U.K. and Australia. Fourth, the way in which NER structures have operated in a range of organizations is examined. In particular, the chapter explores the outcomes and processes of NER forms through survey data and case studies of organizations in the U.K. and Australia. Finally, the conclusion reviews the evidence and offers a synthesis of the findings.

Definitional Problems

The precise structure and level of the NER forms can vary considerably.[3] They may take the form of safety committees, works councils, consultative councils/committees (CCs) or joint consultative committees (JCCs). In addition, the official terminology varies (i.e., CCs and JCCs) between jurisdictions and even among research surveys. But in reality the variations in terminology do not equate to differences of form or function. Importantly, such structures represent all employees[4] at the establishment or workplace. Some structures may have management representation (often as chair) and involve union representatives. This lack of commonality associated with NER structures may be caused by the lack of prescriptive legal requirements and definitions associated with NER structures in the U.K. and Australian workplaces.

Because of the complexity of and variations in NER forms, precise definitions are problematical. But four elements can be identified. First, only employees at the organization can be members of the representative body. Second, there is no or only limited formal linkage to outside trade unions or external employee representative bodies. Third, a degree of resources is supplied by the organization in which the employee representative body is based. Fourth, there is a representation of employees' interests or agency function, as opposed to more direct forms of individual participation and involvement.[5]

In addition, the range of issues considered by a nonunion form of representation varies considerably and is often dependent to some extent on its level and structure in the organization (i.e., ranging from workplace/work-zone safety committees to companywide joint industrial councils—see Taras 1997).

Why Research NER Forms?

Evaluations and generalizations about the impact of NER forms are problematic, which raise a number of questions over their structure, decision-making capacity, issues covered and discussed, and impact of outcomes. The rationale for a representative agency function—union or nonunion—in the workplace can be classified into a number of productivity and equity functions. These include: improved communication and information sharing; effective dispute resolution; enhanced employee bargaining power; fair and just decision making; and improved morale and social cohesion.

Freeman and Medoff (1984) have argued that while unions can provide an effective method of collective employee "voice," there may be an incentive for employers to provide some alternative voice mechanism where workplace union organization is weak or absent.[6] The academic literature has identified the important role of unions in giving employees a voice—enabling them to express dissatisfaction with the working environment without fear of management retaliation. Thus, it is suggested, when unions are weak or nonexistent, this voice effect will be absent, or alternatively an employee may exercise voice through the exit option, although Freeman and Medoff also argue that the exit option may be a less than optimal amount of voice (Freeman and Medoff 1984).

Other commentators have argued that the positive aspects of union voice are counterbalanced by a union's ability to extract a disproportionate share of the total income, decreasing an organization's ability to raise or maintain profits, thereby reducing the public-good aspects of increased employment.

The question remains whether NER forms may approximate "voice" as identified by traditional union structures.[7] Interestingly, as Freeman and Medoff noted, the efficacy of voice depends on the way in which labor and management interact, rather than whether unions exist or not (Sako 1998; Freeman and Medoff 1984). As such, commentators have argued that from a social perspective the role of NER forms as bargaining agents (thus similar to traditional trade union forms) may be desirable for power equality or ethical industrial democracy reasons. Advocates state that this can be achieved only by legal enactment, for example, mandated works councils, because employers will be reluctant to introduce bodies that challenge managerial prerogative and potentially reduce profits due to the additional costs involved.

However, this proposition depends on the wider institutional context. Organizations may create such bodies for the purposes of bargaining to reduce the likelihood of outside involvement by trade unions in organizational decision making, thus ensuring that bargaining processes are contained within the organization. This may be due to the perception that outside influence may distort internal processes and structures, impacting negatively on employee behavior and organizational performance.

Others have argued that structures representing the interests of employees through collective bargaining (legally enforced or not) may give more legitimacy and efficacy to the decision-making process (Hyman 1997), ensuring greater organizational commitment. Some advocates suggest firms voluntarily introduce NER structures, reflecting the culture and norms of a particular workplace. This approach is based on the assumption that by establishing and maintaining effective working employee and employer relationships, employees' rights need to be recognized and respected, encouraging an alignment of interests and promoting mutual respect and responsibility (Walton 1985).

NER and Performance

Fernie and Metcalf's (1995) analysis of the 1990 Workplace Industrial Relations Survey (WIRS3) suggests that where JCCs exist voluntarily, "there is not a single unfavorable association between the presence of a JCC and workplace performance" (Fernie and Metcalf 1995, pp. 397–398). Moreover, they argue that there are weak favorable associations between the existence of a JCC and both increased productivity and a positive employee relations climate. They state that the consultation process implied by the existence of the JCC makes it easier to change working practices and introduce new technology, leading to faster productivity growth both in unionized and nonunion workplaces (Fernie and Metcalf 1995, p. 397).

Additional research in Britain and the United States also suggests that the adoption of a cluster of "best practice" HR practices, which includes some level of indirect employee participation, can increase the market value of organizations by around 15 percent (Fenton-O'Creevy, Wood, and Callerot 1998, p. 9).

They also highlight findings from Denny and Nickell's (1991) research, which show that investment rates are higher in both union and nonunion workplaces with a JCC. Denny and Nickell conclude that the provision of information and consultation appears to lead to more harmonious relations between employees and management than is the case where there is no JCC (Fernie and Metcalf 1995, p. 397). In addition, recent research into the European car components industry has suggested there is positive business performance for those companies adopting more participative employee practices (including representative participation). This has included improvements in quality, communication, and the quality of decision making (Sako 1998). In Australia the latest Australian Workplace Industrial Relations Survey (AWIRS) data also suggest that NER structures through JCCs have a high impact on workplace performance and communications between management and employees, and on encouraging change at the workplace (Morehead et al. 1997, p. 511).

Another study cited in research from the European Works Council Study Group into employee involvement within European multinationals by Addison, Siebert, Wagner, and Wei examined the relationship between unionization and the impact of consultative committees in the U.K. Their findings suggested that consultative committees in unionized workplaces were associated with slightly lower productivity, whereas in nonunion workplaces they were associated with higher productivity (Fenton-O'Creevy, Wood, and Callerot 1998, p. 8).

It was suggested that this conclusion was based on a tendency for committees in union workplaces to consult on minor or "inappropriate" issues (Fenton-O'Creevy, Wood, and Callerot 1998, p. 8). It could also be that unions in such workplaces wish to remain the predominant source of representation over substantive issues and view such committees as talking forums only.

Analysis by Guest and Peccei (1998) of partnership and performance indicates that high levels of direct and representative participation, especially representative participation in policy decisions, have a high impact on employee commitment to the organization and the positive state of the psychological contract between employees and employers. In other words, there was a consistent finding that high levels of employee influence have a positive impact on employee attitudes and behavior (Guest and Peccei 1998, pp. 36–38).

Guest and Peccei conclude, "the level of representative influence over policy was generally very low, so it would seem that there are only a limited number of organisations where management permits representatives to influence policy

decisions; but where they do, either because of the consequences of the input or the underlying trust implied in the process, the pay-offs in terms of positive employee attitudes and behaviour are considerable" (Guest and Peccei 1998, p. 38).

Industrial Democracy

Part of NER debate has centered on the concept of industrial democracy in NER plans. Industrial democracy can be defined as "structures and institutional mechanisms that give workers and their representatives the opportunity to influence organizational decision making in their places of employment" (Hammer 1997, p. 3). Nevertheless, Hammer (1997) has questioned whether mere worker involvement or participation in decision making at the workplace is a sufficient condition for industrial democracy, or whether joint decision making or power sharing between workers and management is necessary before democracy at the workplace can really be achieved. Moreover, labor voice through NER forms can differ in the scope of decisions, the amount of power workers can exercise over management, and the organizational level at which the decisions are made. This results in some forms being purposefully designed to give workers a very modest role in decision making, while others are intended to give the workforce a substantial amount of power in organizational governance (Hammer 1997, p. 3).

The Role of the State

Another dimension in the debate is that of state-imposed as opposed to privately sponsored NER plans. In some continental European countries, NER structures exist within the framework of works councils, where codecision rights reinforce the rights of employees to information and consultation on certain issues. The process of consultation lies within a broader framework of organizational resources (i.e., enterprise and industry bargaining, and union and works council recognition) that, directly or indirectly, shape the process of consultation.

Hammer (1997) has suggested that in the absence of legislation that legitimizes NER, the effectiveness of such programs is dependent on "the good will, trust, and power relationship between the parties." She argues, "trust is a brittle property of any relationship, easily broken and difficult to rebuild" (Hammer 1997, p. 9). In other words, such a relationship based on pure voluntarism is inherently insecure. To reinforce this point, research suggests that trust in the outcomes of nonunion participation structures can be substantial when employees have their group interests protected by general worker rights legislation (Hammer 1997; Hammer, Ingebrigtsen, Karlsen, and Svarva 1994, as cited in Hammer 1997). As Hammer argues, company-specific idiosyncratic representational forms work very well as long as workers believe that the general legislation is sufficient to deter the management from making decisions that can hurt worker interests (Hammer 1997, p. 10).

Recent research into employee involvement within European multinationals by the European Works Council Study Group has suggested that "the principal impact of legislation mandating employee involvement practices is on the channel used to inform and consult employees i.e. via trade union, representative committee or directly with employees" (Fenton-O'Creevy, Wood, and Callerot 1998, p. 3). Moreover, the study also concludes that where limited law and regulation is applied on employee involvement, such as in the U.K., there is a greater diversity of employee

involvement than in countries where employee involvement practices are required by law (Fenton-O'Creevy, Wood, and Callerot 1998, p. 3).

McCallum has added to the debate by suggesting that "if the law does not mandate elected works councils, the coverage and importance of collective labor law will shrink. I venture to think that it is no longer possible for the trade unions to remain the sole repository of collective employee representation in our nation" (McCallum 1997, p. 7).

Conceptual Issues

There is considerable discussion over the functions of NER forms and their outcomes. The debate can be classified into two approaches: first, NER structures are an inherent win-lose or zero-sum game. This is based on the premise that an individual employee is inherently at a disadvantage in the employment relationship due to the monopoly power of the employer. Alternatively, NER structures can be viewed as an instrument through which both sides realize a "win-win" outcome in the employment relationship or positive-sum-game perspective, highlighting common interest between employers and employees promoting a unitarist approached based on shared beliefs and goals, or pluralist "mutual gains" approach based on a cooperative system of employment relations.[8]

Are NER Structures Complementary to or Substitutes for Traditional Decision-Making Structures?

There has been considerable discussion in British and Australian literature on nonunion forms of representation as communication devices or mechanisms for employee involvement, whether

Table 19.1

Strategies and Objectives of Nonunion Forms of Representative Participation

Strategy	Complement	Substitute	
Process	Codetermination/consultation	Representation of employee interests	Cooperation
Power base	Legally imposed or management initiative	Legally imposed or Management initiative	Management initiative
Channel of representation	Dual	Single	Dual
Representative interest	Mutual (win–win)	Conflictual (win–lose)	Mutual (win-win)
Rights	Information, consultation, co-decision making, limited veto powers	Information, consultation limited workplace decision making	Production line information, suggestions, problem identification, and productivity improvement

they are a "complement" to management decision making or, as some commentators have suggested, a "substitute" for unions through the collective bargaining process (see Table 19.1). One notion of a "substitute" is that it serves in place of a union, which presupposes a win-lose employment relationship from an employer's view.[9] It assumes employers create an alternative form of employee representation, which employees will prefer to "union" forms of representation. Alternatively, an entirely different notion is that alternative forms of employee representation make traditional union structures unnecessary, in the sense that they transform the employment relationship, with other high commitment practices, into a win-win relationship. This notion is based on the premise that employees do not desire or need a protective agency through traditional bargaining per se (since this emphasizes the adversarial, distributive element of the employ-

ment relationship) because their basic interests are satisfied. In this approach the purpose of NERs is to encourage and foster an alignment of interests between employer and employees.

Conceptually, the terms "substitute" or "union avoidance" suggest two strategies: first, excluding a union by establishing an NER structure to take its place; second, transforming the employment relationship from a traditional adversarial approach based on conflictual interest of "win-lose" to a "win-win" or mutual gains approach with an alignment of interest, undermining the very reason for a union. This strategy can be described as high-commitment management (HCM) (Walton 1985; Guest 1995; Storey 1992; Wood 1996).

An alternative strategy is evident when traditional trade union structures and alternative forms of employee representation "complement" each other, dovetailing in terms of form and function, as in the case of German works councils in the codetermination process and industrywide trade union bargaining.[10] Some commentators have highlighted the appropriateness of workplace issues discussed by NER forms and industry issues discussed by trade unions, suggesting a linkage between structure and scope of issues. There are two approaches: one based on a European works council model with rights established by law, such as the right to information, the right of consultation in economic and financial matters, and the right of consent in social and personnel affairs. The second approach is through JCCs or labor-management committees, which have more open-ended mandates to deal with issues of common interest to workers and management. They are rarely regulated by law, and their power and role are more limited than those of works councils in the decision-making process.

These strategies seem to be confirmed in research by the European Works Council Study Group, which identified significant differences between the U.K. and other European countries in the issues covered by employee involvement and representative practices. U.K. consultation issues focused on productivity and competitiveness, while in other countries, such as Germany, greater focus was placed on joint decision making and negotiation, such as collective redundancies (Fenton-O'Creevy, Wood, and Callerot 1998, p. 3). Parsons has recently stated that it is not the existence of a particular employee participation structure, but the objectives, strategies, and choices within which it operates.

Environmental Context

To understand the role of NER plans, various dimensions of the environmental context of the U.K. and Australia are next presented. This sec-tion examines the institutional context and historical evolution, the external factors influencing and legal developments underlying NER forms in the U.K. and Australia, allowing identification of the trends emerging in each country.

United Kingdom

Development of NER

In general, British industrial relations has been dominated by voluntary collective bargaining, meaning that employers are under no legal obligation to bargain or recognize trade unions. Historically, however, Britain has had a strong trade union influence in industrial relations, although in recent years this has been reduced, with trade union density declining from 53 percent in 1979 to around 33 percent today.[11]

Notwithstanding the strong trade union influence, there has been a long history of attempts to increase collective employee involvement and participation in the workplace. The first phase was part of a wider movement of industrial democracy that occurred during and just after World War I in Western industrial countries from 1917–20. During this period, so-called Whitley Councils emerged, which were joint employer and employee bodies.

While many councils included a degree of trade union representation, their role was principally representing all employees. Marchington (1994) has suggested that the origins of Whitleyism can be found in a mixture of socioeconomic and political pressures at the time and a desire to integrate workers more closely within the enterprises in which they were employed. In addition to these developments some companies were experimenting with alternative forms of nonunion employee representation. Notably, Spedan Lewis in 1929 set down the principles for creating the John Lewis Partnership. This partnership included extensive employee participation and involvement with the formation of representative structures as foundation. This included a "Branch Council" made up of elected representatives, the managing director, and some of the management team. In addition, a second structure was created at a national level called the "Central Council," of which 80 percent of the 130 members are elected from all parts of the company with management making up the remaining 20 percent. The Central Council also provides the electoral college to appoint five directors to the partnership's Central Board of twelve (More details of the John Lewis Partnership below).

During World War II and the years immediately afterward, the second major phase of collective participation primarily took the form of JCCs at workplace level (Kessler and Bayliss 1992, p. 102) or Joint Production and Advisory Committees (JPACs). Both were part of a drive to stimulate productivity growth and reduce conflict. Marchington (1994) estimates that by the mid-1940s there were over 4,000 committees in existence in engineering alone, covering in excess of 2.5 million workers, with numbers declining during the postwar part of the decade. Marchington suggests (1994) that the reason for the decline of such committees related to their abuse by management as a means to increase power and control and the lack of real management commitment.

The 1960s and early 1970s also witnessed an increase of "staff associations," principally in the finance industry. These representative forms were particularly prevalent in large building societies. This also coincided with a rise in trade unionism in the industry over the same period (IRS 1995, p. 7). In 1992 total membership of such associations stood at 1,166,433 employees (IRS 1995, p. 7). As Industrial Relations Services (IRS) in 1995 reported, the first annual report of the Certification Officer (CO) defined staff associations as "Organizations, usually of white-collar workers, . . . whose membership is confined to the employees of a single employer (or associated employers) in sectors other than central or local government and the nationalized industries." Moreover, while most associations have evolved from employer-inspired bodies, the IRS study found most function as independent trade unions both in terms of the CO legal definition, thus included in the statutory list of trade unions maintained by the CO, and in comparing the activities of conventional trade unions.

The last major phase in collective participation occurred in the 1970s with Britain's accession to the EEC's draft Fifth Directive with its proposals for worker members on boards of directors and harmonization of company law. The entry of Britain into the EEC and the election of a Labour government in 1974 led to the establishment of the Bullock Committee of Inquiry, which proposed a degree of employee representation at board level. However, the subsequent White Paper in 1978 watered down the Bullock majority proposals.

External Influences

A significant external influence on the British industrial relations environment has been the presence of Japanese multinationals, which have demonstrated a more active approach to alternative forms of employee representation.[12] For example, the Nissan motor manufacturer (U.K.), established a Company Council in 1989, which represents all union and nonunion employees at the plant. It acts as a dual channel of employee representation, used primarily as a mechanism for consultation and information purposes. This differs from the union present at the plant, AEEU (Amalgamated Engineering and Electrician's Union), which focuses on traditional union issues of pay and basic conditions for its members.[13] While union members can normally sit on the council, they must represent the views of all employees at the plant, rather than a particular union view. The constitution of the Company Council makes this nonadversarial philosophy clear, "The prime responsibility of all members of the Council is to ensure the prosperity of the Company and by so doing promote the prosperity and security of all staff" (Bargaining Report 1993, p. 12, as cited in Hyman and Mason 1995, p. 130).

In yet another example, Geoffrey Broad's (1994) longitudinal study of a Japanese "greenfield" manufacturing site in the U.K. suggested that employee participation through NER structures remained a highly contentious issue among Japanese transplants, which had arrangements for a "High Involvement Management" (HIM) strategy.[14] Broad states that although Japanese management viewed NER structures as a further step in enhancing long-term employee commitment and participation, British managers at the plant thought that workplace representatives were inexperienced and perceived such bodies as a strategy for staving off unwelcome trade union recognition. Broad (1994) also suggests that Japanese managers were unprepared for the rising expectations of U.K. line workers for further involvement in a range of factory policy matters, such as new products, overtime working, and allocation of work (Broad 1994). As such, the high commitment and participation strategy had raised workers' expectations; however, this resulted in low morale when communication and consultation in the NER forms failed to deliver these expectations, reestablishing "traditional" industrial relations institutions.

However, overall American-style nonunion HRM and OD approaches have had a major effect on U.K. approaches to employee representation. Some American multinationals have used the lack of legal structures as an incentive to introduce innovative NER structures. These firms include Baxter Healthcare, Berol Corporation, Polaroid, Black and Decker, and Pitney Bowes (see below for details).

Legal Developments

Similar to Australia, the U.K. development of statutory employee representation has been conferred only on "recognized trade unions"[15] emphasizing once again the long-standing legal preference for the "single channel" of representation based on trade unions (Terry 1999). Unlike the European continent where works councils are mandatory at most workplaces and, conversely, in the United States, where NER structures are heavily regulated, Australia and the U.K. have traditionally had little state regulation in this area. As a consequence, in the U.K. there has been no legal protection for employees over many issues where employers have chosen not to recognize trade unions. In other areas, such as health and safety, requirements on employers are limited, with employers required only to consult with appointed safety representatives on health and safety matters (Terry 1999, p. 19).

Principally, four pieces of European law have had a direct impact on the nature and impact of employee participation and consultation and the development of NER forms in the U.K. First is the Collective Redundancies Directive, which states under Article 2 (amended in 1992) that an employer contemplating collective redundancies must begin consultations with workers' representatives in good time with a view to reaching agreement.[16] The agreement must cover ways of avoiding or reducing redundancies, and of mitigating consequences through redeployment.[17]

The second piece of European legislation is the Acquired Rights Directive, similar to the Collective Redundancies Directive. In 1994 two decisions in the European Court of Justice (ECJ) held that the U.K. was in breach of its duties under the requirements of the Collective Redundancies and Acquired Rights Directives as transposed into U.K. legislation (Terry 1999, p. 8). As a result, the Collective Redundancies and Transfer of Undertakings (Protection of Employment) (Amendment) Regulations 1995 was introduced.[18]

The third concerns the extension of employee rights to consultation over health and safety matters in nonunion organizations. This has been formulated through the Health and Safety (Consultation with Employees) Regulations 1996 to ensure compliance with the Framework Directive by extending consultation rights to all employees.[19]

Fourth, changes occurring since the election of a Labour government in 1997 have had a profound effect. In particular, the decision by the new government to end the "opt-out" and sign the Social Chapter, including the adoption of the European Works Councils (EWC) directive has had consequences for NER forms. The directive states that any multinational company with more than 1,000 employees and with more than 150 employees in at least two member states is required to implement a EWC, or an equivalent procedure, for the purpose of providing "transnational information and consultation" for its entire workforce (IDS 1997c, p. 1).[20] This obliges the U.K. government to implement any directive of the kind mentioned that sought to provide for the "information and consultation of workers"

under the terms of the Maastricht agreement (Hall 1996, p. 26).[21]

There are limitations to the remit of the EWC directive. The directive does not include rights to negotiate over pay or veto any management decisions. Companies must simply "inform and consult" with worker representatives on issues of "transnational" significance that affect their operations in more than one country. This excludes consultation rights over domestic issues, such as takeovers, closures, large-scale redundancies, and new working practices. Some commentators have suggested that the EWCs will be simply "talking shops" allowing multinationals to claim they engage in worker consultation (*The Observer*, May 11, 1997, p. 4). Nevertheless, this is the first time in the U.K. that employees have statutory backing for consultation over a company's performance and investments, and have the right to meet and question senior management over such decisions.

In addition to these requirements, a potential development of the European Company Statute could further encourage employee involvement and consultation. In May 1997 the European Commission made recommendations for employees' involvement in enterprises incorporated as European companies under the proposed European Company Statute. The key proposal was that all European companies should negotiate a system of worker involvement, which would include issues such as consultation through a group of employee representatives and the representation of employees on the board (IDS 1997a, b, c).

Australia

Development of NER

In contrast to the U.K., Australia's industrial relations system throughout this century has been strongly influenced by the centralized systems of conciliation and arbitration. Arbitration systems in one form or another exist at federal level and in all six states of Australia. Respective federal and state acts of Parliament provide for the establishment of conciliation and arbitration tribunals, the registration and legal recognition of employer and employee associations (unions),[22] and detail the rights and obligations of the parties. The tribunals are empowered to handle industrial disputes and to set wages and conditions of employment embodied in awards (Bamber and Lansbury 1998).

Historically, employer and employee associations together with the industrial tribunals have dominated the wage-setting and dispute-resolution processes. As in the U.K., however, trade union density has declined to around 32 percent of the labor force. Workplace relations involving nonunionized establishments have also been dominated by the centralized system, as awards have a common rule application and cover about 90 percent of the workforce. Individuals performing the category of work specified in an award are covered by the provisions contained in them, irrespective of whether they are members of trade unions. This has created few opportunities for the legal development of NER forms.

As Markey and Reglar (1997) state, employee participation or industrial democracy has been slow to gain acceptance in Australian industry. Furthermore, they argue that "Australian managers have traditionally been wary of any whittling away at their managerial prerogative. . . . Unions were also traditionally suspicious of employee participation schemes as a management plot. For its part, the national level of government had lacked the will or the constitutional authority to implement a widespread system of industry democracy" (Markey and Reglar 1997, p. 358).

Since the mid- to late 1980s a dramatic shift to widespread decentralized arrangements has taken place under wage-fixing principles determined by the Australian Industrial Relations Commission (AIRC). As part of this process, the AIRC required enterprises to establish appropriate mechanisms for consultation and negotiation on matters affecting the organization's efficiency and productivity. But it was not until the Keating government introduced further reforms to extend enterprise bargaining to the nonunion sector under the Industrial Relations Reform Act 1993 that NER structures became a topic of discussion and debate. The legislation gave a renewed focus on nonunion workplace relations, in particular the nature and extent of workplace decision making outside the centralized industrial relations framework, including the influence and role of nonunion forms of employee representation. These nonunion agreements (or Enterprise Flexibility Agreements) were collective in nature and required a high degree of consultation between employees and management in making the agreement.

In 1997, a new phase of industrial relations reform began with the introduction of the Workplace Relations Act 1996, which repealed and replaced the previous industrial relations legislation. The new legislation enabled employers to enter into either a nonunion collective agreement or nonunion individual contracts with their employees, known as Australian Workplace Agreements (AWAs).[23] While these agreements are individually signed, an employer or employee may appoint a person to be his or her bargaining agent in relation to the making, approval, variation, or termination of the AWA (CCH 1998, p. 11), potentially giving NER forms a role in negotiating AWAs.

External Influences

Australian industry has had a high proportion of multinationals, especially from the U.K. and

United States. More recently, Japan and other Asia-Pacific nations have set up workplaces in Australia. The influence of overseas firms on the Australian industrial relations environment has been limited. It has been suggested that this has been partly due to the strong influence and role of tribunals and prescriptive industrial relations legislation (see discussion above).

The centralized industrial relations system has reduced the effect of American-style nonunion HRM and OD approaches to employee representation. While ad hoc developments have occurred in a few multinational organizations, no predominant form of NER has developed in Australia. More recently, however, certain U.S. multinationals have sought to apply nonunion approaches to the Australian context with varying degrees of success (see the case study discussion of The Toys Company below). It has been suggested that recent changes to federal industrial relations legislation has increased the potential for the introduction of more HRM/OD and "mutual gains" approaches in the future. Australia's exposure to such outside influences provides a potential mix and diversity of industrial relations structures, creating a fertile ground for the development of NER forms in the future (Gollan, Pickersgill, and Sullivan 1996, p. 36).

Legal Developments

Australia has not had national or state legislation to support the development of works councils or any other form of NER structures along the lines established in many European countries (Gardner and Palmer 1997, p. 344). Legally, one of the relatively few examples of institutionalized employee participation in management decision-making processes has been the establishment of safety and health committees in organizations with a certain number of employees determined by state occupational health and safety statutes.[24]

In some Australian states, such as New South Wales, some experimentation of NER structures has occurred. In the 1991 Industrial Relations Act (NSW) provisions allowing "works committees" were introduced to facilitate state-based enterprise bargaining. Under Section 119 of the 1991 act, enterprise agreements could be made between an enterprise employer and a works committee to represent persons employed in the enterprise. The act stated that before a works committee could become a party to an enterprise agreement, the proposed agreement must have been approved in a secret ballot by not less than 65 percent of employees in the enterprise. Their role was to represent persons employed at the establishment in negotiating, making, varying, and terminating of enterprise agreements.[25]

Nationally, new consultation requirements were introduced in 1993 as part of the Industrial Relations Reform Act (the Reform Act). In particular, the provisions relating to nonunion agreements, or "EFAs," stated that for an agreement to be approved, it was necessary that during the negotiations "reasonable steps" had been taken to "consult" and "inform" employees about the agreement and its terms. In addition, these terms needed to be "explained" and employees "advised" for approval of the agreement (Mitchell, Naughton, and Sorensen 1997, p. 203).

But these provisions did not prescribe the means (structure or processes) through which such consultation was to occur (Mitchell, Naughton, and Sorensen 1997, p. 203). The provisions stated that as a precondition to approval, the agreement should establish a process for the parties "to consult each other about matters involving changes to the organization or performance of work in any place of work to which the agreement relates" unless "the parties have agreed that it is not appropriate for the agreement to provide" such a process.[26] Importantly, the act only required the establishment of a "process," rather than a "mechanism" or "structure," and therefore did not necessarily envisage a permanent representative body.[27] Nor did the legislation state how employees were to be represented in this process.

Whatever possibility the legislation created for NER forms, the recent Workplace Relations Act 1996 limited this potential. The requirements in the new legislation are limited to ensuring employee "access" to the agreements (up to fourteen days prior to approval), and that the employer took reasonable steps to explain the agreement to employees (PartVIB Section 170LR (2)(a)(b)). Importantly, the legislation did not prescribe a structure or body for consultation.

NER in Practice

This section examines recent and current developments in NER forms, focusing on six interconnected themes—their presence, level, structure, process, agenda, and outcome. The first section examines NER by reviewing the results of large quantitative datasets and national surveys. The second section draws on published and unpublished case studies in the U.K. and Australia and examines the processes, agenda, and outcomes of NER plans. These case studies include Commercial Television Broadcasting, Hotel Industry, Retail Sector, Residential and Commercial Construction Industry, Utilities, Engineering and Maintenance Industry, Healthcare, and Food Industry.

U.K. Evidence

Comparing findings from the 1984 and 1990 Workplace Industrial Relations Surveys (WIRS),[28]

Millward noted that a fundamental change over the period was the proportion of employees *without* access to active NER structures through "functioning consultative committees" (those committees that regularly meet and discuss important issues at the workplace). Overall, fewer than a fifth of workplaces in 1990 had a consultative committee, compared with about a quarter in 1984 (Millward 1994, p. 128). Importantly, the proportion of employees covered by such committees decreased from 43 percent in 1984 to 30 percent in 1990 (Millward 1994, p. 85). (See Table 19.2.) At face value, these figures would indicate that over half of British employees have limited access to any form of effective representative participation, union based or otherwise.

Millward argues that given the origins of many of the practices and much of the philosophy of HRM in the United States, it could be expected that HRM practices in their most developed form would be applied in workplaces (Millward 1994, p. 129). Thus evidence of increased communication in nonunion workplaces might indicate that management was making more effort to secure greater commitment of employees through greater participation and involvement (Millward 1994, p. 127). However, Millward's evidence suggests little widespread use of HRM strategies, and where "fragments of HRM" were found, they were more likely to be found in unionized workplaces than in nonunion workplaces (Millward 1994, p. 129). There was no evidence of an increase in regular meetings between managers and the workforce, systematic use of the management chain, suggestion schemes, or regular newsletters. Nor was there any noticeable increase in the use of multiple channels of communication (as there was in the unionized sector). The two exceptions were the use of regular (usually infrequent) meetings between senior managers and the

Table 19.2

The Extent of Consultative Committees (CC) at Workplace Level in the Union and Nonunion Sectors, 1984 and 1990

	All establishments		Unions recognized		No recognized union	
	1984	1990	1984	1990	1984	1990
CC at workplace	27	21	34	24	21	18
CC meets at least every 3 months	25	19	30	22	20	17
"Functioning CC"	24	18	29	21	19	16

Source: Millward 1994, p. 79.

Notes: Some caution needs to be exercised over these figures. The role and structure of CCs in a unionized setting may be different from those in a nonunion workplace, thus limiting the comparability of the data across the two groups. However, recent case study research suggests that NER structures perform similar roles in unionized and nonunion workplaces. This would indicate that NER forms are not replicating the traditional bargaining role and function of trade unions. A "Functioning CC" is defined as a consultative committee that met at least once every three months and discussed something important in the view of management.

workforce,[29] and a slight increase in the use of newsletters (Millward 1994, p. 90).

Moreover, Millward states "the arrangements at workplace level which managers had put in place to consult, communicate with and inform employees were more widespread and highly developed in unionized workplaces than in the nonunion sector. [Even] briefing groups, the method of communication that showed the fastest increase over the period 1984 to 1990, were much more common in the union sector" (Millward 1994, p. 129). This suggests little evidence of an application of sophisticated nonunion HRM techniques using representative structures in the nonunion workplace.

The first findings from the 1998 Workplace Employee Relations Survey (WERS98) indicate that only 19 percent of private-sector multinational companies operate a European works council (EWC). Of great concern was the finding that 15 percent of managers did not know if they had an EWC. It was suggested that these findings show such structures were far too re-

mote from workplace activity (Cully, Woodland, O'Reilly, Dix, Millward, Bryson, and Forth 1998, p. 12).

Overall, WERS98 indicates that the presence of JCCs from 1990 was stable at 28 percent, with a further 25 percent of workplaces operating a committee at a higher level in the organization. Some 67 percent of employees were covered by these arrangements (Cully et al. 1998, p. 12). Interestingly, only 11 percent of workplaces indicated they had a representative committee at the workplace and at a higher level in the organization (Cully et al. 1998, p. 12). This would suggest only limited adoption of an integrated NER strategy in U.K. organizations, with NER structures either located at workplace level dealing with a narrow range of workplace issues, or NER structures located at higher levels of the organization far removed from workplace involvement. In addition, further analysis of the findings suggests that workplace committees are more likely to be present in larger workplaces (more than 200 employees) and higher-level committees more prevalent in larger organizations (more than 10,000 employees) (Cully et al. 1998, p. 12).

Research by Guest and Peccei (1998) into union-management partnership companies indicated that the presence of representative systems are associated with greater participation in work-related decisions concerning pay, basic work conditions, hours, and staffing levels. But only consultative systems with a specific brief to cover policy and strategic issues indicated high levels of participation on strategic issues such as new technology, reorganization, and development of new products and services (Guest and Peccei 1998, p. 29).

The impression is that U.K. workplaces have not progressed to an integrated approach with their NER plans, with employees having limited involvement, consultation, and negotiation powers and influence. This may be due to the influence of culture, a strong adherence to past custom and practice, and of managerial prerogative. Millward argues that many workplaces without an active union presence have relatively few formal mechanisms through which employees could contribute in a broader context at the workplace than that of their specific job and local work environment. In addition, he argues, "Nor were they as likely to have opportunities to air grievances or to resolve problems in ways that were systematic and designed to ensure fairness of treatment. Broadly speaking, no alternative [or nonunion] models of employee representation—let alone a single alternative model—had emerged as a substitute for trade union representation" (Millward et al. 1992, p. 365).

Australian Evidence

The Australian federal government's Green Paper *Industrial Democracy and Employee Partici-pation*, published in 1986, found "little evidence of the widespread application of employee participation and only a few examples of genuine worker influence on major decision-making" in Australian workplaces both in unionized and nonunion environments (1986, p. 65). Nevertheless, Marchington's analysis of the Australian Workplace Industrial Relations Survey (AWIRS)[30] data reveals a growth in the number of formal joint consultative mechanisms in the latter part of the 1980s, and that generally they were perceived to be quite successful (Marchington 1992, p. 530).

While a large proportion of Australian workplaces reported the existence of various types of employee involvement schemes, however, there were relatively few cases where involvement took the form of representative participation with a genuine opportunity to influence decision making at work. It was found that JCCs existed in only 14 percent of workplaces, although such arrangements covered 30 percent of Australian employees (Mitchell, Naughton, and Sorensen 1997, p. 200; Callus, Morehead, Cully, and Buchanan 1991). As in the U.K., an analysis of unpublished data from AWIRS suggested that NER structures were most common in unionized workplaces (Campling and Gollan 1999).

The release of the latest AWIRS95 data indicates an increasing trend toward NER plans. The 1995 incidence of JCCs was more than double that of 1990, increasing from 14 to 33 percent. The increase for task forces or ad hoc committees was also substantial, up from 25 to 38 percent (Morehead et al. 1997, p. 188). Morehead et al. (1997) state that much of this increase may have come about because of legislative requirements relating to enterprise bargaining or making organizational change initiatives as smooth as possible (Morehead et al. 1997, pp. 189–190).

Judging from this survey evidence, two qualifications should be made regarding the nonunion environment. First, the data indicate that the most common impetus for the introduction of NER plans was management at the workplace. Second, as suggested in the previous AWIRS data and U.K. evidence, NER forms are more likely to occur at unionized workplaces (48 percent), particularly those with an active union presence, compared to workplaces with no union (13 percent) (Morehead et al. 1997, pp. 193–194).

However, research into employee participation of nonunion EFAs by Mitchell, Naughton, and Sorensen (1997)[31] reveals that despite additional legislative requirements for consultation in EFAs under the Industrial Relations Reform Act 1993 (the Reform Act), there has been a poor outcome, with only 59 percent of EFAs containing NER structures such as consultative committees (CCs)[32] (Mitchell, Naughton, and Sorensen 1997, p. 205). In a further analysis, 64 percent of EFAs that included CCs did not indicate a fixed number of meetings, and in 56 percent of EFAs there was no reference to meetings at all (Mitchell, Naughton, and Sorensen 1997, p. 211). In addition, few EFAs that had established NER plans indicated how committees were to be appointed, or stated the committee's jurisdiction (Mitchell, Naughton, and Sorensen 1997, p. 213).

Recent research undertaken in Australia in the nonunion sector by Campling and Gollan (1999) reveals that there is little incentive for most nonunion workplaces to establish any NER structure due to the traditionally centralized nature of Australian industrial relations (see previous discussion on history and legal structures). It can be argued that this is not a failure of NER per se, as bargaining may not be the main purpose of these representative forms. Nevertheless, further research by Campling and Gollan (1999) suggests that even where there have been collective agreements, these have been made without any genuine bargaining or consultation with employees. In addition, management was usually the party that determined whether a more collective relationship was established (Campling and Gollan 1999). This would indicate that NER forms did not complement, but in certain instances undermined, collective forms of wage bargaining.

Additional case study research into JCCs as part of the enterprise bargaining process suggested that many of the committees are limited by management to trivial issues or what McGraw and Palmer term the three Ts—Tea, Towels and Toilets (McGraw and Palmer 1994). They argue that many NER forms have a short life with many issues left unresolved due to limited provision of resources to implement recommendations and inadequate training (McGraw and Palmer 1994, pp. 98–101).

Case Studies

United Kingdom

Table 19.3 details the composition, structures, and processes involved in NER structures. This involves an analysis of eighteen cases, ten in manufacturing and eight in service-based activities[33] with seven British firms, seven subsidiaries of U.S.-based firms, one German, one Japanese, one joint U.K.-French firm (Eurotunnel) and one Australian-owned subsidiary. In total, eighteen cases with NER structures have been identified. All have limited or no union presence.

The majority of firms reported that the main aim of NER forms is to increase consultation and communication. Only two cases (notably Baxter Healthcare) suggest that such structures should have a bargaining role. Most see NER forms as a

Table 19.3

U.K. Cases of NER—Structure and Process

Company	Objective	Coverage	Representativeness of members	Composition	Negotiation/bargaining	Issues for consultation	Frequency of meetings	Dispute/conflict resolution
Allied Colloids (now called Ciba)	Communication channel for employees & managers.	Up to and including middle management.	Elected for two-year rolling terms, employees with one year service. Meetings take place in work time and paid if shift workers (not paid transport cost). No provision to spend further time on council business.	Mix—26 elected representatives and senior management as appropriate. Deputy managing director chairs meetings.	None	Pay, company results, training, OH&S, smoking policy, eye tests, PRP, individual grievances not discussed.	Once every two months.	None specified. Representatives can act as counselors in individual grievance procedures although no formal role.
Baxter Healthcare	Provide collective representation for all nonmanagement sections of workforce.	All employees under middle management.	Secret workplace ballot of all employees. Must have served two years in organization.	Mix—23 employees plus senior management. Chair selected by employees.	Pay and conditions are discussed and agreed through committee.	Any matter, including individual grievances.	Every two months with department meetings held monthly. Special meetings for annual pay review.	ACAS and workforce ballot both used.

Berol	Develop and strengthen existing channels of cooperation and keep employees informed of company policy.	Kings Lynn—hourly paid employees only. Tottenham—all employees except 6 managers.	Elected by secret ballot, must serve two years and have six months' minimum service. Representatives paid full pay for any time spent on council work.	Mix—general works manager (council chair), personnel director, and 6–8 employee representatives.	Pay and conditions; however, makes recommendations to site managers who have right to make final decision.	Working conditions, wages and salaries, holidays, hours of work, health and welfare, output and productivity, safety, manpower policies and procedures, education and training (individual grievances not discussed).	Once every quarter, special meetings any other time with six full working days notice.	No provision—must be "talked to a solution."
Black and Decker	None stated.	All employees except senior managers.	Employee representatives are elected.	Mix—14 employee representatives. 11 production and 3 administration employees and 4 management representatives.	None	Changes to shift patterns and pay.	Meets at least every two months and more frequently if necessary.	None specified.
CECO	Means through which employee views could be gauged. Grievances dealt with and information passed on to workforce.	All employees except senior managers.	Employee representatives are elected.	Mix—11 employee representatives, plus managing director as chair and personnel manager.	None	Any relevant issue.	Meets at least every month.	None specified.

(continued)

Table 19-1 *(continued)*

Company	Objective	Coverage	Representative-ness of members	Composition	Negotiation/ bargaining	Issues for consultation	Frequency of meetings	Dispute/ conflict resolution
Claas UK	Enhance communication and industrial involvement. Means make management more aware of issues; provide increased employee involvement.	All employees except senior managers.	Employee representatives are elected by secret work-place ballot for two terms, need twelve months' service and be over twenty years of age.	Mix—6 elected em-ployee repre-sentatives and 5 nomi-nated management representa-tives. Chief executive acts as chair.	Pay and conditions and any other matters of interest to employees.	PRP, job evaluation, and other matters (individual grievances are not discussed).	Four times a year. Extra-ordinary meetings may be held if any representative wishes.	Provision for arbitration and workforce ballot.
Eurotunnel	Company's only communica-tions forum.	All em-ployees.	Permanent employees with at least one year of service.	Mix—represen-tatives from geographically and functional areas.	None	Organizational change, all terms of employment (including pay), policies and profits, and man-agers' social and welfare budget.	Held once a month.	None specified. Individual councils provide personal representation on individual issues.
Gillette	None stated.	All employees at Reading and Isleworth plants.	Elected em-ployee repre-sentatives; vice-chair elected by employee representatives on the com-mittee, with chair ap-pointed by management.	Mix—employee representatives plus manage-ment-appointed chair and other senior management.	None	Terms of reference include basic conditions of employment and policies for recruit-ment and training.	Held once a month.	None specified.

John Lewis Partnership	Communication of information is an essential part of sharing responsibility.	All employees.	Elected employee representatives regularly brief on progress of company (all employees are shareholders). The national central council provides the electoral college to appoint 5 directors to the Partnership's central board of 12.	Mix—Central council of 135 members, 80% of which is elected from all parts of the partnership with management making up the remaining 20%.	All issues including pay and conditions, redundancy. In practice, agreement must be obtained. Chair can veto capital expenditure proposed if he/she regards it as "too dangerous" to partnership's business interests. Local branch council may deal with local grievances and issues.	All issues including financial information and performance, investment, and company strategy.	Regularly	None specified.
Marks and Spencer	None stated	All employees	Majority of representatives will come from self-nomination and a representative panel of general staff at divisional level will narrow the number down, and divisional teams at national level to decide the actual council representatives.	22 employee representatives meet with management.	At times pay, although not considered as part of council agenda.	Look at issues such as the group financial statement and aspects of business strategy, which include the development of stores and systems.	Not stated.	Issues resolved by local managers or if cannot resolve at this level, the welfare committee.

(continued)

Table 19-1 *(continued)*

Company	Objective	Coverage	Representativeness of members	Composition	Negotiation/bargaining	Issues for consultation	Frequency of meetings	Dispute/conflict resolution
Monarch Group	Continuing viability of the company and hence the job security of all employees of the company.	All employees. Separate representation for engineering and maintenance, supervisory and technical, administration and clerical, cabin crew, and operations staff.	Elections are conducted every two years (on rolling basis) for engineering staff, annually for cabin crew. All meetings take place in company time, shift staff paid (at overtime rate with travel expenses paid). Reasonable amount of time on committee business allowed, including monthly meetings of representatives alone.	Mixed— Engineering, 13 elected —Cabin crew, 4 elected —Operations, 3 appointed —Administration/clerical, 1 appointed all meet with director of personnel and senior divisional directors.	Pay and conditions, grievances, quality and performance of work, OH&S, any other matter appropriate.	Nothing excluded.	—Engineering, once every six weeks. —Cabin crew, once every two months. —Administration/clerical and operations, once a year.	Engineering, ACAS
News International	None stated.	All union eligible employees at three sites.	Wapping council has 25–30 delegates (including some NUJ). Other sites not known.	Mix—Employees and senior management.	Pay and conditions.	Any matter.	None specified.	None specified.
Northumbrian Water	Development and maintenance of "harmonious" relations to ensure prosperity of all employees	All employees, functionally based.	Representatives to seven employee councils are elected by secret ballot for a three-year term. Repre-	Mix—7 representatives, two "advisers" —one from confederation of trade union and one from	Terms and conditions, individual grievances and discipline, OH&S, and other	All issues concerning employee relations.	At least four times a year, on average, five or six times a year.	ACAS

	and the company. In addition, promotion of trust, care, and co-operation in the development and improvement of employee communications, recognition, and reward.		sentatives are allowed reasonable time on company business. Training for representatives at Durham University. Travel and subsistence expenses are paid when necessary.	employee association; 4 appointed managers with managing director in the chair.	company-wide issues.			Aim to discuss issues through to a consensus. No facility for arbitration.
OKI UK	Promote the understanding of company policy and improve job satisfaction.	All nonmanagement employees.	Secret ballot, elections annually, representatives need twelve months' service, reps paid for time spent on council duties and "reasonable time" away from normal duties to seek views of employees.	Mix—8 members elected by secret ballot, 3 managerial members, chair and secretary are nominated by the company.	No—Aim to discuss issues through to a consensus.	Pay and conditions, safety, quality and social issues; individual grievances not discussed.	Held once a month. Subgroups may be formed to discuss specific issues and make recommendations to management.	
Pitney Bowes	Give employees opportunity to contribute, consultation, encourage joint participation and involvement, keep in touch, and encourage atmosphere of mutual cooperation.	All employees.	Elected for two years by workplace secret ballot, in theory need one year of service. Main employee co-chair elected from divisional council representatives for four years full-time, the other co-chair is the managing director.	Mix—main council meetings, 1 elected member from each section, plus employee co-chair. Managing director other co-chair, plus directors and personnel controller.	Pay, including Performance Related Pay (PRP).	General wages, working conditions, and other matters. Individual grievances or individual wages or salaries are not discussed.	Main council meets four times a year. Divisional and sectional councils between four and ten times a year.	ACAS

(continued)

Table 19-1 (continued)

Company	Objective	Coverage	Representativeness of members	Composition	Negotiation/ bargaining	Issues for consultation	Frequency of meetings	Dispute/ conflict resolution
Polaroid	Forum for free exchange of views on all matters of factorywide interest and operating efficiency.	All employees.	Chair (three terms), vice-chair (two years) and other representatives elected by secret ballot, paid for council work, pre-meetings, training is available to all representatives. Also expected to play representation role (e.g. accompany individual workers through grievance or disciplinary procedures).	Mix—representatives drawn on a rotating basis from the body of 23 elected representatives, plus divisional, personnel, and other senior managers.	No—intention of dispersing with the "them and us" attitude.	Make recommendations to management on any subject of concern including wages and conditions, including confidential divisional matters affecting employment and production.	Once a month—extraordinary meetings can be called to discuss particular subjects.	ACAS

| Sainsbury | Give management a new channel for staff suggestions and concerns; create a new means of employee involvement. | All employees | The council is mirrored at branch level by more than 400 local councils, one for each store, regional office, and head office department. Seats on group council divided by 6 U.K. regions and Homebase and Savacentre stores, plus 2 union representatives. Local and group council representatives given time off to brief their constituents and to carry out any other work associated with council, plus paid any traveling time. Group council representatives have three-day induction training in communications, interviewing, time management, and business awareness. | Mix—group council made up of board members, 26 elected employee representatives and 2 union appointees, and group chair (also chairs council) and group personnel director. | None | Discuss matters relating to the structure, activities, and performance of the group where these affect staff, including financial results and general trading and operational issues. Does not discuss individual issues such as pay, promotion, or grievances. | Group council meets twice yearly; Local council meets once a quarter. | Outstanding matters are resolved within four weeks either by chair of committee or district/senior manager. |

(continued)

Table 19-3 *(continued)*

Company	Objective	Coverage	Representative-ness of members	Composition	Negotiation/ bargaining	Issues for consultation	Frequency of meetings	Dispute/ conflict resolution
"Liftco"	Committed to a participa-tive and open approach. Represent the workforce in a total way that many unions split along sectional, craft or work-group character-istics could not.	All employ-ees. Two committees, factory and office.	Employee rep-esentatives elected by workgroups in definable specialism, premeetings one week be-fore full meet-ing to set agenda. Participation encouraged through work-group meet-ings in order that communi-cation reached from bottom to top. Training system in op-eration. Spe-cial rights and privileges to time off, secre-tarial time, information, and facilities regarded by some as su-perior to those in local union-ized plants.	Mix—factory has 22 employee representatives. Office has around 15–20 delegates, plus senior management (management took chair and committee elected secretary).	No consultation/ negotiation distinction.	All issues affecting employees including pay and conditions.	Regularly.	ACAS used when TU recognition issue arose.

Sources: "Liftco" (Cressey, Eldridge & MacInnes 1985; Cressey 1985); "Ceco" (McLoughlin & Gourlay 1994); Gillette (Gollan 1998; IDS 1995); Sainsbury (Littlefield 1996; IRS 1996); News International (Gollan 1998); Black and Decker (Gollan 1998; IDS 1997a); Marks & Spencer (IDS 1995); John Lewis Partnership (Flanders, Pomeranz & Woodward 1968; John Lewis Partnership 1996, 1998; Gollan 1998); and the firms described in the 1994 and 1989 IDS surveys on company councils (IDS 1994, 1989).

more effective channel of communication, stressing more "harmonious" and less conflictual relations with the workforce, thus building and encouraging an atmosphere of mutual cooperation. It would seem from their stated constitutional objectives that managements view NER structures solely as a means to increase company produetivity and efficiency, and to promote an understanding of company policy, rather than as an effective forum of collective representation for the interests of employees, rather than management.[34] In addition, there was considerable variation in the range of employees covered. Committees were either based on geography or function, or a combination of the two. Some included management representatives as well as shopfloor employees.

The most important link between members of NER bodies and those who are being represented is the process and procedures of representatives' appointment. While all these cases have some formal procedures, with most having secret individual ballots organized by the personnel departments for terms up to three years, others had representatives appointed by management. One example is the Monarch committee members, who were appointed by management to both the Operations and the Administrative/Clerical Staff Committees (IDS 1994, p. 12). The majority of the companies operated a qualification period for membership of the committees (usually six months' to two years' service with a minimum age requirement), although this was not always enforced, especially in recently established organizations such as Eurotunnel. The majority also excluded employees involved in disciplinary procedures (IDS 1989, p. 7).

Another important aspect regarding the representativeness of committee members is the interaction of the views of those represented and the representatives themselves. The election process

was the most obvious form of interaction, but other forms of interaction were less clear. While few companies addressed this issue, one company, OKI UK, did allow representatives "reasonable time away from their places of work to seek the views of interest groups concerned with any aspect of their (Committee) meeting." Representatives at Polaroid could address monthly team briefings and with company permission call their own meetings of employees on company time (IDS 1989, pp. 18, 21; Terry 1999, p. 24). The Monarch Group also allowed all meetings to take place on company time and agreed on a "reasonable" amount of time to be spent on committee business, including monthly meetings of representatives alone. In addition, shift employees who attended meetings were paid at overtime rates and had their travel expenses paid.

This was also the case at Liftco (Terry 1999, p. 24), where facilities existed for "premeetings" of elected representatives. In addition, representatives also had access to secretarial time and the use of other facilities regarded by some as superior to those in local unionized plants. Some companies used other incentives, such as time off without loss of pay, and access to training, including accounting, financial, supervisory and managerial skills, and grievance handling. Sainsbury's was the only company to provide a three-day induction program for employee representatives, which included training in communications, interviewing, time management, and business.

In some cases where such resources were said to exist, however, such as Liftco, representatives complained of their lack of training (Cressey 1985, p. 71). Terry's analysis of the Liftco case further suggests that "a conspicuous absence from the list of skills taught was negotiating skills" (Terry 1999, p. 24). The Allied Colloids case demonstrates that, while meetings were allowed to take place on work time, the firm would not pay transport costs for shift workers. In addition, there was no provision to spend further time on committee business, seriously calling into question the effectiveness of such consultation.

Cressey's investigation of Liftco also highlights the issue of participation. He states that "participation was encouraged through the committee system with workgroup meetings in order that communication reached from bottom to top" (Cressey 1985, p. 69). Cressey also highlights a negative aspect of identification with particular work groups. The managerial practice of "going round the table asking each delegate if there was anything to raise . . . engendered a sectional viewpoint which management used professionally in committee deliberations" (Cressey 1985, p. 71).

A crucial issue for NER forms and their representativeness is the number of representatives per employee and the frequency of meetings. The committees varied from 10–12 employees per representative (Northumbrian Water, Berol's Tottenham site) to 200–500 plus (Eurotunnel, Sainsbury, Marks & Spencer). These committees had different levels of representation (workplace, store, division, and company), with the average being around 40–60 employees per representative. This variation in employees to representatives ratio would seem to suggest considerable differences in terms of effectively representing the views of employees. Most committees had a mix of employee and management representation with the majority of committee members representing employees. The majority of committees were chaired by senior management, however, usually the managing director or senior divisional director, who had the authority to veto decisions taken by the committee. In addition, some committees could only make recommendations to management but not formal decisions. Frequency of meetings in the sample ranged from once a month to twice yearly, with the average being around every two months. In addition, some companies made provision for special meetings or meetings of employee representatives only on a more regular basis (Claas UK and OKI UK).

The case studies also reveal two further areas of concern: the attempt to distinguish between negotiation or bargaining and consultation, and the ability of these committees to resolve conflict and "deadlocks." Commentators have suggested these two aspects go to the core of the effectiveness of such bodies (Terry 1999). Others have suggested that nonunion forms of representation may have many functions, purposes, and roles, with negotiation and bargaining a relatively insignificant part of the process. While a sizable minority of cases allowed a degree of negotiation and bargaining, in only two cases were pay and conditions negotiated. In reality, however, the negotiated agreement then takes the form of a recommendation to corporate management, or, as previously mentioned, the chair (most often senior management) has the right of veto.

Notably, there was an absence of matters relating to financial, investment, and company strategy, with only Sainsbury's, Polaroid, the John Lewis Partnership, Northumbrian Water, and Marks and Spencer employees allowed this opportunity. In the case of the John Lewis Partnership, under the Articles of the Constitution, the chair of John Lewis Partnership "has control over all wages and salaries and is the ultimate authority in all matters affecting staff" (Flanders, Pomeranz, and Woodward 1968, p. 37). It must be questioned whether this form of "consultation" and "negotiation" would be able to exist in a unionized environment.

Nearly all the organizations studied allowed

consultation over a number of issues, with pay, occupational health and safety (OH&S), hours, productivity, and training being the most common. Interestingly, few cases allowed consultation over individual grievances, although Polaroid encouraged committee representatives to play a representation role by accompanying individual employees through grievance or disciplinary procedures. The lack of representation over individual grievances would not suggest a true alternative to trade unions' grievance handling role.

Terry (1999, p. 24) also comments on the effectiveness of these bodies in terms of their "weight" to resolve failure to agree or "deadlocks." The cases suggest that many companies use some form of external mechanism for resolving disagreements. It must then be questioned whether these committees have "weight" without the ability to impose sanctions on organizations in the interests of those represented (as is the case with trade unions). This lack of weight would appear to undermine the effectiveness of these committees.

Australia[35]

The following cases are four examples of NER structures that have been established in Australia (Campling and Gollan 1999). The four cases cover commercial television broadcasting (Television Network Company), the hotel industry (The Holiday Hotel), the retail sector (The Toys Company), and the construction industry (Big Block Constructions).[36] Two companies are Australian-owned, one is U.K.-owned, and one is an American subsidiary. All firms have no or limited union presence.

These cases demonstrate the processes involved in NER plans by highlighting the following issues: the objectives, coverage, representativeness of members, composition, level of consultation and negotiation, issues for discussion, frequency of meetings, and type of dispute and conflict resolution.

Of the four organizations, only the Television Network Company allowed their four committees full decision-making authority, while the other three organizations had management right of veto. Three of the four organizations had a mix of employee and management representation. In one organization, Big Block Constructions, management and employees believed that a higher proportion of nonmanagement members would be difficult to achieve due to employees' lack of experience and expertise in meetings. The most important issues discussed in consultative committees were the negotiation of the enterprise agreement, OH&S issues, and general efficiency (see Table 19. 4).

One firm, The Holiday Hotel, established a committee structure representing all areas of the hotel to improve the overall operation of the hotel for both the company and its employees. The committee was established in October 1993 and includes thirteen representatives from all areas of the hotel. The general manager and human resources manager provide facilitation and support. The committee's role includes: commitment to the bargaining process through the enterprise agreement; liaising and listening to team members; dissemination of feedback to hotel departments; cooperation to achieve common goals and enhanced operations and outcomes for the hotel and its employees (Campling and Gollan 1999).

Initially, meetings were held weekly with minutes distributed to each department and posted on a specially designated notice board. As the enterprise bargaining process developed, meetings were held less regularly so that complex issues

438

Table 19.4

Australian Cases of NER—Structure and Process

Company	Objective	Coverage	Representativeness of members	Composition	Negotiation/ bargaining	Issues for consultation	Frequency of meetings	Dispute/conflict resolution
Television Network Company	Attempting to build a "consultative enterprise."	All employees.	Employees elected. Four committees: —Enterprise Agreement Monitoring Committee —Consultative committee (Work environment) —Affirmative Action Committee —Occupational Health and Safety Committee.	Employees only.	Issues include enterprise agreement and work conditions. There is no management right of veto.	Issues: Affirmative Action, OH&S, general efficiency issues, and training.	None specified.	AIRC.
Big Block Constructions	Act as the forum for examining the setting of goals and the measurement of performance. Create a cooperative, mutually beneficial workplace environment that delivers productivity, cost improvements.	All employees.	Employee representatives are elected, union presence at meetings. Personnel manager and training coordinator chair the meetings.	Mix—six employees and two management. However, three employees have supervisory role. Little experience in preparing and running meetings.	Enterprise agreement, set goals and measure performance, job redesign, workplace reform process. Management has right of veto over committee decisions.	Oversee productivity, performance and efficiency issues, job security, individual goal setting, training, quality assurance and control.	At first twice monthly. Now every month.	AIRC and Committee resolution process.

The Holiday Hotel	Commitment to enterprise bargaining process, liaise and listen to team members, dissemination of feedback to hotel departments, unbiased representation, and promotion of a mutual beneficial outcome for the company and employees.	All nonmanagement employees.	Employees elected.	Mix—13 employees plus general manager and human resource manager.	Enterprise agreement, position classifications, flexible hours of work. Management has right of veto over committee decisions.	Performance appraisal system, selecting rosters, annual salary reviews, employee training and development plans.	About once a month.	AIRC.
The Toys Company	Reinforcing the corporate culture inside the organization through management practices and communication.	All nonstaff employees.	Several permanent committees: —Team-talk group with regular rotation to avoid marginalization problems. Management and employees present agenda items for discussion. —Health and safety committee, with six monthly rotation of all positions to ensure as many persons	Mix: —Team-talk group with regular rotation between management and employees —Health and safety committee, three employees and three management, role of chair rotated between employees and management representatives every six months.	Enterprise agreement, position classifications, flexible hours of work. Management has right of veto over committee decisions.	Cross-functional working, store issues, OH&S, loss prevention, and any other general employee-related issues.	—Team-talk group meets weekly. —Health and safety committee meets monthly —Loss prevention committee meets regularly.	AIRC.

(continued)

Table 19.4 (continued)

Company	Objective	Coverage	Representativeness of members	Composition	Negotiation/ bargaining	Issues for consultation	Frequency of meetings	Dispute/conflict resolution
			as possible have input. —Loss-prevention committee, regular rotation of positions.	—Loss-prevention committee, two employees and two management; role of chair rotated between employees and management representatives.				

Source: Campling and Gollan 1999.

could be reviewed before proceeding to the next stage. Notice of future meetings was posted on the notice board, and all staff were invited to these meetings. Between October 1993 and February 1995, twenty-three group meetings were held.

The Toys Company has established two permanent NER bodies since 1994 as part of the enterprise bargaining process (Campling and Gollan 1999). In addition, the Weekly Team-Talk meeting, run by employee representatives, was based on the focus-group concept where management and employee representatives presented agenda items for discussion. Management considered this representative consultative process essential to the successful long-term operation of the enterprise bargaining process.[37] Both senior and store-level management argue that organizational success depends on the cooperative team approach that the enterprise agreement process fosters.

The Health and Safety Committee consists of three employees and three managers, with six-month rotations of all positions to ensure as many staff as possible have input into the process. It meets monthly to oversee health and safety within each store. The role of chairperson rotates between the employees and management members every six months. In addition, a Loss Prevention Committee has also been established in each store to promote an awareness and understanding of loss prevention. The committee consists of two employees and two managers with regular rotation of positions and the rotation of the role of chair between committee members.

Big Block Constructions has also set up a highly developed NER plan through a committee structure, which acts as a forum for setting goals, measuring performance, and addressing a wide range of workplace issues (Campling and Gollan 1999). It is important to acknowledge that the company has recognized the importance of union involvement in the consultative process and actively sought union presence on the committee.

Under the enterprise agreement the committee is required to review, analyze, and promote a wide range of issues. These issues include setting goals and measuring performance; overseeing productivity and efficiency issues; submitting recommendations to management on job security and continuity of employment issues; investigating and implementing a system of job redesign, individual goal setting, and work organization. In addition, the committee assists in the development of the company's overall training plans and develops and implements a system of dispute resolution.

The committee met twenty-three times while the enterprise agreement was concluded from mid-1993 to mid-1995—an average of one meeting per month. The analysis of the consultation process and functions by Campling and Gollan (1999) reveals that the committee is the primary consultative mechanism used by management and is based on the objectives set for it by the enterprise agreement. Analysis of the committee meeting's minutes and of interview data from representatives indicates that the committee has met its stated objectives. First, it met regularly each month since June 1993 and had about an 80 percent attendance record. Second, an examination of the committee's meeting minutes reveals the items requiring action (Table 19.5). It reveals the high priority the company has assigned to training, skill formation, and the introduction of a skills audit and matrix. In summary, the range and frequency of issues covered indicates the committee structure genuinely operates as a forum for focused discussion on the enterprise agreement's operation and related workplace issues (Campling and Gollan 1999).

Table 19.5

Content Analysis of Actionable Items Arising from Big Block Constructions Consultative Committee Meetings, June 1993 to September 1994

Priority	Item/topic	Number of actions arising from meetings
1	Training, skill formation	56
2	Productivity goals/measurement	42
3	Tool allowance/usage/damage	33
4	Quality assurance	24
5	Lost time	19
6	Waste management	18
7	Work area teams	16
8	OH&S	14
9	Rostered days off (RDOs)	13
10	Communications with workforce	11
11	Consultative committee role/goals/ constitution	10
11	Enterprise agreement and pay	10
12	Employee appearance	9
13	Inclement weather	7
13	Working hours	7
13	Employee absenteeism	7
14	Rest periods and crib time	6
14	Daily timings	6
15	Work practices	5
16	Leading hand allowance	4
17	Survey on workforce reform	3

Source: Campling and Gollan 1999.

The effectiveness of the process can be seen from a company-administered questionnaire distributed in early 1994, which revealed that 96 percent of surveyed employees were aware of the committee and 67 percent knew which member on-site represented their interests. Some 55 percent had discussed the outcomes of the meetings with peers, and 60 percent had read and understood the meetings' minutes. This all suggests a high awareness of the committee's workplace role (Campling and Gollan 1999). The survey also indicated that most employees believed the committee provided a "voice" for their opinions and concerns, although some workers believed that management largely controlled the agenda and decisions, limiting its ability to act as a real "voice" for labor.

Some employees believed that management's right to veto the recommendations limited the committee's decision-making power and ability to guarantee the interests of the workforce. Furthermore, in the short term many employees viewed the committee as a mechanism for ensuring that management granted the six-month pay increases. In the long term, however, very few employees felt that it would substantially improve labor-management relations (Campling and Gollan 1999). Many of the employees still viewed the union as necessary for resolving important differences between labor and management. Notwithstanding this, it was considered that the committee's productivity, performance, and monitoring role ensured that its existence was pivotal to the successful operation of the enterprise agreement in the workplace reform process.

Four issues were raised by employees in regard to the actual operation of the committee, diminishing the representative role for employees. First, with only one member of the committee a nonsupervisor, it was not considered sufficiently representative of the workforce. Second, the presence of senior management on the committee was viewed by most nonmanagement members as moderately intimidatory because the expression of views that conflict with senior management's could adversely affect job security. Third, the analysis of the committee meetings' minutes and direct observation of two meetings indicated that the personnel manager and the training coordinator often set the agenda for the meetings and directed proceedings. While neither were officially members of the committee, their active participation in effect increased management representation to four. In fact, this very strong management presence and influence over the agenda resulted in one nonmanagement member resigning from the first committee. Fourth, the nonmanagement members, unlike their management counterparts, had little experience of preparing and running business meetings, which may account for their lack of participation in many of the meetings. It could be concluded that these factors combined to reduce the influence employees had over the committee's direction, decisions and outcomes (Campling and Gollan 1999).

Review and Conclusion

In an environment of what would appear as a widening "representation gap" (Freeman and Rogers 1993, p.14; Towers 1997) developing in many organizations, due to lower trade union presence in recent years, there has been considerable discussion in Australian and British literature on the effectiveness of NER structures as communication devices and mechanisms for employee involvement or, as some commentators have suggested, as a substitute for unions in the collective bargaining process. The underlying debate centers on whether NER forms make trade unions unnecessary or whether NER forms have a different but complementary role to that of unions at the workplace.

To examine these two approaches this research has addressed a number of questions. First, can NER forms act as substitutes for trade unions? Drawing on qualitative and quantitative evidence, this chapter presents the case that NER structures in the U.K. and Australia have been essentially ineffective as substitutes for union representation, due to the very limited role NER structures play in the bargaining process. This has restricted the ability of NER forms to represent employees' interests in the areas of pay and conditions. The evidence also reveals that employee involvement in nonunion workplaces was often structured in a way that minimized the ability of employees to have a significant influence on how and in what form change was introduced.

Therefore, what role do NER forms have and how effective have they been? The evidence available from the U.K. and Australia suggests that NER forms can be very effective in developing greater overall workplace consultation and involvement of employees. In particular, the evidence indicates that in organizations where greater employee participation has been introduced (especially indirect representative participation), it has been good for business in terms of improved performance and productivity.

In addition, it has been suggested that, while the influence of NER structures over policy and strategic issues is limited, where they have influence over such issues, greater organizational outcomes have resulted with higher employee commitment and more positive employee attitudes and behavior toward the organization.

Moreover, the cases examined in this chapter indicate increasing adoption of innovative NER structures as part of sophisticated HRM and OD approaches, which emphasize communication and consultation. However, further analysis questions the longevity of these innovative NER forms in U.K. and Australian workplaces. Evidence suggests that traditional adversarial industrial relations reemerged when raised worker expectations were not met because NER forms failed to deliver the desired outcomes, resulting in low morale and dissatisfaction.

The preceding analysis would suggest that it

is not the formal existence of NER structures that is associated with greater effectiveness and positive performance outcomes. Instead, the nature of the relationship, management style and culture, and trust developed in NER structures, and the degree to which influence over managerial decisions is ceded through such forums, are the most important factors (Fenton-O'Creevy, Wood, and Callerot 1998, p. 27).

In summary, this review raises a number of important points. First, generally these NER structures have limited access to resources (e.g., training) for establishing independence, thus reducing their ability to evaluate effectively the issues discussed at meetings and representing the views of employees. Second, most NER bodies are structured on a mixed basis of employee elected representatives and appointed management delegates, with the latter occupying the most senior position of chair. The case study evidence also suggests that management was usually the party that controls the structure and agenda at meetings. While the election of employee representatives could give the impression of legitimacy to decisions, in reality this must be questioned. Third, most bodies are only given powers of recommendation to management or the chair has the right of veto over decisions. Fourth, unlike unions, few committees have negotiation and bargaining rights, while consultation issues often lack financial, investment, or strategic data. Finally, few of these bodies in practice fulfill the traditional trade union activities of grievance handling and conflict resolution, with such issues being dealt with by local managers or internal dispute-resolution mechanisms. This evidence suggests that most NER structures are used as devices for consultation and communication, rather than acting as bargaining agents. While it can be argued that consultation, not bargaining,

may indeed be their objective, it nevertheless questions the legitimacy of such bodies as true alternatives to unions.

These points highlight an important issue for policymakers, whether in a climate of declining union density should countries seek to redress this decline and close the widening representation gap through supportive union regulation and policies. Or alternatively, if this decline is inevitable or at least if the decline is not likely to be reversed in the short term, is there a role for NER forms in the workplace to represent and enforce the rights of full citizenship in society, encouraged by supportive laws and policies.

In conclusion, while NER structures can be used as mechanisms for more effective means of communication and consultation, in the cases studied here their effectiveness as bodies representing the interests of employees in filling the lack of representation is questionable. This presents the issue whether state-sponsored NER forms with provisions for resources and training could improve the effectiveness of NER forms in representing employees' interests at the workplace. For, as Terry (1999, p. 27) notes, "with no reference to the external agencies of law or trade unions for support, they are perceived—rightly—as managerial emanations subject to managerial whim."

Acknowledgments

The author would like to thank Bruce Kaufman, George Strauss, and John Kelly for comments on previous drafts and Michael Terry for the insightful discussions. The author wishes to thank Susan Bearfield for her insights and comments on the chapter. In addition, the support and assistance from John Campling, Ron Callus, and the Australian Centre for Industrial Relations Research and Training (ACIRRT) was greatly appreciated. The usual disclaimer applies.

Notes

1. Nevertheless, there are in both countries formal requirements that health and safety committees be established in some union and nonunion workplaces.

2. A similar framework has been applied by Hyman (1997) in reviewing the future of employee representation.

3. NER structures can also be referred to as "union independent" forms of employee representation.

4. These structures may include union members where present.

5. Other forms of direct participation may include TQM teams, self-managed work teams, and quality circles. Importantly, these forms of direct participation are not representational in nature as they often include every worker in the work group. Recent research from the European Works Council Study Group has suggested that direct employee involvement is lower in organizations with formal representative structures. This may imply that direct and indirect employee involvement are to some extent acting as substitutes (Fenton-O'Creevy, Wood, and Callerot 1998, p. 24).

6. This view has been challenged because for many employers it is not important whether NER structures can approximate unions as part of the collective bargaining process, since this may not be the objective or desired outcome.

7. This statement presupposes that voice provided by unions is an improvement over the nonunion option. Some commentators have questioned such an assumption, arguing that union-based collective bargaining may have negative aspects, even from a general social and organizational point of view. It is often suggested that union leaders, who represent the union's voice to the firm, may have different agendas than the membership, and thus the voice stated may not actually reflect the members' own interests, or accurately represent the views of the leadership. However, studies in the U.K. have suggested that legal procedural requirements of voting and the strict processes of balloting legislation have legitimized leadership opinions and action, with membership in some unions displacing leadership on the basis of their moderate and accommodating views (Kelly and Heery 1994).

8. This perspective is encapsulated by human resource management (HRM) theorists advocating high-commitment work practices and emphasizing mutual gains in the enterprise (Kochan, Katz, and McKersie 1986; Walton 1985).

9. Unions often claim that both sides can be better off in such a relationship through increased voice benefits and through the union "shock" effect of higher wages. In this situation firms focus on productivity, rather than costs. In addition, advocates of the social partnership model (such as John Monks—general secretary of the TUC) would strongly disagree that union presence presupposes a "win-lose" relationship. Such a perception is based on an assumption about union behavior.

10. A central principle of the German industrial relations model is the dual structure of interest representation: the separation between domestic-level labor relations and collective bargaining at regional or industry level. The former is focused on generating substantive and procedural norms through plant-level agreements, while the latter establishes general conditions of employment and salary and wage levels. This dual system is defined and circumscribed by extensive juridification and legal process (Koch 1995, p. 146).

11. This decline in trade union density is similar to that found in Australia over the same period.

12. Many Japanese firms appear to welcome some form of representative system, both union and nonunion (Guest 1995, p. 135). A report by Incomes Data Services (IDS) also found that NER forms are normally found at Japanese firms with union representation, with a significant number of Japanese firms operating a NER structure alongside a single-union bargaining arrangement (IDS 1998, p. 3).

13. Thus these bodies have different, although complementary, roles at the plant.

14. A strategy emphasizing extensive information sharing and consultation.

15. In Australia and the U.K. there is a system of formal recognition of trade unions. Under such recognition certain rights and responsibilities are conferred, which may include protection from legal prosecution for damages incurred in industrial disputes. In both countries certain conditions need to be satisfied before formal state recognition as a bona fide trade union can be made. In the U.K. the Trade Union and Labour Relations Consolidation Act 1992 states that a "trade union is an organization (whether temporary or permanent) which consists wholly or mainly of workers of one or more descriptions and whose principal purposes include the regulation of relations between workers and employers or employers' associations." In addition, under the criteria of certification, the certification officer must be satisfied that the organization is independent, free from employer interference and control. However, under present U.K. law this does not automatically confer recognition by the employer for the purposes of collective bargaining.

16. While these directives are the individual responsibility of member states to introduce and police, action can be taken against member states if they fail to provide such mechanisms when the employer refuses to recognize such representatives for the purposes outlined above.

17. The directive states that in order to enable workers' representatives to make constructive proposals, the employer must in good time supply them with all relevant information, including detailed reasons for the cuts and the categories and numbers of workers affected.

18. These regulations cover nonunion and union workers, allowing unionized workplaces a dual channel for employee representation. But recent announcements by Ian McCartney, the industry minister, "does not believe employers should be forced to introduce works councils or similar bodies in order to meet the requirements of this legislation" (*Financial Times*, February 16, 1998, p. 12).

19. This is limited to health and safety matters and applies only to nonunion workplaces. Some commentators have argued that these regulations provide a more stable basis for the representation of nonunion employees than those concerning redundancy and transfer. Collective Redundancies Regulations require in principle only the establishment of ad hoc committees in the particular circumstances, while health and safety consultation is a continual process (Terry 1999, p. 11).

20. A survey by Income Data Services (IDS) estimates that a further 130 U.K. firms, and an additional 170 non-U.K. organizations, will now be brought within the scope of the directive (IDS 1997c, p. 1).

21. The U.K. has until December 1999 to introduce relevant national legislation. The firms newly falling within the directive's remit will be given this period in which to reach a voluntary, preemptive agreement if they wish or wait until the directive becomes operational (IDS 1997c, p. 1). In practice this has meant that organizations meeting such criteria must set procedures for establishing a Special Negotiating Body of employee representatives to establish the EWC.

22. In Australia the legal regulation of trade unions is essential to arbitration and conciliation and confers corporate status protection against discrimination, and security and protection against competing unions covering the same industry or occupation (Gardner and Palmer 1992, p. 144). The AIRC needs to be satisfied that "the association is free from control by or improper influence from, an employer, or an association or organization of employers" (Workplace Relations Act 1996 Section 189 (aa)).

23. An AWA is a written agreement between an employer and an employee detailing the employee's terms and conditions of employment. Legally, each agreement between an employee and the employer is a separate AWA, although several AWAs may be included in one document. The rationale for AWAs is to give employers and employees flexibility in setting wages and conditions that suit their individual preferences and situations (Employment Advocate 1998, p. 3).

24. See, for example, Occupational Health and Safety Act 1983 (NSW) ss 23–25; and Occupational Health and Safety Act 1985 (Vic) 37.

25. The purpose of an enterprise agreement is to regulate (wholly or partly) the conditions of employment of employees in a single enterprise.

26. No equivalent provisions to section 170NC(1)(f) appear in the recently enacted Workplace Relations Act.

27. Nor did the act make any reference to the frequency and makeup of this "process" (Mitchell, Naughton, and Sorensen 1997, p. 204).

28. At the time of writing (late 1998) preliminary results were only available. Preliminary results from the latest survey are expected in late 1998. A full source book will be published in 1999.

29. Regular meetings between senior managers and all sections of the workforce became more common, having increased from 29 percent in 1984 to 38 percent in 1990. This growth was largely confined to U.K.-owned private-sector service industries.

30. A national survey in 1990 covering more than 2,000 workplaces and 19,000 employees.

31. All EFAs approved by the AIRC between April 1, 1994 and September 6, 1995 (109 agreements in total).

32. This calls into question the effectiveness of the legislation, which requires a process but does not state the "mechanism" or "structure" by which this should take place.

33. These case studies include "Liftco" (Cressey, Eldridge and MacInnes 1985; Cressey 1985); "Ceco" (McLoughlin and Gourlay 1994); Gillette (Gollan 1998; IDS 1995); Sainsbury (Littlefield 1996; IRS 1996); News International (Gollan 1998); Black and Decker (Gollan 1998; IDS 1997a); Marks and Spencer (IDS 1995); John Lewis Partnership (Flanders, Pomeranz, and Woodward 1968; John Lewis Partnership 1996, 1998; Gollan 1998); and the firms described in the 1994 and 1989 IDS surveys on company councils (IDS 1994, 1989).

34. It can be argued that higher productivity can lead to higher profits leading to higher job security and employee pay. This is dependent, however, on forces that encourage (or enforce) these outcomes on employers, as a firm's main objective is to maximize share value and profits. Thus the positive distribution effects and outcomes may not be realized without such enforcement.

35. The author would like to thank John Campling and Ron Callus for their assistance in this section of the report. This section is based on cases undertaken as part of the ACIRRT project on nonunion and lightly unionized workplaces originally funded by the Australian Department of Industrial Relations. More details of these cases are

published in a book by Campling and Gollan (1999) titled *Bargained Out: Negotiating without Unions in Australia.*

36. For anonymity, fictitious names have been used.

37. This contrasts with a telecommunications company (part of the original study) that dismantled all consultative committee mechanisms believing that this weakened direct individual communication with employees and marginalized those not on the committees. The director of HRM at the company argued, "If you accredit your communication on the basis that all managers should be communicating to all staff, what we don't want is to inadvertently exclude people from that communications process. As far as we are concerned representation-type structures do exclude people. It is naive to think the person that is so-called representing the group is going to be representing everyone in the group because by definition not everyone is going to have the same opinion."

References

Australian Federal Government. 1986. Green Paper, *Industrial Democracy and Employee Participation.* Canberra: Australian Government Publishing Service.

————. 1988. *Industrial Relations Act 1988.* Canberra: Australian Government Publishing Service.

————. 1993. *Industrial Relations Amendment Act 1993.* Canberra: Australian Government Publishing Service.

————. 1993. *Industrial Relations Reform Act 1993.* Canberra: Australian Government Publishing Service.

————. 1996. *Workplace Relations Act 1996.* Canberra: Australian Government Publishing Service.

————. 1996. *Workplace Relations and Other Legislation Amendment Bill 1996.* Canberra: Australian Government Publishing Service.

Bamber, Greg J., and Russell R. Lansbury. 1998. *International and Comparative Industrial Relations.* London: Sage.

Bennett, Laura. 1994. *Making Labour Law in Australia: Industrial Relations, Politics and Law.* Sydney: Law Book.

Broad, Geoffrey. 1994. "Japan in Britain: the dynamics of joint consultation." *Industrial Relations Journal* 25, no. 1: 26–38.

Callus, Ron, Alison Morehead, Mark Cully, and John Buchanan. 1991. *Industrial Relations at Work: The Australian Workplace Industrial Relations Survey.* Canberra: Australian Government Publishing Service.

Campling, John, and Paul J. Gollan. 1999. *Bargained Out: Negotiating Without Unions in Australia.* Sydney: Federation Press (forthcoming).

Campling, John, Paul Gollan, Richard Pickersgill, Mark Short, and Ian Watson. 1995. "The Role of Enterprise Agreements in Lightly Unionized and Nonunionized Workplaces." Unpublished research report prepared for the Australian Commonwealth Department of Industrial Relations, ACIRRT, University of Sydney.

CCH. 1998. *Australian Enterprise Bargaining Update* 22 (March).

Cressey, Peter. 1985. "Recasting Collectivism: Industrial Relations in Two Non-union Plants." In *Trade Unions Today and Tomorrow*, vol. 2, ed. Georges Spyropoulos, pp. 63–83. Maastricht: Presses Interuniversitaires Europeennes.

Cressey, Peter, John Eldridge, and John MacInnes. 1985. *Just Managing: Authority and Democracy in Industry.* Milton Keynes: Open University Press.

Cully, Mark, Stephen Woodland, Andrew O'Reilly, Gill Dix, Neil Millward, Alex Bryson, and John Forth. 1998. *The 1998 Workplace Employee Relations Survey: First Findings.* London: Department of Trade and Industry.

Denny, Kevin, and Stephen Nickell. 1991. "Unions and Investment in British Manufacturing Industry." *British Journal of Industrial Relations* 29: 113–122.

Fenton-O'Creevey, Mark, Stephen Wood, and Emmanuelle Callerot. 1998. *Employee Involvement within European Multinationals.* European Works Council Study Group. Stage 1 Research Report. July.

Fernie, Sue, and David Metcalf. 1995. "Participation, Contingent Pay, Representation and Workplace Performance: Evidence from Great Britain." *British Journal of Industrial Relations* 33, no. 3 (September): 379–415.

Flanders, Allan, Ruth Pomeranz, and Joan Woodward. 1968. *Experiment in Industrial Democracy.* London: Faber and Faber.

Flood, Patrick C., and Judy D. Olian. 1995. "Human Resource Strategies for World-Class Competitive Capability." In *Managing Without Traditional Methods*, ed. Patrick C. Flood, Martin J. Gannon, and Jaap Paauwe, pp. 3–30. Cambridge: Addison-Wesley.

Freeman, Richard B., and James L. Medoff. 1984. *What Do Unions Do?* New York: Basic Books.

Freeman, Richard B., and Joel Rogers. 1993. "Who Speaks for Us? Employee Representation in a Nonunion Labor Market." In *Employee Representation: Alternatives and Future Directions*, ed. Bruce E. Kaufman and Morris M. Kleiner, pp. 13–76. Madison: Industrial Relations Research Association.

Gallie, Duncan, Roger Penn, and Michael Rose. 1996. "The British Debate on Trade Unionism." In *Trade Unionism in Recession*, ed. Duncan Gallie, Roger Penn, and Michael Rose, pp. 1–32. Oxford: Open University Press.

Gallie, Duncan, and Michael White. 1993. *Employment Commitment and the Skills Revolution.* London: PSI.

Gallie, Duncan, Michael White, Yuan Cheng, and Mark Tomlinson. 1998. *Restructuring the Employment Relationship*. Oxford: Oxford University Press.

Gardner, Margaret, and Gill Palmer. 1992. *Employment Relations: Industrial Relations and Human Resource Management in Australia*. Melbourne: Macmillan.

———. 1997. *Employment Relations: Industrial Relations and Human Resource Management in Australia*. 2nd ed. Melbourne: Macmillan.

Gollan, Paul J. 1998. "Alternative Forms of Employees Participation in Nonunion and Lightly Unionized Workplaces." Unpublished discussion paper, London School of Economics and Political Science.

Gollan, Paul J., Richard Pickersgill, and Gabrielle Sullivan. 1996. *Future of Work: Likely Long Term Developments in the Restructuring of Australian Industrial Relations*. ACIRRT Working Paper No. 43.

Gospel, Howard F., and Gill Palmer. 1993. *British Industrial Relations*, 2nd ed. London: Routledge.

Guest, David. 1995. "Human Resource Management, Trade Unions and Industrial Relations." In *Human Resource Management: A Critical Text*, ed. John Storey. London: Routledge.

Guest, David, and Riccardo Peccei. 1998. *The Partnership Company: Benchmarks for the Future*. The Report of the IPA Survey Principles, Practice and Performance. London: Involvement and Participation Association.

Hall, Mark. 1996. "Beyond Recognition? Employee Representation and EU Law." *International Law Journal* 25, no. 1 (March): 15–27.

Hammer, Tove H. 1997. "Nonunion Representational Forms: An Organizational Behavior Perspective." Paper presented at *Nonunion Forms of Employee Representation: History, Contemporary Practice and Policy*. Banff, Canada, September 3–5.

Hammer, Tove H., Bente Ingebrigtsen, Jan I. Karlsen, and A. Svarva. 1994. "Organizational Renewal: The Management of Large Scale Organizational Change in Norwegian Firms." Paper presented at the *Transformation and European Industrial Relations*. Helsinki, Finland.

Hyman, Jeff, and Bob Mason. 1995. *Managing Employee Involvement and Participation*. London: Sage.

Hyman, Richard. 1997. "The Future of Employee Representation." *British Journal of Industrial Relations* 35, no. 3 (September): 309–336.

Income Data Services. 1989. *Company Councils*. Study 437. London.

——— 1994, September. *Company Councils*. Study 561. London.

——— 1995, November. Report 700.

——— 1996, April. *European Works Councils*. Study 600. London.

——— 1997a, June. Report 739. London.

——— 1997b, October. *The End of Voluntarism*. Focus 83. London.

——— 1997c, November. *European Works Councils*. Study 637. London.

——— 1998, April. Report 759. London.

Industrial Relations Services (IRS). 1995. "Staff Associations: Independent Unions or Employer-led Bodies?" *IRS Employment Trends*. 575, January, London.

——— 1996. "Talking Shop: Sainsbury's New Works Councils." *IRS Employment Trends*. 622, December, London.

John Lewis Partnership. 1996. *The (London) Gazette*, September 14.

———. 1998. *The (London) Gazette*, March 17.

Kaufman, Bruce E., and Morris M. Kleiner, ed. 1993. *Employee Representation: Alternatives and Future Directions*. Madison: Industrial relations Research Association.

Kelly, John. 1995. "Works Councils: Union Advance or Marginalisation?" In *The Future of Labour Law*, ed. Aileen McColgan. London: Mansell.

Kelly, John, and Edmund Heery. 1994. *Working for the Union: British Trade Union Officers*. Cambridge and New York: Cambridge University Press.

Kessler, Sid, and Fred Bayliss. 1992. *Contemporary British Industrial Relations*. Basingstoke: Macmillian.

Koch, Karl. 1995. "The German Works Council and Collective Bargaining Development Since Unification." *German Politics* 4, no. 3 (December): 145–155.

Kochan, Thomas A., Harry C. Katz, and Robert B. McKersie. 1986. *The Transformation of American Industrial Relations*. N.Y.: Basic Books.

Littlefield, David. 1996. "Sainsbury's Gets Them All Talking." *People Management*, September 26, p. 9.

McCallum, Ronald C. 1997. *Crafting a New Collective Labour Law for Australia*. The Third Whitlam Lecture, Trade Union Education Foundation, May 14, Newcastle.

McGraw, Peter, and I. Palmer. 1994. "Beyond Tea, Towels and Toilets? Lessons from a Top 500 Company in Using Joint Consultative Committees for Enterprise Bargaining." *Asia Pacific Journal of Human Resources* 32, no. 3: 97–104.

McLoughlin, Ian, and Stephen Gourlay. 1994. *Enterprise without Unions: Industrial Relations in the Non-union Firm*. Buckingham: Open University Press.

Marchington, Mick. 1992. "Surveying the Practice of Joint Consultation in Australia." *Journal of Industrial Relations* 34, no. 4: 530–549.

———. 1994. "The Dynamics of Joint Consultation." In *Personnel Management: A Comprehensive Guide to Theory and Practice in Britain*, ed. Keith Sisson, 2nd ed. Oxford: Blackwell.

———. 1995. "Involvement and Participation." In *Human Resource Management: A critical Text*, ed. John Storey, pp. 280–305. London: Routledge.

Markey, Raymond, and Rosemary Reglar. 1997. "Consultative Committees in the Australian Steel Industry." In *Innovation and Employee Participation through Works Councils: International Case Studies*. Raymond Markey and Jacques Monat, eds. Aldershot: Avebury.

Millward, Neil. 1994. *The New Industrial Relations?* London: Policy Studies Institute.

Mitchell, Richard, Richard Naughton, and Rolf Sorensen. 1996. *The Law and the Propagation of Joint Consultation Mechanisms in Australian Enterprises—Evidence from the Federal Enterprise Agreements Process*. Centre for Employment and Labour Relations Law, University of Melbourne.

———. 1997. "The Law and Employee Participation—Evidence from the Federal Enterprise Agreements Process." *Journal of Industrial Relations* 39, no. 2 (June): 196–217.

Morehead, Alison, Mairi Steele, Michael Alexander, Kerry Stephen, and Linton Duffin. 1997. *Change at Work: The 1995 Australian Workplace Industrial Relations Survey*. Melbourne: Longman.

Office of the Employment Advocate. 1998. *Australian Workplace Agreements: How-to Guide*. March.

Patterson, Malcolm G., Michael A. West, Rebecca Lawthom, and Stephen Nickell. 1997. *Impact of People Management Practices on Business Performance*. Institute of Work Psychology, University of Sheffield and Centre of Economic Performance, London School of Economics, Issues in People Man-

agement No. 22, London: Institute of Personnel and Development.

Rogers, Joel, and Wolfgang Streeck, ed. 1995. *Works Councils: Consultation, Representation and Cooperation in Industrial Relations*. Chicago and London: University of Chicago Press.

Sako, Mari. 1998. "The Nature and Impact of Employee 'Voice' in the European Car Components Industry." *Human Resource Management Journal* 9, no. 1: 5–13.

Storey, John. 1992. *Developments in the Management of Human Resources: An Analytical Review*. Oxford: Blackwell.

Taras, Daphne G. 1997. "Contemporary Experience with the Rockefeller Plan: Imperial Oil's Joint Industrial Councils." Paper presented at the Nonunion Forms of Employee Representation Conference, Banff, Canada, September 3–5.

Terry, Michael. 1999. "Systems of Collective Representation in Non-union Firms in the UK." *Industrial Relations Journal* 30, no. 1: 16–30.

The Observer, May 11, 1997, p. 4.

Towers, Brian. 1997. *The Representation Gap: Change and Reform in the British and American Workplace*. Oxford: Oxford University Press.

"UK: Proposals for Union Rights on Redundancies." February 16, 1998, *Financial Times*, p. 12.

Walton, Richard E. 1985. "From Control to Commitment in the Workplace." *Harvard Business Review* 64, no. 3 (March-April): 77–84.

Wood, Stephen. 1996. "High Commitment Managaement and Unionization in the UK." *The International Journal of Human Resource Management* 7, no. 1 (February): 41–58.

Practitioner Commentary:
Employers

20

Employee Involvement and Section 8(a)(2): EFCO Manufacturing

Chris Fuldner, CEO

As you look at me, you are looking at a target. If you look closely, you'll see that the NLRB has shot many, many holes in this target. To give you an idea of how we became a target and how we got into so much trouble and what we're doing, I think maybe it would be important to give a brief history of our company.

EFCO was founded in 1951 in Monett, Missouri, by my father, Terry Fuldner, and a friend of his named George Eberly. EFCO began as a true "employee involvement" company. Those two gentlemen sold the product. They engineered the product. They would get up from the table, pull material from the warehouse that was just nothing but a rack on the wall, cut the material, fabricate and glaze it, load it into the truck and also drive the truck to the job site, and unload the material at the site.

During the 1960s, the company started to grow, primarily by making and selling residential windows, which were distributed throughout the Middle West. We entered the commercial field in about 1960. Today, we have evolved into a company that manufactures windows and doors and glass curtain wall systems for high-rise buildings, schools, hospitals, and the like. EFCO grew to be about a $3 million company by 1960, and there it remained until about 1977.

My father was very much the epitome of a command-and-control type manager. In fact, I can remember days we'd be sitting in the Engineering Department and could look out across the street to his office, and he would come charging out of that door, virtually running across the street, and when he'd hit the door to the engineering building, which was very small at that time, it would almost come off the hinges. We all sat there wondering who he was going to attack—because attack he would. He would go up to whoever the poor fellow was and just absolutely berate him, just tear him apart. But usually, after he got done and he was blowing the smoke off the end of the barrel, he'd say, "What was it I shot you about?" and it was over, and he would sit down and talk to the individual just like nothing had ever happened.

That type of thing led us into being organized in 1964 by the Carpenters' Union, which we bargained with for eight years. It was a tense and volatile relationship. The employees benefited to the tune of 25 cents an hour over that entire eight-year period. Finally, in 1972 the union was decertified and from that experience we learned that it is best to have happy employees and good employee relationships if we want the company to grow and prosper. At that time, in 1973, we were still a $3 million company.

I moved back to Missouri in 1977 after spending five years in Colorado. At that time, the company was probably at a low point. The 1974–75 recession in the United States just about put us out of business. We had maybe sixty-five employees at that time. The company was worth very little. We had just lost money, and we were a little bit desperate. So we came up with the idea that we wanted to get our employees more involved with the company, to make them feel more a part of EFCO Corporation.

We introduced profit-sharing and followed that up with an employee stock-ownership program. We immediately began to see some growth. Management also began to spend a lot of time with employees on the floor and invited them into the office. By 1980, EFCO had grown to maybe 200 employees.

In the early 1980s, we were still trying to figure out ways to make our employees understand they really had a stake in EFCO, that their livelihood as well as ours was tied to the business. So we started off with sort of a town meeting. We would get all our employees together several times during the year to discuss issues. Whatever they wanted to talk about, wherever they went with their questions, we were willing to go and discuss and to talk to them. We tried to give them an idea of where we thought the company was going, what type of backlog we had, what sort of future we thought the company was going to have in the next year or so—and these things helped. We continued to grow. We probably hit $20 million in 1983, so we were starting to grow fairly rapidly. Our employment climbed to 400 and,

as the numbers grew, we found obviously that it would be very difficult to meet with all our employees at one time. In fact, there's no place in Monett, Missouri, even today, where you can get 400 people together in one spot unless it's the Wal-Mart parking lot. (Monett is a town of about 6,500 people.)

Realizing we had a problem, we tried to have meetings on an ongoing basis. Our management team (of maybe four or five people) would try to meet with each department to discuss its problems, and we soon noticed that most of the questions and most of the things that we ended up discussing were wage issues, benefit issues, policy issues—all the things we now know the NLRA says we're not supposed to talk to employees about.

In 1988 we embarked on a program to implement MRP2 manufacturing techniques on a companywide basis to meet changes in our marketplace. As part of this effort, we implemented teams. Most of them were given a particular target or goal or function to investigate to see if they could come up with something much better than what we were doing. We had some tremendous success. I can give you a few examples.

Our inventory record accuracy went from 60 percent to 98 percent, at a time our business more than tripled. Our inventory turns went from five in 1988 to twenty-six this year. We have some production areas where we're turning our inventory fifty-two times or greater in a year, and that's all directly because of what the teams were able to do for us.

A key indicator of performance for us is factory throughput. In 1988 it was three weeks from the day we pushed our first extrusion to the time we put the product on the truck. Through efforts of a number of teams, that number has dropped to four days. All these examples have had tremendous effects on our bottom line, particularly our cash flow and our cash positions.

As time went by, we discovered that despite our success with these production teams, we still had people who wanted to know more about their benefits, their pay, and asked whether we could make changes or implement new ideas. Meanwhile, the ESOP and profit-sharing programs became so successful that earnings on an annual basis often now far exceed the employees' salaries for the year. We instituted several committees in 1991, one of which we called the Benefits Committee. Another one was the Policy Review Committee. We also had safety committees, which were in place since 1988. We formed the Benefits Committee, for example, primarily for employees to make suggestions that would help modify our benefits package to better fit their needs. They've looked at 401K programs versus our profit-sharing and ESOP programs. They looked at our health programs. They made suggestions on how those are structured, some of which have been implemented. That seemed to be a big problem with the NLRB because we got into the area of dealing with wages and benefits. Our thinking, at the time we put that committee together, was how do you get true involvement of an employee if you can only talk about half the spectrum of issues.

Our various committees were started by management selecting a group of people from all areas of the plant including shopfloor workers, engineering, and estimating. I met with each of these committees the very first day they met, and told them that how they accomplished their reviews or changes, or structured their meetings or committees, was all up to them. They could determine how many members they had, the mem-

bers' terms, how they would be selected in the future, succession issues, and topics. They were free to determine the topics they wished. These committees had no management people in attendance, unless they were specifically invited by the committee. That was to encourage a free exchange of ideas without any fear of intimidation from management or fear that management might take issue with something that was said. The whole hope was to try to entice people to come forward with their ideas.

When the committees made their recommendations, they had choices. They could either submit those directly to the management committee using an individual spokesman, or they could come in as a group, or they could give it to one of our other educational facilitators, and he would then present it to us.

Well, about this time the Carpenters Union decided they wanted to make another run at us. They didn't get to the point where they even had enough signatures to call a vote in the plant. On their way out, however, they took a parting shot. The union filed a complaint with the NLRB and all of a sudden we got cast into the world of Section 8(a)(2), which we didn't know from anything. We were going along in ignorant bliss, and all of a sudden there was a big hole in our ship and we were sinking rapidly.

To make a long story short, the NLRB came in and held a hearing in Monet at the National Guard Building and the administrative law judge (ALJ) said in his opening comment that he couldn't see any difference between us and the *Electromation* company case. And, sure enough, he ruled in 1993 that our committees were illegal and that we had to disband them. These proceedings did not come without significant cost. Aside from the distaste of being treated as though we were criminals, we also spent in the neighborhood of $150,000 in defending ourselves.

We appealed that decision to the full board in Washington, D.C., in February 1995, and expect our legal bills to double if the case goes forward. As of this date [September 1997], we have not heard anything on that appeal from the NLRB. The problem with this is that it's had a very chilling effect on EFCO and our committees and team concepts. Our lawyers have told us to forego establishing any further teams and more or less to let things run their course.

The biggest problem with Section 8(a)(2) is that it deprives the employees of choice. The choice they have now is either come in as individuals or bring in a union so we can have these committee meetings. I think it is the height of arrogance and hypocrisy to suggest that a nonunion company cannot run these committees above-board and that just because somebody has a union card in his pocket, he is all of a sudden capable of participating in such a committee. This seems like a very short-sighted policy to me, and it's why I think the law needs to be changed.

Note from the Editors

On December 31, 1998, the National Labor Relations Board released its decision in *EFCO Corporation and United Brotherhood of Carpenters and Joiners of America, AFL-CIO and Employee Benefit Committee, Employee Policy Review Committee, Safety Committee, Employee Suggestion Screening Committee, Parties-in-Interest* (Case 17-CA-6911, 327 NLRB No. 71). The NLRB order directed EFCO to cease and desist from "dominating, assisting, or otherwise supporting the Employee Benefit Committee, the Employee Policy Review Committee, and the Safety Committee." The board commented that "while the Respondent's stated aim of involving employees in decision making may be commendable, we find with regard to these three committees that the particular means chosen by the Respondent to achieve that end were unlawful." Only EFCO's Employee Suggestion Screening Committee was not disbanded, as it was found not to be a labor organization.

21

Operation of the Production District Joint Industrial Council, Imperial Oil

David J. Boone, Manager of Production Operations

My thoughts are directed to the upstream part of Imperial Oil (the Resources Division). Imperial Oil is Canada's largest integrated petroleum firm. Within our upstream operations, we have an oil sands business unit, which includes the operation of our Cold Lake facilities, and we have a conventional oil and gas business unit.

Our conventional oil and gas operations are based in four primary field-operating areas or districts: Judy Creek (only until April 15, 1998), Norman Wells, Battle River (a district around Edmonton), and Prairie Mountain, which covers a number of oil and gas fields in the more remote areas of Alberta, British Columbia, and Saskatchewan. The majority of our operation is nonunion, with the only exception being Norman Wells, which is represented by the Communication, Energy and Paperworkers Local 777. The Joint Industrial Council (JIC), the nonunion representation vehicle, represents 445 operations employees (people on hourly wages) working for Imperial Oil in the Resources Division.

In addition, we have an alternative nonunion form of representation called an employee forum at Cold Lake, which represents the hourly operations employees plus the professional and administrative employees.

Each of the nonunion operating areas has a number of local JIC councils, which deal primarily with local matters. Where an issue is common across a number of areas or is outside the scope of the local area manager, it will be raised at the JIC district council. The district council typically meets every two months, with a formal agenda developed by elected (worker) and selected (manager) co-chairs. The Cold Lake forum also is represented at district JIC. A premeeting is held by elected delegates the night before to develop their positions on various matters as well as to catch any additional items that need to be added to the district council agenda. Formal minutes are taken and published of the district council discussion. These minutes are distributed to the operating areas throughout Resources Division and are copied to Operations and Human Resources management and the president/CEO of Imperial Oil and the corporate Human Resources group.

All elected employee delegates are chosen from their work units, either by volunteering or by secret ballot. Selected management delegates are appointed and typically are area foremen and area managers. The meetings and proceedings of the district JIC are managed by four co-chairs—two elected and two selected. Assistance is provided by a small Operations Human Resources group.

The district JIC provides a forum for two-way communication and issue resolution. Employees voice concerns, and raise and vigorously debate issues. The company communicates business and employee matters. JIC also is a decision-making body for items that are within its mandate. This mandate has been articulated clearly so that we minimize time spent on matters beyond its scope. For example, the JIC was chartered to design the process by which we fill vacancies in situations where we need skills in one location and have an oversupply of skills in another area. The JIC also has a process by which the management team keeps employees informed regarding the use of contractors in certain roles and the rationale for it.

Some of the more challenging decisions affecting issues, such as pension-plan design and compensation philosophy, are beyond the scope of the JIC and fall within the domain of the board of directors. But we use the JIC as an opportunity to have much earlier input from a broader group into decision making. The district JIC plays an important role in influencing corporate management around policies or decisions that affect employees. The public nature of the meetings, with published and widely circulated minutes, acts to bring issues to the forefront that might not surface under other circumstances. It has been my experience that, in the JIC, we cover broader topics and people get engaged to a greater depth and breadth in things that are important to them in the workplace than what would occur in a union setting.

Delegates are able to discuss and debate issues while providing anonymity to those "constituents" who asked for the issues to be raised. Discussions are articulate, well researched, and well presented, partly due to a training program for new delegates and to ongoing capability development. These discussions also can be frank and hard hitting, but council has earned a high level of respect from senior management and thus plays an input role in policy development. There can be cynicism around level of influence because

it is not always visible to people, but candid feedback and observations from council get passed on directly to the senior vice president of the Resources Division of the company. My management team often jokes that he listens more attentively to the JIC than he does to some of his managers! In many ways, the JIC functions as the "employee conscience," balancing out the purely business side of a variety of decisions.

Key Factors That Determine Effectiveness of Nonunion Representation

Imperial Oil has had a long history of involvement with nonunion forms of employee representation. Over time we have come to recognize a number of key elements that affect the viability of such representation systems. At times, one factor may seem more important; however, where there have been failures, they typically are a result of a combination of factors. Key success factors that we have identified include (1) management values, principles, and leadership style; (2) competitive wages, benefits, and working conditions; (3) impact and ability to influence; (4) formal and informal issue-resolution processes; (5) external labor relations and legal/human rights environment; (6) the will to make it happen and ability to evolve. Each is described below.

Management Values, Principles, Leadership Style

The values and principles of senior management are critical, especially those of senior operations leaders because of their high profile in council. Delegates and employees are sensitive to such questions as these:

• Does the management team believe that employees have a role to play in influencing and setting policy?

- Is open, honest communication valued?
- Is constructive criticism welcomed?
- Are different perspectives respected and valued?
- Do the leaders do what they say they will do?

The values of the company and its leaders/managers translate into behaviors and a management "style" that can make or break the success of any form of representation but is especially key for nonunion representation in which there is no veil behind which management can hide. As the manager responsible for the JIC, if I react very negatively to something with words or body language, that really does shut things down. I have to be quite conscious of my reactions, as do the other operations leaders.

It is crucial that the principles that will guide the JIC are agreed upon and documented, and that *all* members are held accountable for conduct consistent with these principles. An absence of these principles tends to create uncertainty and confusion. Imperial Oil has a well-defined set of corporate industrial relations principles, which were communicated to all employees and are stewarded to on a regular basis.

Imperial takes care to appoint leaders/managers who demonstrate the ability to work well with a diverse workforce and have a proven track record in maintaining positive employee relations. We build this expectation into our management succession planning. A practice of upward promotion of high-performing wage employees into leadership positions has helped to ensure that future supervisors are aware of and understand issues that affect operations employees.

The Competitiveness of Existing Wages, Benefits, and Working Conditions

It is important that a process exist to ensure we remain competitive in our wages, benefits, and working conditions. Let's not be naive. If our compensation package is not competitive, then a nonunion form of representation can break down very quickly. If employees feel they are being given fair and equitable treatment and their issues in these areas are being resolved, they typically see less value in injecting a third party, such as a union, into the process. Our JIC has subcommittees that analyze the regional competitiveness of wages and working conditions. These cooperative processes obviously raise the level of ownership and trust.

Impact and Ability to Influence

As I mentioned earlier, a representation vehicle that has (and is perceived to have) influence over matters within its mandate is more likely to succeed. Where JICs or forums are perceived as ineffective in representing employees, or where there is no formal representative system at all, then employees naturally seek alternative forms of representation. Care is taken to monitor employee perceptions of JIC effectiveness. We do not expect continuous 100 percent satisfaction from all constituents, but we test for the majority view and look for trends.

A related factor is the degree of local autonomy that business unit leaders, site managers, or supervisors have to deal with issues in a timely fashion. Responsiveness is valued and expected. We keep a log of issues to ensure that response time is tracked. Delays without reasonable explanation are flagged for discussion and action.

Having Both Formal and Informal Issues Resolution Processes

The presence of formal and informal issue resolution processes is valued, and the perception as to whether or not they are effective is important to monitor. The existence of a grievance procedure often is cited by people as an advantage of unions, and there is a message in this for nonunion forms of representation. We have provided training for our delegates into how grievances are best handled. Fortunately, our actual incidence of grievances is low, which is an indicator that supervisors are managing the issues promptly and fairly.

Equally important is a working environment where issue resolution can take place and employees are free to voice their opinions without fear of reprisal. We have had numerous discussions on this topic to ensure that all employees understand that they are free to express their opinions. These discussions help reinforce the expectations of operations leaders as well. And, as always, it is most important that we "walk this talk."

External Labor Relations and Legal/ Human Rights Environment

The nature of the outside labor relations and legal/human rights environment also has a bearing on the success of JIC and forum. Our company does not operate nonunion representation in a vacuum. In other words, union actions, whether they be contract settlements, job actions, or grievance/arbitration decisions have some residual effect in nonunion areas. In addition, legal or human rights rulings that affect the workplace require clear understanding by our delegates. Things such as alcohol- and drug-policy implementation have been a hot topic for us. The key in all these areas, from my perspective, is to ensure that we have frank, open discussion of these matters to avoid any misunderstanding, particularly when it relates to a policy decision made by the company.

The Will to Make It Happen and the Ability to Evolve

When all is said and done, JIC works because the people who participate have the will and resolve to make it work. We hire people who are constantly looking to meet challenges and make things work better, and they apply themselves to JIC in the same way. When all the debate has been had, emotionally charged or not, most people will want to work together to go forward constructively and with mutual respect.

This same bias to constructive thinking and action has led Imperial's employees and business leaders to press for continuous improvement in the Joint Industrial Council processes. If this evolution had not occurred, there is no doubt that JIC would not have survived to see its fiftieth anniversary in Imperial Oil's upstream.

I was struck by a comment I overheard that the JIC and nonunion systems are an unstable form of representation. Well, thank goodness. I worry about any form of representation that becomes too stable, given the rate of change in the world around us. The instability of JIC gives us the energy to keep improving and adapting.

Reasons Why Companies Set Up Nonunion Forms of Representation

It is important to be very clear around Imperial's principles in this area. Our company prefers to deal with employee-related challenges and opportunities directly with employees to the greatest possible extent, and where this is not practical, through employee representatives in an open forum. Imperial believes, and I personally believe, that the best relationships can exist without the use of an external third party, such as a union, standing between business leaders and employees. Having said that, we are prepared to deal positively with whomever employees choose to have represent them, as we are doing with the CEP union in Norman Wells.

Major Benefits Companies and Employees Derive from Nonunion Status

I truly believe that better answers and greater understanding can be reached faster with *effective* nonunion representation.

Assuming that the nonunion representation system is functioning well, the traditional wisdom is that companies clearly benefit from an ability to continue to operate with less risk of a work stoppage. But the highest leverage for employers is in the productivity gained.

The business and its shareholders (which in our case includes every employee) benefit from the high productivity and innovation levels of a better work environment created through collaboration, rather than confrontation. This environment attracts positive, results-oriented, innovative people, and this, together with the openness and access to business leaders that it entails, makes for an attractive work environment compared to some alternatives. Employees value this quality of work life, the greater influence and the opportunity that it affords them.

From an employee perspective, I believe it promotes a better understanding of the business, more certainty in the employment arrangement, and more opportunities to learn and progress. If anything, the JIC gives these hourly workers pro-portionately greater influence in the company than is warranted by their numbers alone.

I have heard accusations that the success of our JIC system has a lot to do with the reality of unionization at competitive enterprises, and that Imperial Oil workers are benefiting from the high union dues being paid by other workers in the industry. I see the relationship as being quite the reverse. People in the Joint Industrial Council say, "Those rascals in Norman Wells [who unionized in 1993]! They're riding on the coat-tails of all the work we've done at JIC." They say, "Look, the union is using the same rebalancing process that we developed in council. They are getting the benefit of local policies crafted at JIC and forum, and they lever off the Joint Industrial Council wage rates. They get the same rates, the same wage structure. Jeez, it looks like a Joint Industrial Council with dues."

But this is an important point. This isn't about one approach being right and one being wrong. It is about the fact that there are many approaches to bringing people together. What will work best? Let's make sure there is the choice, the opportunity to go in some different directions and try some different things. There are some extremely progressive unions, and we deal with one of them, which is good for everyone. But there is a spectrum, and let's be open about where we can find new ideas.

Major Disadvantages and Costs

Maintaining an effective nonunion form of representation consumes considerable management and employee effort and has tangible costs. We struggle through gray issues, which, for better or worse, would be black and white in a union agreement. We keep connecting back to guiding principles. This is hard work and comes with a cost.

Even so, there is no doubt in my mind that the effort pays off in terms of better business results and a rewarding collaborative work environment.

Thoughts on Public Policy

This is a bit of a minefield, but I'll give it my best. My eyes have been opened by the American experience. We don't live with anything remotely resembling an 8(a)(2) situation, but it is telling that I felt it prudent to ask one of our lawyers to review my draft notes.

From my perspective, there are numerous examples of how nonunion representation systems can contribute to the success of companies and ultimately to our economy and quality of life. I believe that North America has generally moved beyond the era of employer-dominated employment arrangements, which needed a union presence to counteract "employer abuses." Unfortunately, public policy and, to a certain degree, the academic community have not fully "caught up."

Current policy and legislation generally (though there are exceptions) are biased in favor of unionized representation. There are historical reasons for this that are no longer valid in my view. Most employers, most industries, are very sensitive to offering competitive and attractive compensation, benefits, and working conditions. The benefits of effective nonunion representation seem to have been lost on some policymakers and members of the academic community, and it is timely to reconsider today's bias. This is not to suggest that unions no longer have any place at all, and I want to close by stressing that this is not a matter of right versus wrong. Unions developed for a reason and have contributed positively to society in many ways. It is time to recognize that nonunion representation also has contributed and that this approach, when nurtured properly, offers considerable value (I would argue more value) to all stakeholders.

22

Nonunion Employee Representation at Dofasco

Mark Harshaw, Acting Director of Human Resources

We are a large, well-established Canadian steel company. It is important to put the specific types of formal and informal forms of employee representation at Dofasco into the broader context of our corporate philosophy. The foundation for employee relations is based on respect for each individual. All of our systems or programs or communications are intended to support all employees in representing themselves with both dignity and pride. It is not about being union or nonunion.

I don't think you can discuss Dofasco or its nonunion status without a brief look at its history and consequently its deeply entrenched culture. We have been around since 1912, and we've existed through periods of ups and downs that have stretched our employee relations. Our company founders, the Sherman brothers, established some fundamental values very early in the company's history that became strongly embedded. Because the company initially was run by a family, it came to think of itself as a family and tried to establish that kind of relationship with its employees. As with any family, though, not everything always runs smoothly. Conflict occurs, but we recognized early on that we needed to be open and honest, develop methods to talk out our differences and continue to respect each other.

Over the years, a very strong culture developed, the cornerstone of which was the Golden Rule: "Treat others as you would like to be treated." A sense of entitlement became deeply entrenched. Employees came to expect that they had a job for life, and that the company could look after them, and in the end, they would retire with a sizable nest egg. Working life was stable and change came very slowly. Our employees were comfortable, safe, and happy.

Some innovative practices developed. In many ways the Shermans were ahead of their time in their approach to a number of areas. Contrary to some opinions, union avoidance wasn't the driving force for a lot of our employee relations work, which really began in the early 1920s. The impetus was the company's efforts to take a struggling foundry, a very small company, and turn it into an integrated company. We had a very transient workforce in those days. People came to work, they left, they spent their money and it wasn't on their family, and there were concerns about work performance. The Shermans believed that to build a more stable workforce, the company needed policies that would reinforce long service as well as family values.

In 1938 they introduced profit-sharing. All employees could share in the wealth of the company and at the same time provide them with an incentive to create that wealth through their collective efforts. Later, a savings plan was developed.

The first formal employee representation forum involved the administration of the savings and profit-sharing fund. Employees have input into activities affecting this fund through what are known as "fund reps." The management of the fund is carried out by trustees, who in turn consult with and are answerable to an advisory committee. The committee consists of nineteen members, nine of whom are fund reps voted to the job by other employees. Each rep represents an area of the company. Because fund-rep duties are additional to their normal job requirement, we pay them for the extra time. There usually is competition for the available slots. Each rep holds the job for three years, and elections are staggered for each of three of the nine areas. As a result, there is a fund election every year, and membership in the committee turns over while maintaining some core knowledge of activities in order to avoid a situation where all nine employees are new. This system has been in place for a long time now, and it seems to work to everyone's satisfaction.

Another area where employees are involved and represented in a more formal fashion, and one that's vitally important to us, is our Health and Safety Committee. It was established in 1992 as a support and audit team, and it's an excellent example of management people and the workforce pooling resources, expertise, and experiences to make improvements. The committee consists of nine elected work areas again and six management appointees, and their job is to monitor and facilitate. Members may receive input from fellow employees, or they may be asked to mediate in proceedings between an employee and a safety concern with that employee's area supervision. Committee members regularly tour other facilities to gather information, compare notes, broaden their views, and establish some

benchmarks for Dofasco outside of the traditional steel industry. In the event of a serious accident, the committee members are responsible for assisting in the investigation, liaising with the Ministry of Labour, and helping to develop ways to prevent any recurrence.

With respect to other matters of concern to employees, like wages and conditions of employment, we try to lead rather than follow, and keep the work environment positive to attract and retain people. We regularly benchmark with industry to ensure that we stay competitive. We communicate market and industry comparisons to employees directly through department meetings and indirectly through fund reps. We do make informal use of our fund and health and safety reps to convey such information, but we utilize focus groups of employees to solicit feedback on employment policies and practices. Employees also use reps and focus groups to have greater input to management.

Our company policy manual, which contains all the information on terms and conditions of employment, is made available to all supervisors and employees through the corporate intranet. The intranet is accessible throughout the company, and paper copies still reside in some areas of the company.

Though we have some formal employee representation mechanisms, we believe that the most important representation is on an individual basis. To me, true representation occurs when each employee fully contributes and directly represents himself or herself. For example, when employees have grievances, we try to encourage self-accountability so that employees bring forward their own concerns. Sometimes, grievances may be brought forward by groups or teams as well. Support is available to individuals or groups who have concerns through their supervisors when appropriate, human resources representatives (who are assigned to particular departments and are accessible in each area of the company), employee relations experts, fund reps, and on suitable matters, our health and safety reps. Employees also have access to our medical department or through Family Services, an independent counseling and support organization on contract to Dofasco. Most of our disputes are resolved directly between an employee and supervisor. We do have an open-door policy whereby an employee with any unresolved issue can go to his or her boss's boss and so on right up to the president if resolution can't be achieved along the way. All levels are accessible, and we take every complaint seriously. Nonetheless, it is not a perfect process. We find that it is time-consuming and that it requires trust, empathy, and good communication skills at every level along the way.

To me, representation through employee involvement is key. For Dofasco that means engaging all 7,000 people, not just a few hundred deemed to be the best. Empowerment is about employees being provided with resources in terms of equipment, processes and systems to do the job, being given the skills through training and development to make the most of those resources, and knowing they have the permission to change things, to do things. While empowerment is very trendy, we learned that it has traps: a common one is trying to empower people before they're ready. We've made some good progress but we're still catching up with giving people all the skills and knowledge they need. And of course if employees are encouraged to change things, the company must establish the criteria and the game rules to play in.

Recognizing that, in most cases, two or more heads are better than one, we've emphasized the teaming approach throughout the plant. This meant replacing the old line of progression manufacturing jobs with rotating, multiskilled operating teams that are paid for the competencies they learn and then apply. We also have special-project teams working throughout the entire organization looking at safety issues, quality issues, delivery issues, and so on. The degree to which these teams are representational depends on a lot of things. Do we get the same few people involved all the time? Are they working on real issues? Are they supported? Do they achieve any results? Do they have the tools really to contribute? You can't expect someone to get involved without providing the skills and knowledge necessary to succeed and that includes the soft skills, the meeting skills, the problem-solving skills, the communication skills, and quite often a broader perspective of the customer, of the community, of the shareholders and of the suppliers is required.

We encourage and promote employee involvement in everything from recreation and lifestyle programs, training content, equipment selection and upgrade, job design, product quality improvements, and even customer interaction. We try to match skill and experience to the appropriate areas of representation and this helps involve a broader cross-section of people and it increases the levels of ownership in the results achieved.

Individual representation also occurs regularly through employee focus groups and surveys, even on sensitive items such as compensation system changes and downsizing policies. We also accept and respond to e-mail and voice mail concerns, even at the CEO level. Again, the point is that we respect the individual and we value their input.

Although times have changed since the early days when the Dofasco family was born, our principles and our values have not, and we work very hard to maintain those. We had to downsize and restructure recently in order to survive, but I believe we did it generously and in a way that allowed everyone involved to retain their dignity and pride.

All of this involvement isn't free. There is a cost to it for additional training and time to participate in the meetings or the problem-solving sessions away from the traditional work station and it takes additional time and effort to support an open-book management style and the communication necessary to go along with that. We offered all 7,000 employees a three-day offsite experiential program to set that environment, to teach communications and teaming skills. There was a vice president at every session. John Mayberry, our CEO, attended most of the sessions. Out of those 7,000, we had 6,800 volunteers to attend.

So why do we spend so much effort on employee representation? Because we believe in the value each employee can make to our mutual success, growth, and security. We need all of our employees engaged, motivated, and involved in keeping all our stakeholders satisfied. To us, people really are a competitive advantage but only if you can leverage the capability of all of them and not just the chosen few. Our motto is "Our strength is people, our business is steel," and we develop that strength through appropriate representation and involvement.

Practitioner Commentary:
Employees

23

Delta Personnel Board Council

Cathy Cone, Member, Personnel Board Council

I appreciate the opportunity to discuss a unique experiment in nonunion employee representation at Delta Air Lines, a unique American company. First, I would like to give you a brief overview of our company and then describe the Delta Personnel Board Council and the Flight Attendant Forum as they relate to the issues being presented in this book.

Delta was founded in 1924 and is one of the oldest U.S. airlines. Since its inception, Delta has offered its employees excellent wages, benefits, and one of the best work environments of any business. If you were fortunate enough to be hired by Delta, you were virtually assured that you had a job for life. Over the years, an informal paternalistic philosophy developed regarding the relationship between front-line personnel and management. In fact, Delta's family culture was often cited as one of its strengths and remained so into the early 1990s. This family culture and excellent work environment has given Delta the largest nonunion workforce in the airline industry. Currently, the only two areas of the company represented by unions are the pilots and flight controllers, who are represented respectively by the Air Line Pilots Association and the Professional Airline Flight Controllers Association. Their total membership accounts for approximately 10 percent of our personnel. As you can see, this leaves 90 percent of Delta people who are not represented by a union.

In the 1980s and early 1990s, the effect of growth, deregulation, mergers, and acquisitions moved Delta from a regional carrier to a worldwide airline. The number of employees nearly doubled. This phenomenal growth brought with it the first signs of strain in the family ties that made Delta unique.

Unexpected and uncontrollable events soon caused these Delta family ties to begin to break. The Gulf War and a downturn in the economy in 1991 forced Delta to rethink the way it needed to do business and the way it needed to relate to its people to survive. Forced to downsize and reduce costs by $2 billion a year in order to compete in the industry, Delta's familial culture took a beating. The company reduced headcount by 20 percent, closed offices, cut wages, and reduced benefits. Employee shock and discontent over the radical changes that were made to save the company seem to have forever altered the relationship with management.

As the aggressive cost-reduction program took effect, the economy improved, and Delta rebounded. Today we carry more passengers than any other airline in the world. We estimate that in 1997 we will carry over 100 million passengers. Delta currently employs over 72,000 people worldwide and serves 319 cities in 41 countries. Our total revenue for the fiscal year 1997 was $13.5 billion. However, the people of Delta were changed forever. They began to mistrust management and to express the desire to have a voice in the operation of the company and more control over their future. To try to give employees a voice, the senior vice-president of inflight, Jenny Poole, recommended the creation of the Flight Attendant Forum.

Formed in 1996, this elected body meets quarterly at each flight attendant base to discuss the issues and concerns of the flight attendants. At the local level, representatives are elected on a ratio of 1-to-100 flight attendants. Currently there are 170 forum members representing flight attendants at sixteen bases across the United States. Three times a year, the System Forum meets at Delta's headquarters in Atlanta to bring the most pressing issues forward for discussion with senior management. The System Forum is made up of 26 representatives drawn from the local forum on a ratio of 1-to-1,000 flight attendants. The forum has had success in addressing intradepartmental issues dealing with work rules, per diem compensation, and process improvement. This forum concept may soon be adopted by other departments to address their issues in a similar manner.

While the Flight Attendant Forum could address flight attendant issues, it could not influence companywide decision making. Quite frankly, prior to the downsizing of the company and cut in employee benefits, Delta people were content to be taken care of by management. There was not a serious push for union representation and no thought at all to any form of nonunion employee representation. This changed as Delta began making record profits and profit-sharing and stock options became part of employee benefits. Now, with an ownership stake in the company, pressure began to build for a greater voice in decision making. Employees never wanted to be caught off guard again and forced to endure another round of cost cuts and downsizing.

In May 1996 the pilots, as part of their contract negotiations, requested representation on the board of directors. Management decided that they could not grant the pilots' request without offering the same representation to the other 64,000 employees.

So, in June 1996 the Delta Personnel Board Council was created to be a communication channel between the board of directors and employees. We became the "eyes, ears and voice of Delta people in the boardroom." There are seven members of the council, each representing a different group within the company: Airport Agents (at the ticket counters, gates, ramps, and in cargo), Reservations Sales and city Ticket Offices Representatives; Marketing Representatives; Mechanics, Secretaries and Clerks; Supervisory and Administrative Personnel; and my group, the Flight Attendants. We each serve a two-year term, and there are no term limits. The members of the council are based worldwide, from Amsterdam to San Francisco. All of us were selected by our peers. Management was not involved in the selection process of any group except their own.

I think it is important to keep in mind that we were created simply as a response to the pilot's contract provision for a seat on the board. There was no strategic plan for the council. Our guidelines are very vague and somewhat limiting. We are allowed to have three of the seven council members attend each quarterly board meeting. Training on finance, presentation skills, and any other subject we requested was provided. Only eight days a year were set aside for council and board meetings, but other time was available as needed. It became immediately apparent to us that to represent employee issues and concerns accurately we had to get out and meet with them. We also realized that we needed to know as much about the company and the decision-making process as possible. We therefore initiated a series of city visits to talk to front-line employees, as well as meetings with senior management to understand how decisions were made and what strategic plans were in place for the company.

The council members and the pilot representative (who has the title of Associate Non-Voting Member of the board) are equal in the eyes of the board of directors. The council actively participates in board meetings and can be thought of as lobbyists for all nonpilot employees. We have power to influence but no authority to make changes. We entered into this task with considerable skepticism, knowing that our newly bestowed "rights" were not rights but privileges given at management's discretion. Over the past year this skepticism had given way to the realization that our board and management group want the council to be a means for establishing greater cooperation and integration through improved communication and mutual understanding.

The members of the Delta Personnel Board Council share the opinion that the entire purpose of employee representation is to shift the focus of the front-line and management away from an adversarial struggle over terms and conditions of employment to one of cooperation and mutual gain. While the ability to influence is the key consideration for both sides in an adversarial "we vs. them" relationship, promoting effective teamwork is the key consideration if both sides are to win. To put it another way, the distribution of power is irrelevant if both sides have the same interests and are pulling in the same direction. Given that this is what we believe to be our purpose, it puts us in direct opposition to union's purpose. It also is an alien concept to most management groups, where influence normally is coveted and tightly controlled.

Historically, nonunion employee representa-

tion plans have been attacked as thinly veiled attempts by employers to avoid unions. Was the Delta Personnel Board Council formed to stop unionization? I think there are three things to consider when trying to answer this question. First, the council was not formed as part of any strategic plan. We can be certain of this given the fact that the council has never received any instruction or direction from either the board or management other than to be a means of two-way communication. Second, we have no authority to negotiate wages, work rules, or anything else that is normally the function of a union. Third, and perhaps most compelling, can seven people, working their regular front-line jobs, with no staff and no extra pay, organize 64,000 employees to fight off unionization? I have a hard time believing that anyone could think that this council would be an effective means of keeping unions at bay. If it was Delta's intent to stop the unions with the council, they have chosen a most illogical and ineffective way to do it.

If the council was not formed as a means of union avoidance, then what is our role? I believe that our role and the biggest challenge we have is bridging the communication gap between the front line and management. We have found that the council, being composed of front-line people, has gained the trust of Delta people. We have also gained the respect of the board and senior management. By opening up communication, we have given Delta people a means of expressing their concerns, raising pressing issues, and offering ideas to improve both processes and the workplace.

To give you an idea of the types of issues we have dealt with during our first year in existence, I would like for you to look at this list:

- Automation and Equipment
- Communication

- Training
- Staffing
- Vacation Restoration
- Improved Benefits for Part-Time Employees
- Medical Benefits for Early Retirees
- Enhanced Compensation
- Search for a New CEO

As you can see, most of the issues involved operational considerations, morale, and job skills. Some issues dealt with restoring benefits that were reduced during downsizing. One very significant issue we dealt with was the search for a new CEO. The council met with both the search firm of Spencer Stuart and the three-member Board Search Committee to give input as to the qualities we regarded as essential in a new CEO. This was the first time front-line input had ever been part of the search process for Spencer Stuart or the board. We left the meeting knowing that the Search Committee and Spencer Stuart benefited from our perspective. They told us that they now had a complete picture of the person they needed to find.

As we move into our second year, the council is beginning to focus on work/life issues such as day care, educational assistance, and job sharing.

But regardless of the current issue or concern, the council's most important job is enhancing communication. To that end we have made progress. By giving Delta people a voice, they become partners in building the company. By opening the door to the boardroom, senior management and the board gain a new perspective. Previously, the board relied on management and anecdotal interactions to make then sensitive to what was happening in the field. Information on employee concerns or issues had been neglected, overlooked, or ignored as the company and the board of directors' focus remained in the finan-

cial survival of the company through cost cutting/ revenue-generating initiatives. In addition to offering another perspective on company programs, the Personnel Board Council, with presence in the boardroom, ensures the people that part of our business remains an important consideration of every major decision.

The council also becomes part of a system of checks and balances between the board and management. Issues that may not have gotten the attention or consideration they deserved can now be brought to management and raised to senior management. This helps all levels within the organization, as well as the board of directors, to establish priorities that best benefit the business while supporting our people. We have made three formal presentations to the board dealing with many issues we have discussed and continue to discuss with management.

We have just begun this grand experiment. It is exciting for us, but what does it say about the broader issues raised in this volume? I believe employee input and representation is essential for any company that wants to flourish. To the point of safeguards and legal constraints necessary to protect both employee and employer interests, the council drew up bylaws to govern itself. These were submitted to senior management and our legal department for their input. I believe that such a document should be sufficient to protect everyone's interests. The key to making a council such as ours work is the people. We are blessed with a diverse group of determined people who are not afraid to take a stand on issues in which they believe. We have some rough-and-tumble discussions but always manage to agree on a course that represents the best interests of Delta people and the company. That course may not be popular or politically correct, but if it is in the best interests of the people and the company, we pursue it. There are no filters between us and the people we talk to. What concerns a mechanic at LaGuardia, a gate agent in Los Angeles, and a sales agent in Montreal becomes a concern for management and, if necessary, the board. I believe that many of our problems are exacerbated by too many layers between the front line and upper management. The council cuts out those layers and brings both problems and solutions directly to the top for consideration.

After a year in existence, what are we accomplishing? This is a question every member of the council struggles with each day. Will we make a difference in the long run? We hope so. Have we already made a lasting difference in employee-management relations? I think we have. Our presentations to the board have set the tone and directed attention to many of the process and morale issues that had been neglected. Informal contacts with individual board members further enhance our ability to have front-line concerns as part of an overall strategic plan for the company. Participating in the search for our new CEO was a watershed event in working with the board. The person finally chosen as the new CEO will have an impact on the company for years to come. In a very real way the council is making a difference in employee-management relations.

A postscript: In the weeks since this article was prepared, Leo F. Mullin has been chosen as Delta's new president and CEO. Mr. Mullin has reaffirmed the role of the council at Delta and has asked that all seven council members now attend each board meeting. We look forward to working more closely with the board and management to make Delta a company where everyone is pulling together to reach the goal of mutual understanding and cooperation.

Note from the Editors

The Delta plan falls under the legal purview of the Railway Labor Act of 1926, described in the volume introduction and Appendix 1 of the Estreicher chapter. Not only does the RLA's definition of a labor organization differ from that in the NLRA, more importantly, the RLA only gives the National Mediation Board (NMB) authority to enjoin unfair labor practices, such as employer domination of a labor organization, in the context of an ongoing union representation election. Thus, absent a union election, the NMB has no authority to order disestablishment of a nonunion representational body, such as the Delta Personnel Board Council.

24

Production District Joint Industrial Council at Imperial Oil Ltd.: The Perspective from the Employee's Side

Rod Chiesa and Ken Rhyason, Delegates, Joint Industrial Council

By way of introduction, Ken and I are elected co-chairs of the Joint Industrial Council in the Production Division of the Imperial Oil Company. I am a mechanic by trade and Ken is an operator.

Our own Joint Industrial Council (JIC) has been in operation more than fifty years, and our company has been running JICs for eighty years. We would first like to explain some of its guiding principles.

The JIC has a written mission statement, which is contained in our green JIC handbook. It begins with these words, "The Joint Industrial Council is committed to working together in an open and honest dialogue on any subject of importance to the Employees and the Company. Through trust and cooperation we can all achieve excellence." This statement is what we adhere to in all our meetings. Both management and employees have learned that a key factor in the success of the JIC is trust and cooperation, and that open and honest communication is crucial to achieving these. We also emphasize that the well-being of employees and the company are interdependent and that we all gain from cooperation and collaboration.

As indicated in the mission statement, all issues of concern to the employees can come before the JIC. Major areas we focus on include wages and benefits, safety and health, working conditions, operating efficiency, and company culture. The JIC is divided into local councils and a district council. Purely local issues affecting a particular production site are handled by the local council, while broader issues that concern corporate policy or that affect employees across the division are handled by the district council. Also, local issues that cannot be resolved get passed on to the district council. The district level is the highest tier in the JIC system. The local council tries to act quickly on issues and is generally very effective. At the district level, we try our best to influence corporate issues, but are not always so great at it. From our perspective, that is one of the downfalls of the JIC.

On wages and benefits, the company has a target of being in the seventy-fifth percentile of the industry wage distribution. This is a corporate policy decision and not one negotiated in the JIC. But we have an external wage-review team that surveys the industry and reports back to the council. The council also looks at individual parts of the pay program, such as the allowance for boots or changes in the dental plan. We can also request that a special review team be established to look more closely at a particular issue. We recently did that, for example, on health care costs.

At the district council, the JIC has two selected co-chairs that come from the management side and two elected co-chairs who represent the employees. Right now, that is Rod and myself. Membership on the council is evenly split between management and wage earners. Employee representatives to the local and district JIC are chosen by the wage earners, generally by a secret ballot election in the larger units, but sometimes by a show of hands in the smaller ones. Sometimes, it is very informal, like when someone volunteers, "Yeah, I'll do it," and everybody nods their head and away he goes.

People often ask, "Does the JIC bargain? How does it work?" Well, we are empowered to examine any issue at the local level that doesn't involve corporate policy, and we can take a vote on it. Technically, a majority vote carries the issue, but we try not to approach it that way. Votes are extremely rare. The emphasis is on joint problem solving, on reaching a mutually agreeable solution. To promote this, we do a lot of training. When new delegates come in for their two-year term, they go through a two-day training seminar where they learn skills on making presentations, decision making, fact finding, negotiations, and so on. Also, we have a fifty-year history with the JIC and people on both sides are conscious that they want to make this thing work.

Although we try to reach a consensus on issues, sometimes it just isn't possible, or at least not right off. For example, the company recently proposed changes in the health and dental plan, where there were going to be three options: full

coverage, middle-of-the-road coverage, or none at all. When it was presented to the district council, we looked at it and didn't like it. So we stood up and said, "No, this is no good. We will not accept this." The team took it back, redesigned it, included a fourth and fifth option, and presented it to us again. The JIC then approved it, and the company made the requested modifications, which showed us that it could make a difference and that the JIC works.

One of the most delicate issues the JIC is working on right now is downsizing and the elimination of jobs. Last year, Imperial divested four of its properties. There will probably be more cutbacks. How these are handled is a very sensitive issue. We don't question the business need for doing these things. But we do question the impact on the humans involved and how their needs are handled. There are procedures in place for how these things are supposed to be done, and the JIC will be the watchdog to make sure they are followed.

On the company's part, they are sharing more and more information with us in the JIC so that we can see the business reasons for these decisions and why a particular choice was made. In the past, we got a broad picture at the end of the year, but now we are learning more detailed things on an ongoing basis and the meaning of new terms like "return on capital." When we see a property downsized we know why it was downsized based on these informational sessions.

There is now much more collaboration and information sharing in the JIC, particularly with all the downsizing and other things going on. We spend maybe 50 percent of our time in council meetings on communication and information sharing—where the company is going, its strategy, performance of business units, and so on. Then the delegates go back to their production sites and communicate all of this back to their members, talk about it, get feedback, and take the members' concerns and opinions back to the council. The delegates are supposed to spend about 20 percent of their work time on council business, but these days it could be a full-time job.

When the JIC gets into touchy issues that a particular delegate may feel uneasy in talking about for fear of reprisal or some such thing, Rod or I have a private meeting with the delegate and then present the issue for him or her to the group in our capacity as co-chair.

Which brings us to the subject of discipline and grievances. Our JIC handbook outlines the steps of the grievance process. If a person is not happy with the process, he can get his JIC representatives involved. The final step in the grievance process is at the senior vice president level, but the council remains involved all the way up the line.

We would be lying if we claimed that everything is well and fine with the JIC. There are al-ways problems, and right now, with the downsizing going on, the JIC is facing a very challenging time. And, as some of you already know, since 1993 three facilities at the company have left the JIC and brought in outside representation. These councils at the local level became ineffective. Communication stopped, the two sides weren't being open and honest any longer, and trust disappeared. An easy way out was to bring in a union. That is just our opinion. But it was clear that the employees saw benefits to the union—things like more job security—and the fact that they basically felt powerless when the company didn't fix things on the management side.

We can't speak for anyone else, but we've seen the JIC work and we still believe in it. It promotes better communication, it gives the employees some influence, and it provides both the company and the wage earners with an opportunity to solve mutual problems in a way that is win-win. The JIC has been here over half a century, and we are proud to be part of it.

25

Nonunion Employee Representation at the Royal Canadian Mounted Police

Kevin MacDougall, Representative, Division Staff Relations Program

The Royal Canadian Mounted Police (RCMP) has one officially recognized system of representation. It's called the Division Staff Relations Representative System (DSRR), which we also call the Div-Rep system. The mission statement of the program is as follows:

> The principal goal of the DSRR program is to improve operational and administrative functions while balancing responsibility and authority of management with the rights of RCMP members, particularly the right to good conditions of employment.

Several things are important to note about this mission statement. The first is that it was written by the employee representatives and accepted by management. A second is that it commits management to strike a balance between exercise of its authority to run the organization and its responsibility to involve employees and factor-in their rights and interests. In practice, the approach to be taken is not employer versus employee but mutual consultation.

As far as our workforce is concerned, the RCMP is responsible for federal policing in all of Canada. We are also responsible for provincial policing in eight of ten provinces plus the two territories, and we have contractual obligations with over 200 towns and cities in Canada. We have international responsibilities by way of our embassies. We also perform peacekeeping roles in various countries around the world. All told, the RCMP has 20,000 employees, and 85 percent of them are represented by the DSRR program. The remaining 3,000 employees are represented by a union called the Public Service Alliance of Canada, and their job is to deal directly with the Treasury Board in a collective bargaining environment.

The legal foundation for the DSRR system is contained in Regulation 96(1)(2) of the RCMP Act. The program was established in May 1974, after Force-wide consultation and is designed to provide members of the RCMP with a formal system of elected representation that permits our participation in the decision-making process and a voice in matters that affect our welfare, dignity, and operational effectiveness. The impetus for the system came about as a result of concerns and dissatisfactions expressed by employees in the early 1970s. At that time, the Force addressed employees' issues through managers' strategic placement in certain policy centers such as staffing, finance, and administration. Although top management thought the system was doing well, suddenly it began to crumble and almost overnight large meetings of employees formed across the country to consider unionizing the RCMP.

For a variety of reasons, the government of Canada and the RCMP itself felt unionization was not a viable option and tried to develop an alternative system to address our labor relations problems. There really was no template out there, so we had the unenviable task of developing our own system. We struggled for approximately ten to twelve years and during that time, the DSRR system almost failed. We made a lot of mistakes, and I believe we've learned from our mistakes. Over the last decade or so, we have developed and evolved into a very effective system of representation that is capable of dealing with almost any labor relations problem.

Currently there are twenty-nine employee representatives who are elected by their colleagues in each of the thirteen geographic divisions across the RCMP. Representatives are full-time positions. Twenty-eight are elected divisionally, and divisions normally run along provincial boundaries. In British Columbia, for instance, there are 6 reps because we have 4,700 officers. In Alberta, there are 3, in Manitoba, 2, and so on. There is no fixed formula. I'm the only rep, the twenty-ninth, who is elected nationally. I'm elected by the other reps to serve as chair of their Pay Committee and to work on their newly formed Pay Council, which I'll explain shortly. All together, there are eleven national DSRR standing committees.

We are elected for two-year terms and successive terms are three years. Elections are held in accordance with the Canada Elections Act. There is a specific period for nominations by our peers. There's a specific period to campaign, and votes are by secret ballot with an Election Committee. An interesting point that I should make here is that everyone gets to vote and that anyone can run for the rep job including our commissioner, who is the head of the organization. There is absolutely no separation between management and labor in the DSRR program. This is done to ensure that we all are cognizant of the needs of the organization

and recognize each other's point of view when we are dealing with difficult labor issues.

There are regular meetings, usually in Ottawa. We meet four times a year as a group and with the various policy centers, on an "as and when needed" basis. By and large, reps other than myself come to Ottawa probably once a month to deal with our policy centers. I'm in Ottawa about half the time to do my job.

The DSRR's mandate is to negotiate for members on social, economic, and labor issues. To exemplify how well our system works, currently we have 259 issues on the national agenda, and these are issues that any employee and any member of management can ask the reps to address. So we have everything from travel allowances to discharge on our national agenda, and we try to resolve issues at the lowest level possible. We recently spent five years, for example, in study and negotiation on changing from 38-caliber revolvers to 9-mm revolvers, a $13 million ticket item. Of those 259 issues at our last national conference in Penticton in June, only 10 had to go to the national forum or to the senior management of the Force. When one of these tough chestnuts is being addressed, the commissioner will ask that the reps sit down with the commanding officers in syndicate format and bring him solutions to the problems, and it works very, very effectively.

Even though the program is rooted in legislation, the system's procedures and policies are found in our policy manuals, and there is considerable flexibility and opportunity to make changes. As employee representatives, we favor the flexibility in our system because it permits us to adapt quickly to rapidly changing environments that we all face in the labor relations field. We experienced that through recent cutbacks and job loss, as well as a zero out of our pay for five out of six years. We had to find creative ways of deal-

THE ROYAL CANADIAN MOUNTED POLICE 479

ing with these pressures. One of the setups that exemplifies the flexibility is our newly formed Pay Council.

In 1993, when the federal government began freezing RCMP wages, we met with our commissioner and said we had to find a more effective way of dealing with our labor relations, particularly in the pay and benefits area. He agreed with us. We solicited the help of outside experts, and the recommendation was our newly formed Pay Council.

The Pay Council consists of five people. Two of them are from outside the organization and three of them are from within. The Force puts so much importance on pay and benefits in this council that they put the second highest ranking officer in the organization on the council with myself and the other participants. He has an assistant there to represent senior management and that person is a former assistant commissioner, which is also a very high level in our organization.

I sit on the Pay Council because I am elected by the DSRR system, and I work very closely with two people who are appointed from outside the RCMP. Graham Leslie comes with a tremendous background in finance and negotiations. He's the former deputy minister of labour from British Columbia. The Pay Council chairman and probably the most important person on the council, Paul Lorden, was selected out of 113 applicants in a national competition. We had everyone from former premiers, presidents of the Treasury Board, members of Parliament, and Supreme Court judges apply for this important job. The skills and expertise of the outside members are vital, since the Pay Council works on the basis of consensus.

In assessing the effectiveness of the DSRR system, we need to consider three primary stakeholders. The first is the government of Canada.

If they don't endorse our system, then we'd cease to exist. Several solicitors general that have been around since I've been in the program, which is roughly ten years, have endorsed the DSRR system both publicly and privately. They feel that it is totally appropriate in dealing with labor relations in the RCMP and that it could probably be adapted quite nicely to other organizations.

The second stakeholder, of course, is senior management of the Force. Through their day-to-day actions and examples, we see that they are totally behind the DSRR system. The same holds true for the membership, who I believe, from my perspective at least, is the most important stakeholder in the whole system.

A former DSRR associate and I, when I was a Manitoba division representative, decided to conduct a unique exercise with our employees. We offered to do research into any and all representation systems. We wrote to all our employees, saying, "We will do this research voluntarily for you. We will bring back the results of this research and we will give you an opportunity to vote on changing our system should you wish to do so." This of course includes unionization as we are the only police force in Canada, I believe, that's not unionized. Out of the 1,060 employees in Manitoba, only 15 wanted us to do the research.

Another example is through the CPA, Canadian Police Association's, efforts. They are an umbrella organization for all police or most police forces in Canada, and they have been trying to unionize the RCMP for years and years, I guess because of the size relative to the other Forces. About a year and half ago, the CPA went on a concerted campaign in British Columbia where the bulk of our officers are and offered an informational meeting in the lower mainland where the nucleus of the members work. This meeting was well advertised, and bear in mind, it was only for informational purposes. Out of 4,700 employees in British Columbia, only 156 attended the meeting. Out of the 156 that attended, halfway through the session, approximately half of them failed to return. And when we spoke to them about why they failed to return, they said that they felt that what the CPA was offering was inferior to what we already had. Again, that speaks highly, in my opinion, of the system our Force has set up.

At this point, you may be asking yourself, "Will this lead to unionization?" and my response is, "Absolutely not." It's not intended for that. Our members are not against unionization. They simply feel that the system we have is more effective than the system a union may present or bring. If you think that it's going to lead to unionization, I couldn't fathom how you'd answer the question or the comment that we've been around for twenty-three years, and I fully expect that with the care and nurturing that the Force has given to the DSRR system, we'll be around for at least twenty-three more. And I believe I have to applaud their efforts in that regard.

We use modern labor relations practices in a cooperative approach to resolve our differences. It is a tremendous way to ensure that the grassroots message gets up to the senior management of the Force, where it belongs. We have suggestion boxes. Management can deal directly with the employees themselves. We are not offended or bothered by that, but management admittedly believes that the most effective way of getting that message from the front-line police officer or from that clerk or from that teller, is through the DSRR system. You have a tremendous vehicle as a front-line employee to bring that message up. When senior management makes their decisions, because our system is completely open, honest, and transparent, we as reps generally understand those decisions and then bring the message back down to the front-line employees by way of direct contact, town hall meetings, publications, and so on. So it's a very effective way, and with 20,000 employees out there, there are lots of good ideas that would never normally get to the senior management of the Force. And it's done through our DSRR system.

We have absolutely no binding mechanisms. We have no right to strike, and we have no arbitration, and quite frankly, I cannot see our system working with any of those. If you subscribe to a completely open approach, where your differences are resolved in a professional atmosphere, where each part respects the other, then I do not believe you have to reach back into your bag of tricks for the right to strike. I think we have been successful in resolving many of our issues, not all of them. We still have lots of tough chestnuts to break, and I think we will do it through the system because we keep working on it.

Practitioner Commentary:
Labor Attorney

26

The Section 8(a)(2) Debate: A Management Attorney's Perspective

Andrew M. Kramer, Partner, Jones, Day, Reavis and Pogue

I feel envious of Canadian labor lawyers because they can work with their clients on forms of employee involvement and representation that would clearly be illegal in the United States. I would like to offer a few thoughts on the American situation based on my thirty years of experience as a practicing management labor attorney, and why I believe a change in the National Labor Relations Act is desirable.

I think there are two issues at the center of the debate over reform of the NLRA, such as proposed in the TEAM Act. The first is the presumption by organized labor in the United States that organizing will be more difficult if the TEAM Act, or something like a TEAM Act, is passed. Actually, I would argue that organized labor is dead wrong. If we look at labor history in the United States, we see that many company unions became independent unions, which later became some of the largest locals in our international unions. This was true in shipbuilding and in steel, for example. Also, experience in the public sector supports this view. Two and three decades ago, we had a number of nonunion employee associations in the public sector, and today they are part of AFSCME and other unions.

The second issue is the contention that employers use these committees for antiunion purposes. I would say that employers believe that by treating employees right, they will be less likely to seek union representation. But union avoidance is not the only, or even the main, motivation. Employers are motivated most of all by what is good for the bottom line. They have come to understand that a motivated and productive workforce is good for business.

For example, many employers in the manufacturing area have gone to a team approach. The team approach does not necessarily cover the entire plant. It often covers specific organizational units within the manufacturing enterprise. Team approaches are formed to deal with specific problems in the workplace affecting those employees, the equipment they operate, and meeting the needs of the customer. These organizations, to be effective, must by their very nature deal with things that Section 2(5) of the NLRA says are probably close to being illegal, if not actually over the line. If an employer is going to decide not to violate the law, the employer must step back and tell the employees, "The company cannot deal with you over the very things that are most important. We cannot talk to you about workplace safety. We cannot deal with grievances or disputes about terms and conditions of employment. We cannot talk about shift rotation. We cannot talk about the hours of work or changes in our compensation mode, such as going to a profit-sharing plan instead of a Scanlon plan."

Teams are not the only thing threatened by the

NLRA. Many American workplaces also have adopted the Japanese system of *Kaisan*, or continuous improvement. A continuous-improvement approach generally involves a group of employees either on a representative or rotational basis, meeting with management and talking about processes of work and how those processes can or should be changed. If the employer simply isolates the issue or treats it as a one-way communication opportunity, however, this type of discussion becomes stilted and nonsensical. Should the employer put up a red light to signal "We cannot talk about this" after being advised by a labor lawyer that any further interaction might trigger a violation of the law?

And on top of the prohibitions on topics, there also is considerable confusion in the legal community about what is and is not allowed. For example, the law permits some representation as long as the employer didn't do anything to get the group started, didn't say to the employees, "meet in an office here. I'll give you a Xerox." Actually, there is even confusion about the legal status of photocopying. Apparently according to the Labor Board, maybe Xeroxing is okay, but provision of an office probably is not.

It is foolhardy to believe that employers should operate in such a fashion and yet American labor law clearly requires this today. And it is instructive that several weeks ago a U.S. Court of Appeals apologized for its finding that the employer had violated the NLRA by creating a committee they felt was a clear benefit to employees at the particular workplace. Now that's a sad state of American labor law. It is also a sad state of industrial relations practice because clearly if the issue is union avoidance, there are far better ways to deal with it than saying that employers should be constrained or restricted from doing smart things in the workplace.

This brings me back to the false presumption that creating these workplace teams and employee involvement committees will decrease or diminish the demand for union representation. I claim that employers will just as often be organized whether or not there is a change in this area of the law. Employers organize more unions than unions organize employers. Bad employers tend to get caught. Bad employers will not benefit by any change of the law with respect to the TEAM Act, or similar legislation.

The Section 8(a)(2) issue that bothers me the most is that an employer who is well meaning, who has no antiunion motive whatever, can still be held to violate Section 8(a)(2). What's also important for policymakers and the labor relations community to understand, it's not simply domination and interference that cause or trigger a violation of Section 8(a)(2), it's the mere assistance that causes a violation of Section 8(a)(2). Employers who form workplace teams and provide employees with paid time-off for meeting and office space are most likely in violation of the act. Again, this hardly makes sense. How many employees are going to organize these kinds of meetings on their own time or without pay? Not many.

Despite the enormous attention paid to Section 8(a)(2), I argue that instead of tackling a revision of Section 8(a)(2), the real devil is the too-broad definition of employer organization provided by Section 2(5). A change of Section 2(5) is far more important, and this more significant change should be considered by Congress.

My Canadian colleagues do not have to contend with the restrictions I see in my practice because Canadian law has allowed the legal entry of new forms of work design and managerial practice. In comparison, the current American situation is illogical and counterproductive to providing a smarter and better workplace.

Practitioner Commentary: Organized Labor

27

My Experience with Unionization of Nonunion Employee Representation Plans in Canada*

Reg Basken, Secretary-Treasurer of the Communication, Energy and Paperworkers Union

Just over one-third of the energy segment of the Communication, Energy and Paperworkers Union (CEP) is composed of members who previously belonged to company unions or to independent local unions formed from company unions. We have certified them steadily over the past twenty-five years. At the moment, they are predominantly from Petro-Canada and Imperial Oil, but also from Shell, Gulf (which was purchased by Petro-Canada), and the megaproject Suncor.

Relationship Between Company Unions and the National Union

It is important to point out that we do not necessarily organize employees directly from company councils. The majority go from company councils or nonunion bargaining structures to independent local unions (ILUs), and then we get them to join the national union. But a minority of them we are able to organize directly from councils, without the intermediate step of forming ILUs. To go from a company council to a certified bargaining agent requires a

lot of work, and if councils choose the ILU route, they have to do that work by themselves. If they go directly to my union, then we do the work for them.

We have worked very cooperatively with many company unions over the years. We shared information and met with them frequently. There was, of course, complete variation. Some were honest with us, and some were not. Some started out by saying, we want to join your union, when I knew damned well that they just wanted information. There were others that said, we don't want to join your union, but we want information.

They were most interested in bargaining items, grievances, and how to handle certain labor relations questions. How do you get along with the company if such-and-such occurs. Wages always were a big thing. That was an advantage for us, since they often received more information on wages than we did. They had a 75th percentile clause, or a set figure in most of their council agreements that make sure they monitored other company's wages. We did the bargaining for them anyway, and most of them knew that. This type

---

*Transcribed from an interview with Daphne Gottlieb Taras, December 1997.

of contact happened with joint industrial councils [prevalent in the energy sector] and with ILUs.

We chose to work with company unions because we believed you could catch more flies with honey than with manure. We told them what we thought of them, but we still cooperated—oh, we beat up on them lots of times, but we beat up on them in a sensible way that didn't foreclose communication in the future.

Company unions make it harder for us to bargain because we are bargaining for them, and they provide us with no strength. We cannot count on them for a formal vote, or an informal but important comment to management. They may help us of their own volition, but we cannot count on them in any organized fashion.

Companies bargain with us because they have to. They bargain with the associations because they want to keep them from coming to the union. I don't know what companies gain by it. They treat us differently than they treat the associations. The associations get extras that companies won't give us.

Organizing Company Unions Versus "Greenfield" Sites

There is a marked difference between union organizing where employees have never belonged to a formal structure versus where they have been in a company union. In the site that is "greenfield," we have to contact every member. We have to identify some local leadership in order to buy, borrow, beg, or steal the membership lists so we know how many people are there and who they are and where they live. We have to contact them individually.

With an association, and in many cases, on a greenfield site, many people have the opinion that if they are caught talking to a union guy, they are going to be fired. Frequently, it is pure, unadulterated garbage, since that is not how the petroleum industry operates. For the most part, we have not had a person fired for joining the union in years. We have had some that have been treated rather badly at the worksite, but they haven't been fired.

An association has a preexisting structure, and we just intervene in that structure with our communications and opinions. It is aboveboard. It makes more sense. The problem, though, is that between the time they form an association or council and the time they join our union, twenty-five years might have gone by.

At a greenfield site, we have to find leaders. If we cannot locate a group of people on the inside that are respected, then our organizing campaign won't go anywhere. People don't follow followers.

With regard to organizing strategies, the best ideas for winning company unions involve working with the leadership that is already there. If you go around the leadership, you'll likely fail. When organizing associations or councils, the usual pattern is that the local leaders become frustrated to the degree that they need help, and they call us. It isn't a question of coopting them, or getting in there and nailing them down. They have made the decision that they are ineffective, or could be more effective with a union, and they call us. They know how to call us because we have been meeting with them all the time. When it is time to join the union, they tell us.

The other tactic we have used, with tremendous success, is the affiliation agreement. I discuss this in some detail later.

The few times that we have tried to organize around the association, by bypassing it, we usually lose. If we don't get their leadership, we don't get the union. Whether we like it or not, the council brings forward a certain level of leadership. It doesn't always bring the best leaders, in cases where the best leaders don't like the council but would prefer to join a union right away. These people stay in the background, and don't make the council effective. Once the executive of the council has seen the light and decides to support the union, these other leaders are there for us as well.

The organizing message is about the same. We have more to talk about in a company council arrangement because there are people there who have tried to do things and haven't been successful at getting them done. So we have complex issues and considerable baggage, whereas in a greenfield site, we have people who have worried about things but haven't tried to do anything about it because they figure it is impossible anyway. The myth that it is possible to effect change in a joint industrial council or association is what allows employees to keep a running record that allows them to go back years and years to recall all the ills that have been there, both real and imagined. Actually, mostly imagined.

The Transition Phase and the Tendency for Companies to Punish

In the transition from an association or council to a union there is a very different phenomenon than with the certification of a greenfield site. The difference is hard to explain. When the company council, or "donkey council" as we refer to them, joins the union, they have the impression that all of the ills and bad times they have suffered in the past can now be resolved. They get a hate on for the company like you wouldn't believe. They are angry all the time. It takes years to get them settled down.

And the company says they are traitors. They have double-crossed the company. Then the company, in order to show its anger at these dirty traitors, tries to take away some or all of the things that it gave them to keep them out of the union in the first place. The company says, we gave you all these entitlements to keep you out of the union, and you rotten traitors went and joined the union anyway, so we're taking them back. This is a situation fraught with anger. This was the case at the Strathcona refinery in Edmonton, that went from an Imperial Oil joint industrial council to us, and also at Imperial's Norman Wells refinery.

The role of the union, then, is peacemaker. We spend all our time trying to get the local union officers to understand that the world wasn't made in a day, and all their problems cannot be resolved just because they got a local union number. They still have to deal with their management, who now think they're traitors. We have to try to get both sides to understand what is going on emotionally.

By contrast, when the transition is from greenfield to union, we broker some raised expectations, but there aren't a whole bunch of things at a greenfield site, the entitlements, that employees received in exchange for keeping union-free. The company figured they'd never join the union anyway, and didn't make specialized considerations for them.

Residual Effects on Collective Agreements

In some cases, while the former council members are really angry, they are torn between wanting change but also wanting to preserve what they are used to. This is a common situation because people are creatures of structure and habit. This new bird, the union, has a hard time proving it has a better way. The union is put into an impossible situation. I remember when we were organizing an Imperial Oil refinery in Calgary. I had to negotiate that agreement. The committee was so angry at the company that it was an almost impossible task. All the local wanted to do was "strike the bastards." Of course, it was in our interests to get a collective agreement. It was in the employees' best interests, too. But it was a long, difficult task getting that agreement. They were angry, but because of their past relationship with management, we couldn't write a new collective agreement. There are two reasons: one is the company, and the other is the local. They know how some things worked in the past, and each side wants to change only the things that they didn't like. It is a real inhibiter to early progress in relationships. Often there is a prior written agreement in place that some people are married to.

The union response is to encourage greater participation in the union. Employees come to the union convention and participate in setting the union's national pattern bargaining rates. Yet the problem is that joint industrial council wages are frequently higher than ours, so they want to keep their JIC wage. They write collective agreements that tie them to the JIC, rather than to our union. The local wants to keep everything that their employees received over time that exceeds the union pattern.

Yet the company wants to take things away to punish the new local. For example, the company says, "We will decide how many, and who goes on union business leave of absence." Well, that might be the case in the past, but it isn't the case any longer with the new union certification. We have instances early on in the new relationship where the company might not like the purpose of the request for leave, and might refuse the request. It becomes a grievance, and then a war. Yet, there are so few formal grievances in our industry that I cannot really say whether the grievance rates for former greenfield sites differs from that of former councils or associations.

Because of the very high percentage of our units that once belonged to councils or associations, our collective agreements are badly written. We don't win arbitrations with our agreements very often because too many of them came from company councils. The wording is that "the company may" instead of "the company shall." We are trying to clean up those agreements, but it takes a long time, and we make a little change here, a little change there. But we don't rewrite them. It would be nice if we could. In a sense, they really aren't collective agreements yet. There are too many cases in them where there is a practice of doing it the way they have always done it, and the company is permitted by the language to continue with its past practices.

The new union locals take a long time to recognize these problems. We have to explain to them the significance of "the company may" clauses, and why they cannot win at arbitration. In the case of Imperial Oil's Norman Wells refinery, the company kept the severance policy very loose in the collective agreement and then used that clause to punish workers for unionizing.

Union Loyalty

Regardless of its background, every union local has the same autonomy from the national union. Once a unit certifies with us, we don't make any distinction between former greenfield sites and former associations. They are often pretty independent.

Whether people are able to form attachments and loyalty to the union is complex. The tone on the question of attachment to the union is more set by the company than set by the individuals in the locals. Usually the companies help us out because they are so antiunion that they make people draw loyalties. Companies claim that you cannot be loyal to the company and to the union both. Employees have to pick. Early on, because they are so new to the union, they pick the union, and then it is our job to say, "But you can be loyal to the company and the union at the same time." Not that they have the same objectives, but there is common ground.

If a company decided not to have any reprisals or clawbacks after a council unionizes, then the situation is different. The company could win back the loyalty of its workers much more easily. But in my experience, I have found that most companies have a tendency to punish, without even realizing that they are punishing, and they don't anticipate the unpleasant effects.

In this industry, more so than in most, there is a hatred for the head office. The only time that the local management and the local union get together on something, it is to hate a move made by the national office of the company or the union. For example, it is a Toronto head office that makes all the bad decisions, but it is the local manager that makes all the good ones. (But the facts are more likely that the local manager has made the decision and asked Toronto to back him up, and then he rallies support by badmouthing Toronto.) Dual loyalties to the union and the company develop with this common stance against the head office.

Unfair Labor Practices

My union doesn't aggressively pursue company union complaints to labor boards. Partly, this is because we don't win organizing campaigns that way. But also, we haven't relied on the law for much. In most cases, all of our working conditions are well beyond the statutory requirements. We do things ourselves. We haven't found labor board intervention to be useful, and they usually are not on our side. We wait and say we'll fight another day. In the early days of Syncrude [an

Alberta megaproject], we did charge the company, the government, and all the owners, of having an antiunion bias in running their company union. It was sort of a huge, informal JIC, which is not surprising, since Imperial Oil calls the shots at Syncrude. Sometimes it is formal, sometimes less so. I didn't get anywhere with the case, but it was fun. There were nineteen lawyers, all before the Alberta Labour Board. This was sometime between 1975 and 1979. I went to the Labour Board half a dozen times. The premier's lawyer asked whether it was my intention to put the premier of Alberta in jail. I said, "No, of course not." He said, "Good, then I can go golfing today." (He was the lawyer who set up the Suncor company union and all the other councils.) We lost the case. And they are still nonunion. And we are still trying to organize them. I cannot recall another instance of going to labor boards.

Views on Company Unions

There are no benefits to company unions. They just keep the trade union movement figures lower. If there were no unions, company unions would have to become unions because somebody has to set the patterns, the tone, and bring in change. The difference with the union is that the membership has to vote on things, so they have to have a certain level of commitment to doing something. In an association, the level of commitment is less. They don't have to care as much because they cannot do much to alter their condition anyway. Our people have to make a decision that an association doesn't. Our people have to decide whether to go on strike or settle. An association can decide not to settle, but to wait until somebody else does.

Of course, company unions are a bad thing, by their very existence, but if you take advantage of them properly, they become a good thing for union organizing. But I don't want that comment to take away from the central fact that they don't deserve to exist. They have nothing to offer, and they are protection for the company, not protection for the workers.

Whether company unions increase or decrease the propensity of workers to unionize is a very difficult question. In the very early days of the formation of a joint industrial council or association, the chances of joining a union are relatively limited because they still have the feeling that the company will do the right thing. Over time, the company might disappoint them, and they will join the union. That is a long way down the road, though.

When companies pay nonunion workers in order to keep them out of unions, the whole process is delayed. Early on, Imperial Oil paid five cents an hour more on a two-dollar wage in order to pay workers to stay out of a union. They still pay an incentive on top of a premium wage.

The company councils established in the United States in the 1920s and 1930s just didn't work very well down there. Roosevelt wanted to help out the union movement, so company unions were banned. The unions organized a lot of members then. Canada decided not to go in that direction because the government thought we'd never be successful in organizing unions anyway. William Lyon Mackenzie King decided on a strategy of doing nothing at all. The companies said that company unions and associations will help keep unions out. But in many cases, companies found that small, fragmented, weak unions are very difficult to deal with because there is no leadership to talk to outside the organization. An advantage that we have with the national union today is that if the CEO of a company gets angry at one of its local unions and wants to talk to me,

he will call me and say, "Get your guys in line here, buddy." Too often that happens. For example, plant closures are a very difficult thing, and we often get accused of being on the company side when what we are really doing is trying to get an orderly close-down because we cannot change the decision.

The only good thing about the company union movement in the petroleum industry is that we were able to use the high wages paid by non-union companies to avoid unions in a way that ratcheted up wages for the union members. The industry does not allow us to write benefits into the collective agreements. The industry would see us in hell, would take massive strikes, rather than bargain benefits. With regard to pension plans, they were developed and given out in order to decrease the potential for unionization. Then, when they didn't decrease unionization, pensions became issues all over the country. Companies had to increase pensions gradually all across the country. This industry is very proud. It either makes a huge amount of money or loses a huge amount of money. It is a strong part of the economy. It wants to be able to say, "We're better than everyone else at everything, including being antiunion." They don't want to kill union officers, but they have this altruistic view that they can do better than unions.

And it is psychologically unnerving to find out that their workers are traitors. It is hard on them. I see it in the eyes, and in the conversations, with CEOs that finally get a union. "Where did we go wrong," they say, almost with tears in their eyes. Sometimes the answer is so simple, really. The plant manager has become a dictator, and the company doesn't know it. Even though companies are thinking that they have improved the people skills of managers, they are completely wrong. Managers remain just as autocratic. They may speak softer, but they are carrying a bigger stick. The soft touch doesn't last long.

Often there is a grand canyon between what company officers think they have, and what they actually get, when they hire lower-level management. Often the managers report up the hierarchy that labor relations are harmonious, in control. But privately, I have lunch and find out that labor relations might be only a three out of ten, but the head office is under the impression that they are a nine. The manager in nonunion plants has the ability to report to the CEO and tell the CEO only what he wants to hear. Errors are made. The insulation process is more than R-40. With a union, at least the company gets a great reality check. It is more honest, and the company has a better chance to respond in a way that matches the information.

JICs always have had the ability to draw from the strengths and experiences of unionized sites. That is why the Sarnia [sociotechnical plant, built in the 1970s by Shell, in a unionized environment] thing became so popular in the industry. They used it to learn from, and applied the lessons to nonunion sites.

We don't find that we have much to learn from in the operations of nonunion councils. It is hard to say, though, because sometimes items appear in bargaining, and we don't know where they come from. There are practices that management sees, and tries to drive into union relationships. Sometimes they are of value, and sometimes they are not. But it is management that benefits, not us. In terms of overall managerial flexibility, they have the total ability to demand, and require, and expect and attain and achieve, flexibility because the nonunion council is no encumbrance.

Collective agreements are sometimes an encumbrance, but more often in this industry, it is not the collective agreement but rather the will of the people. Our industry agreements are much more flexible than those negotiated in other industries. But, many times, matters are handled by unions that don't appear in collective agreements. For example, sometimes workers just balk at doing something, and a union can sometimes communicate and then enforce a good part of that sentiment. A company has to tread lightly and walk on eggs.

Management keeps trying to adjust its culture, believing incorrectly that there is such a thing as a single perfect culture. But culture is even department by department. Imperial Oil destroyed the unanimity of the culture they had built up over the years when they broke the tacit agreement that when you were hired at Imperial Oil, you'd work there for life. You would retire at Imperial Oil. When they destroyed that by laying people off, they destroyed their own culture, but they still think it is there, and management thinks that Norman Wells is exactly the same as Sarnia, is exactly the same as Edmonton. And they are going union. The company cannot figure it out.

Importance of Affiliation Agreements in Organizing Company Unions

More than two decades ago, my union developed tactics for organizing company unions and independents. This was a significant departure from our then international union (Oil, Chemical, and Atomic Workers) because it was something we in Canada needed. (We were the Canadian district of OCAW at the time.) We had so many independent unions and associations that were wanting to come into the union. For independent local unions, the affiliation strategy worked more easily than a raid.

With the affiliation agreement, all the local

would need to do is hold a meeting and pass a motion. They didn't have to have a labor board supervised vote. It didn't put any pressure on individuals because they could come to a meeting and argue and fight, all in the open. They didn't have to go into the church basement in the dark. OCAW was aware of the affiliation agreement strategy, and would have liked to have had it in the United States, but the legislation worked differently. In effect, because the Wagner Act banned company unions, you couldn't use their structures on which to build your own structure. The difference in Canadian law helped us. We were smart enough to work within the law and find a process that was simple for the workers.

We used the affiliation agreement more on an ad hoc basis in the 1960s and 1970s, but in 1980 it started seriously. We had a friendly separation from OCAW and formed the national Energy and Chemical Workers Union (ECWU). We put affiliation provisions into our constitution. Under the authority of the union president, we could bring in different bargaining units, and with the approval of the union executive, we could grant them different conditions.

To illustrate how the affiliation agreement strategy worked in practice, let me use the example of the separate school board support staff association in Edmonton. There were 350 of them, totally out of our jurisdiction. The officers of the support staff organization got me drunk one night over dinner, and I made a commitment to do their bargaining for them. I didn't want to see them having to pay a lawyer. I didn't ask them to come into the union because they were only paying a dollar a month in dues, and they didn't have any money, and really didn't fit our organization. They really belonged to the Canadian Union of Public Employees (CUPE). I said, I'll do your bargaining this year (in about 1979). Bargaining was easy

for me because it was a walk down the street from my office, and the bargaining happened after school hours, which fit nicely into my schedule. I made them go through the process of inviting me to a meeting of their membership, so their membership could see what I was doing, that I was a union officer, and that they wouldn't be afraid of it. I told them then that I wasn't going to push them to join the union, and that I was going to do it only once. Well, I did it once, and then once again, and then again, and again. Finally, when I became president of the ECWU in 1984, I said, look, this is all over, I cannot do it anymore. They begged for someone else from the ECWU to bargain. I went to them and said, look, we've got to formalize this a bit more. The executive and I drafted an affiliation agreement, which was approved by the membership. We took only a small part of the union's regulations and rules. They were the loosest arrangement of all the affiliations we ever agreed to. It was cancelable at any time. Over the years, the school unit rejected CUPE a dozen times. When they came to our union conventions, they were frequently accused of not being a union. They weren't paying full dues, and the affiliation agreement was so loose. A few years ago, they got their membership to vote to affiliate fully with the union, and graduated their per capita tax over a two- or three-year period, and now they are fully in CEP as Local 52. Their local leadership structure remained intact.

Actually, although few affiliation agreements are as loose as Local 52's, most of the agreements do allow affiliated members to withdraw at any time. If they don't like what they are getting, all they have to do is move a motion in order to leave us. I think we have had only one that pulled out.

The Suncor experience is interesting. Suncor began with a company union structure in the

1960s (the Great Canadian Oil Sands Collective Bargaining Association, set up by the company's lawyer, who later admitted he set it up and brought supervisors from Sarnia to be the officers and work in the bargaining unit, and later they got promoted back to be supervisors). Over the years, it gradually transformed into a full-fledged antagonistic, confrontational independent union (Fort McMurray Independent Oil Workers Union). The company and the independent union were at war in the 1980s. In 1986 the company locked them out, and they refused to be locked out, so they went on strike. We had tried to unionize them for twenty years. We were working on an affiliation arrangement with them, but had not concluded it as the May 1 strike/lockout date loomed. I was in Geneva when they phoned me to say they were on strike, and asked if they could conclude the affiliation agreement. I said yes. Before their strike, they had insisted they would not pay anything into the union strike fund. When they phoned me, they said they had made a mistake, and they would participate in the strike fund. They originally wanted to save money, but when the strike happened, they needed the fund. After the dust settled, and the strike was over, they were fully part of the ECWU, and our membership jumped by about 800 people.

The affiliation agreement starts off with exactly the same conditions as under the union constitution for a regular local union but our constitution allows us to vary that in any way we want. I do not think there is any other union that uses this strategy. We may be the only example in existence in the union movement. It works well, and I would not change a thing. It was completely misunderstood by the other two unions (Communication and Paperworkers) when we merged in 1992 to form the CEP. They thought it was a confounded, convoluted, disgraceful arrangement. I hung in there, advocating for affiliation agreements, and said the merger would not occur without it. Fortunately, shortly after that, in 1993, we had an affiliation, and it had to go before the merged executive board. It gave me an opportunity to explain the benefits of affiliations. We were getting 150 members coming in, paying less per capita tax than our other members for a few years, but if we do a good job, they'll join us. That debate at the board took half a day because nobody understood it. It finally passed, with an awful lot of abstentions, but nobody voted against it.

At every board meeting now, we have an affiliation decision. The CEP has been using the affiliation strategy in the past few years to organize outside the energy sector. A sawmill here, the public school support staff in Toronto, a number of them, not huge, but a number.

The affiliation strategy has to be all out in the open. You tell the prospective members that if they do not like it, they can get out of it, but if they do like it, in a few years they will be full-fledged members of the union. It is a straight, very rational decision. I have always had the preference for two years before affiliates must fully join the union, but Local 52 went for more than twelve years. But, generally, if a unit cannot make up its mind in two years, they will not make it up at all. Since the other membership starts out paying full dues, and even many affiliation agreement members also pay fully, so the full members do not want to see that many new locals coming in without financial advantage for a long period of time.

I have been dealing with the smooth transition from ILU to our union, but there is a slightly different process for signing up company councils. The first situation is that of the ILU. In the case of Gulf Oil refinery workers in Edmonton (now owned by Petro-Canada), I had a bunch of meetings with their independent union officers in my basement, and they decided that they had better join the union. They had some membership meetings, and then we conducted our own vote. We conducted the vote, not the labor board. After winning the vote, we applied to the labor board to change the name from the Gas and Oil Workers Union of Canada, to Local 501 of the ECWU. It was merely a matter of changing the name.

But for joint industrial councils, since they are not recognized by legislation, we have to apply to the labor board for a vote in order to bargain. We get an agreement to work with the JIC, we get the affiliation agreement in place, and then another vote sometime later on to apply for certification by the labor board. The JIC can affiliate with us at any time without being recognized as a bargaining unit, but when they join us for bargaining, they have to be certified by the labor board. If they are not certified, there is no requirement for the company management to meet and bargain with me.

We have had only one example of a company that refused to bargain with us after an affiliation agreement was signed with an ILU. That was Texaco in Edmonton, in the mid-1970s. We had recourse; we called a meeting of the bargaining unit. They formally voted to appoint me as the chief spokesman. They were in the throes of going on strike, and they really needed help. When I walked into the bargaining meeting, the company's guy from Toronto did not know I was going to be there. His local management had not warned him. When I walked in, he just about died. He refused to bargain with me. The mediator of the day sent us into another room, and we waited for about four hours. I said, "Look, I do not have a problem. If they do not want to recognize me, the union bargaining committee can go in there alone, and I'll advise from the outside." But they said, "No damned way. We had a vote that you

are the spokesperson and you are going in." Later on that day, we went in, and I was spokesman. The company recognized that they had a strike on their hands, and the mediator convinced them that I was not there to have a strike, but to get a settlement. We did!

Applying My Thinking to the U.S. Situation

I think a mistake is made of trying to make too much of the difference between Canadian and American law on company unions. The problem is broader. Americans grew up with a very antiunion political movement. In Canada, we had enough governments like the CCF and then the NDP that tried to keep a balance between labor and management issues. Also, the United States is far more monolithic in its labor laws. In Canada we have been able to whipsaw good labor legislation into the individual provinces.

One thing did not come out of your conference at Banff [on Nonunion Forms of Employee Representation, September 1997], and it is a very important thing. The antiunion companies in Canada always says they want to stay nonunion because once they get to be union, they cannot consult their employees, they cannot speak to their employees. What a dishonest distortion! They talk to them all the time. It is just that they cannot always set the bottom line for the discussion. Somebody else's opinion is expressed and it might not always agree with theirs. In a nonunion setting, management consults with workers in order to confirm management opinion, not to get their opinion so you can confirm theirs. Nonunion workers simply fine-tune decisions management has already made. Managers use company unions to answer the question, "How can I make it possible to do what I already intend to do?"

The case is often made that in some situations in the United States, workers genuinely do not want to join the union, for whatever reason. Perhaps they dislike the aims of the particular union in the industry. Yet they cannot legally be represented. They cannot set up their own structure. But I do not think this is a concern. If you take the individual who just does not want a union, why would he want a nonunion union? You cannot be half pregnant. That is what company unions are. We are going to have a baby, but we did not make love. It is divine conception in the labor relations sense. What is so wonderful and altruistic about someone who does not want to join a union, yet wants to have some say in the workplace. What makes that person better than a person who wants to join a union, and when he gets a majority of his fellow workers, he can be honest about his situation. But in the United States you can get a majority with the rest of them being free riders. What the American management people do not realize, and many working people, is that unions are the truest form of stabilization in a democracy. In the countries in the world with dictatorships, on the left or on the right, true unionism disappears. On the left, because everyone joins so there really is no such thing as the union; and on the right, union leaders get shot or disappear.

Having had dozens of years of experience in Canada, I have these thoughts for an American audience. We in Canada have lived with, and worked with, company unions. It is part of our culture. In the United States, they have developed an entirely different culture. You cannot take one thing in isolation and say that it will make any difference. I would prefer that American company unions come out of the closet so that other unions could go and organize them. But you cannot do just that one thing in isolation. The unions would immediately object to it because they clearly see it as an attack. Given the current difficulties for unions with right-to-work legislation, why should not unions object to loosening the restrictions against company unions? On the other hand, if you got rid of right-to-work at the same time as allowing company unions to exist legally, you might have an entirely different view as to what was worthwhile.

If I were in the American labor movement, I would not want to see just one single change. I want them to fight like crazy against the incrementalism and try to change the whole package. It is only the companies that want this 8(a)(2) change. It is not a demand of their councils, or donkey unions. Of course the unions see it as just one more antiunion right-to-work piece of legislation, and that is exactly what it would be in the short run. Industry in the United States would be absolutely shocked to find out that once those company unions come out of the closet, the American union movement and labor-management relations would gain from it. But certainly under the circumstances with right-to-work legislation and everything else, I do not blame the American labor movement for saying, "No. Stick it up your nose."

28

Employer-Employee Committees: A Union Perspective

Jonathan P. Hiatt and Laurence E. Gold, General Counsel and Assistant General Counsel, AFL-CIO

The renewed focus in recent years on employee involvement committees in nonunion workplaces reflects the convergence of several trends that became acutely felt and widely reported in the early 1990s: the declining portion of the union-represented workforce; the ascendance of a Republican Congress eager to undermine the role of organized labor further; widespread worker dissatisfaction with traditionally hierarchical workplace structures; and American business's realization that restructuring workplace relationships could increase productivity and profitability.

It has been reported often that unions oppose employee involvement initiatives and disdain cooperative mechanisms because we fear structures that "compete" with unions, and we are locked into a mentality of antagonism about worker relationships with employers. These facile characterizations simply do not square with the labor movement's record and aspirations. Meanwhile, the legislative approach that has been repeatedly offered for the ostensible purpose of enhancing worker-management collaborations—the TEAM bill—would undermine fundamental workplace protections and is unnecessary given the considerable range of cooperative arrangements that national labor law already accommodates.

Dominant Structures of Work Organization

For most of the twentieth century, work in American factories and offices—from the largest government agencies to the smallest of businesses, and from the most complex and technical professions to those jobs considered to be the least skilled—has followed a rigid, hierarchical model that has demeaned, rather than uplifted, workers.

Under this system, the tasks of thinking, planning, and decision making are performed by an elite corps of owners, executives, managers, industrial engineers, policy planners, and others who centralize knowledge about, and control over, the workplace. The individual worker is to perform assigned tasks in an assigned manner, archetypically through a high degree of specialization and division of labor with each worker repeating a small, fixed task. The worker requires and develops expertise in that task, rather than broader knowledge or more variable skills. Frederick Winslow Taylor—who is generally regarded as the father of this system of work organization and after whom the term "Taylorism" was coined to describe it—advocated this critical division between the elite's "brain work" that laid the plans and the workers' rote execution of them.

In this system, work functions are implemented in a regimented environment in which layers of management assure that the decisions of the thinker/planners are correctly executed by the workers, who are instructed and closely monitored in carrying them out. Questions or problems are raised in a military-style chain of command to the appropriate level of supervision for decision. Indeed, the workers are little more than "inputs" into the production process, much like raw materials and other factors, from which it is the employer's aim to secure the maximum output at the lowest possible cost.

This work system, of course, is most commonly associated with the assembly line and mass production. But its principles permeate work organization in many American industries. Banks and insurance companies, for example, typically operate what amount to paper assembly lines in which an application, a payment, or a claim is passed from station to station so that workers in each area can successively perform a quite limited function until the transaction is fully processed. Franchised enterprises such as fast-food restaurants emphasize standardized systems and results. Even government agencies have adopted a similar approach in delivering their services.

Organized Labor's Efforts to Ameliorate and Transform the Traditional Work System

As has become painfully more evident over the past generation, the dominant American model of work organization does not meet the needs of working men and women. It drives down wages and working conditions by demeaning skills and disregarding safe and healthful workplaces, job security, protection of worker rights, and humane working conditions. It denies workers the free-dom to use and develop their talents fully; stifles initiative and discretionary effort; and deprives workers of a sense of satisfaction and fulfillment that work can and should provide.

Advantageous as this system historically was for American employers when the United States dominated the world economy, it now disserves their interests in a globally more competitive economy where multinational enterprises originating in many countries exert tremendous economic and political power. The traditional work system inefficiently requires superfluous management layers that add substantially to the cost of products and services. Hierarchical bureaucratic structures do not respond flexibly or quickly to new marketplace developments. Meanwhile, foreign businesses have challenged America's economic supremacy through both innovative workplace arrangements and cheap labor.

Although the traditional work system is well entrenched in modern American culture, it is an industrial-age departure from the period in our history when workers were extensively trained in their crafts and were expected to—and did, in fact—exercise judgment, discretion, and initiative on the job. The earliest forms of American trade unionism sought to protect the interests of highly skilled workers and their crafts. This approach still survives, most notably in the unionized sector of the construction industry, which depends upon apprenticeship and training programs to develop workers who understand the total operation, work processes, and work organization, and who apply their skills with minimal managerial direction.

America's unions have long opposed antiquated arrangements in which employers hire employees from the neck down, and require them to do what they are told, and only what they are told, while on the job. The modern American labor movement arose in large measure to end the degrading and authoritarian structure of employer-employee relations, and it has strived to achieve dignity and an independent voice for millions of workers in thousands of occupations.

Since its earliest days, the labor movement has sought to improve the quality of worklife, enhance the opportunities for workers to participate in the workplace, and create industrial democracy. Its efforts have changed the basic power relationships between workers and employers, and established wage standards creating a vast middle class. The labor movement pioneered our system of employer-paid health insurance and private pensions, which are typically administered by joint labor-management funds authorized under Section 302 of the Labor-Management Relations Act, 29 U.S.C. Section 186. And the labor movement introduced such innovations as protections from discharge without just cause; guarantees of occupational safety and health; and limits on the number of hours employees can be required to work.

Organized labor's commitment to infusing dignity and meaning to work has produced broad-based training programs that enable workers both to perform their existing jobs better and to develop the skills and abilities to handle new and more challenging jobs. Indeed, in many industries unions have negotiated for joint control over, as well as adequate funding of, such training programs. Unions have resisted efforts at deskilling work and have negotiated for promotional systems and lines of progression that afford workers the opportunity to advance to more skilled and responsible jobs.

In many industries and workplaces, labor unions have been taking the lead for years in creating new partnerships with management to transform the way work is accomplished and the way labor and management relate to each other. Among the best-known partners in such ventures that have flourished on a large scale are Kaiser Permanente and an eight-union coalition; Harley-Davidson and the International Association of Machinists and the Paper, Allied-Industrial, Chemical and Energy Workers International Union; and Detroit Diesel and the United Automobile Workers. Indeed, employee involvement is most effective, and most durable, when it is nurtured through collective bargaining, where workers speak with an independent voice, secure in the law's protection of their rights, and on actual equal terms with their employers.

In fact, the entire structure of collective bargaining facilitates meaningful interactions and mutual decision making in the workplace. Unions and employers over the years have refined their relationships to address mutual needs, redress abuses, and respond to evolving worker interests and demands. One of the labor movement's goals is to create more sustainable workplaces that guarantee good jobs and employment security, preferably in partnership with management. Where such partnership cannot be achieved, unions nonetheless seek to influence management decision making regarding productivity, quality, and competitiveness.

Principles to Underlie the Organization of Work in the New Century

In 1995, the AFL-CIO Executive Council issued a white paper entitled *The New American Workplace: A Labor Perspective* that strongly endorsed new cooperative and participatory workplace arrangements. That paper set forth five principles that ought to guide the transition to a new model of workplace relationships for the twenty-first century.

First, we must reject the traditional dichotomy between conception and execution. Workers are in the best position to decide how their work can most efficiently and effectively be accomplished. This process requires a fundamental redistribution of decision-making authority from management to teams of workers who develop and refine analytical and problem-solving skills in order to make the best possible decisions.

Second, jobs must be redesigned to include a greater variety of skills and tasks and, more importantly, greater responsibility for the ultimate output of the organization. Workers should be trained not merely in a particular task but in the overall process of producing a good or service, and they should work in teams that exercise discretion, judgment, and creativity in doing the right thing, not the prescribed thing.

Third, a flatter management structure must replace the traditional multilayered hierarchy. Workers must become self-managers who are responsible for their own performance, scheduling work, ordering materials, hiring other workers, and the like. There must be fewer managers, and they must lead, rather than command.

Fourth, workers must exercise a decision-making role at all levels of the enterprise. Just as workers understand best how the work should be organized, workers have expertise to contribute to strategic decisions as well, such as what new technologies to acquire or how to change products or services. As stakeholders in the enterprise, workers have a vital interest in these decisions, and their experiences enable them to promote policies designed to ensure that businesses can both enjoy long-term futures and provide long-term employment at decent compensation.

Finally, the rewards realized from transforming work organization must be distributed on equitable terms agreed upon through negotiations between workers and management. Under our legal system this is the only effective way to forge a true workplace partnership. Such a partnership does not mean that the relationship is "cooperative," rather than "adversarial." That simplistic dichotomy pretends that employees and employers have no inherently conflicting interests. In fact, they do, most obviously regarding the basic distributive issue—how the wealth created by the enterprise is shared. But mutual dealing on equal terms can peaceably resolve inherent tensions and maximize productivity and collaboration.

The Legislative Goal of the TEAM Bill

In the nonunion sector of our economy, where most workers are employed, many private employers have also experimented with numerous forms of workplace structures, engaging workers in various participatory initiatives. These ventures have had mixed results, and absent the "empowerment" of workers that rarely occurs absent union representation, they have attained only limited scope and objectives.

Four years ago, Congress began to give active consideration to a legislative proposal, the Teamwork for Employees and Managers (TEAM) bill that, its proponents claim, would provide necessary legal space for these nonunion ventures to be undertaken. The TEAM bill would carve out major exemptions from Section 8(a)(2) of the National Labor Relations Act (NLRA), 29 U.S.C. Section 158(a)(2), the sixty-year-old ban on employer-dominated labor organizations. In 1996 both houses of Congress passed a version of that bill, but a presidential veto blocked its enactment. That bill was reintroduced in 1997, but made no progress in the 105th Congress. At this writing, it has not yet been introduced in the 106th Congress. It likely will be, and will then face highly uncertain prospects.

The AFL-CIO has vigorously opposed the TEAM proposal, for it would mark an unwise and counterproductive step backward in employer-employee relations.

Congress enacted Section 8(a)(2) as part of the NLRA in 1935 in order to end rampant abuses by employers in exploiting an unintended flaw in the NLRA's predecessor, the National Industrial Recovery Act (NIRA) of 1933. That statute first accorded federal protection of workers' "right to organize and bargain collectively through representatives of their own choosing." But the NIRA did not preclude employers from involvement with the formation or administration of labor organizations; and immediately after the NIRA went into effect, employers created company unions and "employee committees" literally by the hundreds of thousands to squelch the truly independent unions that now enjoyed legal sanction.

Section 8(a)(2) invalidated that stratagem by rendering it unlawful for an employer to "dominate or interfere with the formation or administration of any labor organization or contribute financial or other support to it"—a legal guarantee of independence for unions from employer control and manipulation. The NLRA in turn defined a "labor organization" as

> any organization of any kind, or any agency or employee representation committee or plan, in which employees participate and which exists for the purpose, in whole or in part, of dealing with employers concerning grievances, labor disputes, wages, rates of pay, hours of employment, or conditions of work. (NLRA Section 2[5] 29 U.S.C. Section 152[5])

Section 8(a) carried out Congress's legislative judgment—which it had previously rendered for railway labor relations in enacting the Railway Labor Act of 1926—that throughout the private sector the opportunity of employees to attain true representation and self-organization would be thwarted if employer-dominated organizations were permitted to operate (*NLRB* v. *Pennsylvania Greyhound Lines, Inc.*, 303 U.S. 261, 266-268, 271 [1938]).

Later, in 1947, the Labor Management Relations Act ("Taft-Hartley") significantly curtailed the power and prerogatives of labor unions by, among other things, recognizing union unfair labor practices (Section 8[b]), prohibiting secondary strikes, threats to strike and boycotts (Section 8[b][4][A]), barring such actions to pressure work assignments to employees in a particular union or craft (Section 8[b][4][D]), creating union decertification procedures (Section 9[c][1][A][ii]), stripping supervisors of an enforceable right to organize (Sections 2[3] and 14[a]), and authorizing states to enact so-called "right-to-work" laws (Section 14[b]). But Congress refused to enact proposed NLRA amendments that would have weakened the statute's prohibition of employer-dominated employee groups. (See *NLRB* v. *Cabot Carbon Co.*, 360 U.S. 203, 214–218. 1959). That prohibition became even more critical to sound industrial relations in the wake of Taft-Hartley's radical shakeup of the NLRA's balance between labor and management.

In short, the NLRA guarantees the integrity of both formally constituted unions and any employee committees established for representational purposes to deal with working conditions, and that guarantee is a basic and vital pillar of American labor law.

In its form to date, the TEAM bill would amend Section 8(a)(2) to grant employers carte blanche to "establish, assist, maintain or participate in" employee organizations. Management would have the right to create—and disband—employee organizations at will. And, for each organization management chose to create, management could determine its governing structure and operating procedures; write its bylaws; and even hand-pick the employees' "representatives" on it. In short, the employee "involvement" that the TEAM bill would enable is employee subjection to management-created and management-controlled processes taking the form—but not the substance—of joint decision making.

Equally important, the bill would enable management to dictate the organization's mission and jurisdiction. The bill does not limit the scope of issues the group could address; the operative language is "matters of mutual interest, *including, but not limited to*, issues of quality, productivity, efficiency, and safety and health" (emphasis added). That means such an employer-controlled group could lawfully deal with "grievances, labor disputes, wages, rates of pay, hours of employment, or conditions of work," the very subjects with which a "labor organization" under NLRA Section 2(5) by definition is engaged.

Employee Involvement Under the National Labor Relations Act

The 1996 Senate committee majority report on the TEAM bill contended that the NLRA poses a barrier to employee involvement initiatives based on worker-management cooperation. The committee identified five common forms of employee involvement: joint union-management committees; quality circles; quality of worklife programs; self-directed work teams; and gain-sharing programs. The committee acknowledged that most of these initiatives commonly occur in unionized settings, and it suggested that without TEAM none legally could exist in nonunion workplaces. But over sixty years of case law under Section

8(a)(2) proves that suggestion wrong—a TEAM Act could do nothing to guarantee a legal "safe harbor" for new forms of work organization in unionized *or* nonunionized workplaces because Section 8(a)(2) does not now preclude them.

Analysis of whether an employee committee is lawful begins with the question of whether it is a "labor organization" within the meaning of NLRA Section 2(5) of the NLRA. As noted earlier, Section 2(5) defines a labor organization as any body "in which employees participate" and whose purposes include "dealing with employers concerning grievances, labor disputes, wages, rates of pay, hours of employment, or conditions of work." NLRA Section 8(d), 29 U.S.C. Section 158(d), defines an employer's collective bargaining obligation as extending to "wages, hours, and other terms and conditions of employment." And, NLRA Section 8(a)(5) provides the means of enforcing that obligation, by defining as an unfair labor practice an employer's refusal to bargain in good faith with the lawful representative of its employees.

The matters the National Labor Relations Board (NLRB) and the courts have determined to be mandatory subjects of bargaining for Section 8(a)(5) and Section 8(d) purposes are included in the Section 2(5) definitional listing. But merely because an employee committee addresses terms and conditions of employment does not necessarily render the committee a "labor organization," and even if it is a labor organization, it is not necessarily unlawful under Section 8(a)(2).

In fact, under Section 8(a)(2) there are no subjects that are illegal for teams of employees in nonunion settings to discuss. The nature of the matters discussed by worker committees is relevant only to the inquiry of whether the committee is a Section 2(5) "labor organization." And, even if the committee does address "grievances, labor disputes, wages, rates of pay, hours of employment, or conditions of work," the committee will not be considered a statutory labor organization unless (1) "employees," as defined by the NLRA, "participate" in the committee; (2) the committee is "dealing with" the employer over these issues, and (3) the committee acts in a collective and representative capacity. *Electromation, Inc.*, 309 NLRB 990, 994 (1992), *enf'd*, 35 F.3d 1148 (7th Cir. 1994). (See, generally, *NLRB* v. *Cabot Carbon Co.*)

In turn, the committee's "dealing" with management must be more than occasional activity; "the concept of 'dealing with' essentially involves a bilateral process, ordinarily entailing a pattern or practice by which a group of employees makes proposals to management, and management responds to these proposals by acceptance or rejection by word or deed" (*EFCO Corp.*, 327 NLRB No. 71. 1998). This requirement "strikes a proper balance which permits experimentation with employee participation but protects against the danger of an employer-dominated labor organization which Section 8(a)(2) was designed to address" (*Stoody Co.*, 320 NLRB 18, 20. 1995).

Further, even if all these preconditions to qualifying as a "labor organization" are met, no Section 8(a)(2) violation will be found unless the employer's actions toward that organization constitute interference, domination or illegal support, making the committee not truly autonomous, democratic, and representative of employee interests (*Electromation, Inc.*, 309 NLRB at 994–996).

Applying these principles, the NLRB and the courts have afforded ample opportunity for non-union employers to consult their employees on workplace issues, and for employees to meet with their employers, in order to promote greater workplace democracy and productivity. Under the NLRA, for example, a "labor organization" is not a group created to perform a managerial or adjudicative function, such as:

- A committee or team upon which an employer confers "the power to decide matters for itself." *E.I. Du Pont de Nemours & Co.*, 311 NLRB 893, 895 (1993).
- A division of employees divided into work crews as part of an employer-created job enrichment program, where formerly managerial functions such as scheduling have been entirely delegated to the employee teams. *General Foods Corp.*, 231 NLRB 1232 (1977).
- A group of employees, including some managerial employees, that investigates or determines the merits of employee grievances without negotiating with the employer. *John Ascuaga's Nugget*, 230 NLRB 275 (1977), *m'fied*, 623 F.2d 571 (9th Cir. 1980), *cert. denied*, 451 U.S. 906 (1981); *Mercy-Memorial Hospital*, 231 NLRB 1108 (1977).
- A communications committee used as a management tool to increase company efficiency or improve quality, which occasionally touches upon a subject within Section 2(5). *Sears, Roebuck & Co.*, 274 NLRB 230 (1985).
- A joint apprenticeship program established to train apprentices properly. *National Electrical Contractors Assn., Sacramento Valley Chapter* v. *Wallace*, 114 LRRM 3037 (E.D. Cal. 1983).
- A "Corrective Action Team" consisting of employees who meet management in improving product quality and operational efficiency. *Simmons Industries*, 321 NLRB 228 (1996).

Nor, under current law, is a "labor organization" a group whose activities do not constitute "dealing with" the employer, including:

- "A unilateral mechanism such as a 'suggestion box,' or 'brainstorming groups' or meetings or analogous information exchanges." *Electromation, Inc.*, 309 NLRB at 995 n.21. See also *E.I. Du Pont de Nemours & Co.*; *Modern Merchandising*, 284 NLRB 1377 (1987).
- An "Employee Suggestion Screening Committee" that reviews and forwards employee suggestions to the appropriate management committee after screening out frivolous and "unreasonable" ones. *EFCO Corp.*
- A committee that serves to provide better employee-employer communications. *Sears, Roebuck & Co.*, 274 NLRB 230 (1985).
- "Isolated instances in which the [employee] group makes ad hoc proposals to management followed by a management response." *E.I. Du Pont de Nemours & Co.*, 311 NLRB at 894.
- A social action group advocating the rights of workers, women, minorities, and consumers, that supports strikes and pickets against targeted employers. *Center for United Labor Action*, 219 NLRB 873 (1975).
- Isolated incidents of proposals from a professional employee association concerning working conditions, which do not rise to the level of a "pattern or practice." *NLRB* v. *Peninsula General Hospital Medical Center*, 36 F.3d 1262 (4th Cir. 1994), *denying enforcement of* 312 NLRB 582 (1993).
- The participation of management as facilitators or observers of an employee committee without the right to vote on employee proposals. *E.I. Du Pont de Nemours & Co.*, 311 NLRB at 895.
- A handbook committee that meets once for a specific task. *Stoody Co.*, 320 NLRB 18 (1995).
- A "quality circle group," formed to address operational concerns, which in one isolated instance makes a proposal to management about a dress code. *Vons Grocery Co.*, 320 NLRB 53 (1995).

And, under the NLRA, a labor organization is not a group that does not serve in a representative capacity, such as:

- An open meeting for all employees (a "committee of the whole") where they have an opportunity to present issues and concerns to the employer. *General Foods Corp.*
- Work teams in which each employee participates and speaks and acts as an individual. *General Foods Corp.*
- A committee whose membership continually rotates so that it resembles "employee groups speaking directly to management on an individual, rather than a representative, basis." *NLRB* v. *Scott & Fetzer Co.*, 691 F.2d 288, 295 (6th Cir. 1982), *denying enforcement of* 249 NLRB 396 (1980).
- A communications committee on which all employees serve as members at some point and do not represent the interests of other employees during their tenure. *Sears, Roebuck & Co.*, 274 NLRB 230 (1985).
- An individual or group of employees meeting once or twice with management to ask questions about an employer's new benefits policy. *Fiber Materials, Inc.*, 228 NLRB 933 (1977).

Further, under current law, the requisite employer domination, interference, or support is not established by:

- Minimal conduct such as suggesting to employees that they form a committee or organize a union. *Electromation, Inc.*, 309 NLRB at 993.

- Payment of employees for the time spent at committee meetings, or the provision of meeting space and supplies, where the committee is a legitimate, independent employee organization. *Electromation, Inc.*, 309 NLRB at 998 n.31; *Duquesne Univ.*, 198 NLRB 891 (1972).
- Cooperation between the employer and the organization, including the use of space or services, that does not have the effect of inhibiting self-organization and free collective bargaining. *Federal-Mogul Corp.* v. *NLRB*, 394 F.2d 915 (6th Cir. 1968); *Chicago Rawhide Mfg. Co.* v. *NLRB*, 221 F.2d 165 (7th Cir. 1955); *BASF Wyandotte Corp.*, 274 NLRB 978 (1985), *enf'd*, 798 F.2d 849 (5th Cir. 1986).
- The participation of supervisors in an employee committee if they are in the minority and exercise no veto power over decisions of the group, which is governed by majority rule. *E.I. Du Pont de Nemours & Co.*, 311 NLRB at 893.

Indeed, it is beyond dispute that Section 8(a)(2) does not mandate command-and-control management (or any other form of management, for that matter), but leaves management in unionized and nonunionized settings alike entirely free to move as much, or as little, "brain work" to front-line employees as management deems appropriate. The NLRB's 1977 decision in *General Foods Corp.*, referred to above, makes this plain. In *General Foods* the "nub of the issue," as the NLRB stated, was whether work "teams" were Section 2(5) "labor organizations" (231 NLRB at 1234). The NLRB decided they were not, for they were "created for the purpose of performing the various jobs that must be done"; they reflected "the judgment of . . . management" as to "the best way to organize the work force to get the work done"; and employee team meetings were "occasions for management to communicate directly with its employees and vice versa" that did not "serve to transform the teams into either de facto or de jure labor organizations" (ibid., at 1234–1235).

The NLRB has demonstrated a capacity to discern distinctions among an employer's various employee committees. In *Simmons Industries, Inc.*, 321 NLRB 228 (1996), for example, the board held that several "Safety Committees" at a nonunion poultry processing company, which were established and controlled by management and composed of appointed employees, were statutory labor organizations because they purported to represent employees in dealing with safety and health matters; and a "Total Quality Management/Fast Food Committee," structured and operated in the same manner but dealing with incentive bonuses, discipline, hours of work, and other such matters, was also unlawful. But the NLRB upheld the lawfulness of similar committees that were informational mechanisms on matters of product quality and operational efficiency, even though they occasionally and incidentally directly addressed some terms and conditions of employment (ibid., at 249–255).

We do not necessarily subscribe to the conclusions reached in all of the decisions noted above. But the fact is that they reflect the legal climate within which the TEAM debate has been waged.

The Dangers of the TEAM Proposal

The evidence of actual employer practice bolsters what this case recitation suggests. According to the Senate committee's 1996 report, 75 percent of all employers use employee involvement programs, and 96 percent of employers with 5,000 or more employees do so. These findings hardly suggest a chilling effect of Section 8(a)(2), a heavy-handed NLRB stamping out employee participation programs left and right, or a retrograde labor movement flooding the NLRB with charges to put a stop to these programs. Instead, it seems clear, Section 8(a)(2) and the new American workplace coexist in harmony.

Against this legal backdrop, the public record and the text of the TEAM bill point to the conclusion that this bill has been devised to allow employers to establish and maintain employer-dominated systems of employee representation in the workplace—and to wield them to discourage or defeat the formation of truly independent workplace representatives: unions. As the 1996 Senate committee minority report concluded, the bill "is destructive of rights fundamental to a democratic society and is inherently antiunion." Indeed, the misuse of employer-created committees to foil union organizing efforts remains all too prevalent. For example, see *Electromation, Inc.*; *Aero Detroit, Inc.*, 321 NLRB 1101 (1996), *modified sub nom. APX International, Inc.* v. *NLRB*, 144 F.3d 995 (6th Cir. 1998); *Vic Koenig Chevrolet, Inc.*, 321 NLRB 1255, 1282–83 (1996), *enf'd in relevant part*, 126 F.3d 947 (7th Cir. 1997); *Webcor Packaging, Inc.*, 319 NLRB 1203 (1995), *modified*, 118 F. 3d 1115 (6th Cir. 1997), *cert. denied*, 118 S. Ct. 1035 (1998). In reviewing post-*Electromation* decisions in which the NLRB found that employers unlawfully dominated labor organizations, we found that in 80 percent of these cases, either union organizing was under way or union representation was already in place.

During the initial congressional consideration of the TEAM bill in 1995, an employer group called the "TEAM Coalition" circulated a memorandum that identified two "critical components" of the bill that, the coalition argued, "should not be compromised": (1) allowing employers to create structures "to deal directly *and exclusively* with terms and conditions of employment," and (2) leaving the "formation, composition and operation" of these structures in the hands of the employer (emphasis added). As narrowly approved by the 104th Congress—and as reintroduced since then—the TEAM bill meets both objectives.

It was not long ago that two major national employer groups—the National Association of Manufacturers and the Labor Policy Association—went on record that current law posed no impediments to the pursuit of employee participation and other worker-management cooperation programs (see U.S. Department of Labor, *U.S. Labor Law and the Future of Labor-Management Cooperation*, 119 BLMR 84, 88. 1987). That law remains intact, but the legislative sea change brought about by the 1994 national election has tempted some employers to seek new advantages. Others, however, have forthrightly eschewed such opportunism. For example, former NLRB chairman and current management attorney Edward Miller strongly affirmed to the president's Commission on Worker-Management Relations in 1993 that "the so-called *Electromation* problem . . . is [a] myth," that "it is indeed possible to have effective [employee involvement] programs . . . in both union and nonunion companies without the necessity of any changes in current law," and that repeal of Section 8(a)(2) would lead to the recurrence of "sham company unions" (201 *Daily Labor Report* A-5, October 20, 1993).

It is no solace, then, that the TEAM bill withholds legal protection from the employer where the employee committee undertakes formal action to act as the "exclusive bargaining representative" or to "negotiate or enter into collective bargaining agreements." There is no need for an employer to set up so crass a construct as the blatant company unions of the 1930s when it can achieve the same end—the creation of a potent unionization-deterring palliative—by more subtle and flexible means. Nor is the bill's destructive aim blunted by its exemption of workplaces where a union has been established under Section 9(a) of the act (29 U.S.C. Section 159[a]); inasmuch as the bill's likely impact would be the preservation of employers' nonunion status; exempting unionized workplaces little improves the legislation.

As proposed, then, the TEAM bill would revert the law to its old NIRA status and could generate an explosion of employer-sponsored organizations that deal with terms and conditions of employment but stop short of meaningful employee representation, and the conversion of legitimate and currently lawful employee involvement structures to take advantage of the new TEAM loophole. Cynical management consultants would accurately hype TEAM's usefulness as a union-avoidance scheme. In short, employer control of statutory labor organizations would be legitimized, and such domination could soon become the norm.

Some have argued that TEAM-like legislative changes, if coupled with NLRA revisions easing worker efforts to select unions of their own choosing, would enhance employee free choice, bona fide employer workplace initiatives, and union organizing itself. (See, for example, the Kaufman chapter in this volume.) Although we are constrained to acknowledge that there must be some theoretical point at which such a tradeoff would be desirable, NLRA revisions in exchange for a TEAM bill would have to be quite dramatic to justify the risk involved.

The suggested premise of such a bargain is that employees who could easily organize into a union independent of the employer would not long remain captive of an abusive company union, and employers would be deterred from imposing improper structures lest their workers rebel and secure true union representation. While there is surface logic in this, it underappreciates some real workplace factors.

First and foremost is the inherent sway of the employer that creates the committee and coopts its workforce by a dominated mechanism. Section 8(a)(2) is intended not just to preclude the most exploitative employer gambits but also the more seemingly benign ones that deter through half-measures the impulse to engage on a basis of true equality. It is difficult to discern what employer-dominated arrangements would be deterred when all would enjoy the imprimatur of the law. Organized labor is unwilling to concede an employer safe harbor to effect such programs, which would proliferate and pretermit true independent action.

A second and related factor is that fear of the employer and ignorance of individual and group rights still pervade the nonunion workplace. Even in the best of times, most workers can't relax about pleasing their superiors, and pursuing a real union rarely does. Meanwhile, the lack of popular knowledge about rights under current law contributes significantly to the lack of genuine organizing activity; there is no reason to believe that amending the law will remedy this. A right that's little known will be as little exercised; meanwhile, employers—aided by lawyers, trade publications, and their own relative permanence—will learn about their new options and have the wherewithal to exercise them.

In short, the Section 8(a)(2) protection is fundamental to maintaining balance in the workplace;

and NLRA rights, remedies, and procedures concerning the choice of true union representation would have to be overhauled so greatly to balance a gutted Section 8(a)(2) as to suggest little point in pursuing such an approach in the foreseeable legislative and political environment.

A Look at the Canadian Experience

Canadian labor-management law, which, unlike American labor-management law, includes both federal law and autonomous provincial law, does not precisely match the NLRA's treatment of employee involvement arrangements in the nonunion setting. Canadian law does universally proscribe employer-initiated or -dominated unions, and precludes their public certification as bargaining representatives, much as American law does. And Canadian law, like American law, similarly proscribes employer-initiated employee committees that are intended to foil union organizing efforts (Adams 1999, 6.700, 10.200–10.347; Taras 1997).

However, it does not appear that Canadian courts have squarely addressed the legal treatment of employer-dominated employee involvement arrangements in the nonunion context and in the absence of a union-avoidance motive, which in the Untied States would breach NLRA Section 8(a)(2). This may be a function of a lack of labor board jurisdiction over these situations, a paucity of prospective complainants with the means and awareness to initiate a legal challenge, and an overall employer culture that is less antiunion than in the United States.

Regardless of how this legal issue would be addressed in Canada, we are unaware of any empirical study that quantifies the incidence of such Section 8(a)(2)-incompatible arrangements in either country. That makes it difficult to evaluate how nonunion employee involvement programs in Canada affect the exercise of employee rights or the degree of union organizing and density. And, of course, there are significant differences between more well-developed Canadian and American legal rules governing union organizing efforts; for example, automatic certification on the basis of particular percentages of employee execution of union authorization cards is available in most provinces, and Canadian law generally restricts employer tactics to influence employee choice of representation to a greater degree than does the NLRA (Adams 1999, 7.900–7.960, 10.720–10.950; Taras 1997, pp. 318–326).

Overall, union members constitute about 14 percent of eligible, nonagricultural workers in the United States and 34 percent of such workers in Canada. These figures and the differing cultures and legal rules in the two countries are at least suggestive that some combination of loosening Section 8(a)(2) and importing Canadian-style regulation of the union organizing and election process might make an acceptable legal regime. But it remains necessary to ask, with respect to the TEAM proposal or outright Section 8(a)(2) repeal, to what end? As we have shown, the NLRA gives employers free reign to pursue many approaches to employee involvement. All that's left is the establishment of quasi-union systems that employers control, which in the United States is almost always driven, at least in part, by a union-deterrent motivation.

Conclusion

No argument that has been offered for the TEAM proposal has successfully challenged the straightforward and fundamental premise that underlies Section 8(a)(2): employer-dominated representation is inherently illegitimate and inimical to the exercise of full freedom of association in unionized and nonunionized workplaces alike. Employers should have nothing to say about who will represent the interests of workers to those employers, or how, when, and for what purposes such representatives are selected. Where employers select the employee representatives or establish the employee representation system, the employee representatives will, by definition, be creatures of the employer. Such representatives can have no real independent existence, let alone independent power; true independence means that representatives enjoy the "unfettered power . . . to determine [their] own actions" (*NLRB* v. *Electromation, Inc.*, 35 F. 3d at 1170).

That insight answers TEAM proponents' oft-stated mantra that changing Section 8(a)(2) is necessary so that employers can "empower" their employees. True empowerment requires a workforce that can deal with the employer on an equal and independent footing in determining the terms and conditions of employment. Instead, the thrust of the TEAM legislation is to further management's unilateral control over those terms and conditions. Indeed, the TEAM bill mandates that whatever plans or ideas employer-established workplace organizations devise cannot bind the employer. If "empowerment" is the aim, the NLRA as now written poses no obstacle; indeed, that is the very purpose of the act.

Sixty years ago, Senator Robert F. Wagner, the author of the NLRA, observed that while some of the company unions of that day had done some things well, they "failed dismally to standardize or improve wage levels," goals that required industrywide or national mechanisms. "Without wider areas of cooperation among employees there can be no protection against the nibbling tactics of the unfair employer or of the worker who is willing to degrade standards by serving for a pittance."

Now, in this age of multinational enterprises and mammoth corporate mergers, when wages are stagnant and inequality is rising despite relatively low unemployment and a booming economy, and when workers are unlawfully fired with virtual impunity in one out of every four union organizing campaigns, it would be foolish to erect, or resurrect, another obstacle to workers seeking to improve their lot. A profusion of employer-employee committees freely operates under current law, and they should. Union representation best guarantees their effectiveness. We are hopeful that Congress will see fit to take no backward steps and that workers and enlightened employers will engage their best efforts on the basis of true equality in the new workplace.

References

Adams, George W. 1999. *Canadian Labour Law.* 2nd ed. Aurora, Ont.: Canada Law Book.

AFL-CIO Executive Council, 1995. *The New American Workplace: A Labor Perspective.*

Taras, Daphne Gottlieb, 1997. "Collective Bargaining Regulation in Canada and the United States: Divergent Cultures, Divergent Outcomes." In *Government Regulation of the Employment Relationship*, ed. Bruce Kaufman, pp. 295–341. Madison, Wis.: Industrial Relations Research Association.

United States Department of Labor, 1997. *U.S. Labor Law and the Future of Labor-Management Cooperation*, 119 BLMR 84. Washington, D.C.: Government Printing Office.

Policymaker Commentary

29

Electromation:
An Opportunity Lost or Just Postponed?

John N. Raudabaugh, Former Member, National Labor Relations Board

The significance of *Electromation, Inc.*, 309 NLRB 990 (1992), *enfd.* 35 F.3d 1148 (7th Cir. 1994), while appreciated by many, has depreciated over time, due in part to legislative wrangling, prosecutorial politics, and, more recently, anecdotal reports that some employee involvement activities may not always deliver. Why is this so? Is a different result important? Can a better outcome still be realized? To answer these questions, a little history may help.

Presumably, management and government are interested in employee participation programs because of reported reduced costs and cycle times, improved product quality and customer service, improved workplace relationships, and more employee self-fulfillment. Now, whether these programs do, in fact, achieve the intended goals is not easily answered. There is still a dearth of good analysis and reporting. Most studies are collections of anecdotal reports or small sample econometric studies yielding limited conclusions. But whether employee participation results in enhanced productivity, dollar savings, or increased sales is not the sole measure of success or failure of the programs themselves and is not relevant to the legal inquiry. Even if there is only marginal economic value added, there may well be social value that cannot be measured in dollars. For example, employee participation programs may reach beyond a productivity or quality

focus to matters of training, dispute resolution, or skills enhancement, programs for which value is indirect and not easily measurable.

During the 1970s and 1980s much was reported about Japanese management style. Indeed, the concepts of lean production, *kaizen* or continuous improvement, and team-based organizations were aggressively marketed by management consultants. Labor Secretary Brock, on behalf of the Reagan administration, issued a report urging teamwork and employee involvement. Notably, the report acknowledged that employee participation initiatives may trigger issues under the National Labor Relations Act ("Act").

By 1990, I was serving as a Member of the National Labor Relations Board. I arrived at the Board after years of working with primarily southern clients to achieve something more creative than mere legal compliance or union avoidance— enhanced relationships among managers, supervisors, and employees to recognize mutuality of interests in the workplace. Within a few months of beginning my new duties, along comes a case that apparently escaped the attention of the General Counsel's office since we received no notice that it was of any particular policy interest to the General Counsel.

Upon first reading, I recognized that the case had all the trappings of a "real world" effort to improve employee communications and establish rudimentary employee participation initiatives in order to enrich workplace relationships and enhance productivity and the "bottom line." It seemed to me that the case presented the very issues confronting employers generally—how to involve employees in a multitude of workplace issues, as advocated by the U.S. Department of Labor, yet without clear guidance as to whether such employee participation activities are lawful under the Act.

Thinking that we, the Board, should clarify the "metes and bounds" of Sections 2(5) and 8(a)(2) of the Act as applied to this now common and much touted "new age" management phenomenon, I sought out my colleagues to agree to schedule the case for oral argument—an event that intentionally invites greater participation in the debate and signals a heightened policy interest and a possible change in case law. My two Republican colleagues opposed the idea; my two Democrat colleagues embraced it. For the first time in anyone's institutional memory, those who opposed the suggestion for oral argument went so far as to threaten to ignore Board tradition and issue written dissents to any call for formal public debate.

Of course, as events unfolded, our three votes prevailed, no dissents to oral argument were issued, the case was heard, and, as they say, "the rest is history." Nevertheless, my two Republican colleagues continued for years to say that the case was unimportant and that the Board should have waited for the elusive "better" case. By relying on the lack of charge filing and prosecutorial inaction, I believe that they probably preferred to leave well enough alone, choosing not to attack "modern" management methods and not to draw attention to the lurking legal threat to participative workplace initiatives. By contrast, one Democrat colleague and I reasoned that the case before us raised questions about an apparent conflict between government policy regarding a necessary response to global competition and extant law. Moreover, it seemed timely to attempt some guidance should management proceed too far down the road in investing in team-based organizations only one day to have their wings clipped by some future General Counsel using the law as a sword to protect unions from what may be seen by them as yet another inroad on their already waning appeal.

Electromation received much attention initially. Representatives Gingrich and Gunderson and Senator Kassebaum expressed concern for the decision's likely impact on a host of employee participation programs. Legislation was introduced to amend Section 8(a)(2), but change was not forthcoming. New Labor Secretary Reich invited us to his office, as did Secretary Martin before him, to sound out whether *Electromation* had a broad or narrow reach.

Then the much ballyhooed Dunlop Commission charted the Clinton administration's labor agenda only to have the mid-term Republican election victory make moot the recommendations—namely, to promote employee participation programs provided employee choice to select "independent representation" is not compromised. Although the Commission supported employee involvement programs if limited to topics of production, quality, safety and health, training, and dispute resolution, the Commission also would support the current prohibition on any program that goes beyond "incidental involvement in issues traditionally reserved to independent labor organizations." Notably, the Commission also proposed quick elections, increased use of injunctions, and arbitration to ensure first-time contracts, all to enhance employee opportunity to choose "independent representation."

After returning to private practice, I was contacted by Congressman Fawell. I forwarded written recommendations on January 30, and February 19, 1995 for amending Section 2(5), rather than tinker with Section 8(a)(2), recognizing that the term "labor organization" appears elsewhere in the statute as well as in the Labor-Management Reporting and Disclosure Act (LMRDA). One option would limit "labor organization" to a representational entity, rather than "any organization of any kind." A second option would not only clarify the essential representational element but would restrict the definition to "bargaining" and eliminate the broader concept of "dealing with." An additional variation would modify a labor organization's purpose of "dealing with" (or, under the second option, "bargaining with") an employer to be its "sole" purpose, rather than "a" purpose or "a purpose in whole or in part."

As a less preferred alternative, I offered language amending Section 8(a)(2) but different from the proposed TEAM Act. It seemed to me that the TEAM proposal failed to address adequately the representational issue, unnecessarily limited mutual-interest subject matter, would not resolve significant LMRDA issues, and ignored potential problems of financial or "other support." To avoid these shortcomings, I suggested a proviso to Section 8(a)(2) that would expressly permit employer formation, administration, and support of any *nonrepresentative* employee group that "deals with" an employer concerning any matter of mutual interest. Congressman Fawell and others chose to support the TEAM proposal, which, so far, remains just that. Other than this one inquiry, no *Electromation* author, to my knowledge, was approached by the Commission or any congressional committee regarding the issues in the case despite our many months of research and debate.

In the years since *Electromation*, there has been little prosecution of cooperative programs. Why? Is it because employers heeded the teachings of *Electromation* and *Du Pont* and stopped all such activities? Or, is it because union charging parties, and perhaps the NLRB General Council too, thought it best to "cool" their objectives and rhetoric lest the TEAM Act or other legislative action solve the problem and then some.

To address the issues raised by participative management, I believe you must begin and end with a core value: employee free choice. To this end, the preamble of the National Labor Relations Act speaks volumes. It talks in terms of the economic rationale behind the law and clearly anchors the legal structure and bargaining process in the principle of free choice. Free choice—to elect or reject representation—is a precondition to all that follows. Without election, there is no legitimate representation. And, without representation, there is no statutorily mandated collective bargaining process. Nevertheless, the debate continues, and not just in the academic community, as to whether employee free choice is a necessary *precondition* to whether there will be any collective bargaining or merely an ancillary factor to consider while ensuring and encouraging a collective bargaining outcome that some advocates call the "level playing field."

The question of employee free choice should weigh heavily in any discussion regarding the issues flowing from the *Electromation* decision and should dictate the core structure of any future legislative "adjustment." For example, does participative management threaten employee free choice or merely make the union's job of selling the benefits of representation more difficult? On the other hand, if free choice is threatened, can whatever skews free choice be remedied short of rejecting all forms of employee participation?

And, if free choice is not compromised by employee involvement activities, then what is all the fuss? One would think that employees in a participative environment should be able to choose, like employees in a traditional workplace, between the status quo and union representation. Finally, even if we could agree on what the policy choice should be, what are we going to do to enforce it?

In my view, the Dunlop Commission and TEAM Act advocates avoided these questions and the critical task of benchmarking employee free choice and employee participation. Rather than offer substantive answers to facilitate serious legislative reform, we saw short-of-the-mark executive agendas, legislative proposals, and high-profile lobbying campaigns.

My hunch is that employees, more often than not, view as legitimate the longer-running participative programs and, faced with a choice, would consider them objectively. Restricting or prohibiting such programs amounts to nothing more than shoring up the union option at the expense of employee choice. It simply cannot be that well-subscribed, mature, long-term participative programs necessarily coopt free choice. As to those participative activities that allegedly impede free choice, field research may assist in identifying the contributing factors that need to be addressed by legislative change. Alternatively, amending and limiting the "labor organization" definition to a representative entity only would free most forms of employee involvement activities.

The law also is concerned with employer domination and support or assistance of "labor organizations." It seems to me that these issues really turn back to the question whether employees in an employer initiated cooperative program can still freely choose other forms of representation.

As long as employees can continue to make a free choice to select or reject a third party, even after the cooperative committee fails or succeeds, why should we care about it, and what is the problem with the form or manner or means of employer initiation of or support for such activities?

We also need to consider questions about individual versus collective rights. Should federal labor policy favor collective protections over individual protections? What does "cooperation" mean? Is it somehow wrong to have cooperation among unorganized, nonrepresented people in a workplace? And, if collective bargaining is allowed to enhance only "good" cooperative relationships, then we need to study and reach consensus as to what are the "good" as opposed to the "bad" cooperative programs so that we can understand what the true factors are for defining such differences.

Let's talk further about employee free choice. Does it mean something or are we just giving lip service to it? In an effort to wrestle with the statutory polemics of "dealing with," should we truly be concerned that some simple two-way communication device may pose a threat to collective bargaining? Are team meetings, as opposed to focus groups or "brainstorming" sessions, really going to coopt people from making choices regarding third parties whose real purpose ought to be holding out the promise of the upper hand when it comes to distributive issues?

I simply don't believe that all the dealing in the world is going to shut down by brute force or coopt an employee's ability to choose how best to increase the chances for "distributive justice." The issue of whether a third party can really win the upper hand and increase wages and benefits on the margin is, and always has been, a matter of economic power, which is not going to be significantly enhanced or diminished by cooperative programs. Information and the distribution of information by third parties is not compromised by cooperative programs and is protected activity anyway. I doubt that an employee's ability to read, evaluate, and choose which of several options will yield increased rewards on the margin can be compromised by the presence of workplace cooperation.

In the final analysis, unions as "labor organizations" are representative, political institutions. Labor policy must continue to protect an employee's right to form, join, or assist unions. The problem facing cooperative initiatives is the present, overreaching "labor organization" definition. Employee participation programs and committees should be freed of current regulation. The right to inform employees of and the ability to offer a record of workplace protections and economic rewards is what drives employee choice. The opportunity to participate in nonrepresentative employee involvement activities and to choose between such programs over representative unions should not be restricted. Under the law, employees and unions can campaign and solicit support. Under the law, employer overreaching can be addressed. What is there to fear? Given a choice, employees will choose the option that they believe offers them the greater economic benefit and workplace protection.

30

A Canadian Policymaker's Perspective on Nonunion Representation

Andrew Sims, Chair, Canadian Federal Task Force on Part I of the Canada Labour Code

Canadian and American Differences

My colleagues in this volume have written about employee representation in the context of the U.S. debate over Section 8(a)(2) of the NLRA. The history and intricacies of that section lead me to make two preliminary observations about the difference between U.S. and Canadian labor relations law. The U.S. law has achieved a high level of complexity. One has visions of workers and employers walking around their plants with their attendant lawyers, ready to advise them at every turn, looking much like pirates with parrots perched on their shoulders. Laws can reach such a high degree of refined complexity that they cease to serve the parties they were meant to serve.

As a policymaker, I would like to point to an advantage Canada has over the United States. We Canadians actually change our collective bargaining laws occasionally. Not a year goes by without one government or another passing a new variant of collective bargaining law. In contrast, Americans dip their toes in the legislative pool by occasionally proposing bills in Congress, through they rarely actually dive in and pass amending legislation. As former Alberta Labour Board chair, I had the privilege of being involved in a couple of major reviews of Alberta legislation. More recently, I headed a review that led to the new draft of the Canada Labour Code. Throughout Canada, there is a very healthy debate as to how legislation should keep abreast of current industrial practice and how it affects our competitive position. As a result, the question of employee representation in Canada has been the subject of significantly more experimentation. In Canada, therefore, it is realistic to believe law and legislation can keep pace with the needs of our workforce.

A Broader Focus on Employee Representation

When we talk about employee representation, our tendency is to focus on the employee's voice within the workplace. I want to broaden out from there, for two reasons.

First, the concept of enterprise-based employee representation is getting a little frayed at the edges. Moving to bolster employee representation at the enterprise level relies on an outdated presumption that workers will continue to have long-term employment relationships with single employers.

Second, workers have far more fundamental needs than simply enhancing their voice with an employer. This is particularly so as the lifelong employment relationship withers away, leaving employees to face a career that will involve several employers; the need to make some difficult transitions; and a need to retrain and acquire new skills to keep pace with industrial change. Needs such as income and benefit security and retraining create a demand for more outward-looking forms of representation. Thus, the "enterprise focus" concentrates upon representation with too narrow a set of actors and over too narrow a set of issues.

Structures

Form follows function. Existing organizations engaged in employee representation have historically (in the past fifty years or so) followed the functions they have been assigned by legislation, which is mostly to bargain collectively. So, for example, unions in the health care industry have been as much molded by labor board bargaining unit policies as by employee choice. More recently, in Canada, our unions have begun changing quite drastically. They have merged into much bigger entities. They have "morphed" themselves from enterprise-based representatives to sectoral organizations. They have bolstered their quasi-political social advocacy role. They have had to increase their size and scope of activities to handle these added functions and responsibilities. Partly, this has been a response to the heightened sectoral attention necessary to meet global competition.

Nonunion employee representation has not offered employees any ability to group together across firms or industries, nor has it taken on any significant public policy advocacy role.

A guiding principle for me as a policymaker in the dispute resolution area is "Let the forum fit the fuss." When we are talking about employee representation, what we need is effective representation, where employees have available to them the resources that enable them to meet the challenges they are facing at the time. This does not mean a trip to the Supreme Court every time

there is a workplace incident to be resolved. Elaborate processes may resolve complex legal issues, but over time they effectively deny the employee true representation. We need speedy, efficient, fair, and independent adjudication, appropriate, in terms of time and cost, to the nature of the issue being addressed.

Different Perspectives

The debate about nonunion employee representation usually involves two different perspectives. First, some argue that it is a good thing to afford employees rights and processes over and above those available at common law. This should be so even though those employees have not or cannot choose collective bargaining. The second and contrary perspective cautions that it would be a bad thing for nonunion forms of representation to interfere with the free, effective ability to select a trade union. That is really what the Section 8(a)(2) debate is about.

I think it is useful to look at employee representation at three different levels. How might employee representation be enhanced at each of these levels?

- The individual employee's tenure
- Bargaining unit—enterprise-level representation
- Sectoral representation

The Individual Employee's Tenure

The first level is the most intimate from the employees' point of view. Representation here usually involves an adjustment to the common law to allow protection in respect to job security. The need for representation is most urgently felt at the point of dismissal. The central question is whether we want to reverse the common-law rule that says the courts cannot reinstate a dismissed employee. Collective bargaining in a unionized setting almost universally reverses this rule by the negotiated just-cause provision and the grievance procedure. I have absolutely no difficulty with reinstatement in collective agreement circumstances. Is it a viable option outside of unionization? The United States and Canada each come from a different starting point. The American law begins with "employment-at-will" subject to some more recent statutory incursions, arising for example, from antidiscrimination statutes. Canadian law begins with the right to reasonable notice of termination, or damages in lieu.

Canada, in the federal sphere, has implemented a statutory right to grieve a termination. This applies to any employee under federal jurisdiction (union or nonunion, managerial or not) once he or she has a year on the job. My own experience with this federal law is that it is less effective than it might be, for both employees and employers. The difficulty is not so much the right itself, but the process that gives effect to that right. Part of the problem is that the legislators and subsequently adjudicators modeled the option on the unionized arbitration system.

While I am philosophically inclined to favor reinstatement as a remedy, I am skeptical about the efficacy of moving toward a system where every person has the right to grieve and seek reinstatement. Without unions or some similar and cost-effective form of lay representation to back it up, it is difficult to make such a system work. People cannot access or prosecute the right effectively without representation of some form.

The system also lacks a filtering mechanism. The right to grieve in a collective agreement situation is not absolute. It is really only the right of the union to grieve, subject to the duty of fair representation. One of the things a union does,

which is very important to the employer's interest in the process, is sort out the wheat from the chaff. Although unions get little credit for it, they cull out or settle, at an early stage, many of the cases unworthy of adjudication.

We tend to romanticize about the right to a job. Most jobs in this economy are lost not through arbitrary termination but through workplace change. Making a change in representation at the worksite level fails to address the problems of those who have been displaced rather than arbitrarily treated.

Bargaining Unit—Enterprise Level Representation

The second level is the bargaining unit, which, in our North American system, essentially means at the enterprise level. The focus of the public debate has been on what unions do now. There has been little useful discussion of their role as it will emerge over the next twenty years. Our unions, which are currently our most effective vehicles for employee representation, are structured around our current enterprise-based collective bargaining system. Unions try to be active beyond their collective bargaining role, but they, and we as public policymakers, have to recognize that our present labor relations structure limits their activities. The only way unions can formally collect dues and raise money for what they do is by negotiating dues checkoffs or union or closed shops. In return, they must represent those people within the enterprise, which is, of itself, an expensive proposition. This is particularly so as unions become more involved in joint labor-management initiatives.

Efforts to extend activities beyond the areas encompassed by the terms and conditions of employment contained in the collective agreement are always at the expense of the organization's core functions.

An area of concern in the United States is the degree to which the prohibitions in labor law on employer-dominated unions restrain the type of employee-employer communication necessary in a flexible competitive workplace. Our federal task force was concerned to ask this question for Canada. Despite our raising this for comment, neither labor nor management considered it a serious problem. In nonunion environments, our laws are far less restrictive than those in the United States. In the unionized environment, few problems were raised with us about restraints on employer-employee communication. The issue appears to be less of a problem in Canada than the United States for several reasons.

First, our boards have avoided the strictures of the per se violation approach in favor of a more case-specific analysis focusing on intention. Second, Canadian labor law, and perhaps behind that, the Canadian approach to governance generally, has had less of a concern over strict conflict-of-interest protections and concepts like the separation of powers. Such matters are more likely to be left to be dealt with on the basis of personal ethics and ad hoc arrangements that suit the particular situation than through elaborate rules and procedures. Third, many unions have shown a willingness to adapt their form of representation to fit new forms of work and work organization, particularly where employers are prepared to offer a meaningful role in workplace decision making.

The things that matter to employees are not just the traditional "terms and conditions of employment" encompassed by the collective agreement. One of the things that has happened in Canada, particularly when we have followed the American example, is that we have assigned a whole series of workplace disputes away from true collective bargaining, using statutory schemes that apply universally, regardless of whether the workplace is unionized.

Employee workplace interests include such things as employment insurance, workplace readjustment, occupational health and safety, third-party disability plans, training, and the recognition of qualifications. Benefit plans, income security, safety, and antidiscrimination protections have become increasingly important in the workplace. Such matters often focus workers' attention toward legislative protections and away from the collective agreement as the source of rights and remedies.

Many of these matters are legislated universal plans. I believe we have made a mistake in not giving unions a more formal role in these broader statutory processes. The existence of nonunion workplaces originally led legislators to favor the "government service agency" model. If individuals needed help accessing programs, the responsible agency would provide that help, obviating the need for employee representation. More recently, however, cutbacks in government expenditures have undermined that model's effectiveness. As a result, individuals are underrepresented in a lot of areas where representation is truly useful. This has left a void.

In a way, our Wagner Act model has (by tying union access to resources specifically to the workplace) sapped the incentive for labor organizations to represent all workers. Canada's central trade union organizations, like the Canadian Labour Congress, work hard at the political level to represent the workforce on a broad basis. But they lack the resources or the statutory authority to provide representation in the proliferation of statutory schemes that affect workers. There are strong lobby groups for drivers and travelers, and for the elderly. We have vigorous organizations representing the interests of women. We have a profusion of advocates for equity-seeking groups. I find it alarming that the one "interest group" that really lacks vigorous representation is workers. By this, I mean workers as a whole, as opposed to those who are represented specifically through collective bargaining.

In my view, some of this broader representation is in fact more interesting and important. This is so, both in terms of bringing about change in the rights of employees and, more importantly, in moving Canada toward an effective and competitive industrial relations system.

Sometimes the arguments about alternate forms of employee representation are simply a reflection of the inefficiency of our current certification processes. If employees have the right to certify, my strongly held view is that we should remove the procedural impediments that distort that right to choose. We must not make unionization a right that is attainable only after a four-year obstacle race. It should be a right that is obtainable quickly by a process that is efficient and "on the ground."

In Alberta, for example, we committed to a certification process that had an average turnaround of fourteen days. In the Federal Task Force, we recommended that certification take about thirty days, recognizing that Canada is a big country. When you achieve time frames like this, a lot of the arguments about employer involvement in employee representation (such as unfair labor practice complaints of various kinds) wash away. This is because the process for selecting a trade union has become easier to achieve, and the frustrations that give opportunities for unfair employer intervention have no time to grow. Similarly, the argument that unionization is an ineffective method of representation loses at least some of its vigor when the process of selection (and revocation) are fair and expeditious.

Sectoral Representation

The third level of representation has to be examined through the lens of public policy and the public interest. Let's look at the full scope of employee interests, particularly as our economy seems to be emerging. What do employees need, and what does public policy demand for the public interest?

Individually, workplace disruption can have tragic consequences as savings get eaten up, older workers lose access to opportunities, and the disabled lose any chance of a fair place in the workforce. Workers who have very little connection to their society, who have very little tenure in their jobs, and who are periodically thrust out on the street without security also create a social problem. Supporting such people and their dependents during their transition is a drain on public resources. The loss of their productive capacity is a waste of a valuable social asset. If their displacement reflects outdated skills, it points to a lack of focus or efficiency in our training and continuing education programs. Whether the impact is looked at from the personal or social perspective, the potential for harm is still evident.

There is a public interest in providing mechanisms, through employee representation of some form, to help smooth the transitional displacement difficulties that our new, faster economy generates. Some unions have moved in the direction of providing training centers to ensure their members retain relevant skills for changing job markets. Employee representation organizations are better suited to this than individual employers because the employees can retain their connection to the organization despite disruptions in their employment. Similarly, unions are often more effective at devising readjustment programs because their focus is broader than that of the departing or shrinking employer. There are constraints on unions because of their history and structure that makes adapting to such new forms of representation difficult. Nonetheless, I think there are tremendous opportunities in such areas, particularly in partnership with government.

What form of representation will employees need in the new economy? They will need advocacy with government, because a lot of the changes affecting workers are determined by statutory schemes. Workers also need advocacy in respect to the allocation of public funds, for example, to workplace readjustment, training programs, and matters of this nature. I believe that workers need to be effectively represented in the processes within the statutory schemes that impact on the workplace, not just in the areas of dismissal and discipline, but in compensation, insurance, qualifications, and similar matters. I do not mean by this putting a lawyer on every worker's shoulder. What I do mean is representation through available clear information and advice on how to handle the very complex legislation that surrounds the workplace.

I also believe that, as the connection between employers and employees breaks down and where lifetime employment is no longer a realistic expectation, employees should increasingly look to organizations of workers for the type of income-security programs that have been traditionally attached to employment.

Medical, pension, and disability schemes all fall into this category. While employees increasingly change employers over a career, by and large they still maintain an affiliation to a sector or industry, because of their basic skill sets and experience. This suggests to me that it may be timely for employee organizations to partner with the third-party benefit providers and begin taking over the role of benefits provider. I see no reason why an employee's affiliation to an employee organization is not as good or better a source of such services as the (increasingly impermanent) employer. The superficial answer is that it is the employer who pays the premiums. But there is no reason why that cannot be preserved while shifting the administration (and thus the qualification and continuity issues) from the employer to an employee-focused institution.

Similar arguments apply to how employees access retraining programs. I do not think we should rely on employers, who may be facing going out of business, to provide that kind of continuity of training. In the area of pension reform, I cannot understand why, if we have the technology to track things like airline frequent-flyer points, we cannot use similar technology to provide pension portability to meet the needs of an increasingly mobile workforce.

Employees organizations, whether they be unions, or "morphed unions," or whatever else they may be called, will have a role in these areas. The same will be true in income maintenance programs, in representation in a variety of other needs that workers have for advice, direction, lobbying, advocacy, and these broader forms of representation.

It is for these reasons that I think it is unduly narrow to examine employee representation at the enterprise level alone. Employer-promulgated non-union representation plans are not capable of meeting the needs of employees, because they are designed only to achieve gains at the point where employees interact with their employer, which is becoming an outmoded model of the employment relationship. Effective public policy for the future must examine the realities of the job market, of the complex statutory regime that touches on employment concerns, and the needs of employees as they confront the dissolution of the notion of lifelong attachment to a single employer.

Conclusion

31

Nonunion Employee Representation: Findings and Conclusions

Bruce E. Kaufman and Daphne Gottlieb Taras

Almost anything that may be said about employee representation will be true.

—William Leiserson, 1928

In this concluding chapter we review and synthesize the findings and conclusions on nonunion employee representation (NER) contained in the preceding chapters with respect to three principal themes: history, practice, and public policy. This job is unusually difficult because of the large number of authors, the diversity of perspectives, and the breadth and depth of topics covered. Nonetheless, presented below are what we consider to be the major lessons learned and continuing points of debate. We end the chapter and volume with our recommendations concerning reform of the American National Labor Relations Act and the treatment therein of employer-created representation committees.

NER: A Brief Typology

We start with a brief recapitulation of the form and function of nonunion employee representation. As noted in the introductory chapter, employee representation is any organizational structure that has one or more employees in it and represents in an agency capacity the opin-

ions and interests of other employees to management. The organizational form of employee representation traditionally focused on is the labor union. In this volume attention is shifted to nonunion forms of representation—a subject that has heretofore received little attention in the modern literature of industrial relations and human resource management (HRM).

The individual chapters in this volume reveal a tremendous diversity in the forms and functions of NER. Authors grappled with what in practice are often fine distinctions between participation systems (direct employee involvement) and representation systems (workers channeling their concerns through their representatives), between on-line (production-related) and off-line (working and employment conditions) topics, and between formal and informal systems. Likewise, NER has many different purposes, which include improving communication between management and employees, serving as the organizational vehicle for employee participation and involvement, negotiating or bargaining (overtly or covertly) on behalf of employees over terms and conditions of employment, raising and resolving employment disputes, facilitating joint problem solving, enhancing quality control, and continuous improvement in production processes, providing a method for power balancing between management and labor, and fostering a greater sense of organizational justice, morale, and shared enterprise. Another purpose of NER is to blunt the threat of unionization.

A similar range of diversity is found in the structure of NER. Some nonunion employee representation plans (NERPs) are small-scale, informal bodies representing a single work group or dealing with a specific issue, such as a production coordination committee or a joint safety committee; others cover all the employees in a multifacility company, have written constitutions and employment agreements, and deal with a wide array of strategic and tactical business issues. In North America NERPs are generally established voluntarily by employers, although some states and provinces mandate joint safety and health committees. In a number of European countries, by way of contrast, a form of NER—typically an enterprise-level works council—is mandated or highly encouraged by law and covers most of the workforce.

NER in some cases serves as a substitute for independent unions, but in others is a complement. In North America the substitute role predominates, since workers covered by a form of NER typically are not also covered under a collective bargaining contract (and vice versa). Indeed, many employers use NER as part of a union-avoidance strategy, a motivation that most starkly illustrates the substitution effect. In most European countries, by contrast, unions and NER often are complementary methods of employee representation. German employees, for example, often are represented by a nonunion works council at their workplace and by a trade union in industry or regional-level collective bargaining.

As a generalization, NERPs emphasize cooperation, advancing the interests of the enterprise, and "growing the pie." Unions emphasize bargaining, advancing worker interests, and "dividing the pie." Common elements are also found in both, as when a trade union works with employers to improve productivity in the workplace and a NER body presents a demand to management for improved pay or benefits.

Firms are motivated to adopt NER for a variety of reasons: bottom-line considerations of profit and loss, philosophical and ethical considerations, and, in certain crisis periods, such as the two world wars, because government mandates it as an antidote to industrial unrest. From a bottom-line perspective, the decision to invest resources in operating a form of NER, and the breadth and depth of duties and powers delegated to it, is in principle the same as the decision to invest in any other human resource management activity: are the additional profits created from improved communication, enhanced employee morale, and keeping the firm union-free greater than the additional costs? In many instances the answer is no, either because the benefits of NER are nil, the costs are too large, or there are judged to be more effective ways to reach the same end. Other companies, however, will see some form of NER as a worthwhile investment—sometimes on a small-scale basis for a narrow or well-defined problem, in other cases as a response to a union organizing drive, and yet in others as part of a broader, strategically driven effort to create a high-performance work system. A firm's (voluntary) decision to adopt NER is not only a function of profit and loss, however, but also is influenced by management's underlying ethical values and employment relations philosophy. NER will more likely be made part of a firm's human resource management program if senior executives either value a "family culture" with close employee-manager interaction, implement new forms of work design that depend on employee input, or strongly desire to maintain non-union status.

Employer-created forms of employee representation—the primary NER type examined in this volume—are almost always enterprise based. NER neither provides a mechanism for diffusion of wage and employment standards across firms nor for political action by workers. Unlike labor unions, employer-created forms of NER are established, structured, and operated by the company. NER bodies focus on integrative approaches to workplace issues; typically have no independent treasury or outside resources, such as legal counsel; and do not strike or use other overt economic sanctions to win demands. The mandate given to a NERP is delegated by management, can be altered at management's discretion, and terms and conditions of employment remain management's to determine unilaterally. As a worker representative at Delta Air Lines put it, "We have power to influence but no authority to make changes" (see Cone, chapter 23 in this volume).*

Research Findings: History

Five chapters of the volume described the historical aspects of nonunion employee representation, while several others touched on these issues at various places. Important findings and points of debate include the following:

The Emergence of NER

Employer-created works councils, plant committees, and other such groups first appeared in North America at a few scattered companies around the turn of the twentieth century (see Kaufman, chapter 2). Labor unions, by contrast, emerged more than a century earlier. A seminal event in the development and spread of NERPs was the establishment of the "Rockefeller plan" at the Colorado Fuel & Iron Co. in 1915 (see Taras, chapter 11). Although the Rockefeller plan gained considerable national publicity, it was during World War I that NERPs proliferated as a result of a confluence of factors, including a marked increase in union organizing and strikes, the breakdown of authoritarian "drive" methods of employment management in the full-employment wartime economy, the edicts of the War Labor Board (U.S.) that mandated formation of employee representation committees in several hundred plants, and the "industrial democracy" movement inspired by the war's drive to "make the world safe for democracy." NERPs also were adopted at the same time in England and in much of continental Europe, and legislation mandating enterprise-level works councils was enacted in several countries.

The Motives of Employers

The conventional wisdom among contemporary labor historians and legal scholars is that NERPs—often called "company unions" with some degree of opprobrium and in many cases inaccuracy—were established by employers as a union-avoidance device and a method to forestall greater government intervention in the workplace (Brandes 1976; Gitelman 1988; Morris 1994). The historical record reveals a more complex set of motives, animated by both positive and negative purposes. Especially during periods of crisis, such as World War I or the New Deal years of 1933–35 in the United States, when employers saw their interests threatened by organized labor

---

*Unless otherwise indicated, all references to specific chapters refer to essays in this volume.

or government, many reacted with a defensive strategy meant to buy time, maintain control, and ward off union organizers or unwanted labor legislation (Jacoby 1997; see also Kaufman, chapter 2; Sefton MacDowell, chapter 5; and Taras, chapter 6). These hastily erected NERPs tended to last only as long as the crisis. Most served only as window-dressing and accomplished little. Frequently they were used to manipulate, deceive, or coerce employees so they would not organize an independent union. Widely excoriated as "shams," many NERPs deserved this epithet.

There is also a positive side to the early history of NERPs. A minority of employers with NERPs were animated by virtuous religious, political, or philosophical beliefs and saw the plans as a means to maintain personal contact with employees and maintain a family culture (Smith 1960). While highly paternalistic, these employers nonetheless used NERPs largely for positive purposes, such as the equitable resolution of employment disputes, obtaining employee input on company policies, and involving employees in company housing and recreation programs.

Pragmatic business considerations and calculations of profit and loss figured more often, however, in the decision of forward-thinking employers to install and maintain some form of NERP. World War I saw the emergence and spread of a new model of employment relations, variously called personnel management, employment management, and industrial relations management. As described by early proponents—including the notable academic John R. Commons (1919), this new model sought to accomplish the employer's objective of maximum profit by replacing authoritarian, inefficient, and unjust management methods and a commodity concept of labor with an alternative model that viewed workers as human resources and citizens of an indus-

trial government. Employers were attentive to methods that promoted cooperation, goodwill, and a unity of interest between capital and labor (Kaufman, chapter 2). Most of the progressive employers of the 1920s—a distinct but highly visible and influential minority of the business community—adopted some form of plant- or companywide NERP. In many respects, these employers were pioneering an early prototype of today's much-touted "high-performance" workplace model. These employers, of course, desired to remain union-free and maintain management control, but their panoply of progressive employment practices, of which NERPS were widely viewed as the crown jewel, accomplished this end largely by giving workers better treatment and terms and conditions of employment than unions could deliver (Leiserson 1928). Had overt union avoidance been the primary motive, many of these employers would have abandoned NERPs after the union (and government) scare of the late 1910s subsided, but the evidence indicates that, instead, the number of employees covered by a NERP steadily increased in the 1920s, reaching a figure of nearly a million in the latter part of the decade.

The Attitude of Organized Labor

Organized labor expressed varying degrees of support and hostility toward NERPs, depending on the country and time involved. The overriding consideration appears to be labor's judgment concerning the degree to which NERPs are, on net, complements to or substitutes for union organization.

In the United States the American Federation of Labor initially supported the spread of nonunion works councils during World War I, based on the belief that they would serve as a springboard to union organization; shortly thereafter, however, the Federation became quite hostile once it appeared that employers were successfully using the councils to remain union-free (see Nelson, chapter 3). Unions were not, in fact, active during the 1920s and early 1930s in most of the industries where NER was concentrated (e.g., durable manufacturing, utilities), but the success of employers in replacing unionism with NER in certain high-profile cases, such as the railroad industry, coupled with the inability of unions to make inroads in the mass-production industries, convinced union leaders that NERPs were a mortal threat. As a result of events associated with the Great Depression and the New Deal economic program of the Roosevelt administration, in 1935 American labor succeeded in obtaining legislation—the National Labor Relations Act (NLRA, or Wagner Act)—that effectively banned company unions and heavily restricted most other NER forms. (Amendments to this effect were made a year earlier to the Railway Labor Act, originally enacted in 1926.) The AFL-CIO today remains quite resistant to any liberalization of these legal prohibitions, in the belief that NER will largely be used to thwart independent union organization (see Hiatt and Gold, chapter 28).

Unions in Canada, Great Britain, and Germany have taken different tacks on the issue of NER. Organized labor in Canada initially followed the American pattern (initial openness followed by hostility) on the company union issue, reflecting in part the American origins of both many of the trade unions and large corporate employers (see Sefton MacDowell, chapter 5; and Taras, chapter 6). But the hostility of Canadian labor toward NER never reached fever pitch as in the United States—in part because of the political influence of Mackenzie King, who was one of the preeminent architects of NER, and because of the different historical experiences of the two countries.

When finally Canada passed equivalent labor legislation to the Wagner Act at the end of World War II (a decade later than the NLRA), organized labor—with reluctance in some·quarters to be sure—acquiesced to language that allowed employers to continue to operate NERPs. But since Canadian federal and provincial labor laws went further than American law in facilitating union organizing, most Canadian unions did not feel as threatened by employer-created representation plans (indeed, some have found them to be fertile ground for new organizing) and largely ignored them as an issue of labor policy (see Basken, chapter 27; and Sims, chapter 30).

Nonunion employee representation plans also proliferated in Germany and Great Britain after World War I, but in both cases unions had much greater success in absorbing or coopting them. In Germany, for example, the nonunion works councils after the war largely became plant-level adjuncts of unions, a pattern repeated after the works council system was reconstituted after World War II (see Addison, Schnabel, and Wagner, chapter 17). The British system of Whitley Councils established shortly after World War I also came under trade union sway (see Gollan, chapter 19). In both cases, unions saw that NERPs could be complementary to their activities, rather than overtly competitive, and thus a more accommodative stance developed.

Accomplishments and Shortcomings of NER

During the 1920s, most informed observers of the American industrial relations scene wrote approvingly of NERPs, albeit with qualifications (see Kaufman, chapter 2). Some plans accomplished little, and others disappeared when employers lost their initial enthusiasm—a pattern witnessed with nearly all new management fads and innovations. Certainly a number of workers chafed at management's control of the agenda and decision making and felt the plans gave them little independent power to advance broader issues related to wage levels and hours of work. Workers' fear of reprisal for speaking up or taking an unpopular stand with management also undercut the effectiveness of many NERPs and caused some to degenerate into relatively torpid bodies.

On the positive side, on net employee representation—and the progressive Welfare Capitalist employment model of which it was part—represented a notable advance over the drive methods and autocracy of the traditional employment system. As Nelson reminds us in chapter 3, the choice facing most employees at this time—given the confinement of trade unionism to a narrow range of industries and their exclusionary, craft-based membership policies—was working for a traditionally managed company where the foreman ruled with unquestioned authority, personnel practices were administered capriciously, and employment was "at will," versus a Welfare Capitalist employer with some form of NER for purposes of voice and dispute resolution, as well as a formally constituted personnel department and a policy of secure employment for good performance. Suddenly the advantages of the latter loomed larger and the faults smaller.

On the shopfloor, NER improved employees' work lives by providing a check to the foremen's unilateral and often arbitrary power—a fact that explains why foremen and other first-line managers often stoutly resisted NER (see Kaufman, chapter 2; and Sefton MacDowell, chapter 5). In addition, in the better-run plans hundreds of grievances were funneled through worker representatives, and well over half of them were settled in favor of the employees. NERPs also resulted in numerous suggestions for improvements in working conditions and production processes, and served as a direct communications channel between top management and shopfloor workers. Some employers also turned over part of the management of company housing and recreation programs to the employee representatives. By common agreement, NER's greatest benefit to the employer was that it forced the company to improve substantially the quality, professionalism, and sensitivity of its management cadre and to adopt more systematic and humane personnel practices. While there is significant controversy in our volume over the relative advantage of trade unions and NERPs, widespread agreement exists that NERPs provided workers with benefits that exceeded those available in individual-based employment relationships.

A controversial aspect of NER concerned its impact on wages and other "bread and butter" issues. Critics of employee representation (e.g., Dunn 1926; Gitelman 1988; Basken, chapter 27) argue that NERPs were relatively powerless organizations ("toothless dogs") that gave employees little effective say in the determination of the terms and conditions of employment ("collective begging") and existed largely to manipulate employees into approving what management had already decided to do. The literature of the 1920s suggests a modestly more positive picture.

NERPs were not intended by their management creators to serve as independent bargaining organizations. Workers did not have the collective leverage that goes with striking and other union pressure tactics, and managers often refused to accede to demands for a general wage increase or shorter hours. But NERPs often conferred on workers a measure of indirect bargaining power nonetheless, since firms that installed NER were most often seeking to gain employee cooperation and goodwill and willingly paid the "price tag" that went with this in terms of higher pay, better benefits, and so on. Also operative in this regard was employers' knowledge that the NERP would wither and possibly open the door to union organization if workers did not receive some "wins." These suppositions are supported by the fact that wages and employment conditions at the employers with NER in the 1920s were typically superior to those of other firms in the labor market. During the Great Depression years of 1929–31, when smaller and less progressive employers quickly instituted wage cuts and layoffs, the bulk of the Welfare Capitalist firms, despite severe financial exigency in many cases, for two years maintained wages and minimized layoffs through work sharing in order to protect their costly investments in employee morale and cooperation (see Kaufman, chapter 2). Thus, it may be concluded that NERPs by themselves often did not produce more than marginal improvements in wages and hours, but, taken as a package, the Welfare Capitalist human resource management (HRM) model did give workers definite, tangible gains.

The Demise of NERPs in the United States

Nonunion employee representation plans fell into disrepute in the 1930s in the United States, and many were effectively banned in that decade (Nelson, chapter 3; Estreicher, chapter 9). The downfall of NER came about through the combined influence of the Great Depression and the New Deal economic recovery program of the Roosevelt administration (see Kaufman, chapter 2). Employees became disillusioned with NERPs, and the Welfare Capitalist model in general, because they proved incapable of stanching the wage cuts, layoffs, speed-ups, and arbitrary and rough treatment unleashed by the depression. Then, in June 1933, a newly elected president, Franklin Roosevelt, launched the National Industrial Recovery Act (NIRA), which sought to end the deflationary spiral by stabilizing wages and prices and, at the same time, to promote economic recovery by redistributing income from capital to labor in order to boost household purchasing power, spending, and production. One method chosen to accomplish these goals was to promote greater unionization and collective bargaining. The new law resulted in an unprecedented boom in union organizing, membership, and strikes.

Many nonunion employers quickly established NERPs, partly from the belief that the NIRA either required or encouraged collective representation, but more often as a way to forestall union organization. To foreclose this option, Senator Robert Wagner wrote into the 1935 National Labor Relations Act language that made it an unfair labor practice for an employer to operate a nonunion representation plan or committee that engaged in any type of bilateral dealing with employees over terms and conditions of employment. The rationale was that company unions were a threat to the New Deal's economic recovery program (because they lacked bargaining power to take wages out of competition and redistribute income from capital to labor) and a sham form of collective bargaining used by employers to thwart workers' legitimate aspirations for union representation (Kaufman 1996).

The Disappearance of NERPs and ILUs

Membership in company unionlike organizations at the time of passage of the Wagner Act stood at roughly 2.5 million. Six years later, membership in plant-level employee organizations had fallen to less than 20 percent of this level (see Jacoby, chapter 4). Immediately upon enactment of the NLRA, the newly created National Labor Relations Board quickly and zealously attacked employer-operated representation committees and ordered scores of them disestablished, even when the employer had ceased all support of the committees and the employees in a secret ballot had voted to maintain the company organization. Seeing the handwriting on the wall—particularly after the Supreme Court in 1937 upheld the board's rulings—many employers voluntarily disbanded their NERPs. Another option chosen by some companies was to transform the NERP into an independent labor union (ILU), a plant-level union independent of the employer but also unaffiliated with any national or international union. In 1940 about 1,100 ILUs existed, a number that gradually grew during the 1940s and most of the 1950s and then sharply declined in the 1960s and beyond. ILUs were favored by a number of employees because they allowed greater local membership control and involvement, charged much lower dues, and were less adversarial and strike prone than AFL- and CIO-affiliated unions. Likewise, a number of employers opted for ILUs because they provided many of the benefits of NER (e.g., improved communication, a formal mechanism for grievance resolution) and at the same time helped keep out traditional unions. Employers gradually lost interest in ILUs, however, as the union threat subsided in the late 1950s, and they discovered alternative HRM strategies and programs that could promote and maintain positive employee relations at a lower cost in terms of money, bureaucracy, and independence of management control. By the early 1960s, therefore, the options for workplace representation in the United States had narrowed considerably,

given the evisceration of NER by the Wagner Act and NLRB and the sharp decline in the attractiveness and viability of the ILU alternative to the traditional trade union.

Canada Takes a Different Road

The Great Depression also hit the Canadian economy hard, but it did not foster a new national labor policy (Sefton MacDowell, chapter 5; Taras, chapter 6). Union organizing and labor conflict increased noticeably in Canada in the 1930s, but not nearly to the degree experienced by its southern neighbor. There was therefore less pressure and less of a political/economic rationale for restricting NER than in the United States and no legislation along this line was enacted until 1944 when PC 1003—Canada's version of the NLRA at the federal level—was put in place. Behind PC 1003 was the Canadian government's fear of disruptions to wartime production and the electoral danger posed by the developing alliance between unions and an emergent social democratic party. The legislation (and similar legislation at the provincial level), like the NLRA, banned employer-dominated unions. But, unlike the NLRA, the Canadian law prohibited only employer domination of a *union*—meaning an independent organization of workers formed for purposes of collective bargaining—rather than the much broader American prohibition of all forms of representation committees that in some respect dealt with employers over terms and conditions of employment. The effect was to allow employers to maintain NERPs as long as they did not seek to utilize the committees for purposes of collective bargaining or overt methods of union avoidance. Although many NERPs were eventually organized by Canadian- or American-based unions, a number survived and continue to operate today (see Taras, chapters 6, 11). A number of others have been established in more recent years in both the private and public sectors. ILUs, on the other hand, never grew to more than a fringe movement in Canada.

Research Findings: Contemporary Practice

In addition to history, this volume also explores at length the role of NER in the contemporary practice of industrial relations and human resource management. Here are some of the most important points that emerge from the individual chapters.

Extent of NER

The extent of NER in modern industry has until recently been unknown. This volume reports new evidence on the subject. The first point to stress—and one that is often overlooked—is that employer-created teams and councils for purposes of employee involvement and participation (EIP) overlap but are not coterminous with nonunion employee representation groups. A number of EIP forms, such as self-managed work teams and quality circles, are typically "committees of the whole" and are thus not representational. Chapter 10 by Lipset and Meltz reports that in the United States and Canada roughly half the workers (50 percent in the United States, 51 percent in Canada) say that their employers have established new methods of decision making in order to promote employee involvement and participation—a figure that rises to 90 percent in the United States for people working in firms with 5,000 or more employees (71 percent in Canada). The extent of EIP in the United States reported by Lipset and Meltz, it should be noted, matches closely with the figure of 56 percent reported by Freeman and Rogers (1999).

Lipset and Meltz then asked workers about the presence of formal systems of NER at their workplace. They found that in both the United States and Canada approximately 20 percent of nonunion workers were employed in companies having a formal system of employee representation and about 12 percent of U.S. nonunion workers were covered by such a system (9 percent in Canada). Approximately one out of ten nonunion workers in both countries reported that their firm had a NER body that discussed with management issues related to, respectively, safety and compensation and benefits, and approximately 5 percent of these workers said their firm had a NER group that bargained with management over such issues. For purposes of comparison, Freeman and Rogers (1999) found that 28 percent of the employees they interviewed who participated in an EIP group reported that the group discussed matters related to wages and benefits. Given a U.S. employment level in 1998 of approximately 97 million nonunion wage and salary workers in nonagricultural industries, the Lipset and Meltz results indicate that roughly 19 million American workers are employed in companies with some type of formal NER, and 10 million have a NER that discusses some aspect of "terms and conditions of employment." The latter finding suggests that noncompliance with the company union prohibitions of the NLRA may be far more widespread than previously thought.

The extent of nonunion employee representation varies in other countries. In chapter 17, Addison, Schnabel, and Wagner report that roughly 20 percent of German firms have a works council but that three-fourths of workers are covered (indicating that works councils are disproportionately found in large firms). Although the works councils are employer-financed and organizationally independent of trade unions, a majority of elected council delegates are union members. In chapter 18, Morishima and Tsuru report that the two most important forms of NER in Japan are joint consultation committees and nonunion employee associations. The former are found in approximately 30 percent of nonunion firms, the latter in over 50 percent of nonunion firms (but only one-third of these discuss terms and conditions of employment, the other two-thirds focus on social and recreational activities). In Britain, Gollan reports that roughly one out of five nonunion workplaces has some type of formal joint-consultation committee, covering about 30 percent of nonunion workers (see chapter 19). He reports that roughly 30 percent of workplaces in Australia have a form of NER committee or consultative body, although in a number of cases these operate in firms that also have collective bargaining (similar to Great Britain).

Heterogeneity of NER Forms

Reported in this volume are over forty case studies of NER in modern-day firms. One facet of NER that is immediately apparent from these case studies is the tremendous variation and heterogeneity in the structure and scope of NER forms. There is no "one size fits all" form of nonunion representation, and the "company union" label often attached to NERPs is frequently an inaccurate descriptor.

The chapters in this volume—and particularly the evidence from Canada, where employers have relative freedom to operate whatever form of NER they desire—suggest that the majority of nonunion employers favor smaller-scale, decentralized forms of NER that serve as communication, consultation, and coordination devices and that focus primarily on a small subset of well-defined topics primarily related to matters concerning production, quality, and cost containment (see Taras, chapter 6; Verma, chapter 14). Specific aspects of employment and human resource practice, such as work scheduling, incentive pay rates, and grievances, may be discussed, but most employers desire to keep companywide policies regarding terms and conditions of employment "off the table." Their preference in these matters is guided by a number of factors, including a belief that relatively narrow, targeted forms of NER deliver the most tangible benefits at the least cost; decentralized NERPs promote faster decision making, flexibility in operations, and less bureaucracy; and the fear that broader, more formal types of NER will increase employee bargaining power, foster a collective identity among the employees, and open the door to union organizing.

A minority of nonunion companies, however, for both business and philosophical reasons, desire to operate larger-scale, more formalized employee representation councils and committees—in some cases resembling rather closely the NERPs of the 1920s (see chapters 6, 12, 21–25). The reasons for doing so are also varied, but typically they rest on a company culture that values employee voice, a strong preference to remain union-free, and a belief that employee input can help identify significant production efficiencies, achieve better coordination and implementation of enterprise-level employment practices, and serve as a stimulus to improved management.

Most examples of NER in North America are found in situations where collective bargaining is absent—which is to say that NER and unions function largely as substitutes. But exceptions occur. One notable example is in the Canadian federal sector, where employees are represented by both public-sector labor unions and a NERP—the National Joint Council (NJC) of the Public Service of Canada (see Chaykowski, chapter 15).

Although many observers expected the NJC, originally founded in 1944 as the representational agent for federal government employees, to wither and die when public-sector collective bargaining was legalized in 1967, it has not only survived but now plays an important role within the heavily unionized public sector. In effect, the two forms of representation complement each other. Unions handle traditional distributive bargaining issues and the NJC handles integrative or intraorganizational issues where a collaborative problem-solving approach is suitable.

The same bifurcation of roles is found in many European countries, Australia, and Japan. In chapter 19, Gollan cites examples in the U.K. and Australia where nonunion joint committees function in the same enterprise side by side with trade unions, and in chapter 18 Morishima and Tsuru report that 83 percent of firms with collective bargaining also have joint consultation committees. Similarly, in Germany and many other continental countries, plant-level human resource issues are dealt with by nonunion works councils and broader, market- or industry-level issues are handled by national trade unions and employer associations (see Addison, Schnabel, and Wagner, chapter 17). In the 1920s a number of observers anticipated (or hoped) that this two-tier system of representation would develop in North America, but such has not been the case (see Kaufman, chapter 2). The principal explanation is that this type of complementarity and peaceful coexistence among representational forms requires that union organization be widespread, institutionally secure, and relatively centralized in the relevant market or industry (otherwise unions and NER become rivals), a set of conditions never realized in North America.

NER as a Component of High-Performance HRM Practices

Beginning in the early 1970s, much attention in both the academic and practitioner worlds has focused on the development and spread of a new model of work and employment, often referred to as the "high-performance" workplace (Pfeffer 1994; Kochan and Osterman 1994). A number of the features of the high-performance workplace have antecedents in the Welfare Capitalist experiment of the 1920s, but the model itself originates from post–World War II ideas and events—such as the development of sociotechnical theory of work systems, behavioral science theories of employee motivation and involvement, Japanese "lean production" methods, and the popularization of total quality management concepts (Kaufman 2000, Nadler and Gerstein 1992). The high-performance workplace model seeks competitive advantage through redesign of work and employment processes. Crucial ingredients of the system are teams, employee involvement, enlarged jobs and greater self-management, gain-sharing reward systems, egalitarian company cultures, extensive two-way communication and information sharing, and cross-functional training. While only a small minority of firms have implemented the entire package of high-performance practices, a much larger proportion—including a high percentage of the nation's largest 1,000 employers—have adopted portions of it, particularly with regard to programs aimed at fostering greater employee involvement and participation (Lawler, Ledford, and Albers 1992; Osterman 1994).

For many employment and production issues and in larger-size workplaces, direct forms of participation are too cumbersome and costly and have to be replaced with indirect forms of participation—which is to say with some form of employee representational team, council, or committee (see Fuldner, chapter 20). Most previous research studies on employee involvement and participation programs in North America have glossed over the difference between participation and representation and have devoted little attention to the role of NER in EIP programs and as an important human resource management (HRM) practice in the high-performance workplace model. The work contained in several of the chapters in this volume suggests, however, that this neglect is ill considered.

The field research, survey evidence, and testimony of employers and employees contained herein suggest that NER forms are widespread in companies with well-developed, sophisticated EIP programs and are likely to spread even further in future years (see chapters 12–14, 20–22). Examples of EIP activities that utilize a form of NER include production coordination teams, joint safety committees, a plant employee council, an employee representational group that reports to the board of directors, a companywide joint industrial council, a gain-sharing committee, and project teams formed to make recommendations on changes in company human resource practices. Not only is this an important finding in its own right, but attention is also drawn to an important paradox in American labor policy. The virtues of employee involvement and high-performance workplace practices are widely and routinely proclaimed by academic scholars, management consultants and practitioners, labor leaders, and policymakers, yet, on the other hand, the nation's labor law—principally the National Labor Relations Act and the Railway Labor Act—tightly restrict the range and form of NER that nonunion companies can operate (see chapters 20, 26, 29; see also Commission on the Future of Worker-Management Relations 1994a; Kaufman 1999).

Benefits and Costs of NER for Employers

Adoption of NER, at least in a North American context, is typically an employer decision and is thus made with employer interests uppermost. These interests are largely related to increased profit, but maintenance of effective power and control in the organization is also salient. NER provides a number of potential and actual benefits to companies, as described in the individual chapters in this volume.

One benefit of NER, for example, is motivational—to improve levels of employee morale, commitment, and loyalty to the organization and thus achieve higher work effort, lower turnover, fewer grievances, and so on (see Hammer, chapter 8; Boone, chapter 21). Motivation can be improved by giving employees greater opportunity for participation in decision making, by sharing more information with them, giving employees a sense of ownership in the enterprise, and fostering greater perceived equity and dignity. Often these motivational purposes are best served by small-scale, decentralized forms of NER (and direct forms of participation), since they give employees the most opportunity to get involved personally, a psychological precondition for becoming more emotionally energized (Cappelli and Rogovsky 1998). But larger-scale NERPs also promote motivation, for example, by helping management install and fine-tune more responsive and procedurally fair employment practices.

Nonunion forms of employee representation also serve management's profit goal by improving the coordination and performance of activities in the firm (see chapters 7, 20, 21, 23). Partly this occurs by facilitating an improved two-way flow of communication and information between management and employees—separated as they often are in large organizations by numerous layers of hierarchy and location in different facilities and states. A plant- or companywide NERP, for example, can provide top management with a direct, relatively unfiltered method both to learn what employee concerns are and to communicate to employees the company's perspective or rationale on important matters. Coordination can also be improved where there are important interdependencies in production or administration across functional areas or departments. A paper mill, for example, may form a NERP with representatives from both the pulp and paper departments in order to coordinate production levels and resolve quality problems. Finally, NER can promote improved organizational performance by allowing firms to delegate more tasks and responsibilities to employees, thus permitting a reduction in first-line supervisory staff.

Another benefit of NER for companies is union avoidance. This topic, because of its importance and its controversial nature, is considered separately below.

NER also entails a variety of costs for business firms of both a direct and indirect nature. Direct costs include management and employee time used for NER meetings, activities, and oversight; costs of legal counsel and management consultants in setting up the program; and office space, supplies, travel, and other expenses. Indirect costs of NER include potential loss in the speed of decision making, less flexibility in employment practices, higher labor cost (due to pressure on management to grant more generous wages and benefits), and creation of a potential in-house organizing committee for an outside union. Evidence from both historical and contemporary case studies indicates that successfully operating a companywide NERP often entails a large investment of money and management time

and in some instances costs the firm more than if it dealt with a traditional union (see Kaufman, chapter 2; Taras, chapter 6; and Boone, chapter 21). Generally, labor costs are equal to, and in some instances higher, than they would have been with a large national union (see Jacoby, chapter 4; and Taras, chapter 11). Though NERPs rarely overtly bargain with management, their power to extract "entitlements" for their nonunion status increases dramatically in the shadow of a union organizing presence.

NERPs also require a different style of management. In chapter 21, David Boone, a senior Canadian manager, lists the management practices that are crucial for the successful operation of a large-scale NERP—a list that many managers will find daunting. These practices include continuous vigilance, hypersensitivity to discontent, brokering open communications across multiple hierarchical levels, and balancing the desire of employees for greater rewards and influence with the need of management to maintain decision-making authority and a competitive cost structure. Without the shelter offered by explicit management-rights clauses found in union-management collective agreements, management is in a vulnerable position, having to justify its decisions to an often skeptical workforce. As Boone puts it, there is "no veil behind which management can hide." Taras has nicknamed NERPs "pet bears" because they require their "trainer" to keep sweets in his pockets and never turn his back for long (Taras and Copping 1996). Enterprise-level NERPs are not an easy substitute for unions, and employers who believe they can use NER for this purpose are seriously deluding themselves.

The uncertain profit impact of NER is further suggested by the econometric evidence reviewed by Addison, Schnabel, and Wagner in chapter 17.

They report that works councils in Germany are associated with higher wages, higher levels of productivity in large firms, and lower profits overall.

The size of both the benefits and costs of NER varies across firms, industries, and time periods (see Kaufman and Levine, chapter 7). Benefits, for example, are likely to be higher in large firms, in firms with more technologically interdependent or knowledge-intensive production processes, where employees are regarded as strategic assets, within imperfectly competitive product markets (where profits are typically higher and employers can afford more generous compensation for workers), in firms with well-developed internal labor markets and/or high-performance work practices, and in a macroeconomy characterized by full employment and stable growth. The latter considerations—full employment and stable growth—are particularly important for successful NER, as less than full employment provides firms with a cheaper and easier method to motivate employees (through fear of job loss), and declines in product demand necessitate layoffs and other "give backs" that erode the spirit of trust and cooperation so essential to a successful NER.

Benefits and Costs for Employees

NER also entails a number of benefits and costs for employees. These benefits and costs are important not only in their own right as they affect the well-being of employees but also because they indirectly determine the extent of NER in the workplace by influencing the desire of employees for outside union representation.

On the benefit side, NER can provide employees with greater opportunities for participation, involvement, and voice in the workplace, both individually and as a group (see Cone, chapter 23; Chiesa and Rhyason, chapter 24; and MacDougall, chapter 25). Where the representational body is small and decentralized, such as a production coordination team or a joint safety committee, the scope for participation and involvement may be restricted largely to immediate production-related issues or a specific workplace problem, but where the NERP spans an entire plant or company, workers have the opportunity to influence broader, sometimes strategic issues affecting basic aspects of financial, production, and employment policy. NER also provides employees with an opportunity to learn new skills, take on greater leadership roles, and broaden the range of day-to-day tasks and activities on the job. Case studies and anecdotal reports indicate that employees in well-functioning NERPs have higher levels of job satisfaction and often become loyal "company men" (or "company women"). A cautionary note is introduced, however, by the statistical results reported by Morishima and Tsuru in chapter 18 that no difference, on average, exists in reported employee job satisfaction among Japanese workers in firms with and without NER.

In many cases NER also leads to concrete improvement in the terms and conditions of employment for workers. Often cited as among the most important is providing a check to the arbitrary, sometimes petty, and discriminatory authority of supervisors and foremen. Another benefit often cited is that NERPs allow workers to communicate to management various changes in production methods and working conditions (e.g., a new exhaust fan, an ergonomic improvement in a work process) that not only increases productivity but also makes workers' lives easier and safer.

As noted in the historical section, a contentious issue is the impact of NER on basic bread-

and-butter aspects of the employment relation, such as wages and hours. Critics argue that the NER effect is close to zero and, in some cases, actually works against employee interests (see Hiatt and Gold, chapter 28). Their position is based on three suppositions: NERPs lack bargaining power to advance employee interests because employees are controlled by management and have no right to strike or other type of leverage; any wage increase or other benefit delivered by a NERP is an illusion because management would have taken the same action anyway but is using the NERP to create a false image of worker empowerment; and management uses NERPs to "soften up" employees to accept the necessity of wage cuts and other concessions.

The evidence from contemporary sources—like that from historical studies—suggests a mixed verdict on this matter. To begin, it has to be recognized that many forms of NER are small-scale, decentralized employee groups, and so, by design, they are not intended to affect companywide terms and conditions of employment. Most employers desire to keep distributive issues, such as wages, hours and benefits, off the table and so avoid larger-scale NERPs along the lines of the company unions of the 1920s. Among the minority of employers who do establish (or would like to establish) a companywide NERP, several generalizations seem supportable.

First, to echo a theme developed when union avoidance is discussed, the motives of the employer are crucial. When employers use NER as part of a positive, "high-road" HRM strategy, they are endeavoring to win employee commitment, cooperation, and hard work by creating employment conditions superior to those found at most competing firms. Part of the way these firms achieve high employee satisfaction and commitment is by providing above-market wages, benefits, and conditions—often as high or higher than at similar unionized firms. On the other hand, when employers are pursuing a "low road" HRM strategy of below-market pay and substandard benefits and conditions, the impact of NER is more often illusionary or negative in the long run. Often, these firms do not implement a system of NER until a tangible threat of union organization appears, and then a NERP is quickly established as a reactive, defensive measure intended to buy time and beat back the union threat. In this instance, any wage increase or improvement in conditions is most likely a short-run, opportunistic action that will disappear once the crisis has passed or that may be promised but never delivered.

A second generalization is that the degree of influence NER has on wages and other terms and conditions of employment depends heavily on the pressures management feels from external sources such as unions, government, and the labor market (see Kaufman and Levine, chapter 7; Taras 1997a, b). NER works to the advantage of employees in direct proportion to the degree management perceives "doing right" by workers promotes the company's interests. A number of external pressures can lead to this conclusion, such as a strong union threat effect, the prospect of new government labor regulation or legislation, and full employment conditions in labor markets that make employee attraction and retention a strategic concern. When these pressures are absent, NER loses a considerable amount of its vitality and force for protecting and advancing employee interests except among the small elite of firms most dedicated to progressive employee relations (see chapters 2, 3, 6, 11, 21). Nonunion representation groups formed by employees, such as the diversity networks and advocacy groups studied by Helfgott (see chapter 16), suffer from the same problem, only instead of lack of external pressure, it is lack of salience to the firm's business objectives that leads to their relative ineffectiveness.

Nonunion systems of representation impose negligible direct costs on employees, as they pay no dues, incur no lost time from strikes, and are usually paid for their time devoted to NERP business. Indirect costs can be substantial, however, to the degree NER is a successful instrument for union avoidance among workers who genuinely want and need independent representation. Individual workers can also experience large costs from NER if they are fired or otherwise discriminated against for saying or doing things through an NER-related activity that displease management.

Social Benefits and Costs

Public policy toward NER must take into account not only the benefits and costs that accrue to individual employers and employees but also those that fall upon the broad economy and society.

Two issues are most important in this regard. The first is whether the private decisions of employers lead to the optimal amount of NER in the economy. This issue is considered in chapter 7 by Kaufman and Levine. They conclude that while no definitive statement can be made solely on theoretical grounds, a probable case exists that a free-market economy will underproduce the socially optimal amount of NER. Thus, a rationale is provided for modest, selective encouragement of NER by government, such as tax incentives and legislation that mandates a form of NER in specific cases where the net social benefits are large and compelling. An example is joint safety and health committees in high-risk industries.

The second issue concerning the social benefits and costs of NER concerns the relative encouragement (or discouragement) public policy should give to union versus nonunion forms of employee representation. As noted previously, union forms of representation typically give workers more direct forms of bargaining power and as a consequence have a greater impact on improving terms and conditions of employment for workers. Unions, for example, raise wages on the average of 15–25 percent above the nonunion level (Freeman and Medoff 1984), and a recent study by Weil (1999) finds that mandated joint safety committees in unionized firms lead to higher safety levels (through more stringent OSHA enforcement) than those in nonunion firms. It is arguably the case, however, that NER forms of representation perform better at promoting productivity and productivity growth (a "grow the pie" as opposed to "divide the pie" outcome) because they do not impose as many restrictive work rules on employers, do not discourage capital investment through high wage demands, and do better at promoting collaborative EIP efforts. (The union effect on productivity and productivity growth, judged in the latter case to be negative, is surveyed in Addison and Hirsch 1997).

Kaufman argues that the preference in public policy toward union versus nonunion forms of employee representation depends, in this regard, on microeconomic and macroeconomic considerations. At a microeconomic level, economic theory shows that economic welfare is maximized when wages and other terms and conditions of employment are set at full employment, competitive levels. To the degree various imperfections in labor markets, such as monopsony, externalities and public goods, result in wages and conditions that are below competitive levels, welfare can be improved by fostering through public policy forms of employee representation (Kaufman 1999; Kaufman and Lewin 1998). It follows that the more severe and widespread are labor market imperfections, the more public policy should give encouragement to unionized forms of representation, given that unions have more bargaining power and thus the ability to offset market failures. But if the extent of market failure is modest to negligible, union bargaining power may well be excessive, and public policy should tilt more in favor of NER, given that it pushes wages up a smaller degree and, arguably, has a greater positive effect on productivity growth. At a macroeconomic level, the major argument advanced by proponents of unions is that they help promote greater macroeconomic stability (by taking wages out of competition) and economic growth (by stimulating aggregate demand through income redistribution from high-income to low-income households). Proponents of NER dismiss such "underconsumption" arguments and instead stress the more favorable impact nonunion forms of representation have on productivity growth and expansion of aggregate supply.

Few modern economists subscribe to the macroeconomic rationale for unions and this conclusion thus undercuts the ban on most forms of NER contained in the NLRA (Kaufman and Levine, chapter 7). It is also fair to say that most economists believe that labor markets are, on net, more competitive than they were several decades ago (Boal and Ransom 1997; Kaufman 1997). This also points in the direction of greater use of NER, although the case is not ironclad because one must consider the *degree* to which labor-market outcomes—even if more nearly competitive—still diverge from the competitive ideal.

Policy toward unions and NER should be based, of course, on more than economic considerations. A wide range of noneconomic social benefits and costs must also be included. Kaufman

and Levine note, for example, that one commonly cited noneconomic argument in favor of union representation is "industrial democracy"—that workers should have a formally constituted and independent form of voice and protection in the workplace. Similarly, Taras (1997b) argues that there are social justice arguments to be made for the existence of organizations that engage the citizenry in the democratic life of the state. In chapter 30, Sims argues that NER, because it is restricted in coverage to the plant or company, is unable to address adequately many concerns (e.g., portability of health care and pensions) of today's workers, who are likely to be employed at a number of different companies over their work careers. A final consideration to note of a noneconomic nature is that unions engage in considerable political action and legislative lobbying and thus provide workers (or at least a subset thereof) with a greater voice in the political process than occurs through NERPs (Delaney and Schwochau 1993).

Union Avoidance

The most controversial aspect of nonunion employee representation plans is their alleged use by employers to thwart the desire of employees for independent union representation. Indeed, the use of NERPs as a union-avoidance device provided the major rationale for the heavily restrictive stance taken toward them in America in the National Labor Relations Act.

The chapters in this volume point to several conclusions on this subject. First, certainly in a North American context it is true that nearly all employers desire to remain union-free, although the strength of this desire and the degree to which it reflects issues of principle versus pragmatic business policy vary considerably by firm, industry, region, and country (see Fuldner, Boone, and

Harshaw, chapters 20–22). Toward this end, employers craft various legal and human resource management strategies that either reduce employees' preferences for union representation or in some way impede their ability to organize. Among those firms that adopt some form of NER, the evidence is overwhelming that one motive—but not necessarily the only motive or the most important—that guides them is the expectation that a NERP can help maintain their union-free status.

A second conclusion, however, is that union avoidance per se is not necessarily antisocial or to be condemned out-of-hand but, rather, must be judged by the way it is accomplished and the effect on the employees and broader society (see Kaufman, chapter 2; Kramer, chapter 26; and Raudabaugh, chapter 29). To explain our view, it is useful for purposes of generalization to follow Kochan and Katz (1988) and reduce firms' union-avoidance strategies to two basic types: what they call a strategy of *union substitution* and *union suppression.*

A strategy of union substitution endeavors to keep out unions by making employees feel satisfied, well-treated, and loyal to the firm through a variety of positive employment practices, including fair treatment, opportunities for participation and involvement, and provision of terms and conditions of employment that equal or exceed what unions can win through collective bargaining (see Boone, chapter 21; and Cone, chapter 23; see also Foulkes 1980). This may also be called a "high-road" employment strategy. The opposite is a union-suppression strategy. The hallmark of union suppression is the use of negative and often unethical and/or illegal sanctions and methods, such as spreading false rumors about union financial malfeasance or company plans to close the plant, provoking racial polarization among the workers, and firing union activists, which keep the

workers from organizing through fear, intimidation, and misinformation (see Basken, chapter 27; Hiatt and Gold, chapter 28; see also Hurd and Uehlein 1994). Frequently, union-suppression tactics are used by low-road employers who tend to view labor as a commodity and short-run expense to be minimized, who manage employees through "command and control" tactics that are unilateral and sometimes arbitrary and capricious, and who provide only the minimum necessary in wages, benefits, safety, and other amenities. High-road employers, however, can also resort to union suppression tactics when more benign methods of union avoidance fail.

Some form of NER will often (but not always) be used by both groups of employers as part of their union-avoidance strategy. But the purpose of the NERP, its impact and ultimate effect on the workers, and the social implications thereof, differ greatly depending on whether the strategy is one of union substitution or suppression. Firms practicing a high-road, union-substitution strategy put in place high wages, job security, methods of fair dealing, and opportunities for employee involvement as a proactive method to build employee satisfaction, morale, and commitment—all with an eye to obtaining greater profit through reduced turnover, greater work effort, higher-level customer relations, and greater operational flexibility. Not all these firms will decide to establish one or more forms of NER, particularly of a more formal, centralized nature, but many will do so as a vehicle for employee involvement, grievance resolution, safety improvement, and so on. The hallmark of a high-road employer is that the NERPs and other accoutrements of a union-substitution strategy are put in place and built up over time as a proactive investment in employee goodwill and are abandoned or circumscribed only in reaction to fundamental threats to profitability or a far-reaching change in top management. Thus, even though the high wages, generous benefits, and "in-house union" are likely to be condemned by union activists as morally suspect products of paternalism and union avoidance, to most workers and to the public at large the end result appears to be a win-win outcome where the firm prospers, in part because of its dedicated, hard-working employees, and the workers enjoy terms and conditions of employment—and opportunities for voice and involvement through various forms of NER—that are unobtainable at many other companies.

Firms that endeavor to remain union-free through a union suppression strategy, in contrast, will typically use some form of NER in a defensive, short-run, and socially illegitimate manner. The purpose of the NERP, in this instance, is not to make a forward-looking investment in employee goodwill but to nip in the bud an incipient union organizing campaign or to defeat one already in progress (see LeRoy, chapter 13). The fact that the employees are ripe for union organization typically means they are dissatisfied with employment conditions in the firm, be it the level of wages or benefits, the lack of due process in the resolution of grievances, or insensitive or discriminatory treatment by first-line management (Freeman and Rogers 1999). The employer, once cognizant of the threat of unionization, reacts in a variety of ways, depending on the amount of time and range of tactics the law and business considerations allow. In most cases, for example, the employer will hire a labor attorney to provide legal advice and possibly initiate court or labor board appeals in order to buy extra time; in addition, the employer may hire a union-avoidance consultant to take charge of the company's countercampaign. The employer will also endeavor to determine the sources of dissatisfaction and convince the employees that improvements will be made; will try to identify the union supporters among the workforce and may, in some instances, fire some of them; and will make promises or threats to workers that in some way seek to reduce the perceived gains from unionizing or raise the costs (Lawler 1990; Kaufman and Stephan 1995). Some firms will practice union suppression without adopting some form of NER—fearing that a NERP may too easily be turned into an in-house organizing committee for the union. If unconstrained by the law, however, many employers will quickly erect some form of employee council or committee system as part of their union-avoidance effort (see LeRoy, chapter 13).

On the positive side, these NERPs will often provide employers with a better, more informed picture of why employees are dissatisfied and may contribute to some improvement in terms and conditions of employment. Nevertheless, the negative aspects of NER, in this situation, loom larger. By creating a NERP, for example, the employer can buy time to defeat the union by temporarily addressing employee concerns, only to go back to "business as usual" when the union is defeated or loses majority support. Likewise, a NERP can be used by employers as a vehicle for funneling disinformation to workers about the union or for making false or illegal promises and threats. Finally, a NERP can aid the employer's effort to identify the union activists and discriminate against them, or provide an organizational vehicle that pro-company employees can use to spread propaganda or bestow favors. The specific uses of NER vary in each of these examples, but the net effect is the same—to serve as a short-run instrument of union avoidance so that employees do not organize to gain better treatment and improved wages and conditions through collective bargaining. Since unionization of low-road employers can often promote both social justice and economic efficiency, the use of NER for union-suppression purposes is condemnatory on both economic and ethical grounds (Kaufman 1999).

In sum, the evidence provided in this volume suggests that NER is, indeed, frequently utilized for purposes of union avoidance but that a judgment on its social and economic merits must consider the manner in which union avoidance is practiced and its impact on employees. When it is of a union-substitution form, a system of NER largely promotes win-win outcomes for firms and workers and should be permitted by law; while if it is of a union-suppression nature, a system of NER retards economic progress and works against social justice and should be restricted or banned by law. Of course, in the real world many companies have elements of both high- and low-road employment practices and adopt an amalgam of union-substitution and union-suppression strategies, so public policy has the difficult task of drawing the line on legitimate and illegitimate uses of NER.

Another conclusion emanating from this volume concerns the actual effect of NER on union organizing and growth. In the short run, the preponderance of evidence points to a negative impact, but over the medium to long term NER may—at least in countries with strong protections of the right to organize and vibrant labor movements—actually promote greater unionization rather than retard it (see Kaufman, chapter 2; Sefton MacDowell, chapter 5; and Kramer, chapter 26; see also Taras 1998; Kaufman 1999). In the short run, adoption of NER probably deflects worker interest away from trade unions because it provides an alternative channel for worker voice, provides employees with at least a modicum of influence (or hopes thereof) in improving terms and conditions of employment, at least temporarily strengthens employee identification and allegiance to the company, and serves as a useful device for union suppression. The long-run effects are contradictory, however. In firms that successfully practice a high-road or "high-performance" employment strategy, a NERP effectively serves as a substitute for a trade union, and the employees will shun the latter because they are, on one hand, relatively satisfied with the in-house system of representation and, on the other, repelled by the adversarialism, bureaucracy, "big labor" image, and costs associated with a regular union.

In a number of other instances, however, employers who adopt a form of NER will, in the end, be more likely to be organized by a trade union than if they had avoided NER altogether. The reason is that when employers put in place a system of NER, they inevitably raise worker expectations about the degree to which employees are to have influence in management decision making and company policy with respect to both the process of production and the terms and conditions of employment. Research evidence strongly indicates that as long as companies behave in ways that fulfill these expectations the employees reciprocate by providing behaviors management desires—such as hard work, good customer service, low turnover, and disinterest in union organization (Akerlof 1990; Wheeler and McClendon 1991; Taras and Copping 1998). But if these expectations are seriously violated and not rectified in a speedy, good-faith manner, then a NER system leads to the opposite emotional effect on employees: they feel intensified negative feelings of anger, betrayal, and injustice (relative to a situation where the employer had not installed a NER system) and more aggressively seek ways to punish the employer for breaking the psychological contract. One of the most visible and potent ways to punish the employer is to organize a union.

It is for this reason that many employers decide not to utilize systems of NER in the first place (and particularly the formal, companywide systems), as they conclude that the potential upside gain from raising employee morale and commitment is not worth the downside risk that they will have to break the psychological contract later and reap the negative consequences thereof. Still, a number of other employers, if unconstrained by the law, will conclude that the gains of NER are worth the costs and will establish some form of NERP. Whatever their motive, these employers run a larger risk of unionization to the extent that they do not operate their NERPs in ways that meet employee expectations. Thus, a low road employer may successfully defeat a union organizing campaign by using a NERP, but if the NERP is a sham form of empowerment the employees will come to feel—absent employer efforts to correct the underlying sources of dissatisfaction (and egregious unfair labor practices, such as closure of the plant)—an even greater sense of disillusionment and hence a desire for union representation. Likewise, a high road employer may have successfully operated a NERP for several decades, but if adverse market or financial conditions force it to downsize, and the downsizing is done in a manner that bypasses the NERP or violates established norms of shared decision making and equality of sacrifice, the employees may quickly react by threatening to bring in an outside union.

The evidence from the case studies reported in this volume, and the experience of unions and companies in Canada, strongly support these suppositions. As Taras describes in chapter 6, most of the NERPs established in the 1930s and 1940s in Canada were subsequently organized by independent unions, although sometimes only after many years. Likewise, in chapter 27 Basken, formerly president of Canada's Energy and Chemical Workers Union until its merger with two other large national unions, states that approximately one-third of the new members organized by his union in recent years have come from raids on employer-created representation plans. Also noteworthy in this regard is that union density in Canada—approximately one-third of the nonagricultural workforce—is double the American level, even though Canada permits nonunion employers relatively unrestricted ability to operate NERPs.

But Canadian experience also shows that some companies successfully operate NERPs for many years and that their employees, despite repeated organizing efforts by unions, prefer the employer-created plans to independent representation. Examples provided in this volume include Imperial Oil and Dofasco. A clear lesson, however, is that this accomplishment does not come easily or cheaply for the company and its managers. According to the case study evidence provided here, a prerequisite of successful NER (particularly a more formal, companywide form) is that the employer provide wages, benefits, and conditions that match or exceed the union level (see Taras, chapter 11; and Boone, chapter 21). A successful NER also sets in motion dynamics in the employment relationship that make managing the workforce more difficult and time-consuming. These dynamics become particularly difficult to manage, as previously noted, when companies are forced by deteriorating profits or heightened competitive pressure to downsize, merge, or consolidate, or in other ways retrench and belt-tighten (see Chiesa and Rhyason, chapter 24; Cone, chapter 23; and MacDougall, chapter 25). As a union-avoidance device, therefore, a formal, large-scale system of NER can be successful, but over the longer run most companies are likely to conclude that less expensive and demanding methods will accomplish the same end. This conclusion is supported by Verma's finding in chapter 14 that even though Canadian law is permissive with regard to NER, the large majority of firms choose to utilize it only on a small-scale, relatively informal and narrowly focused manner, particularly with regard to issues related to terms and conditions of employment.

Research Findings: Policy

The third subject considered at length in this volume is public policy toward nonunion employee representation. Here are some of the major points that emerge from the chapters.

Diversity in National Policy

National policy on NER varies considerably. At one end of the spectrum are countries such as Germany where national law either mandates or highly encourages enterprise-level forms of NER, usually in the form of a works council (described in Addison, Schnabel, and Wagner, chapter 17). At the other end is the United States, which takes the most restrictive public policy stance toward NER of any major industrialized country.

Other countries leave NER largely unregulated, or mandate only certain forms of NER, such as health and safety committees. For example, Gollan reports in chapter 19 a virtual absence of legislation regarding NER in the United Kingdom—a fact he finds congruent with that country's long tradition of voluntarism regarding recognition of trade unions. As a result, employers have largely unrestricted freedom to establish, structure, and operate NER forms as

they choose (except for the impact of Britain's 1997 decision to comply with the European Works Council Directive). According to Gollan, until the 1990s Australia also left NER largely uncovered by statute law. Since the mid-to-late 1980s, however, Australian industrial relations policy has attempted to move the locus of decision making from highly centralized structures toward the enterprise level and, in that effort, NER has been encouraged in several statutes.

Japanese policy toward NER is examined in chapter 18 by Morishima and Tsuru. Although Japanese companies use a wide variety of NER forms, the authors note that legal regulation of NER is, in their words, "almost nonexistent." They go on to say that "there is virtually no law regulating or governing the forms or functions of employee representation in Japan."

Canadian policy on NER is examined by Taras (chapter 6). She notes that Canadian industrial relations law at both the federal and provincial levels stipulates that in order to gain certification from a government labor board, any organization formed for purpose of collective bargaining on behalf of employees must demonstrate majority support, and subsequently enjoys exclusive representation rights—provisions broadly similar to the American approach. Also similar is the provision in federal and provincial Canadian laws that prohibits employer support or interference in the establishment and operation of a labor organization. The key difference between Canadian and American laws is that Canada has adopted a more narrow definition of what constitutes a "labor organization," a subtlety that allows for the continuing legality of NERPs in Canada.

The American approach is to define a "labor organization" broadly as any kind of employee representational group that in some manner engages in bilateral dealings with the employer over terms and conditions of employment. This expansive definition, in conjunction with the prohibition on employer domination or support of a labor organization, effectively bans many forms of NER in the United States. Canadian law, by way of contrast, adopts a different standard. The relevant provincial legislation in the province of Saskatchewan, for example, states: "'labour organization' means an organization of employees, not necessarily employees of one employer, that has bargaining collectively among its purposes." Thus, the effect of Canadian law is to prohibit employer interference with the establishment and operation of bona fide trade unions, but it leaves nonunion employers free to operate whatever forms of NER they desire (Taras, chapter 6)—as long as these employee bodies do not interfere with employees' statutorily protected rights to organize (say, by offering inducements or threats to workers during a union organizing campaign). Company-dominated NERPs that are readily disestablished in the United States thus face no similar legal challenge in Canada.

American treatment of NER is the most restrictive in the industrial world for reasons that go back to the 1930s and the events surrounding the Great Depression and New Deal legislative program. The two relevant pieces of legislation affecting NER in the private sector are the National Labor Relations Act (NLRA) and the Railway Labor Act (RLA). (Public-sector laws are quite diverse, but many adopt the restrictive approach of the NLRA and RLA. See Estreicher, chapter 9.) We focus on the NLRA, since it covers a far larger part of private employment than the RLA.

Section 8(a)(2) of the NLRA states that it is an unfair labor practice for a company "to dominate or interfere with the formation or administration of any labor organization or contribute financial or other support to it." Section 2(5) of the NLRA, in turn, defines a labor organization as "any organization of any kind, or any agency or employee representation committee or plan in which employees participate and which exists for the purpose, in whole or in part, of dealing with employees concerning grievances, labor disputes, wages, rates of pay, hours of employment, or conditions of work."

The effect of Section 2(5) of the NLRA is to put off-limits most forms of employer-created NER. This restrictive treatment applies not only to formally elected plant- or companywide bodies, such as the employee representation plans or company unions of the 1920s, but also a variety of smaller, more decentralized forms of NER, such as joint safety committees, peer-review panels, and gain-sharing committees. More detailed evidence on this matter is discussed next.

Effects of the NLRA on Nonunion Employers

Considerable controversy exists in the United States regarding the degree to which the provisions of the NLRA (and RLA) actually constrain nonunion employers in their ability to operate various forms of employee collectives. The focal point for this controversy was the National Labor Relations Board 1992 decision in the *Electromation, Inc.* case (see chapters 9, 12, 13, and 29). The board's decision ordered a nonunion company to disband five "action committees" established to provide management with suggestions for changes in various company HRM practices (e.g., smoking policy, pay progression) because they were found to be employer-dominated labor organizations, as defined in the

NLRA. (The complainant Teamsters Union later won a representation election at the company.)

Critics of the *Electromation* decision claim that it seriously restricts the ability of nonunion employers to operate effective employee involvement and participation programs—a restriction that not only is detrimental to the public interest because it undercuts the competitiveness of American employers in the global marketplace but also because it reduces the opportunities of workers for more meaningful and rewarding jobs (see Raudabaugh, chapter 29; Kramer, chapter 26; and Fuldner, chapter 20). Supporters maintain, on the other hand, that the NLRA in no way prevents nonunion employers from operating NERPs as long as the focus is on productivity and quality issues; relatively few Section 8(a)(2) cases are filed each year so the negative impact is negligible in practice; and it remains in the social interest to restrict employer-dominated NERPs heavily because their principal purpose is union avoidance (see Hiatt and Gold, chapter 28).

Several chapters in this volume present empirical evidence on these issues. For example, in chapter 13, LeRoy obtained data from six nonunion Fortune 500 companies on the number of employee participation groups utilized in one or more of their production facilities and the characteristics and purposes of these groups. He found that most of the participation groups were small (fourteen employees, on average), were classified as "teams," and nearly always were created and operated with substantial employer input. Roughly half of the participation groups dealt with subjects related to terms and conditions of employment—principally work scheduling and safety but also in some cases matters related to vacations, pay, grievances, and so on—and the large majority used a method of decision making that involved more than just employee sugges-

tions and information sharing. He concludes that a large number of these participation groups have potential compliance problems with the NLRA, but that in practice the constraining effect is mitigated by a combination of factors: the modest "on the margin" nature of many of the potential violations, the ability of many of the employers to effect revisions that can pass legal muster (e.g., drop discussions of work scheduling), and uncertainty about NLRB doctrine on numerous "fuzzy" aspects of the groups' structure and operation.

Based on these survey results, LeRoy concludes that there is scant evidence of the presence of old-style company unions in modern nonunion employee involvement programs—suggesting that the company union restrictions in the NLRA may no longer be as relevant. But this conclusion is tempered when he examines individual Section 8 (a)(2) cases that have come before the NLRB since *Electromation*. In the majority of these cases, nonunion employers were found to have established, often coincident with the onset of union organizing activity, some formally constituted NER system to represent employees in a more ongoing, substantive way.

A second perspective on the contemporary use of NER by American nonunion employers is provided in chapter 12 by Kaufman, Lewin, and Fossum. They look at eight nonunion companies that have advanced employee involvement and participation programs, describe their EIP activities and employee representation bodies, and examine these forms of NER in relation to legal barriers imposed by the NLRA. The large majority of these companies use one or more forms of NER that in some respect deal with management over terms and conditions of employment, thus raising significant legal compliance issues. While LeRoy found that most participation groups in the companies he surveyed are small-scale "teams," Kaufman, Lewin, and Fossum find that a number of the companies they examined have more formal, often larger-scale NER bodies.

From extensive personal interviews with executives, management attorneys, and consultants, Kaufman, Lewin, and Fossum conclude that companies with EIP programs fall into one of three groups. The first group uses direct forms of participation (e.g., autonomous work teams) or confines EIP mostly to production and quality issues and thus is largely unconstrained by the NLRA. The second group is modestly constrained by the NLRA in that employers currently use (or want to use) NER forms, report a desire to have more extensive joint dealings with employees and more latitude than the law currently permits, but if given freedom on the matter would expand their NER programs only selectively in terms of breadth and depth. They would not likely adopt formal, plant- or companywide NER bodies with peer-selected employee representatives. The third group already stretch the limits of the law with regard to the use of NER in their EIP programs and, if unconstrained by the NLRA (or RLA), would go considerably further.

It is also worth noting that both LeRoy and Kaufman, Lewin, and Fossum report similar conclusions from interviews with management attorneys on two issues. The first is that the *Electromation* decision initially cast a significant chill on employer EIP programs but that employer concerns have since moderated— due in part to the low probability of being charged with a Section 8(a)(2) violation, the weak penalties if found guilty (a cease-and-desist order), a decision by some employers to proceed with certain EIP activities despite legal uncertainties, and the discovery by others of ways to conduct EIP that may be modestly inconvenient but that are nonetheless serviceable. The second conclusion is that

many employers remain leery of proceeding very far with forms of NER out of fear that they will later provide an entrée for union organization.

Evidence from Canada

Evidence on the constraining effect of the NLRA (and RLA) on EIP programs among American nonunion employers can be extrapolated from chapters 11 and 14 by Taras and Verma that examine NER in present-day Canadian firms. Since Canadian labor law allows nonunion firms wide latitude in setting up and running NERPs, Canada provides a particularly useful illustration of what might happen in America if the company union provisions of the NLRA and RLA were liberalized. Two conclusions seem warranted. The first is that even with no legal impediments, only a modest number of firms use formal, relatively centralized plans of employee representation. Such elected plant committees, industrial councils, and so on, are sprinkled across the public and private sectors in Canada—per the findings of the Taras chapter—but are not an overwhelming presence in the employment landscape. The second inference—per the findings of the Verma chapter—is that most often employers choose to operate their EIP programs and associated forms of NER in a smaller-scale, more decentralized manner. However, these more modest programs frequently do discuss (but not negotiate) with employees regarding workplace subjects broadly related to the terms and conditions of employment.

If there is a remarkable aspect of the cross-country pattern of NER between the United States and Canada, it is the finding of Lipset and Meltz (chapter 10) that the penetration rate of NER is almost identical (20 percent) in the two countries despite the differences in legal treatments (Canada being permissive, the United States restrictive).

One possible interpretation is that differences in legal treatment have, in the aggregate, little impact on firms' demand for NER and ability to operationalize it. Another is that the roughly equivalent rates of NER density reflect offsetting factors—for example, fewer legal restrictions in Canada (a "plus" for Canada) but greater breadth and depth of EIP activity (compare the case studies in Kaufman, Lewin, and Fossum, chapter 12; and Verma, chapter 14) among American companies (a "plus" for the United States). We cautiously believe that adoption of the Canadian legal regime in the United States would, indeed, promote greater NER in the short run, but that the long-term impact (once the less committed employers drop NER plans or have them unionized) would be a modest expansion in terms of both breadth and depth of activity.

In concluding, we note that the evidence from all the countries considered in this volume suggests that roughly one-fifth to one-quarter of nonunion employees, give or take five percentage points, work at companies that have a strong disposition to adopt some form of NER. Since approximately half of American employees report that they desire some form of collective employee representation at the workplace (Freeman and Rogers 1999), we must conclude, as others have (e.g., Towers 1997), that a substantial "representation gap" is likely to persist even if American labor law is liberalized regarding NER. Apparently, the amount of NER employers find optimal for business reasons is substantially less than the amount employees want, or at least say they want.

Policy Recommendations for American Labor Law

In this final section we briefly outline our suggestions for revision in American labor policy regarding nonunion employee representation. The discussion is framed in terms of the National Labor Relations Act but is equally applicable to the Railway Labor Act and other relevant public-sector statutes. What follows is solely the opinion of the authors and does not necessarily reflect the views of the other contributors to this volume.

We start with several normative assumptions. The first is that public policy should provide as much free choice as possible for both employers and employees regarding use of a representational agent or organizational body in the workplace. The second is that providing employees with an organizational vehicle for voice, participation, and due process is desirable for noneconomic reasons related to self-actualization, democracy, and justice and thus should be encouraged by public policy, but that all efforts in this regard must be done in ways that minimize raising business costs, creating new regulatory bureaucracies, or promoting additional litigation. A third is that the right to organize for purposes of collective bargaining is a fundamental freedom and should be fully protected by law. Employer practices of a coercive or punitive nature that infringe on this right should be prohibited.

With these thoughts in mind, the evidence presented in this volume leads us to the following conclusions. The American ban on most forms of NER was a poor long-term policy decision. It was the product of unique economic and political events associated with the Great Depression and the Roosevelt administration's New Deal economic recovery program. Promoting greater collective bargaining and banning most forms of NER as an economic recovery method was ill considered, and the other unfair labor practice provisions of the NLRA (possibly further strengthened) would have largely prevented employers from using NER for illegitimate union-suppression purposes.

The second conclusion we reach is that the ban on most forms of NER is overbroad, and contrary to a continued spread in the breadth and depth of employee involvement and participation programs in American industry—a trend that many observers welcome and believe public policy should encourage (Lawler, Ledford, and Albers 1992; Commission on the Future of Worker–Management Relations 1994a). In this regard, restricting the agenda of employee representational committees and teams to nonemployment-related issues is both impractical and detrimental to employee interests. It is impractical because many aspects of productivity and quality improvement inevitably involve employment-related subjects, such as safety, work scheduling, and skill-based pay (see chapters 12 through 14 and chapter 26); and it is detrimental to employee interests because companies are given an excuse to focus committee meetings only on issues most germane to management's concerns (higher output, lower cost, etc.) while avoiding for legalistic reasons issues of greatest concern to employees, such as pay rates, vacation scheduling, and health insurance. Furthermore, we note, recent survey evidence of American employees (Freeman and Rogers 1999) reveals that the majority express a strong desire for additional voice and participation in the workplace and most often want this to take place through some form of cooperative, joint management-worker committee—exactly the form of NER that the NLRA heavily restricts.

A third conclusion we reach is that NER has both a positive "face," as described above, and a negative face. The negative face is when NER is used as an overt suppressive tool for union avoidance. When NER is used by employers as an aboveboard mechanism to increase involvement, information, and effective dispute resolution, the result can often be that the employees are relatively satisfied with their jobs and have no desire for union representation (see Cone, chapter 23; Chiesa and Rhyason, chapter 24; and MacDougall, chapter 25). We do not believe this form of indirect union avoidance is detrimental to the public interest. We recognize that well-run, successful EI programs tend substantially to reduce employee interest in independent representation and thus are useful to employers as union-avoidance devices, but this practice seems largely benign and even beneficial to the extent that the employer provides wages and conditions of work that meet or exceed what a union might deliver. But when employers use a form of NER as a reactive, defensive method to forestall or squash the legitimate desire of their employees for independent union representation, we believe equally strongly that such action is antisocial and should be prevented by law. The same survey evidence cited above (Freeman and Rogers 1999) reveals, for example, that approximately one-third of American employees are dissatisfied with conditions at their workplace and, if given the choice, would vote for union representation. Often, employee dissatisfaction arises when management practices and policies are regarded as exploitative, unjust, or arbitrary and capricious. Relatively unobstructed access to union representation is an efficacious means for employees to redress these problems (see Basken, chapter 27; Hiatt and Gold, chapter 28), and evidence indicates that unionization of such employers often improves both the economic and social performance of the workplace. Thus, the challenge for public policy is to promote (or at least not obstruct) employer use of the positive face of NER for generating mutual gain outcomes but, at the same time, prevent employer use of the negative face of NER for union-avoidance purposes.

The best approach to accomplish this task, in our opinion, is to recast the National Labor Relations Act so it more closely parallels Canadian federal and provincial labor law. This proposed restructuring represents, in effect, an amalgamation of the proposals for labor law reform contained in the recommendations of the Dunlop Commission and the TEAM Act (see Kaufman, Lewin, and Fossum, chapter 12; and Kaufman 1999, for greater detail). Specifically, we propose the following:

Nonunion employers should be permitted to establish and operate whatever kinds of employee representation committees are desired—including no committee. These committees should be allowed to deal with any and all kinds of workplace issues. To accomplish this end, the definition of a "labor organization" in Section 2(5) of the NLRA should be revised to include only independent associations of workers organized for purposes of collective bargaining. (The definition of a labor organization would also have to be collaterally changed in other relevant parts of the statute law, such as the Landrum-Griffin amendments to the NLRA, in order to make the law consistent.)

Employers should be given as much latitude as possible in terms of how they choose to structure and operate nonunion representation committees in order to encourage their adoption and most effective deployment. Thus, contrary to proposals made by some scholars (e.g., Weiler 1993), we do not believe it is wise public policy to mandate that all employers adopt some form of NER, since the benefits to workers, firms, and society are in many cases less than the costs (see Kaufman and Levine, chapter 7; and Addison, Schnabel, and Wagner, chapter 17). Employers should, accordingly, be left to decide whether to adopt any type of NER. We amend this general principle

with the caveat that in certain selective, well-targeted situations a legal mandate has merits (per our second normative proposition, stated above), such as mandated joint safety and health committees in certain industries.

In a similar vein, other scholars (e.g., Summers 1993; Morris 1996) have argued that companies should be given wider latitude to establish nonunion representation committees but only if representatives are chosen by secret ballot election, employees have the right to vote for acceptance or rejection of the employer's plan, and/or employee representatives have guaranteed access to outside expert counsel. We also believe these restrictions are counterproductive, as they introduce needless bureaucracy, inflexibility, politics, and potential adversarialism into employer-employee relations in nonunion workplaces and mistake the form of democracy (voting) for the substance of democracy (uncoerced choice, due process).

Our position is that employers will be induced to operate nonunion committees in a mutual gain, procedurally fair manner to the extent they face three "threats": (1) a viable union threat effect, (2) a viable employee "exit" effect (quitting for a job elsewhere), and (3) well-enforced legislative and judicial restrictions on discriminatory and otherwise antisocial employment practices. When labor law gives workers relatively unobstructed access to union representation, and this is supplemented by full-employment labor markets that give workers other readily available employment opportunities and access to courts and regulatory agencies for redress of employer acts of discrimination and opportunism, firms will be motivated by self-interest to structure and operate NERPs in an aboveboard way in order to keep employees relatively satisfied. To the degree that these three types of threat effects can be institutionalized, nonunion employer committees do not need more extensive regulation and control, such as those just cited. Toward this end, we propose below substantial changes to the NLRA to reduce the impediments workers now face in organizing independent unions. Maintaining full employment is more problematic and not easily addressed by law, but we note that considerable progress has been made on this front in recent years. Much progress has also been made through law and judicial oversight in heavily circumscribing employment discrimination and other abuses of employee rights and interests.

We are mindful, however, that employers often possess a power advantage over individual employees in a nonunion context and that the threat of unionization, employee turnover, and court action can never prevent all employer abuse. The form of employer abuse most inimical to successful, aboveboard NER is employee fear of retribution and discrimination for speaking up or taking actions in ways that are unpopular with management. Thus we believe one compromise in our general principle of deregulation toward NER has considerable merit. This compromise is a stipulation that whenever an employer-created form of NER in some way deals with the resolution of employment disputes that minimum standards of procedural equity must be followed, such as outlined in the final report of the Dunlop Commission (Commission on the Future of Worker-Management Relations 1994b) or the "Protocol" promulgated by the National Academy of Arbitrators (1998). A more sweeping provision would be to mandate that companies choosing to operate any kind of NER must have a dispute-resolution mechanism in conformance with these standards or, going even further, that all companies over a certain size have such a system. These broader options have merit, but so does gradualism.

Moving on in our list of recommendations, Section 8(a)(2) should remain unchanged so that bona fide agencies of collective bargaining remain free of employer interference and domination. Such a provision is essential in order to prevent "rat unions" (which really represent management interests) and "sweetheart" contracts. Section 8(a)(2) is a clear, precise, and cogent directive that prohibits an unfair labor practice and allows the Labor Board to exercise its power. Without exception, every Canadian jurisdiction has the equivalent of a strong 8(a)(2). Given our revised definition of a labor organization in Section 2(5), the reach of Section 8(a)(2) would be limited to independent worker organizations (i.e., labor unions). Note that both the Dunlop Commission recommendations and the TEAM Act legislation propose to modify Section 8(a)(2) in order to give employers more flexibility in operating NER forms, when in fact the fundamental source of the problem is the overly broad Section 2(5) definition of a labor organization.

In order to ensure that nonunion employers do not use NER for suppressive, illegitimate union-avoidance purposes, and collaterally to ensure that nonunion employers have strong incentives to operate NERPs in an aboveboard, win-win manner, legal and administrative changes should be made to the NLRA that collectively lower the impediments to union organization. A viable union threat is a powerful guarantor of fair dealings. Thus, we recommend that the time delays in holding union representation elections be substantially reduced. The present median time between union petition and election in the United States is six to seven weeks. In comparison, the Canadian province of Ontario requires that representation elections be held within five days of petition. We believe the American law gives employers an undue ability to chill a union's campaign, but that it is not necessary to hurry the election process to the degree done in Ontario to solve this problem. Thus, we recommend an intermediate position in which the NLRA is revised to require an election within one month of petition. Financial penalties levied against employers for acts of antiunion discrimination should be increased, and the NLRB should be given greater latitude to seek injunctive relief on behalf of employees harmed by employer discrimination. Finally, it should be declared an unfair labor practice for an employer to establish a new employee representation committee, or to modify an existing one, once a union has commenced organizing.

We believe adoption of these proposals will promote the economic and social interests of the United States and move its national labor policy closer to that of other countries. They allow nonunion employers greater latitude to establish and operate employee committees and teams, provide greater opportunities for nonunion workers to have voice and participation in the workplace, and strengthen the right to organize so that the union option is readily available to workers. Although adoption of these proposals may be difficult to achieve in the current atmosphere of political partisanship and polarization, they are in broad outline the direction for labor law reform favored by the majority of Americans and are consistent with much of the research and investigation contained in this volume.

References

Addison, John, and Barry Hirsch. 1997. "The Economic Effects of Employment Regulation: What Are the Limits?" In *Government Regulation of the Employment Relationship*, ed. Bruce Kaufman, pp. 125–178. Madison, Wis.: Industrial Relations Research Association.

Akerlof, George. 1990. "The Fair-Wage Effort Hypothesis and Unemployment." *Quarterly Journal of Economics* 105 (May): 255–284.

Boal, William, and Michael Ransom. 1997. "Monopsony in the Labor Market." *Journal of Economic Literature* 35, no. 1: 86–112.

Brandes, Stuart. 1976. *American Welfare Capitalism, 1880–1940.* Chicago: University of Chicago Press.

Cappelli, Peter, and Nikolai Rogovsky. 1998. "Employee Involvement and Organizational Citizenship: Implications for Labor Law and 'Lean Production,'" *Industrial and Labor Relations Review* 51, no. 4: 633–653.

Commission on the Future of Worker-Management Relations. 1994a. *Fact-finding Report.* Washington, D.C.: U.S. Department of Labor and U.S. Department of Commerce.

———. 1994b. *Report and Recommendations.* Washington, D.C.: U.S. Department of Labor and U.S. Department of Commerce.

Commons, John. 1919. *Industrial Goodwill.* New York: McGraw-Hill.

Delaney, John, and Susan Schwochau. 1993. "Employee Representation through the Political Process." In *Employee Representation: Alternatives and Future Directions*, ed. Bruce Kaufman and Morris Kleiner, pp. 265–304. Madison, Wis.: Industrial Relations Research Association.

Dunn, Robert. 1926. *American Company Unions.* Chicago: Trade Union Education League.

Foulkes, Fred. 1980. *Personnel Policies in Large Nonunion Companies.* Englewood Cliffs, N.J.: Prentice Hall.

Freeman, Richard, and James Medoff. 1984. *What Do Unions Do?* New York: Basic Books.

Freeman, Richard, and Joel Rogers. 1999. *What Workers Want.* Ithaca, N.Y.: Cornell University Press.

Gitelman, H. 1988. *The Legacy of the Ludlow Massacre.* Philadelphia: University of Pennsylvania Press.

Hurd, Richard, and Joseph Uehlein. 1994. "Patterned Responses to Organizing: Case Studies of the Union-Busting Convention." In *Restoring the Promise of American Labor Law*, ed. Sheldon Friedman et al., pp. 61–74. Ithaca, N.Y.: ILR Press.

Jacoby, Sanford M. 1997. *Modern Manors: Welfare Capitalism Since the New Deal.* Princeton: Princeton University Press.

Kaufman, Bruce. 1996. "Why the Wagner Act? Reestablishing Contact with Its Original Purpose." In *Advances in Industrial and Labor Relations*, ed. David Lewin, Bruce Kaufman, and Donna Sockell, vol. 7, pp. 15–68. Greenwich, Conn.: JAI Press.

———. 1997. "Labor Markets and Employment Regulation: The View of the Old Institutionalists." In *Government Regulation of the Employment Relationship*, ed.

Bruce Kaufman, pp. 11–55. Madison, Wis.: Industrial Relations Research Association.

———. 1999. "Does the NLRA Constrain Employee Involvement and Participation Programs in Nonunion Companies? A Reassessment." *Yale Law and Policy Review* 17 no. 2: 729–811.

———. 2001. "The Theory and Practice of Strategic HRM and Participative Management: Antecedents in Early Industrial Relations." *HRM Review* (forthcoming).

Kaufman, Bruce, and David Lewin. 1998. "Is the NLRA Still Relevant to Today's Economy and Workplace?" *Labor Law Journal* 49 (September): 113–1126.

Kaufman, Bruce, and Paula Stephan. 1995. "The Role of Management Attorneys in Union Organizing Campaigns." *Journal of Labor Research* 16, no. 4: 439–454.

Kochan, Thomas, and Harry Katz. 1988. *Collective Bargaining and Industrial Relations*, 2nd ed. Homewood, Ill.: Irwin.

Kochan, Thomas, Harry Katz, and Robert McKersie. 1986. *The Transformation of American Industrial Relations.* New York: Basic Books.

Kochan, Thomas, and Paul Osterman. 1994. *The Mutual Gains Enterprise.* Cambridge: Harvard Business School Press.

Lawler, Edward, Gerald Ledford, and Susan Albers. 1992. *Employee Involvement and Total Quality Management: Practices and Results from Fortune 1000 Companies.* San Francisco: Jossey-Bass.

Lawler, John. 1990. *Unionization and Deunionization.* Columbia: University of South Carolina Press.

Leiserson, William. 1928. "The Accomplishments and Significance of Employee Representation." *Personnel* 4 (February): 119–135.

Morris, Charles. 1994. "Deja vu and 8(a)(2): What Is Really Being Chilled by Electromation." *Cornell Journal of Law and Public Policy* 4, no. 3: 25–32.

———. 1996. "Will There Be a New Direction for American Industrial Relations? A Hard Look at the Team Bill, the Sawyer Substitute Bill, and the Employee Involvement Bill." *Labor Law Journal* 47, no. 2: 89–95.

Nadler, David, and Marc Gerstein. 1992. "Designing High-Performance Work Systems: Organizing People, Work, and Technology." In *Organizational Architecture*, ed. David Nadler, Marc Gerstein, and Robert Shaw, pp. 110–132. San Francisco: Jossey-Bass.

National Academy of Arbitrators. 1998. "A Due Process Protocol for Mediation and Arbitration of Statutory Disputes Arising Out of the Employment Relationship." *Proceedings of the 48th Annual Meeting of the National Academy of Arbitrators*, ed. Joyce M. Najita. Washington, D.C.: Bureau of National Affairs.

Osterman, Paul. 1994. "How Common Is Workplace Transformation and Who Adopts It?" *Industrial and Labor Relations Review* 47, no. 2: 173–188.

Pfeffer, Jeffrey. 1994. *Competitive Advantage Through People: Unleashing the Power of the Workforce.* Cambridge: Harvard Business School Press.

Smith, Robert. 1960. *Mill on the Dan: A History of Dan River Mills, 1882–1950.* Durham, N.C.: Duke University Press.

Summers, Clyde. 1993. "Employee Voice and Employer Choice: A Structural Exception to Section 8(a)(2)." *Chicago-Kent Law Review* 69: 129–148.

Taras, Daphne Gottlieb. 1997a. "Managerial Intentions and Wage Determination in the Canadian Petroleum Industry." *Industrial Relations* 36, no. 2: 178–205.

———. 1997b. "Collective Bargaining Regulation in Canada and the US: Divergent Cultures, Divergent Outcomes." In *Government Regulation of the Employment Relationship*, ed. Bruce Kaufman, pp. 295–341. Madison, Wis.: Industrial Relations Research Association.

———. 1998. "Nonunion Representation: Complement or Threat to Trade Unions?" In *Proceedings of the Fiftieth Annual Meeting*, pp. 281–290. Madison, Wis.: Industrial Relations Research Association.

Taras, Daphne Gottlieb, and Jason Copping. 1996. "When Pet Bears Go Wild." Paper presented to the Annual Canadian Industrial Relations Association Conference, St. Catharines, Ontario.

———. 1998. "Transition from Nonunion Employee Representation to Unionization: A Case Study." *Industrial and Labor Relations Review* 52, no. 1: 22–44.

Towers, Brian. 1997. *The Representation Gap.* New York: Oxford University Press.

Weil, David. 1999. "Are Mandated Health and Safety Committees Substitutes for or Complements to Labor Unions?" *Industrial and Labor Relations Review* 52, no. 3: 339–360.

Weiler, Paul. 1993. "Governing the Workplace: Employee Representation in the Eyes of the Law." In *Employee Representation: Alternatives and Future Directions*, eds. Bruce Kaufman and Morris Kleiner, pp. 81–104. Madison: Industrial Relations Research Association.

Wheeler, Hoyt, and John McClendon. 1991. "The Individual Decision to Unionize." In *The State of the Unions*, ed. George Strauss et al., pp. 47–83. Madison, Wis.: Industrial Relations Research Association.

Index

About the Contributors

John T. Addison is professor of economics at the Darla Moore School of Business, University of South Carolina, and senior research fellow at the University of Birmingham, England.

Reg Basken is recently retired secretary-treasurer of the Communications, Energy and Paperworkers Union in Ottawa, Ontario, and former president of the Energy and Chemical Workers Union.

David J. Boone is manager of the Production Operations Divisions of Imperial Oil in Calgary, Alberta, and is president of the Cynthia Gas Gathering Co. Ltd. and Redwater Water Disposal Company Ltd.

Richard P. Chaykowski is associate professor at the School of Industrial Relations, Queen's University in Kingston, Ontario.

Rod Chiesa is an employee of Imperial Oil's Bonnie Glen Decision Unit and lives in Leduc, Alberta.

Cathy Cone is an employee of Delta Air Lines, headquartered in Atlanta.

Samuel Estreicher is professor of law and director of the Center for Labor and Employment Law at NYU School of Law, New York University.

John A. Fossum is professor of industrial relations in the Industrial Relations Center, Carlson School of Management, University of Minnesota.

Chris Fuldner is president and chief executive officer of EFCO Corporation in Monett, Missouri.

Laurence E. Gold is associate general counsel of the AFL-CIO.

Paul J. Gollan is a teacher and doctoral student at the London School of Economics and Political Science.

Tove Helland Hammer is professor of organizational behavior in the New York State School of Industrial and Labor Relations, Cornell University.

Mark Harshaw is interim director of human resources of Dofasco Inc. of Hamilton, Ontario.

Roy B. Helfgott is Distinguished Professor of Economics Emeritus, School of Management, New Jersey Institute of Technology, and president of the Industrial Relations Counselors, Inc.

Jonathan P. Hiatt is general counsel of the AFL-CIO.

Sanford M. Jacoby is professor of management,

history and policy studies at the University of California at Los Angeles (UCLA).

Bruce E. Kaufman is professor of economics and senior associate, and former director, of the W.T. Beebe Institute of Personnel and Employment Relations at Georgia State University.

Andrew M. Kramer is partner-in-charge of client affairs at Jones, Day, Reavis & Pogue in Cleveland, Ohio.

Michael H. LeRoy is associate professor of labor and industrial relations, College of Law, at the University of Illinois at Urbana-Champaign.

David Levine is associate professor at the Haas School of Business, University of California at Berkeley.

David Lewin is professor at the Anderson Graduate School of Management, University of California at Los Angeles (UCLA).

Seymour Martin Lipset is a senior fellow at the Hoover Institution and Hazel Professor of Public Policy at George Mason University.

Kevin MacDougall is a member of the Royal Canadian Mounted Police and lives in Winnipeg, Manitoba.

Laurel Sefton MacDowell is professor of history at the University of Toronto, Ontario.

Noah M. Meltz is professor of economics at the University of Toronto, Ontario.

Motohiro Morishima is associate professor at the Graduate School of Business Administration, Keio University, Japan.

Daniel Nelson is professor of history and chair of the Department of History at the University of Akron.

John N. Raudabaugh is attorney and partner with Matkov, Salzman, Madoff and Gunn in Chicago. He was a member of the National Labor Relations Board from 1990 to 1993.

Ken Rhyason is an employee of Imperial Oil's Rainbow Lake Decision Unit and lives in Rainbow Lake, Alberta.

Claus Schnabel is head of industrial relations research at the Institut der Deutschen Wirtschaft in Köln, Germany. He is also *privatdozent* in labor economics at Tuhr University, Bochum.

Andrew Sims is a labor lawyer and arbitrator in private practice with the Sims Group in Edmonton, Alberta.

Daphne Gottlieb Taras is associate professor of industrial relations in the Faculty of Management at the University of Calgary, Alberta.

Tsuyoshi Tsuru is professor of economics at the Institute of Economic Research of Hitotsubashi University, Japan.

Anil Verma is professor at the Rotman School of Management and at the Centre for Industrial Relations, University of Toronto. He is a research associate with the Canadian Policy Research Networks.

Joachim Wagner is professor of economics at the Institut für Volkswirtschaftslehre, Universität Lüneberg, in Germany.